THE GARDENER'S GUIDE TO COMMON-SENSE

PEST CONTROL

COMPLETELY REVISED & UPDATED

THE GARDENER'S GUIDE TO COMMON-SENSE

PEST CONTROL

COMPLETELY REVISED & UPDATED

WILLIAM OLKOWSKI
SHEILA DAAR
HELGA OLKOWSKI

Coauthored and edited by
STEVEN ASH

The Taunton Press

The Taunton Press
Inspiration for hands-on living®

The Taunton Press, Inc.
63 South Main Street
PO Box 5506
Newtown, CT 06470-5506
e-mail: tp@taunton.com

Editors: Steven Ash, Christina Glennon
Project manager: Pam Weatherford
Copy editor: Seth Reichgott
Indexer: Jim Curtis
Jacket/Cover design: Stacy Wakefield Forte
Interior design/Layout: Stacy Wakefield Forte
Illustrator: Steve Buchanan

Fine Gardening® is a trademark of The Taunton Press, Inc., registered in
the U.S. Patent and Trademark Office.

The following names/manufacturers appearing in *The Gardener's Guide
to Common-Sense Pest Control* are trademarks: 3M®, AAtrex®, AQ10®,
Actino-Iron®, Actinovate®, Altosid®, Apex®, Baygon®, Benlate®,
Biolure®, BotaniGuard®, CLV-LC®, CYD-X®, CideTrak®, Collego®,
Combat®, Decyde®, DeVine®, Dianex®, Dimilin®, Dipel®, Dirt
Squad™, Doom®, Dr. Bronner's®, Elcar®, Enstar®, Enstar®, Entrust®,
Fels Naptha®, Flea Trol®, Flexinet®, FruitGuard®, Galltrol-A®,
GemStar®, Gentrol®, Green Magic®, Gypchek®, Husqvarna®, Kabat®,
Kaligreen®, Kryocide®, Lawn Restore®, Lysol®, M-One®, Marvelous
Marianne's SkinSafer®, Masonite®, Matsukemin®, Minex®, Mycotal®,
Mycotrol O®, Nash®, Norbac 84®, Orthene®, Osmocote®, Out O'Sight®,
Pharoid®, Pramitol®, Precor®, Princep®, RootShield®, Roundup®, Saf-
er®, Sevin®, Serenade®, Seventh Generation™, Sharpshooter®, Sluggo®
Snailproof®, Soil Aid®, StaFresh® 460, Strengthen & Renew®, SunSpray®,
Tangle-Trap®, Tanglefoot®, Tecnu®, Tilt®, Tomcat®, Tyvek®, Vapor
Gard®, Velcro®, Vertalec®, Victor®, Virosoft®, Wilt Pruf®.

Library of Congress Cataloging-in-Publication Data
Olkowski, William.
   The gardener's guide to common-sense pest control : completely revised
and updated / William Olkowski, Sheila Daar, Helga Olkowski ; coau-
thored and edited by Steven Ash. -- Rev. and updated.
      p. cm.
   Includes bibliographical references and index.
   ISBN 978-1-60085-500-9
1. Garden pests--Integrated control. I. Daar, Sheila. II. Olkowski, Helga.
III. Ash, Steven A. IV. Title.
   SB603.5.O45 2013
   635--dc23
                          2012043015

Printed in the United States of America
10 9 8 7 6 5 4 3 2 1

ACKNOWLEDGMENTS

Mary O'Malley, for nearly 40 years you've been by my side. Your personal and professional integrity have inspired me all these years, and you are my hero; I love you. Sheila Daar for the opportunity to work with you over the years and to do this book. Bill and Helga Olkowski for taking a chance on me. Pam Weatherford, I could not have done this without your help; even if I could have, it would not have been as much fun. As Sheila Daar always said about IPM knowledge, "We all stand on each other's shoulders in IPM." I'd like to say thanks to the following people from whom I've learned so much, the proverbial "shoulders" on which I stand: Debbie Raphael, Chris Geiger, Pavel Svihra, Debi Tidd, Anne Joseph, Teresa Eade, Ralph Montana, Fred Crowder, Bob Fiorello, Ellie Rilla, Jerilyn Downing, Luis Agurto, Sr., Luis Agurto, Jr., Guido Ciardi, Tonya Drlik, Bill Quarles, Don Thomas, Jessian Choy, Cynthia Havstad, Laurel Thomassin, Linda Novy, Stacy Carlsen, Deshelia "Nikki" Mixon, my brother John Ash the architect, and, of course, my Mom and Dad. I know I've missed some people, so I thank all of those I've worked with over the years, too. Thanks to Peter Chapman and everyone at Taunton.

Steven A. Ash
San Rafael, California

DEDICATION

To the memory of Helga Olkowski, companion and wife to Bill Olkowski for 42 years. Helga passed away during the revision of this book, but she provided many key ideas for the original and made additions to this edition, where her contributions will have further life.

Helga was first among this book's authors to campaign for pesticide reduction, long before there was much interest in the topic. She was a true pioneer, in the spirit of Rachel Carson.

PART TWO

PESTS IN THE GARDEN

PREFACE

OUR INSPIRATION

The inspiration for *The Gardener's Guide to Common-Sense Pest Control* was the groundbreaking book *Silent Spring*, written by Rachel Carson. Published in 1962, it gave rise to widespread concern over global contamination of soil, water, air, and biological food chains from the use of newly developed, highly toxic chlorinated hydrocarbon pesticides. Initially, the popularity of these new materials was spurred by the need to fight insect-borne pathogens during World War II. The heavy-metal-based insecticides, such as lead and arsenic used for decades before the war, were hazardous to people and not very effective against insects. New, more potent insecticides were needed.

The alleged reduction in hazards of the new broad-spectrum chlorinated hydrocarbon insecticides, their profitability, and their apparent effectiveness in the short term all contributed to their rapid widespread adoption. DDT was the most commonly used of these new insecticides, and it became the first global chemical pollutant. Although banned in the United States in 1972, DDT residues are still found in humans and food chains throughout the planet. DDT also became the first to reveal another major drawback of these chlorinated hydrocarbons and other widely used materials: the rapid growth of insect resistance.

INTEGRATED CONTROL

When we began our pest management careers in the early 1970s, routine calendar treatments for pest problems were the rule. At that time, one of us, William Olkowski, had just received his PhD in biological control of insects, having seen firsthand how an introduced parasitoid successfully controlled an aphid. Thus, we started out with a bias toward the use of and conservation of natural enemies such as predators and parasitoids. Gradu-

ally we realized that the use of natural enemies had to be embedded within a total ecosystem management program, because pesticides dominated pest control applications.

The development of "Integrated Control" in agriculture (Stern *Integrated Control Concept,* 1959) inspired us. After effectively applying this approach to street trees in Berkeley, California, we realized this multifaceted approach could be adapted to urban pest situations. We then expanded the same concepts in other settings.

"Integrated Control" developed into "Integrated Pest Management," or IPM. An IPM-based federal policy followed during the Carter years (1977–1981). Because IPM had the potential to reduce toxic material use, the term became synonymous with "good" pest management. Many pest control practitioners jumped on the bandwagon and began to call what they were already doing "IPM." In reality, however, it was just business as usual.

From our perspective, a pest management system should not be called IPM unless it contains certain key features: (a) monitoring (checking on a regular basis to see where the problem is most severe and whether applied treatments are successful), (b) use of "injury levels" to trigger treatments (to reduce the energy and cost of treatments for problems that can be tolerated), and (c) a spectrum of treatments such as redesign of the management system, education, habitat management, and horticultural, physical, biological, and least-toxic chemical controls (the latter is especially important to conserve natural enemies).

The temptation to co-opt the phrase IPM slowly started to fade with the development of true IPM programs in various government agencies, private pest control companies, and pilot IPM programs in agricultural colleges. The Environmental Protection Agency (EPA) took the lead in funding some of our

THE DIFFERENCES BETWEEN IPM AND CONVENTIONAL PEST CONTROL

ELEMENT	CONVENTIONAL PEST CONTROL	INTEGRATED PEST MANAGEMENT
Education, knowledge	Minimal	Extensive
Inspection and monitoring	Minimal	Extensive
Emphasis	Treat symptoms of problem; routine pesticide application	Treat sources of problem; pesticides used only when nonchemical methods inadequate
Insects in managed areas	Insecticides: sprays, granulars, baits, and drenches	Combinations: baits, biologicals, botanicals, beneficials, cultural, physical/mechanical, etc.
Application of sprays	Broadcast treatments	Generally avoided or spot treatments
Weeds	Herbicides	Mulches, barriers, manual, mechanical, grazing, flaming, competitive planting, etc.
Soil and media management	Minimal, soil testing	Extensive: feed the soil, soil testing, compost, grasscycling, organic fertilizer, etc.
Fungal diseases	Emphasis on fungicides	Emphasis on resistant plants, cultural, irrigation, diagnostics, least-toxic fungicides
Vertebrate control	Emphasis on toxic baits	Emphasis on exclusion, resistant plants, trapping, repellents
Program strategy	Reactive	Preventive
Potential liability	High	Low

Adapted from *IPM in and around Buildings*. Armed Forces Pest Management Board Technical Guide #29, July 1994.

early work. The National Parks Service (NPS) was the first federal agency to institutionalize IPM, applying the approach throughout its parks.

One of the most useful products from this federally sponsored work was a course and training manual we developed that was adapted and built upon by other agencies. We also produced a range of publications through the nonprofit institution we founded: The Bio Integral Resource Center (BIRC). Some of our publications were aimed at pest management professionals, such as the monthly journal *The IPM Practitioner* (first issue January 1978, continuing to the present). Others, such as the original *Common-Sense Pest Control* and its follow-up *The Gardener's Guide to Common-Sense Pest Control*, *The Common-Sense Pest Control Quarterly* (1975–present), and numerous fliers, articles, and booklets on managing household, garden, and community pest problems, were produced for the general public.

WHY A NEW EDITION OF THE GARDENER'S GUIDE?

The first decade of the 21st century has seen IPM concepts and compatible products and services establish a significant foothold in the pest management mainstream. This slow but steady shift toward a less-toxic approach has emerged as conventional pesticides have become less effective and substantially more expensive, while at the same time there has been reduced consumer confidence in them due to health and environmental concerns.

Today, as more people seek green living ideas, move toward growing their own food, and work to reduce negative environmental impacts, an updated version of the *Guide* is needed more than ever.

The first edition of the *Guide* was published at a time when there was no other user-friendly comprehensive introduction to least-toxic IPM targeted to the general public as well as professionals.

And it has remained in demand long after it went out of print.

With each pest covered, the biology of the pest is briefly summarized and then the means for designing an IPM program are outlined. The *Guide* can function as a text for students and a reference for those involved in urban pest control, such as (a) homeowners and home gardeners, (b) professional pest control personnel who want to minimize the risk posed by daily exposures to poisons for their customers and for themselves, (c) maintenance workers whose jobs require knowledge of pest control but have few places to learn about IPM, and (d) people who serve the public by selling pest control products in garden shops, nurseries, supermarkets, hardware stores, and online mail-order sources.

Over the years, many people have thanked us for the tips we have provided on handling difficult common pest problems. However, from our own point of view, the book's greatest contribution is its presentation of least-toxic IPM concepts and example programs. IPM places emphasis on a decision-making process rather than a product-oriented solution. It is based on the fact that every organism requires a certain range of biotic (living) and abiotic (non-living) factors to survive. By reading about the problem and/or direct observation of the precise circumstances of the problem, one can find means to modify the life-support system of the pest and its natural enemies either positively or negatively. Rarely can you do just one thing to solve a problem for lasting positive change.

Since publication of the original edition, there has been continued growth of public interest in reducing unnecessary exposures to toxic materials. This has encouraged the rise of many new companies and products. The first edition of this book included a "products and services" resource appendix. These pages have been dropped in this edition because constant growth and change within the pest control industry requires regular updating. You may now find this information at our companion website, FineGardening.com/common-sense-pest-control, along with further references and readings.

INTRODUCTION

This book is about ways to manage your encounters with other living organisms you regard as pests. The emphasis is on concepts and techniques that help you to do so in a manner that is in harmony with the health of humans, pets, other domestic animals, wildlife, and the general environment. Chances are good you are reading this book because you want help solving a specific pest problem. Below we suggest various ways you can use the book for that purpose.

MAGIC, SCIENCE, AND SIMPLE SOLUTIONS: DISTINGUISHING COINCIDENCE FROM CAUSE

In all the information we present, we make a concerted effort to distinguish science from "magic" and to guide you in the art of applying sound scientific principles to the solving of pest problems. For many people actively seeking a less ecologically disruptive pest control technology, magic holds a strong attraction. Most likely this is because they have become disillusioned with science and the often destructive products they associate with it, including toxic pesticides. This may be one major reason why until recently much of the commonly available advice on nontoxic pest control contained such a heavy dose of magic.

Magical thinking can be entertaining. It can also lead to creative insights through intuitive processes beyond conscious control. But as a source of practical pest management techniques it is not very reliable. Magical thinking often concludes that one event was caused by another just because the events followed each other in time. It does not distinguish between coincidence and cause. For example, someone tells you that planting marigolds in your garden keeps bad bugs away. You try it. That year it seems as though the pest problem is less

severe. Were the marigolds responsible? Magical thinking would instantly conclude that they were.

But we might ask a few more questions before jumping to that conclusion. What was the mechanism by which the marigolds kept the bad bugs away? Is the effect repeatable? Magical thinking does not deal with mechanisms; in fact, much of its appeal lies in the mysterious, unexplainable ways in which it operates. Like other human pursuits of mystery, such as religion, it requires unquestioning faith.

However, when you persist in questioning magical explanations—exactly how is it that marigolds reduce pest problems in the garden—suddenly the magic disappears and you find yourself in the world of science. In this book you might find a statement like this:

> Certain marigolds, including *Tagetes patula* and *Tagetes erecta* (the universal scientific names for these particular species), have a root exudate that can reduce the number of plant-parasitic nematodes in the soil. To obtain this effect, the area where the problem is known to exist must be planted solidly with marigolds for an entire season. Then the plant must be chopped up and incorporated into the soil.

This statement is specific as to pest, species of plant, technique, and pest control mechanism—in this case, a substance exuded from the roots that suppresses pest nematode populations.

WHAT WE MEAN BY THE SCIENTIFIC PROCESS

Science is a loaded word in our society because it means different things to different people. Often the word is used in contexts involving emotional and political issues. In this book, we use science to refer to the process by which an effort is made to discover the mechanisms underlying phenomena observed in the natural world. We also use it to distinguish between causal relationships and events that follow one another in time but probably are associated only by coincidence.

The scientific process goes something like this. First an idea occurs to someone—you, us, or perhaps a professional scientist. If it has to do with the subject of this book, it is probably a new and better way of managing a particular pest problem. We call this a treatment, or because treatment to some people means applying a chemical material, we call it more formally a treatment action.

Next, that idea, or treatment, is tested in an experiment. In a sound experiment, the new treatment action is repeated several times and/or in different places. The experiment includes an untreated control group, also called a check. (Control is a confusing word. In a scientific investigation, the control is the group on which you do *not* carry out the treatment action. To the layperson, however, the word seems to suggest just the opposite, so we prefer the term "check.")

To return to the marigold example, we might conduct an experiment by selecting three areas where pest nematodes are known to occur at similar concentrations in the soil. We would plant Area 1 solidly for a season with what was said to be the "right" species of marigolds and then plow them under, as suggested previously. In Area 2, we might interplant a few marigolds with other plants. Or, as some people do, we might run a border of marigolds around the entire bed and plant other things within the bed. Area 3, our check area, would contain no marigolds. The following season, we would plant all three areas with a species of plant known to be susceptible to the pest nematode that was originally present in the soil. Then we would compare levels of harmful nematode infection in each area by pulling out plants and examining their roots.

By carrying out just such an experiment, investigators at the Connecticut Agricultural Experiment Station determined how planting marigolds might reduce nematode pests infesting susceptible plants. The recommendation given above is based on our reading of the literature published on the experiment station studies.

HOW RELIABLE ARE OUR RECOMMENDED TREATMENT ACTIONS?

When one has completed a scientific investigation such as that just described, the best one can say is that the treatment action works under the specified circumstances a certain amount of the time. To say that an idea is scientifically valid means that the same result will be achieved under the same conditions at least 95 out of 100 times it is tried, or 95 percent of the time.

The key words are "under the same conditions." It is important to realize that while conditions can be duplicated in the laboratory, no two pest situations are identical in the real world. This has important consequences for applying pest management advice. You can't simply repeat a recommended treatment by rote and get the predicted results, as you can under laboratory conditions (or as you supposedly can using magic formulas).

To the contrary, your key to success in applying the scientifically derived pest management advice we offer in this book is to follow a three-part process that involves your own judgment, intelligence, and even a little creativity. First, you must understand the underlying concepts. Then, you must familiarize yourself with circumstances under which the desired results have been achieved elsewhere. Last, you must adapt the general techniques recommended in this book to the precise situation you are trying to manage.

This adaptation to your own circumstances is where the art comes in. You must become part biologist, carefully observing the various life forms you are attempting to manipulate, and part ecologist, observing the environment in which they live. Because so many conditions—soil, microclimate, and plant or pest variety (or strain), to name a few— vary from place to place even in your own house, yard, or greenhouse, you may need to carry out a few experiments of your own before you can figure out how the prescribed technique will work for you.

FEW SIMPLE SOLUTIONS

Does that sound simple? Most people say no. That is why pesticides are so popular. Their use seems simple. They offer what appears to be a simple solution to a complex problem. This apparent simplicity is also the reason why pesticides are limited in their usefulness. They are too simple to solve the problem in a permanent way. It's a bit like kicking the television when it stops working. You may get lucky, and the sudden jarring could get things working again . . . for a while. But finding a permanent solution to the problem requires that you take the trouble to educate yourself on the subject, put your attention to it, diagnose the problem, and then apply the appropriate remedy. With complex systems, something more subtle than a sledgehammer is required.

THE HARDEST PART OF ALL

Minimizing your dependence on pesticides takes a little more time and effort initially. But the rewards include less trouble in the long run and reduced personal and environmental contamination with toxic materials. Because the alternatives to toxic chemicals require learning new things and changing behavior, they also require a greater commitment than applying the same old simple but temporary chemical solutions. In fact, you may find that modification of your own behavior is the hardest part of all.

We sympathize. Having changed our own lives substantially to try to bring them into harmony with our ideals, we know how long it takes to break old patterns and make new ones automatic. For those of you who would like to learn more about how to change individual, family, or institutional behavior, we recommend these two books: *Communication of Innovations: A Cross-Cultural Approach* by E. Rogers and F. F. Shoemaker (Free Press, 1971) and *Diffusion of Innovations, 5th Edition* by Everett M. Rogers and E. Rogers (Free Press, 2003).

WHAT YOU NEED TO KNOW AND HOW TO FIND IT IN THIS BOOK

Two quite different types of information are needed to achieve good pest management. The first is gen-

eral. You need a procedure for analyzing the problem and you need criteria for selecting the right treatment. The second is highly specific. You must know about the life cycle of the particular organism, the role it plays in the larger scheme of things, and the role you or other humans play in creating or supporting the problem.

Accordingly, the first part of the book covers basic concepts. Part 1 should help you take the right approach in thinking about existing pest problems and their solutions. In so doing, it should also provide you with a preventive approach to pest management. The second part of the book tackles specific problems, providing some of the specific pest control solutions many people are seeking. We present them as programs with diverse elements. In truth, however, there are so many garden pests that to address them all specifically would take a multivolume encyclopedia. So even in Part 2 it will sometimes be necessary for you to generalize from specific examples to other closely related species whose management is similar.

AFTER THE EMERGENCY IS OVER

We suspect most readers will reach for this book after a pest problem has assumed emergency proportions and no longer responds to previously tried methods. The sense of urgency about the problem is often made worse by a fear of the pest organism itself or of the rapid damage it may cause. That is to say, when the house appears to be burning down, one wants fire-fighting equipment, not a learned discussion on making the house fireproof. So, understandably enough, there will be a temptation to skip the background material and get right to specifics. However, we hope that once you have applied the "band-aid" suggestions we include under each specific pest, you will take the time to consider the deeper and wider perspective on the problem the book also provides. In our own experience, band-aid solutions, where available, are usually only temporary. If you want to avoid similar crises in the future, you should develop long-term, nontoxic preventive-management strategies before the emergencies arise again.

HOW WE DECIDED WHICH PESTS TO INCLUDE

In deciding which pests to include, we asked ourselves several questions: Is the pest common enough so that people in a large part of the country are familiar with it? Are reliable less-toxic alternatives to toxic methods of control now in common use? If a pest species is only regionally important, is it typical of a group of pests elsewhere whose least-toxic management is similar? Does the management program for the pest—or the common mismanagement of it—illustrate some important concept?

IF IT'S NOT IN THIS BOOK: USING THE REFERENCES

You may be disappointed to find that some less-common pests are not in the book. Don't be discouraged. If you are serious about finding a relatively nontoxic solution, read Part 1. Armed with the information on basic approaches and analogous situations you'll find there, you can turn to the section of the book that covers pests that fall into the same biological category or physical environment as yours. You can then adapt the recommendations to fit your situation. If you still have questions, the reference materials at the end of the book and on our website will help you understand more about the biology and ecology of your pest.

A word about these references. We are always uneasy with information provided to the public by so-called experts who give no indication of where they found it. If you are skeptical about some new idea you encounter in this book, you have the right to ask, "Who says so?" You should be able to determine whether our suggestions are based on our personal experience, technical literature, anecdotes from others, or some other source. We have tried to make our sources clear.

On the other hand, to reference this book formally would require a citation for almost every statement and it would become a cumbersome scientific treatise—just the opposite of what we want it to be. Thus, we have limited ourselves to citing in the text only those books and articles we particularly want to draw to your attention; we also include some technical papers needed to substantiate recommendations that may be especially nontraditional or controversial.

YOU CAN HELP US, TOO

Much information in this book is the direct product of our own experience in pest management, but we learned most of what we know from the existing literature and from people we have tried to help. We have always appreciated feedback from our readers, and we do not hesitate to test and pass on novel approaches or techniques you suggest. If you are frustrated because your pest problem isn't addressed in this book, or if you have a comment on our recommendations, write to our nonprofit organization, the Bio-Integral Resource Center, P.O. Box 7414, Berkeley, CA 94707.

We established BIRC in 1978 to identify and publicize scientifically based information on least-toxic pest management. We draw upon our staff's decades of field work and applied research in IPM, an extensive IPM database, and an international network of scientists, innovative farmers, and other pest control professionals. BIRC members—membership is open to anyone who is interested—are kept up-to-date on least-toxic pest control through our magazine, *Common-Sense Pest Control Quarterly*, and our international journal for pest control professionals, *The IPM Practitioner*. Members also use our consulting services by telephone or through correspondence for specific pest problems.

This book was written first and foremost for laypersons—gardeners, homeowners, and other individuals. We have done our very best to use nontechnical, everyday language and to explain things as completely as possible. Yet we realize we may not always have been successful in this and welcome your suggestions as to how the book might be improved.

PART ONE
THE BASICS

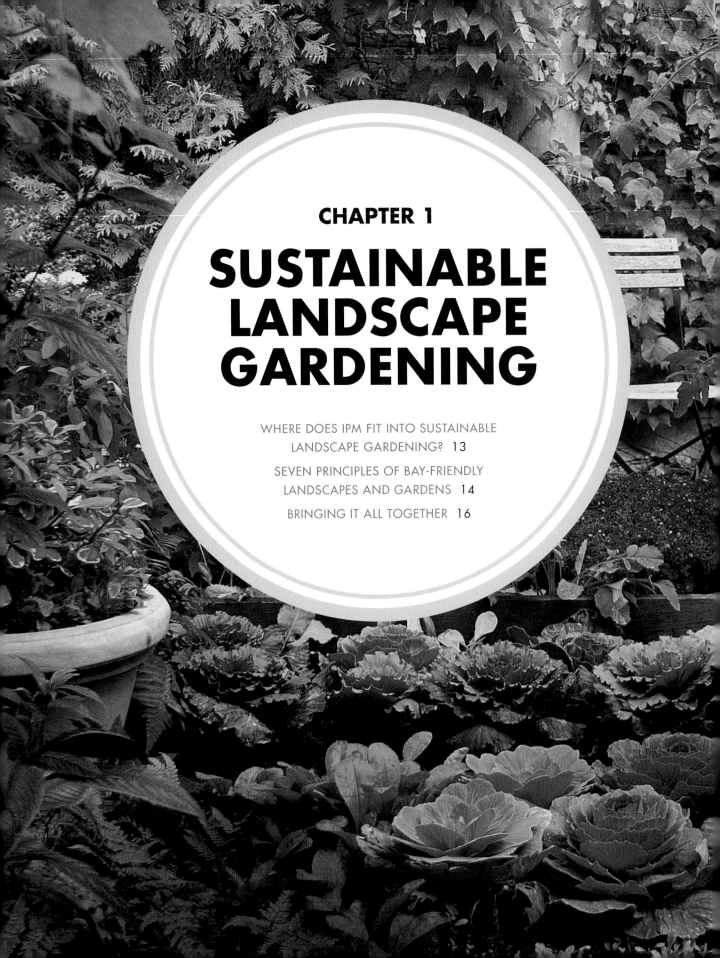

CHAPTER 1
SUSTAINABLE LANDSCAPE GARDENING

In April 1987, in a report entitled "Our Common Future," the U.N. World Commission on Environment and Development defined sustainability as "meeting the needs of the present without compromising the ability of future generations to meet their own needs." It is a concept we fully support. When Dr. William Olkowski (Bill) started exploring Integrated Pest Management (IPM) and established the Integral Urban House in Berkeley, California, over 40 years ago, it was to make the present safe and the future safer.

Sustainability expanded that early concept of IPM into an all-encompassing standard. It combined a variety of disciplines under one roof: water conservation, recycling, soil conservation, construction, energy conservation, and many others. We see this today in the LEED (Leadership in Energy and Environmental Design) program of the Green Building Council. In fact, the LEED certification program requires that IPM be part of the structural and landscape design, construction, and maintenance plans.

Our purpose here is to speak to gardeners about IPM. Just how does IPM fit into sustainability? Through sustainable landscape practices.

Since 2008, we have been involved with the Bay-Friendly Landscape (BFL) and Gardening program. This sustainable landscape program was established by stopwaste.org (their name is their web address). Stopwaste.org is a public agency made by combining the Alameda County (in the San Francisco Bay Area) Waste Management Authority and the Alameda County Source Reduction and Recycling Board. It operates as one integrated public agency that includes the county, its fourteen cities, and two sanitary districts. Its funding comes primarily from waste-disposal and import-mitigation fees collected at the county's three landfill sites; it receives no general tax fund dollars. We love the idea of waste paying for its own solutions.

We've adopted the program ourselves because it is an excellent program that brings together amateurs and experts from all of the many landscape garden disciplines. The Integral Urban House was

INTEGRATED PEST MANAGEMENT

Integrated Pest Management is a decision-making-systems approach to pest control that utilizes regular monitoring to determine if and when treatments are needed and employs physical, mechanical, cultural, biological, and educational tactics to keep pest numbers low enough to prevent intolerable damage or annoyance. Least-toxic chemical controls are used as a last resort.

In IPM programs, treatments are not made according to a predetermined schedule; they are made only when and where monitoring has indicated that the pest will cause unacceptable economic, medical, or aesthetic damage. Treatments are chosen and timed to be most effective and least disruptive to natural pest controls.

Bill and Helga Olkowski's early attempt (in the 1970s) at experimenting with sustainability. All of us involved with writing this book have had many ideas over the years on how to integrate (we use that word often) all of our knowledge from various disciplines into one overarching concept. None were quite as elegant and comprehensive as Stop Waste.Org's Bay-Friendly Landscape and Gardening program.

WHERE DOES IPM FIT INTO SUSTAINABLE LANDSCAPE GARDENING?

Over fifty years ago, *Silent Spring* (Fawcett, 1962) by Rachel Carson, the ground-breaking book that first brought national attention to the dangers of pesticides, was published. By 1970, most scientists, swayed by the evidence, were convinced Carson was right. Action needed to be taken, and in 1972, the U.S. Environmental Protection Agency (EPA) was born. When urban IPM developed over 40 years ago, it was really the only comprehensive environmental game in town. It addressed a serious pesticide use and abuse problem and, most important, provided a coherent science-based solution. We have watched it grow over these many years and have seen it adopted by the National Park Service in the 1970s, followed by other agencies. In the fall of 1996, the City and County of San Francisco was the first major urban center to adopt IPM, which is when we first became involved in that ground-breaking program. Sheila Daar was the lead person from BIRC (Bio-Integral Resource Center), our non-profit, there to stimulate this program's development. Steven Ash was there as an independent IPM Consultant and Licensed Pest Control Advisor; he was doing contract work for the San Francisco Municipal Transportation Agency at the time.

In 1990, *Common-Sense Pest Control* (CSPC) was published, and five years later the first *Gardener's Guide to Common-Sense Pest Control*, adapted from CSPC, was published. These two books became the proverbial "bibles of IPM" and are still in use and in demand over 20 years after publication. These books helped encourage gardeners, pest managers, and others to think in broader terms about the environment in a systematic way. Ideas came from many disciplines and sources and eventually began to coalesce into the sustainable-development movement we see today with programs like LEED and stopwaste.org.

We support the Bay-Friendly Landscape and Garden Coalition, a nonprofit established to promote BFL educational and practical goals. We will use their model for our discussion here. For further information and some fine literature on Bay-Friendly Landscaping (www.BayFriendlyCoalition.org) and other stopwaste.org programs, we recommend you visit their websites.

The BFL program is based on seven principles of sustainable landscaping. It is geared toward the San Francisco Bay Area's nine counties, but this material is easily adapted to your location; just substitute your local information for San Francisco Bay Area specifics.

SEVEN PRINCIPLES OF BAY-FRIENDLY LANDSCAPES AND GARDENS

The seven principles form a comprehensive sustainable landscape standard. Below is a list, followed by our short interpretation based on IPM. The seven best practices are as follows:

1. Landscape locally
2. Nurture the soil
3. Create and protect wildlife habitat
4. Landscape for less to the landfill
5. Conserve water
6. Conserve energy
7. Protect water and air quality

Landscape Locally. This has two meanings: (a) landscape using native plants when possible, and 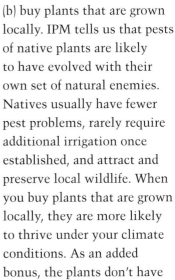 (b) buy plants that are grown locally. IPM tells us that pests of native plants are likely to have evolved with their own set of natural enemies. Natives usually have fewer pest problems, rarely require additional irrigation once established, and attract and preserve local wildlife. When you buy plants that are grown locally, they are more likely to thrive under your climate conditions. As an added bonus, the plants don't have to travel as far from the grower to the nursery; energy and time saved.

Nurture the Soil. Compost, mulches, and organic fertilizers are surefire ways to maintain a healthy soil food web. A healthy soil, especially the microbial component, promotes healthy plants and discourages pathogens. Healthy soils promote soil insects and other invertebrates that feed on pest insects and other soil-borne pests. Mulch not only helps retain moisture but also mitigates soil temperatures, both important for soil and plant health.

Mulch also provides shelter for beetles, centipedes, salamanders, lizards, and other beneficial surface predators.

Create and Protect Wildlife Habitat. When we think of wildlife, we think of everything from bacteria to deer to fungi to birds to insects to worms and beyond. We want every beneficial and aesthetic wildlife species to visit our gardens. You will see in later chapters how important it is to attract and keep beneficials in and around your garden and, oddly enough, even some pest species. Wildlife is a part of the garden, not an intruder. OK, sometimes wildlife is an intruder, as when deer come up the driveway and eat a half-dozen rose buds about to bloom.

Landscape for Less to the Landfill. Plant debris and green waste, or your fertilizer dollar, as we prefer to call this resource, are an ever-present part of garden maintenance. Compost it, use it as mulch, but for heaven's sake don't discard this valuable resource unless absolutely necessary. Selecting and installing plants where they can grow naturally makes for healthier plants that thrive. Constant shearing and pruning not only weakens the plant, but allows access for pathogens, and the injury can alert insects that the plant is weakened and vulnerable to attack. The bark beetles are an example of insects that attack wounded or other-wise unhealthy trees. Trips to and from the land-fill, especially by professional landscape gardeners, use substantial amounts of energy. Twenty-three states have banned or limited the disposal of plant debris in their landfills. Alameda County, popula-tion just over 1.5 million (seventh in California), has reduced plant debris going to landfills from a high in 1995 of 170,000 tons per year to 110,000 tons in 2000. Plant debris was banned from county landfills in 2010.

Conserve water. Less than 1 percent of the water in the world is potable water; that alone is a reason to conserve it. Since the authors were born, the U.S. population has more than doubled and the world population has tripled. A gallon of water "allotted" to each of us when we were born now needs to be shared with two more people. That is reason enough for concern, and yet in gardens and landscapes we continue to waste water through over-watering and runoff. Overwatering alone is the biggest single cause of biotic and abiotic disorders. Root-rotting fungi and molds thrive in soil that is too wet, which is why managing water has always been an important IPM tool. Using drip irrigation reduces the overhead water that weed seeds need to germinate, resulting in less weed-control effort. Keeping water off of leaves reduces the opportunities for pathogens to gain a foothold and cause disease.

Conserve Energy. We already discussed the gas used in hauling debris, but what about the energy used to create it? Fertilizer to push growth, pesticide

PLANT DEBRIS IN LANDFILLS

To give a little better perspective on the huge quantities of plant debris that were landfilled in the past in Alameda, and maybe where you live, let's break down the 110,000 tons per year in 2000 to numbers we can better understand. We chose the 110,000 tons because it is the number that appears as an example in the BFL landscape manual's 2010 online edition (p. 5).

Some interesting conversions of that 110,000 tons of green debris are as follows:

- 220,000,000 lb.
- 880,000 trips to the dump with a 250-lb. load each trip
- 602,740 lb. of debris generated per day
- 7 lb. of debris per second
- 20 miles roundtrip to the dump means 17,600,000 miles traveled
- Gas at 20 mpg and $4 per gal. comes to a staggering $3,520,000.

Over 3.5 million dollars per year to haul away a resource is mind-boggling. What are the numbers for your county? Information available at stopwaste.org can help you begin a similar program where you live.

applications of all types, and power equipment to prune and mow plants and to clean up debris are all energy intensive. Plants should be a source of energy conservation rather than an energy sink. Using trees and shrubs to shade ground-level air-conditioning units improves their efficiency. Shading parking buildings, sidewalks, and other hardscape areas reduces the heat island effect, reducing cooling needs. Shading parking lots, especially on the south and west, keeps cars cooler. When cars are cooler, they don't need to run the air-conditioning as much. Auto and truck air-conditioning reduces gas mileage, which means more gasoline used for a trip. That tree that shaded the car in the parking lot is also absorbing pollution from the car beneath. The trees and shrubs that are providing these shade benefits are also adding to the biological diversity of the site. Increased biodiversity means healthier plants and gardens overall. Conventional pesticides are very energy intensive to produce and transport. The diversity on site helps reduce the need for the pesticide group of energy hogs. Mitigation of temperatures through shading, whether from plants or mulch, also keeps pest populations, which thrive on wide temperature swings, in check.

Protect Water and Air Quality. Last, we come to protecting water and air quality. In the BFL model, this is where IPM fits. As you can see from the previous six principles, IPM touches them all. It is, however, fitting that IPM goes here. In a simplified example, we spray pesticides through the air; some goes into the air as vapor and mist, some lands on the plant, and then some of that is washed off by irrigation or rain, which in turn runs off into the gutter and down the storm drain and winds up in the nearest creek, river, pond, lake, bay, harbor, or other body of water. That body of water is used for drinking water, fishing, swimming, and other ecological, recreational, community, and commercial uses. When we reduce pesticide use, we are actively making a contribution to cleaning the air and water for our family, friends, neighbors, and ourselves.

BRINGING IT ALL TOGETHER

One important point we have always understood is that pest problems and solutions require "many hands." That is why we use the term "Integrated Pest Management." We never expected to know everything ourselves—well, not seriously, anyway. We have always wanted to integrate the knowledge of all of the stakeholders when solving a pest problem.

We come back to the statement at the beginning of the chapter. "Sustainable development is meeting the needs of the present without compromising the ability of future generations to meet their own needs." It turns out that knowing there is help available from experts and professionals, in a variety of landscape garden disciplines, is a revelation to many people. Bringing them together, or just gathering some of their knowledge, can make all the difference in the success of your gardening endeavors.

The fact that IPM and sustainable landscaping, doing what's right for the environment, is the *common-sense,* moral, and ethical thing to do is not the surprise. The surprise is realizing that it is just plain *common courtesy* to your family, your friends, and your neighbors.

Monarch butterfly on sweet alyssum. (Photo by BHamms/Shutterstock)

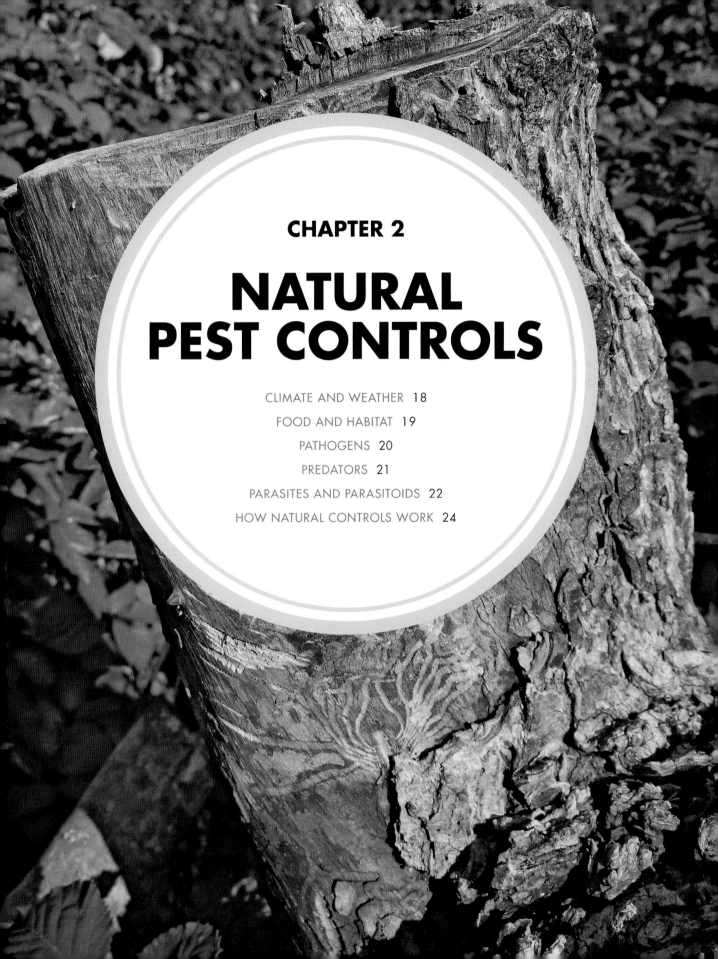

CHAPTER 2

NATURAL PEST CONTROLS

n this chapter, we look at the balance of nature and some of the fundamental ways in which living organisms control their own populations as well as populations of other living organisms. This aspect of sustainable landscaping is especially important, because we want to create habitat for wildlife, especially natural enemies. Obviously, when we look at all living organisms, we are including that subset of organisms we regard as "pests." Therefore, included in this chapter is an examination of truly natural pest control— pest control that occurs in nature without any prompting from humankind. We humans have disturbed this great system and must now learn how to reestablish its effects using sustainable landscape practices. As a sustainability guideline, we regularly say we will use any methods that meet our criteria of least toxic, sustainable over the short and long term, and most cost-effective.

Many of the microenvironments in which pest problems occur today are at least partially human-made or controlled, but the biological principles at work are still dictated by nature. Thus, understanding the natural principles discussed here will aid you tremendously in managing pest problems. Furthermore, many of the concepts in this chapter are critical to the development of a successful IPM program, the subject of the next chapter.

Many animal and plant populations are capable of expanding very rapidly. For example, crabgrass (*Digitaria* spp.) can produce 2,000 seeds per square foot in a single season. The common housefly can lay 600 eggs, which mature in about six days in hot weather. Given that reproductive rate, over the course of one summer, one original pair of flies could eventually lead to a layer of flies thousands of feet thick around the entire planet.

This has never happened, of course, because insects, like all other animal and plant populations, are under natural controls. The most important controls are climate and weather, food and habitat, pathogens (disease-causing organisms), predators, parasites, and parasitoids. We now examine each of these factors in turn.

> **TIP** If a plant is constantly being attacked by an insect or other pest species, it is best in the long run to remove the infested plant and replace it with a species or variety that is resistant to the insects and diseases common in your area.

CLIMATE AND WEATHER

Climate is the long-term overview of temperature and humidity changes in a region; weather is the local and short-term variation in climate. Extremes of heat, cold, rainfall, dew, or fog can limit a living population and influence its seasonal distribution. For example, whether the tomato hornworm (shown at left) is a pest in your area may be a function of climate, as warm summers favor the hornworm. But the weather in a given year—wet or

The head on this larval tomato hornworm, *Manduca sexta*, is on the right, but the horn on the left also appears to be the head, which misleads predators. (Photo courtesy of Beth Sands)

dry—will determine whether the hornworm breaks out early or late in the season, and, to some extent, how large the outbreak is.

The development of all insects, within certain upper and lower limits, is tied to temperature variations. Warm weather speeds maturation from larvae to adult; cool weather retards it. Thus, weather can influence how quickly a population builds. Green bottle flies illustrate this well. As long as there is ample food, the flies can progress from egg to adult and be ready to mate and lay new eggs in as few as six days if the temperature is over 95°F (35°C). This means that in the summertime, a generation can easily mature in the garbage can between refuse collections without the householder being aware of it, particularly if garbage collection occurs only once a week.

FOOD AND HABITAT

Food and habitat can also be important limiting factors upon the growth of a pest population. It is obvious that without food, no organism can survive. Yet when confronted with a pest problem, it is not always so obvious that limiting the pest's access to food can be the simplest nontoxic method of control.

"It has been our experience, and the experience of many environmentally conscious gardeners, that toxic pesticides are rarely, if ever, needed in a home garden."

There are many pest control tactics that are based on the premise that food is a limiting factor. For example, placing barriers around the stems of new transplants can protect them from cutworm damage. Transplants, at this early stage in their development, have stems that are still tender and succulent. As the plant matures, the barrier can be removed because the stem is no longer suitable food for cutworms. Barriers are important tools, often underutilized due to the easy availability of

HOW THE NUTRIENT BALANCE CAN ATTRACT PESTS

The nutrient balance within a plant may affect the selection of habitat by plant-feeding insects. Deciduous-tree insects, such as the aphid, may go through two population peaks each season. These correspond to the periods when nitrogen levels are highest in the foliage. The first peak occurs in spring when the leaves unfold; the second comes in fall when the leaves are ready to drop. The insects need the nitrogen to form new tissue and produce young. It is important to bear this in mind when you use quick-release, synthetic, nitrogen-containing fertilizer, because you may unintentionally encourage aphids and other nitrogen-loving pests. Compost, compost tea, and organic and slow-release fertilizers release nitrogen at a slow, even rate, so there is no nitrogen-rich flush of new growth. It is this lush and succulent growth that is favored by most insects and plant pathogens.

pesticides. It has been our experience, and the experience of many environmentally conscious gardeners, that toxic pesticides are rarely, if ever, needed in a home garden. Remember that garden design criteria should be more about how the garden *works* than how the garden *looks*. It usually turns out that if the design works, then the garden looks good, too.

To a pest, availability of habitat is as important as food. For example, in some areas of California, the ash aphid *(Prociphilus fraxinifolii)* is a common pest on Modesto ash trees. For reasons that are not entirely clear, the aphids' preferred habitat is the sucker growth around the base of the tree as well as suckers that grow from the trunk within the inner tree canopy. When these suckers are pruned away, the remaining aphid population may be so small as to be rarely noticed.

On the other hand, if the main outer branches are pruned severely in such a way as to encourage rapid, extensive sucker growth in the canopy, the pest problem may become severe. The aphids will curl up in the leaves and shower honeydew on cars and sidewalks beneath the trees. (Honeydew is a sticky substance derived from the sap of the tree and excreted by the aphids. It is as harmless to animals and plants as maple syrup, but the mold that grows on it may harm the finish on vehicles.)

PATHOGENS

The effect of disease-causing pathogens on human populations over the centuries has been chronicled in *Plagues and Peoples* (Anchor Press/Doubleday, 1976), in which William McNeill writes, "One can properly think of most human lives as caught in a precarious equilibrium between the microparasitism of disease organisms and the macroparasitism of large-bodied predators, chief among which have been other human beings." Overpopulation, leading to resource depletion, malnutrition, and competition for habitat, has always led to disease and war,

and clearly this model was well worked out in the plant and animal kingdoms before humans evolved.

That plants and animals commonly die of disease without human intervention is obvious to gardeners (see the drawing below). It is the basis for the folk pest control recipe for grinding up sick or dead insects and spraying the bug juice to spread the pathogens (microorganisms that cause disease) and kill more pest insects. However, spraying homemade bug juice around your house may not be a good idea, as some microorganisms and fungi found on the dead bodies of insects are pathogenic to humans and might get into the "juice." But the idea of using microbes that cause disease in plants and insects to control pests is not a bad one. A number of such microbial products are available commercially. They are examined in

THE WAYS IN WHICH PATHOGENS INJURE PLANTS

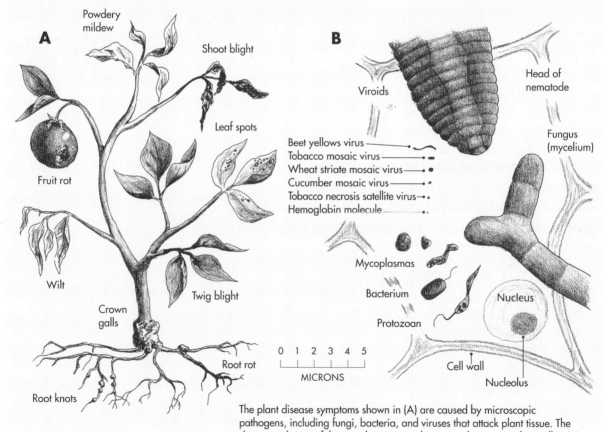

The plant disease symptoms shown in (A) are caused by microscopic pathogens, including fungi, bacteria, and viruses that attack plant tissue. The shapes and sizes of these pathogens are shown in relation to a plant cell in (B).

Redrawn from *Plant Pathology* Agrios, 1978.

detail in Chapter 8 and are mentioned throughout the book where they are applicable as controls for specific pests.

PREDATORS

Agricultural entomologist Carl Huffaker said it best: "When you destroy the natural enemies, you inherit their work." Once you are aware of the tremendous amount of work that natural enemies do for you, and do it for free no less, you are likely to do what you can to protect them and help ensure their survival.

Predators are often critical in the suppression of natural populations of animals and plants. Together with pathogens and parasitoids, they make up the fascinating study of biological control, discussed in greater detail in Chapter 4.

For the purposes of this book, predators, which can be mammals, arthropods, or microorganisms such as nematodes (see the drawing on the facing page), are defined as free-living, general feeders. Predators may eat a single prey at a meal, as do peregrine falcons when they feed on pigeons or coyotes when they eat mice. Or they may consume many individuals, as does the convergent lady beetle (*Hippodamia convergens*).

Predatory insects in the larval (worm, grub, or nymph) stage often must consume several prey to attain maturity. Therefore, predator adults usually lay their eggs near populations of their prey, where the hatching young have a good chance of obtaining adequate food. Syrphid flies lay their eggs near aphid colonies so that their maggot larvae can eat aphids and grow. You can sometimes discover their eggs when examining small groups of aphids. Look for a white egg lying near the aphids, but not within the group.

> **TIP** Selecting plants that beneficials use as alternative and supplemental food sources should be part of your garden design or redesign. This will attract and keep beneficials in your garden when pest numbers are too low to support a healthy population of beneficials.

Spiders are an exception to this rule, however. They are among the most important predators of insects, and their role in controlling insect pests is often underappreciated by humans. Rather than lay eggs near prey populations, many web-building spiders establish themselves in an environment in which their prey is likely to encounter them by accident. For example, one spider species likes to construct its webs over the holes of inverted flowerpots. Insects emerging from pupation in the soil fly toward the light and are caught by the spider as they come through the hole. Other spiders hunt by night, stalking their prey. Chinese farmers move bundles of stalks into newly planted fields in order to repopulate the growing plants with spiders. Spiders can live a long time with very little food and will resort to cannibalism when food becomes scarce. They commonly drift into the garden by extending

(Photo by Brian Stone thenatural/stone .blogspot.com)

FLYING VERSUS NONFLYING PREDATORS

The problem with flying predators such as lady beetles as pest control agents is that they frequently skim off the top of an abundant pest population and then move on without providing sufficient pest suppression. In enclosed environments such as screened greenhouses, however, their effectiveness can be substantial. We have had success with nonflying predators, such as lacewing larvae pictured here, in landscape situations. Predatory mites may also be used successfully, out of doors, to control pest mites and thrips. Such organisms can be purchased from commercial sources or attracted to and raised in the garden by planting plants the beneficials need to survive. Leaving small populations of pests in the garden provides a constant food source that will keep beneficials nearby.

a strand of silk into the air until it is long enough to catch the wind and carry them off on the breeze. This mode of distribution is called "ballooning." Spiders are precious: finding out how to encourage them can be important for keeping pest populations within tolerable bounds.

PARASITES AND PARASITOIDS

The difference between parasitoids, which are parasite-like organisms, and parasites is that parasitoids kill their hosts whereas parasites do not. Hence, parasitoids provide more effective pest control. An example of an internal parasite is the ubiquitous pinworm *(Enterobius vermicularis)*, a common pest of young children. While the symptoms are annoying and in severely malnourished children may have serious consequences, they often come and go unnoticed and are not thought of as causing a serious affliction. Parasites cannot regulate a pest population, but they can debilitate it and slow down its growth rate. There are many mite species that fit this category. They are difficult to detect, but widely present on many insects and other organisms.

Parasitoids are the unsung heroes of naturally occurring insect pest control. Because they often are so tiny, their presence is generally not recognized and their effect is undervalued. They frequently have no common names, and their scientific names are long and difficult to pronounce and spell, so it is often hard to remember them even when they are noticed. We discuss them here at slightly greater length than predators because of their importance and the fact that they are generally not well-known.

"Parasitoids are the unsung heroes of naturally occurring insect pest control."

Many parasitoids are members of the insect order Hymenoptera, along with bees and wasps. Indeed, they look like minute wasps and are called miniwasps. Parasitoids often provide good control of an insect population, even when the pest is present at very low densities, because many parasitoids are restricted in the number of species they can attack. Thus, they are called host-specific, which is, however, a relative term. Some parasitoids attack one or just a few species that are closely related. Others are restricted to a genus, or a larger group, within a family. Seldom is the host range of a parasitoid as wide as that of a predator. For example, many lady beetles feed on certain pest groups, like aphids, mites, scales, and others. There is no one species of lady beetle that will feed on all of these. There are other lady beetles that eat molds growing on the surface of leaves, and nectar and pollen from flowers and extrafloral nectaries.

The advantage of host-specific parasitoids is that when they do find a population of the pest, they attempt to kill every last one they encounter. The adult parasitoid

The adult syrphid fly, also called the hover or flower fly, lays eggs near an aphid colony so its larvae can easily find aphids to eat. The adults feed on flowers and are obvious in their hovering, which is very different from the bees that they mimic. (Photo by Peter Cristofono © 2012)

aggressively searches for prey. Unless it is confined to a cage with the pests, however, it never finds every last one. There are always a few prey that escape the parasitoid or wander in from outside the immediate area. This is not necessarily a bad thing. These prey reproduce and maintain enough of a population to ensure that the beneficial parasitoids have something to eat; otherwise, the parasitoids would perish. Under ideal conditions, populations of parasitoid and prey rise and fall in natural cycles, just like local populations of coyotes and rabbits, for example.

As shown in the drawing below, a common parasitoid life cycle starts with an adult female miniwasp laying her egg in or on another insect. Various parasitoids lay their eggs at various stages of the host's development. For example, one parasitoid lays its eggs in the eggs of the elm leaf beetle, another lays its eggs in the pupal (cocoon) stage. These parasitoids do not attack any other insect species; hence, they are species-specific and stage-specific biological controls.

Parasitoids such as those in the family Aphelinidae may feed upon and kill several aphids while selecting the one in which to lay an egg. They operate like predators, wounding the host with an egg-laying stinger without depositing an egg. They then feed on this wound, killing their host. This is called host-feeding.

Some parasitoids lay many eggs in or on the body of the host; others lay only one. Either way, the eggs develop into maggot-like larvae that begin to eat away at the prey and sooner or later cause its death. After killing the host, the larva of the miniwasp changes into a pupa. Aphid parasitoids may do

this within the body of the aphid. These dead, parasitized aphids can be spotted easily among a colony of living ones because they are usually stiff, shiny, and of a slightly different color than the live ones.

Other parasitoids may leave the dead host to spin a cocoon nearby. Within the pupal case, the insect changes, or metamorphoses, from a maggot-like form to a wasp-like adult form, as a caterpillar changes to a butterfly. In some species of parasitoids, the newly emerged female adults must find males to mate with before they can lay fertile eggs, starting the cycle again; with others, mating is unnecessary, and with still others, males are unknown or are rarely found. We offer further details on these beneficial insects in Chapter 5.

For the layperson, the only clue that these fascinating natural controls exist may be the sight of a dead insect with tiny pinholes in it where the parasitoids have emerged. This is frequently seen in aphids and scales. Sometimes, too, a child will put

PARASITOIDS OF INSECTS

Parasitoids attack their hosts by laying eggs on or inside a specific developmental stage of the insect: egg, larva, pupa, or adult. For example, *Tetrastichus galerucae* (A) lays its egg inside the egg stage of the elm leaf beetle, where it hatches and eats the beetle embryo. *Aphidius* species parasitoids (B) lay their eggs inside the adult stage of aphids. Each egg develops into a larva, which eats the aphid from the inside, metamorphoses into an adult, cuts a hole in the dead aphid's body, and then emerges (C). You can recognize a parasitized aphid by its hard, shiny body and the hole in its posterior.

a caterpillar cocoon or other insect in a jar, only to find some quite different and unexpected insects inside the jar later. These are the natural enemies of the original specimen that have emerged as adults to search for prey.

HOW NATURAL CONTROLS WORK

"If natural controls are so great, why aren't they working?" you may well ask if you are battling some damaging or annoying pest. The answer is that natural controls do work, all the time. In fact, the number of species of plant-feeding insects is so great, and the number of individuals in each species so large, that if most of these herbivores were not under good natural control, they would have denuded the earth of plant life long ago, making their own further survival—along with ours— impossible. However, at certain times in certain places, specific insect, plant, or animal populations grow so large that they become a problem. Why?

One reason is that sometimes their predators and parasitoids cannot find them. For example, aphids, mealybugs, whiteflies, and spider mites can become a problem when plants are kept

indoors. If the house plants are set outdoors for a few days during warm weather, however, the natural enemies of the pests may find them and clean up the infestation.

All animal and herbaceous plant pest populations tend to fluctuate, rising and falling due to the natural controls we have just discussed (see the graph below). This fluctuation is particularly noticeable among insects. Occasionally, a native insect will become numerous enough outdoors during one or more seasons to cause aesthetic or economic damage. Then the outbreak will subside due to natural controls and the insect may hardly be noticed for a few or many years. Examples of

"It is the goal of sustainable landscape design, installation, and maintenance to bring wildlife back into urban landscapes."

insects that are famous for this kind of fluctuation are the southern pine beetle, eastern tent caterpillars, and caterpillars of the gypsy moth and California oak moth. These insects do have pathogens, parasitoids, and predators that usually keep them in check as long as the plants they live on are not routinely treated with broad-spectrum insecticides.

THE BALANCE OF POPULATIONS IN NATURE

Populations of all living organisms fluctuate in size over the short term. But over the long term—seasons or years— the average population size remains fairly stable.

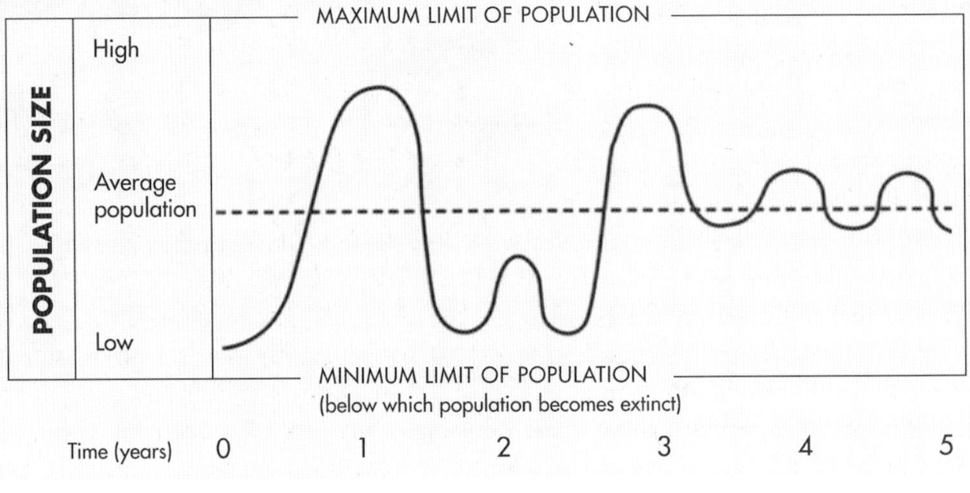

MAXIMUM LIMIT OF POPULATION

POPULATION SIZE

High

Average population

Low

MINIMUM LIMIT OF POPULATION
(below which population becomes extinct)

Time (years)   0   1   2   3   4   5

Even with these natural controls, however, the populations of herbivores periodically rise to great numbers. For example, a native shade-tree insect such as the California oak moth (see the photo at right) is capable of completely defoliating oak trees during the one or two seasons when its populations are high. If this happens on trees near the house or in other highly visible locations, people may become upset, either because they believe something is wrong if the tree isn't green or because they object to the sight of the caterpillars and their droppings. An infestation of this sort is hard to accept as a natural phenomenon.

Examining the California oak moth situation a little more, we see that the defoliation just described occurs in California's dry season, and thus reduces water loss through the leaves of these trees. Furthermore, the caterpillars process the leaves, which in many California native oak species are otherwise very slow to decompose. When the caterpillars eat the leaves, they leave behind their own droppings, a kind of "caterpillar manure" that releases the nutrients back to the tree when winter rains come. Thus, periodic defoliation of these native oaks may actually be more beneficial than harmful.

Similarly, deeper investigation into the rise and fall of other native animal pests usually reveals that these fluctuations are part of a natural cycle of events in their ecosystems. Consequently, we need to learn more about the ecological role these "pests" are playing and adjust our aesthetic opinions and reactions accordingly.

Another factor that may account for high pest populations on a particular plant is its greater genetic susceptibility to the pest than related strains or the plant's wild ancestors. "Old roses," for example, are far more disease-resistant than modern hybrid tea roses. In general, as traits that satisfy particular human desires and tastes are bred into vegetables,

Periodic outbreaks of the California oak moth, *Phryganidia Californica* family Dioptidae, can defoliate entire trees. This defoliation does not kill healthy trees and may even be beneficial by reducing water loss during dry summers. (Photo courtesy of Aaron Schusteff)

a number of traits that served to discourage insect attack may be eliminated. Strong oils, terpines, resins, and hairiness are examples of such traits. A similar loss of pest resistance may occur as ornamentals are bred for aesthetic characteristics. As the new variety was developed, little or no emphasis was placed on retaining the plant's resistance to insects, pathogens, and other pests. Thankfully, this practice is changing and plant breeders are again selecting for disease and insect resistance. We support traditional plant breeding and selection methods. We do not support the use of plants that are genetically modified organisms (GMOs), at this point in time, for two reasons. First, evidence that GMOs are safe and equal to traditionally bred plants in the long term is lacking. Second, GMO plants will inevitably breed with non-GMO plants

Elm bark beetle larval galleries (tunnels) are shown when the bark is removed. Elm bark beetle is the vector for the Dutch Elm disease fungus (*Ophiostoma ulmi*). (Photo by L.C. Benefield)

INTRODUCED PESTS

A native insect population may fluctuate from year to year, but the invasion of a foreign insect may result in high populations every year. Our common indoor cockroaches, the gypsy moth, the Japanese beetle, and the Mediterranean fruit fly are pests of exotic origin made familiar to nearly all citizens through first-hand experience or media attention. In these cases, the invading insect has usually left its most important natural enemies behind in its native area. Although in some cases predators and parasitoids of closely related insects may consume small numbers of the new invaders, the absence of specific controls usually permits the introduced species to reach population levels regarded as aesthetically or economically damaging. In the exotic pest's native range, it may not be well known because it is under good control naturally.

Other well-known examples of introduced pests are the pathogens that cause Dutch elm disease and chestnut blight; rapidly spreading plants such as dandelions, kudzu, and water hyacinth; and vertebrates like the English sparrow and the common rat and house mouse. In fact, as you will see throughout this book, many of our most serious pest problems arise through accidental—and occasionally deliberate but misguided—introductions of exotic species.

in the wild, resulting in genetic pollution in natural ecosystems.

Potential pest populations also may be encouraged, or their natural enemies discouraged, by attempting to grow a particular variety of plant in an environment not suited to it. It may simply be too hot, cold, wet, or dry for the plant compared to its native home. Stressed by the new environment, the plant may be more susceptible to insect attack or less able to overcome insect damage when it occurs. For example, a London plane tree (*Platanus acerifolia*) planted in an unfavorable site is far more susceptible to anthracnose disease caused by the fungus *Gnomonia platani* than it would be if it were planted in a more favorable setting.

In horticultural plantings, species from many continents are often combined in close proximity, frequently with insufficient consideration of their individual native requirements. Even less thought is given to the requirements of the natural enemies of potential pests of the plant species selected. For example, free water from sprinklers, dew, and other sources during dry periods, and nectar and pollen from shallow-throated flowers, are required by parasitic insects, particularly the tiny ichneumonid wasps that parasitize many caterpillar species. Without this liquid and protein, the lives of many natural pest enemies are shortened, allowing pest numbers to rise. Given the wide lack of attention to the importance of natural controls and the details of how they relate to specific pest problems, it is not surprising that a stable mix of insect and other wildlife populations is rarely achieved in human-contrived landscapes. It is the goal of sustainable landscape design, installation, and maintenance to bring wildlife back into urban landscapes.

Finally, the methods used to deal with pests may themselves cause the problem to become worse, or they may create entirely new problems. These undesirable results of human actions—which we hope to help you avoid—are discussed throughout the book under specific pest problems.

CHAPTER 3

INTRODUCTION TO INTEGRATED PEST MANAGEMENT (IPM)

In Chapter 2, we looked at some of the ways in which various organisms manage and control each other and themselves in nature. That understanding will help you immeasurably as you approach specific pest problems in your garden. Chapter 2 was also important in showing you that many of the techniques used in Integrated Pest Management, an increasingly familiar term, are in fact nothing new at all. We are simply borrowing and adapting processes that have existed in nature since time immemorial. With that in mind, we introduce the concept of Integrated Pest Management, the cornerstone of this book.

WHAT IS IPM?

Integrated Pest Management (IPM) is a decision-making systems approach to pest control that uses regular monitoring to determine if and when treatments are needed, and employs physical, mechanical, cultural, biological, and educational tactics to keep pest numbers low enough to prevent intolerable damage or annoyance. Least-toxic chemical controls are used as a last resort.

In IPM programs, treatments are not made according to a predetermined schedule; they are made only when and where monitoring has indicated that the pest will cause unacceptable economic, medical, or aesthetic damage. Treatments are chosen and timed to be most effective and least disruptive to natural pest controls.

IPM: THE REAL DEAL

The strategies for managing specific pests outlined later in this book are based on the IPM concept defined above. There are now many definitions of IPM (see www.ipmnet.org/IPMdefinitions/defineIII.html); in fact, there are 67 at this website alone. It is the decision-making process, and the emphasis on non-pesticidal controls, that separates true IPM from a "greenwashed" version. The *American Heritage Dictionary*, 4th ed., defines "greenwash" as "The dissemination of misleading information by an organization to conceal its abuse of the environment in order to present a positive public image."

IPM, developed initially for agriculture, provides a process for identifying and reducing the factors causing pest problems; it is also designed to determine whether the cost of a particular pest management action is worth the result. Determining economic damage to a crop, where you have yield amounts and marketplace returns against which to measure results, is relatively straightforward. But putting a dollar amount on the revulsion or fear caused by a particular organism or on the media-inspired need for a "perfect lawn" is much more difficult. You must ask yourself whether preventing the damage is worth exposing your family and pets to the potentially health-impairing chemicals in "conventional" pesticides, or, alternatively, whether you are willing to put the requisite time and effort into less-toxic alternatives.

"No animal in itself is a pest. The way each of us feels about a visitor determines whether the animal is welcome or not, whether it is a pet or a pest."

Clearly these are not straightforward questions, because both the costs and the benefits are harder to quantify than in traditional agriculture. Even in agriculture, the evaluation is becoming more difficult as costs that once were considered external to production—groundwater contamination, pesticide residues on and in food, regulatory requirements, educational activities, the purchase and use of safety equipment, occupational exposure to toxic materials—are beginning to be factored into the calculations.

The kinds of pest problems, the environments in which they occur, and the personal values and community standards of those experiencing the problems vary enormously and change over time. The best we can do in this book is introduce you to some evaluative criteria and sources of information that will help you make up your own mind about when pest control is warranted and which methods to use.

Ultimately, the decision about what is tolerable, either in terms of pest numbers or exposure to potentially hazardous materials, is yours. These decisions are not so very different from deciding whether you want to allow smoking in your house or whether riders in your car must buckle their seat belts.

PEST OR GUEST?

The question of when an organism becomes a pest is central to IPM. In *Unbidden House Guests* (Hartnack Publishing, 1943), the brilliant, if eccentric, German pest management specialist Hugo Hartnack eloquently and sometimes humorously points out the thin line between when a specific creature is a valued member of the household and when it is despised. For example, the pet mouse is adored, but as a pantry visitor it is abhorred. Mealworms are purchased to feed tropical fish, but when they are found in the flour they precipitate a domestic crisis. In Hartnack's words, "No animal in itself is a pest. The way each of us feels about a visitor determines whether the animal is welcome or not, whether it is a pet or a pest, or, in the old Latin words, *hospes* or *hostis*, a guest or a foe."

A number of classic cases demonstrate how the same species may be regarded differently by various groups of people in the same society. This can precipitate lawsuits, legislative intervention, and media attention. For example, some years ago, we were consultants to the National Park Service and learned of a situation where the politically powerful and wealthy members of a suburban golf club adjacent to one of the parks petitioned the park to undertake mosquito control in a stream that bordered both properties. Club members complained that they were being bitten while pursuing their favorite recreational activities.

The Park Service proposed solving the problem by killing mosquito larvae in the stream with the microbial insecticide *Bacillus thuringiensis*, toxic only to mosquitoes and blackflies. When local farmers and low-income residents in the area learned about the plan, however, they strongly and loudly opposed it and threatened to sue. Mosquito larvae were the primary source of food for the fish local residents caught to supplement their diet. Although Park Service personnel were conscientious in their choice of the least-toxic method of pest control, and were trying their best to be sensitive to the needs of all parties involved, the incident received much local press coverage that did not always cast the Park Service in the most favorable light.

It is plain from this and many other examples that we will discuss later in the book that there are few intrinsic characteristics that universally distinguish "good" from "bad" species of plants and animals. It is the human social context in which the organisms exist that determines whether a population is considered a pest. Moreover, it is almost always the size of that population, not merely the presence of an individual organism, which matters.

IS THE DAMAGE TOLERABLE?

Whether or not an organism is viewed as a pest is really an issue of whether its damage or annoyance is considered tolerable. Thus, when someone reports to us that they have observed a "pest" in their environment, our first impulse is to ask, "How bad is the damage?" or, "How badly are you bothered by it?" As we just mentioned, it is important to realize that there is almost always some tolerable level of a pest population—even with organisms, such as rats, that are known to pose medical and public health risks. For most pest problems you are likely to experience, complete elimination of the pest is neither economically nor biologically feasible. Even if it were, the cost of eradication in terms of human health and environmental contamination would be prohibitive. Thus, the question of how large of a pest population can or should be tolerated is a very important and practical one.

For example, the definition of what an area or site is used for is critical to setting a tolerance level or treatment threshold. Turfgrass in a median on an interstate highway and turfgrass on a golf green are both grassy areas, but the definition of the site

PEST TOLERANCE

We have come across what some would call rather extreme examples of pest tolerance. We saw aesthetic damage by an aphid population on a hedge in Berkeley, California. It was an obvious and very large infestation, but nobody seemed to care. The hedge surrounded a house on a corner and was high, at about 5 ft. The infestation was already damaging the hedge, which could easily have been treated with a water spray or a soap-and-water solution. This would have been easy, cheap, and sustainable. But from our viewpoint it was a good food source for many beneficials. So we did nothing and watched the population crash after a few weeks, primarily from lady beetle predation. The hedge recovered shortly after the aphid population crashed.

and its use is what leads us to determine the weed tolerance. The weed tolerance on a golf green is essentially zero. It is an athletic turf and the game requires that the green be as uniform as possible. At the other extreme is the interstate median, where the turfgrass need only be drive-by-scenic. How many lawn weeds can you see driving by at 65 mph, with your eyes on the road to boot?

In between these extremes we helped eliminate the use of broadleaf weed herbicides in a city park. The primary park users were toddlers and lawn bowlers as well as some ducks and geese. Parents were appropriately concerned and complained about the use of herbicides around such young children. The park gardeners wanted the park turf to look like the bowling greens, an unrealistic expectation. We suggested that they think of the park lawns as a meadow and weeds as wildflowers. They took to the suggestion immediately. By redefining the park turfgrass as a grassy meadow, the need for herbicides instantly disappeared.

TYPES OF INJURY OR DAMAGE CAUSED BY PESTS

The broad categories of pest injury or damage include economic damage, medical damage, aesthetic damage, and nuisance problems.

ECONOMIC DAMAGE

Economic damage is most easily assessed in agriculture, forestry, and similar occupational settings where pest activity affects the production of economic goods. Examples in and around the home might include boards that are so termite-eaten they must be replaced, cabbage seedlings that wilt and die from cabbage maggot infestations in the roots, a valuable wall hanging that has been destroyed by clothes moths, or an old elm in your front yard that dies from Dutch elm disease, reducing the value of your property.

MEDICAL DAMAGE

Even in the United States, there remain serious pathogens that can be transmitted to humans by common wildlife. For example, the bubonic plague bacillus can be passed from certain wild rodents to humans, cats, and domestic rats via species of fleas that carry the bacteria or through the coughs or sneezes of infected animals. Ground squirrels, chipmunks, and wild rabbits can also pass plague bacilli to humans.

The spirochete that causes Lyme disease is passed from wild mice, lizards, and deer to cats, dogs, farm animals, and humans. In this case, the disease vector (the organism that transmits the pathogen causing the disease) is a tick. Mosquitoes can transmit encephalitis and may pick up malaria brought in by travelers from areas of the world where it is common. Even the ubiquitous pigeon can spread the causal agents of histoplasmosis (an internal fungus infection), toxoplasmosis (an affliction of the central nervous system), and a host of other nasty pathogens. As you can see, the potential for passing pathogens to humans and domestic animals may be reason enough to control certain otherwise desirable wildlife species.

AESTHETIC DAMAGE

Aesthetic damage occurs when the mere presence of a plant or animal causes an undesirable change in the appearance of something. What constitutes an undesirable change is highly personal—one person

The boxelder bug *(Leptocoris trivittatus)* is an example of a harmless organism that is nonetheless considered a pest. Its tendency to aggregate en masse on the exterior of homes near female boxelder trees, where it feeds on the seeds, makes some people fearful of it despite its harmlessness. (Photo © Melinda Fawver/Shutterstock)

en masse have led people to fear large numbers of even innocuous organisms. We have observed that a small infestation of tent caterpillars can cause near hysteria in some people.

Often it is the fear of future damage that causes concern. For example, although most aphids feed on plants only in one or a few closely related genera, some people worry that the aphids on their maple tree (genus *Acer)* will move onto their roses (genus *Rosa)* and damage the blossoms. Learning about the biology and ecology of the pest in question usually relieves these fears.

Sometimes the aesthetic problem is a product of the animal's activity. A dusty spider web along the ceiling (a sign that the web is no longer in use), aphids' honeydew drips on a parked car, or scales on a tree are all examples. These problems can be solved by cleaning away the offending evidence but leaving the animal alone. That way the spider can continue to catch houseflies and other indoor pests, and the aphids can remain as food for the predators that keep the aphids and other plant-sucking insects under control.

In extreme cases, the fear engendered by the mere sight of insects can turn an aesthetic problem into a medical one, called entomophobia. This

may be repelled by a head of cabbage with signs of insect damage on its outer leaves, whereas another finds it a welcome indication that the food is probably not covered with poisonous pesticide residues.

Sometimes the chief aesthetic complaint is the appearance of the pest itself. Insects and spiders often fall victim to this aesthetic judgment. Even though most spiders can be counted on to kill insect pests such as garbage flies in the house and plant-eating pests in the garden, many people kill them on sight simply because they find their appearance unappealing. Another example is the boxelder bug (see the photo above), which some people simply don't like to look at despite the fact that it causes negligible damage to plants.

In some cases, people are frightened because insects like the boxelder bug are found massed together on walls, under foundation plantings, or in other locations. Perhaps movies of insects attacking

FEAR OF NATURE

Concerns about aesthetic damage are in part a reflection of two prevalent attitudes in our society: the perception that nature is messy and needs to be cleaned up by humans in order to look beautiful, and a fear or lack of understanding of the natural world. For example, we don't like to see a leaf with a hole in it or a damaged bud, yet the plant itself may easily tolerate that damage without any measurable or noticeable loss of health. Many pest problems affecting ornamental plants fall into this category.

BURROWING ANIMALS

Rabbits and gophers can ruin many vegetables. In home gardens these losses may be tolerable. If such damage is common, it may be a good idea to plant extra plants to allow for this type of loss, particularly when space is not a major limiting factor. Another option is to use barriers, such as root cages made from hardware cloth, to keep gophers and other burrowing animals away from roots. Root cages can be extended above ground and combined with bird netting to exclude rabbits, mice, rats, voles, birds, and other animals intent on eating your garden plants. It seems to be a truism that animals find your garden produce ripened to perfection a day or two before you do.

Wire cages around garden plants protect them from rabbits and other herbivores. (Photo by Juliette Wade/GAP)

condition is surprisingly common. Public health personnel, who must sort out the real from the imaginary, recount many examples of people who complain that their houses are infested with insects and that they are being attacked and bitten repeatedly. But careful sleuthing fails to turn up any offending organism. Luckily, fear of insects—like other phobias—can be cured. In one case, we were able to help someone overcome a mild case of entomophobia simply by giving her a paper we had written on the subject.

NUISANCE PROBLEMS

Because cities were created for humans with little thought given to the wildlife and domestic animals that colonize such areas, many annoying pest problems arise when these three groups of animals attempt to coexist. Examples are fungus gnats that breed in houseplant soil, sparrows or swallows that nest in eaves and befoul buildings, squirrels that dig up lawns to bury nuts, and free-roaming dogs that knock over garbage cans and defecate on the sidewalk. These organisms or the damage they cause may not be terribly destructive, but if you feel the nuisance strongly enough, you may take considerable pains to manage the problem.

Plants can become nuisances, too. For example, a generally desirable ornamental plant or vegetable may tend to "take over" and establish itself everywhere. This often happens in mild climates with calendulas, nasturtiums, and chard. Seedling trees may pop up in your vegetable bed or lawn, as is often the case with elms, boxelders, and maples.

DETERMINING TOLERABLE DAMAGE OR INJURY LEVELS

Total eradication of pest organisms is virtually impossible, and as mentioned earlier, it is usually undesirable because it often spells the demise of the pests' natural enemies and can upset the broader ecological balance. Although there are situations in which eradication is warranted, such as with newly invading species, it is usually better to determine the level of pest presence or pest-related damage you can tolerate without harm to your health and plants. This is called the injury or damage level.

Determining this level is a three-step process. First, you decide how much aesthetic, medical, or economic damage can be tolerated. Second, you find out how large the pest population can grow before it causes that level of damage. Third, you establish a treatment level that keeps the pest population small enough so it does not cause an unacceptable level of damage.

We can apply these three steps to the management of a familiar household pest: the common cat flea. Let's assume that your cat (or dog) is scratching noticeably. You begin combing the cat with a flea comb once a day, and you count the fleas you flick into a bowl of soapy water. You make a note of how many fleas you catch each day. After a week or so, it gets harder to find fleas, and the cat scratches much less. Now you comb every second or third day. Eventually you switch to once-a-week or once-a-month combing, still keeping track of the fleas. Suddenly, a comparison of your recent flea catch with the earliest counts shows the infestation is recurring. The time has come to increase combing frequency and possibly institute other measures.

In this example, the amount of scratching the cat was doing and the number of fleas you removed with the comb constituted the damage or injury level. But you might also define the injury level as the impact the fleas have on you. As with all injury levels, this varies from pet to pet, household to household, season to season, and owner to owner. Some pet owners ignore almost constant scratching by their pets; others become alarmed at a mere indication the pet is itching. Some people hardly notice a flea bite or two, others scratch persistently afterward or feel discomfort after one bite.

In the cat example, the daily combing provides an approximate count of fleas. These numbers serve as a damage index and can suggest a level of fleas the cat can tolerate without much suffering. Efforts to eliminate all the fleas, however, may be more hazardous than helpful. Even if you do get rid of the fleas completely, others will ride in on the pet unless the pet is kept permanently indoors. And even that may not prevent humans from carrying in fleas.

The comb in the example functions much like a trap that allows you to approximate the flea population and ascertain whether it is rising or falling. This knowledge is essential to determining whether your control methods are working. A variety of traps for the same purpose are available commercially for fleas. The use of monitoring traps is discussed in later chapters, along with the specific problems for which they are appropriate. In many cases, however, using traps is not necessary or even possible. Instead, you can learn to correlate numbers of a given pest with levels of damage by regularly observing pest activity or damage and recording this information mentally or on paper. This process is called monitoring.

MONITORING THE PEST: RECORDS, TOOLS, TIMING, STRATEGIES

Being good at noticing things is critical to pest management. You particularly need to observe the connections among various elements of the environments in which you are working or living. You must become aware of how your own activities affect the other organisms, desirable and troublesome, with which you share your indoor and outdoor space.

Monitoring can vary from extremely casual to statistically strict, depending on how serious you feel the problem is. The levels of effort, listed from casual to strict, are as follows:

1. Hearsay or other people's casual observation
2. Casual looking with no record keeping
3. Casual looking with written observations
4. Careful inspection with written observations
5. Regular written observations and quantitative descriptions
6. Quantitative sampling on a regular basis
7. Statistically valid quantitative sampling

"When serious pest problems are encountered, it is essential to keep written or electronic records rather than rely entirely on memory."

The idea is that you match the level of monitoring effort to the importance of the problem. Levels 1 and 2 are the most common and least helpful; levels 3, 4, and 5 are most useful in the house or garden. Usually you start at level 3 and progress to level 5 only if you think the problem will become serious or recur. Level 6 is appropriate to situations like a greenhouse, where you may be releasing beneficial insects and need to know where pest "hot spots" are and how effective beneficial insects have been in preying upon and controlling the pests.

TO CATCH A PEST

The difference in hours of activity between humans and pests is one of the common causes of misidentified pests. A great deal of effort may be expended with no reward. For example, when we started a garden for students at the University of California at Berkeley in 1970, we regularly blamed the substantial damage to our spring greens on snails and slugs, two pests common in our area. We were at our wits' end because no amount of hand removal of these pests could make a dent in the problem. The lettuce was being eaten to the nub.

In this particular instance, our early-evening examinations with a flashlight proved insufficient. Finally, one adventurous student took her sleeping bag to the garden and stayed there overnight. In the early morning she found birds raiding the vegetable patch with a vengeance. Our response was to place netting over the beds, which solved the problem immediately.

Often, instead of recording numbers, you can use estimates such as "small," "medium," or "large" to describe the extent of the problem and the size of the pest population. Whether you use numbers or estimates, the important things are to get out and assess the situation, to do so at regular intervals, and to make some record, no matter how informal, of what you see. When serious pest problems are encountered, it is essential to keep written or electronic records rather than rely entirely on memory.

Unfortunately, monitoring may be complicated by the fact that pests and people don't always keep the same hours. Pests may be just becoming active when you're going to bed. In fact, the survival of a pest species in close proximity to humans may be partially dependent on the fact that our daily schedules are dissimilar. For this reason, a flashlight is often one of the most valuable monitoring tools you can have.

Another useful monitoring tool is a magnifying glass or hand lens (see the photo below), as many pests and their natural enemies are difficult to see without enlargement. A lens that provides at least 5× enlargement is usually adequate, and a 15× lens allows you to distinguish among various mite species and other similarly small garden pests.

Don't forget a notebook and pencil for keeping records. You can also use the convenient Monitoring Record form on the facing page. Another option is to use a smartphone, tablet, or laptop computer to record your field observations on the spot and to enter "monitoring reminders" for areas that will need additional tracking. In the past, we have used phone features like voicemail, camera, video, email, voice recording, texting, and calendar programs and applications to record our observations and reminders. You can also use GPS and other mapping apps to record exact locations in parks, wildlands, and large landscapes.

Use plastic bags and/or small jars for holding specimens you want to examine more closely or have already identified.

Monitoring kit: digital camera, smart phone, hand lenses, field microscope, pruners (small and large), plastic bags, specimen bottles, collapsible trowel, rubbing alcohol, gardening multi-tool, and a carrier box. (Photo by Steven Ash)

MONITORING RECORD

Name of Plant	Date	Condition of Plant	Presence of Natural Enemies	Abundance of Pests	Abundance of Plant Damage	Weather	Management Activities	Evaluation Remarks

Monitoring information is an important and integral part of the IPM process. Entries don't need to be long or complex; simple entries, along with photos, can provide all the information you need.

If you want to get really sophisticated, you can buy an aspirator or small vacuum for collecting specimens. These and other tools are discussed at appropriate points throughout the book; they can be purchased from garden and horticultural supply houses online.

A maximum/minimum thermometer is another useful monitoring tool, because outdoor pests are greatly influenced by the weather. High temperatures may speed the development of certain pest populations or do just the opposite, causing them to go into a state of suspended activity (called *aestivation* in mammals and *diapause* in insects). An early or late freeze can affect the activity of pest organisms.

A wetter, or drier, than usual spring or late summer can have a tremendous impact on pests, especially insects and fungi. A rain gauge is helpful for monitoring rainfall and for planning watering activities. Is your expected seasonal rainfall greater than average or below average? More watering is needed during droughts, for example. Keep track of long-range weather forecasts, longer than seven days, to see if rain is expected soon, so that irrigation can be postponed if possible. It is always a little disconcerting to irrigate thoroughly and have it rain a day or two later. By reading the appropriate reference works recommended in this book and through careful observation, you can learn to anticipate these effects and put that knowledge to work in your management program.

MONITORING THE PEST: WHAT YOU SHOULD LOOK FOR

In one sense, the question of what to look for presents a "chicken-and-egg" dilemma: To know where to look for the pest you must know something about its biology and ecology. But to find out more about its biology and ecology, you need to know what the pest is. Which comes first? It depends on what you already know.

If you are reasonably certain what the pest is, do a web search and read about it. View online images to verify the pest's identity (two good sites for this are www.bugguide.net and www.amentsoc. org/insects/what-bug-is-this). This can also tell you more specifically what to look for when monitoring, if you don't know the precise identification. On the other hand, if the main thing you find is the pest's damage and not the pest itself, a sleuthing job is in order. Try to answer as many of these questions as are relevant to the problem.

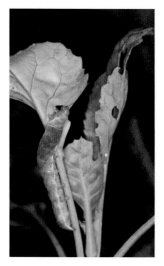

Noctuid caterpillar "cutworm" feeding on young cabbage plant at night. (Photo by Dave Bevan/GAP)

WHERE TO LOOK

The question of where to look for pests is not always as simple as it seems. It can depend on the time of day you look. For example, you can spot a cutworm or armyworm quite easily when it is munching in the open at night. But during the day, you would have to search in the first few inches of the soil or in the mulch closest to its last meal. A suddenly wilted plant can indicate root damage, requiring pulling of the plant in order to inspect the root mass for maggots, sow bugs, or another species. If no insects are present, it could be a fungus or other microscopic pests attacking the plant.

Ants, cockroaches, and certain other insects often like to lay eggs or nest near electrical devices, where the electric current generates warmth. Looking for them inside electric irrigation time clocks, HVAC units, outdoor switches and timers, and other electronic equipment may prove useful. Some years back, we were called in to check an irrigation system that was not functioning properly. We went to the time clock, which appeared normal from the outside, opened it, and found it filled with thousands of ants. The ants had caused an electrical short in the circuit board. When we took the timer in for repairs, we found out this is a fairly common occurrence. Just as you must learn about the impact of weather on a pest's activity, so you must learn where to look for the pest by reading about its life cycle and behavior and by making careful observations.

Evidence of Damage. If insects, weeds, or pathogens are visible, are they causing any apparent damage? If so, what is the nature of the damage (honeydew drippings on the sidewalk, holes in the rose petals, brown spots in the lawn)? Where is the damage found (on buds, leaves, stems)? What is the nature of the microenvironment (shady, damp, warm—near heater)? How many pests are present? This last piece of information might be recorded as precisely as "10 caterpillars on 1 ft. of branch 5 ft. off the ground on the north side of tree," or as generally as "many more than I can count along the branches."

If insects or other organisms are present but there is no apparent damage, record the date, site or plant, and presence of the organism. If you don't know the exact identity of the organism, use the general category—insect, for example—that best describes it. The entry might look something like this: "June 4—Many aphids on undersides of leaves of cucumber on fence by the driveway." Make a mental note to check again a few days later in hot weather, or in a week in cool weather, to see if the population has gotten larger or smaller and if natural enemies are present.

Presence of Natural Enemies. Do you have any sense of what feeds on the pest or competes with it? Can you tell how many types of enemies are there and where they live? If you were to look at the cucumber plant in the example above a week later, the aphids you had observed might have disappeared altogether, or their numbers might have fallen dramatically if they were eaten by natural enemies such as lady beetles or syrphid (hover) fly larvae. Or they might have been parasitized by miniwasps (discussed in detail on pp. 76–77). In this case, the dead aphids would have turned into bronze "mummies," indicating that a miniwasp is—or was—inside them. You would record any evidence of natural enemies, the date, whether or not the numbers of live aphids had dropped, and whether any damage was apparent.

Relevant Human Activities. What regular human activities might be encouraging the pest? For example, how are plants watered, pruned, and fertilized; how are wastes managed?

Other Potentially Contributing Activities. Are there any random or out-of-the-ordinary human or other events that might affect pest levels? For example, if you backed out of your garage and scraped some bark off your tree several months ago, it may explain why wood-boring insects are attacking it now.

Weather and Microclimate. How hot, cold, wet, dry, or windy is it? How long has it been that way? Are there specific local variations? For example, is it windier outside the fence where the problem occurs, or is there less air circulation there?

WHERE AND WHEN TO TREAT

So far we have talked about monitoring as a means of helping initially to identify a pest problem and its significance. However, the long-term success of any treatment depends on its being timed and located properly. Ongoing monitoring tells you whether this is happening and lets you know if you are achieving your pest control objectives.

In timing treatment activities, you often need to consider the life cycles and seasonal variations of both the pest and its natural enemies. As we saw in the flea example earlier, there is a time of year when fleas are more likely to be a problem. No

IT'S ALL IN THE TIMING

Correct timing is crucial in the application of the many newer, less-toxic commercial pesticide products, such as microbial controls and insect hormones. For example, *Bacillus thuringiensis*, known generically as BT and sold as Dipel® and other products, is a bacterial product originally found to be potent in controlling various caterpillars without harming other insects or mammals.

Caterpillars are the young of moths and butterflies, and the BT must be eaten by the caterpillar to be effective. Thus, applying the material when the moths are flying is worthless. Even during the caterpillar stage, the insect is more susceptible to BT at certain times than at others. This important biological/chemical tool is discussed further on pp. 138–143, along with other microbial pesticides and insect growth regulators. Other examples illustrating the importance of proper timing of treatments are presented throughout the book.

doubt you have noticed the same is true with other pests. But you must also note the generation time of a pest, the time it takes to grow from seed or egg to adult. You can do this through firsthand observation or by reading about the pest. Generation time

Waterlily aphid, *Rhopalosiphum nymphaeae*, colony on a pond-lily pad. Most of those in the foreground are mummies, parasitized by an *Aphidius* spp. braconid wasp. (Photo by Whitney Cranshaw, Colorado State University, Bugwood.org)

SPOT TREATMENT

In every pest situation there are likely to be locations where the problem is more severe or less severe. Outdoors, where it is not possible to eliminate pests completely because more pests can walk, fly, or be blown in, it is crucial to apply treatment specifically where the problem is worst. That way you leave a small, local, untreated residue of pests to feed the beneficial natural enemies of the pest, and the natural enemies are more likely to be around the next time the pest migrates into the area.

This very important basic approach—treating only the critical area—is known in IPM as *spot treatment*. This concept applies to cultural, physical, mechanical, biological, and, most important, chemical controls. Obviously, it is far more conservative than the traditional approach of blanketing an area with a commercial pesticide. If you try to spot-treat with a commercial pesticide, you may run into problems. You may have to buy a gallon of pesticide when all you need is a cup's worth. What do you do with the rest, often considered "hazardous household waste" because it poses a threat to the environment? Even if your town has hazardous-waste collection days, what can they do with it? It is tempting to use it up by spraying it around for preventive purposes. Sadly, this is often just what town or county agencies suggest. From an environmental point of view and from a pest control perspective, this is often the worst thing to do.

may be shorter or longer than the seasons, and this has a bearing on the treatment schedule.

Bagworms, for example, should be treated before they have constructed their bags. Similarly, Japanese beetles are treated most effectively when they are still grubs in the lawn rather than once they have become beetles and feed on the roses. Mosquitoes should be managed as larvae in their water source, not fogged after they emerge in the flying stage, as is still the practice in many commu-

"The long-term success of any treatment depends on its being timed and located properly."

nities. Soap-and-water treatments can be effective in reducing scale populations, but only if applied when young scales, called crawlers, are moving about on the plant. When predatory lady beetles are in the pupal stage, they are less vulnerable to soap-and-water sprays than when they are young larvae out on the leaves and actively eating aphids.

Where you apply management tactics is also important, and it, too, hinges on knowledge of the biology and ecology of the pest. Treatment should be applied only where the problem is most severe and your actions will have the greatest impact. To illustrate this, we return to the flea example. The immature fleas are not on the pet, they are in its bedding and in the general household environment. Therefore, tactics that focus exclusively on the pet are bound to be less effective in the long run.

Biological and environmental problems associated with spraying large quantities of pesticides over an area are discussed in Chapter 6. Fortunately, there are many alternative management options for pests. These are the subjects of the next chapter.

Close up of the bagworm, *Thyridopteryx ephemeraeformis*, full-grown larval stage. In late summer, it permanently attaches itself to the host tree on a small branch. (Photo by Eric R. Day, Virginia Polytechnic Institute and State University, Bugwood.org)

CHAPTER 4

PEST TREATMENT STRATEGIES AND TACTICS

A mulch layer keeps weeds down, mitigates soil temperature, and reduces evaporation from the soil surface. The mow strip, made with pavers, makes mowing the lawn edge easy and eliminates the need for an edger or weed whip to keep the edge neat. The mow strip also keeps the turfgrass from growing into the garden bed. (Photo by Virginia Small, courtesy of *Fine Gardening*)

Within the broad programs presented throughout this book for managing pests in the garden, we recommend specific treatment strategies and tactics. If Integrated Pest Management is to work for you, it is critical that you understand the terminology involved and approach your particular pest problem with a solid knowledge of all the strategies and tactics available.

It's not as imposing as it sounds. We're really talking about six strategies and fifteen tactics, and it is not necessary at this point for you to jot them down or commit them to memory. The purpose of this chapter is to give you an idea of what kinds of tools are in the IPM practitioner's toolbox. This knowledge will make you far more resourceful when it comes to selecting the least-toxic methods for solving a specific pest problem.

CRITERIA FOR SELECTING A TREATMENT STRATEGY

A strategy is an overall approach to a problem, such as using habitat management to suppress a pest. A tactic is a specific action or series of actions within that strategy. For a landscape example, draining water from a depression in a field or cleaning out a clogged gutter that is retaining rainwater are tactics that might be part of a habitat-management strategy for mosquitoes. A garden example is mulching. It moderates soil temperatures, conserves moisture, shades the soil preventing some weed seed germination, and provides hiding places for spiders, ground beetles, and other beneficials.

An examination of the ecosystem of which the pest is part, as well as careful consideration of the natural control processes discussed in Chapter 2, usually suggests a variety of strategies and tactics you might use to suppress the target pest population below the intolerable injury or damage level. The objective is to design a program that uses more than one strategy. In doing this, we suggest you choose strategies that meet the following criteria:

- Least disruptive of natural controls
- Least hazardous to human health
- Least toxic to nontarget organisms
- Least damaging to the garden and general environment
- Most likely to produce a permanent reduction of the pest population
- Easiest to carry out effectively
- Most cost-effective over the short and long terms

These are the criteria we have applied throughout the book in making treatment recommendations. Frequently, we also indicate why certain popular methods fall short of one or more of these criteria.

IPM IS PROACTIVE

Integrated Pest Management is proactive. The first objective of IPM is to design, or redesign, pests out of the system whenever possible and to take the action most likely to produce a permanent reduction of the pest population. Its second objective is to prevent pests from exceeding damage/action thresholds through monitoring, preventive measures, and least-disruptive pest management actions. In acute pest situations, IPM can treat the immediate problem and, with the information gathered, provide you with the knowledge and tools you need to be prepared for the pest's next appearance. This facilitates the redesign of the garden, whether it is replacing just a few plants or renovating the entire landscape. Always evaluate your program and adjust it to benefit desirable plants and other species and to discourage pests. Once you've established an IPM and sustainable landscape program, you can spend more time enjoying the garden instead of always battling pests.

IPM PROGRAM COMPONENTS AND THEIR INTERRELATIONSHIPS

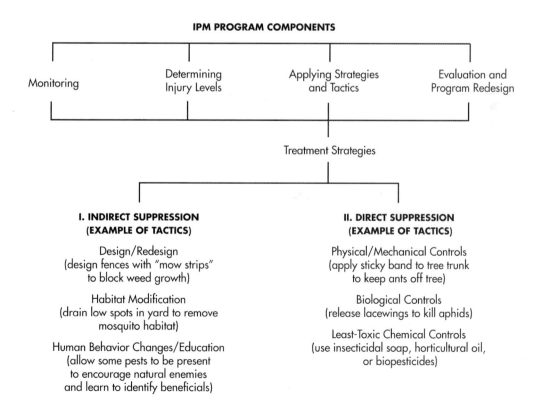

IPM PROGRAM COMPONENTS

Monitoring — Determining Injury Levels — Applying Strategies and Tactics — Evaluation and Program Redesign

Treatment Strategies

I. INDIRECT SUPPRESSION (EXAMPLE OF TACTICS)

Design/Redesign (design fences with "mow strips" to block weed growth)

Habitat Modification (drain low spots in yard to remove mosquito habitat)

Human Behavior Changes/Education (allow some pests to be present to encourage natural enemies and learn to identify beneficials)

II. DIRECT SUPPRESSION (EXAMPLE OF TACTICS)

Physical/Mechanical Controls (apply sticky band to tree trunk to keep ants off tree)

Biological Controls (release lacewings to kill aphids)

Least-Toxic Chemical Controls (use insecticidal soap, horticultural oil, or biopesticides)

THE MAJOR TREATMENT STRATEGIES AVAILABLE

There are many strategies available to the pest manager who has a broad perspective. We outline these strategies in the chart on p. 41 and provide many examples under specific pest discussions in later chapters. As you read through these options, bear in mind one of the most important tenets of IPM: For most pest management problems, combined strategies are more effective in the long run than any one strategy used by itself.

To give you an idea of how we have organized things, there are two broad treatment strategy categories: Category I, indirect suppression, and Category II, direct suppression. Within these categories are specific strategies, which we have given letter designations; under these are various tactics, which we have numbered.

We should also say in advance that a seemingly disproportionate amount of space in this chapter is devoted to one particular direct treatment strategy: biological control. We feel this reflects its relative importance in Integrated Pest Management.

TREATMENT CATEGORY I: INDIRECT SUPPRESSION OF PESTS

Within this category are three strategies: design/redesign of the garden and landscape, modification of the habitat, and changing human behavior.

STRATEGY A: DESIGNING/ REDESIGNING THE GARDEN AND LANDSCAPE

The purpose of this strategy is to "design the pest out" of the system.

Tactic 1. *Selection of plant species and/or structural features that resist pests, aid natural enemies, and support and enhance ecosystem diversity and processes; and the use of barriers that prevent the passage of pests.* Examples are plants resistant to disease or attractive to beneficials; permanent barriers of wire, concrete, wood, and so on; walkway materials that minimize compaction such as sawdust and wood shavings; and birdbaths to encourage insect-eating birds.

Tactic 2. *Use of landscape designs/ redesigns that promote the health of the host plant or animal; are appropriate to the weather, soil, minerals, water, energy resources, and systems (irriga-*

Nasturtiums interplanted with brussels sprouts. Nasturtiums can attract aphids away from other plants, and their flowers make an excellent addition to salads. (Photo by Leigh Clapp/GAP)

tion, waste management) at the site; and alter the microclimate to retard pests or enhance natural pest enemy populations. Examples include creating improved water infiltration by changing soil slopes or channeling rainfall to more appropriate locations, and replacing plants that have continual pest problems or whose fast and aggressive growth makes them weedy.

We use the word and concept of "redesign" because so often pest-free maintenance is not emphasized in the original designs of new landscapes, gardens, hardscapes, or garden structures. Professional landscape and building architects and designers are often woefully untrained in or insensitive to the maintenance implications of various designs. Where potential pest problems were not considered at the outset it usually means some redesigning must be done once the unanticipated difficulties surface. Realistically, the garden design is always in flux as you learn, decide on new plants, and respond to environmental changes from year to year. The garden, especially the food-producing garden, is and must be dynamic.

In some cases, it almost seems as though the pest problems were deliberately designed into the landscape. You still see wood porch stairs built in direct contact with the soil or very close to it—an open dinner invitation to termites. Even more frequently you see gardens where vegetables of the same kind are grown in the same area, have barren

IN PRAISE OF WILDNESS

Bare soil is an open invitation to weeds. And if all plants of the same kind are clustered together, it makes it easy for plant-specific pests to find new hosts and multiply. If all plant debris is cleaned away, there is no buffer against extremes of temperature at the soil surface and no hiding place for hunting spiders, lizards, and toads, all of which are important predators of insect pests. Beneficial parasitoids often pupate inside the remains of dead pests while the pest is still attached to the leaf on the plant. When this leaf grows old, it may fall to the ground with the parasitoid still in place inside the pest. When the fallen leaves are swept away, the parasitoids emerge far from where they can continue to help in the garden by parasitizing more insect pests.

Contrast this "neat and clean" garden design with the gardens of many indigenous peoples. In *Plants, Man and Life* (University of California Press, 1971), Edgar Anderson provides a vivid description of the gardens of Central American Indians. In the chapter entitled "Dump Heaps and the Origin of Agriculture," he writes:

The garden…was a small affair about the size of a small city lot in the United States. It was covered with a riotous growth so luxuriant and so apparently planless that any ordinary American or European visitor, accustomed to the puritanical primness of north European gardens, would have supposed (if he even chanced to realize that it was indeed a garden) that it must be a deserted one.

The garden was a vegetable garden, an orchard, a medicinal garden, a dump heap, and a bee yard. There was no problem of erosion though it was at the top of a steep slope; the soil surface was practically all covered and apparently would be during most of the year . . . . In addition to the waste from the house, mature plants were being buried in between the rows when their usefulness was over . . . . Plants of the same sort were so isolated from one another by intervening vegetation that pests and diseases could not readily spread from plant to plant.

Apparently the large number of plant species and varieties in these early Indian gardens, as well as the appropriateness of the species to the microclimate, soils, and horticultural techniques of the gardeners, helped create a stable situation that was well buffered against the wild fluctuations associated with damaging pest and disease outbreaks. Two basic principles seem to underlie the design of such landscapes: (a) avoiding bare soil and (b) encouraging a diversity of organisms. Diversity is accomplished by applying ample organic materials to the soil to encourage soil organisms of all kinds and by growing a variety of plants, which also encourages wildlife of all sizes to visit the garden.

soil between the crop rows, with fallen leaves and other debris cleaned away, as if the levels of neatness and cleanliness appropriate to a human dining room were equally desirable in the garden.

STRATEGY B: MODIFYING THE HABITAT

This strategy involves changing the biophysical environment to reduce its carrying capacity with regard to the pest population. Carrying capacity describes the ability of an environment to support a population.

Tactic 1. *Reduction of the pest's food, water, shelter, growing room, and other needs.* Examples include improved drainage to reduce habitat for

THE CONCEPT OF LIMITING FACTORS

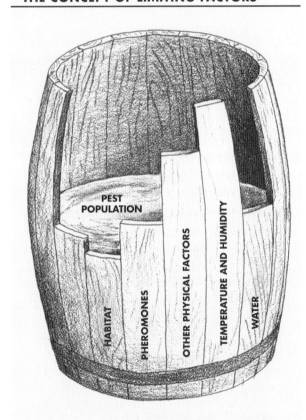

The shortest barrel stave—the limiting factor—is the one that dictates how much water the barrel can hold, despite the fact that the other staves are much taller. In this representation, limited habitat is restricting the size of the pest population despite a relative abundance of food, water, and other factors.

root pathogens, and monitoring and correcting soil pH to maximize mineral absorption and the soil food web. Another, used extensively in agriculture and too seldom in the garden, is cover cropping. This technique is used to "rest the soil" and grow plants not susceptible to the insects or pathogens of the food crop that was planted there.

Tactic 2. *Enhancement of the environment required by the pest's predators, parasitoids, and pathogens.* An example is planting wildflower and garden plants that attract beneficial insects to the garden and encourage them to stay. These plants, which have a variety of flower sizes and blooming periods, provide beneficials with alternative food sources that are often needed to complete their life cycles. The variety of plants also attracts beneficials to the garden and provides refuge for them during their active season. Rincon-Vitova Insectaries (www.rinconvitova.com) and other suppliers carry several seed mixtures designed for specific garden, farm, and wildland interface applications. One can also consult with seed suppliers directly for specific plants and flowers that attract beneficials. For example, white sweet alyssum flowers are preferred by the predatory minute pirate bug *(Orius* spp.). Be certain that the seed mix that you select will thrive in your local garden climate and conditions.

A companion to the concept of carrying capacity is that of limiting factors (see the drawing at left). A site can support only a certain number of pests because one or more of the key requirements—food, water, shelter—is limited. When you are faced with a pest problem in a specific environment, the challenge is to decide which essential element(s) of the pest's life-support system can be modified to reduce the presence of the pest.

Conversely, you can raise the limit on certain limiting factors to promote populations of the pest's natural enemies. For example, many parasitoids of insect pests need free water. Although adult parasitoids get some water from dew drops and from the food they consume, they may not satisfy all their water needs from these sources, particularly where it is arid. Thus, in the dry summer of the Mediterranean climate, such as exists in parts of the western and southwestern United States, an occasional sprinkling of garden plants with a hose provides water droplets from which the parasitoids can drink. This can increase the number of parasitoids in a specific location and lead to better control of certain plant pests such as aphids.

Temperature is a limiting factor in using certain parasitoids to control whiteflies in the greenhouse. The parasitoids work best at warmer temperatures than many unheated greenhouses maintain in winter, especially at night. Realizing that temperature is a limiting factor, you can figure out how to modify the habitat against the pest and in favor of its natural enemies. For example, you might use drums of water in the greenhouse, which absorb solar radiation during the day and release it at night.

STRATEGY C: CHANGING HUMAN BEHAVIOR

Tactic 1. *Modification of horticultural practices.* In pest management literature, this tactic is usually referred to as using "cultural controls," an abbreviation of the phrase "horticultural controls." It involves changing such practices as cultivating, mowing, watering, fertilizing, pruning, mulching, and planting methods and techniques.

Tactic 2. *Modification of waste-management and sanitation processes.* This means adjusting the way cleaning is performed and the manner in which garbage and other wastes are managed. For example, don't toss leaves into the garbage; use them as mulch or add them to your compost. Be careful about selecting manures: Use only well-composted

TIP Many beginning gardeners need to shed insect and creepy-crawly phobias imprinted on them by their peers, parents, and science fiction and horror movies. For example, learn to identify and appreciate good non-poisonous snakes, which eat gophers and local venomous snake species.

manures. "Raw" or incompletely composted manures may carry weed seeds, pathogens, and even drug residues and metabolites from antibiotics and hormones fed to livestock to hasten weight gain.

Tactic 3. *Inspection and quarantining of new plants, pets, and materials that have the potential to transport pests.* Inspection can prevent the importation of greenhouse pests into the garden, pests from other gardens via transplants, or house plant pests on newly acquired interior plants.

Tactic 4. *Education.* By educating yourself and others about pests and about the benefits of certain wildlife such as spiders and paper wasps, you can modify your own and others' perception, taste, and judgment to avoid the unfortunate consequences of overzealous efforts to control organisms that are causing no harm. This may involve altering your definition of what constitutes cosmetic damage or readjusting your judgment as to how heavily manicured or defect-free a landscape must be before it is acceptable. Education can also influence how strongly one fears or is revolted by the physical appearance of a certain animal or plant.

TREATMENT CATEGORY II: DIRECT SUPPRESSION OF PESTS

Direct methods of destroying or excluding pests include physical and mechanical controls, biological controls, and least-toxic chemical controls.

STRATEGY A: PHYSICAL AND MECHANICAL CONTROLS

Tactic 1. *Manual removal, squashing, collecting, or mechanical killing of pests. Examples include vacuuming up insects; hoeing or hand removing weeds; and collecting snails and slugs at night.*

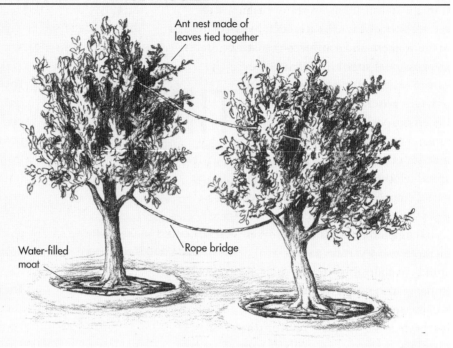

The oldest example of the deliberate manipulation of a natural enemy species comes from ancient China. It involves collecting nests of yellow ants (*Oecophylla smaragdina*) and placing them on citrus trees to control caterpillars and other pests. Rope bridges allow the ants to commute from tree to tree. Moat barriers on the ground force these predatory ants to stay in the trees.

Ant nest made of leaves tied together

Water-filled moat

Rope bridge

Tactic 2. *The use of barriers, including screens, nets, and caulking designed to exclude the particular pest, or group of pests, that are problematic.* Some examples include adding thick straw mulches under developing strawberries to protect the fruit from sowbugs; and using sawdust, very high in carbon (C) and low in nitrogen (N) (high C to N ratio), in walkways to reduce weed growth (the extra carbon robs the immediate soil of the nitrogen weeds need to grow).

Tactic 3. *The setting of traps. Examples include pit traps, sticky traps, water traps, and electric and light traps.*

Tactic 4. *The use of heat or cold to destroy pests.* This tactic includes the use of flamers in weed control, soil solarization to pasteurize the soil, heating wood structures (like garden sheds) to kill wood-boring pests, microwaving silverfish in books to kill them (although not for too long or the book could catch fire!), refrigerated storage of bulbs to meet their cooling needs and suppress pests, and similar strategies.

STRATEGY B: BIOLOGICAL CONTROLS

This very important strategy, discussed at some length here, involves maximizing the impact of the pest's natural enemies, including predators, parasitoids, pathogens, antagonists, and other competitors. The study and application of biological control techniques is most advanced in relation to the control of arthropods, specifically insects and mites.

Examples of the use of this strategy in agriculture and forestry are extensive and go back centuries, particularly in China (as shown in the drawing above).

The deliberate use of biological control techniques to manage agricultural pests in the United States can be traced to 1888, perhaps the most significant date in the early history of pest control in this country. In that year, the U.S. Department of Agriculture (USDA) imported the Vedalia lady beetle *(Rodolia cardinalis)* into California from Australia to control the cottony-cushion scale, which had been brought accidentally to the United States from Australia and was devastating the citrus industry in southern California. The lady beetle was so successful in permanently controlling this pest that the citrus industry to this day is a strong supporter of biological controls. This early and important event is discussed further in the sidebar at right. It is an example of "classical" biological control involving the release of natural enemies of pests, as distinguished from the recently developed biotechnological approaches in which tissue, cellular material, or DNA from different species is manipulated.

The Vedalia importation project is a classic example of the many benefits of biological control as a pest management tool. The few thousand dollars the USDA spent to import the beetles was a far smaller investment than that required of farmers using insecticides in their fruitless effort to control the scale. Pest management researchers Paul DeBach and David Pimentel have documented that for every $1 invested in biological control, $30 is earned in preserved crop yields and savings on conventional pesticides. By contrast, for every $1 invested in conventional pesticides, only $4 is earned in preserved crop yields. This is a common-sense point: Do you want a 30-fold increase on your

> **"For every $1 invested in biological control, $30 is earned in preserved crop yields and savings on conventional pesticides."**

investment or a 4-fold increase? Common sense, as well as financial "cents," says take the 30-fold increase.

Another advantage of biological control is that it can produce permanent pest suppression, as contrasted with pesticides, which must be reapplied on a regular basis. Except where pesticide use has killed the Vedalia beetles, they have kept pest

This Vedalia beetle, *Rhodolia cardinalis*, is attacking cottony cushion scale (Icerya purchase). (Photo by Mark Hoddle, Center for Invasive Species Research, University of California, Riverside)

HOW A LADY BEETLE SAVED THE AMERICAN CITRUS INDUSTRY

Although the Chinese have cultured and moved predatory ant species around for thousands of years, the modern importation of natural enemies to control insect pests began in late 1888, when USDA entomologist Albert Koebele shipped the Vedalia beetle *(Rhodolia cardinalis)* from its native Australia to California to combat the cottony-cushion scale *(Icerya purchasi)*. In his account of this project, Paul DeBach likens the establishment of the Vedalia beetle to the "shot heard around the world."

In the 1880s, the cottony-cushion scale was devastating the booming citrus industry in southern California. Various insecticides, including cyanide gas, were used in attempts to control the scale, but with little effect and at great cost. The initial objective of Koebele's trip to Australia was the acquisition of the scale-eating parasitic fly *Cryptochaetum iceryae*, which Australian entomologist Frazer Crawford had discovered in 1886.

Koebele sent thousands of the flies back to the United States, and they were soon established in California. But he also sent back 524 Vedalia beetles, and they were used to start a series of field cultures in southern California. Through the efforts of farmers, insectaries (insect producers), government workers, and researchers, the beetles were distributed throughout California, and later to other states and more than 50 countries.

Within a few weeks of introducing the beetles into citrus orchards, the scale population was reduced to negligible levels, and within one year, virtually no cottony-cushion scale could be found in the state. (The parasitic fly also helped suppress scales, especially in coastal areas.) Today, it is difficult to locate either the pest or the beetles in citrus orchards. The pest is evident only when there is heavy insecticide use or when an especially cold winter in the northern areas of its range kills the few predators needed to keep scale populations low.

scales under biological control in California citrus groves for the past 100 years.

We should also point at that the Vedalia project was undertaken by a nonprofit government agency, the USDA, acting in the interest of society at large. Because successful biological control importations generally produce permanent pest controls, farmers profit from the introduction of beneficial organisms, but the importers of the beneficials receive no direct monetary reward once the new organism becomes established in the environment. Pesticides, on the other hand, are generally developed by private industry, which expects to realize substantial profits from continuing sales and repeated use of their products. Absence of the long-term profit motive explains the relative neglect of the biological control strategy. It also emphasizes the need for the public to pressure the state and federal departments of agriculture as well as universities to undertake and fund such projects and support the commercial insectary industry that produces beneficial organisms for sale.

The application of the science of biological control to weed pests is more recent, and its application to plant pathogens is most recent of all. In general, research into biological control is vastly underappreciated; therefore, it is also underfunded.

This is unfortunate, because the potential economic, social, and ecological benefits are so substantial. You should actively support funding for biological control research if you are concerned about the use of pesticides on your food, public and private landscapes, rights-of-way, public buildings (inside and out), homes and apartments, and public transportation conveyances.

"Biological control can produce permanent pest suppression, as contrasted with pesticides, which must be reapplied on a regular basis."

Under the overall strategy of biological control we can identify four distinct tactics.

Tactic 1. *Conservation of biological controls.* This involves protection of those biological controls already present in the environment. Because the natural enemies of the pest need some low level of prey in order to maintain their own numbers, complete elimination of the pest should almost never be your objective. Conservation is the approach of most importance to the layperson, and several very important guidelines are summarized here.

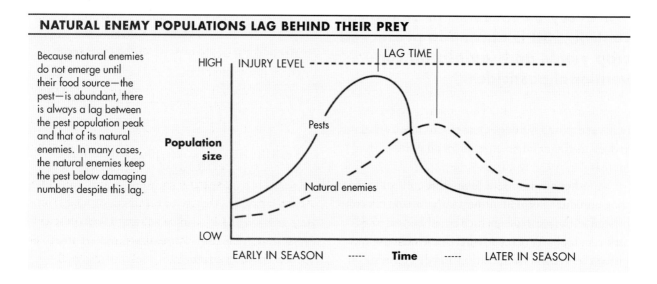

NATURAL ENEMY POPULATIONS LAG BEHIND THEIR PREY

Because natural enemies do not emerge until their food source—the pest—is abundant, there is always a lag between the pest population peak and that of its natural enemies. In many cases, the natural enemies keep the pest below damaging numbers despite this lag.

HIGH · INJURY LEVEL

LAG TIME

Pests

Population size

Natural enemies

LOW

EARLY IN SEASON ----- **Time** ----- LATER IN SEASON

A. *Use plants that attract and support beneficial insects.* Seed mixes that support beneficials are available through specialty sites like Rincon-Vitova Insectaries, big box stores like Home Depot, nurseries, and even some hardware stores. These plants provide alternative food sources, especially for predators and parasitoids. For example, certain beneficials, like lacewing adults, eat only pollen and nectar from easily accessible flowers like bachelor's buttons, alyssum, crimson clover, daisies, fennel, and many others. Keeping the adults around means they will continue to lay eggs on your plants and their hungry larvae will consume almost any insect or insect egg.

B. *Treat only if injury levels will be exceeded.* The size of the predator and parasitoid populations will always lag slightly behind that of the pest (see the graph on the facing page). This is only natural, because predators multiply as a result of finding food, not in anticipation of it. When their prey becomes plentiful, their own numbers increase. Thus, it is just before the pest reaches damaging numbers that the beneficials become abundant. If you apply a pesticide before you are certain treatment is necessary, it will damage natural enemy populations no matter how nontoxic the pesticide is to humans and pets. This can actually cause the pest problem to worsen.

C. *Spot-treat to reduce the impact on the natural enemies of the pest.* Restricting treatment to the very spot where the problem is serious and leaving adjacent areas untreated preserves the natural enemies of the pest. This ensures that some of these natural enemies survive to react quickly when the pests begin to multiply again.

D. *Time treatments so they are least disruptive.* Timing should take into account both the season and the life cycle of the pest's natural enemies. Because timing depends on a number of factors, such as the organisms involved, the host plant or site, and the geographic area, it is difficult to gen-

This braconid "miniwasp," *Aleiodes indiscretus,* is laying an egg in a gypsy moth caterpillar. You have to be patient to see this seldom-observed activity, as it occurs in less than a second. (Photo by Scott Bauer/USDA Agricultural Research Service)

eralize about it. This is why it is so important to learn about the biology of the plant or animal and make careful observations of it. Record keeping in a notebook, in a calendar, or with an app for your smartphone will become your site memory. This historical site information will be one key to the success of your IPM program.

E. *Select the most species-specific, least broadly damaging treatment.* Although few other techniques can match the specificity of traps, hand removal of pests, or host-specific parasitoids, this guideline does not exclude the use of certain pesticides. Some degree of specificity can be achieved with pesticides by carefully selecting compounds that are relatively focused in their effects and break down rapidly into nontoxic compounds. This is discussed at greater length in later chapters. Of course, pesticides should be used under the guidelines suggested here. If these guidelines are followed scrupulously, the specificity of the chemical compound may become less important. For example, when an herbicide is painted only on the cut stem of an offending plant rather than sprayed all over the weed and its surroundings, the application method itself is selective even though the herbicide is broad-spectrum or nonselective.

Tactic 2. *Augmentation of natural enemies.* This is the process of artificially increasing the numbers of specific predators, parasitoids, or pathogens already present at the site in low numbers. Although augmentation has been used extensively in agriculture, it also has much to offer in many other situations. For example, pest mite outbreaks are common, especially when pesticides have been used that kill beneficial mites or when plants are dusty, which benefits pests. Releasing predatory mites onto plants can reestablish control of pest mites. In the case of thrips insects, predatory mites *(Amblysieus cucumeris)* are available in sachets that can be hung from branchlets for easy release. We've used beneficial mites successfully in urban landscapes of all descriptions.

Microbial controls developed from naturally occurring caterpillar pathogens have long been used for caterpillar control on ornamental plants and vegetables. A feature of some of these microbial pesticides, and to a lesser degree of augmentative releases generally, is that once released, the beneficial organisms may maintain themselves in the natural environment for several years. Two examples are *Bacillus popilliae,* a bacterium used to treat lawns for Japanese beetle grubs, and *Nosema locustae,* a protozoan

used to control grasshoppers and locusts.

The variety of commercially available beneficial biological controls, including insects, mites, nematodes, and various microbial species, is already quite large and can be expected to increase considerably in coming years.

TIP Although you as a private citizen cannot import beneficial insects from outside the country, you can prompt government agencies and nonprofit organizations to do so by encouraging your legislators to support expenditures for research and development of importation.

Tactic 3. *Inoculation with natural enemies.* This involves releasing natural enemies of the pest at the beginning of the season when they are not normally present and will not permanently colonize an area. Generally, natural enemies are not present early in the season because winter temperatures are too severe. As summer progresses, they fly in or get blown in. When unfavorable weather conditions return, they die off and do not reappear until the warm season is well underway the next year. By inoculating the pest population with beneficials earlier in the season year after year, both the current year's problem and the overwintering pest population can be reduced safely.

What distinguishes inoculation from augmentation is that natural enemies are released early in relatively low numbers before the pest population has

"The size of the predator and parasitoid populations will always lag slightly behind that of the pest."

built up rather than after the number of pests is already large. This procedure assumes that releases must be repeated regularly—at least once a season if not more often—because for some reason peculiar to the site or geographic location, the natural enemies are unlikely to establish themselves permanently.

Sometimes the natural enemy species native to the area where the pest occurs is not the species released. Instead, a related species is used because it is felt to be more effective or is more readily available. In China, Russia, and many eastern European countries, inoculative releases of *Trichogramma* miniwasps are routinely used on a very large scale to control caterpillar pests in agriculture. A number of species of *Trichogramma* wasps, which parasitize the eggs of their hosts, are available commercially in the United States. We hope that augmentative releases of these beneficials will continue to become more common here in the future.

Tactic 4. *Importation of natural enemies.*
This involves bringing in and permanently establishing the appropriate natural enemies of a pest that has invaded a new area. The introduction of the new pest is usually accidental. Examples are the fruit flies that occasionally hitchhike onto the American mainland on produce from Hawaii, and the chestnut blight fungus, which came to North America on plants imported from Europe.

Insects as well as terrestrial and aquatic weeds have been suppressed by using the tactic of importation. We have already mentioned the Vedalia beetle, the most famous and earliest example of the use of this approach against insect pests in the United States. The classic case in the field of weed management occurred in the 1940s with the control of Klamath weed (St. John's wort), *Hypericum perforatum.* This plant, which is poisonous to cattle and sheep, was crowding out forage plants in the rangelands of the Northwest. Importation and establishment of other beetles, but especially the Klamath beetle *(Chrysolina quadrigemina),* wiped out 99 percent of the Klamath weed over millions of acres of rangeland in less than a decade.

Of all the approaches that come under the heading of biological control, importation, when successful, is probably the most spectacular in terms of results and the most economical in terms of money invested in research. Despite its obvious benefits, however, importation is greatly underutilized for a number of reasons. Perhaps the most important is the lack of potential for future commercial benefit. If the right natural enemy or combination of enemies is found and introduced, the pest problem virtually disappears. The natural enemies become established in the new area, and the beneficial result is permanent. Thus, the controlling organism cannot be sold regularly for profit. In fact, once the biocontrol organism is working, few people even remember the prior pest problem or

The importation of the Klamath weed beetle, *Chrysolina quadrigemina*, is a classic case of biological control of a weed species. (Photo by Eric Coombs, Oregon Department of Agriculture, Bugwood.org)

BE CAREFUL WHAT YOU WISH FOR

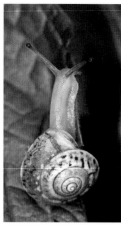

The brown garden snail was originally brought from France to the United States as a culinary delicacy, escargot. (Photo by Sailesh Patel/Shutterstock)

Occasionally, organisms that become pests are introduced deliberately by people who are nostalgic for old-country wildlife (the English starling, for example) or by people who want to study a species for possible commercial use. The most famous example of the latter is the importation of the gypsy moth in the hope that its silk would prove commercially valuable. A few moths escaped from their enclosures, and the species is now a major pest of trees in much of the northeastern United States.

The brown garden snail, *Cornu aspersum* (formerly *Helix aspersa*), was originally brought from France to the United States in the 1850s as a culinary delicacy, escargot. It escaped (slowly) into the wild and became the common garden pest it is today. It takes about 2 to 2½ weeks of being fed a special cleansing diet of grain and lettuce before the snails are ready for the kitchen. Snail recipes and preparation methods can be found online. As with all wild foods, make sure you have accurately identified the species before eating.

When pet store customers tire of their exotic flora and fauna, they sometimes dump them in the nearest body of water or let them go free. Hydrilla and water hyacinth, both serious water weed pests, were originally sold as aquarium plants, and flocks of fruit-eating parakeets, probably descendants of former household pets, have naturalized themselves in some southern areas of the United States.

the fact that the natural enemy is still present and working.

We can illustrate this from our own experience. Bill Olkowski released *Trioxys tenuicaudus,* an aphid parasitoid, to control aphids infesting elm trees in Berkeley, California. At the beginning of the project, the sticky honeydew exudate from the aphids was so thick on the sidewalk and on cars parked under the trees that people frequently complained about the problem. The fallen leaves, dirty from the mold that grows on the honeydew, stuck to shoes and were dragged into houses, soiling floors and carpets. The honeydew also covered windshields and damaged the finish on cars.

The parasitoid was obtained from Czechoslovakia by the late Robert van den Bosch, who chaired the Division of Biological Control at the University of California at Berkeley. After it was released in the elms lining one city street, the site was monitored regularly during the growing season for several years to see if the parasitoid had become established. During the first and second years, we found no sign of the parasitoids, although we searched the trees regularly, riding high in the bucket of a city lift truck. At the beginning of the third year, however, parasitized aphids were found on the tree where the initial releases had been made. Within a year, the aphid pests all but disappeared from the initial release site. As the parasitoid extended its range season by season, control was obtained block by block. As the aphid numbers declined, so did the sticky exudate, and to this day the sidewalks and cars beneath these trees remain free of honeydew. No further control action against aphids has ever been needed. Amazingly, no one seems to remember the honeydew problem!

Several important points can be drawn from this example. First, biological control importation projects must nearly always be supported by government agencies, commodity groups, such as the citrus farmers' cooperative mentioned earlier, or similar groups that stand to benefit directly from the result. Thus, there was no likelihood a business would have undertaken the Berkeley project. However, having been far-sighted enough to invest a few thousand dollars in importation, Berkeley has reaped the benefits of many years of cost-free, nonpolluting pest control.

A second point is the length of time it took for the project's results to appear. During the two years that passed before it became evident that the parasitoid would be effective, residents had to endure sticky sidewalks and cars. Conventional pesticides could not be sprayed on the trees for fear of damaging the natural enemies. Thus, a considerable effort to educate residents was needed to persuade them to be patient—something people are not often willing to do when pest problems seem as severe as this one.

Although not a problem in our example, it should also be noted that it is often necessary to repeat an importation experiment several times before a strain of parasitoid appropriate to the local climate can be identified or before the right combination of natural enemies can be selected. The decades of ongoing effort by the federal government to find the best combination of natural enemies to control the gypsy moth is a good example.

Finally, it is important to note that imported natural enemies are host-specific; that is, they live within one particular pest species but in no other. Because they depend on that single host species for survival, they are very good at seeking it out, even when populations are low. This is what makes them so effective.

We should also take a moment in this introductory discussion to answer the most commonly asked question about importation: What if an imported natural enemy starts feeding on something besides the pest and becomes a problem itself?

The first part of the answer is that the predators, parasitoids, and pathogens used in biological control have adapted through eons of evolution to feed upon a specific pest or group of closely related pests. They are good at suppression of that particular pest exactly because they are unable to feed on anything else. Furthermore, to ensure that imported organisms do not become pests, an elaborate protocol is followed. Permits to import the species must first be obtained from the USDA's Animal and Plant Health Inspection Service (APHIS). Then the living material is reared in a federal quarantine laboratory with special drains, windows, and doors to prevent accidental escape of the organisms. If there is any doubt about the identity of the organism being imported, it is tested in the laboratory by making sure it attacks the right host.

Projects involving the biological control of weeds operate under even more complex protocols because they deal with herbivores—organisms that eat plants and could possibly harm agriculture. An insect or mite found feeding and reproducing on a pest weed in its native country is a candidate for controlling the weed in a new area. But first it is tested against related horticultural and agricultural plants grown in the new area to make sure it is incapable of feeding on them. Only when it is clear that the herbivore depends for survival on the pest plant alone is it considered for the new area.

DID YOU KNOW?

One pesticide class, the microbials, is made up of fungi or bacteria that are antagonistic or lethal to pests. Although these beneficial microbes are technically beneficial organisms, legally they are registered pesticides.

STRATEGY C: LEAST-TOXIC CHEMICAL CONTROLS

Chemical compounds of various sorts have an important role to play in many environmentally sound pest management efforts. If you disagree, perhaps you are defining the word "chemical" more narrowly than we are. It is important to realize that "chemical" describes not only the traditional, conventional pesticides that often find their way into soil, water, air, wildlife, food, and us, but also other less harmful compounds that are derived from plants and other "natural" sources or are synthesized in imitation of these compounds. The line between what constitutes a nontoxic or less-toxic chemical compound and one that is too toxic to be acceptable may be drawn differently by different people. This complex and sensitive topic is covered in detail in Chapters 6, 7, and 8.

CHAPTER 5

MEET "THE BENEFICIALS"

I n this chapter, we introduce you to many of the beneficial organisms that help keep pest populations at low levels. The list starts with the non-insect arthropods—spiders, predatory mites, and centipedes—then moves to the beneficial insects—lady beetles, ground beetles, rove beetles, lacewings, hover flies, predacious bugs, ants, bees, and wasps—and finally to the "odd one out," the night-flying mammals, bats. (Note that the discussion of beneficial nematodes is reserved for Chapter 8, on microbial insecticides.)

If you take a planetary view, the terms *beneficial insect* and *beneficial organism* (or "bennie," as we often say informally), frequently used when referring to insect biological control agents, are really misnomers. The larger perspective makes plain that all organisms are beneficial, just as are all other forms of life. Insects, mites, and spiders are essential parts of the complex food webs of the ecosystems that support life on earth. The larvae of mosquitoes, which are generally considered pests of humans, feed fish; the berries of mistletoe, which we often consider a plant pest, feed songbirds; bats eat night-flying insects and produce guano (bat feces), which has been harvested for centuries as an agricultural fertilizer; and so on. In fact, everything feeds something else so that the great wheel of life can keep turning.

But, being human, sooner or later we want to know whether an organism furthers or hinders our human pursuits. It is very well to take the larger view and say that all species are beneficial, but what happens closer to home? When it comes right down to it, we might rewrite the old adage about equality: Some arthropods are more beneficial than others. We'll save our discussion of bats, the "least equal of the mammals," for the last section of this chapter.

There are some groups, genera, and species of arthropods that you really should become familiar with because of their great importance in controlling pest

insects and mites. We introduce you to them here, but the number of species is so great and they are often so abundant in home and garden environments that we cannot do them complete justice. We hope that your interest in controlling pests naturally will motivate you to continue learning on your own.

A number of beneficial organisms are available commercially for release in various situations. Many more organisms previously available only to large agricultural enterprises, or only in Canada and Europe, are now widely available in the United States as the home-level market for nontoxic products grows.

We should also note that some of these commercially available insects that make charming pets or educational subjects for school projects—such as the praying mantid shown below may have little impact on garden pest populations. Research on use of mantids in North America is still undeveloped compared to use in China, where we reviewed the research literature a few years back. In China (and elsewhere), mantids are field collected as overwintering "cocoons," which are really eggs cases of 50 or more tiny mantids (they look identical to

The European praying mantid (*Mantis religiosa*), introduced into North America from Europe, has been widely distributed throughout the United States by insect collectors. (Actual size: 2 in. to 2½ in./5 cm to 6.5 cm) (Photo by Kristina Postnikova/Shutterstock)

adults of the species). They are used to seed into a crop in which an expected early-season aphid population can feed the tiny mantids while they develop. As adults they eat a wide range of insects. There are two common North American species: *Mantis religiosa* is an import from Europe and Africa, and *Tenodera sinensis* is naturalized in America from an early import from China.

PREDATORS AND PARASITOIDS: HOW MANY ARE THERE?

During the discussion of natural and biological controls earlier in the book, we distinguished between parasitoids and predators. To give you some feeling for the numbers and importance of these groups of organisms, we quote from *An Introduction to Biological Control* (Plenum Press, 1982) by the great biological control specialist Robert van den Bosch, his colleague P. S. Messenger, and former student A. P. Gutierrez:

> Parasitoids are recorded from five insect orders, with the bulk of species occurring in the Diptera [flies] and Hymenoptera [wasps] . . . . Despite their restriction to only five orders, there are tremendous numbers of parasitoid species worldwide . . . Extrapolating from the numbers of described Coleoptera [beetles] and parasitic Hymenoptera in the well-studied British fauna (4,000 beetle species and 5,000 species of parasitic Hymenoptera),…up to 500,000 parasitic Hymenoptera might be described worldwide if that fauna were to be as well-studied as that of beetles. . . .
>
> Predatory insects are the lions, wolves, sharks, barracudas, hawks and shrikes of

This lynx spider is said to "hunt like a cat," and does not build nests or webs but captures prey by pouncing upon them. All spiders are predators, and hence are beneficial. Don't kill them. (Photo by Wong Hock Weng/123RF)

> the insect world.…From the standpoint of feeding habit, there are two kinds of predators: those with chewing mouthparts, e.g., lady beetles (Coccinellidae) and ground beetles (Carabidae), which simply chew up and bolt down their victims—legs, bristles, antennae, and all—and those with piercing mouthparts, e.g., assassin bugs (Reduviidae), lacewing larvae (Chrysopidae), and hover fly larvae (Syrphidae), which suck juices from their victims . . . .
>
> Predatory species occur in most insect orders, with the greatest number of species occurring in the order Coleoptera. Dragonflies (order Odonata) are exclusively predacious, and others are nearly so. Predators may be polyphagous, having a broad host range (e.g., the green lacewing, *Chrysoperla carnea* and *C. rufilabris*); oligophagous, having a restricted host range (e.g., aphid-feeding coccinellids and syrphids); or essentially monophagous, that is, highly prey specific (e.g., the Vedalia beetle, *Rodolia cardinalis*, which feeds only on cottony-cushion scale, *Icerya purchasi*, and its close relatives).

The greatest predators of the arthropods are not insects at all but spiders. It is with these that we begin our discussion of beneficial organisms.

SPIDERS

(Class Arachnida, order Araneae)

One day only! Greatest troupe of trained animals in the world! Don't miss this opportunity to see: death-defying parachutists, skilled performers on the flying trapeze, graceful and original dancers. These clever animals make their own apparatus for they are skilled engineers. See them spin and weave. Nothing like this has ever been presented before on any stage!

So begins *How to Know the Spiders* by B. J. Kaston (Wm. C. Brown, 1972). This magnificent spider show goes on all the time. Unfortunately, many people harbor unnecessary fears of spiders and don't appreciate the beneficial role they play in most settings. W. Gertsch, in his classic work *American Spiders* (Van Nostrand Reinhold, 1979), discusses the enormous economic importance of spiders:

> Spiders are among the dominant predators of any terrestrial community. When the fauna of the soil and its plant cover is analyzed, they come to light in vast numbers, in such convincing abundance that it is evident that they play a significant part in the life of every habitat.

Gertsch provides some very impressive figures. For example, there were approximately 64,000 spiders per acre in a meadow near Washington, D.C., and 2,265,000 in a single acre of undisturbed grassland in England. That is about one spider in every three square inches!

The primary food of most spiders is insects. Gertsch points out that although spiders are not often viewed as efficient agents of biological control, they can act that way. He cites a case where a predacious spider was credited with eradicating bedbugs in Greek refugee camps. Hundreds of years later, he says, the same species was imported in a successful effort to control the same pest in German animal-rearing laboratories. There

are examples of spiders controlling stored-grain pests, a caterpillar pest of the coconut palm, cotton worms, rice planthoppers, gypsy moths, pea aphids, and others.

> **"Unfortunately, many people harbor unnecessary fears of spiders and don't appreciate the beneficial role they play in most settings."**

PREDATORY MITES

(Class Arachnida, order Acari)

Many people are familiar with pest mites that feed on plant leaves, but few are aware of the many species of beneficial mites that feed on pest mites, thrips, and other organisms. Of the more than 200 mite families, predatory species are found in 13.

This orange predatory mite, *Phytoseiulus persimilis,* is attacking a spider mite. The species is so voracious that it usually clears up a spider mite infestation and then starves because it has no more food. (Photo by Martin Dohrn/ Science Photo Library)

Like pest mites, predatory mites are small (usually less than 1/25 in./1 mm long) and tend to move rapidly. Some are white or cream-colored; a few are brightly colored. One of the most effective predators of pest mites on ornamental and food plants, *Phytoseiulus persimilis,* has a brilliant orange-red color. During the warm months, *P. persimilis* can complete its life cycle in just seven days—reproducing almost twice as fast as some pest mites (see the drawing on p. 58). This reproductive advantage enables the predator to keep pest mite populations at low levels. *P. persimilis* will eventually eat up the entire pest population and then die off from lack of food. With beneficial mites, as with other species, diversity is an attribute. We recommend that you release a combination of beneficial mites and monitor the results regularly.

When temperatures reach 70°F (21°C), many predatory mite species can reproduce twice as fast as pests such as the two-spotted spider mite *(Tetranychus urticae)*. It takes the two-spotted mite two weeks to mature from egg to adult, whereas its predator *Phytoseiulus persimilis* can go through two generations in the same time.

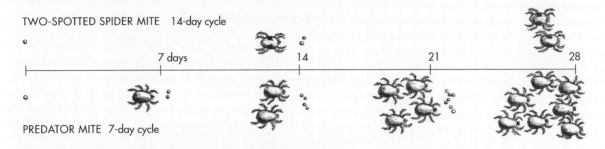

TWO-SPOTTED SPIDER MITE   14-day cycle

7 days   14   21   28

PREDATOR MITE 7-day cycle

Redrawn from N. V. Tonks's *Pest Problems in Small Greenhouses and Indoor Plantings* (Ministry of Agriculture and Food, 1982)

Predatory mite species are abundant in the upper layers of soil and in moss, humus, and animal manures, where they feed on insects and mites. Other mites are found on plants, where they primarily consume pest mites and their eggs. Still others inhabit aquatic systems (including hot springs!), where they feed on other mites, small crustaceans, isopods, and insects. A few species occupy grain-storage facilities, where they attack a large number of insect species that damage the stored grain.

Predatory mites are used widely to control mites and thrips on food and ornamental crops in commercial greenhouses in Europe. The interior landscape and greenhouse nursery industries in North America use these beneficials, but not to the extent that they do in Europe. Predatory mites are also being used to control pests in orchards and vineyards in the United States, Canada, and elsewhere. We became familiar with predatory mites while designing IPM programs for pests of interior plants, greenhouses, and landscape shrubs and shade trees. Fortunately, many predatory mite species can now be purchased from commercial insectaries for release on indoor plants, the garden, landscapes, and orchards.

CENTIPEDES

(Class Chilopoda)

The chilopods, or centipedes, have one pair of legs per body segment, whereas millipedes, with which they are often confused, have two pairs of legs per body segment. All centipedes are predators, whereas millipedes are primarily detritivores (animals that break down dead plant materials). Both are commonly seen in the garden under boards resting on damp soil or when the soil or compost is turned.

About 3,000 centipede species are known. All have poison glands that open through the jaws. Although none are dangerous, the bite of some southwestern species is painful temporarily. Some

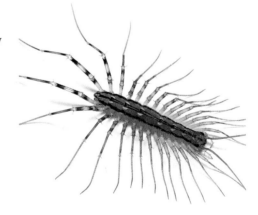

The house centipede, *Scutigera coleoptrata*, eats cockroaches and flies inside the house. It moves so rapidly that it can be mistaken for a roach and is seldom detected because it eats at night. (Photo by Marcouliana/Dreamstime.com)

centipedes are blind; all are predacious. A centipede frequently encountered indoors is the common house centipede, *Scutigera coleoptrata*. It is also found outdoors throughout the southern United States and Europe. It has 15 pairs of legs and long antennae, is about 1 in. (2.5 cm) long, and can move rapidly along walls and floors when hunting flies and other insects, which it usually does at night. There are no reports of this species biting humans. Some people kill centipedes without realizing they provide good household insect control; other people are not even aware they are in the house. If you see a centipede indoors or out, don't kill it; let it help you control pest insects.

DID YOU KNOW?

Centipedes can generally move much faster than millipedes. The fastest centipedes have the fewest legs.

and tigers (more on that in a moment). Two other families are also seen regularly by gardeners and composters: the ground beetles (family Carabidae), and the rove beetles (family Staphylinidae). Some other families and their prey groups are listed in the chart below.

Nearly everyone knows what a lady beetle looks like, but few of us know more than that. The Coccinellidae include about 400 North American beetle species and about 4,000 species worldwide. Except for one small subfamily, all members of this family prey in their larval and adult stages on aphids, mealybugs, scales, psyllids (jumping plant lice), whiteflies, mites, and other insects.

Some of the more common predacious lady beetle species in the family Coccinellidae are listed in the chart on p. 61. Probably the most common beneficial species in North America is the convergent lady beetle *(Hippodamia convergens)*. All the lady beetles have similar life cycles. Eggs are laid in the early spring, producing larvae that feed for several weeks, pupate, and then emerge as adults. The adults feed through the fall, then either lay eggs and

LADY BEETLES

(Order Coleoptera, family Coccinellidae)

Most predatory insects are beetles. The best known of these are the lady beetles in the family Coccinellidae, which children call ladybugs, not realizing that bugs and beetles are as different as elephants

PREDACIOUS BEETLES AND THEIR PREY

COMMON NAME	FAMILY NAME	PREY
lady beetles	Coccinellidae	aphids, scales, mealybugs, whiteflies, mites
ground beetles	Carabidae	a wide variety of insects found in the same niche
rove beetles	Staphylinidae	scavengers; also prey on a variety of insects and mites; some are parasitic, others occur in ant and termite nests
tiger beetles	Cicindelidae	ants, flies, small beetles, bugs, caterpillars, spiders, aphids, fiddler crabs, marine fleas, grasshoppers
predacious diving beetles	Dytiscidae	tadpoles, snails, small frogs, fish, earthworms, immature dragonflies, mayflies, water bugs
whirligig beetles	Gyrinidae	dead and dying insects around water
carrion beetles	Silphidae	snails, caterpillars, fly larvae
hister beetles	Histeridae	principally scavengers; also prey upon beetles, flies, ants
lightning beetles	Lampyridae	cannibalistic; also prey upon snails and earthworms

Listed in order of approximate effectiveness as predators. For further information on predacious beetles, see W. V. Balduf's *The Bionomics of Entomophagous Coleoptera* (E. W. Classey Ltd., 1969).

die or hibernate over winter, emerging in spring to deposit eggs and die. The prey of the most common lady beetle species are listed in the chart below.

THE CONVERGENT LADY BEETLE
(Hippodamia convergens)

"Ladybug, ladybug fly away home." So goes the children's rhyme about the most popular insect of all. Only the ladybug isn't a bug at all—it's a beetle. There is a big difference between the chewing insects of the order Coleoptera and the sucking insects of the order Hemiptera. Not only do members of these two groups have different ways of eating, and thus differently shaped mouthparts, but they also have a distinctly different first pair of wings. Beetles have a hardened first pair or wings, whereas bugs have a half-hardened, half-membranous set, giving rise to the name Hemiptera ("hemi" means "half").

This lady beetle, *Coccinella californicus*, is preparing to eat an aphid. The markings on the thorax are different from the other common lady beetles, *Hippodamia convergens*. (Photo © Joseph Calev/iStockphoto)

The distinguishing characteristic of the convergent lady beetle is the two oblique, converging white lines on its thorax. The thorax is the second body segment, located behind the head and before the abdomen. You must look carefully for these markings, as the head of this beetle is partially hidden when viewed from above. This species may occur with orange, red, or yellow wing covers and black circular spots. The number of black spots varies—sometimes they are absent entirely—so the white thoracic lines must be relied on for positive field identification.

The convergent lady beetle is a migrating species. Many individuals fly hundreds of miles to hibernating sites at higher elevations in the late spring after feeding. They return to the valleys the following early spring. For most of the year, they remain in a quiescent state in large, spectacular aggregations. The aggregations shift during the year from the sides of creeks during the summer to mountainsides in fall and winter. During the aggregating phase, the beetles feed very little but do drink water. They live largely off fat stored during the spring feeding phase.

If you find such an aggregation in the wild, stop to appreciate it but don't disturb or harvest it. There is a cottage industry that collects and sells these hibernating beetles for pest control purposes. Once released, many if not most of the hibernating beetles fly away. Those that remain are sluggish and may even form aggregations again as if they were still hibernating. Several studies confirm what we have observed ourselves: Released hibernating beetles do not feed. They must fly to burn off the stored fat before they can feed again. Thus, many may leave the area where released without benefiting the person who purchased them.

THE PREY OF COMMON LADY BEETLES

LADY BEETLES GENUS	COMMON NAME OF PREY GROUP
Adalia	aphids, scales
Anatis	aphids
Chilocorus	scales
Coccinella	aphids
Cryptolaemus	mealybugs, aphids, scales
Hippodamia	aphids
Olla	aphids
Rhizobius	mealybugs, soft and armored scales
Rodolia	scales (cottony-cushion scale)
Stethorus	spider mites

From L. A. Swan and C. S Papp's *The Common Insects of North America* (Harper & Row, 1972).

COMMON NORTH AMERICAN LADY BEETLES

COMMON NAME	SCIENTIFIC NAME	DISTINGUISHING CHARACTERISTICS
ash-grey lady beetle	*Olla abdominalis*	ash grey to pale yellow with black spots
black lady beetle	*Rhizobius ventralis*	shiny velvety black; reddish abdomen
California lady beetle	*Coccinella californica*	lateral white marks on thorax
convergent lady beetle	*Hippodamia convergens*	yellow-whitish slash marks on thorax
fifteen-spotted lady beetle	*Anatis quindecimpunctata*	head black, abdomen reddish-brown with 15 black spots
mealybug destroyer	*Cryptolaemus montrouzieri*	black head, reddish abdomen
red mite destroyer	*Stethorus picipes*	shiny black with white hairs
twice-stabbed lady beetle	*Chilocorus stigma*	shiny black with two red spots
two-spotted lady beetle	*Adalia bipunctata*	head black, two black spots on reddish abdomen
Vedalia lady beetle	*Rodolia cardinalis*	red, with irregular black marks

From L. A. Swan and C. S. Papp's *The Common Insects of North America* (Harper & Row, 1972).
The term "abdomen" is used in place of "elytra," which means wing covers. The first pair of wings of the beetles is hardened, and technically called the elytra. Distinguishing marks occur on these covers rather than on the abdomen proper.

The life cycle of the convergent lady beetle, *Hippodamia convergens*, is shown here. Top to bottom: pupa, teneral (recently formed) pupa, and prepupa. (Photo by Whitney Cranshaw, Colorado State University, Bugwood.org)

Moreover, many of these beetles die soon after being relocated or even during storage prior to purchase.

In some areas, at the same time that purchased hibernating beetles are being released in gardens, naturally occurring beetles are also flying in from their hibernating sites. Although the artificially released beetles fly away, successful control of the aphid pests may result from predation by the naturally occurring beetles that have come out of hibernation and flown in themselves. The homeowner often mistakenly assumes that the released beetles are solely responsible for the improvement, and this helps explain why the business of collecting hibernating beetles for sale persists.

Some commercial insectaries do sell adult convergent lady beetles that have been gathered in the spring during the feeding phase. These will feed heavily on an aphid population. When the number of aphid pests has been reduced to the point where there is no longer sufficient food for the beetles, they fly away to areas with more aphids. Proper timing of releases and the use of beetles that have used up their stored fat and are ready to feed are very important.

Outdoors, convergent lady beetles may not arrive until after plant damage has occurred. They are opportunistic, skimming off the top of the large aphid population but not staying long enough to do a good job of cleaning up the pests. Thus, successful aphid control with purchased convergent lady beetles is more likely to be achieved inside a screened greenhouse than in a garden.

In addition to their aphid prey, convergent lady beetles should have access to a simulated honeydew or artificial yeast/sugar mixture. We generally do not recommend releasing adult lady beetles in the house because they fly to windows and tend to die in large numbers there. You can, however, import young beetle larvae from the garden and place them on aphid-infested house plants for some temporary help.

Hippodamia convergens females can lay eggs from spring to late fall if there are adequate numbers of aphids and the temperature is high enough; usually, however, they and the males migrate by late spring. The yellow eggs are laid in groups of 5 to 50. (The maximum number of eggs laid by a female in the laboratory under ideal conditions is 2,500.) Eggs stand on end, each attached to the underside of a leaf, and they hatch in warm weather in about three to five days. The tiny black larvae that emerge cluster around the eggshells, some-

TIP If you are washing aphids off a tree or shrub (see pp. 305–306), timing the washing with the period when the lady beetles are in the pupal stage rather than in the larval or adult stages ensures that more of them remain on the tree. Lady beetle larvae that are washed to the ground may be damaged or eaten by predators; if they do survive, they may never find their way back to the infested plant.

times eating the empty shells—and some of their brothers and sisters that are late in emerging.

When the dark, alligator-like larvae are very young, they have no conspicuous markings. But after they mature somewhat, colored markings begin to appear. Each coccinellid species in the larval stage has a characteristic design. *H. convergens* larvae have orange markings on a black background on the thoracic segment, and on the third, fourth, and fifth abdominal segments.

After the larva has eaten 300 to 400 aphids and molted three times, a pupa (a quiescent, transitional stage between the larva and adult) forms. This pupa is black with reddish markings, and is usually found on upper leaf surfaces with its head pointing downward. Although attached to the leaf, the pupa is still capable of some movement. If you touch it with your finger or the end of a pencil, you will see it jerk. In five to seven days, the adult emerges from the pupal skin. The whole cycle from egg to adult takes about one month during the spring, and slightly less in summer. Mating, which is usually conspicuous, occurs several days after emergence from the pupa. After feeding on 200 to 500 medium-size aphids, females produce their first eggs.

AN INDIRECT BENEFIT

Perhaps the most important beneficial effect of releasing feeding convergent lady beetles in the garden is an indirect one: People who release beneficial insects are less likely to use disruptive pesticides in the same areas. This allows other less-visible or lesser-known biological controls to survive and provide the desirable control (even if the beetle does get all the credit).

GROUND BEETLES

(Order Coleoptera, family Carabidae)

Ground beetles, all of which are predacious in their larval and adult stages, are sometimes mistaken by the layperson for cockroaches, particularly in the warm, moist areas of the United States where cockroaches commonly occur outdoors in spring and summer. But cockroaches have long antennae and a different overall shape when seen from above.

As the common name implies, ground beetles are usually found on the ground. But they also tunnel under objects and surface debris, and search for prey on leaves and flowers. They are mostly nocturnal, preferring to hide during the day. Although sometimes seen flying to lights at night, they usually run rapidly, rather than fly, when disturbed.

Both larvae and adults—which usually occur in the same habitat—prey on a wide variety of organisms, from mites, snails, and earthworms to many of the insect orders. The well-known and rather large (1 in./2.5 cm) caterpillar hunter *Calosoma sycophanta* was introduced from Europe to control the gypsy moth. Although it does feed on this pest, it cannot by itself control gypsy-moth outbreaks. It also feeds on a wide variety of other pest caterpillar species, including the satin moth, the brown-tailed moth, and tussock moths. The adults have shiny iridescent coloration. Compared to most insects, these beetles are long-lived, sometimes surviving as long as four years.

Ground beetle, *Carabus granulatus*, will eat almost any organism they can find on the ground surface, including earthworms, and are frequently killed out of fear and ignorance. (Photo by Alslutsky/Shutterstock)

GROUND BEETLES: WHAT THEY EAT

Learning about the feeding habits of predatory beetles is difficult, because they leave so little evidence of what they ate after they're done. Specially contrived laboratory or field studies are needed to determine their diet. In feeding experiments, *Pterostichus malidus* larvae (a European species of the common large black carabid genus beetles that occur widely throughout Europe and North America) consumed the following: nematodes, isopods (crustaceans), earthworms, thrips, bugs (Jassidae), caterpillars, larval craneflies and marchflies (Tipulidae and Bibionidae), ground-beetle eggs, larval water scavenger beetles, rove beetles, and weevils. They also ate some species within the following groups: aphids, adult flies, springtails (Collembola), larval fruit flies and soldier flies, mites, spiders, silverfish and bristletails, slugs, larval ground beetles and soldier beetles, adult beetles,

ROVE BEETLES

(Order Coleoptera, family Staphylinidae)

Most rove beetles are predators of other insects found in decaying organic matter such as dung and carrion. One group in the subfamily Aleocharinae has species that are parasitic on fleas, ants, and termites. Rove beetles are easy to spot because they have wing covers so short that most of their abdominal segments are visible from above. Frequently, these beetles carry their abdomen pointing upward.

Although rove beetles comprise one of the largest families of beetles, with about 3,000 North American species and 30,000 worldwide, they are poorly studied. They are found in a wide variety of habitats: in decaying vegetable matter; under stones; at the edges of creeks; in moss, fungi, dung, and seaweed; on carrion; under bark; in caves; and in the nests of birds and mammals. In the garden they can be seen in

and others. However, they would not touch slug eggs, larval flower flies (Syrphidae), plant seeds, leaves of grasses and moss, strawberry, or apples. The studies indicate that this genus will eat a wide variety of other organisms—including its own species—that live within the same soil surface zone.

A few ground beetles are highly specific feeders that attack only certain arthropod groups; others feed on a range of plants. Many ground beetles are carrion feeders, some others are parasitic. An example of the latter is the large genus *Lebia*, which has species that parasitize the elm leaf beetle in southern Europe and the Colorado potato beetle.

Ground beetles are fed upon by an equally wide range of parasitic microorganisms and predators, including insectivores (hedgehogs, shrews, moles), bats, mice, birds, frogs, toads, spiders, predacious robber flies (Asilidae), and ants.

compost piles, in and under mulches, and on flowers.

One large black species, *Ocypus olens*, with the ominous-sounding common name of devil's coachman, has been explored as a control for the brown garden snail *(Helix aspersa)*. This snail was introduced quite deliberately into California in the 1850s by a Frenchman who wanted to encourage its consumption by Americans. The snail never really did catch on as food here, but it has become a major pest in citrus groves and in domestic ornamental and food gardens (see Chapter 14). *Ocypus olens* preys on snails and other organisms in both the larval and adult stages. Where the beetle occurs, snail populations are lower. The devil's coachman is difficult to spot, but its presence can be detected by the small (⅛ in./3 mm) holes it leaves in empty snail shells.

This rove beetle in the family Staphylinidae is easily distinguished from other beetles: its abdominal segments are visible behind its short wings. (Photo by Katarina Christenson/Shutterstock)

We should note that research on this beetle species as a control for snails was eclipsed by newer work on the predatory decollate snail *(Rumina decollata)*, a beneficial snail that has been shown in field studies to be effective against the brown garden snail (see pp. 343–344). *R. decollata* is easier to rear than the staphylinid beetle. Nevertheless, where the beetle is present, it provides a valuable service in reducing snail populations, as damage to snails in our own area shows. It turns out that decollate snails not only prey on the brown garden and other snails, but they are omnivores and will eat seedlings, too. In California, shipments of decollate snails are limited by law to areas south of the Tehachapi Mountains. In areas north of the mountains, the decollate snail feeds on endangered native snails. There are no shipping limitations in other states.

The cabbage root maggot *(Delia [=Hylema] brassicae)*, an accidentally introduced pest of brassicas (cabbage, turnips, broccoli, etc.), is preyed on by a staphylinid beetle, *Aleochara bilineata*. The beetle was also accidentally introduced, probably about the same time as the pest. Adult staphylinid beetles lay their eggs in the soil near the roots of brassicas already infested by the pest root maggot. The young beetle larvae hatch in about 12 days and search out the maggot pupae, which by this time have left the roots. The beetles gnaw a hole in the pupal shell and feed on the developing pupae within. The beetles then pupate within the pupal shell (the entrance hole they chewed is sealed by their waste, called frass), and later emerge and mate. The adult beetles are strongly predacious on both the eggs and larvae of the root maggot.

LACEWINGS

(Order Neuroptera, families Chrysopidae and Hemerobiidae)

As the common name indicates, lacewings have two pairs of delicate lace-like wings in the adult stage. Another common name, aphid lions, implies that the lacewing's sole food is aphids, which is not so. Although many lacewings do feed on aphids, they also attack other pest insects, including scales, mealybugs, whiteflies, caterpillars, leafhoppers, thrips, mites, and others. The relatively well-known "ant lions" that dig a pit to capture ants are not lacewings at all, but related neuropterans (family Myrmeleontidae). There are at least nine other families in the order Neuroptera. Most of these species are only known and identified by specialists. If you already know and recognize species in the two common families of lacewings, you can also recognize many of the others. All of the adults have "nerve-like wings," the common family characteristic from which the name is derived. The family name Neuroptera combines the word "neuro" meaning "nerve" and "optera" for "wing."

Two families of lacewings are known: the green lacewings (*Chrysopidae*) and the brown lacewings (Hemerobiidae). Chrysopidae, with over 1,500 species in 90 genera, is the largest neuropteran family and occurs on all the temperate continents and islands. The green lacewings are sometimes called golden-eyes. They lay eggs on the end of a thread of silk to protect them from predators, whereas brown lacewings lay eggs directly on leaves. Both families are widely distributed and are commonly seen by gardeners. Adults are sometimes observed flying to lights at night or against the outside of screened windows. Larvae are harder to find and frequently camouflage themselves by attaching debris to their backs.

Adult lacewings in the family Chrysopidae are commonly attracted to lights and on warm summer evenings, congregate on window screens. (Photo by Sergeytoronto/Dreamstime.com)

THE GREEN LACEWING
(*Chrysoperla carnea* and *C. rufilabris*)

The green lacewing has become important as a commercial pest control agent; it is mass-produced and released for control of aphids on many landscape, garden, and greenhouse plants, and on many horticultural and agricultural crops.

Adult green lacewings are beautiful green or yellow-green insects about ¾ in. (1.9 cm) long with golden eyes. In the adult stage, this species of lacewing feeds only on pollen or honeydew (a sweet exudate of aphids, scales, mealybugs, and some other hymenopterans derived from plant sap) or honeydew substitute, which we discuss further below. The larval stages prey on many types of soft-bodied insects and eggs of even more insects and mites. The larvae are very active and look like flat alligators, but with large, piercing, laterally opposed tusks. These hollow tusks, or mandibles, are used

THE LIFE CYCLE OF THE GREEN LACEWING

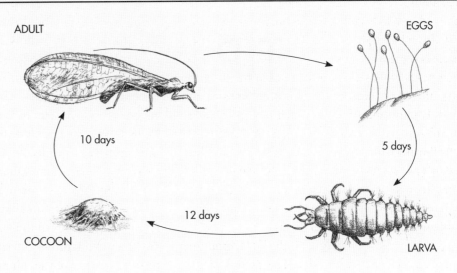

The lacewing adult (*Chrysoperla carnea*), which lives 20 to 40 days, feeds on pollen and honeydew. Each female lays 10 to 30 eggs per day. The larvae that emerge in about five days are general predators of aphids, psyllids, mealybugs, moth eggs, and larvae.

Redrawn from R. L. Tassen and K.S. Hagen's *Culturing Green Lacewings in the Home and School* (University of California Cooperative Extension Service, 1970).

ADULT

EGGS

10 days

5 days

12 days

COCOON

LARVA

An adult common green lacewing, *Chrysoperla carnea*, feeds on pollen and nectar. The larva stage is predatory. (Photo by Kodo34/Dreamstime.com)

to pierce prey and suck out body fluids. The larger larvae do not hesitate to attack considerably larger pest insects, such as caterpillars. But they also eat smaller prey, such as pest mites.

The lacewing pupa is white and shaped like a small pearl. The strands of silk in the pupa are visible to the naked eye. After pupating for approximately two weeks, depending on the temperature, the adults emerge and look for mates. After mating, the females lay their eggs on short silky stalks, presumably to protect the late hatchers from being eaten by the early ones, which are cannibalistic. The life cycle of the green lacewing is depicted in the drawing on p. 65.

TIP Like the bees whose markings and color they imitate, valuable hover flies are especially at risk from insecticides used on flowering plants. You should let the hover flies eat your aphids; if you feel you must take further action against the aphids, try the plain water or soap-and-water wash described on pp. 305–306 before using something more toxic that might harm the hover flies.

HOVER FLIES

(Order Diptera, family Syrphidae)

Syrphids, or hover flies, are also called flower flies, because they frequently visit flowers. They are nectar- and pollen-feeders, and are important pollinators. For protection, many adults are brightly colored with yellow, black, or metallic-looking markings that mimic the markings of wasps and bees. The range of feeding habits in this family is great. Syrphidae include plant-feeders, decomposers, predators, and flies that live in ant, bee, or wasp nests as inquilines (predators that enjoy the protection of the prey colony while feeding on the immature stages of the prey) or scavengers. The predacious species feed on aphids, caterpillars, beetles, thrips, and larval sawflies.

Adults of the predacious species can usually be observed hovering around flowers or aphid colonies. They are easily mistaken for bees or wasps, but their hovering habit is steadier and more intense than members of these two groups. As dipterans, they have a single pair of wings. This distinguishes them from hymenopterans, or true bees, which have two pairs of wings. The males can be distinguished from the females (even while hovering) by the large eyes that cover most of their heads.

After feeding on pollen for protein, the females are capable of laying eggs. Their white eggs are laid singly in a horizontal plane attached to leaf surfaces. (With a hand lens, these eggs can be distinguished from brown lacewing eggs, which have a short, raised cylindrical knob on one end.) The larvae that emerge are the important stage if you are relying on hover flies for aphid control. These larvae, which lack jointed legs and are brownish or greenish in color, can frequently be seen moving about in aphid colonies, attacking aphids by puncturing their skins and sucking out the liquid contents.

After feeding and molting a number of times, the larvae form into tear- or barrel-shaped pupae, which are glued to the leaf. These pupae often resemble grape seeds. If you place one in a jar and let it emerge from its pupa, you can get a good look at an adult. But sometimes shiny, metallic-green miniwasps emerge instead of the adult hover fly. These are parasitic insects that have killed the developing hover-fly pupae;

This adult hover fly, or flower fly, in the family Syrphidae, feeds only on flowers and aphid honeydew. (Photo by DtguyDreamstime.com)

DID YOU KNOW?

The computer term "bug" was popularized by computer pioneer Rear Admiral Grace Hopper when a real bug, a moth in this instance, was trapped and shorted a relay in the Harvard Mark II computer in 1947.

they belong to the hymenopteran genus *Diplazon* (family Ichneumonidae), and are sometimes called hyperparasites, or secondary parasitoids.

PREDACIOUS BUGS

(Order Hemiptera)

"Bug off," "You bug me"—bugs have found their way into the English language in many ways. And now they have invaded computer programs, which sometimes need debugging. We use the term loosely, even pejoratively, in everyday language. But what does bug mean in the strict biological sense? As you have just read, ladybugs are not bugs at all, but beetles.

Scientifically speaking, hemipterans are the true bugs. But even the true bugs have suffered a confusing shift in nomenclature. Originally there were two orders, Hemiptera for bugs and Homoptera for aphids, scales, whiteflies, mealybugs, leafhoppers, etc. Now both have been combined in a single large order, the Hemiptera, and the bugs that were in the original Hemiptera order now occupy the suborder Heteroptera, the true bugs.

More important than these fine points of nomenclature, however, is the fact that many Heteroptera are very important beneficial insects. For example, the spined soldier bug *(Podisus maculiventris)* is an important predator of the Mexican bean beetle and the Colorado potato beetle, two serious farm and garden pests that are largely resistant to insecticides. This suborder also contains phytophagous (plant-eating)

The spined soldier bug, *Podisus maculiventris*, is a predatory stinkbug. This one is feeding on a fall armyworm, *Spodoptera frugiperda* (most stinkbugs are herbivores; this is an exception). (Photo by Frank Peairs, Colorado State University, Bugwood.org)

ANTS, BEES, AND WASPS

(Order Hymenoptera)

After spiders, probably no group of arthropods is as feared and under-appreciated as the organisms in the order Hymenoptera. Sadly, this may be an indication of how far we have moved away from our agricultural roots and how much we now control and limit our interaction with the natural systems that surround us.

The bad name is undeserved. In fact, hymenopterans comprise the greatest number of species that control pest insects through predation and parasitism. They are the most important plant pollinators, and many are detritivores. The hymenopterans in the latter group are particularly significant, as they break animal and plant tissues into smaller particles that eventually release nutrients crucial to the continued maintenance of life.

species. Some important Heteroptera families containing predatory species, together with their prey (if they are specific), are listed in the chart below. The entire order contains more than 61 families.

IMPORTANT FAMILIES OF PREDATORY HETEROPTERA

FAMILY	COMMON NAME	PREY AND/OR HABITAT
Anthocoridae *Orius* spp.	minute pirate bugs or flower bugs	thrips, homopterans, hemipterans, lepidopterans, mites
Dipsocoridae	(none)	found in moss, leaf litter, and ant nests
Enicocephalidae	(none)	found in litter, under stones, and in rotting logs
Lygaeidae *Geocoris* spp.	big-eyed bugs	mites, Diptera larvae, aphids, leaf hoppers
Miridae *Deraeocoris* spp.	plant bugs	pentatomids, syrphid larvae, aphids
Nabidae *Nabis* spp.	damsel bugs	aphids, leaf hoppers
Pentatomidae	shield or stink bugs	lepidopterans, beetle larvae, bed bugs
Reduviidae	assassin bugs	aphids, leaf hoppers, caterpillars, fly larvae, bed bugs, other reduviids, bees

Adapted from R. W. Merritt and K. W. Cummins's *An Introduction to the Aquatic Insects of North America* (Kendall/Hunt, 1978).
Another nine families occur in this order; all aquatic species, consult the source document for further details.

Hymenoptera get their order name from "hymen" (membrane) and "ptera" (wings). They have two pairs of wings, but the second pair is often hard to see. This order is so big that it is difficult to capture its diversity in a brief review. Some of its species are virtually unnoticed and unstudied; others are so large or so common that most of us are very familiar with them. In fact, by the time most children reach kindergarten they have received so many warnings about bees and wasps that their curiosity has been replaced by fear of these marvelous creatures.

We can start by sorting the various Hymenoptera into ants, bees, and wasps. But it is important to remember that their taxonomical grouping is more complicated. Technically, the Hymenoptera are grouped into two large suborders. The first suborder contains sawflies and horntails, which are primarily plant-feeders, although one family is entirely parasitic on wood-boring beetles and the adults of other families are predators on other insects. The second suborder contains two divisions, one composed of the parasitoids, the other containing the ants, bees, and predacious wasps.

It is important to understand that the few species of ants, bees, and wasps that are considered pests also perform important predacious services. The chart at right lists the superfamilies in the three hymenopteran suborders.

ANTS
(Superfamily Formicoidea)

"Go to the ant . . . and consider her ways, and be wise" (Proverbs 6:68). The problem is, there are over 9,000 species of ants in nine subfamilies. Which one is the Bible suggesting we visit? George and Jeanette Wheeler actually try to answer this question (among others) in *The Ants of North Dakota* (University of North Dakota Press, 1963). After surveying various ants' modes of living, they concluded that the Bible must be talking about the harvest ant.

THE SUPERFAMILIES OF THE HYMENOPTERA

SUPERFAMILIES	COMMON NAMES/DESCRIPTION
SUBORDER SYMPHYTA	SAWFLIES; HORNTAILS; STEM, WOOD, AND LEAF WASPS
Cephoidea	All these feed on plant and plant products except for some carnivorous adults in Tenthredinoidea, and one family in Siricoidea (Orussidae) that contains parasitoidic species that attack flat-headed wood-boring beetles in the family Buprestidae.
Megalodontoidea	
Siricoidea	
Tenthredinoidea	
Xyeloidea	
SUBORDER APOCRITA	
Division: Parasitica	
Chalcidoidea	parasitoids and gall-makers
Cynipoidea	one family, Cynipidae, contains gall-makers or gall inquilines
Evanioidea	one family, Evaniidae, contains cockroach egg capsule parasitoids
Ichneumonoidea	parasitoids; largest Hymnopteran family
Megalyroidea	parasitoids of wood-boring beetles
Proctotrupoidea	parasitoids with a diverse range of hosts
Trigonaloidea	hyperparasitoids of sawfly and caterpillar larvae
Division: Aculeata	
Chrysidoidea	parasitoids of wasps and bees; Chrysididae comprises the cukoo wasps
Apoidea	contains 11 families of bees
Bethyloidea	mostly parasitoids
Formicoidea	only one family, Formicidae, the ants
Pompiloidea	spider wasps, with one spider per nest cell
Scolioidea	parasitoids of beetles
Sphecoidea	digger wasps, the largest group of predatory wasps
Vespoidea	social wasps, yellowjackets, hornets, paper wasps

From Krombein et al.'s *Catalog of Hymenoptera in America North of Mexico*, vol. 2 (Smithsonian Institute Press, 1979).
Gall-makers produce external growths on plants. Gall inquilines live inside galls. Hyperparasitoids attach and develop on primary parasitoids.

Some ants form associations with aphids, raising them like dairy cattle. The aphids produce honeydew for the ants, and the ants in turn protect the aphids from predators. (Photo by Johann Viloria/Shutterstock)

The ability to provide for the winter is just one reason ants deserve our respect. They are also very useful scavengers that not only clean up dead animals and debris in the garden (and house, if permitted), but also aerate the soil and prey on other insects. Certain ant species are used to control caterpillars in Chinese citrus orchards, and red ants are used in forest management in Europe because of their predatory habits. The fire ant kills boll weevils in U.S. cotton fields.

We have witnessed the power of Argentine ants *(Iridomyrmex humilis)* in killing subterranean termites. These ants, which are common through-out the southern United States from the eastern seaboard to California, can wipe out entire termite colonies overnight if humans allow them to enter the termite nest by opening the tunnels for them.

It seems clear that some measure of protection from new termite invasions is provided when the boundaries of a home or other wooden structure are patrolled constantly by ant species such as this one.

Of course, the Argentine ant and other ant species can be pests, too. Outdoors, Argentine ants protect honeydew-producing pests such as aphids from their natural enemies, and indoors they can become

DID YOU KNOW?

If hymenoptera had not evolved well before humans and other mammals, plant-feeding insects probably would have devoured everything in sight, making it impossible for us and many other species to have evolved.

nuisances in the kitchen. Fire ants feed directly on plants and can inflict painful stings when they bite humans. The different ant subfamilies and their feeding habits are outlined in the chart below.

BEES
(Superfamily Apoidea)

In *Beekeeping in the United States* (United States Department of Agriculture, 1971), M. D. Levin states:

> Many of our fruits, vegetables, legumes, and oilseed crops are insect-pollinated. Although many kinds of insects visit flowers and effect accidental pollination, the amount is small. Bees are the most efficient and only dependable pollinators, because they visit flowers methodically to collect nectar and pollen and they do not destroy the plant by feeding on it in the pollination process. Although various species of bees contribute to the pollination of our crops, an estimated 80 percent

of this pollination is done by the domesticated honeybee.

More than 100 American crops, about one-third of our diet with a total yearly value exceeding $20 billion, rely solely on honeybees for pollination or are pollinated by a combination of honeybees and wild bees. Also, the stings people fear so much usually result from stepping on bees, inadvertently threatening their hive, or brushing them away violently when they come to drink. (The sole

"More than 100 American crops, about one-third of our diet with a total yearly value exceeding $20 billion, rely solely on honeybees for pollination or are pollinated by a combination of honeybees and wild bees."

intention of sweat bees in the family Halictidae, for example, is to drink moisture from your body.)

Although most bees are solitary, the common honeybee (*Apis mellifera*) is a social insect. The honeybee is one of the oldest domesticated animals; its honey and wax are still valuable commodities in

SUBFAMILIES OF NORTH AMERICAN ANTS

SUBFAMILY	FEEDING HABITS AND OTHER CHARACTERISTICS
Dolichoderinae	These ants are omnivorous, feeding on living and dead insects and honeydew, nectar, and sugar. They include the Argentine ant (*Iridomyrmex humilis*) and the odorous house ant (*Tapinoma sessile*).
Dorylinae (army ants)	The only army ants in North America are two species of *Neivamyrmex* that prey exclusively on other ants in the southern United States from coast to coast.
Formicinae	This subfamily contains the largest ant genus, *Camponotus,* the carpenter ants, which live in decayed wood.
Myrmicinae	The harvester ants in this subfamily harvest seeds and grow fungi; some are parasitic. The largest subfamily, *Pogonomyrmex* spp., are serious agricultural pests and have vicious stings; the fire ants, *Solenopsis* spp., are in this subfamily.
Ponerinae	These ants are monomorphic (the reproductives and workers look alike) and carnivorous. They comprise 25 species found mostly in the southern United States.
Pseudomyrmecinae	These ants nest in plant cavities formed by other organisms or events. The five North American species are confined to the southern states.

From C. G. Wheeler and J. Wheeler's *Ants of Deep Canyon* (Philip L. Boyd Deep Canyon Desert Research Center, University of California, 1973).

This large bumblebee is collecting pollen from a hebe bush to feed its young. Notice the bristles on the abdomen, which distinguish this bee from a carpenter bee, which has a shiny abdomen. Both are relatively docile. (Photo by Ian Grainger/123RF)

societies that lack modern sugar- and oil-refining technology. Because of this bee's great value to humans and our fascination with its complex social behavior, a great deal is known about it.

Honeybees are considered the most highly evolved of the Hymenoptera. The key to the success of their complex, highly regulated society is that reproductive activities are delegated to a single member of the society: the queen. This theme—the segregation of reproductive functions among females—is the subject of a fascinating and groundbreaking book by Edward O. Wilson, *The Insect*

Societies (Harvard University Press, 1971), which describes in great detail the biology and sociology of bees and the other major social insects: wasps, ants, and termites.

SOCIAL WASPS
(Superfamily Vespoidea)

The social wasps are the insects people think of when they hear the term wasp, and they generate the same frightened reaction in some people that spiders do. All social wasps are predators; some are also scavengers. Thus, they are beneficial insects despite the fact that they can and occasionally do sting people.

The social wasps comprise the yellowjackets, hornets, and paper wasps. The yellowjackets and hornets are great opportunists, feeding on almost any soft-bodied insect, spider, or small animal, alive or dead. Yellowjackets have been seen preying on flies where the flies occur in large concentrations, as on cattle ranches. They also feed on economically injurious agricultural pests, including Lygus bugs, spittle bugs, various caterpillars, earwigs, beetles, grasshoppers, and psyllids (jumping plant lice). However, studies documenting yellowjackets' prey habits and overall beneficial impact are few compared to those assessing damage caused by the injurious species.

All social wasps live in colonies, building their nests from a mixture of wood pulp, saliva, and, sometimes, mud. They have worker castes that gather food, build, and guard the nest and tend a queen and the young. The queen lays all the eggs for the colony; if a queen dies, a worker can take over the egg-laying function until a new queen is produced by the colony.

These social species only occur in Vespidae, one of the three families in the superfamily Vespoidea (see the chart below). The other two families, Masaridae and Eumenidae, are solitary or subsocial wasps. These wasps and the paper wasps (subfamily Polistinae, family Vespidae) are much more docile than the aggressive yellowjackets and hornets in the subfamily Vespinae (family Vespidae).

CLASSIFICATION OF THE SOCIAL WASPS

TAXON	CHARACTERISTICS
Superfamily Vespoidea	
Family Eumenidae	nonaggressive, solitary or subsocial; predacious on various insects, most often caterpillars
Family Masaridae	nonaggressive, solitary or subsocial; primarily pollen- and nectar-feeders; one genus predacious
Family Vespidae	aggressive and docile species; social; predacious
SUBFAMILY POLISTINAE	docile
Tribe Polistini	worldwide distribution
Genus *Polistes*	docile paper wasps
Tribe Polybiini	found in tropical South America and Africa
Tribe Ropalidiini	found in tropics of the Old World
SUBFAMILY STENOGASTRINAE	docile
SUBFAMILY VESPINAE	generally aggressive
Genus *Dolichovespula*	very aggressive hornets; four North American species; aerial nesting
Genus *Provespa*	nocturnal; three Southeast Asian species
Genus *Vespa*	only one North American species, the docile giant hornet (*Vespa crabro*)
Genus *Vespula*	aggressive yellowjackets; 12 North American species; large colonies

From R. Edwards's *Social Wasps* (Rentokil, 1980).

The beneficial role of the paper, or umbrella, wasps has received more attention. Researchers have attempted to increase their numbers by building artificial nesting locations and measuring their predation rates. Studies have shown that more nesting sites can increase their impact on garden and agricultural pests, such as the cabbage butterfly *(Pieris rapae)* and tobacco hornworm *(Manduca sexta)*. Predation rates can be very high. For example, in starting up a new colony, individual wasp queens killed between one and eight cabbage-butterfly caterpillars a day. By the time the workers emerged in the new colony, the queens had already killed a total of 152 caterpillars on average. And after the workers emerged, the total caterpillars killed per wasp colony soared to 2,000.

The relatively docile paper wasps have thin waists that distinguish them from the more aggressive yellowjackets and hornets. Those found in the garden or around the house probably belong to the paper wasp genus *Polistes*. If the waist is thin and long with bright yellow and black markings, the wasp is probably a mud-dauber, especially if it is seen flying to a mud nest. Mud-daubers prey on spiders.

Yellowjackets (subfamily Vespinae) are wasps about the size of bees (½ in. to ¾ in./13 mm to 19 mm long) with thick waists (or seemingly no waists at all) and yellow markings. They are often seen flying near garbage cans or picnic tables in search of food. These wasps can be quite troublesome and may bite as well as sting. Fortunately, the bite is not as painful as the sting, and the effects are not as long-lasting.

Hornets *(Dolichovespula* spp.) also have thick waists, and their behavior is similar to that of yellowjackets; however, unlike yellowjackets, they usually live in aerial nests. The European hornet *(Vespa crabro)* was introduced accidentally from Europe. It is the largest vespine species, almost an inch long. Unlike yellowjackets, it is not pestiferous.

This large predatory paper wasp is tending its nest. Paper wasps are relatively docile compared to yellow jackets, with which they are commonly confused. They make a nest by chewing bark and other materials and gluing them together. Paper wasps are predators of caterpillars and are beneficial in the garden. (Photo by Jahoo/Dreamstime.com)

THE PREY OF THE IMPORTANT CHALCID FAMILIES

FAMILY NAME	PARASITIC ON
Aphelinidaea	scales, aphids
Chalcididae	lepidopteran pupae and Diptera (flies, most species), Hymenoptera (ants, wasps, etc.), and Coleoptera (beetles, some species)
Encyrtidae	most insect orders, ticks, and spider eggs
Eucharidae	immature ants within nests
Eulophidae	Coleoptera, Lepidoptera, Diptera, Hymenoptera, mites, spider egg cases, Thysanoptera (thrips), and Homoptera; Eulopidae are primary and secondary parasitoids
Eurytomidae	insect and spider eggs, gall-formers, Lepidoptera, Coleoptera, Diptera, Hymenoptera, and psyllids in Homoptera; some are phytophagous (plant-feeders)
Eutrichosomatidae	weevils
Leucospidae	solitary bees
Mymaridae (fairy flies)	eggs of many species
Ormyridae	gall-forming Hymenoptera
Perilampidae	dipteran and hymenopteran parasitoids of Lepidoptera, Coleoptera, Neuroptera; Perilampidae are primary and secondary parasitoids
Pteromalidae	Lepidoptera, Coleoptera, Diptera, Hymenoptera; Pteromalidae are primary and seconday parasitoids
Spalangiidae	muscoid, calliphorid, and drosophilid flies exclusively; attack pupae
Torymidae	gall-formers in Cynipidae, Cecidomyiidae, Diptera, Coleoptera, Lepidoptera, Hymenoptera, Orthoptera; plant-feeders and carnivorous
Trichogrammatidae	eggs of many Lepidoptera, Homoptera, Hemiptera, Orthoptera, Thysanoptera

Aphelinidae, the most important family in classical biological control, is sometimes included in Encyrtidae. Some authors include the Eucharidae, Perilampidae, and Spalangiidae families as subfamilies in Pteromalidae.

This species is predacious, capturing large grasshoppers, horseflies, flies, bees, and yellowjackets. Its workers fly at night and are sometimes attracted to lighted windows, causing unwarranted alarm to the people inside.

This hornet has been reported to girdle (damage the cambium layer under the bark) twigs and branches of many trees and shrubs, including lilac, birch, ash, horsechestnut, dogwood, dahlia, rhododendron, and boxwood, probably to obtain sap. Sometimes the plants are killed. *V. crabro* is also a pest of beehives, but it does not attack en masse like its relative *V. mandariia,* a major pest of honeybees in the Mediterranean. In the United States, *V. crabro* is more beneficial than troublesome, so it should be tolerated where possible.

SOLITARY PREDATORY WASPS

About 90 percent of predatory wasps are solitary species that hunt and sting insects in various groups. They provision their nest with the paralyzed prey, upon which they lay their own eggs. After hatching, the predatory wasp grub devours the prey, pupates, and metamorphoses into an adult. The adults mate and the adult female provisions her nest with insects, starting the cycle again. Generally, the males do not hunt; they feed on nectar and pollen.

The females hunt and feed on specific insect groups. With a few exceptions, these are pest species. Evaniids, for example, attack only cockroaches; pompilids attack spiders. One well-known pompilid often seen in the southwestern United

HOST SPECIFICITY

Certain parasitoid groups attack certain types of prey (or hosts). Host specificity is the key to successful use of these parasitoids against pests. The more host-specific a parasitoid is, the more it depends for survival on finding every individual of the pest species. But this also means that it will not switch to another pest species once it has decimated the first. It is obligated biologically to complete its life cycle on the particular host to which it is specific.

States is the large, striking, metallic-blue tarantula hawk *(Pepsis mildei)*. This species, with its fiery red wings, is a favorite subject of nature films, which show the females attacking and paralyzing the much larger tarantula and then provisioning their nests with it.

The mud-dauber wasps that build clay nests belong to the largest predatory family, Sphecidae. They are also called thread wasps for their thin waist, which occurs between the thorax and abdomen. They are often seen around wooden buildings. They ferry mud to their nests, which they build in cavities, in attics, and even on stored clothes. Wasps like these are fun to watch; they are so docile and so preoccupied with their work that they pose little hazard.

PARASITIC WASPS
(Division Parasitica)

Parasitic wasps are miniwasps that are busy controlling pest species all around you, indoors and out. You probably don't even notice them, but once someone with a trained eye points them out, you'll find them easy to spot, especially in the garden.

A common miniwasp nationwide is *Diaterella rapae,* a parasitoid of a common aphid that attacks brassicas. Because it is one of the larger miniwasps found on garden plants, chances are good you can spot it. Try watching a colony of aphids on any plants in the cabbage family for five minutes or so on a sunny day. Sooner or later, you will notice tiny winged insects flying and walking about among the aphids, jabbing their ovipositors into the aphids and

laying eggs. In a very quick movement, the parasitoid curves the end of her abdomen under her body toward her head each time she deposits an egg.

The parasitic wasps fall mainly into two superfamilies: Ichneumonoidea and Chalcidoidea. Ichneumonoidea is divided into five families, three of which are minor. Most of the species in the two large families, Ichneumonidae and Braconidae, attack specific pest insect groups. They have been of major importance in the biological control of agricultural pests that have invaded from elsewhere.

The ichneumonids have been studied extensively by Henry and Marjorie Townes, who have amassed what is probably the largest collection of worldwide parasitic wasp species and have published a long series of volumes on the family. According to the first volume, "The Ichneumoni-

An ichneumonid parasitoid drilling down with its ovipositor to lay an egg in a wood boring beetle. Ichneumonids are among the most common insects; because of their small size, few people know they exist. (Photo by Jason S/ Shutterstock)

dae is one of the largest of all animal groups; it includes more species than the entire Vertebrata and more than any other family, with the possible exception of the Curculionidae [weevils]."

The ichneumonids comprise 5 percent to 10 percent of the insects in a particular geographical area and about 20 percent of all parasitic insects. Most of the world's species probably still remain to be described. Ichneumonids are mainly primary parasitoids—with a few hyperparasitoids—of all major insect orders. Some attack adult spiders as well as the egg sacs of spiders and pseudoscorpions. They also attack larvae and pupae of other insects, but not the adults or nymphs (the immature stage of orders that do not have pupae). The usual hosts are lepidopterans (caterpillars), sawflies, and wood-boring beetles.

The braconids are primary internal parasitoids of caterpillars, but they attack most insect groups that undergo complete metamorphosis—Coleoptera (beetles), Diptera (flies), and Hymenoptera (bees and wasps), for example—as well as spiders. Worldwide, there are perhaps 40,000 species. Some species are hyperparasitoids, but these are relatively rare. Braconids have been used extensively in biological control projects. A former braconid subfamily that has been raised to family status (the family name is only used by Europeans), Aphidiidae, is important in the biological control of aphids.

The chalcids are the other large assemblage of hymenopterous parasitoids, with over 100,000 species worldwide. The superfamily Chalcidoidea includes some of the gall-formers; the fig wasps (without which some fig trees would not be pollinated); the well-known, commercially available parasitoids of caterpillar eggs in the family Trichogrammatidae; the fairy flies (Mymaridae), which are among the smallest known insects (all are egg parasitoids); and many other parasitoids.

One of the better-known chalcids is the whitefly parasitoid *Encarsia Formosa,* along with the genus *Aphytis* in the family Aphelinidae, which is important in the biological control of scales. The chart on p. 75 summarizes the prey groups of the important chalcid families.

BATS

(Order Chiroptera)

Bats have an undeserved bad reputation. Of all the animals in nature, we probably get more direct assistance from the 1,200 known species of bats worldwide than any other animal. Most bats eat insects that fly at night, many of which directly affect gardening, agriculture, and people. The little brown bat *(Myotis lucifugus)* can eat up to 1,000 mosquitoes per hour and up to about 4,500 insects per night, which is greater than its body weight. A single colony of 150 big brown bats *(Eptesicus fuscus)* can protect farmers from 33 million or more rootworms each summer. The estimated 50 million Mexican free-tailed bats at Bracken Cave in Texas, the largest known bat colony in the world, can consume upward of 1,250,000 lb. of insects per night. This is a prodigious number of insects, and most are pest species.

Bats are the most important mammalian predators of insects. The pallid bat shown here has just captured a grasshopper. (Photo © Merlin D. Tuttle, Bat Conservation International, www.batcon.org)

Insects eaten by bats include mosquitoes, corn earworm, codling moth, grasshoppers, spotted cucumber beetles, leafhoppers, flies, tomato hornworm, termites, moths, and stink bugs, to name just a few. Many of these insects are economically important pests of food and fiber crops in gardens and agriculture. Some, such as mosquitoes, flies, termites, and others, also have a direct impact on people.

Bat populations are declining precipitously for a number of reasons, primarily habitat loss, but also from people killing bats. Providing habitat in the form of bat houses is one way to slow the population decline and maybe even reverse it locally. One new problem is the lethal fungal disease called White-Nose Syndrome, so-named because of the white fungus that grows on the noses and sometimes wings, ears, and tails of bats. Discovered in February 2006 in New York State, the pathogen has spread rapidly and, as of February 2012, has been documented in 19 U.S. states and four Canadian provinces. The causal pathogen of White-Nose Syndrome is the fungus *Geomyces destructans.* The species name "destructans" is apt, as it is so destructive to bat populations. Although bat-to-bat contact is probably the primary means of transmission, there is evidence to suggest that people may be moving the pathogen from infected sites to clean sites.

It is important that we do what we can to help preserve an animal that provides us with so much free insect pest control assistance. Construct bat houses in your neighborhood and community. As bats move in, night-flying insects decline. Collect the guano under the bat houses and use it as an organic fertilizer, being sure to wear rubber gloves and a dust mask when handling guano between the collecting point and soil incorporation. Refrain from using persistent broad-spectrum insecticides, which can bio-accumulate in bats. Please visit the Bat Conservation International website (www.batcon.org) and find out more about these fascinating mammals.

If you have bats roosting in your attic, garage, or other building, you need to call an exclusion expert. Bat Conservation International can provide names of reliable experts in your area and give you information on what you can do before, during, and after exclusion. Putting up a bat house near a structure where bats are roosting gives them an attractive alternative residence.

If you handle a bat and are bitten, see a doctor immediately. Infections from bat bites, and any animal for that matter, are not uncommon. Rabies from bats is extremely rare, 15 cases in 50 years. Trap and save the bat that bit you and take it with you to the doctor's office so it can be checked for rabies or other infections.

This bat house for roosting bats is nailed to a tree trunk. (Photo by Nancy Hixson/123RF)

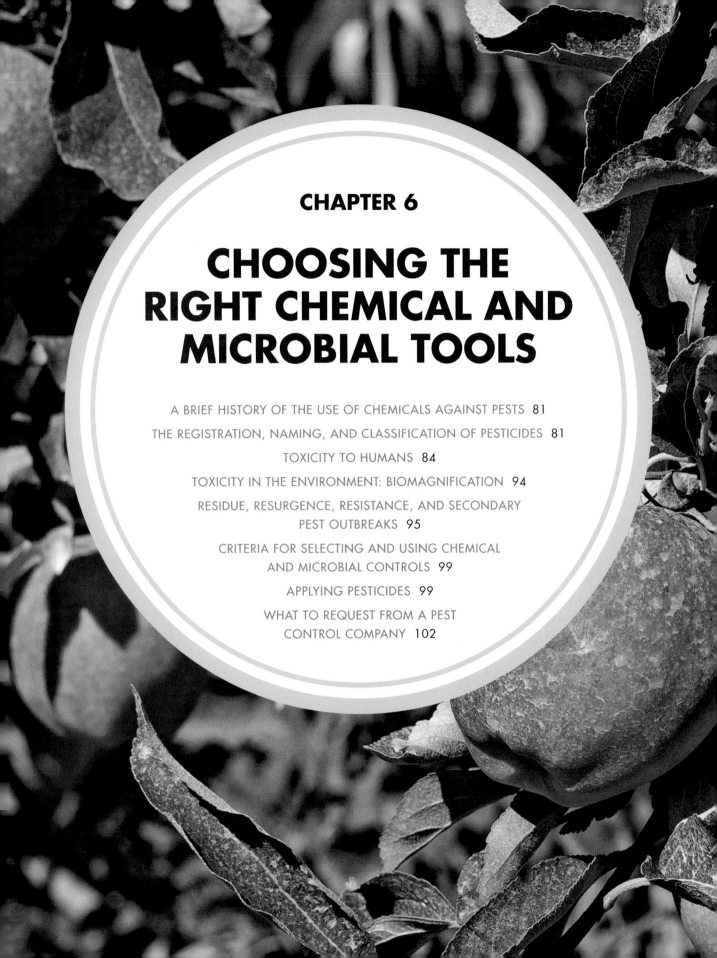

CHAPTER 6

CHOOSING THE RIGHT CHEMICAL AND MICROBIAL TOOLS

The use of chemical compounds as tools in the competition among species predates the rise of humans. Plants have evolved chemical defenses against other plants (allelopathy) that are often expressed as root exudates or compounds leached from the leaves. Leaves or other tissues can also produce chemicals that repel or damage organisms that attempt to feed on them. Many familiar animals, such as toads, snakes, and skunks, have incorporated repellent or poisonous materials into their skins, saliva, or other fluids. And, among animals without backbones (invertebrates), the use of poisons against enemies is commonplace. Thus, it seems entirely natural that humans should also resort to chemical tools to rid themselves of their pests.

However, the primary focus of this book is on nonchemical methods. We are not trying to cover everything there is to know about pesticides; our goal is to provide enough information to enable you to select the safest, most effective material, and apply it in a manner that protects both you and the general environment. Instead of discussing common insecticides such as malathion, herbicides like 2, 4-D, or fungicides such as chlorothalonil, we focus on the least-toxic pesticidal products, such as pesticidal soaps, horticultural oils, and botanical

"Our goal is to provide enough information to enable you to select the safest, most effective material, and apply it in a manner that protects both you and the general environment."

A sampling of pest control products: 1. lady beetle adults, 2. milky spore powder, 3. grasshopper pathogen, 4. beneficial nematode powder, 5. predatory mites, 6. trichogramma wasps, 7. green lacewings, 8. praying mantis egg cases, 9. BT dunks. (Photo by Jennifer Brown, courtesy of *Fine Gardening*)

compounds, as well as on insect growth regulators and microbes used to kill pests. This chapter and the next two chapters provide background information on the composition, application, and impact of various pesticides, including the innovative botanical and microbial materials we often recommend when pesticides are necessary.

A BRIEF HISTORY OF THE USE OF CHEMICALS AGAINST PESTS

Before World War II, the pesticides in common use in the United States were predominantly inorganic materials, such as sulfur, lead, copper, arsenic, boron, and mercury, as well as botanical (plant-derived) compounds, such as nicotine, pyrethrum, derris, rotenone, ryania, and sabadilla.

The emergence of DDT, a "miracle" insecticide developed by the Swiss just before World War II, changed the nature of pest control worldwide. The extraordinary effectiveness of DDT and the related materials that followed it in rapid succession—lindane, dieldrin, chlordane, 2, 4-D, and others—greatly slowed research and development of other, less-toxic methods of pest control, particularly biological controls (the use of pests' natural enemies to control the pests). Even the gradual accumulation of evidence that the entire planet was becoming contaminated with these newly created materials and their breakdown products failed to impress upon many responsible people the real threat posed by this type of pollution. The first systematic accumulation of information on the organochlorine insecticides and other pesticides, especially DDT, is found in the book *Silent Spring* (Fawcett, 1962) by Rachel Carson. Reading the book today is an education on how far we have and have not come since its publication in 1962, over a half-century ago.

Today there is a great deal of confusion about the toxicity of and necessity for pesticides. The good news is that there are some pesticides already on the market that are highly selective, meaning they kill only certain groups of pests, and are relatively harmless to humans and other nontarget organisms. They also biodegrade rapidly. These materials, discussed in detail in Chapters 7 and 8, are far more benign than such broad-spectrum insecticides as carbaryl, malathion, and acephate, which kill a wide range of organisms, including beneficial insects and microbes. Many broad-spectrum insecticides and other pesticides do not biodegrade readily into harmless materials and can contaminate groundwater and other resources.

THE REGISTRATION, NAMING, AND CLASSIFICATION OF PESTICIDES

Pesticide selection is often complicated by technical terminology. This section should help clarify some of the important terms used by pest control personnel and researchers.

REGISTRATION

The word "pesticide" is an umbrella term for all the subcategories of materials used to suppress pests. These include insecticides, herbicides, fungicides, and rodenticides. At present, a wide variety of commercially available chemical tools is used to control pests. Most are legally considered pesticides, although some are not. For example, when you use a spray solution of liquid dishwashing detergent against aphids, it is acting as a pesticide; however, it is not legally registered as such.

TRUST THE FACTS

"Facts are stubborn things; and whatever may be our wishes, our inclinations, or the dictates of our passions, they cannot alter the state of facts and evidence." That statement was made by John Adams in 1770, while acting as the defense attorney at the trial of the British soldiers involved in the Boston Massacre. We use it here to remind you that when you evaluate a pesticide, or any method or tactic, you rely on facts and evidence, not on "wishes, [your] inclinations, or the dictates of [your] passions." IPM is fact-based and depends on thorough and reliable facts for success. Always check your facts and, remember, sometimes you will be making decisions based on the preponderance of evidence, rather than on a clear-cut set of facts.

"MINIMUM-RISK" PESTICIDES

A relatively new class of pesticides is made from extracts derived from food-grade materials. These products are known formally as the Minimum Risk Pesticide Products Exempted Under Section 25(b) of FIFRA (Federal Insecticide, Fungicide, Rodenticide Act). Exempt pesticides are commonly called 25(b) pesticides, for the regulation governing them. Some examples are castor oil, cloves, corn gluten meal, garlic, mint oil, sesame oil, sodium chloride (table salt), sodium laurel sulfate, and white pepper, to name a few. A list of inert ingredients that may be combined with 25(b) exempt pesticides are the GRAS (Generally Recognized As Safe) materials, also in the Pesticide Registration Notice. Our one concern about the 25(b) exemption is that these materials do not have EPA registration numbers, as all other pesticides do. Use reporting is not required, or even possible, because the EPA registration number is used for reporting and tracking. We feel that any material in the commercial sector, used for pest control of any kind, should have its own unique EPA registration number for easy identification of the exact material in case of poisoning, spills, or other mishaps. We also feel that all pesticides used should be reported; this gives researchers important information when compiling pesticide use data and efficacy statistics.

For more information on section 25(b) pesticides, go to the EPA website, www.epa.gov/PR_Notices/pr2000-6.pdf.

If a product is sold as a pesticide, it must be registered at the federal level by the Environmental Protection Agency and at the state level by an agency such as the state's department of agriculture, environmental protection agency, department of pesticide regulation, or similar state agency. EPA-registered pesticides must carry labels describing the proper dosage and frequency of application for the control of specific pests. The label must also contain a list of the active ingredients (but not necessarily the "inert" ingredients, whose importance is discussed below), information about the product's relative toxicity to mammals, the name and address of the manufacturer, the net contents, an EPA registration number, and cautions regarding hazards to humans and the environment.

EPA registration implies that the pesticide has met standards set for health and environmental safety, although this is the subject of considerable controversy. Many people maintain that safety standards, testing methodology, and testing compliance are far from adequate. These shortcomings are discussed more completely on pp. 91–92. There is no doubt, however, that the registration process is more stringent now than it was in the 1950s and 1960s, when most of the 62,000 pesticide products and over 600 active ingredients currently used as pesticides were registered. Unfortunately, the newer standards are still problematic. They are not comprehensive enough for those concerned about the hazards of pesticides, and they are too costly and too fraught with bureaucratic delays to suit manufacturers, particularly the small, innovative companies attempting to secure registration for novel, less-toxic pesticides.

MODE OF ACTION AND FORMULATION

Before exploring some of the ways in which pesticides are classified, it helps to understand two important terms: *mode of action* (MOA) and *formulation*. The mode of action of a pesticide is the physiological mechanism by which it affects the pest. Many least-toxic pesticides operate physi-

PESTICIDE GROUPS BY TARGET PEST

PESTICIDE GROUP	PRESUMED TARGET PEST
algicide	algae
bactericide	bacteria
fungicide	fungi
herbicide	plants
insecticide	insects
miticide	mites
molluscicide	snails, slugs
rodenticide	rodents

Many pesticides, although labeled as confined in their activity to a particular group of pests, may actually have broad toxicity over many types of organisms. Herbicides, for example, can damage insects and microbes.

cally or mechanically on the pest. For example, sorptive dusts like silica aerogel or diatomaceous earth disrupt the waxy coating on the cuticle of insects, causing them to dehydrate and die. Insecticidal soap penetrates the waxy coating and disrupts the membranes surrounding the cells, allowing the cell contents to leak out, resulting in dehydration and death of the insect.

Other pesticides, including most conventional synthetic functions, have a biochemical mode of action. They disrupt enzymes, hormones, nervous system functions, or other biophysical processes of the target pest. The effect on the organism and the total impact on the environment from a pesticide with a biochemical MOA are often difficult to predict. Unanticipated side effects are more often encountered with pesticides that operate this way than with pesticides whose mode of action is primarily physical and/or mechanical.

The formulation of a pesticide refers to the mixture of its active ingredient and the other ingredients that affect the active ingredient's solubility, its ability to stick to vegetation or insect bodies, and other functions. Substances other than the active ingredient are referred to as adjuvants. An example of an adjuvant is a surfactant, also called a wetting agent or spreader. A surfactant enhances the coverage of a sprayed-on pesticide by reducing the surface tension of the spray droplets and allowing greater pesticide contact, enhancing the toxicity of the material. On the pesticide label these adjuvants are called inert substances, certainly a misnomer because they generally are not inert and usually act synergistically. In some cases, the inerts are more toxic than the active ingredient itself.

CLASSIFICATION

Pesticides can be classified by their target pest group (see the chart on the facing page), formulation (see the chart on p. 85), chemical category (see the chart on p. 86), or function (see the chart on p. 87). Insecticides can also be classified according to the stage in the target insect's development at which they are effective. Most insects go through four develop-

HOW TO GET MORE INFORMATION

A layperson may have considerable trouble obtaining and understanding information about pesticides, because each compound generally has at least two or three names. The generic name—carbaryl, for example—is the term used to refer to the chemical compound. It is frequently the name by which you must search online in order to get the technical literature you need to find out about its toxicity and effectiveness. There is also the chemical name, which describes the molecule. The chemical name for carbaryl, for example, is 1-naphthalenyl methylcarbamate. Sometimes there is more than one chemical name for a compound, depending on the conventions used to describe the molecule.

The trade or brand name is what you ask for in the store; it is also the name pest control professionals generally use when talking with the public. To continue the example, the best-known brand name for carbaryl is Sevin®. To confuse the issue even more, a substance may have several brand names when it is marketed in slightly different formulations.

The following are six websites where you can obtain reliable information that goes into greater depth regarding safety and environmental impacts than do the labels and Material Safety Data Sheets MSDSs/(I) of pesticides.

When searching for pesticide information, use the common chemical name, such as carbaryl in the example above. If you do a search for the brand name Sevin you will most often be directed to websites that sell the product.

- National Pesticide Information Center (NPIC) at Oregon State University: www.npic.orst.edu

- Extension Toxicology Network (Extoxnet): extoxnet.orst.edu

- Pesticide Action Network of North America (PANNA): www.panna.org

- EPA Fact Sheets: www.epa.gov/pesticides/factsheets

- Organic Materials Review Institute (OMRI): www.omri.org

- C&P Press Greenbook (for labels, MSDSs, and additional pesticide information): www.greenbook.net

mental stages: egg, larva (caterpillar, worm, grub, or nymph), pupa (cocoon), and adult. Thus, an ovicide attacks eggs, a larvicide attacks the young, and an adulticide attacks mature individuals. (Note that there are no pupicides.)

Another major point about pesticide classification is that within the major categories (insecticides, herbicides, fungicides, etc.) there are often subgroups peculiar to that group. For example, herbicides are frequently classified according to when they are applied in the life cycle of weeds. Pre-emergent herbicides are applied before the weed germinates; post-emergent herbicides are applied after weed growth is underway. Herbicides can also

THE TRUTH ABOUT INERTS

The complete formulation of a pesticide—the active and inert ingredients together—is now tested, by the EPA and other registration agencies, for all new pesticides and also during re-registration of older pesticides. In the past, only the active ingredient (A.I.) was tested for toxicity, not the formulation sold commercially. The controversy now is that pesticide companies can keep the inert ingredients secret by calling them proprietary ingredients. In other words, they are a trade secret. It is hard to imagine that pesticide manufacturers' chemists don't know exactly what is in a competitor's product. The only parties from whom this information on inerts is kept are the general public, professional pest managers, pesticide applicators, and farmers. So, while pesticide manufacturers and distributors ask us to make our own informed decisions on pesticide use, they continue to refuse to provide us with all of the information we need to make that informed decision.

We must know everything that is contained in pesticides, not just what the companies find convenient. Write to your state and federal legislators and regulators and let them know that you want complete disclosure of pesticide ingredients. Vote with your wallet, by purchasing least-toxic and organic products; increased demand will increase supply. Demand-side economics is the only system that can really make a change. Remember, sometimes the inert ingredients are more toxic than the pesticide's active ingredient. Inerts are inert as far as the pest is concerned— not for you, your family, your pets, or the environment.

be classified according to their selectivity. A selective herbicide is intended to kill certain weeds but leave desirable plants. A nonselective herbicide is toxic to most plant material it encounters.

"All toxicity testing is done by the manufacturer, not the Environmental Protection Agency."

Herbicides classified according to their mode of activity usually fall into one of three main categories: contact, translocated, or residual. Contact herbicides injure or kill plants on contact with their foliage. They are called "chemical mowers," because, like a lawn mower, they kill only that part of the plant with which they come into contact. The 25(b) exempt post-emergent herbicides are all contact herbicides.

Translocated herbicides move through the entire plant system carried by water and food streams to the plant's active growth centers, which they damage or destroy. They can be applied to the soil around the plant or to the plant's foliage, and are usually selective in the range of plants they affect. Soil-residual herbicides are those that remain active in the soil for relatively long periods, depending on the dosage. To be effective, they must be sprayed directly on emerging plant shoots or washed into the soil, where they are taken up by the roots and carried to the leaves; they are relatively ineffective when sprayed on mature foliage.

Similar subcategories exist for all the major pesticide groups. Rodenticides, for example, are separated into single- and multiple-dose groups, fungicides into preventive and curative categories.

TOXICITY TO HUMANS

All toxicity testing is done by the manufacturer, not the Environmental Protection Agency. Pesticides registered by the EPA do not need to meet any safety standards. In fact, the EPA will take

PESTICIDES BY FORMULATION

FORMULATION	EXAMPLES
Baits (poison mixed with food or other attractant)	most rodenticides; ant baits such as boric acid in mint jelly for control of pharaoh ants
Dusts (finely ground mineral or pesticide combined with a dry carrier)	boric acid, diatomaceous earth, pyrethrum, silica aerogel, sulfur
Fumigants (poison gas)	CO_2
Granules (pesticide and carrier combined with a binding agent)	many insecticides and herbicides
Sprays	
Aerosols (very fine liquid droplets delivered from a pressurized can)	pyrethrins
Emulsifiable concentrates (petroleum-based liquid plus emulsifiers that enable it to mix with water)	many pesticides, either ready-to-use or concentrated
Flowables (combine the qualities of emulsifiable concentrates and wettable powders; require agitation when mixed and sprayed)	sulfur; copper compounds
Microencapsulated materials (pesticide particles surrounded by a plastic coating; active ingredients are released slowly as the plastic coating breaks down)	many pesticides
Slurry (thin, watery mixture of finely ground dusts)	Bordeaux mixture (hydrated lime and copper sulfate)
Water-soluble concentrates (liquid pesticides that dissolve in water)	insecticidal soaps
Wettable powders (water-insoluble active ingredient plus mineral clay ground into fine powder that can be mixed with water)	*Bacillus thuringiensis*
Oils (petroleum or botanical)	horticultural oil; weed oil

Note: These materials are discussed in greater detail in this and the next two chapters, and in later portions of the book are recommended in certain situations against specific pests.

INSECTICIDES BY CHEMICAL CATEGORY

CATEGORY	EXAMPLES
Inorganic	boric acid, borates, chlorates, copper, cryolite, diatomaceous earth, silica aerogel
Organic	
botanical	garlic, limonene, neem, pyrethrum, rotenone, ryania, sabadilla
microbial	*Bacillus thuringiensis, B. popilliae, Cephalasporium lecanii, Nosema locustae*
Carbamates	carbaryl (Sevin), propoxur (Baygon®)
Chlorinated hydrocarbons	aldrin, chlordane, kelthane, lindane, pentachlorophenol
Organophosphates	acephate (Orthene®), diazinon, malathion
Synthetic pyrethroids	permethrin, resmethrin
Neonicotinoids	clothianidin, imidacloprid, thiacloprid, thiamethoxam
Miscellaneous	horticultural oils, insect growth regulators, insecticidal soaps, insect pheromones

Note: Most of these materials are discussed in greater detail in this and the next two chapters, and in later portions of the book are recommended in certain situations against specific pests. The names in parentheses are trade names that have become so common that the chemical or generic name is less known.

action against an entity that claims EPA registration means the pesticide is safe. Testing determines toxicity of a material based on selected tests. It also determines what steps should be taken (i.e., what kind of safety equipment is needed) to minimize the hazards when using the pesticide.

Toxicity questions about poisons usually fall into several broad categories: toxicity to humans; toxicity to plants (phytotoxicity); toxicity to organisms that may be exposed to the poison accidentally through drift, soil contamination, water contamination, or magnification in the food chain (biomagnification); effectiveness against the pest; and procedures for using the poison as a pest management tool. We examine human toxicity first.

MEASURING TOXICITY

There are two general kinds of toxicity: acute and chronic. A given dose of a poison is said to have acute toxicity if it affects human health adversely after a relatively short term of exposure; it has chronic toxicity if it has an adverse impact after long-term exposure. Long-term exposure can range from days to years. A poison may be chronically toxic even at relatively low doses if there is prolonged exposure. Dizziness and, in more extreme cases, anaphylactic shock or a heart attack that occurs right after an individual sprays a pesticide indoors are examples of acutely toxic responses. The development of cancer or neurological problems from occupational exposure to pesticides over several decades is an example of a chronic toxicological response.

The most common method of measuring the acute toxicity of a pesticide is by giving test animals known doses of the poison and observing the results. This is the method by which the lethal dose, referred to as the LD_{50}, or the lethal concentration, commonly called the LC_{50}, of a compound is established. These measurements are used to predict the hazards to people and other non-target organisms. Given the choice between two compounds, the higher LD_{50} rating indicates the less acutely poisonous—that is, the "safer"—compound.

The "50" in this expression refers to the dose of a given substance that kills 50 percent of the organisms exposed to it in tests (see the graph on p. 88).

The LD$_{50}$ rating is usually expressed in milligrams of poison per kilogram of body weight, or mg/kg. For example, if a particular poison has an LD$_{50}$ rating of 1.0 mg/kg and each individual in a group of 150-lb. (68-kg) men consumes approximately 68 mg of the pesticide, presumably half the individuals will die immediately. Here's how we arrive at that number mathematically: 1 mg/kg (the LD$_{50}$ rating for the poison) $\times$ 150 lb. (the weight of each man) $\times$ 0.45 kg/lb. (the number of kilograms in each pound) = 68 mg, the dose that will kill one out of two men. However, this measurement has some serious limitations, as discussed on p. 90.

Acute toxicity can also be measured by the amount of pesticide vapor or dust in a given volume of air, or the amount diluted in waterways, that will cause the death of any specific proportion of a test-animal population. This measurement is the lethal concentration, or LC$_{50}$, and it is expressed in micrograms (one microgram equals one millionth of a gram) per liter of air or water mixture or solution.

The LD$_{50}$ and LC$_{50}$ are important numbers for comparing the acute toxicity of one pesticide to another, but let's step back for a moment and look at what this means in real terms. "Lethal dose or concentration" to 50 percent of the test animals should raise red flags as a matter of common sense. To any toxic material, there is usually a wide range of responses, complications, and side effects between being healthy and being dead. Under any definition or consideration, death is a pretty severe complica-

PESTICIDES BY FUNCTION

CATEGORY	EXAMPLES
Attractants	compounds that attract pests to traps or poisons, including sex-based and food-based attractants (e.g., the food attractant in some cockroach traps)
Repellents	compounds that repel the target pest, e.g., neem oil from the neem tree of India, which repels the Japanese beetle
Desiccants	compounds that kill by disrupting insect cuticle, thus drying out the insect, (e.g., diatomaceous earth, silica aerogel)
Insect growth regulators (juvenile hormones)	compounds that mimic insect hormones that regulate development (e.g., methoprene, which prevents fleas from maturing)
Poisons	
contact poisons	materials that penetrate the skin or outer membranes and disrupt the physiology of the organism (e.g., insecticidal soap, pyrethrins)
stomach poisons	materials that attack the pest after it has ingested the poison (e.g., the microbial insecticide *Bacillus thuringiensis*, boric acid)
fumigants	respiratory poisons that kill by suffocation (e.g., CO_2, used to kill storage pests)
pass-throughs or feed-throughs	poisons that pass through an animal's digestive system and kill insects that attempt to inhabit the dung
systemics	materials that are first absorbed by the plant or animal, then kill any organism that feeds upon the poisoned tissues (e.g., the insecticide metasystox-R, the fungicide benomyl)
Sterilants	
insect	materials (in various stages of research) that sterilize an insect without killing it; no commercial products available at present
soil	compounds that kill many forms of life in the soil (e.g., methyl bromide, which is used to fumigate the soil where plant-infesting nematodes are a problem)

THE PRECAUTIONARY PRINCIPLE

We support the Precautionary Principle as it was defined and passed into law by the City and County of San Francisco. "The Precautionary Principle requires that if an activity raises threats of harm to human health or the environment, precautionary measures should be taken even if cause and effect relationships are not fully established scientifically." For more information on the San Francisco Precautionary Principle, go to www.sfenvironment.org.

tion. Review the "Hazards to Humans and Domestic Animals," "Environmental Hazards," and the "Physical or Chemical Hazards" sections of the label to determine effects, other than death, that may occur from exposure to the pesticide. These three sections are legally required to appear on every pesticide label. Read the MSDS thoroughly for additional information on hazards to humans, pets, wildlife, and the environment. The label and MSDS will also provide information on steps you can take to prevent exposure, and what first aid and/or remedial actions you can take in case of exposure or accidental release of the pesticide. This is also the time to refer to the National Pesticide Information Center, Extoxnet, PANNA, EPA Factsheets, and other reliable sources of information on the pesticide and/ or the active ingredient you are considering for use.

An additional point regarding the LD_{50} and LC_{50} method and results is the relative health of the 50 percent that survived the testing. The surviving animals were not healthy. In fact, as you might have guessed, they were very near death themselves. They merely survived within the time limits of the experiment's protocol.

CAUTIONS ON PESTICIDE LABELS

If you look at a pesticide label—and you should always look at the label very carefully if you plan to use any pesticide—you will see one of these signal words: caution, warning, or danger. By law, a signal word must be included on every pesticide label to give the user some indication of the acute toxicity of the material. The chart on p. 90 gives you an idea of what the various signal words mean. The word "caution" indicates a Category III or IV pesticide. Materials in this category are least-toxic based on their LD_{50}. Category I pesticides, as indicated by the signal word "danger," are the most toxic or hazardous and are generally restricted to use by professional pest control operators.

It is important to remember that the tests that determine these ratings are performed primarily on rats and to a lesser degree on dogs, chickens, rabbits, monkeys, pheasants, ducks, sparrows, and other animals. The reason for conducting the tests this way is obvious, but remember that humans may not react to the poison exactly as other animals do.

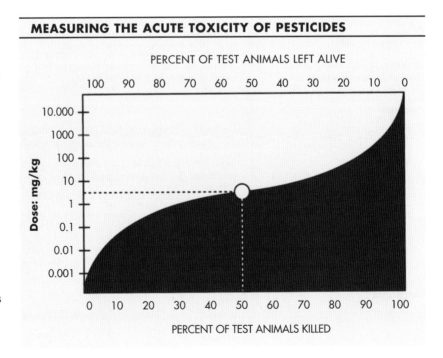

MEASURING THE ACUTE TOXICITY OF PESTICIDES

This apple crop is coated with residue from an insecticide spray. Always wash your produce thoroughly (or, a better alternative, grow your own without pesticides). (Photo by Phil Augustavo/iStockphoto)

ROUTES OF PESTICIDE EXPOSURE

The four routes of entry of pesticides into an organism are as follows:

- oral (swallowed or not)
- dermal (on or absorbed by the skin)
- respiratory (breathing exposure to the lungs and all air passages)
- optical (in the eye or on or around the eyelid)

Usually LD_{50} data is based on oral exposure as determined by feeding pesticides to test animals, but there can be large differences in the LD_{50} with different routes of entry. For example, the common organophosphate insecticide malathion has an oral LD_{50} (using rats as the test animal) of 2,800 mg/kg, but the dermal LD_{50} is only 4,100 mg/kg. Of the two exposure routes, the oral is the more toxic because it takes less material to kill 50 percent of the animals tested.

The respiratory route of entry is usually the most toxic of all, because pesticides are absorbed most rapidly through the lungs. Absorption through the lungs is roughly equivalent to intravenous injection. The pesticide is quickly distributed throughout the body in the bloodstream, causing all organs and tissues to be exposed within minutes after inhalation. Unfortunately, studies of lung exposure to pesticides have been relatively few to date, and little or no comparative data are available.

The chart on p. 92 illustrates the susceptibility of body parts to the absorption of pesticides. Note that the scalp and scrotum are more susceptible than the hands. This is why we are concerned about the use of pesticides on the heads of young children to control head lice, as well as their use in the pubic area of children and adults to control pubic lice.

PESTICIDE TOXICITY SCALE

HAZARD LEVEL (CATEGORY) SIGNAL WORD	I DANGER EXTREMELY TOXIC	II WARNING MODERATELY TOXIC	III CAUTION SLIGHTLY TOXIC	IV CAUTION NEARLY NONTOXIC
Oral LD_{50}	Up to 50 mg/kg	50 to 500 mg/kg	500 to 5,000 mg/kg	> 5,000 mg/kg
Inhalation LC_{50}	Up to 0.2 micrograms/liter	0.2 to 2 micrograms/liter	2 to 20 micrograms/liter	> 20 micrograms/liter
Dermal LD_{50}	Up to 200 mg/kg	200 to 2,000 mg/kg	2,000 to 20,000 mg/kg	> 20,000 mg/kg
Eye effects	CORROSIVE! Corneal opacity not reversible within 7 days; probable blindness	Corneal opacity reversible within 7 days; irritation persists for 7 days	No corneal opacity; irritation reversible within 7 days	Slight or transient irritation
Skin effects	CORROSIVE! Chemical burning of skin	Severe irritation at 72 hours	Moderate irritation at 72 hours	Mild or no irritation
Probable lethal dose to a 150-lb. man	A drop to a teaspoonful	A teaspoonful to 1 oz.	1 oz. to 1 pint (1 lb.)	> 1 pint (1 lb.)

THE LIMITATIONS OF TOXICITY RATINGS

The LD_{50} rating as a measure of how hazardous a material is has severe limitations because chronic, or long-term, effects are not indicated. Chronic effects may be carcinogenic (causing cancer), mutagenic (causing genetic changes), or teratogenic (causing birth defects). Furthermore, there is substantial variation in the impact of a toxic substance from individual to individual and from developmental stage to developmental stage in the same individual. For example, children, the elderly, pregnant women, and the sick are more vulnerable than a younger but mature 150-lb. man in the peak of health. Yet it is the latter for whom toxicity test data on animals are extrapolated.

Poisons can also produce a number of miscellaneous symptoms such as rashes, sleepiness, or restlessness in sensitive individuals exposed over a period of time. Doctors do not easily associate many of these symptoms with pesticide poisoning because they mimic other conditions. Often only the person suffering makes the connection. For example, the subject may observe that he or she is regularly exposed to pesticide treatments for cockroaches in the office or aphids in the garden, and that this coincides with headaches, rashes, or other problems.

"Data on chronic toxicity is woefully inadequate or completely missing for many of the more than 800 registered active ingredients in pesticide products."

Many pesticides, especially the organophosphates (malathion, acephate) and carbamates (Sevin), may also mimic symptoms of heat-related illnesses, like heat stress, heat cramps, and heat stroke. Awareness of this is especially important when wearing personal protective equipment (PPE) and applying pesticides during hot weather. PPE is, of necessity, water repellent or waterproof and doesn't "breathe" like ordinary clothing. When clothing doesn't breathe, heat builds up inside the protective suit and equipment. Perspiration has no way to evaporate and cool the body; consequently, the body sweats even more heavily, trying, in vain, to cool down. Large quantities of water and electrolytes can be lost from the body, to the point where heat-related symptoms and illness can occur. Our personal experience wearing full protective equipment in greenhouses in Florida substantiates this phenomenon. Following a 1-hour pesticide application in a greenhouse, 1½ pints of sweat was poured out of a pair of rubber boots. We exhibited symptoms of heat stress and heat cramps for about an hour after the application and cleanup.

DATA GAPS

Whereas data on acute toxicity is available for most of the 17,000 registered pesticides, data on chronic toxicity is woefully inadequate or completely missing for many of the more than 800 registered active ingredients in pesticide products. It wasn't until the mid-1970s that chronic toxicity data was required by law, and the new legislation allowed all pesticides to remain on the market despite major data gaps on chronic toxicity. Although pesticide manufacturers are now required to produce the missing data, the EPA acknowledges that it will take many years to complete all of the testing.

This is not a small problem. Every year in the United States alone over 2.2 billion pounds of pesticides are applied around homes and in agriculture. This huge number doesn't even include water purification pesticides, germicidal soaps and detergents, swimming pool chemicals, chlorine bleach, or other antibacterial and antibiotic cleaners and medications. Many of these products end up being flushed or poured down drains and travel in our sewers down to our sewerage treatment plants. Many of these chemicals are *not* broken down during sewerage treatment and usually can only be removed from treated water using a reverse osmosis process. Currently, the effluent, which still may contain hazardous materials, is released back into surface or ground water. Even though these materials are diluted during the treatment process, there is the very real concern of low-level chronic exposure.

Chronic exposure apparently begins at conception, as environmental chemicals and pesticides are now routinely found in sperm samples. Exposure goes on for the full nine months of fetal development because some environmental pollutants can and do pass from the mother through the placenta to the developing embryo.

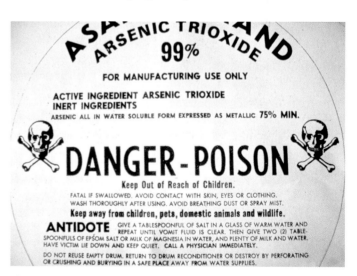

All pesticides carry a signal word, in this case it is "danger-poison" with a skull and crossbones. This means the pesticide is highly poisonous. If it had the word danger alone it would mean that it is highly corrosive to the skin and eyes. The other signal words are "warning" for moderate toxicity and "caution" for low toxicity. (Photo courtesy of USDA Forest Service - Region 8 - Southern Archive, USDA Forest Service, Bugwood.org)

RATES OF ABSORPTION OF PESTICIDES INTO THE HUMAN BODY

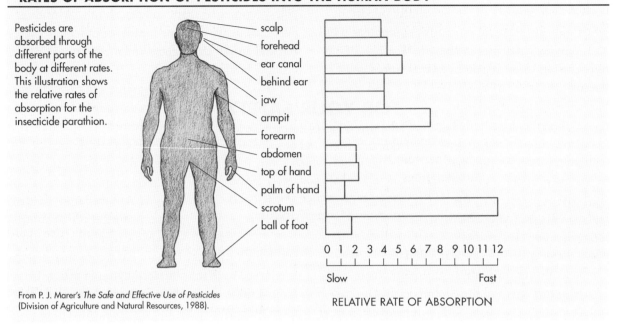

Pesticides are absorbed through different parts of the body at different rates. This illustration shows the relative rates of absorption for the insecticide parathion.

scalp
forehead
ear canal
behind ear
jaw
armpit
forearm
abdomen
top of hand
palm of hand
scrotum
ball of foot

0 1 2 3 4 5 6 7 8 9 10 11 12
Slow   Fast

RELATIVE RATE OF ABSORPTION

From P. J. Marer's *The Safe and Effective Use of Pesticides* (Division of Agriculture and Natural Resources, 1988).

Another major problem is lack of toxicity data on the so-called inert ingredients in pesticide formulations. If you examine a pesticide label, you will see that these inert ingredients can represent as much as 90 percent to over 99 percent of the volume of the material in the package. In general, the inert ingredients are not identified, and there is little or no data on their toxicity. With the growing recognition that many inert ingredients are not inert at all, and in some cases may be more toxic than the pesticide's active ingredient (for example, the surfactant in the herbicide Roundup® is more toxic than its active ingredient, glyphosate), the EPA is beginning to require the listing of inert ingredients on the label and some level of testing. As with chronic-toxicity data, however, significant data on the impact of inert ingredients is still years away.

SYNERGISM

Another potential danger not reflected in the LD_{50} rating is synergism. Synergism occurs when one compound enhances the effect of another many times beyond what would be experienced if either were encountered alone. This is why, for example, alcohol should not be combined with certain drugs. The interaction of the two substances can produce effects that are amplified in a totally unexpected manner.

To understand the implications of synergism, we must understand something about the nature and frequency of our exposure to various toxic sub-

> "The growing number of 'chemically sensitive' individuals and individuals who believe or can document that they are suffering damage to their immune systems from chronic exposure to synthetic compounds, such as pesticides, is of increasing concern to health professionals."

stances. There have always been natural hazards in the environment, and over the millennia it took for humans to evolve, man slowly developed various means of adapting to or managing these hazards.

But now, suddenly, we live in a "soup" of human-created compounds. In a single morning you may knowingly or unknowingly expose yourself to a wide variety of pesticides: flea collars and clothes-moth repellents at home, tree sprays on the way to work, cockroach treatment residues on the bus or in the office, and so on.

In addition, we may expose ourselves deliberately or passively to many other chemical hazards: alcohol; tars, nicotine, and other compounds in tobacco and other recreational drugs; food preservatives; prescription and nonprescription antibiotics and drugs; and various cleaning agents. Finally, inside the house, at school, at work, in the garden, and on the street we are unwillingly or unknowingly exposed to a vast variety of toxic materials that are by-products of our industrial world. This is especially true of air and water contaminants, such as toxic gases that are emitted by synthetic building materials and furnishings or are the breakdown products of water-treatment chemicals and various aerosols. The list of pollutants in the air and drinking water is growing.

No one is examining, in any systematic way, how these many compounds, combined in the manner in which we are actually exposed to them, might produce undesirable health effects. Furthermore, the laboratory methods used to determine pesticide toxicity do not take into account the impact of mixtures of several pesticides and their additives, or pesticides plus other environmental toxicants. The human body can detoxify many poisons, but how much can be processed safely by different individuals cannot be stated clearly.

The growing number of "chemically sensitive" individuals and individuals who believe or can

ACUTE TOXICITY MEASUREMENTS FOR SOME COMMON PESTICIDES

GENERIC NAME	LD$_{50}$ (MG/KG)	ROUTE	TEST ANIMAL	HONEYBEES
acephate	866–945	oral	rats	toxic
Bacillus thuringiensis	10,000	oral	rats	—
boric acid	3,200	oral	rats	—
carbaryl	800	oral	rats	very toxic
diazinon	300,850	oral	rats	toxic
diphacinone	3	oral	rats	—
	3.0–7.5	oral	dogs	—
	14.7	oral	cats	—
insecticidal soap	>10,000	oral	rats	—
malathion	2,800	oral	rats	toxic
methoprene	5,100	oral	rats	very toxic
neem oil	>13,000	oral	rats	slightly toxic
pyrethrin aerosol	584	oral	rats	toxic
pyrethroid	430	oral	rats	toxic
pyrethrum	>18,000	dermal	rats	slightly toxic
silica aerogel	4,400	oral	rats	—
sodium octaborate	2,000	oral	rats	—

From G. Berg's *Farm Chemicals Handbook* (Meister Publishing, 1980); W. J. Wiswesser's *Pesticide Index* 5th ed. (Entomological Society of America, 1976); and C. R. Worthing's *The Pesticide Manual* (BCPC Publication Sales, 1979).
Because LD$_{50}$ values may vary with the formulation, these values are given for comparative purposes only. Column 5 indicates toxicity to honeybees and other beneficial insects in the order Hymenoptera.

document that they are suffering damage to their immune systems from chronic exposure to synthetic compounds, such as pesticides, is of increasing concern to health professionals. In fact, the medical practice known as clinical ecology is developing to address this question.

Despite its limitations, and even though much research remains to be done, information on acute toxicity is nonetheless valuable. The chart on p. 93 lists some common pesticides and their LD_{50} ratings.

MATERIAL SAFETY DATA SHEETS

Pesticide regulations require that manufacturers provide a material safety data sheet (MSDS) for each pesticide they produce. MSDSs are actually required for all chemical products. The MSDS describes the chemical characteristics of the active and other hazardous ingredients, and lists fire and explosion hazards, health hazards, reactivity and incompatibility characteristics, and types of protective equipment needed for handling and storing the pesticide and cleaning up spills. It also gives first-aid information to treat exposure to the material. LD_{50} ratings are given for various test animals, and manufacturers' emergency phone numbers are listed. The MSDS is a valuable source of information and should be obtained for any hazardous material you may use, not just pesticides.

In too many cases the scope of the toxicity information on the MSDS still leaves much to be desired. In some cases, especially with older pesticides, the data on chronic health effects and environmental impacts are minimal, or may be missing entirely. There is, at least, much more detail in an MSDS than is provided on a pesticide label. The manufacturer is required to provide an MSDS to anyone selling or using the material. If your local pesticide supplier does not have an MSDS for the pesticide you are considering, obtain one from the manufacturer whose name and address are listed on the pesticide label. Most MSDSs and labels can be obtained online by going to the manufacturers' websites and directly downloading the documents.

There are some websites that are dedicated solely to providing MSDSs; some of these sites also provide labels and other documentation. In some instances, you must send an email or other written request to obtain an MSDS. We think that the law should be strengthened to require manufacturers, distributors, and sellers to have labels and MSDSs available for anyone to download on their sites without having to request a copy.

DID YOU KNOW?

Most pesticide applications contaminate adjacent areas. Landing on non-target organisms, plants, other animals, the soil, and outdoor furniture. Because a healthy garden is teeming with life, all kinds of undesired side effects can arise.

TOXICITY IN THE ENVIRONMENT: BIOMAGNIFICATION

When considering how safe a material is, you must also look at its effects on the environment. With the exception of poison baits, which usually attract and kill just the pest, the application of most pesticides results in only a small amount—often less than 1 percent—of the poison actually reaching the target pest. This is especially true of insecticides. Most of the material lands in adjacent areas. Outdoors, this means it falls on non-target organisms, plants, other animals, the soil, and outdoor furniture.

Because a healthy garden is teeming with life above and in the soil, all kinds of undesired side effects can arise. For example, fungicides used against a plant disease may fall on and become incorporated into the soil. This may inhibit the growth of the beneficial fungi called mycorrhizae that are associated with plant roots and are important in helping the plant obtain nutrients. Decompose microorganisms and invertebrates, which break down dead plant and animal litter so the nutrients are once again available for plant growth, may also be affected by pesticides that fall on garden soil.

Some pesticides accumulate in food chains. Small amounts of poison distributed over plants or plant-eating animals can become concentrated in the bodies of the organisms that eat those plants or animals. For example, organisms such as earthworms that are low on the food chain may eat many fallen leaves. Even though each leaf holds only a small amount of pesticide residue, the pesticide is concentrated in the earthworm's body because of the number of leaves it consumes. This concentrated dose is then passed on to the earthworm's predators, such as birds. Because a single bird eats many earthworms, the pesticide reaches even higher concentrations in the bird's body. Finally, at the top of the food chain, predators such as cats may ingest such high concentrations of poison that they become sick or suffer an impaired ability to reproduce.

In one classic case, plankton absorbed pesticides from contaminated waters through the microorganisms they fed upon. The plankton were eaten by small fish, and these were in turn fed upon by larger fish. The brown pelican, a fish-eating bird at the top of the food chain, suffered a serious population decline due to the effects of these accumulated poisons. Other fish- and rodent-eating birds, such as bald eagles and peregrine falcons, were also suffering declines. This is one reason why a whole series of long-lasting compounds, starting with DDT, was withdrawn from use by the federal government.

RESIDUE, RESURGENCE, RESISTANCE, AND SECONDARY PEST OUTBREAKS

"Three Rs and an S" is a mnemonic device we learned from Dr. Donald Dahlsten, an entomologist at the University of California at Berkeley, which helps you remember the main problems associated with pesticide use.

Residue is the first R. Biomagnification is one aspect of the residue problem. But residues can also be a more direct problem. This is true in the house, for example, when pesticide sprays fall on dishes and other surfaces or mix with the air we breathe.

(Photo from the archives of USDA APHIS Pest Survey Detection and Exclusion Laboratory)

DDT AND THE DANGERS OF BIOMAGNIFICATION

Because humans are at the top of numerous food chains on this planet, the long-term health consequences of using pesticides are feared. DDT is a good example of a substance whose direct toxicity, when expressed as an LD_{50} measurement, does not reflect its tendency to biomagnify. If we consider its LD_{50} alone, we might be misled into thinking that DDT is not as potentially dangerous as it really is. Unfortunately, the current EPA registration process does not exclude substances that biomagnify. Even though DDT was banned in the United States in 1972, it can still be found in soil and sediments. Researchers are still finding DDT and its metabolites in human fatty tissue and mother's milk in countries that banned DDT over 30 years ago. DDT is also found on every continent, including Antarctica, where it has never been used. Despite its many negative environmental effects, DDT continues to be used in some countries.

Outdoors, pesticides often get into the groundwater or rivers. From there they can contaminate wells or have undesired effects on aquatic life. Over 50 percent of Americans rely on wells for drinking water. As of 1988, the EPA found groundwater in 38 states contaminated by 74 pesticides.

The EPA has set guidelines for permitted levels of residue for specific pesticides—a concept unacceptable to many clean-water advocates—and the pesticide levels in a significant number of the wells tested exceeded these levels. Even in wells where residues from a specific pesticide fall within the guidelines, there may still be a problem, because the guidelines fail to take into account the synergistic effect of the residues of several pesticides in the same well.

Residues constitute the one negative aspect of pesticide use that has most captured the public's attention. It is primarily the residue problem that inspired Rachel Carson's book, *Silent Spring*. The book is still very relevant to today's pesticide controversies. However, it is the other two Rs, resurgence and resistance, and the S, secondary pest outbreaks, that are of greater direct concern to the pest manager.

Resurgence, the second R. Resurgence occurs when the predators, parasitoids, or pathogens that would naturally control the pests are temporarily removed, drastically reduced in number, or killed off completely. The home gardener often experiences this phenomenon without realizing what is happening. In treating aphids on shrubs, for example, the first spraying may kill predators such as lacewings and syrphid flies, as well as the tiny parasitoids (miniwasps) that kill the aphids from within. Initially the aphids appear to have been wiped out by the pesticide. But some always escape the poison and others fly in from neighboring areas. In fact, it is quite possible that what the gardener has thoroughly decimated is not the aphids, but their natural enemies. There are always fewer of these and they have lower reproductive rates than the pests.

Because of their greater mobility, natural enemies are also more likely to come in contact with higher doses of the poison. The remaining aphids can now multiply with fewer restraints. After a time, the aphid problem is even worse. Horrified at this new and more serious infestation, the gardener may spray a second time. This time, the aphids bounce back even more quickly; their population has resurged. But the population of natural enemies does not bounce back to catch up with the pest; in fact, it is knocked down again by the second application. This process is often repeated a number of times. This is what we call the pesticide treadmill. It sells pesticides, but it's not good for us or the environment.

Generally, there is a time lag between the appearance of the first noticeable populations of the pest and the development of sufficient numbers of their parasitoids or predators to reduce the pest population satisfactorily. This makes biological sense. The predators have evolved life cycles that ensure that when they emerge or are lured into an area, there is enough prey for them to eat. Populations of predators and parasitoids often take longer to build up than the pest because they produce fewer generations per season. The predators may compensate for this by living longer, as in the case of predacious ground beetles and spiders, by having more young, as with the parasitoids of caterpillars that produce multiple young from a single host, or by taking better care of their young, as with social insects such as wasps, ants, and many mammalian predators.

To illustrate this, we return to the example of the aphids and their predators. Aphids don't need to mate during the growing season. The insects you see on the plants are likely to be females carrying female embryos ready to be born in a short time. The parasitoids of aphids, however, must find a member of the opposite sex, mate, search out an aphid of the right kind, and lay an egg within it to survive. Obviously this is a much slower, more complicated process than aphid reproduction. But eventually the parasitoids have a substantial impact on the pest population because each female parasitoid is capable of laying hundreds of eggs. If most of these beneficial insects have been killed by pesticides, however, it takes a long time for their population to recover.

There is another factor that explains why predators and parasitoids frequently do not bounce back as quickly as their prey after pesticide treatments. Sometimes the compounds used are more toxic to the predators than to the pests. This is true, for example, of carbaryl (Sevin), which is still popular with home gardeners and pest control professionals even though it is toxic to honeybees and the many beneficial insects closely related to them in the order Hymenoptera.

Resistance is the third R. In some ways, resistance is even more awesome in its potential for causing problems than residue or resurgence. Each time a pesticide is applied, some of the pests that survive to produce the next generation develop a means of avoiding or detoxifying the poison. This is very different from immunity, wherein the body develops antibodies to a disease organism (e.g., the polio virus) so that on subsequent exposure the body is far less or not at all susceptible to it. The resistance we are referring to is one of forced genetic selection. By creating a situation where only those organisms that can tolerate a pesticide survive and reproduce, we humans effectively select certain groups to continue that species. Normal genetic processes take centuries or longer to produce measurable differences in the gene pool; the changes produced in pest populations by pesticide applications over a few short years are a form of accelerated genetic selection.

With each treatment, the pests whose genetic composition allows them to tolerate the poison increase in number while those that are still susceptible to the poison die (see the drawing on p. 98). Gradually, it becomes harder to reduce pest numbers through applications of the poison. In response, many people increase the frequency of treatment and the strength of the dose, only to have the pest population bounce back sooner and in greater numbers than before. This often happens with aphids, whiteflies, and other garden, household, and body pests that are treated frequently with pesticides. Today, over 440 insects and mites and more than 70 fungi are now resistant to pesticides.

In agriculture, resistance to pesticides has become a matter of worldwide concern. According to Marvin J. Levine, the author of *Pesticides: A Toxic Time Bomb in Our Midst* (Praeger, 2007), crop losses due to pests in the United States alone actually increased from 30 percent in 1945 to about 37 percent in 1990. This occurred even though pesticide use has increased 33 times during that same period. The development of insect, weed, and fungus resistance to pesticides is a major factor in this increase.

Switching to a new compound may help, but the success may be short-lived due to the phenomenon known as cross-resistance. Once a pest has developed resistance to one class of chemicals, it usually develops resistance to others as well, often in a shorter time than it did to the first. This is the "pesticide treadmill" described vividly by Robert van den Bosch in *The Pesticide Conspiracy* (University of California Press, 1989), in which sole reliance on pesticides leads to ever-increasing use until at some point no pesticide is effective against the pest.

The implications of this phenomenon for the field of public health are particularly important. As with the antibiotics used to control human infections, casual or overly frequent use of powerful pesticides can render them powerless when they are really needed. For example, resistance has become a problem among certain mosquito species that carry the causal agents of malaria and encephalitis,

HONEYBEES AND PESTICIDES

There is a new condition affecting honeybees called Colony Collapse Disorder (CCD) that is wiping out huge numbers of bee colonies all over the country. Pesticide use is considered to be one of the factors contributing to this tragedy. It is considered a tragedy, because most of our fruit and vegetable crops require pollination by honeybees. It is estimated that honeybees provide about $20 billion per year in pollination services in the United States alone. In some areas of China, honeybees have been wiped out and pollination services are done by people by hand. Imagine pollinating all of the flowers on an apple tree by hand. We ask that you limit, or eliminate if possible, the use of any pesticide that is toxic to honeybees. If you must use a pesticide toxic to bees, use it only when bees are not actively foraging (evening applications) and avoid treating flowers if possible.

We recommend that you visit the Partners for Sustainable Pollination website (www.pfspbees.org) for information on what you can do as a gardener to help honeybees that pollinate your tomatoes, squash, fruits, and other flowering food plants.

and among rats whose fleas vector bubonic plague. There are always some cases of these diseases in humans in the United States, and as a nation we could face a major emergency if serious outbreaks of such diseases should occur.

More than 600 pest insects, weeds, and plant pathogens are now resistant to one or more pesticides. Because pesticides cost much to develop and test, the loss of their use just when they are needed most is a double tragedy for the society that has invested so much in them.

It is important to understand that the problem of resistance is not related to the toxicity of the compound to humans, other non-target animals, or the environment. Resistance can be expected to show up in any population of pests that is regularly exposed to a pesticide. This is because a chemical compound cannot change or adjust in response to genetic changes in the pest population that help the pest tolerate the chemical. This is quite different from biological controls, where pest and predator or parasitoid have evolved together over millions of years, the population of each adjusting to changes in the other.

For this reason, chemical tools must always be regarded as temporary solutions to be resorted to only when other methods have failed and the pest problem truly threatens to become intolerable. Designing your home, garden, and work environments to maximize the effect of natural enemies on the pest is always a more permanent and ultimately more cost-effective approach.

Secondary pests. Secondary pests often emerge from obscurity when pesticide use decimates their natural enemies. These previously unimportant insect pests are called secondary pests—the S in the "3 Rs and an S." These multiply rapidly in the absence of their former competitor or other natural control organisms that have been killed by the chemicals. Although the gardener may be aware of only one or two types of insects present in large numbers on a particular plant, in actuality many other potential pest species are likely to be feeding there also. They are not obvious because their natural enemies keep their populations low.

When a pesticide is sprayed to kill pests such as caterpillars, the natural enemies of other potential pests may also be killed. Thus, the caterpillar problem is soon replaced, for example, by a damaging and sometimes more serious mite problem. As with the natural enemies of aphids, the natural enemies

PESTICIDE RESISTANCE

This drawing shows how pesticide resistance builds up in a pest population. In (A), some individuals (shown in black) in the pest population have genetic traits that allow them to survive the pesticide spraying. In (B), a certain portion of these survivors' offspring has inherited the pesticide resistance trait. These individuals survive the next spraying. If spraying is frequent, the population soon consists mainly of resistant individuals (C).

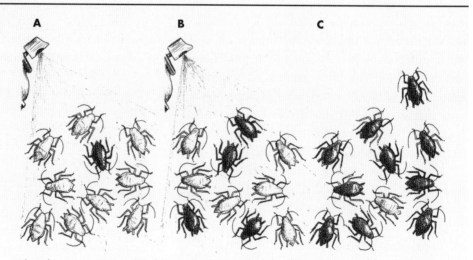

Redrawn from P. J. Marer's *The Safe and Effective Use of Pesticides* (Division of Agriculture and Natural Resources, 1988).

> **"Secondary pests often emerge from obscurity when pesticide use decimates their natural enemies."**

of mites (usually other, carnivorous mites) are very susceptible to many pesticides, often more so than are the pests.

CRITERIA FOR SELECTING AND USING CHEMICAL AND MICROBIAL CONTROLS

As we mentioned earlier, a wide variety of new chemical tools are appearing on the market, largely in response to an increased understanding of the "3 Rs and an S." Some of these are believed to be far less toxic to humans and other mammals than the more traditional pesticides still in use. In this respect, the new materials are more acceptable for application around the home and garden. Nevertheless, most have not been around long enough for us to fully understand the long-term implications of their use, so caution is in order. We don't want to wait 10 or 30 years to find out that something has gone wrong, possibly irreversibly. Leukemia, for example, will develop 15 years or more after exposures. Other carcinogens exhibit lag times making causal linkages difficult, or certainly questionable.

You can minimize the hazards to yourself and the environment and maximize the immediate desired effect upon the pest and the long-term usefulness of the material. To do this, select the least-toxic, most species-specific, most effective microbial (or chemical) material with the shortest residual life available. The sidebar on pp. 100–101 describes the kind of information you should have about any pesticide before buying or using it.

It is important to remember that pesticides are *not* a substitute for good horticultural practices. If you design your garden and select plants so that you can take care of them efficiently and effectively, your need for pesticides of any kind can be reduced or even completely eliminated.

This gardener is fully outfitted in personal protective equipment (PPE) for a pesticide application. (Photo by Mary O'Malley)

APPLYING PESTICIDES

The pesticides recommended for use in this book can be applied by laypersons or professional pest control operators. The next section describes safety precautions you should follow whenever you use these pesticides.

WHAT YOU SHOULD KNOW BEFORE USING A PESTICIDE

SAFETY

This means safety to you, other humans, pets, livestock, wildlife, and the overall environment.

- Acute and chronic toxicity. What is the LD_{50} of the substance? Can or might it be carcinogenic (cancer-causing), mutagenic (causing genetic changes), or teratogenic (causing birth defects)?

- Mobility. Is the compound volatile, so that it moves into the air breathed by a building's occupants? Can it move through the soil into the groundwater?

- Residual life. How long does the compound remain toxic?

SPECIES-SPECIFICITY

The best materials are species-specific; that is, they affect just the group of animals or plants you are trying to suppress. Avoid broad-spectrum materials because they are nonselective and can cause resurgence and secondary pest outbreaks in the long run. Where broad-spectrum materials must be used, apply them in as selective a way as possible (for more on this, see the discussion of spot treatment on p. 38).

EFFECTIVENESS

This issue is not as straightforward as it might seem, because it depends on how the effectiveness is being tested. For example, a pesticide can appear to be very effective in laboratory tests because it kills 99 percent of the test insects. But in field tests under more realistic conditions it may also kill 100 percent of the pest's natural enemies. This will lead to serious pest outbreaks at a later date.

ENDURANCE

A pesticide may have been effective against its target pest at the time it was registered, but if the pest problem is now recurring frequently, it may be a sign that the pest has developed resistance to the pesticide or, stated otherwise, that the pesticide has lost its endurance.

SPEED

A quick-acting, short-lived, more acutely toxic material might be useful in emergencies; a slow-acting, longer-lasting, less-toxic material might be preferable for a chronic pest problem.

REPELLENCY

Some insecticides are effective more because of their repellency to insects than their ability to kill them. This is an important consideration in cockroach and subterranean termite control.

COST

This is usually measured as cost per volume of active ingredient used. You can find the percentage of active ingredient in the mixture by reading the product label. By multiplying the percentage of active ingredient by the

PROTECTING YOURSELF WHEN APPLYING PESTICIDES

The pesticides we discuss are the least-toxic pesticides currently available, but we nevertheless strongly recommend that you wear personal protective equipment whenever applying any pesticide. A great deal of additional excellent advice on safety issues surrounding use of pesticides is contained in *The Safe and Effective Use of Pesticides*, 2nd ed. (Agriculture & Natural Resources, 2000) by Patrick Marer. This book, a study guide for professional applicators, is easy for the lay-gardener to understand. It is available from the University of California Agriculture and Natural Resources Communication Services; refer to, or search for, Publication #3324. The UC-ANR catalog is available at www.anrcatalog.ucdavis.edu.

Anyone planning to apply a pesticide should have on hand the following gear at the minimum:

- Full-length pants and a long-sleeved shirt made from tightly woven cotton fabric. Cotton or Tyvek® overalls on top of these garments provide added protection and can be removed easily if there is a spill.

- A water-resistant or plastic wide-brimmed hat or a hooded waterproof jacket. Remember, the scalp readily absorbs pesticides.

- Waterproof gloves made from nitrile, natural rubber, butyl, or neoprene. Do not use lined gloves because the fabric used for lining may absorb pesticides. Avoid latex gloves, as they will dissolve in the presence of petroleum-based products and solvents. Make sure the number of times you need to apply the material and then multiplying this product by the cost per volume of active ingredient, you can determine the cost-effectiveness of the pesticide.

Some of the newer, less-toxic microbial insecticides and insect growth regulators discussed later in the book may appear to be more expensive than some older, more-toxic pesticides. But the newer materials tend to be effective in far smaller doses than the older materials—one container goes a long way. This factor, together with their lower impact on the environment, often makes them more cost-effective.

OTHER CONSIDERATIONS

In addition to informing yourself about the characteristics of the material itself, it is important to do the following:

- Observe all application directions on the label.

- Clothe yourself in neoprene gloves, goggles, respirator, hat, and other protective clothing as necessary (see the discussion of protective clothing below).

- Confine your use of the material to the area requiring treatment (see the discussion of spot treatment on p. 38).

- Store all materials under lock and key.

SOURCES OF INFORMATION

Authoritative information on pesticides, including acute and chronic toxicity data, are available at the following websites:

- Beyond Pesticides: www.beyondpesticides.org

- National Pesticide Information Center: www.npic.orst.edu

- Extension Toxicology Network: extoxnet.orst.edu

- Pesticide Action Network of North America: www.panna.org

- EPA Pesticide Factsheets: www.epa.gov/pesticides/factsheets

- The Greenbook Group (a commercial site for labels, MSDSs, and other information): www.greenbook.net

- California Office of Environmental Health Hazard Assessment: www.oehha.ca.gov/pesticides.html

cuffs of the gloves are long enough to extend to the mid-forearm. Wear sleeves on the outside of gloves to keep pesticides from getting inside (unless spraying overhead, in which case sleeves should be tucked inside the gloves).

- Footwear made of rubber, nitrile, neoprene, or butyl. Do not wear leather or fabric shoes because they absorb most pesticides.

- Goggles, a full faceshield, or safety glasses with brow and temple shielding for protection from pesticides that can cause eye injuries. In some cases, this damage is irreversible. Eyes are another highly absorptive area of the body.

- A respirator or disposable paper dust mask to protect the lungs and respiratory tract from airborne pesticides. Dust masks should be worn when applying pesticidal dusts. Buy masks that are capable of screening out micron-sized particles.

When liquid sprays are being applied, a cartridge respirator should be worn. The cartridge contains activated charcoal, which removes pesticide vapors when the wearer inhales. It is essential that respirators fit properly (i.e., seal tightly to the face). You should record the amount of time a cartridge is used so you know when to replace it. Store the record book with the respirator. Because beards and long sideburns impede a good seal, persons with facial hair should consider finding someone else to apply the pesticide.

Using a respirator can give you a false sense of security. Proper fit can be problematic. In professional situations, applicators are professionally fitted and tested annually to make sure that they can use a respirator properly and that it is functioning properly. There are now dust-type disposable masks impregnated with charcoal that are sufficient for short exposures expected by home gardeners. This is an instance when we prefer the disposable model to the reusable type for the amateur pesticide applicator. Keep any respirator model, whether reusable of disposable, in an airtight, sealed plastic bag or container. The activated charcoal present in pesticide cartridges and masks will absorb moisture and air pollutants when just sitting on a shelf. Never store safety equipment (PPE), especially respirators, with pesticides or any volatile materials.

In the end, if you feel that a pesticide is so toxic that you must wear full-body-protecting PPE, consider replacing the plant. If plant replacement is not an option, hire a professional to do the pesticide application for you. But watch the applicator and put a stop to any behavior that is not appropriate. Just because he or she is a professional does not mean they will always do what's correct or even legal.

TIP With each use, dispose of the respirator storage bag, as it could be toxic from contact with the respirator, which is contaminated from being in the aerosol zone produced by application.

WHAT TO REQUEST FROM A PEST CONTROL COMPANY

If you choose to hire a pest control company to solve your pest problem, it is important that you retain control over the methods and products used on your property. Try to find a company that is familiar with Integrated Pest Management approaches and will work cooperatively with you in selecting the least-toxic methods available. We have been helping an increasing number of pest control providers in both the public and private sectors throughout the United States to develop IPM services, and it is becoming easier for consumers to find local firms offering this approach.

"If you design your garden and select plants so that you can take care of them efficiently and effectively, your need for pesticides of any kind can be reduced or even completely eliminated."

Traditionally, pest control companies have offered routine spray services, often on a monthly basis. This service is based on the idea that regular applications of pesticides, whether or not a pest is present, prevent pest problems. Today, there is both a need and a great opportunity for IPM services where the consumer pays a pest control professional to provide regular monitoring rather than regular spraying. This is especially the case now that so many cities, counties, states, and even the federal government are adopting IPM. The City and County of San Francisco and the National Park Service are good examples of government implementing IPM.

Biweekly or monthly monitoring reports from a pest control company reassure the consumer that a professional is overseeing pest prevention and management. Pest treatments occur only if the monitoring data shows a developing problem. Because monitoring serves as an early warning system, there is usually time to act preventively with non-chemical methods before pest numbers become high. Spot treatment with a least-toxic pesticide can be used as a backup.

If you have a pest emergency and cannot find a company that uses an IPM approach, show the company you hire the chapter in this book on managing the pest in question, then ask the company to use the methods described. Whichever you choose, insist that they treat with the least-toxic substances recommended in this book. Remember that virtually all the least-toxic pesticides described here are available commercially, so even if the pest control operator (PCO) is not familiar with the material, he or she can order it from local or online pesticide suppliers. Information on all available pesticides is also available online.

If the PCO is not willing to apply the materials suggested in this book, or similar substitutes, do not hire them. If they recommend a substitute, request the material safety data sheet, described on p. 94, and ask to see the label for the pesticide(s) the operator plans to use. Both the MSDS and the label contain the generic and chemical names for the material. With this information in hand, do a search online to find information on the pesticide(s). This will at least give you some background for choosing among the pesticides offered by the PCO. If you have any questions about the information conveyed by the PCO, call your county agricultural commissioner, the local cooperative extension office, or your public-health agency to verify the information. The agricultural commissioner's office or state consumer protection agency can also tell you if there have been any complaints filed against the pest control company you are contemplating hiring. Be sure to ask the pest control company representative to provide you with references that you can contact to get feedback on their services.

When the pesticide is applied in your garden, insist that the spot-treatment approach described on p. 38 be used so that the pesticide is applied only where it is absolutely needed. Take indoor plants outside to treat with pesticides. If the plant must be treated indoors, open your windows and doors and thoroughly air out the house for as long as possible after the indoor pesticide application. Most liquid pesticide formulations volatilize in the air, leading to respiratory exposure for the occupants.

If you or a PCO is going to apply a pesticide in your yard, it is a courtesy to give your neighbors advance warning. In some places this is a legal requirement; check with your local agricultural commissioner's office or the county extension service office. Many people suffer from chemical sensitivities to synthetic materials, including conventional pesticides. The inevitable drift of pesticides in the air can cause sufferers of this syndrome intense physical discomfort for long periods. If they know of the intended spraying in advance, they can take the necessary precautions. In some cases people with chemical sensitivities may know some alternatives to pesticide applications about which you or your pest control applicator may not be aware. Sharing information with other gardeners on nontoxic and least-toxic solutions to pest problems is one of the best and most enjoyable aspects of Integrated Pest Management.

TIP Virtually every pest control company in the United States has at least a passing familiarity with IPM, through their licensing training and their continuing education requirements. If they resist and will only apply a pesticide, hire another company.

FOR YOUR SAFETY

Remember that if you can smell a pesticide, your lungs are absorbing it. And the respiratory route of entry is usually the most toxic of all, because pesticides are absorbed most rapidly through the lungs. Absorption through the lungs is roughly equivalent to intravenous injection.

CHAPTER 7

SOME USEFUL INORGANICS, ORGANICS, AND BOTANICALS

Now that we have given you abundant warnings about pest resistance, human health hazards, and other potential problems associated with pesticide use, let's look at a variety of chemical tools we have found exceedingly useful in our work. We will also discuss others that we think will be very valuable once they arrive on the marketplace. In some cases, registered products we think are still cutting-edge materials have been "canceled," or not re-registered, by the manufacturer. We hope that by increasing the general knowledge about these products, we will help increase the demand for them. This, in turn, should increase their availability and use in place of more toxic materials. The greatest single motivator to get environmentally friendly green products, practices, and services to the market is your commitment to spend your money for them. "Green" begets "green."

In this and the following chapter, we introduce you to the least-toxic pesticides. It is often difficult for the average consumer to obtain accurate information on their composition and use. Even though you may already be aware of some of the older pesticides, such as sulfur and oils, you may not be familiar with their full spectrum of use. This chapter focuses on inorganic materials, including sulfur and copper; insecticidal dusts, including silica aerogel, diatomaceous earth, and boron; sodium hypochlorite, pesticidal soaps, and horticultural oils; and botanicals, including pyrethrum, neem, limonene/linalool, and garlic.

Chapter 8 discusses the frontiers of pesticide development, focusing on microbials, pheromones, and insect growth regulators. It covers newer materials that have become commercially available, as well as materials that are in the future. It also touches on some microbials that have been available for a long time but should be better known.

When reading about these pesticides, it is very important to remember that they should be used only within an overall IPM program that includes nontoxic methods. By taking this approach, you will maximize the effectiveness of your pest control efforts and minimize use of toxic materials.

Note that we do not take the space here to discuss many of the conventionally available pesticides, including the organophosphates such as malathion, acephate, and the carbamates such as carbaryl (Sevin). There is already a large body of literature on these pesticides, and almost any cooperative extension publication on the subject of pest control will provide you with a surfeit of recommendations on their use. Only if one of these pesticides is commonly used for a specific pest problem and there is no alternative to it will we mention it in the section discussing the pest for which it is appropriate.

LEAST-TOXIC CHEMICAL TOOLS: SPECIAL CHARACTERISTICS

Least-toxic pesticides have a number of special characteristics that must be kept in mind when using them. The first is the duration of effective action against the target pest. Although it is true that these substances may be more benign in relation to mammals (including humans) and less of a threat to the environment at large, the very qualities that make them better in that respect often mean they are not likely to last. Some are broken down quickly by sunlight and microbes. This is

> **"The greatest single motivator to get environmentally friendly green products, practices, and services to the market is your commitment to spend your money for them."**

particularly true of the insecticidal soaps and many botanicals. For example, if you treat a plant for aphids with a soap-and-water spray, you will probably have to treat again after a shorter interval than if you used a more poisonous material. On the other hand, you won't have to take the same risks and safety precautions as with the more toxic substances and it is less damaging to your garden ecosystem.

A second apparent drawback is that least-toxic chemicals can be slower to show results than more commonly used pesticides—although they may be every bit as effective against the pest in the long run. Boric acid, for example, is a far more permanent control than most of the other insecticides used against cockroaches. But the roaches do not keel over the first day boric acid is used. Because most customers want to see roaches die immediately, pest control professionals have been reluctant to use boric acid. In addition, most boric acid is formulated as a powder or dust that is somewhat less convenient to apply than a liquid spray. This is why individuals who do their own pest control seem more willing to buy and use boric-acid dust than do pest control professionals. However, an aerosol formulation that has recently become available may increase the use of this less-toxic compound among professionals.

A third apparent drawback concerns the selectivity of the pesticide. The fact that a material is less toxic to mammals is no guarantee of selective toxicity to the pest alone. In fact, many of the materials discussed below—pyrethrum, for example—have a very broad spectrum of impact on insects. Some of these materials kill the natural enemies of the pest or the enemies of other potential pests just as much as more toxic materials do. With the pests' natural enemies decimated, the pest problem may actually become worse. However, when the material's residual life is short—meaning it is effectively gone in hours—the overall impact on the general living community in your garden and landscape can be minimized.

TIP Before you use any pesticide, read the label. Do not exceed the recommended dosage and observe all the listed precautions.

How you integrate these materials into a comprehensive program that includes nontoxic tactics first or simultaneously, and when and where you use least-toxic chemicals, are questions that are just as important as they are with more conventional pesticides. We discuss this issue in later chapters devoted to specific pests.

The old adage, "If a little pesticide is good, a lot must be better," is absolute nonsense. Improper use and overdosing with almost any pesticide can lead to damaged plants or belongings, at best. At worst, misuse can lead to serious harm to people, pets, and the environment. Remember what Albert Einstein said: "The environment is everything that isn't me." If you protect yourself and the environment, you'll have all your bases covered.

INORGANIC PESTICIDES

Inorganic pesticides are those that do not contain carbon. They are among the oldest known pesticides and may include the following elements: arsenic, boron, copper, lead, sulfur, barium, mercury, thallium, antimony, selenium, or fluorine. Inorganic pesticides also include such sorptive dusts as silica aerogel, diatomaceous earth, and the fluorine compound cryolite (sodium fluoraluminate, sold as Kryocide®). Many inorganic pesticides take the form of tiny white crystals that resemble common table salt. They are very stable, do not volatilize, and are often soluble in water.

The only elemental inorganic pesticides still in wide use today are arsenic, boron, copper, and sulfur. Arsenic is used in herbicides (e.g., MSMA), but EPA registrations for most other materials, including ant baits, have been withdrawn because

FOR YOUR SAFETY
Keep in mind, even though arsenic is registered for certain uses, extreme caution should be used when handling it, because it can be absorbed readily through the skin.

SULFUR

Elemental sulfur without additives is probably the oldest effective pesticide in use today, and it remains popular because of its low toxicity to humans. Sulfur smoke was used to fumigate trees for aphids in the 1700s, and candles made from sulfur were burned in the late 1800s as a fumigant for bedbugs and as a general household disinfectant. Sulfur sprays for mildew control also became common in the 1800s. Today, sulfur is used widely as a fungicide and sometimes as a miticide. Gardeners can purchase finely ground sulfur products in most plant nurseries.

Properties. Sulfur is used as a pesticide both in its elemental form and as an important component of other pesticide compounds. The organosulfur compounds, which contain carbon and sulfur, are widely used as fungicides and miticides, but elemental sulfur, which occurs in nature as a yellow powder or crystal and produces a powerful odor when heated, has even wider use.

Mode of Action. Sulfur disrupts the metabolic processes of fungi and other target pests that absorb it and try to use it in place of oxygen.

Formulations. Sulfur is available in four major formulations. The first is sulfur dust, which has particles small enough to pass through a 325-mesh screen. It is mixed with 1 percent to 5 percent clay or talc to enhance the spread and adhesion of the

Sulfur is one of the oldest fungicides and miticides still in use. (Photo by jakawan_k/Fololia.com)

of the potential for environmental contamination and the threat to human and animal health. For these reasons, we suggest you do not use arsenic-containing compounds. Arsenic, mercury, and lead are heavy metals that are potent disrupting agents in all living systems. They are especially hazardous to children, pregnant women, the sick, and the elderly. These heavy metals are much more directly toxic than the lighter metals such as boron, copper, and sulfur. Heavy metals can also become methylated or alkylated. When they do, they are more soluble and mobile in living systems, which only increases their threat to health. With the exception of boron, copper, and sulfur, the inorganic light metals are no longer used because more effective, less-toxic substitutes are now available.

> **"Elemental sulfur without additives is probably the oldest effective pesticide in use today, and it remains popular because of its low toxicity to humans."**

dust. The second is wettable sulfur, which is composed of finely ground sulfur particles and a wetting agent to make the sulfur soluble in water. The third is colloidal sulfur, which has particle sizes so small it is formulated as a wet paste so it can be mixed with water. The fourth is a liquid, in both concentrate and ready-to-use formulations. The small particle size is important in dispersing the sulfur evenly over the surface of a leaf so it can affect fungal pathogens before they penetrate the leaf tissue. Sulfur in large particles—crystalline "flowers of sulfur," for example—leaves spaces between particles through which fungi can attack the plant.

ber boots should be worn when applying sulfur in any of its formulations.

TIP Because sulfur has a tendency to settle out when in liquid form, the spray bottle or tank must be agitated frequently during application. Sulfur materials are abrasive to metal, so plastic sprayers should be used.

Safety. Sulfur is less toxic to humans than many conventional synthetic fungicides and miticides. However, precautions should be taken to prevent inhalation of the dust and skin or eye contact with sulfur compounds. Sulfur compounds can damage the lungs and are strong eye and skin irritants. A dust mask, goggles, impervious gloves, long sleeved shirt, long pants, and rub-

Uses and Application. Sulfur is effective against powdery mildews, rusts, apple scab, brown rot of stone fruits, rose black spot, and other plant diseases. Copper and oils can have a synergistic effect when used with sulfur that causes the sulfur to be more potent against plant pathogens. But this enhanced toxicity also increases the likelihood that the sulfur will burn the plant tissue. For this reason, sulfur sprays or dusts should not be applied within a month of an oil spray. Because heated sulfur can burn leaf tissue, it should not be applied when the air temperature is above 90°F (32°C).

Sulfur is toxic to arthropods, although mites are far more susceptible than insects. This relative selectivity means that sulfur can be used without causing undue disruption of many species of beneficial insects. We have used sulfur dusts to hold down populations of the broad mite *(Polyphagotarsenomus latus)* on gerberas in the greenhouse. However, we found a predatory mite, *Amblyseius limonicus,* more effective than sulfur.

COPPER

The growth of modern plant pathology was stimulated by a copper and lime combination called Bordeaux mixture. This mixture was used for the first time in 1878 by French viticulturists, whose grapes were being pilfered, particularly where they grew along roadways. In an attempt to discourage theft, the growers applied a poisonous-looking mixture of lime

Copper sulfate pentahydrate is an algicide and fungicide. When mixed with lime it is called Bordeaux mixture and used as a fungicide. (Photo by Radu Razvan Gheorghe/Dreamstime.com)

and copper sulfate to the roadside plants. A. Millardet, a researcher at the nearby Academy of Sciences in Bordeaux, noticed that the vines painted with this mixture suffered little or no downy mildew disease, which had been introduced inadvertently into Europe from America. But the vines without the compound were being defoliated. This observation led to widespread use of what became known as Bordeaux mixture. The fungicide was introduced into the United States in 1885.

Properties. Copper compounds in their solid state are blue, green, red, or yellow powders that are virtually insoluble in water.

Mode of Action. The toxic action of copper is attributed to its ability to denature (change) the properties of cellular proteins and to deactivate enzyme systems in fungi and algae.

Formulations. Many copper compounds are used as fungicides. Among the most common is copper sulfate, also known as bluestone. It is available as a crystalline solid, wettable powder, liquid concentrate, or dust. Bordeaux mixture, which in its solid state is a pale blue powder, is prepared by combining copper sulfate and hydrated lime. It can be purchased as a wettable powder at most plant nurseries.

Safety. Dilute copper solutions are considered to have moderately acute toxicity to humans; the LD_{50} of copper hydroxide in rats is 1,000 mg/kg. However, copper compounds are strong eye and skin irritants, so you should always wear protective clothing when applying these materials. Copper compounds are highly toxic to fish and aquatic invertebrates.

Uses and Application. Copper sulfate, which is corrosive to the eyes and skin, is primarily used as an algicide in lakes, ponds, reservoirs, and irrigation systems, although it is also applied as a foliar fungicidal spray on fruit, nut, vegetable, and ornamental plants. Copper hydroxide, cuprous oxide, and other formulations are also used for this purpose.

Bordeaux mixture is used primarily as a fungicide, but it also has insecticidal and repellent properties. It was used in the 1940s to repel flea beetles on potatoes and tomatoes. It is also used to control common plant diseases, such as peach leaf curl, powdery mildew, black spot, rust, anthracnose, fire blight, and bacterial leaf spots and wilts.

Because copper compounds can be toxic to plant tissue, the timing of Bordeaux mixture applications is very important. For example, if the mixture is used to prevent peach leaf curl—and it is still the best treatment for this problem—it should be applied just before leafing out occurs. If it is applied afterward, it can damage the leaves. It is not safe to use on peaches during the growing season, and it may burn apples and cause them to russet. On rose leaves, it can cause red spotting, yellowing, and leaf loss, symptoms that may be confused with black spot, an important disease of roses (see pp. 327–337). It may also defoliate Japanese plums. Injury is most prominent when the temperature drops below 50°F (10°C) and the humidity is high. Read the label for additional cautions, and consult *Westcott's Plant Disease Handbook* (Springer, 2008).

Copper is also commonly used in sheet form as a barrier against snails, as discussed on p. 341. Copper "tape" for snail barriers is available at nurseries and online garden suppliers.

TIP Late summer use of Bordeaux mixture may increase the plant's susceptibility to early fall frosts.

INSECTICIDAL DUSTS

Many insects are repelled by dusts. Birds and animals know the value of dust in ridding themselves of lice, fleas, and other ectoparasites. Powdered clay is used by some human tribes for the same purpose. Sulfur, which we have already discussed, is often applied as a dust to control fungi and mites on food and ornamental crops.

Certain dusts known as sorptive dusts have the ability to cling to or be absorbed by the waxy layer on the outside of the cuticle of insects. This waxy layer, which is the chief barrier to excessive loss of water, averages about 0.25 microns in thickness in most insects. Some sorptive dusts are abrasive and scratch off the waxy material, whereas others remove the wax by absorbing it. Either way, the insect eventually dies through dehydration.

Among the many substances proven effective in disrupting the solid wax coating on the outside of the insect cuticle are activated gas-mask charcoal, alumina (aluminum oxide), diatomaceous earth, montmorillonite, and kaolin acid-activated clays, amorphous precipitated silica, and silica aerogels.

Below we discuss the active ingredients of three dusts that are particularly useful as insecticides around the house: silica aerogel, diatomaceous earth, and boric acid and borate compounds. These insecticidal dusts are now receiving the attention they have long deserved from the public and from pest control professionals. Special application equipment is often needed to apply dusts uniformly to plant surfaces. These dusts can be less toxic and more effective against certain insect groups.

Remember, however, that if you use dusts of any kind in your pest management programs, even dusts safe enough to eat, you should avoid getting them in your lungs or eyes. Protect yourself with goggles and a dust mask. Once in place, these materials no longer pose the same hazard potential, unless they are stirred up. Because sorptive dusts are inorganic and nonvolatile, they can remain active for years if kept dry and undisturbed.

SILICA AEROGEL

Silica aerogels are amorphous, non-abrasive, chemically inert materials that are used as insecticides and dehydrating agents. You have probably seen, for example, the small bags of silica aerogel that are put in electrical equipment packages to prevent the accumulation of moisture during shipping or storage.

Properties. Silica aerogels are formed by a reaction of sodium silicate and sulfuric acid to form fluffy aerogels, whose small particles can absorb three times their weight in linseed oil—a substance similar to the waxy material on the cuticles of insects—and 5 percent to 100 percent of their weight in water.

Mode of Action. These aerogels absorb the waxy protective coating on an insect's cuticle, causing the insect to dehydrate and die.

Formulations. There are several formulations of silica-aerogel on the market, often in a mixture with pyrethrum or pyrethroids. Piperonyl butoxide, a synergist and insecticide, is also a frequent ingredient. Silica aerogel insecticides are labeled for indoor and structural pest control, so we will not delve further into them here.

It should be noted, however, that there is some controversy over the safety of piperonyl butoxide (see p. 123), which is still being resolved. The EPA has categorized piperonyl butoxide as a group C carcinogen, a possible human carcinogen, based on limited evidence of cancer in laboratory animals.

DIATOMACEOUS EARTH

Properties. Diatomaceous earth is mined from the fossilized silica shell remains of unicellular or colonial algae in the class Bacillariophyceae, better known as diatoms. It has both abrasive and sorptive qualities.

Mode of Action. Like the silica aerogels, although to a lesser extent, diatomaceous earth absorbs the waxy layer on the surface of insect skins, causing

> ## FOR YOUR SAFETY
> Pyrethrum is an organic insecticide that can be toxic to humans when one is exposed to large doses. Handle all pesticides with care; organic does not mean nontoxic.

the insect to desiccate (dry out). In addition to its desiccant action, it works abrasively to rupture insect cuticles, allowing cell sap to leak out.

Formulation. Diatomaceous earth is formulated as a dust, either alone or in combination with pyrethrin.

Safety. Diatomaceous earth is virtually nontoxic to mammals. The oral LD_{50} in rats is between 3,160 and 8,000 mg/kg, depending on the formulation. It is safe for human consumption in the small amounts that are mixed with grains for insect control. However, treated grain should be rinsed before cooking.

Both swimming-pool-grade (used as a filtering agent) and natural diatomaceous earth come from the same fossil sources, but they are processed differently. The natural grades are mined, dried, ground, sifted, and bagged. The pool-grade diatomaceous earth is chemically treated and partially melted; consequently, it contains crystalline silica, which is a respiratory hazard. Thus, it is imperative that only natural diatomaceous earth be used for insect control. The human body is not harmed by this noncrystalline form of silica. It can, however, irritate the eyes and lungs, so wear goggles and a dust mask when applying it.

Uses and Application. Diatomaceous earth is used as a border around vegetable and ornamental plant beds to discourage slugs and snails. It also helps control ants, earwigs, silverfish, cockroaches, fleas,

Compounds made from boron are used as least-toxic insecticides and wood preservatives. (Photo by hdagli/iStockphoto)

millipedes, and other crawling arthropods in and around the garden, planters, and garden structures.

BORON

Boron is probably best known for the compounds borax and boric acid, which have many uses. Early Asian artisans used borax—the most common compound of elemental boron—in welding and brazing and in glazing pottery. It was also used in drugs and pharmaceuticals. Borax has long served as a mild antiseptic and fungicide, and boric acid is commonly used as an eyewash. Today, boron finds use primarily in glass-making, but it is also used in cleaners, soaps, contact-lens solutions, flame retardants, metal flux, control rods in atomic reactors, and agricultural and wood-preservative chemicals.

FOR YOUR SAFETY

Crystalline silica is the form of silica that is associated with silicosis. Never use swimming-pool-grade diatomaceous earth for insect control because of the silicosis hazard. Moreover, it is less effective against insects than the natural insecticide grade of diatomaceous earth.

Properties. It is important to understand the difference between boron, borate, borax, and boric acid. Boron, an element, is found naturally in combination with sodium, calcium, or magnesium and oxygen as borates. Borax, or sodium tetraborate, is a combination of sodium, boron, and oxygen, and is mined from the soil in its crude form. Boric acid is a crystalline material derived from borax.

Mode of Action. Boric acid acts as a stomach poison when ingested. The exact mechanism is not fully understood, but some researchers think boric acid disrupts the action of protozoa or bacteria in the insect's gut, inhibiting the functioning of the enzymes that break down food. This causes the insect to starve to death.

Formulations. Borate products used in pest control (primarily boric acid) come in many formulations, including powders, pastes, aerosols, tablets, and liquid solutions.

Safety. Judging from their LD_{50} rating in rats (from 3,200 to 6,000 mg/kg depending on the formulation), borate products have low toxicity to humans and other mammals. Boric acid has been used for over 80 years in low doses as an eyewash, and is found in many contact-lens cleaners. When ingested in high doses, however, boric acid can be harmful. Therefore, it must be kept away from food, children, and pets. When inhaled, boric acid powder can irritate the nose, throat, and lungs. Boric acid and other borate compounds can also be absorbed through skin lesions and burns. You should wear a dust mask, gloves, and eye protection when applying it. Keep boric acid in its original container and store in a safe place.

Uses and Application. Boron-based pesticides are registered almost exclusively for insect and fungal pests associated with structures. These boron-containing compounds are widely used in the United

States as insecticides against ants, cockroaches, fleas, silverfish, and other insects. Borates are also gaining favor as wood preservatives in the United States and around the world.

Because the boron-based pesticides are labeled primarily for structural use, we will not go into deeper detail here.

SODIUM HYPOCHLORITE

Most people are familiar with sodium hypochlorite as household bleach and use it to "whiten" their clothes or to keep their swimming pools and hot tubs free of algae. It is widely used as a disinfectant in water supplies, medical facilities, and food-processing plants. Sodium hypochlorite also serves as a fungicide in the nursery industry, and it is this application we focus on here.

Properties. Sodium hypochlorite is caustic in a water solution.

Mode of Action. Sodium hypochlorite is a strong oxidizing agent that kills organisms by chemically "burning," or oxidizing, their tissue. Hypochlorite compounds act by releasing chlorine-oxygen radicals.

Formulation. Sodium hypochlorite (chlorine) is sold as a 5-percent solution that has a slightly yellow color. Chlorine is also sold at 6-percent solutions for household uses and at 10 percent to 12 percent for swimming pool and water-purification use. The quantities used in the bleach solution recipes below are based on a 5-percent bleach solution.

Safety. In the dilute solution in which it is used, sodium hypochlorite is relatively safe for human use, although the undiluted material is quite toxic.

> **TIP** Be careful when using bleach; wear old clothing. Chlorine, even diluted, will bleach natural fabrics, leaving permanent "light spots" on the fabric. Clothing is especially in danger when dipping hand clippers during pruning.

Its oral LD$_{50}$ in rats is 150 mg/kg. Bleach is a caustic eye and skin irritant, so it is important to wear gloves and eye protection when mixing it. Because it is highly reactive, it breaks down rapidly in soil.

Uses and Application. Bleach solutions are used to disinfect greenhouse benches, seedling flats and pots, and pruning tools to prevent fungal and bacterial infection of plants. They are also used to protect cuttings from disease organisms. In commercial nurseries, for example, the stems of rose and grape cuttings are dipped for 20 minutes in a 0.5-percent sodium hypochlorite solution (household bleach diluted at 1 part bleach to 9 parts water) to eliminate crown gall bacteria (*Agrobacterium tumefaciens*), which may be carried on the surface of the cuttings. A drench of 2-percent solution of household bleach (2½ oz. of bleach to 1 gal. of water) can also be used to arrest the development of damping-off fungi in flats of cuttings or seedlings.

PESTICIDAL SOAPS

Fish-oil soaps, the most widely used early insecticidal soaps, included those made with whale oil until public awareness that whales are endangered curtailed their use. Vegetable-oil soaps, which did not have as disagreeable an odor as fish-oil soaps, were made with coconut, corn, linseed, or soybean oil. "Green soap," a potassium/coconut-oil soap used widely as a liquid hand soap in public restrooms years ago, has been used to control many soft-bodied insects such as aphids. Although the term "green soap" is no longer used, similar potassium/coconut-oil soaps are still available on the market as hand soaps and shampoos.

Most of the research on and use of insecticidal soaps halted abruptly during World War II due to the increasing availability of inexpensive chlorinated hydrocarbon pesticides, such as DDT, which had broad toxicity. The soaps, though virtually nontoxic to humans, were relatively short-lived and

Insecticidal soap is sprayed on aphids feeding on a green pepper plant. (Photo by John Swithinbank/GAP)

could not match the persistence of the chlorinated hydrocarbons. Unfortunately, the long-term human health and environmental effects of the chlorinated hydrocarbons were not understood until years after their introduction. Today, pesticidal soaps are extremely popular with gardeners.

Properties. A soap is a substance made from the action of an alkali such as sodium or potassium hydroxide on a fat. The principal components of fats are fatty acids. The old-fashioned way of making soap was by boiling animal fat and lye (sodium hydroxide). This converted the normally water-insoluble fat into a water-soluble soap. Commercial insecticidal soaps that are manufactured today contain a blend of selected fatty-acid chain lengths.

Mode of Action. When pesticidal soap touches the cuticle (outer body) of a susceptible insect, the fatty acids penetrate the insect's covering and dissolve into the membranes around its cells, disrupting their integrity. The cells leak and collapse, resulting in the dehydration and death of the insect. Susceptible insects become instantly paralyzed on contact with the soap; other insects become paralyzed for a short time, then recover. Soap can also penetrate the protective coating on plant tissue and fungi, causing dehydration and death.

Formulations. Pesticidal soaps are formulated as liquid concentrates and ready-to-use liquid sprays.

Safety. The principal value of soaps as pesticides is that they are virtually nontoxic to the user unless

TIP Because bleach breaks down rapidly in soils, it provides little or no residual protection. Moreover, it is strongly alkaline and can raise the pH of soil. Therefore, you should apply an acidic drench of tea (the beverage type) or 25-percent vinegar (acetic acid) solution after every third bleach drench to counteract the alkaline effect.

ingested in high doses. Even at high doses they have no serious systemic effects, although they can cause vomiting and general stomach upset. The LD_{50} in rats of Safer® Insecticidal Soap is greater than 16,500 mg/kg, and Safer's other soap products show similarly large margins of safety. At the doses found in commercial formulations, including concentrates, no mortality has been observed in test animals. Pesticidal soaps biodegrade rapidly in the soil. Always wear appropriate safety equipment, especially eye protection, when applying soap-based pesticides.

Soaps show relative selectivity in the range of insects they affect. Soft-bodied mites and sucking insects such as aphids, scale crawlers, whiteflies, and thrips are the most susceptible. Some insects, including adult beetles, wasps, flies, and grasshoppers, are relatively unaffected, apparently due to resistance factors in the chemical composition of their outer coverings. Slow-moving insects are more susceptible than highly mobile ones that can fly away from the spray. Thus, the adult forms of many beneficial insects, such as lady beetles, rapidly moving lacewings, and syrphid flies, are not very susceptible; the flightless, soft-bodied pre-adult forms of these insects are more susceptible.

DID YOU KNOW?
Soaps, which are sodium or potassium salts combined with fish or vegetable oil, have been used as insecticides since the late 1700s and perhaps even earlier.

Uses and Application. Specific uses of soap sprays are discussed throughout the book under various pest problems. The chart on the facing page lists the organisms that are susceptible to insecticidal soap.

One limitation of earlier insecticidal soaps was the fact that their active ingredients and dosages varied widely due to a lack of standardization.

Many of the insecticidal soaps were obtained from the commercial soap trade, where the blend of fatty acids was not quality-controlled. Therefore, there was little consistency from one batch to the next. A 1-percent to 2-percent solution of regular household soap or detergent can be used to kill insects, but its reliability is less predictable than soaps formulated as insecticides. Such solutions are also more likely to "burn" plants than are the commercial insecticidal products. Modern soap insecticide formulations are far less phytotoxic than their predecessors. However, if soaps are applied too frequently or with too short an interval between applications, the result will be leaf scorch and possibly defoliation. Although the home gardener is free to use "homemade" pesticides, professional pest control applicators may only use soaps registered by the EPA for pest control.

In recent years, the standardization of insecticidal soap has improved considerably, largely through the work of Dr. G. S. Puritch of Safer, Inc. In the 1970s, his published research indicated that the toxicity of fatty-acid salts (soaps) peaked when the saturated fatty-acid molecule contained about 10 carbon atoms, or 18 in an unsaturated molecule. Insecticidal soaps marketed today are standardized to maximize the number of 10-carbon or 18-carbon fatty acids in their formulations.

Insects with relatively soft bodies, including aphids, adelgids (a type of aphid), mealybugs, whiteflies, and pear psylla, are the most sensitive to these fatty acids. The lepidopteran defoliators, such as gypsy moths and winter moths, are less sensitive. Least affected of all are the beetles, including lady beetles, spruce beetles, and black vine beetles. Pesticidal soaps are particularly useful indoors, where the toxicity of other pest control materials can pose a safety threat.

Safer, Inc., has also introduced a soap-based fungicide composed of fatty-acid salts and sulfur. It is effective against a variety of fungi that attack ornamental and food plants, including powdery mildew, black spot, brown canker, leaf spot, and rust. It also controls mites, chiggers, and ticks.

SOME ORGANISMS SUSCEPTIBLE TO SAFER INSECTICIDAL SOAP

GENERAL GROUP	SPECIFIC ORGANISMS
aphids	cabbage, pea, bean, balsam wooly, spruce gall, many others
caterpillars	hemlock looper, tent caterpillars, Douglas-fir tussock moth
crickets	
earwigs	European earwig
fleas	cat flea, dog flea adults
flies	adult fruit flies, fungus gnats
grasshoppers	
lacebugs	
leafhoppers	
mealybugs	
mites	two-spotted spider mite, red spider mite, bird mites, others
mosses, algae, lichens, liverworts	plant bugs
psyllids	pear psylla
sawflies	cherry, pear, and rose slugs (actually sawflies, not slugs)
scales	brown soft scale, some others
spittlebugs	
springtails	
thrips	
whiteflies	greenhouse whiteflies, other whiteflies

Sources: Product labels and research papers provided by Safer, Inc. Specific organisms listed if identified in the literature. Efficacy on leafhoppers is highly variable.

The fungicide has both a preventive and an eradicant action on fungi. For example, properly timed sprays can prevent powdery mildew and rust from germinating, or they can eradicate existing infections. The fungicide also prevents the germination of black spot, but it cannot remove the damage symptoms (black spots) from individual leaves because the tissue is already dead.

Safer, Inc., markets a fatty-acid herbicide, a nonselective material that kills or damages any plant it touches. The fatty acids are decomposed by

USING INSECTICIDAL SOAP SAFELY

When using an insecticidal or fungicidal soap, test the dosage on a small number of plants or on the portion of the plant to be treated to evaluate its toxic effects. When used as directed, paying special attention to the recommended interval between applications, insecticidal soap is not phytotoxic. Applications made at too short an interval result in the insecticidal soap acting as a contact herbicide, which can damage leaves to the point of defoliation of the plant. Plants that have hairy leaves, such as African violets, tend to hold the soap solution on their leaf surfaces, where it can cause leaf burn and scorching. You can minimize this effect by rinsing the soap off the plant after the pests have died. This should be done within ten minutes to several hours after application, depending on the sensitivity of the plant, the temperature (the higher the temperature, the more likely the plant is to react negatively), and the strength of the soap solution. You will have to experiment to discover what works best.

soil microbes within 48 hours. This product is most effective when used against weeds in the seedling stage. Because it does not translocate to the roots it is not very effective against mature perennial plants, particularly those with tap roots.

HORTICULTURAL OILS

Written records of the use of oils as pesticides date from as early as the first century A.D., when the Roman scholar Pliny the Elder wrote that mineral oil controlled certain plant pests. It was also recognized that oils could damage plant tissue. By 1763, petroleum oil and turpentine were in common use as insecticides. Whale oil was used against scales as early as 1800 in the United States, and an oil mixture of kerosene, soap, and water was used against caterpillars in the 1860s.

Oils can be petroleum-based (that is, they come from fossilized plants), they can be derived from living plants, as with the vegetable oils or botanicals described in the next section, or they can come

from animal fat. Most pesticidal oils in use today are petroleum-based, and there has been a resurgence in their use as insecticides as a result of new refining techniques that reduce plant damage. Horticultural oils (which are insecticides), creosote (which is a fungicide/ insecticide), and weed oil (a herbicide) are examples of petroleum oils used as pesticides. Petroleum-based oils are considered to be synthetic organic chemicals because they have been highly purified compared to the crude state in which they were extracted from underground oil deposits.

In recent years, insecticidal oils extracted from safflower, corn, and other crop plants have become more common. Research shows these materials to be effective insecticides, particularly against pests that have developed resistance to common chemical insecticides. Vegetable oils are also being used as spreader stickers, a type of spray adjuvant.

Properties. Horticultural oils are a complex mixture of hydrocarbons containing traces of nitrogen- and sulfur-linked compounds.

Mode of Action. In general, oils kill all stages of insects by blocking their breathing apparatus and smothering them. Oils kill eggs by penetrating the shells and interfering with metabolic processes, or by preventing respiration through the shells.

Formulation. Horticultural oils are sold as emulsified liquid concentrates. Because oils and water do not mix, a third material (such as soap) must be introduced to bring them together. Such materials are called emulsifiers. When oil and water are mixed by means of an emulsifier, the product is called an oil emulsion. It is made up of very minute and separate globules of oil surrounded by thin films of water.

Prior to the 1970s, most horticultural oils were "heavy," that is, they had a viscosity range of 100 to 220. They were used primarily as "dormant oils" on fruit and shade trees that had shed their leaves for the winter, mostly against scales and overwintering aphids. When these heavy oils were used on trees in leaf, however, the oil would clog the stomata (breathing pores on leaves) and lenticles (breathing pores on stems), reducing the trees' ability to exchange gases with the air. This often resulted in burning of tissues and other damage, particularly if the tree was under water stress at the time of spraying.

Research between 1930 and 1970 identified the source of the phytotoxicity problem as the aromatic, unsaturated sulfonated compounds in crude oils. A new class of "superior" horticultural oils was developed to overcome the problem. These oils have had most of the sulfur compounds removed, and are lighter, with viscosities between 60 and 80. Under appropriate conditions, they can be applied to most verdant plants without harm. Virtually all the horticultural oil sprays on the market today are these newer, highly refined oils, although they may be marketed under the old names, such as dormant oil and summer oil.

Safety. Oil operates physically on a plant or insect rather than by disrupting biochemical pathways, as do many other synthetic pesticides. Oil's mode of

FOR YOUR SAFETY

"Written records of the use of oils as pesticides date from as early as the first century A.D., when the Roman scholar Pliny the Elder wrote that mineral oil controlled certain plant pests."

action places it toxicologically in a much safer class than a material that blocks biochemical processes similar to processes that occur in humans and other mammals. Oils also have a relatively short residual life and less impact on natural enemy populations than other synthetic products.

Uses. Oils are used against a wide range of insects and mites, weeds, and, to a lesser extent, certain fungi. The insects susceptible to horticultural oils are listed in the chart on p. 119.

OILS AS INSECTICIDES

Oils are commonly used on ornamental plants and fruit trees to combat adelgids, aphids, cankerworms, leafhoppers, leafrollers, leaftiers, mealybugs, mites, mosquitoes, psyllids, scales, tent caterpillars, and webworms, particularly the overwintering stages. Until recently, horticultural oils were most commonly used as dormant sprays applied during fall or winter when deciduous trees are leafless and insects and mites cling to the bark in their egg or other overwintering stage. This is when they are most susceptible to suffocation.

The labels on many dormant oils caution against spraying certain thin-barked species, such as maples, beeches, and birches, and certain evergreen conifers with waxy or powdery (glaucous) leaves. According to Warren T. Johnson, an authority on horticultural oil sprays from whose work much of the information in this discussion is drawn, these precautions are unfortunate holdovers from the days of heavy oils. The dormant oils available on the market today are the lighter "superior" type, and Johnson says he had found "no published literature that claims phytotoxicity to any species of deciduous tree or shrub, in the U.S. or Canada, from using a superior oil in the dormant stage." According to Johnson, the same is true of conifers, except for those such as blue spruces in which the oil removes the bluish frosted material from the needles. It takes two or three years before the normal color returns.

Johnson also disputes the label precautions against using oils on plants when temperatures fall below 40°F (4°C). "Field studies at the New York

Agricultural Experiment Station have yielded no evidence that low temperature oil applications, per se, will cause damage to dormant fruit trees. Any superior oil that remains in the liquid state at 20°F [–6.5°C] should be safe for all routine field applications."

The new horticultural oils can also be sprayed as a 2-percent solution against insects and mites on plants in full leaf if environmental conditions are right. Field tests of summer applications of oils on trees, shrubs, and greenhouse-grown bedding and foliage plants have shown that the new oils can safely be applied to most common ornamental plants even at high temperature (see the chart on p. 121). The key is making sure that the plants are not under water stress when they are sprayed and that the relative humidity is low to moderate (45 percent to 65 percent) so the oil spray evaporates from the leaves fairly quickly.

"There are plenty of examples where oil has been applied to shade trees when the temperature was over 90°F [32°C] without injury symptoms," Johnson writes. He points out that it is not the high temperature itself that should be of concern, but the combination of high temperature and moisture stress. If oils are sprayed on foliated trees at high temperatures, damage (e.g., scorched leaves) will probably occur only if the trees do not have access to sufficient water to replace respired moisture. However, research by University of Maryland entomologists John Davidson, Stanton Gill, and Mike Raupp during drought periods demonstrated that even under moisture stress, shade trees have a surprisingly high tolerance for oil sprays at high temperatures. They sprayed oils on over 50 genera of trees and found very little damage to the leaves and other plant parts.

Horticultural oils are used in commercial nurseries to control pests on bedding and house plants, and have become more common in the home garden for use on food and ornamental plants. Whether mineral- or vegetable-based, horticultural oils are available at nurseries and online garden suppliers. As with any insecticide, you should always test the material on a small portion of the plant before treating the entire specimen. The cooler and shadier the conditions when the oil is applied, the better.

Oils are also used to kill mosquito larvae. The oil is spread on the surface of water in which mosquitoes develop. When the larvae, sometimes called "wigglers," push their breathing tubes through the surface of the water to take in oxygen, the oil adheres to the tubes, clogging them and suffocating the mosquitoes.

Recent changes in formulation have made commercial oils used against mosquitoes less toxic to other forms of wildlife than they were a decade or so ago. However, oils applied to the surface of water also kill or otherwise interfere with certain beneficial insects that inhabit the water surface, including water striders, which prey on mosquito larvae and pupae. Even so, most other mosquito larvicides kill a much wider range of aquatic species. Thus, oils can serve as one of the less-toxic insecticides in an overall mosquito control program. Oils are especially effective in storm-sewer catch basins, where standing water often lingers long after the last rain storm and creates perfect breeding environments for mosquitoes.

OILS AS HERBICIDES

Unlike the highly refined horticultural oils used on trees and shrubs, the best weed oils are cruder oils with a high percentage of the aromatic, unsaturated sulfonated compounds that are toxic to plants. Cruder diesel oils are used as nonselective herbicides on railroad beds, roadsides, and paths; however, these materials are potential soil contaminants, so we do not recommend them for this purpose.

In *Weed Science* (John Wiley and Sons, 1975), weed specialists Glenn Klingman and Floyd Ashton discuss the ways in which herbicidal oils act on plants. Oils penetrate the leaves, bark, and roots, and move into intercellular spaces where they apparently dissolve the constituents of cell walls. This allows the cell sap to leak out, causing collapse of the cell. As a result, leaves sprayed with oil often look as if they are water-soaked.

INSECTS AND MITES KILLED OR REPELLED BY HORTICULTURAL OIL SPRAYS

SCIENTIFIC NAME	COMMON NAME	SCIENTIFIC NAME	COMMON NAME
Aphids and Adelgids		**Mites (continued)**	
Aphis citricola	citrus aphid	*Oligonychus bicolor*	oak mite
A. fabae	bean aphid	*O. ununguis*	spruce spider mite
A. pomi	apple aphid	*Panonychus ulmi*	European red mite
Cinara spp.	pine aphids	*Phytoptus pyri*	pear leaf blister mite
Eulachnus agilis	pine needle aphid	*Tetranychus urticae*	two-spotted spider mite
Hormaphis hamamelidis	witch hazel leaf gall aphid	*Vasates aceriscrumena*	spindle gall mite
Illinoia (Macrosiphum) liriodendri	tuliptree aphid	*V. quadripedes*	bladder gall mite
Macrosiphum rosae	rose aphid	**Phylloxera and Psyllids**	
Myzocallis granovsky	hemlock wooly adelgid	*Phylloxera* spp.	pecan phylloxera
Beetles		*Psylla pyricola*	pear psylla
Diabrotica spp.	corn rootworms	**Sawflies**	
Pyrrhalta luteola	elm leaf beetle	*Amauronemalus* spp.	locust sawflies
Bugs		**Scales**	
Stephanitis pyrioides	azalea lace bug	*Aonidiella aurantii*	California red scale
Caterpillars		*Asterolecanium* spp.	pit scales
Archips spp.	leafrollers	*Carulaspis juniperi*	juniper scale
Heliothis zea	corn earworm	*Chionaspis pinifoliae*	pine needle scale
Malacosoma americanum	eastern tent caterpillar	*Coccoidea* spp.	scales
Spodoptera frugiperda	fall armyworm	*Coccus hesperidum*	brown soft scale
Yponomeuta multipunctella	euonymus webworm	*Gossyparia spuria*	European elm scale
Fungus Gnats and Leafminers		*Lecanium corni*	lecanium scale
Liriomyza spp.	leafminers	*Lepidosaphes gloveri*	Glover scale
Lycoriella mali	fungus gnat	*Macrosiphum liriodendri*	tuliptree scale
Mealybugs		*Melanaspis obscura*	obscure scale
Dysmicoccus wistariae	taxus mealybug	*Neolecanium cornuparvum*	magnolia scale
Planococcus citri	citrus mealybug	*Pulvinaria amygdali*	cottony peach scale
Mites		*P. innumerabilis*	viburnum cottony scale
Aculus ligustri	privet rust mite	*Saissetia oleae*	black scale
Eotetranychus tillarum	linden spider mite	*Unaspis euonymi*	euonymus scale
Epitrimerus pyri	pear rust mite	**Whiteflies**	
		Bemesia tabaci	sweet-potato whitefly
		Trialeurodes vaporariorum	greenhouse whitefly

Note: This list of species has been assembled from a number of research papers on the effectiveness of oils on various pest species. Many other insects and mites are no doubt also susceptible to oil sprays, so experimentation is encouraged.

BOTANICALS

Botanical pesticides are derived from plants. Common examples include pyrethrum, which is derived from a species of chrysanthemum, and azadirachtin, derived from the neem tree. There are several basic ways in which botanicals are derived from their source plants.

- Preparations made from the crude plant material. These are the dusts or powders made from ground and dried plant parts that have not been extracted or treated extensively. They are marketed at full strength or are diluted with carriers such as clays, talc, or diatomaceous earth. Examples include dusts or wettable powders of cubé roots (rotenone), pyrethrum flowers, sabadilla seeds, ryania stems, and neem leaves, fruits, and bark.

- Plant extracts or resins. These are water or solvent extracts that concentrate the plant's insecticidal components. Such extracts or resins are formulated as liquid concentrates or are combined with dusts or wettable powders. Examples include pyrethrins, cubé resins (rotenone), citronella and other essential oils, and neem seed extracts or oils.

- Pure chemicals isolated from plants. These are purified insecticidal compounds that are isolated and refined through a series of extractions, distillations, and/or other processes, and are formulated as concentrates. They include d-limonene and linalool, and pyrethrin. Nicotine sulfate, an extremely toxic insecticide that falls into this category, is no longer registered for use in the United States.

TIP Despite the apparent safety of oils, during hot weather plants should be irrigated before spraying to minimize the potential for phytotoxicity. This is true for any pesticide application. It is also wise to spray in the early morning or on cloudy days, when it is cooler, to reduce the likelihood of damage.

Hundreds of plants are known to have insecticidal properties, and the number of separate compounds is probably in the thousands. Like the inorganic pesticides described earlier, botanicals were in common use until the 1940s when they, too, were displaced by modern synthetic pesticides that seemed cheaper, easier to apply, and longer-lasting. Pyrethrum, nicotine, and rotenone continued to be used in small amounts by organic farmers and home gardeners, but sabadilla and ryania virtually disappeared from use. As awareness of the health and environmental hazards of synthetic petrochemical-based pesticides increases, however, and as pests become resistant to more and more of the synthetic compounds, interest in plant-derived pesticides is increasing.

It is important to realize, however, that just because a pesticide is derived from a plant does not mean that it is safe for humans and other mammals or that it cannot kill a wide variety of other life. For example, the botanical insecticide nicotine is a very poisonous compound that impedes neuromuscular functioning, causing insects to convulse and die. But the same fate can befall humans exposed to high doses of nicotine. Commercial nicotine insecticides are no longer registered in the United States, and we discourage the

"Regardless of how poisonous they are, botanicals tend to break down into harmless compounds within hours or days in the presence of sunlight."

use of homemade nicotine preparations. Ryanodine, the active ingredient in the botanical insecticide ryania, is 20 times more toxic to mammals than to most insects. Strychnine, a botanical widely used against gophers and birds, is very dangerous if

ORNAMENTAL PLANTS THAT TOLERATE SUMMER OIL SPRAYS

SCIENTIFIC NAME	COMMON NAME	SCIENTIFIC NAME	COMMON NAME
Trees and Shrubs		P. serrulata 'Kwanzan', 'Tibetica'	Japanese flowering cherry
Acer griseum	paperback maple	P. subhirtella 'Pendula'	higan cherry
A. palmatum	Japanese maple	P. yedoensis 'Yoshino'	Japanese flowering cherry
A. platanoides 'Crimson King', 'Debbie'	Norway maple	Pyrus calleryana 'Aristocrat', 'Bradford', 'Redspire'	ornamental pear
A. rubrum 'Embers'	red maple	Quercus palustris	pin oak
Betula pendula	weeping birch	Syringa chinensis 'Expansa'	Chinese lilac
Cedrus atlantica 'Glauca'	blue atlas cedar	S. vulgaris	common lilac
Cornus florida	pink flowering dogwood, white flowering dogwood	Taxus cuspidata 'Intermedia'	Japanese yew
		T. media 'Hicksii'	Hicks yew
Cryptomeria japonica	Japanese cedar	Tilia cordata 'Greenspire'	linden tree
Cupressocyparis leylandii	Leyland cyprus	Tsuga canadensis	Canadian hemlock
Euonymus alata 'Compacta'	winged spindle tree	Zelkova serrata 'Green Vase', 'Village Green'	zelkova
Fraxinus pennsylvanica 'Marshall Seedless', 'Autumn Applause'	green ash	**Bedding and Potted Plants**	
Ginkgo biloba 'Prince Century'	maidenhair tree	Ageratum houstonianum 'Blue Puffs,' 'Madison'	floss flower
Gleditsia triacanthos inermis 'Shademaster'	honeylocust	Impatiens 'Red Dazzler', 'Dazzler White'	busy Lizzie
Ilex crenata 'Convexa'	Japanese holly	Petunia 'Plum Madness', 'White Dancer'	petunia
I. opaca	American holly	Poinsettia spp.	poinsettia
Juniperus chinensis 'Pfitzerana-Glauca'	blue pfitzer juniper	Salvia 'Red Carabiniese', 'Blue Carabiniese'	sage
Laburnum anagyroides	golden chain tree	Tagetes 'Bonanza Harmony', 'Hero Flame'	marigold
Magnolia stellata	star magnolia	Vinca 'Little Bright Eyes', 'Little Linda'	periwinkle
Malus 'Indian Summer'	crab apple		
Oxydendrum arboreum	sourwood		
Platanus acerifolia 'Bloodgood'	London plane tree		
Prunus laurocerasus	cherry laurel		

Note: In tests conducted by University of Maryland researchers, these plants were sprayed one or more times with a 2-percent SunSpray® UltraFine or SunSpray 6E Plus oil during summer months when temperatures ranged from 70°F to 100°F (21°C to 38°C). Plants were evaluated for phytoxic reactions, including leaf spotting, discoloration, marginal burn, and distortion.

Plants in this table showed little or no phytotoxic reaction, and none of the trees and shrubs listed showed damage. Among the bedding and potted plants listed, impatiens showed minor spotting or pitting on leaves or buds, but subsequent growth was unaffected and quickly covered the damage. Poinsettias showed no damage if sprayed prior to bract expansion. Additional oil-tolerant potted and bedding plants listed on the SunSpray label include azaleas, camellias, crowns of thorn, dieffenbachias, some ferns, gardenias, jade plants, some palms, philodendrons, portulacas, and zinnias.

SOME WELL-KNOWN BOTANICAL PESTICIDES

ACTIVE INGREDIENT	PLANT SOURCE	LD$_{50}$ (MG/KG)	ROUTE	TEST ANIMAL
derris, cubé, rotenone	*Derris* spp., *Lonchocarpus* spp.	132–1,500	oral	rats
hellebore	*Veratrum viride*	—	—	—
nicotine	*Nicotiana tabacum*	50–60	oral	rats
		50	dermal	rabbits
pyrethrum	*Chrysanthemum cinerariaefolium*	200	oral	rats
		>18,000	dermal	rats
quassia	*Quassia* spp.	low toxicity to mammals	—	—
red squill	*Urginea maritima*	0.7	oral	male rats
		0.43	oral	female rats
ryania	*Ryania speciosa*	750–1,000	oral	rats
		750	oral	dogs
sabadilla	*Schoenocaulon officinale*	>10,000	oral	rats

Compiled in part from H. H. Shepard's *The Chemistry and Toxicology of Insecticides* (Burgess, 1939). All but red squill, which is a rodenticide, are insecticides. Toxicity ratings primarily from C. R. Worthing's *The Pesticide Manual: A World Compendium*, 6th ed. (British Crop Protection Council Publications, 1979).

ingested by humans or other vertebrates. If the carcasses of strychnine-poisoned rodents are eaten by birds or other animals, they in turn can be killed. This secondary poisoning of hawks, owls, and animal predators and scavengers, including pet cats and dogs, is well documented. The newer anti-coagulant rodenticides, especially the single-feed baits, have resulted in deaths to hawks, eagles, owls, and other animals in numbers large enough for the EPA to take notice. The EPA is trying to remove single-feed baits from the retail market, but some manufacturers are resisting. Visit the San Francisco Department of the Environment website at www.sfenvironment.org and search for "Don't Take the Bait" for more information on the EPA and San Francisco's efforts to remove highly toxic rodent baits from store shelves.

Regardless of how poisonous they are, botanicals tend to break down into harmless compounds within hours or days in the presence of sunlight. Because they are chemically very close to the plants from which they are derived, they are also easily decomposed by a variety of microbes common in most soils. A list of common botanical pesticides is provided in the chart above, along with the names of their plant sources and their toxicity ratings.

> **"Just because a pesticide is derived from a plant does not mean that it is safe for humans and other mammals or that it cannot kill a wide variety of other life."**

SYNERGISTS

Many botanical insecticides are formulated with synergists. Synergists have no insecticidal effect of their own, but serve to enhance the insecticidal effect of the botanicals. Synergists help deactivate the enzymes in the bodies of insects and mammals that break down a wide variety of toxic substances. This increases the impact of the insecticide and reduces the amount of raw active ingredient needed to do the job. Synergists are usually combined with insecticides in ratios of from 2:1 to 10:1

(synergist:insecticide). In the presence of a synergist, a little active ingredient can go a long way.

Piperonyl butoxide (PBO), which is derived from sesame, is the most common synergist. It is used in most products containing pyrethrins but is also formulated with rotenone, ryania, sabadilla, citrus-oil derivatives, and some synthetic pyrethroids. PBO is somewhat controversial because there are indications that chronic levels of human exposure to PBO can affect the nervous system and it may be an endocrine disruptor. Thus, PBO-containing materials are often not allowed for use in organic certification programs. PBO is now registered as a pesticide in its own right.

The botanicals described in detail below are the least toxic and most versatile currently available.

The dried Chrysanthemum flowers of *Tanacetum cinerariaefolium*, are the source of pyrethrum insecticide. (Photo by Martin Pateman/123RF)

PYRETHRUM AND ITS DERIVATIVES

Pyrethrum is probably the most important insecticide ever developed. Details about the discovery and early commercial development of insecticidal powders from flowers of chrysanthemum species remain obscure, but peasants in Persia and the Caucasus made an insecticidal powder from the dried flowers of *Chrysanthemum roseum* and *C. carneum*. China, however, was probably the earlier source. In 1886, serious cultivation of *C. cinerariaefolium*, from which "Dalmatian powder" was prepared, was begun in Europe. This expanded until World War I, when Japan became the major supplier. Later, the growing of pyrethrum shifted to Kenya and Tanzania in eastern Africa, which remain the major sources today.

It will help you considerably throughout this book if you are clear about the meaning of the three names that relate to materials derived from the chrysanthemum flower. *Pyrethrum* refers to the dried, powdered flower heads of the plant. *Pyrethrin* refers to the active-ingredient compounds that occur in the flowers derived by chemical extraction. *Pyrethroid* refers to synthetic compounds that resemble pyrethrins in chemical structure but are more toxic to insects. They are also far more stable in the presence of sunlight. Some formulations persist in the environment longer than either pyrethrum or pyrethrin, often lasting 10 days or more, compared to a few hours or days for the natural botanicals. The newer generations of pyrethroids have been found in streams and other surface water, especially in urban areas.

Properties. Pyrethrum is a mixture of compounds, including pyrethrins I and II and cinerin I and II. Pyrethrins comprise 0.9 percent to 1.3 percent of dried pyrethrum flowers. Pyrethroids are composed of synthetic compounds similar to pyrethrins.

Mode of Action. The toxic effect of pyrethrin, the active ingredient of natural pyrethrum, is attributed to its disruption of normal transmission of nerve impulses, causing virtually instant paralysis

Extracts from the leaves and fruit of the neem tree, *Azadirachta indica*, are used in pesticides, medicines, and other products. (Photo by Unclesam/Fololia.com)

where they destroy the protective ozone layer. The propellant in most products has been changed to CO_2 or nitrogen. Many pyrethrin and pyrethroid products are still packaged as aerosols for home use.

In general, we do not recommend aerosol formulations, because so much material is released into the general environment rather than directly onto the target pest. In addition, the mist created by an aerosol is composed of very fine particles that stay suspended in the air longer than those from liquid applications. Thus, indoor aerosol sprays cause unnecessary respiratory exposure. Unfortunately, many aerosols contain pleasant perfume additives rather than the unpleasant odors that would alert people that they have just taken a breath of poison.

Some formulations contain micro-encapsulated pyrethrins that release their active ingredient slowly, prolonging the life of the insecticide when used indoors. Other pyrethrins are formulated with inorganic or other botanical insecticides so the quick knockdown from the pyrethrins is combined with slower but longer-term control from the other ingredients.

in insects. Some insects can detoxify pyrethrin and recover from the initial knockdown, so most pyrethrins are combined with the synergist PBO, which blocks the ability of insects to break down the toxin. Synthetic pyrethroids have a similar mode of action.

FOR YOUR SAFETY
Pyrethrin can be toxic to cats at doses above 0.04 percent, so you should follow the label directions closely when treating cats for fleas.

Formulations. Pyrethrum is available as a powder or, like pyrethrin and the pyrethroids, can be purchased as a liquid concentrate, wettable powder, or aerosol "bug bomb." Aerosols with fluorocarbon propellants, created during the World War II era, soon became so popular that almost every home in the United States had them. Today, fluorocarbons are banned for use as aerosol propellants because fluorocarbons are now known to contaminate the upper atmosphere,

Safety. Pyrethrum, pyrethrin, and some pyrethroids are low in mammalian toxicity; the oral LD_{50} of pyrethrin in rats is 1,200 to 1,500 mg/kg. In rats fed synthetic pyrethroids, acute toxicity ranged between 430 and 4,000 mg/kg for permethrin, depending on the solvent used as a carrier, and was 3,000 mg/kg for resmethrin. No genetic mutations or birth defects were found during the chronic-exposure tests. However, repeated contact with dusts may cause skin irritation or allergic reactions in humans.

Wear gloves, goggles, and a respirator when applying these compounds, because inhalation places the poison directly in the bloodstream. (See pp. 100–102 for details on protective equipment.)

Uses and Application. Pyrethrum and related compounds are toxic to a wide range of household and garden insects, including ants, aphids, beetles, caterpillars, cockroaches, fleas, flies, leafhoppers, lice, and mosquitoes.

NEEM

The tropical neem tree *(Azadirachta indica)* is widely distributed in Africa and Asia and is grown as a beautiful ornamental shade tree in the southern United States and other subtropical regions of the continent. Neem-oil extracts have been used as medicinal preparations and pest control products in Asia and Africa for centuries. Neem's insecticidal, fungicidal, and bactericidal properties and its safety to mammals aroused interest among researchers in Europe and the United States, leading to the development of commercial insecticide and fungicide products with neem oil and neem derivatives as the active ingredients. These ready-to-use and concentrated neem products are widely available at nurseries and online sources.

Properties. Neem oil is composed of a complex mixture of biologically active compounds. It has a strong, unpleasant odor and a bitter taste.

Mode of Action. The complex structure of neem oil makes it difficult to pinpoint its mode of action. The principal active ingredient is azadirachtin, but more than 25 other active compounds, including deacetylazadirachtinol, meliantriol, vepol, and salannin, have also been isolated. Its various active ingredients act as repellents, feeding inhibitors, egg-laying deterrents, growth retardants, sterilants, and direct toxins. These multiple modes of action make it unlikely that insects or pathogens will develop resistance to neem compounds because they affect the pests in so many ways.

Neem has both contact and systemic action in plants. When it is applied to the soil, some species absorb it through their roots and distribute (translocate) it throughout the plant. When sprayed on plant foliage, neem is only somewhat systemic, but

ORGANISMS AFFECTED BY NEEM EXTRACTS

SCIENTIFIC NAME	COMMON NAME
Aphis fabae	bean aphid
Culex pipiens	northern house mosquito
Dacus dorsalis	oriental fruit fly
Diabrotica undecimpunctata	spotted cucumber beetle
Epilachna varivestis	Mexican bean beetle
Heliothis zea	corn earworm, bollworm
Leptinotarsa decemlineata	Colorado potato beetle
Liriomyza trifolii	serpentine leafminer
Locusta migratoria	migratory locust
Meloidogyne incognita	root-knot nematode
Nilaparvata lugens	brown planthopper
Oncopeltus fasciatus	large milkweed bug
Pectinophora gossypiella	pink bollworm
Plutella xylostella	diamondback moth
Podagrica uniforma	flea beetle
Schistocera gregaria	desert locust
Spodoptera frugiperda	fall armyworm
Tetranychus urticae	two-spotted spider mite
Trichoplusia ni	cabbage looper

only in certain species. Generally, flushes of new foliage must be sprayed periodically to ensure adequate protection.

Formulations. A number of registered neem products are currently available for use on ornamental and food crops.

Safety. Neem-oil extracts show very low toxicity to mammals. The oral LD_{50} in rats is greater than 13,000 mg/kg. According to the Ames test, which uses bacteria as test organisms, neem oil is not mutagenic. Seed dust can irritate the lungs, but in most forms neem is not irritating to the skin. The active ingredients biodegrade rapidly in sunlight and within a few weeks in the soil.

Uses and Application. Neem extracts affect a wide variety of insects in various ways. Extracts have inhibited feeding in more than 170 insect species in seven orders. They have inhibited normal growth in species in four orders and have proven directly toxic to aphids, termites, and various caterpillars. In a review of neem as an antifeedant and growth inhibitor, at least 20 species of Coleoptera (beetles), 5 species of Diptera (flies), 14 species of Hemiptera (bugs), 3 species of Homoptera (scales, mealybugs, and whiteflies), 2 species of Isoptera (termites), 25 species of Lepidoptera (caterpillars), 5 species of Orthoptera (locusts and crickets), and 1 mite species showed responses to neem extracts. The chart on p. 125 lists some major household and garden pests that are affected by neem.

Studies also indicate that certain beneficial insects such as hymenopteran parasitoids and predatory mites escape the effects of neem.

Limonene is a citrus peel extract that is used in least-toxic insecticides and cleaning products. (Photo by Scott Phillips, courtesy of *Fine Cooking*)

LIMONENE AND LINALOOL (CITRUS PEEL EXTRACT)

Tons of citrus peel are discarded regularly by the juice industry, yet they contain insecticidal compounds that are of low toxicity to mammals. These insect-killing properties were brought to the attention of Dr. Craig Sheppard, an entomologist at the Coastal Plains Experiment Station in Georgia, by a

> **"Tons of citrus peel are discarded regularly by the juice industry, yet they contain insecticidal compounds that are of low toxicity to mammals."**

group of auto mechanics, who reported that a hand cleaner called Dirt Squad™ killed fire ants. This hand cleaner contained orange-peel liquids, so Sheppard designed experiments to investigate the insecticidal properties of oil extracts from citrus peels.

The two most effective insecticidal compounds are d-limonene, a terpene that constitutes about 90 percent of crude citrus oil, and linalool, a terpene alcohol. Terpenes are hydrocarbons found in essential oils. They are used as solvents, fragrances, and flavors in cosmetics and beverages. Linalool can also be extracted from pine wood.

Properties. Citrus oils have a fresh floral odor and an oily consistency.

Mode of Action. Limonene and linalool are contact poisons, but research on their properties and modes of action is ongoing. It is thought that limonene heightens sensory nerve activity in insects, causing massive overstimulation of motor nerves that leads to convulsion and paralysis. Some insects, such as adult fleas, recover from the paralysis unless limonene is synergized by piperonyl butoxide, a controversial material discussed on p. 123. The effectiveness of linalool as an insecticide or insect repellent has not been clearly demonstrated.

Formulation. Limonene is available in aerosol and liquid products. They are marketed primarily as insecticides, flea dips, and shampoos but are also formulated with insecticidal soap for use as contact poisons against aphids and mites.

Safety. Limonene and linalool are used extensively in cosmetics, foods, soaps, and perfumes. At low doses such as these, they are regarded as safe by the U.S. Food and Drug Administration. Limonene has an oral LD_{50} of more than 5,000 mg/kg in rats; linalool has an oral LD_{50} in male rats of 4,858 mg/kg and in female rats of 4,127 mg/kg. At the higher doses found in insecticides, greater caution is called for.

In summarizing preliminary toxicology literature on these materials, Henn and Weinzierl (University of Illinois Office of Agricultural Entomology, circular 1296, 1989) reported that when applied topically to some laboratory animals, both compounds could irritate the skin, eyes, and mucous membranes. They also found that at both moderate and high doses these substances could cause tremors, excess salivation, lack of coordination, and muscle weakness. However, even at the higher doses the symptoms were temporary, lasting several hours to several days, and the animals recovered fully. Some cats may experience minor tremors and excess salivation for up to one hour after applications of limonene at recommended rates. Limonene was shown to promote tumor formation in mouse skin that had been previously sensitized to tumor initiation.

Uses and Application. Limonene and associated citrus compounds are registered for use against fleas, aphids, and mites. However, studies by Dr. Sheppard have shown that these compounds also kill fire ants, houseflies, stable flies, black soldier flies, paper wasps, and house crickets. In a test using scarified (grated) limes, all the fruit flies were immobilized in 15 minutes, and all were dead in two hours. Flies on unscarified limes appeared to be unaffected after two hours. In California, tests of citrus oils on Argentine ants have shown them to be very effective in immediate toxicity, although they degrade rapidly.

Citrus oils have been incorporated into general-purpose insecticides, botanical herbicides, flea-control products, termite treatments, and household cleaners.

GARLIC OIL

Garlic *(Allium sativum)*, a member of the lily family, has been used for thousands of years in treating coughs, colds, chronic bronchitis, toothache, earache, dandruff, high blood pressure, arteriosclerosis, and other ailments. The first detailed description of garlic as a medicinal plant was made by the Greek physician Dioscorides, who recommended it for destroying or expelling intestinal worms and as a diuretic. Chinese medicine uses garlic for diarrhea, amebic and bacterial dysentery, pulmonary tuberculosis, bloody urine, diphtheria, whooping cough, typhoid, hepatitis, trachoma, scalp ringworm, vaginal trichomoniasis, and other disorders. Modern studies confirm that garlic oil exhibits antibacterial, antifungal, amebicidal, and insecticidal qualities, although whether garlic is indeed effective against all the ailments listed above requires further research.

Encouraged by recommendations and anecdotes in the organic-gardening literature, gardeners have been using homemade garlic preparations as insecticides for many years. Take note, however, that although garlic does kill pest insects and some pathogens, it also kills beneficial insects and microbes. Thus, we do not recommend it as an all-purpose spray for garden use. We include it in the list of botanical materials discussed here due to its popularity with gardeners and the fact that interest in botanicals among pesticide researchers has led to the marketing of commercial garlic-based pesticides.

Properties. Garlic is a strong-scented plant whose bulb contains the volatile oil alliin (S-allyl-L-cysteine sulfoxide) and other compounds. Com-

Formulation and Uses. Garlic is toxic to a broad range of organisms. Laboratory studies have shown various extracts to be effective against two nematodes, *Aphelenchoides sacchari,* which attacks commercial mushrooms, and *Tylenchulus sempenetrans,* which attacks citrus. Garlic chips fed to baby chickens prevented the establishment of candidiasis, caused by the yeast *Candida albicans.* Aqueous extracts of commercially prepared garlic powder were shown in laboratory studies to inhibit clinical isolates of the yeast *Candida albicans* and the fungus *Cryptococcus neoformans.*

Garlic solutions have been reported to destroy four species of larval mosquitoes in the genera *Culex* and *Aedes,* as well as aphids, the cabbage-butterfly caterpillar *(Pieris brassicae,* a European species), and larvae of the Colorado potato beetle *(Leptinotarsa decemlineata).* They have also been reported to be toxic to the natural aphid enemies *Syrphus corollae,* a syrphid fly; *Chrysoperla carnea,* the green lacewing; and *Coccinella septempunctata,* a lady beetle. See Chapter 5 for a more complete discussion of these important beneficial insects.

Garlic, *Allium sativum,* has pesticidal and medicinal uses as well as its familiar role in the kitchen. (Photo by Amy Albert, courtesy of *Fine Cooking*)

mercial garlic oil is obtained by steam distillation of crushed fresh bulbs; powdered garlic is derived from dried bulbs.

Mode of Action. Although the chemical structure of garlic compounds is not well studied, diallyl disulfide and diallyl trisulfide, both present in garlic oil, have been identified as causing mortality in mosquito larvae. Both natural and synthetic samples of these active ingredients were lethal at a dosage of five parts per million in water. Garlic oil also contains the volatile compounds allicin, citral, geraniol, and linalool, which are known to have insecticidal properties. Extracts obtained with a water and alcohol mixture appear to have more fungicidal and bactericidal effects than does the essential oil.

Safety. Because garlic is a culinary staple, it is presumed safe for humans. When used as an insecticide, however, it has a broad-spectrum effect, killing both pests and beneficials. Because it is a naturally occurring plant, it can be presumed to biodegrade rapidly in the soil.

> **"Although garlic does kill pest insects and some pathogens, it also kills beneficial insects and microbes. Thus, we do not recommend it as an all-purpose spray for garden use."**

We do not recommend garlic for aphid control because it kills the natural enemies of the aphids as well as the pests. Insecticidal soaps are preferable. Because garlic seems to have broad-spectrum insecticidal effects, it should be limited to those home and garden applications where natural controls are rarely present.

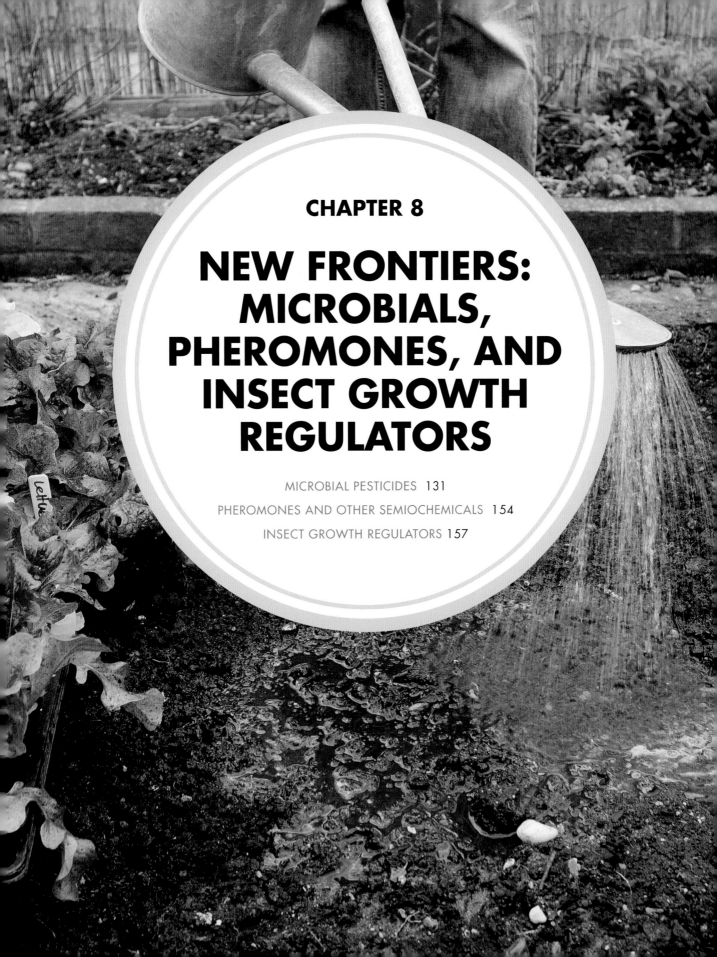

During the 1970s and 1980s, exponentially rising rates of pest resistance to conventional chemical controls, which we discussed in Chapter 6, and widespread public concern about the health and environmental hazards of many pesticides led researchers to seek novel materials that were effective against the pests but posed fewer hazards to other components of the ecosystem. As a result, three categories of biopesticides entered—or re-entered—the marketplace: microbials, insect pheromones, and insect growth regulators (IGRs). Microbial pesticides are used to suppress weeds and plant diseases as well as insects; pheromones and IGRs are used only against insects.

The biological pesticides discussed in this chapter deserve the special attention of those who are interested in less-toxic pest control, as they are at the forefront of improved pest management tools. They combine increased effectiveness, safety, and biodegradability with novel active ingredients and modes of action. In general, however, they also require greater sophistication and knowledge on the part of the user.

After defining the terms used to refer to the three groups of biopesticides, we examine each in turn, including how it works, the pests it controls, its special characteristics, its potential role in IPM programs, and what developments must take place before it fulfills that potential.

Microbial pesticides. Microbial pesticides contain living microorganisms or the toxins they produce as active ingredients. Algae, bacteria, fungi, mycoplasms, parasitic nematodes, protozoa, rickettsia, viroids, and viruses that kill their host organisms are referred to as microbials within the pesticide industry.

Many microbials are cultured in large industrial vats in much the same way as yeasts used to brew beer are cultured. They are collected at a certain stage of their development, such as the spore stage in the case of the microbial *Bacillus thuringiensis* and the infective juvenile stage in the case of nematodes. They are mixed with compounds that make them compatible with water and enhance their shelf life, and are then packaged for sale.

Microbials are formulated as sprays, dusts, and granules, and are applied with the same equipment as conventional pesticides. Although we don't recommend it, if absolutely necessary, some microbials can be used in conjunction with syn-

> **"Biological pesticides combine increased effectiveness, safety, and biodegradability with novel active ingredients and modes of action. However, they also require greater sophistication and knowledge on the part of the user."**

thetic chemical pesticides. The label indicates when this is the case. When the mixing and application of more than one pesticide is necessary to bring a pest species under control, it is important to ask yourself this question: Do the hassle, the pesticide and safety equipment costs, and the environmental impacts and safety hazards of multiple plant treatments exceed the value? Plant replacement may be the best option in many such cases.

Pheromones. Pheromones are chemical signals emitted by insects and other organisms that enable the organisms to communicate with other members of the same species. Pheromones are sometimes referred to as "perfumes," particularly those pheromones used to attract members of the opposite sex for purposes of mating. In insect control, pheromones can be used to attract insects to traps. Or they can be applied in artificially large amounts over a crop to so confuse insects that they fail to find mates and thus fail to reproduce.

Insect growth regulators. Insect growth regulators are compounds that mimic or interfere with the natural hormones that regulate an insect's developmental stages: egg, larva, pupa, and adult. These hormones affect only physiological processes unique to certain arthropods (insects, spiders, mites). Chitin inhibitors can also have an effect on aquatic invertebrates with chitin exoskeletons, such as crabs, shrimp, lobsters, and others. Hazards to nontarget species are the main reason that outdoor use of IGRs is limited.

MICROBIAL PESTICIDES

The microbes currently marketed as insecticides, fungicides, and herbicides are very effective against their target pests but are virtually nontoxic to humans, domestic animals, wildlife, and the natural enemies of the pests. In other words, they are highly selective in their action. Selectivity refers to the ability of a pesticide to affect a pest organism but not the rest of the ecosystem. It is a very important factor in choosing pest control tools. For example, because currently available microbials are nontoxic to humans and other animals, they can be applied to food crops right before or during harvest.

Microbial pesticides have other advantages. First, they have less potential for environmental contamination than conventional pesticides because they are much more biologically fragile and are therefore more biodegradable. The use of microbials is also far less likely to produce pest resistance or pest resurgence, the twin banes of conventional pesticide technology that were discussed in Chapter 6. The explanation lies in their selectivity.

Most chemical pesticides are designed to kill insects on contact. Most microbials must be consumed before they become active. Thus, consumption determines which insects die from a microbial, whereas only resistant individuals will survive treatment with a chemical insecticide, which also tends to decimate the pest's natural enemies. Because microbials are generally harmless to a pest's natural enemies, pests that survive the microbial application are often subsequently killed by their existing predators or parasitoids, preventing resurgence. The microbial pesticide does not kill as high a proportion of a pest population, which ensures that the pest's gene pool contains individuals susceptible to the microbial, thereby slowing or preventing development of resistant pest populations.

Although microbial pesticides are often referred to as biological controls, they must be distinguished from the predators and parasitoids used to control pests in the kind of classical biological control programs described in Chapter 4. Many predator and parasitoid populations become established on a self-sustaining basis in the natural environment; they increase or decrease their numbers in response to the population density of their prey. In contrast, most microbial pesticides require repeated applications just like conventional pesticides.

There are a few cases in which the introduction of a microbial species did suppress a pest with the same permanence shown by introduced parasitoids or predators. The classic example is the introduction of the myxoma virus *(Leporipoxvirus)* into Australia and France to control the European rabbit *(Oryctolagus cuniculus)*, which had become a serious pest in these countries. The virus became permanently established as one control element for these rabbits. The microbial insecticide *Bacillus popilliae,* also known as milky spore disease, is applied to turf to kill beetle grubs and can remain active in the soil for more than 25 years before another application is needed. Even this, however, does not equal the permanence of many successfully established predators or parasitoids.

Microbials have many advantages, but their use may require special care. For instance, many micro-

> **TIP** You should buy only the amount of microbial you can use during its effective storage life; don't keep a supply on hand for the long term, as is often done with chemical products.

bials are highly vulnerable to unfavorable environmental conditions. Although most are effective if applied in warm, moist conditions, coolness, insufficient moisture, or exposure to ultraviolet radiation from sunlight can deactivate or kill them. It is important to pay close attention to the application directions on the label.

The fact that microbials are living organisms means that some have shorter shelf lives than some synthetic chemicals. Containers of synthetic pesticides can usually be stored for several years under a wide range of temperatures, whereas microbials are most effective when fresh. Their storage lives may be limited to a few weeks or months under optimum conditions, which may include refrigeration. In fact, some microbials must be kept in portable ice chests while being transported to the site where they will be used.

With microbials, the timing of applications to coincide with the vulnerable stage of the pest is usually far more critical than it is with synthetic chemical products. The latter are more likely to damage several or all life stages of the pest, whereas many microbials affect only one life stage. For example, the bacterial insecticide *Bacillus thuringiensis* var. *kurstaki* (BTK) kills only the caterpillar, or larval stage, of moths and butterflies. If it is sprayed when adult moths are seen, it does nothing to prevent damage by the next generation of caterpillars that emerges from eggs laid by the moths.

Because a single microbial pesticide is toxic to a narrow range of pest species, only a portion of the pests occurring in a crop or garden will be affected by the application. Pests unaffected by the microbial will continue to cause damage unless additional measures are used to combat them. A single chemical pesticide does not kill all groups of pests either, but the range of host species killed is much greater than with microbials.

TIP Because a single microbial pesticide is toxic to a narrow range of pest species, it is very important that microbials be combined with cultural, physical, mechanical, and biological controls so that a wide range of mortality factors are brought to bear on any particular pest species.

REGISTRATION OF BIOPESTICIDES

In the United States, the EPA has responsibility for registration of pesticides. The Biopesticides and Pollution Prevention Division (BPPD), created in 1994, regulates biopesticides. Compared to the registration requirements for synthetic pesticides, biopesticide registration is usually quicker and less complex and can be less expensive. This is especially true when extensive information on the material already exists and it is presented to the BPPD in a manner that can be used in a risk-assessment process. However, the process can still be quite lengthy and expensive and has limited the number of biopesticides developed for the marketplace.

The term *biopesticides*, as used by the EPA, refers to pesticides composed of or analogous to naturally occurring organisms or substances and includes most microbials, analogs of certain chemicals produced by pests (e.g., pheromones and juvenile hormones), and other naturally occurring biochemicals, such as allelotoxins (natural herbicides), that differ in their mode of action from most conventional pesticides.

The EPA includes pesticidal substances produced by plants containing genetic material not found in the plant's natural gene pool. These substances are called plant-incorporated protectants, or PIPs. These are highly controversial, and in some countries they are illegal.

BT corn, which is corn genetically modified to force the plant to manufacture the BT toxin, is an example of a PIP. The BT toxin gene is derived from the bacteria *Bacillus thuringiensis*, a naturally occurring bacteria. BT, discussed below, is used as a biopesticide in its own right.

The registration process has been streamlined somewhat at the EPA level, but high production costs associated with the research and testing required for registration have prevented the registration of many seemingly benign microbial pesticides that could play an important role in least-toxic pest control. Thus, fewer new microbial products have reached the market than we might expect. Those that have tend to be biotechnologically altered microbes or their by-products. Currently, engineered organisms seem to be favored by the pesticide industry because they can be patented. We examine this issue next.

The EPA website has extensive information on biopesticides at www.epa.gov/pesticides/biopesticides. The Biopesticide Active Ingredient Fact Sheets page can be found at www.epa.gov/pesticides/biopesticides/#factsheet.

MICROBIAL PESTICIDES AND BIOTECHNOLOGY

In the past, most microbial pesticides were formulated with naturally occurring microorganisms. With the advent of the biotechnology industry and its concomitant drive for profits from genetically altered and patented organisms, research emphasis shifted. Rather than selecting the most effective pesticidal strain of bacteria or fungus from among the dozens or hundreds occurring naturally within a single species, researchers are focusing more time and research dollars on artificially enhancing the toxicity of microbes by altering their genetic material. The organic gardening and farming markets have kept active the search for, and registration of, naturally occurring biopesticides. This reaffirms the role you play in the direction that research goes, based on what you purchase and what you accept. Genetically altered biopesticides, including plant-incorporated protectants, are not allowed for use in organic production.

Genetic modification has both potential advantages and drawbacks. The focus of much of this research is on increasing the speed with which microbials kill insects. Thus, a number of safe and effective microbial products may result from biotechnology. However, the PIP line of research creates plants that will kill insects that eat any part of the crop plant. This could lead to the development of insect resistance to microbes, a subject discussed further below.

One of the first bioengineered microbials registered for use was a *Bacillus thuringiensis*–based insecticide toxic to the Colorado potato beetle (*Leptinotarsa decemlineata*) and to the elm leaf beetle (*Pyrrhalta luteola*). The product, called M-One®, consisted of a natural plant bacterium whose genetic material is deliberately altered to contain genes from a BT strain that naturally kills beetles. The bacterium was killed prior to formulation so there was no danger of the engineered organism reproducing in the environment. It was incorporated into an improved formulation that was more persistent than the natural bacterium alone, yet is no more likely to encourage

The Colorado potato beetle, *Leptinotarsa decemlineata*, is native to the eastern slopes of the Rocky Mountains. Originally a weed-eater, it changed to potatoes when settlers introduced the root vegetable in the late 1800s. It is the most common beetle seen in most areas of the U.S. (Photo by Scott Bauer, USDA Agricultural Research Service, Bugwood.org)

development of insect resistance than is natural *Bacillus thuringiensis.*

We were involved in a project that used M-One for the control of elm leaf beetle. The results were excellent. Mycogen Corporation, maker of M-One bioinsecticide, received the "Most Innovative Product Award for 1988" from CONNECT for its development and marketing of M-One. Affiliated with the University of California at San Diego at the time, CONNECT is a research advancement organization. The CONNECT Association spun off from U.C. San Diego as an independent organization in 2005. (M-One is no longer registered in the United States; Mycogen Corporation was bought by Dow AgroSciences in 1998.)

In tests, other engineered microbials have been released live onto target pests or incorporated into the genetic makeup of crop plants. These approaches are far more controversial because it is not known how the altered organisms will affect the environment in the long term. Of immediate concern is the incorporation of *Bacillus thuringiensis* genes into crop plants that may lead to insect resistance to this safe, naturally occurring insecticide. The gene code for the BT toxin active against caterpillars has been inserted into corn plants by researchers at Monsanto, Inc., a leading pesticide manufacturer. The resulting transgenic (genetically altered) plants produce their own BT toxin and are protected from feeding by moth larvae that die from feeding upon the plant.

Critics worry that the wide use of genetically altered plants will rapidly lead to the rise of insects that are resistant to the BT toxin. As this book goes to press, University of Illinois researchers announced that they found and confirmed BT resistance in

"Critics worry that the wide use of genetically altered plants will rapidly lead to the rise of insects that are resistant to the BT toxin."

corn rootworm on two separate Illinois farms. Our prediction that incorporating BT toxin into GMO crops would lead to BT resistance in the field has come to pass. This and other cautions about the impact of biotechnology on pest control research are discussed further in the sidebar on p. 136.

A disturbing application of transgenic science is the incorporation of genes into food crops so that they resist the application of herbicides. Currently, glyphosate-resistant varieties of corn, soybean, and cotton are in cultivation in the United States. In fact, 90 percent of the soybeans grown in the United States are GMO glyphosate-resistant plants. Pesticide companies are now seeking approval for crops that are resistant to 2, 4-D and Dicamba herbicides. Dicamba and 2, 4-D are both controversial herbicides. We recommend that you do a web search for information on these two herbicides, which are commonly used to control broadleaf weeds in turfgrass.

BotaniGard®, *Beauveria bassiana* spores in dry granular formulation. BotaniGard targets many soft-bodied sucking insects. Thorough spray coverage of the plant is required as the spores are most effective when they come in direct contact with the insect. (Photo by Rincon-Vitova Insectaries)

At a time when people are increasingly concerned about the effects of pesticides on themselves and the environment, these transgenic crops encourage the increased use of herbicides. Common sense tells us that this increase in herbicide use can't be good for farm families, farm workers, the watershed, and groundwater. We are especially concerned about health and environmental complications to people, pets, and wildlife that may arise from chronic exposure to these herbicides.

One current and future environmental complication is the creation of "superweeds" from the continual use of the same herbicide. Superweeds is the term given to weeds that have developed a resistance to one or more herbicides. Below is an excerpt from an article published by the German Federal Ministry of Education and Research on the cultivation of herbicide-resistant crops. The article, "USA: 'Superweeds' encouraged by GM plants?" appears on the European Union's GMO Safety website.

> Farmers in the U.S. are increasingly facing problems with weeds that have developed resistance to certain herbicides. A recent study blames the problem on the large-scale cultivation of genetically modified crops.

> The fact that, sooner or later, the use of herbicides leads to the emergence of resistant weeds has been known since the 1970s. The emergence of resistant weeds is documented in a publicly accessible database by the Weed Science Society of America. The database currently documents 194 species with 341 biotypes—local populations of a species—around the world that are resistant to at least one herbicide. Most herbicide-resistant weeds occur in the US.

> In a study published in November 2009 in the U.S., the author Charles Benbrook presents the view that the cultivation of genetically modified herbicide-resistant crops exacerbates the problem of resistant weeds. The U.S. grows around half of the world's genetically modified crops. The majority are crops that are resistant to the broad-spectrum herbicide glyphosate (known under the brand name Roundup).

> Although glyphosate has been used since the 1970s, in the mid-1990s there was no record of any glyphosate-resistant weeds. By 2009 there were 16 species worldwide, nine of them in the US.

The entire text of the article is available, with web links, at the GMO Safety website: www.gmo-safety.eu/news/653.usa-superweeds-encouraged-plants.html.

MICROBIAL INSECTICIDES: CURRENTLY REGISTERED ORGANISMS

Of all the pest groups being studied for possible control with microbial pesticides, insects have received the greatest attention. The knowledge that fungi can attack and kill insects has been established for over 175 years. Agostino Bassi spent 30 years studying "white muscsardine disease" that was killing silkworms. In 1835 he discovered and described the entomophagous (insect-eating) fungus *Beauveria bassiana.* The species "bassiana" is named in his honor. His work with this fungus also inspired Pasteur, Koch, and other microbiology pioneers in the early and mid-1800s.

> **"Transgenic crops encourage the increased use of herbicides. Common sense tells us that this increase in herbicide use can't be good."**

There are more than 1,850 naturally occurring microorganisms or their by-products that hold promise for the control of major insect pests. These pathogens, found within insects, include nearly 100 species of bacteria, over 700 viruses, more than 750 fungi, and at least 300 protozoan species. Currently, over 75 microbial pesticides, genetically

GMO FOODS ANYONE? OUR 2013 PERSPECTIVE

Biotechnology will bring some important changes and benefits to agriculture, medicine, and other fields. But in the years since we wrote the first edition of this book, when we mentioned the potential promise of this subject, history has told a different story in at least one arena: transgenics. The recent creation, registration, and use of GMOs and transgenic products, a subcategory of GMOs, raises important concerns and troubling questions.

One case in point, relevant to this book, is transgenic plants, specifically those created to carry the toxin derived from *Bacillus thuringiensis* as a kind of internal pesticide. As a microbial insecticide, BT is a highly selective product, which is a rarity. The market for these products is limited to those managing the few select groups of insects affected by BT (see p. 138).

Genetically modified crops do not lead to less pesticide use.

We know that any continuously dispensed pest control substance will fail. This is because pests repeatedly exposed to the same toxin will develop resistance more quickly than they would from the episodic exposures they get from spray applications. Continuous use of the same toxin puts the pest population under greater selection pressure; all the susceptible insects die off, whereas those immune to the toxin survive and reproduce. The susceptible population is no longer part of the gene pool. In contrast, the episodic spray regimen doesn't kill all of the pests, even those susceptible to the pesticide. The susceptible genes remain in the gene pool. As a result, the pesticide, BT in this instance, remains a viable tool in the IPM toolbox. This is an argument based on genetic reasoning and experimental evidence.

Weed resistance has happened because glyphosate (Roundup) is used continuously; it is a classic case of resistance buildup in a pest population from overuse of the same pesticide. Crops genetically modified to tolerate herbicides, for example, have now been shown to create superweeds because of the overuse of one herbicide. As weeds develop their resistance to these herbicides, farmers must use stronger herbicide concentrations to kill the same weed species. Eventually the weeds are totally immune: Currently, 16 weeds are completely immune to glyphosate, 9 of which are in the United States.

Genetically modified crops are not necessary.

People produced food, lots of it, without such crops. There are alternatives to cultivation besides GMO crops and herbicides. Alternative cover crops, used to suppress weeds, are underutilized. Crop rotation and cover crop alternatives don't pollute surface water and groundwater as herbicides do. Herbicide pollution is bad, but not necessarily permanent. GMO crops give us genetic pollution, something far worse because it is now part of the plant DNA.

In addition, once a company manufactures such a product it defends it with all its corporate powers. Crops belonging to organic and conventional farmers but raised near GMO crops can become contaminated with GMO crop genes during pollination. Those foreign genes are then expressed in the seeds of the formerly normal crop. Big producers of GMO crops contend that the crop, now contaminated with GMO genes, is corporate property. When this occurs the corporation often sues the farmer for royalties. The costs and time involved in litigation can easily put a family farmer in financial jeopardy.

Genetically modified crops are an ecologically inferior food source with contaminated genetic material.

Such crops have unknown health and environmental consequences. All pest control products sold on the market should be first proven to be safe before being registered; we don't need any more hazards in our food supply, or anywhere else on our planet.

Almost 50 countries—including Russia, China, Japan, and the European Union—require labeling of genetically engineered food and ingredients. Far from the disastrous results that some corporations would have us believe, labeling has not significantly increased food costs, nor are consumers in those countries confused. What has happened is this: Once labeling was required by law, millions of consumers rejected GMO-tainted food products. Consequently, food manufacturers and retailers stopped selling GMOs. Farmers stopped growing them. Sales of organic products increased significantly. Consumers, empowered with their "right to know," became more knowledgeable and healthier. Farms and fields became less contaminated. Small farmers are doing just fine.

We need to protect our environment. As Albert Einstein said, "The environment is everything that isn't me."

modified organisms, and plant-incorporated pro-tectants have been registered for use in the United States (see the chart on p. 138). More microbials are in the pipeline; there is even the promise of a bio-herbicidal replacement for glyphosate (Roundup).

The manufacture of microbial pesticides is often expensive. Because microbials tend to be very host-specific, it is often not cost-effective for a company to manufacture a product, due to a very limited group of consumers. So the number of "reg-istered" microbials doesn't match the number of products being marketed. Often, registered microbi-als are produced when the need reaches a point that makes manufacturing profitable. In these cases a limited quantity is available for a limited amount of time. The U.S. Forest Service maintains cultures of some microbials that are important to forest health, such as the Gypsy Moth Nucleopolyhedro-sis Virus (NPV) Gypchek, and produces the patho-gen only when the need arises.

BACTERIAL INSECTICIDES

The active ingredients in most bacterial insecti-cides are rod-shaped bacteria in the genus *Bacillus*. Most of these bacterial species belong primarily to the families Enterobacteriaceae, Micrococcaceae, Pseudomonadaceae, and Bacillaceae. About 100 species are reported to attack insects, and four of them—*Bacillus thuringiensis*, *B. popilliae*, *B. lentimorbus*, and *B. sphaericus*—have been stud-ied extensively as insect control agents. The chief advantages of bacterial species are their narrow host range and their lack of toxic effects on non-target species, including humans and the natural enemies of the pests.

Bacterial species were the first commercial microbial pest control products. The earliest, called Doom® or milky spore disease, was registered in 1948 for use against Japanese beetle grubs. Com-posed of two bacterial species, *Bacillus lentimorbus* and *B. popilliae*, milky spore disease is still mar-keted today. The second species to be marketed was *B. thuringiensis*, variety *kurstaki*, which is active against caterpillars. Since then, additional BT strains have been discovered and formulated commercially for use against a variety of insects, and many others show potential. The highly effective mosquito pathogens *B. sphaericus* and *B. thuringiensis* var. *israelensis* are available com-mercially for control of mosquito larvae. *B. thuring-iensis* subsp. 'tenebrionis' is effective against the Colorado potato beetle and the elm leaf beetle.

These *Bacillus* species are commonly found in soils, and all are spore-forming. The spore is the stage that tides the bacteria over from one favor-able period to the next, and it has the ability to

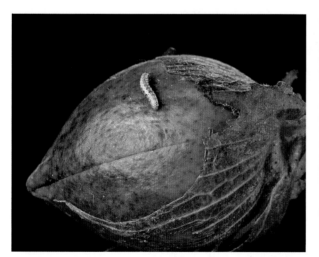
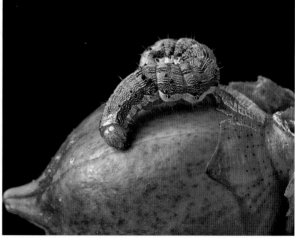

In studies to track the development of BT resistance, the undersize, 12-day-old larva (photo at left) was fed a diet containing BT proteins. The photo at right is a normal 12 day-old cotton bollworm larva raised on a control diet. (Photos by Peggy Greb, USDA Agricultural Research Service, Bugwood.org)

withstand degradation by ultraviolet light rays, drought, and other unfavorable environmental conditions, at least for a short time. *B. thuringiensis* and *B. popilliae* also produce protein crystals within their sporulating cells. These crystals are their important toxic agents. Bacteria that do not form spores usually do not persist long enough to control pests once applied to a crop; consequently, they are considered poor candidates for development as insecticides.

Bacillus thuringiensis.

Bacillus thuringiensis is a commercially available bacterial species that causes disease in certain insects. It was first discovered in 1901 by the Japanese biologist Shigetane Ishiwatari as the agent that was killing silkworm larvae. It was "rediscovered" in 1911, by Ernst Berliner, as the causal agent in killed Mediterranean flour moths. *B. thuringiensis* is named after Thuringia, the town in Germany where Ernst Berliner rediscovered the pathogen in the diseased Mediterranean flour moths. Berliner got to name the bacteria because, at that time, scientific institutions were centered in Europe in general, and Germany in particular. Ishiwatari named the bacterium *Bacillus sotto* in his 1901 description, but that name was later ruled invalid by European scientific authorities. At least 35 BT varieties have now been identified, each of which attacks different groups of insect hosts via the toxic protein crystals contained in their spores. The total number of strains under investigation and isolates being held in culture for

MICROBIAL INSECTICIDES

PATHOGEN	HOST RANGE
Bacteria	
Bacillus thuringiensis var. *kurstaki* (BTK)	caterpillars
B. thuringiensis var. *israelensis*	mosquito larvae (*Aedes* and *Psorophora* spp.), black flies, fungus gnats
B. thuringiensis var. *san diego*	larvae of Colorado potato beetle, elm leaf beetle adults
B. thuringiensis var. *tenebrionis*	larvae of Colorado potato beetle
B. thuringiensis var. *aizawai*	wax moth larvae
B. popilliae and *B. lentimorbus*	Japanese beetle larvae and certain other lawn grubs
B. sphaericus	mosquito larvae (*Culex, Psorophora, Culiseta* spp.)
Fungi	
Beauveria bassiana	many soil-dwelling insects
Lagenidium giganteum	mosquito larvae (most genera)
Protozoa	
Nosema locustae	grasshoppers, crickets
Viruses	
Gypsy moth nuclear polyhedrosis virus	gypsy moth caterpillars
Tussock moth NPV	tussock moth caterpillars
Pine sawfly NPV	pine sawfly larvae
Codling moth granulosis virus (GV)	codling moth larvae
Nematodes	
Steinernema feltiae	many larvae of soil-dwellers and wood-borers
Heterorhabditis bacteriophora	many soil-dwelling insects

various uses is increasing as commercial interest grows. Some companies maintain hundreds or more cultures.

According to University of Florida entomologists Rick Weinzierl and Tess Henn, authors of the excellent pamphlet "Microbial Insecticides."

BT products are produced commercially in large industrial fermentation tanks. As the bacteria live and multiply in the right conditions, each cell produces (internally) a spore and a crystalline protein toxin called an endotoxin. Most commercial BT products contain the protein toxin and spores, but some are cultured in a manner that yields only the toxin component....The nature of the crystalline protein endotoxin differs among BT subspecies and isolates, and it is the characteristics of these specific endotoxins that determine which insects will be poisoned by each BT product.

An excellent factsheet, originally published through the University of Illinois, can be found at www.edis.ifas.ufl.edu/in081.

The first commercial BT product entered the market in 1958. It was formulated from the variety *kurstaki* and was effective only against the caterpillar (larval) stage of moths and butterflies in the insect order Lepidoptera. Over the years, improved BTK strains have been formulated as a variety of products. In the 1980s, additional BT strains that kill insects in other orders were registered with the EPA. These include BT variety *israelensis* (BTI), which kills the larvae of certain mosquitoes, black flies, and fungus gnats in the insect order Diptera, and BT varieties *san diego* and *tenebrionis*, which are toxic to certain beetles in the insect order Coleoptera.

TIP We recommend treating your plants with BT in the late afternoon or early evening. Most caterpillars feed at night to avoid predators. The BT will remain effective during the night, before it can be broken down by ultraviolet light from the sun. Treating on a cloudy day, when no rain is expected, is another option to maximize the effectiveness of BT.

Properties. BT appears as a fine tan to brown powder or reddish-orange granules consisting of spores or toxic crystals and inert ingredients. In liquid concentrate form it is light brown to tan in color, with a thick consistency.

Mode of Action. BT is a bacterial stomach poison that must be eaten by an insect to be toxic. All commercial BT products have similar modes of action. When the crystal endotoxin is ingested by an insect with a highly alkaline gut that contains appropriate enzymes, the crystal dissolves. The components of the crystal attach to the gut wall, blocking the enzyme systems that protect the insect's gut from its own digestive juices. In a very short time, holes appear in the gut wall, allowing the gut's contents to enter the insect's body cavity and bloodstream. This initial poisoning causes the insect to stop feeding and may also lead to paralysis. Then bacterial spores themselves invade the insect's body cavity through these holes, producing septicemia (blood poisoning), which may kill the insect immediately or take a few days to do so.

A caterpillar that ingests BT may live for several days. However, it does not continue feeding and therefore causes no further damage to plants. Dead and dying caterpillars turn a dark color, remaining attached to leaves for a few days, usually hanging at a 90-degree angle toward the ground.

Although the BT multiplies within the body of the infected insect, spores and toxic crystals are almost never produced. Consequently, insects killed by BT do not serve as sources of new infections, and several applications of BT may be required to control an insect infestation, much as with a conventional insecticide. Also, when sprayed outdoors, BT is broken down within one to several days by

CATERPILLAR PESTS SUSCEPTIBLE TO *BACILLUS THURINGIENSIS* VAR. *KURSTAKI* (BTK)

COMMON NAME	SCIENTIFIC NAME
Susceptible	
bagworm	*Thyridopteryx ephemeraeformis*
cabbage looper	*Trichoplusia ni*
diamondback moth	*Plutella xylostella*
fall cankerworm	*Alsophila pometaria*
fall webworm	*Hyphantria cunea*
gypsy moth	*Lymantria dispar*
imported cabbageworm	*Pieris rapae*
Indianmeal moth	*Plodia interpunctella*
mimosa webworm	*Momadaula anisocentra*
spring cankerworm	*Paleacrita vernata*
spruce budworm	*Choristoneura fumiferana*
tent caterpillars	*Malacosoma spp.*
tomato/tobacco hornworm	*Manduca sexta*
Not susceptible	
codling moth	*Cydia pomonella*
peachtree borer	*Synanthedon exitiosa*
squash vine borer	*Melittia curcurbitae*

From R. Weinzierl and T. Henn's *Microbial Insecticides* (Office of Agricultural Entomology, University of Illinois, 1989). Species that are not susceptible live in the plant interior and thus are not reached by BT spray.

ultraviolet radiation, another reason repeated applications may be necessary.

BT is nontoxic to the natural enemies of BT-susceptible insects. Thus, target pests that escape the effects of a BT application are often attacked afterward by their predators and parasitoids, further lowering the pest population and reducing the amount of pesticide needed.

Formulations. BT products are formulated as liquid concentrates, wettable powders, ready-to-use sprays and dusts, granules, and briquettes. Advances in formulation promote adherence to leaves, increase drop density per unit of foliage sur-

face area to improve coverage, reduce evaporation during application, enhance palatability to pests, increase resistance to breakdown in sunlight, and increase the ease of mixing. These improvements may mean that older studies suggesting that BT is ineffective against certain pests should not be relied on; instead, there should be new tests against such species using the improved formulations.

Safety. BT is generally considered harmless to humans and other species. The acute oral toxicity rating in rats varies from an LD_{50} of 400 mg/kg for BT technical grade (preformulation) powder to 8,100 mg/kg for the formulated product Dipel 2X. After thorough testing for toxicity to humans, the Food and Drug Administration granted an "exemption from tolerance" for the use of BT on food crops. This means that there is virtually no level that causes toxicity in test animals, and BT can be sprayed on food crops without harm to humans. There is one report of a lab technician inadvertently getting BT solution in his eye, but no dire consequences developed, and the infection was cleared up with an antibiotic.

It is only common sense that you should wear a respirator or mask to avoid breathing mist from the spray or dust of various BT products (which have a variety of carriers). Goggles are also recommended, because mist or dust can irritate your eyes. Wear gloves, long-sleeved shirts, and trousers when applying any pesticide, including microbials.

Uses and Application. Because BT is a living organism, it must be protected from high temperature during storage. Ideally, BT packages should be stored in a refrigerator or cooler until used. When kept at 70°F to 75°F (21°C to 24°C), BT powders remain active for two to three years; storage at lower temperatures presumably prolongs their shelf life somewhat. When transporting BT, keep packages shaded and ventilated. BT should not be exposed to direct sunlight, and the container should not be left in a car trunk or other enclosed space on a hot day.

Because storage temperatures affect the viability and effectiveness of the product, be certain the package is fresh from the manufacturer through the distributor. Look on the package for an expiration or "use by" date. Some distributors resell BT that has languished on retail shelves, where it may have been subjected to high temperatures and other conditions that reduce its effectiveness. If you have any doubt as to the product's age, note the batch number on the package and call or email the manufacturer directly.

Most BT formulations are mixed with water and applied as sprays. When mixing wettable powders, be sure to start with the water and add the BT while constantly stirring the mixture. Use water that is adjusted to pH 7 or less (making it more acidic), because an alkaline suspension of pH 8 or more destroys the toxic effect of the crystal. However, most formulations are buffered to minimize pH problems. The addition of a spreader-sticker, available at garden centers, nurseries, and online, will improve the flow of BT onto leaf surfaces. Spreader-stickers (spray adjuvants) break the surface tension of the water, so that the spray doesn't bead up on the leaves. It also helps the BT to adhere to the leaf surface. If you don't have a spreader-sticker, you can add soap or detergent to the spray mix. This lesser substitute will achieve similar results. If you use soap or detergent, test the spray mixture on a small area of the plant to check for phytotoxicity. Mix only the amount you will need to treat the plants for caterpillars. Mix a fresh batch of BT for

each use; mixtures lose their effectiveness in 12 to 72 hours, depending on which formulation you use. Shake the container of spray constantly during application to ensure that the BT remains in suspension.

Treating Caterpillars.

Hundreds of species of caterpillars that feed on plants are susceptible to *Bacillus thuringiensis* var. *kurstaki*, including the "worms" that attack vegetables such as broccoli, cabbage, corn, and tomatoes, the "loopers" found on melons and lettuce, the armyworms and webworms that eat the leaves of lawn grasses, the oakworms, bagmoths, gypsy moth larvae, and tent caterpillars found on trees and shrubs, and the larvae of moths that attack stored grains and infest beehives. The chart on the facing page lists some of the more common caterpillar pests that are susceptible to BT.

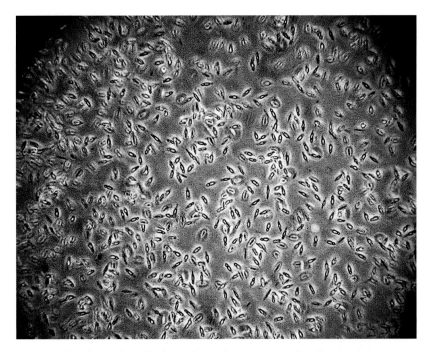

The spores of *Bacillus popillae* and *B. lentimorbus* are the causative agent for milky spore disease, lethal to Japanese beetle larvae. Milky spore disease was the first microbial insecticide developed commercially. (Photo by David Cappaert, Michigan State University, Bugwood.org)

The chart also lists some caterpillars that cannot be controlled effectively by BT products currently available, primarily because they feed little or not at all on the treated surfaces of plants. These pests include larvae that live in the soil (e.g., certain cutworms), those that bore inside plant stems (e.g., fruit tree borers), and those that attack the inside of fruits (e.g., codling moths in apples and walnuts).

The labels on BTK products list many, but not all, the common caterpillars susceptible to the material. Additions to the label of susceptible species often lag months or years behind tests demonstrating efficacy against them. Therefore, if your caterpillar pest is not listed on the BTK product label, contact the manufacturer whose address is on the label.

As we mentioned earlier, BTK is a stomach poison and must be ingested by caterpillars to kill them. Because caterpillars often feed on different sides of leaves or locations on leaves at different developmental stages, thorough coverage of both the upper and lower surfaces of leaves is necessary for good control. BTK degrades fairly rapidly in the presence of sunlight, so spray in the late afternoon

FOR YOUR SAFETY

Remember, natural or organic does not mean "harmless." Always use care when handling pesticides of any kind, and be sure to keep all pesticides out of the reach of children and pets.

or on cloudy (but not rainy) days to prolong the effectiveness. Special materials are added to most BT formulations to help them adhere to plants during rainfall.

BTK is most effective when applied while caterpillars are small, during their first and second instars. Here, as with all safe, effective pest management, learning how to monitor your plants and recognize when insects are at various stages and most susceptible to various controls is critical. General monitoring techniques were introduced in Chapter 3; methods specific to garden caterpillars (pp. 251–256) and caterpillars on shade trees (pp. 368–370) are discussed in later chapters. When we treated oak moth populations with BT, we monitored the hatch rate of egg masses, which are easy to see. We treated when monitoring determined that about 90 percent of the eggs had hatched.

Treating Mosquitoes, Blackflies, and Fungus Gnats. *Bacillus thuringiensis* var. *israelensis* is most effective against larval mosquitoes in the genera *Aedes* and *Psorophora*; higher than normal doses are required to kill *Anopheles* and *Culex*

IPM AT WORK

As part of their IPM program, the City and County of San Francisco's IPM team has recruited bicycle messengers to distribute mosquito larvicide dunks or packets to storm-sewer catch basins. The San Francisco Department of Environment's IPM Team and Pestec, the city's IPM Contractor, along with SFPUC and SFDPH, created the MAC Team (Mosquito Abatement Courier Team) to monitor the city's more than 23,000 storm-drain basins by bicycle every month during the mosquito season. When necessary, MAC technicians treat the drains with the approved mosquito larvicides. The dunks and packets are safer and easier to use and handle than sprays and reduce the risk to the technicians and the environment alike. The MAC techs are trained and supervised by Luis Agurto Jr. at Pestec.

San Francisco has trained bicycle messengers to distribute mosquito dunks (briquettes) to storm sewer catch basins. (Photo courtesy of Carlos I. Argurto of PESTEC) species. BTI's effectiveness against flies is limited to larval stages of aquatic blackflies in the family Simuliidae and fungus gnats in the genera *Megaselia, Lycoriella,* and others. BTI does not affect common houseflies or stable flies. This is perhaps because it is not available to their larval stages, which live in manure and other organically active environments in which BTI spores quickly decompose.

BTI can be applied to water sources where mosquitoes develop, such as ditches, standing ponds, catch basins, storm drains, pastures, salt marshes, and rice fields, and to streams inhabited by blackfly larvae. It is most effective when used by mosquito-abatement districts on a community-wide basis.

BTI formulated with corncob granules is commonly used to control mosquitoes breeding in tree cavities, tires, and other containers. The granules are more resistant to degradation by sunlight and can be blown efficiently into piles of tires and other breeding sites where good penetration and coverage are difficult to achieve by other means. BTI should be applied to clear, calm water, as turbidity and high levels of organic pollutants reduce its effectiveness.

For treating fungus-gnat larvae in greenhouses, BTI is mixed with water and applied as a drench to potted soil. Drenches can also be applied to the soil under greenhouse benches or in large planter boxes.

Treating Beetles. *Bacillus thuringiensis* var. *tenebrionis* (BTT) is toxic to a limited range of leaf-feeding beetle species, including larvae of the Colorado potato beetle (*Leptinotarsus decemlineata*) and the elm leaf beetle (*Pyrrhalta luteola*). However, products containing BTT cannot control other common beetle larvae, such as corn rootworms and wood-boring beetles, which live in hidden, difficult to penetrate sites. The application techniques are similar to those already discussed for the other BT products. See the package label for further details.

Other Insecticidal Bacterial Species. The milky spore disease of the Japanese beetle (*Popillia japonica*) was the first microbial control to be

An insect killed by the Entomophthorales fungus, a pathogen of insects. Notice the wrinkled, dried abdomen, which indicates fungal attack. (Photo by Dariusz Majgier/Dreamstime.com)

developed commercially. Milky spore is the name of the disease to which Japanese beetle larvae succumb when attacked by *Bacillus popilliae* and *B. lentimorbus.* These species combine to kill the larvae, and in so doing turn them milky white.

Between 1939 and 1951, the USDA applied milky spore powder to turf in 14 states and the District of Columbia in a successful effort to suppress the newly invaded Japanese beetle. At least 13 other species of beetle grubs that feed on turf are also known to be susceptible to various strains of *B. popilliae* and *B. lentimorbus.* At present, however, only products effective against Japanese beetles are available. For details on using milky spore disease to control Japanese beetle grubs, see pp. 261–263.

FUNGAL PESTICIDES

Fungi are probably the most numerous insect and plant pathogens, so it seems logical to search among the fungal species for commercial possibilities for insecticides, fungicides, herbicides, and other microbial pesticides. More than 750 fungal species representing approximately 100 genera have been reported to infect insects alone. Nearly all fungal groups and virtually every insect group is represented. Insect-attacking fungi have been found in approximately 175 host insect species in North America (see the chart on p. 146).

Mode of Action. Most of the fungi that attack insects and other organisms spread by means of asexual spores called *conidia*. Free water or high humidity is usually required before conidia can germinate and attack a susceptible host. Unlike bacterial spores or virus particles, fungi can penetrate the insect cuticle directly, so they don't have to be ingested to infect insects. Thus they can be useful against sucking insects as well as against those that chew foliage. Likewise, fungi can enter plant tissues or other fungal organisms. The infected hosts die from toxins produced by the fungus.

FUNGAL INSECTICIDES

In nature, fungal pathogens persist at low levels within insect populations, causing some amount of sickness and/or death in each insect generation. When conditions are optimal—meaning a high population of susceptible insects and appropriate temperature and humidity—the fungal pathogens multiply rapidly and explode into a disease outbreak called an epizootic by insect pathologists. In 12 hours to two weeks or so, this outbreak kills tens of thousands of insects. This phenomenon is common among many caterpillar pests of forest and ornamental trees, chinch bugs that attack grain crops and lawn grasses, beetles that attack potatoes and other food crops, and many other insect groups.

Unfortunately, epizootics generally don't occur until insect populations are high, which is often too late to prevent extensive plant damage. In theory, fungal pesticide products that can be sprayed directly onto pests could trigger disease outbreaks when pest numbers are still low, before there is significant damage to plants.

Vertalec® and Mycotal® are microbial insecticides that contain spores of the fungus *Cephalosporium* (=*Verticillium*) *lecanii*. Natural epidemics of this fungus occur in insect populations in the trop-

Melanoplus grasshoppers killed by the fungus *Beauveria bassiana*. (Photo by Stefan Jaronski)

ics and subtropics. Both products have been registered in Europe for some years, and are used in the greenhouse industry to control pests such as aphids and whiteflies. Vertalec and Mycotal were available in the United States in the 1980s, but unfortunately they were discontinued for reasons that are unclear.

Lagenidium giganteum, a fungus that attacks the larvae of pest mosquitoes, is registered in the United States, but is currently not being manufactured.

Beauveria bassiana. The fungal species *Beauveria bassiana*, discovered in 1835 by Agostino Bassi, has been applied against insect pests in field tests more frequently than any other fungus. This bioinsecticide is available under the brand name Mycotrol O®, which is OMRI (Organic Materials Review Institute) listed. It is also available under several other brand names, not all of which are OMRI listed. *Beauveria bassiana* is used extensively in the Soviet Union, Eastern Europe, and China. Currently, the Soviet Union applies over five tons of *B. bassiana* each year, mostly against the Colorado potato beetle (*Leptinotarsa decemlineata*). *Beauveria* is now used extensively in the United States, especially in organic gardening and farming.

Properties. *B. bassiana* is a naturally occurring soil fungus, found throughout the world. In formulations it appears as an amber-colored oil with mild odor, or a white powder with a dusty odor.

Mode of Action. The spores infect the insect's cuticle, producing enzymes that dissolve the cuticle. The fungus enters the insect's body through these breaks in the "skin" and continues to grow inside the insect's body, eventually filling the body with a fungal mass. The insect will change color as it is dying, usually turning a pink to brown color, depending on the species. A white fungal mass will usually appear on the outside of the insect. The parasitized insect will sometimes move off to die in some other place, so if you find a fuzzy insect attached to the garage door, it's probably dead from a fungus.

Formulations. *B. bassiana* comes primarily in liquid concentrate formulations. There is also a wettable powder formulation that is not OMRI listed.

Safety. *B. bassiana* is considered nontoxic to mammals, birds, and plants; it can be toxic to bees. The formulations and mixed spray solutions of these pesticides can be irritating to the eyes, skin, and lungs. Take proper precautions to prevent exposure, being sure to use personal protective equipment when mixing and applying, and during cleanup.

Uses and Application. Preparations of *B. bassiana* contain live spores of the fungus. Store in a cool, dry, and secure location. Avoid temperatures below freezing and above 85°F. Stability and viability of the product decreases over time at temperatures above 85°F (29°C). The fungus degrades almost completely within 24 hours of contact with water, so mix only what you need for the application. Always treat all plant surfaces, especially the upper and lower surfaces of leaves. Look for and treat "hiding spots" on plants, including branch unions and leaf nodes where mealybugs and certain other pests may hide.

Pests. Pests controlled by *B. bassiana* include whiteflies, aphids, thrips, psyllids, mealybugs, leafhoppers, weevils, plant bugs, borers, grasshoppers, Mormon crickets, and leaf-feeding insects. It is also registered for use on vegetables and ornamentals grown indoors, outdoors, in nurseries, greenhouses, and shadehouses, and in field, agronomic, and orchard crops.

TIP *Beauveria bassiana* can be toxic to bees, so don't apply when honeybees are actively foraging. They do so during the day, beginning shortly after sunrise and continuing until shortly before sunset.

Spinosad. Fermentation of the actinomycete *Saccharopolyspora spinosa* produces about 20 spinosyn compounds. Of those, two of the compounds, spinosyn A and D, combined at 85 percent to 15 percent respectively, had the best insecticidal results. The name Spinosad was created by combining "spinosyn" with the "A" and "D" component terms, hence "Spinosad." Spinosad is considered to be nonsynthetic, with some formulations allowed under the USDA-NOP (National Organic Program). They are also OMRI listed. Actinomycetes are filamentous soil-inhabiting bacteria that give soil and mature compost that healthy garden-soil smell. *S. spinosa* is considered rare, but was found in soil samples from a Caribbean island in 1975. Spinosad was registered with the EPA in 1997, primarily for garden/landscape use. It is now approved for most edible crops; check the label for a full listing of treatable plants. Spinosad is also labeled for control of fire ants.

Properties. Spinosad is produced as a white to off-white powder that has a latex-like odor.

Mode of Action. Spinosad has three modes of action. It is a contact poison, it has stomach activity, and it has nervous system effects. Spinosad acts as a nicotinic acetylcholine receptor agonist. Although this unique mechanism is not completely understood, it causes the insect to lose muscle control and die within one to two days. Because Spinosad has a unique mode of action and has shown no cross-resistance with other pesticide classes, it is recommended as an option in a pesticide-resistance management program.

Formulation. Spinosad comes in ready-to-use liquid spray and liquid concentrate.

Safety. Spinosad has very low acute toxicity in mammals. No cancer, mutagenicity, teratology, or neurotoxicity was found in chronic feeding studies. Spinosad breaks down quickly in sunlight (photolysis); it can, however, be persistent in the soil and

water. Spinosyn and its metabolites can build up in the soil. Check the label for maximum annual application rates. Always wear eye protection, a particle mask, waterproof gloves, long-sleeved shirt, long pants, and waterproof boots when mixing or applying pesticides. Keep all pesticides out of the reach of children and pets.

Uses and Application. There is concern about insect resistance when using Spinosad on a regular basis. Diamondback moths have developed resistance to spinosyns when the product was used intensively.

Pests. Spinosad is a fairly broad-spectrum insecticide. It controls caterpillars, leafminers, thrips, and Colorado potato beetle larvae and has shown variable control on aphids, whiteflies, adult flea beetles, and all stages of striped and spotted cucumber beetles. It has excellent action against caterpil-

FUNGI BEING DEVELOPED AS MICROBIAL INSECTICIDES

FUNGUS	INFECTIVE STAGE	HOST INSECT
Chytridiomycetes		
Coelomomyces	motile zoospores	mosquitoes
Oomycetes		
Lagenidium	motile zoospores	mosquitoes
Zygomycetes		
Entomophthora	conidia	caterpillars, aphids, flies
Deuteromycetes		
Ashersonia	conidia	whiteflies
Beauveria	conidia	beetles, caterpillars
Culincimomyces		
Clavosporus	conidia	mosquitoes, other diptera
Hirsutellia	conidia	mites
Metarhizium	conidia	leafhoppers, beetles, mites
Nomuraea	conidia	caterpillars
Paecilomyces	conidia	beetles
Cephalosporium (=Verticillium)	conidia	aphids, whiteflies, scales

From *Microbial Insect Control Agents* (National Academy of Sciences, 1979). Conidia are asexual spores of fungi.

lars and should be considered as an alternative in a pesticide-resistance management program.

MICROBIALS THAT PROTECT AGAINST PLANT DISEASE

Microbial products that control plant pathogens have reached the marketable stage. Galltrol-A® and Norbac 84® have been registered for use for over 20 years. These products contain the active ingredient *Agrobacterium radiobacter*, which is a bacterial antagonist of the crown gall disease that affects many species of fruit and nut trees. Several other biofungicides have also been registered, including *Trichoderma harzianum*, *Bacillus subtilis*, and *Streptomyces lydicus*.

Trichoderma harzianum. This fungus is registered as a soil-applied biofungicide. *T. harzianum* protects crops from *Pythium* spp., *Rhizoctonia solani*, and *Sclerotium rolfsii*. It may also control *Sclerotium cepivorum*, *Verticillium dahliae*, and several other soil-borne pathogens. It can be mixed into potting or backfill soil to treat individual plants and reduce transplant complications. *T. harzianum* can be broadcast-applied in either a granular or spray formulation. The fungus works at temperatures above 50°F (10°C), and for maximum efficacy must be applied before the onset of disease. Store products in a cool dry place, as product quality will drop when stored above 75°F (23°C) for prolonged periods.

Bacillus subtilis. This bacteria commonly comes in two naturally occurring strains that are OMRI listed. The QST713 strain was isolated in 1995 from soil in a California orchard and is applied to foliage. It is used primarily to control powdery mildew but has shown some effect on *Botrytis cinerea*, downey mildew, bacterial spot, fire blight, walnut blight, grape sour rot, and *Sclerotinia* leaf-drop. The GB03 strain was discovered in Australia in the 1930s and is applied to seed or directly to the soil to suppress root-infecting fungi, including *Fusarium*, *Rhizoctonia*, and possibly *Verticillium*.

Monterey Garden Insect Spray with Spinosad is an OMRI-listed organic insecticide. Spinosad works on contact or when ingested by leaf-feeding insects; it is not effective for sucking insects or mites. (Photo by Rincon-Vitova Insectaries)

Two other non-OMRI listed strains are commercially available, *B. subtilis* var. *amyloliquefaciens* strain FZB 24 and *B. subtilis* strain MBI 600.

Serenade® Garden Disease Control is available at garden centers, nurseries, and online garden supply sites. It is used to control powdery mildew, bacterial spot, rust, grey mold, leaf blight, scab, and more. If you purchase Serenade, we recommend that you purchase the RTU (ready-to-use) formulation unless you have a large area to treat. This is a living organism and improper storage can reduce effectiveness significantly.

Streptomyces lydicus. This is one of the newer Actinomycete bacteria that is moving into the marketplace. Several other strains are currently being investigated. Actinovate® and Actino-Iron® contain *S. lydicus* strain WYEC 108, which suppresses or controls *Pythium*, *Phytophthora*, *Fusarium*, *Rhizoctonia*, *Verticillium*, *Postia*, *Geotrichum*, *Sclerotinia*, and other root infecting fungi. Applied to foliage it is used to suppress or control powdery mildew, downey mildew, *Botrytis, Alternaria,* and other foliar fungi. Currently, *S. lydicus* comes in two formulations: a soluble powder and a granular form with added iron. The mode of action appears to be a combination of colonization of the root tips, parasitizing of root decay fungi, and production of antibiotics that are active against nearby pathogens.

MICROBIAL HERBICIDES

Microbial herbicides are living organisms or their products that are useful in suppressing weed populations. They offer the same advantages as microbial insecticides: They are relatively selective in their impact on plants and are safe to the user and the environment. Most of the microbial herbicides studied to date have been fungi. Thus, the term *mycoherbicide* ("myco" = fungus) has gained popularity as a label for the class of microbial products that uses fungi to suppress weeds. When a fungus is not the active agent, however, the proper term is bioherbicide.

Nematodes and other microbes are also under study as bioherbicides. The use of fungi as herbicides seems reasonable, because fungi exhibit great selectivity in the range of species they attack. Many rust fungi, for example, attack only one plant species. Two bioherbicides that were commercially available are DeVine® for controlling milkweed vine (*Morrenia odorata*) and Collego® for controlling northern jointvetch (*Aeschynomene virginica*).

The initial emphasis was on the development of herbicides for control of weeds in rangeland and agriculture. But scientists are now also trying to find ways to use bioherbicides to control the aquatic weeds that clog ponds, canals, drainage ditches, and recreational lakes, as well as the artificial bodies of water that have become common features in urban residential and commercial developments. Eventually, we should have products that are more directly useful in lawn and other landscape care, particularly if there is increased interest in microbial controls among landscape maintenance professionals and home gardeners.

According to a 2010 report by the International Organization for Biological Control (IOBC), there are five bioherbicides that are currently EPA registered but not currently (at the time of this writing) in production. One is a bacteria, *Bacillus cereus BP01*, which acts as a plant growth regulator. The remaining four bioherbicides are fungi: *Alternaria desturens 059* controls dodder, *Chondrostereum purpureum PFC2139* is a stump sprout inhibitor, *Colletotrichum gloeosporioides* f.sp. *aeschynomene ATCC202358* suppresses northern jointvetch, and *Puccinia thlaspeos* is a rust that controls Dyer's woad.

VIRAL INSECTICIDES

Insects, particularly in the larval stage, are susceptible to major outbreaks of viral diseases. Over 700 types of viruses have been found to infect insects, most of which fall into one of the following major viral groups: nucleopolyhedrosis, cytoplasmic polyhedrosis (CPV), granulosis (GV), entomopox (EPV), and noninclusion viruses (NIV).

Like fungal diseases, viruses tend to be highly specific, attacking only a single insect genus or even a single species. The NPV and GV viral groups are the most promising candidates for development as commercial insecticides due to their specificity, stability, virulence to insects, and low toxicity to mammals and nontarget species. These virus groups infect caterpillars and the larval stages of sawflies. No hazards to nontarget organisms were found when these viruses were subjected to toxicological tests.

Mode of Action. Insects must ingest viruses to become infected. The viral particles (protein-coated bundles of DNA) can move into insect cells and

TIP Always store microbials in a cool dry place away from sunlight. Refrigeration can extend their shelf life.

lodge in the nucleus, thereby taking charge of genetic synthesis. Entomologists Rick Weinzierl and Tess Henn, in their pamphlet "Microbial Insecticides," explain how these viruses act on susceptible insects.

In sawfly larvae, virus infections are limited to the gut, and disease symptoms are not as obvious as they are in caterpillars. In caterpillars, virus particles pass through the insect's gut wall and infect other body tissues. As an infection progresses, the caterpillar's internal organs are liquefied, and its cuticle (body covering) discolors and eventually ruptures.

Caterpillars killed by virus infection appear limp and soggy. They often remain attached to foliage or twigs for several days, releasing virus particles that may be consumed by other larvae. The pathogen can be spread throughout an insect population in this way (especially when raindrops help to splash the virus particles to adjacent foliage) and by infected adult females depositing virus-contaminated eggs. Dissemination of viral pathogens is deterred by exposure to direct sunlight, because direct ultraviolet radiation destroys virus particles. Although naturally occurring epidemics do control certain pests, these epidemics rarely occur before pest populations have reached outbreak levels.

Uses and Application. With the exception of the codling moth CPV and the bollworm NPV, viral insecticides registered in the United States are produced exclusively by the U.S. Forest Service and are used to treat forest pests. Other viruses that infect agricultural pests like cabbage loopers and worms, soybean and alfalfa loopers, and armyworms have been effective in field tests, but have not been registered commercially.

Several obstacles are hindering greater commercial development of viral insecticides. First, they must be produced in live hosts, which is commonly

REGISTERED VIRAL INSECTICIDES

Seven insect-attacking viruses are currently registered in the United States:

- GemStar®, the NPV of the cotton bollworm, (*Helicoverpa zea*)

- CLV-LC®, the NPV of the Lepidopteran larvae

- Gypchek®, the NPV of the gypsy moth (*Lymantria* [=*Porthetria*] *dispar*)

- CYD-X®, the GV of codling moth

- FruitGuard®, the GV of Indian meal moth

- Virosoft®, NPV of Bertha armyworm

- Spod-X, the NPV of beet armyworm

Elcar®, an NPV registered in 1975 for cotton bollworm, was the first virus to receive EPA registration in the United States, and it is a landmark in microbial control.

In Japan, Matsukemin®, a CPV of the pine caterpillar (*Dendrolimus spectabilis*), was registered in 1974.

Decyde®, a CPV of the codling moth (*Cydia pomonella*), was registered in the United States for a brief time in the 1980s but is no longer on the market.

thought to be an expensive process. Second, the fact that they are genus- or species-specific greatly limits their market. Moreover, they rapidly decompose in sunlight, do not tolerate high temperatures, and tend to kill slowly. We hope that improvements in artificial media for rearing insect viruses as well as formulations that increase their residual life in the field are forthcoming and that more of these highly selective insecticides will become commercially available.

PROTOZOAN INSECTICIDES

Of the 35,000 protozoan species known, the approximately 300 insect-attacking species are in the orders Microspordia and Neogregarinida. Protozoan

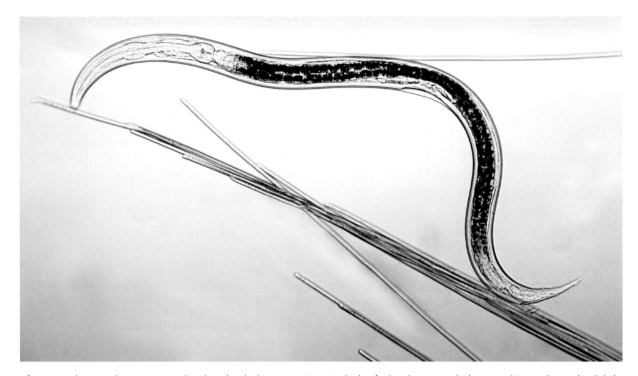

Infective juvenile nematodes enter an insect host through its body openings. Once inside, they feed on the insect and release toxic bacteria that produce lethal blood poisoning. (Photo by N Nehring/istockphoto)

pathogens tend to produce chronic but not always fatal diseases in insects. Chronic infections generally result in reduced feeding and reproduction, although death can also occur. In toxicological tests, insect-attacking protozoa have shown no effect on humans or other mammals.

Like insect viruses, almost all protozoa of potential use as insecticides must be produced in living hosts, which is thought to make them too expensive. This is one factor accounting for the slow pace at which protozoan insecticides are being developed.

At present, only one protozoan insecticide has been registered by the U.S. EPA. It is *Nosema locustae,* a pathogen of grasshoppers. It is marketed by several companies under various trade names.

Mode of Action. After being eaten by a grasshopper, *Nosema locustae* infects the fat tissue. Infection then spreads throughout the body of the grasshopper, disrupting circulation, excretion, and reproduction, and leads to disfigurement and/or death. Infected eggs carry the disease from one generation to the next.

Uses. This protozoa species is known to infect 58 species of grasshoppers as well as the mormon cricket (*Anabrus simplex*), a black field cricket (*Gryllus* spp.), and a species of pygmy locust.

INSECT-ATTACKING NEMATODES

Although nematodes are not microbials in the same sense as the bacteria, fungi, viruses, and protozoa described above, their microscopic size and the fact that they release toxic bacteria into host insects have led to their being grouped with microbials in pest control terminology. Nematodes are tiny, mostly microscopic roundworms that belong to the phylum Nematoda. They are also called threadworms (*nema* in Greek means "thread"). Nematodes occupy all the basic habitats of the earth. They live in marine and fresh-water environments, in soil as free-living saprophytes (decomposers), in and on plants, on other animals, and on humans.

Nematodes are well known as pests of plants and humans, but there are also a large number of predatory nematode species that are natural enemies of insects and pest nematodes. These nematodes are useful against the grubs (insect larvae) that attack lawns, shrubs, trees, and agricultural crops. Over 400 pest insect species have proven susceptible to parasitic nematodes in laboratory and field studies; the major groups in the phylum Nematoda are listed and described in the chart on p. 153.

Species of nematodes that have been mass-produced in quantities sufficient for use in field trials as insecticides fall into the following genera: *Delademus, Romanomermis, Heterorhabditis, Heterotylenchus,* and *Steinernema (=Neoaplectana). Romanomermis culicivorax* was used widely against mosquito larvae in the 1950s but was displaced by synthetic insecticides. *Heterotylenchus autumnalis* has been used widely and successfully against the face fly (*Musca autumnalis*). Most current research on and commercial development of parasitic nematodes is focused on species in the genera *Heterorhabditis* and *Steinernema*, especially the latter. Commercial products containing *H. bacteriophora* (=*H. heliothidis*), *H.megidis, S. carpocapsae, S. riobravis, S. feltiae, S. kraussei,* and *S. scapterisci* are usually available at local nurseries, and can be purchased from insectaries and other online sources.

Mode of Action. Parasitic nematodes kill their hosts by infecting them with bacteria that poison the blood. The hardy third-stage infectious juveniles (J3), which can survive without feeding for long periods in moist soil, actively search for insect hosts by standing on their tails and waving back and forth. When they sense the presence of a host, they swim on a film of soil moisture to invade the host's body. They can jump many times the length of their bodies, which also helps them find a host.

Steinernema nematodes enter the host via the mouth, anus, or other natural opening; *Heterorhabditis* nematodes enter through the same openings or use a hook-like appendage to bore directly into the insect cuticle. Once inside the host, they develop into adult males and females, mate, and lay eggs. The eggs hatch and the nematodes continue reproducing inside the insect until crowding, lack of food, or other unfavorable situation arises. At that point, the young nematodes develop into the J3 stage and exit the dead insect to seek a new host.

These infectious juvenile nematodes have mutually beneficial relationships with the bacteria *Xenorhabdus nematophilus* and *X. luminescens,* which they carry in their gut. Once inside the host, the bacteria are released from the anus of the nematode and multiply rapidly in the host's bloodstream. The insect host dies within 24 hours from blood poisoning caused by the bacteria, and the nematodes continue to use the bacteria as a food source within the insect's body.

DID YOU KNOW?

Nematodes are among the oldest living multicellular life forms, dating from the Cambrian period 500 million years ago.

Formulations. Mass production of nematodes has resulted in a number of commercial products containing J3 infective nematodes. These are mixed with water and are applied as drenches or sprays to the soil or other moist environments. The major factor limiting wider use of parasitic nematode species was the lack of a formulation that allowed nematodes to survive for long periods under adverse—particularly dry—conditions. Encapsulation processes, whereby nematodes are enclosed in a polyacrylamide gel material, are now used to increase shelf-life. OMRI-listed nematodes are packed in a carrier of diatomaceous earth. New developments in mass-rearing have lowered production costs, so that nematodes are now commercially feasible for use in the garden.

Safety. After extensive toxicological testing, these nematodes and their bacteria have been found to be nontoxic to humans, animals, and other nontarget organisms.

Uses and Application. At their present stage of development, parasitic nematodes are most effective when applied to moist soil to kill insects in the ground or in plant containers, or when injected into holes bored by insects in trees. Because commercial nematode species cannot survive naturally in dry environments, current formulations are not highly effective when sprayed on the leaves of plants. Nematodes applied this way quickly desiccate and usually die before finding a host.

Steinernema carpocapsae, the most widely available commercial nematode, has been shown to infect and kill about 300 species of insects in 17 families of Coleoptera (beetles), nine families of Diptera (flies), five families of Heteroptera (bugs), four families of Homoptera (aphids, scales, mealybugs, whiteflies), eight families of Lepidoptera (caterpillars), one family of Neuroptera (lacewings), and five families of Orthoptera (grasshoppers, crickets). With an organism that has such a wide host range, it may be necessary to devise baits, carriers, and other delivery systems that ensure the nematode attacks the target pest selectively.

The same nematode has been shown to attack subterreanean termites (*Reticulitermes* spp.) in laboratory cultures. However, field testing of this and other nematode products against subterranean termites is still underway. A number of private termite companies have been using the nematodes for several years and report success; however, data from controlled studies of treatments applied to struc-

> **TIP** According to directions from Rincon-Vitova Insectaries, you should in all cases hold nematodes in a refrigerator at 40°F to 45°F (4°C to 7°C) until release. If it is necessary to hold the nematodes longer than three or four days, check with the supplier for maximum storage lengths. Various packaging and species combinations have different maximum storage lengths.

tures is needed before scientifically accurate assessments of nematode effectiveness can be made.

Parasitic nematodes have been shown to kill many horticultural and agricultural insect species in laboratory tests; however, when applied to plants or soil in field experiments, *S. carpocapsae* was effective in controlling only a few plant-boring insects, including carpenterworms (moths of the family Sesiidae) in figs, oak, and other trees, and the wood-boring larvae of the western poplar clearwing moth (*Prionoxystus robinae*) in birches and willows in California. In these cases, the nematodes were mixed with water and pumped directly into the hole made by the borer, using either an oil-can applicator or a hand-operated plastic spray bottle. The nematodes can also be applied with traditional spraying equipment.

Another *Steinernema* species has been found effective in controlling a borer of currants in Australia; when used in conjunction with one or more species of *Heterorhabditis*, it has also been successful in controlling a few soil-inhabiting insects. Commercial cranberry growers have controlled the strawberry root weevil in cranberry bogs through aerial applications of nematodes. In lawns, nematodes have controlled white grubs such as the Japanese beetle (see p. 263), other beetles, cutworms, and mole crickets. *Steinernema* and *Heterorhabditis* are effective against root weevils, such as the strawberry root weevil (*O. ovatus*) and the black vine weevil (*Otiorhynchus sulcatus*). We did one treatment to a residential garden with a combination of *Steinernema carpocapsae* and *Heterorhabditis bacteriophora* (=*H. Heliothedis*) to control an infestation of black vine weevil. The result was no weevil damage in the garden for eight years, whereas previously it was a regular problem.

MAJOR CATEGORIES OF THE PHYLUM NEMATODA WITH THEIR HABITATS AND/OR PREY

TAXONOMIC CATEGORY		HABITAT AND/OR PREY
Class Adenophorea		
Subclass Chromadoria		mostly marine forms
Subclass Enoplia		soil, aquatic; plant and animal parasites
Order Mermithida		
Superfamily Mermithoidea		
Family Mermithidae	*Romanomermis culicivorax*	mosquitoes
	Mermis nigrescens	Orthoptera and others
	Pheromermis pachysoma	yellowjackets
	Pheromermis myopis	horseflies
	Hydromermis conopophaga	chironomid midges
	Mesomermis flumenalis	blackflies
	Filipjevimermis leipsandra	diabrotica beetles, other Coleoptera
Family Tetradonematidae	*Tetradonema plicans*	fungus gnats in Sciaridae and Mycetophilidae
	Heterogonema ovomasculis	nitidulid beetle
Class Secernentea		
Order Rhabditida		soil, aquatic; insects, mollusks, annelid and vertebrate parasites
Superfamily Diplogasteroidea		
Family Diplogasteridae	*Mikoletzkya aerivora*	termites, white-fringed beetle
Superfamily Rhabditoidea		
Family Rhabditidae	*Rhabditis insectivora*	cerambycid beetles
Family Steinernematidae	*Steinernema carpocapsae*	Coleoptera, Diptera, Heteroptera, Homoptera, Hymenoptera, Isoptera, Lepidoptera, Neuroptera, Odonata, and Orthoptera
Family Heterorhabditidae	*Heterorhabditis bacteriophora, H. heliothidis*	originally found in Lepidoptera; experimental infections also occur in Coleoptera, Diptera, and Orthoptera
Order Tylenchida		mostly plant parasites, some invertebrate parasites
Superfamily Neotylenchoidea		
Family Neotylenchidae		weevils and woodwasps
	Deladenus siricidicola	Hymenoptera, Siricidae, Coleoptera, Melandryidae
Superfamily Allantonematoidea		
Family Allantonematidae		Coleoptera, Diptera, Siphonaptera, Thysanoptera, Heteroptera
	Heterotylenchus autumnalis	face flies (*Musca autumnalis*)
	Howardula husseyi	mushroom phorid (*Megasalia halterata*)
Superfamily Sphaerularioidea		
Family Sphaerulariidae	*Tripius sciarae*	fungus gnats in the family Sciaridae
Order Strongylida		vertebrates
Order Ascaridida		vertebrates
Order Oxyurida		vertebrates and invertebrates
Order Spirurida		vertebrates

From G. O. Poinar Jr.'s *The Natural History of Nematodes* (Prentice-Hall, 1983).

PHEROMONES AND OTHER SEMIOCHEMICALS

Various pheromone products have had a great impact on pest control to date and offer great promise for the future. Pheromones are chemicals secreted and emitted by an organism that elicit responses in other individuals of the same species. The insect sex pheromones are the most widely known, probably because they have enjoyed good press and have captured the interest of the public. Large-scale detection programs for the gypsy moth that use sticky cardboard traps baited with their sex pheromones familiarized the public in many areas of the country with this new class of chemicals for manipulating pest populations.

There are other types of pheromones and related substances with potential for insect control. These include alarm pheromones, aggregation pheromones, food attractants, food stimulants, and various repellents, deterrents, and arrestants. In fact, pheromones are only one of at least three classes of chemicals called semiochemicals (see the sidebar below) that are used by organisms to communicate with other species and the inanimate environment.

Awareness of the importance of semiochemicals is still relatively new, but research in this area may have a great impact on world affairs if it continues to grow and mature. After all, if human sex pheromones can influence human behavior just as insect sex pheromones affect insects—and there is now good evidence of this in humans as well as in other mammals—then a whole range of other classes of pheromones and semiochemicals may also be affecting humans without our being aware of it. This means that a whole new set of substances awaits discovery, industrial use, and market exploitation.

PHEROMONES USED IN INSECT CONTROL

The ability to synthesize insect pheromones in the laboratory has given rise to the seductive vision of total, species-specific pest control in a bottle. If we sound skeptical, it is not because we doubt the usefulness of these materials in pest control programs; it simply seems unwise to put too much faith in a chemical control that is used repeatedly and in isolation. The likelihood of insect resistance or tolerance is too great. It is obvious to us that the value of these materials is as a complement to programs that integrate many strategies to make the habitat less desirable for pests. Using many strategies is, after all, the very heart of Integrated Pest Management.

Mode of Action. Insects can communicate via chemical stimuli produced in their bodies and emitted into the air. They detect these compounds by way of their chemoreceptors, which detect messenger compounds at extremely low concentrations. Once a chemical message is detected, it may trigger a specific behavior or development process. Most pheromones currently used in pest control are synthetic versions of natural insect chemical compounds, chiefly sex pheromones, aggregation pheromones, or feeding attractants.

CHEMICAL-RELEASING STIMULI

Semiochemical: A substance produced by an organism or inanimate object that elicits a response in another organism.

Pheromone: A substance produced by an organism that elicits a response in another individual of the same species.

Allelochemic: A substance produced by an organism that elicits a response in an individual of a different species.

Allomone: A type of allelochemic that favors the emitter over the receiver.

Kairomone: A type of allelochemic that favors the receiver over the emitter.

Synomone: A type of allelochemic that favors both emitter and receiver.

Apneumonic: A substance produced by a nonliving thing that elicits a response from a living organism.

From D. A. Nordlund et al., *Semiochemicals: Their Role in Pest Control* (John Wiley and Sons, 1981).

Use a watering can or hose-end sprayer to apply beneficial nematodes to the soil in water. Lightly cultivate the soil surface to help the nematodes enter the soil and irrigate following the application. (Photo by Paul Debois/GAP)

Formulations. Pheromones are used as lures to attract insects to traps or baits containing insecticides. The most commonly used pheromones are the attractant chemicals that one insect gender uses to attract the other. For example, a pheromone secreted by female moths is placed in a trap to capture males of the same species (or vice versa). The chemical attractant is usually impregnated into or enclosed within a rubber or plastic lure or hollow tube that slowly releases the pheromone over a period of days or weeks. Sometimes several pheromones are combined in the lure. The lures are then placed in cardboard or plastic traps (see the drawing on p. 156) that use an adhesive-coated surface or funnel-shaped entrance to capture the target insect.

Uses and Application. Pheromone traps are used to monitor for the presence of pests, as control tools to capture insects, as confusants to disrupt insect mating, and as lures to attract insects to insecticidal baits. Currently, the most important use of pheromones is as detection and monitoring tools. They make it possible to look for pests with a "chemical searchlight" that points out where and when the pest is occurring so other measures can be brought to bear on the pest and its environment. An excellent example is the use of traps for gypsy moth detection and eradication programs.

Different pheromone-baited traps also attract a large variety of other pest species indoors and in the garden. We mention these species in the discussions of pests of lawns and ornamental plants in Chapters 12, 13, and 14. But some general cautions about using pheromone-baited traps are in order here.

First, the synthesized materials are usually not perfect replicas of the natural product. Because the substances that insects and plants manufacture themselves are so complex, it is extremely difficult to copy them exactly. This means that the natural pheromones emitted by the living organism "out-compete" the human products in attractiveness to other members of the same species. The pulsed timing of the normal release and the need for a target with normal behaviors (a live partner) are also factors that make attractant traps less than effective in some species. Thus, what works on a very small scale, for example in one fruit tree in a backyard, may not necessarily be successful on a larger scale, such as in a suburban lot or small home orchard. In the latter situations, it may be difficult to provide an artificial scent in a trap that is as powerful as that emitted by live members of the same pest species.

Second, there is always the possibility that you will attract a pest into the area that was not already there, or attract it in greater numbers than would otherwise have been present. Thus, strategies have to be applied to limit drawing pests to an area, especially small-scale plantings. To do this, you must place the traps around the perimeter of the area being sampled, attaching the traps to plants that would not normally be attacked by the pest. For example, a codling-moth trap should be placed on a linden or elm tree, because these trees lack the fruit on which the moth normally lays its eggs. Apple or walnut trees, of which the moth is a pest, would be bad choices because traps set in them may attract more moths than they can catch. In such cases, the traps would actually exacerbate the pest problem.

The important exception to the above is the use of pheromone confusant systems. These are hollow plastic fibers that contain a pheromone sex attractant distributed en masse over many acres, usually by aircraft. Results to date have been very promising in large-scale agriculture and forestry against the pink bollworm (*Pectinophora gossypiella*), the tomato pinworm (*Keiferia lycopersicella*), the artichoke plume moth (*Platyptilia carduidactyla*), and the western pine shoot borer (*Eucosma sonomana*). The same approach has also been used against the gypsy moth (*Lymantria* [=*Porthetria*] *dispar*).

A slightly different type of pheromone system combines an aggregation stimulant, or a bio-irritant, and a conventional pesticide. The irritant encourages the pest insect to travel farther; the insect is thereby exposed to higher dosages of the insecticide than it would be without the stimulant. This system has proven effective against the boll weevil (*Anthonomus grandis*) and two tobacco and cotton pests, *Heliothis virescens* and *H. zea,* which are also vegetable pests in home gardens. This approach offers the potential for the reduction of the amount of insecticide applied tovarious crops.

Although most pheromone trap systems have been developed for the larger agricultural pest control market, they may also find use in home gardens. But gardeners troubled with agricultural pest problems on a small scale will have to do their own experimentation. Once you have accurately identified the pest, search online for "lures," "baits," and/or "traps." Always use the scientific name for

PHEROMONE LURES AND TRAPS

Pheromones are impregnated in lures that slowly release the active ingredients over a period of days or weeks. Lures are placed in a variety of traps designed to attract specific groups of insects. Trap styles include wing traps (A), delta traps (B), which also shows a cross section of the Biolure® pheromone dispenser), square cardboard traps (C), and funnel traps (D).

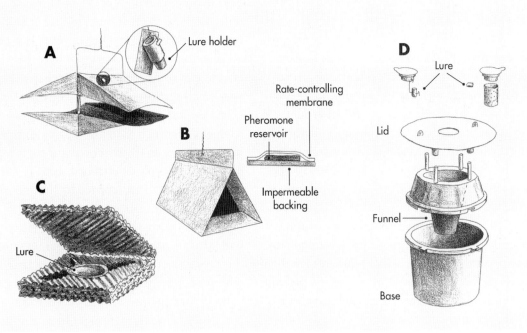

the pest first during searches: This is more likely to be successful. If not, give the common name a try. Check with your county cooperative extension service or agricultural commissioner's office to see if they have traps available for the pest(s) with which you are concerned. Cooperative extension main offices can usually be found at state land-grant universities. You may be asked to "enlist" as a volunteer monitor for pests common to your area, which is a great learning opportunity and a chance to help your community.

A few pheromones attract an entire insect family instead of just one species or a few members of a single genus. For example, the pheromone that attracts the ash borer (*Podosesia syringae*) also attracts other members of the same family, the Sesiidae (Lepidoptera). If your web search for the pest is not successful, try to find another pest in the same genus; the pheromone that works against it may also work against your pest.

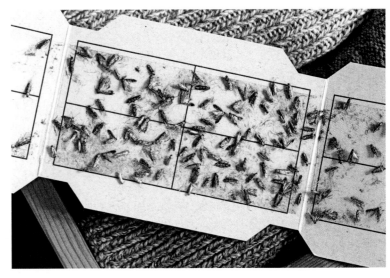

Male clothing moths, *Tineola bisselliella*, stuck to a pheromone trap. (Photo by Ingo Bartussek/Fololia.com)

INSECT GROWTH REGULATORS

Insect growth regulators (IGRs) are the insect hormones (or their synthetic mimics) that govern an insect's maturation processes and other vital functions. IGRs are sometimes referred to as third-generation insecticides. The first generation consisted of stomach poisons such as arsenic compounds. The second generation included the commonly used contact organochlorines, organophosphates, and carbamates. The third generation, the IGRs, are still the newest compounds on the scene, and there are still great hopes for this class of pesticide, with its promise of selectivity of target pests and safety to nontarget organisms.

Insects, like other animals, can be viewed as biochemical factories, with each of their various glands producing specific compounds. These compounds function in reproduction, coordination of the nervous system, tissue protection and repair, molting, and metamorphosis. Insects, like many other forms of life, are biochemically similar to humans and other mammals in certain ways, but differ significantly in other ways. The search for less-toxic insecticides has focused on substances such as IGRs that affect biochemical processes unique to arthropods, so that the potential negative effects on humans and other mammals are minimized.

This motivation, coupled with adequate research support, has so far facilitated the exploitation of two classes of important insect hormones: ecdysone, which is responsible for insect molting, and juvenile hormones (JH) that prevent metamorphosis (the change from larva to adult). Scientists have mapped the biochemical pathways involved in their production and their impact on target tissues. Of the two, the juvenile hormones continue to receive more commercial attention. The application of a natural JH and its synthetic mimics to juvenile insects in many orders arrests their development enough so that they cannot complete their life cycles and either die at an immature stage or mature into sterile adults.

Formulations. Available IGRs are formulated as liquid concentrates or as aerosol sprays or foggers. The concentrates can be mixed and applied with standard spray equipment.

Safety. Because mammals do not molt or metamorphose as insects do, the chemical compounds in IGRs are unlikely to affect them. The LD_{50} of methoprene, the most widely used IGR, is greater than 34,000 mg/kg, indicating its wide margin of safety to humans and other mammals. In addition, the relatively narrow range of species affected by a given IGR results in low or zero toxicity to beneficial insects.

Uses. At least five IGRs have been registered: the JH analogs methoprene, hydroprene, kinoprene, and fenoxycarb, and the chitin inhibitor diflubenzuron. The chart on the facing page lists the target pests affected by these IGRs.

Methoprene. Methoprene impedes insect maturation, causing sterility and death before insects can mature. Thus, like most JHs, it is useful only on insects such as fleas that are pests when adults but whose immature stages are not troublesome. Methoprene is used widely against fleas, mosquitoes, some ant species, fungus gnats, pests, chrysanthemum leafminers, and a few other economically important insects. The list of target pests should increase because methoprene has a relatively large host range.

Hydroprene. Hydroprene is marketed specifically for cockroach control. After being applied to young roaches, the JH eventually produces sterile adults with twisted wings.

Kinoprene. Kinoprene, which is toxic to both adult and larval insects, is an effective IGR for common pests of houseplants and greenhouse-grown crops (e.g, aphids and scales). It was marketed in the 1970s under the brand name Enstar®, then dropped from the market in the 1980s. An

Delta traps for gypsy moths contain pheromones to attract moths to the sticky trap interior. (Photo by Terry S. Price, Georgia Forestry Commission, Bugwood.org)

improved formulation is currently available. This product could be very important in commercial greenhouses in helping make the transition to biological controls, because it does little damage to natural enemies.

Fenoxycarb. Fenoxycarb, through its JH analog activity, causes distortion of the wings and other parts of an insect, which indicates that it has caused the insect to become sterile. Part of fenoxycarb's molecular structure resembles a carbamate, but it does not inhibit cholinesterase (nerve transmission) as do carbamate insecticides. Fenoxycarb, which is more persistent in the environment than other JH analogs, is registered for use against cockroaches, fire ants, fleas, and stored-product pests.

Diflubenzuron. This material is a chyttyitin inhibitor. Chitin, a polysaccharide similar in structure to cellulose, is the main ingredient of insect skin. Because all insects contain chitin, concerns over the potential negative impact of the indiscriminate use of diflubenzuron on beneficial insects as well as its unusual stability have led the EPA to restrict its use to licensed pest control professionals.

INSECTICIDES CONTAINING INSECT GROWTH REGULATORS

PRODUCT	TARGET PEST (SCIENTIFIC NAME)	AFFECTED CROP/TARGET AREA
Methoprene		
Altosid®	mosquitoes *(Culex, Culiseta)*	
Apex®	darkwinged fungus gnats *(Sciaridae)*	mushrooms
Dianex®	almond moth *(Ephestia cautella)*	stored products
	Indianmeal moth *(Plodia interpunctella)*	
	lesser grain borer *(Rhyzopertha dominica)*	
	sawtooth grain beetle *(Oryzaephilus mercator)*	
	red flour beetle *(Tribolium castaneum)*	
	confused flour beetle *(T. confusum)*	
Kabat®	cigarette beetle *(Lasioderma serricorne)*	tobacco
	tobacco moth *(Ephestia elutella)*	
Minex®	chrysanthemum leafminer *(Liriomyza trifolii)*	
Pharorid®	pharaoh ants *(Monomorium pharaonis)*	
Precor®, Flea Trol®	cat flea *(Ctenocephalides felis)*	
Kinoprene		
Enstar	whiteflies *(Trialeuroides* spp.)	greenhouses
	aphids (many species)	indoor plants
	soft and armored scales (many species)	
	mealybugs *(Planococcus)*	
Hydroprene		
Gentrol®	Used exclusively for cockroach control	buildings and yards
	German cockroach *(Blattella germanica)*	
Diflubenzuron		
Dimilin®	gypsy moth *(Lymantria dispar)*	
	forest tent caterpillar *(Malacosoma disstria)*	
	Nantucket pine tip moth *(Rhyacionia frustrana)*	
	boll weevil *(Anthonomus grandis)*	
	mosquitoes (many species)	
	mushroom flies (many species)	
	darkwinged fungus gnats (many species)	
	beet armyworm *(Spodoptera exigua)*	

From labels and other information supplied by Zoecon Corporation and Uniroyal Chemical Company.

PART TWO
PESTS IN THE GARDEN

CHAPTER 9

GARDEN DESIGN AND MAINTENANCE

The late Steve Jobs said, "Design is a funny word. Some people think design means how it looks. But of course, if you dig deeper, it is really how it works." He said this to garden designer Penelope Hobhouse, grande dame of British garden designers and writers, when they discussed the redesign of his garden at Palo Alto. "How it works" is the key to a successful garden design.

In Chapter 1 we discussed sustainable gardening design and the Bay-Friendly Landscape Gardening program model. In this chapter, our focus will be on designing pests out of the garden, based on those seven principles (see the sidebar below).

It seems to be human nature to respond to emergencies rather than to plan ahead and avoid them. Once a pest problem becomes intolerable, most people will seek and follow advice on pest control. But they are far less motivated to do so when there is no problem in sight. This is unfortunate, because most pest problems in food-producing and ornamental home gardens can be prevented or greatly reduced during the initial design or through regular maintenance of the garden.

When we speak of garden design, we mean the selection of the parts of the system. These include the individual plants, their placement in relation to each other, and the microclimate and soils of the site.

There are two elementary rules of good garden design:

1. Select plants that require no more maintenance time and skill than you can give them, are generally suited to the climate and soils of your area, and are most resistant to the common diseases or other pests of your area.
2. Place plants in relation to each other and the site in a way that provides the necessary growing space, light, drainage, and wind protection.

If you look at human-designed landscapes, you will discover that these two rules are often broken. Amateur and professional landscapers tend to focus on aesthetics to the exclusion of maintenance. In so doing, they build in pest problems from the start. If you want to manage your garden with a minimum of hazardous pesticides, you cannot afford to overlook these basic rules.

There are other considerations, too. Nearly everyone would agree that ideal garden design should preserve the balance of nature—the harmonious coexistence of plants, birds, insects, and other organisms. Most of us also want as much beauty

"Most of us want as much beauty or food as possible from our gardens with as little effort as possible. Designing a garden system that largely maintains its own balance of pests and controls is the only way to achieve this goal."

or food as possible from our gardens with as little effort as possible. Designing a garden system that largely maintains its own balance of pests and controls is the only way to achieve this goal. It's best to think of design as a continuous process, so as problems and successes are identified, appropriate adjustments can be made to the garden. Design, like IPM, must be dynamic. When an existing garden comes under your "new management," consider a sustainable IPM redesign.

THE SEVEN PRINCIPLES AND PRACTICES OF BAY-FRIENDLY SUSTAINABLE GARDENING

1. Landscape locally
2. Nurture the soil
3. Create and protect wildlife habitat
4. Landscape for less to the landfill
5. Conserve water
6. Conserve energy
7. Protect water and air quality

THE DIFFERENCE BETWEEN HUMAN-DESIGNED AND NATURAL SYSTEMS

Without arguing whether a balance of nature still exists in natural areas undisturbed by human activities, you will doubtless agree that some very striking and relevant characteristics distinguish those environments from the ones we humans create. The most noticeable difference is that human-designed systems are greatly simplified in the number and arrangement of species they support compared to the complexity of undisturbed natural environments.

Ecologists may debate the extent to which species diversity contributes to ecosystem stability in specific settings. Nonetheless, it is clear that the young, simplified systems typical of the common garden lack some of the protective mechanisms of more complex natural systems. Simplified systems are more subject to the wide fluctuations in pest and pathogen numbers we have come to expect in the cultivated plot. These fluctuations manifest themselves as pest emergencies that send us scrambling to the closest neighbor or plant nursery for advice on what to use to kill the offending organism.

This is the result of the simplified way in which we plan and care for our gardens. We assume that a healthy garden consists of a specific number of specimens of identifiable, desirable species of plants and animals. This notion, which focuses on individual organisms we recognize as desirable—for example, a rose bush, a cabbage plant, a honeybee, or a lady beetle—inevitably leads to the assumption that all other organisms are undesirable and should be excluded. In our minds, these other organisms are now pests. As a consequence, we make a continuous effort to eliminate them, in most cases before careful observation and analysis suggest that they really deserve this fate.

Organisms live in communities. The complex interactions within these communities are the most reliable mechanisms for achieving and maintaining stability in an ecosystem. It is not just the presence or absence of a particular pest insect, plant pathogen, or weed seed that determines the health of the garden. It is the composition and interaction of all these communities of organisms that ultimately determine the absence or presence of pest problems.

These communities are in the air surrounding the plants, on all the surfaces of the plants, above and below the ground, on the ground surface, and between soil particles. Often they form extremely

HEALTHY GARDENS HAVE GREAT DIVERSITY

Gardens with a high degree of ecological diversity are healthier and more productive than those with a limited number of plant and animal species. In this garden, a variety of flowering plants provides nectar to a wide range of beneficial insects. Birds help control pest insects, and mulch inhibits weeds and provides a rich organic medium for the growth of beneficial microbes that aid in nutrient uptake by plant roots and compete against pathogens.

intimate internal associations with the plants, such as the relationship between plants and the mycorrhizal fungi or nitrogen-producing bacteria that assist plants in acquiring nutrients. A myriad of life forms, most too small to notice with the naked eye, most without common names, and many difficult to identify, make up the true plant and garden environment. Any garden model that does not recognize the desirability of this natural complexity dooms the gardener to an endless battle against one plague after another.

DEVELOPING AN ECOSYSTEM PERSPECTIVE

A more complex, more realistic ecosystem perspective suggests a different approach to garden design and maintenance. It tends to evoke curiosity about and respect for the life forms encountered in the garden, and it fosters the American ideal of an innocent-unless-proven-guilty attitude toward new organisms. Ultimately, it leads to fewer pest emergencies and less frantic pest control.

This belief in the benefits of diversity is by no means a new discovery by modern ecologists. It was the intuitive agricultural practice of numerous "primitive" cultures, and today it is a basic tenet of the organic or biological agricultural movement. Unfortunately, recognition of this basic idea in no way lessens the disdain with which the latter movement has been regarded until recently by scientific horticulturalists and agronomists in the scientific community.

A 1960 USDA home and garden pamphlet pictures rows of vegetables spaced neatly apart in bare earth containing relatively little organic matter. A thin veneer of regularly applied preventive pesticide sprays ensures plastic-perfect foliage and the virtual absence of creepy-crawlies and nasty weeds. Now, by contrast, envision the heavily mulched, low-maintenance plots depicted in American organic garden literature or the densely planted beds of the much-publicized European and Asian intensive agricultural systems.

DUMP HEAP GARDENS

Consider the native Latin American "dump heap" gardens so eloquently described by Edgar Anderson in *Plants, Man and Life* (University of California Press, 1952). In such native gardens, vegetables and flowers are mixed together and cover almost every available surface. After examining one Guatemalan plot in detail, Anderson concluded:

> In terms of our American and European equivalents the garden was a vegetable garden, an orchard, a medicinal garden, a dump heap, a compost heap, and a bee yard. There was no problem of erosion, though it was at the top of a steep slope; the soil surface was practically all covered and apparently would be during most of the year. Humidity would be kept up during the dry season and plants of the same sort were so isolated from one another by intervening vegetation that pests and diseases could not readily spread from plant to plant. The fertility was being conserved; in addition to the waste from the house, mature plants were being buried between the rows when their usefulness was over.

Even without the benefit of scientific research, these gardeners intuitively understood the importance of several basic assumptions that flow from a sustainable ecosystem perspective.

1. LANDSCAPE LOCALLY

Diversity in the garden is a good thing, uniformity is not. In fact uniformity of plants increases the chances of pest problems. It is desirable to grow a variety of flowering plants and mix them among or bordering the vegetable patch, because of the many benefits a diversified garden community provides. Try to have one plant or another flowering throughout the growing season.

In his well-researched book, *Designing and Maintaining Your Edible Landscape Naturally* (Metamorphic Press, 1986), Robert Kourik notes that plants in the parsley family (Apiaceae, formerly Umbelliferae) and in the sunflower family (Asteraceae, formerly Compositae) are especially accessible to beneficial insects. Plants in the parsley family include carrots, celeriac, Florence fennel, dill, cumin, anise, coriander, and caraway.

INTEGRATED PEST MANAGEMENT AND THE SEVEN BASIC PRINCIPLES OF SUSTAINABLE LANDSCAPING

1. LANDSCAPE LOCALLY

Diversity in the garden should be encouraged.

- Plant locally grown native species wherever possible.

- Introduce a wide variety of locally grown flowering and fruiting plants.

- Select species so that something is in bloom at all times, even in the food garden.

- Plant "naturalized" non-native plants that come from a similar climate.

- Check with master gardeners at the county extension service office for food and ornamental species and varieties that do best in your area.

2. NURTURE THE SOIL

Bare soils are undesirable because they invite weeds, are subject to compaction by rain and foot traffic, and tend to lose organic matter through wind and exposure to sunlight.

- Mulch the soil surface to provide a residue of organic matter at the soil surface.

- Shade the soil through correct plant spacing, cover cropping, interplanting, and multiple cropping strategies.

- Incorporate organic matter— microbes' food source—into the soil.

- Use organic fertilizers, compost, and manures; avoid using synthetic quick-release fertilizers.

3. CREATE AND PROTECT WILDLIFE HABITAT

A variety of desirable macro- and microorganisms live in the soil and in your garden. They not only add practical benefit; they are also fun to watch.

- Protect and encourage a variety of recognizable predatory garden wildlife, such as toads, frogs, spiders, lizards, snakes, and ground beetles.

- Promote microbial wildlife in the soil.

- Include bird habitat, like a birdbath, birdhouses, and feeders.

- Add owl boxes and raptor perches to help with rodent control.

- Create a wildlife section to your landscape, if room permits.

Sunflower family plants include artichoke, lettuce, endive, daisy, dandelion, edible chrysanthemum, sunflower, yarrow, artemisia, marigold, zinnia, aster, and gazania.

The chart on p. 168 summarizes Kourik's suggestions for potential insectary plants (plants that feed beneficial insects). However, Kourik adds a caution: "While we may be able to somewhat shape the insect ecology of our yards by the types of flowering plants we grow, keep in mind that there is very little research on the subject, and I run the risk of starting new myths by mentioning specific plants and specific insects."

Kourik recommends that you observe flowers planted in your area to see which attract such easily recognized predators as syrphid or hover flies, which are important aphid controls, or the larger

Strawberries mulched with straw in raised beds helps reduce weeds, moderate soil temperature and moisture, and keep fruit clean. (Photo by Suzie Gibbons, Chelsea 2011/GAP)

4. LANDSCAPE FOR LESS TO THE LANDFILL

- Allow enough space for plants to grow with minimal pruning.

- Use a mulching mower on turfgrass.

- Compost all plant debris; this is a resource, not garbage.

- Hauling compostable plant debris to the dump wastes the nutrients contained in the debris.

5. CONSERVE WATER

- Create hydrozones by grouping plants that have the same water requirements.

- Add some drought-tolerant plants.

- Plant natives—they need no irrigation once established.

- Use mulches to reduce evaporation from the soil surface.

- Water deep and infrequently rather than shallow and often.

- Install drip irrigation to reduce foliar pathogens and weeds while conserving water.

6. PROTECT WATER AND AIR QUALITY

Some damage from pests is natural and desirable.

- Avoid the area-wide use of any pesticide, no matter how selective or nontoxic it is to humans, pets, and wildlife.

- Take pest control action only if the amount of damage is or will become intolerable.

- Deliberately allow the presence of some pest insects so their natural enemies will also be present.

- Install companion plants: plants that complement each other and groundcovers under and between shrubs, for example.

- Plant groundcovers to crowd out weeds.

7. CONSERVE ENERGY

- Have less lawn.

- Use manual gardening tools and equipment.

- Use corded electrical or battery-powered equipment instead of gas powered.

- Use less water.

- Avoid synthetic fertilizers and chemicals; their production is energy intensive.

We look at these seven basic ideas in greater detail beginning on p. 165, with our focus on Integrated Pest Management.

---

wasps that prey on caterpillars. A book like *Garden Insects of North America: The Ultimate Guide to Backyard Bugs* (Princeton University Press, 2004), by Whitney Cranshaw, pictures each insect clearly and summarizes its habits and prey, can be a great help. Leaf through the sections of the book devoted to those insect groups containing the largest number of important natural enemies of common insect pests. Gradually you can become quite knowledgeable about the various types of insects likely to be predators of pests, even if you never learn their scientific names or identify their species. You should also consult Chapter 5 of this book for further help in recognizing the beneficials in your garden.

2. NURTURE THE SOIL

Mulching is one way to add diversity to the garden while protecting the soil surface. The advantages are many. Bare soils are subject to erosion from wind and water runoff, extreme temperature fluctuations, and rapid reduction in organic matter due to exposure to the sun and compaction from rainfall. Bare earth provides little or no habitat for a variety of permanently or periodically ground-dwelling natural enemies of plant pests. And it invites colonization by less-desired plants commonly called "weeds."

The best mulch is your homemade compost, with chipped and shredded clippings from the garden an excellent alternative. Mulches can be as simple as weeds pulled from the beds and left to die where they fall, or as elegant as purchased materials such as cocoa bean hulls. Either way, they serve to protect the soil surface from sun, rain, and wind, and

PLANTS THAT ATTRACT BENEFICIAL INSECTS

COMMON NAME	SCIENTIFIC NAME	BENEFICIAL INSECTS ATTRACTED
alfalfa	*Medicago sativa*	minute pirate bugs, big-eyed bugs, damsel bugs, assassin bugs, lady beetles, parasitic wasps
angelica	*Angelica* spp.	lady beetles, lacewings, sand wasps
baby-blue-eyes	*Nemophila menziesii*	syrphid flies
buckwheat	*Fagopyrum esculentum*	syrphid flies
California buckwheat	*Eriogonum* spp.	sand wasps; tachinid, chloropid, and syrphid flies; minute pirate bugs
California coffeeberry	*Rhamnus californica*	tachinid and syrphid flies; lady beetles; sand, ichneumonid and braconid wasps; lacewings
camphorweed	*Heterotheca subaxillaris*	tachinid and syrphid flies, lady beetles, ichneumonid, and braconid wasps, lacewings
candytuft	*Iberis umbellata*	syrphid flies
carrot	*Daucus carota*	minute pirate bugs, big-eyed bugs, assassin bugs, lacewings, parasitic and predacious wasps
coriander	*Coriandrum sativum*	tachinid flies
coyote brush	*Baccharis pilularis*	syrphid, chloropid, and tachinid flies; braconid, ichneumonid, sand, and chalcid wasps
evening primrose	*Oenothera laciniata* and *Oenothera biennis*	ground beetles
evergreen euonymus	*Euonymus japonica*	lacewings; chloropid, tachinid, and syrphid flies; chalcid, braconid, sand, and ichneumonid wasps; lady beetles
fennel	*Foeniculum vulgare*	braconid and sand wasps, syrphid and tachinid flies
goldenrod	*Solidago altissima*	predacious beetles, big-eyed bugs, lady beetles, spiders, parasitic wasps, long-legged flies, assassin bugs
ivy	*Hedera* spp.	flower and tachinid flies; braconid, sand, hornet, and yellowjacket wasps

discourage the germination of weed seeds, which generally need bright light and exposed soils. Consult p. 194 for a comprehensive list of mulch materials and methods. Inorganic materials like plastic sheeting and synthetic fabrics should be avoided, as they add nothing to the soil and can't be recycled.

Incorporate organic matter, such as compost, into the soil when preparing the garden beds and when transplanting. Don't use too much compost in backfill soil as this can create a flowerpot effect. That is

TIP Synthetic fertilizers and pesticides have an overall negative effect on the soil food web. Synthetic fertilizers increase the salt index, which plays havoc with soil microbes and invertebrates. Salts can be especially damaging to clay soil structure.

when the roots of the transplant stay in the "good soil" in the planting hole and don't grow out into the native soil. Regular compost topdressing will add organic matter to the soil, thanks to the action of worms, insects, and other soil creatures that eat the organic matter in and on the soil below ground. There they eat the organic matter and generate their waste, which is mixed with the lower layers (horizons) of the soil.

Use organic fertilizers, compost, and manures for

COMMON NAME	SCIENTIFIC NAME	BENEFICIAL INSECTS ATTRACTED
meadow foam	*Limnanthes douglasii*	syrphid flies
Mediterranean umble	*Bupleurum fruticosum*	tachinid flies; sand wasps
Mexican tea	*Chenopodium ambrosi-oides*	assassin bugs, big-eyed bugs, lady beetles
morningglory	*Convolvulus minor*	syrphid flies, lady beetles
oleander	*Nerium oleander*	minute pirate bugs, big-eyed bugs, assassin bugs, lady beetles, soft-winged flower beetles, lacewings, syrphid flies, parasitic wasps
pigweed	*Amaranthus* spp.	ground beetles
ragweed	*Ambrosia artemisiifolia*	lady beetles, assassin bugs, spiders
rue	*Ruta graveolens*	ichneumonid wasps
saltbush	*Atriplex* spp.	sand wasps
silver lace vine	*Polygonum aubertii*	tachinid and syrphid flies
snowberry	*Symphoricarpos* spp.	flower and tachinid flies
soapbark tree	*Quillaja saponaria*	syrphid and chloropid flies; lacewings; lady beetles; ichneumonid, chalcid, and braconid wasps
tree-of-heaven	*Ailanthus altissima*	syrphid and chloropid flies, braconid and ichneumonid wasps, lacewings
white clover	*Trifolium repens*	parasitic wasps of aphids, scales, and whiteflies
white sweet clover	*Melilotus alba*	tachinid flies; sand, hornet, and yellowjacket wasps
wild lettuce	*Lactuca canadensis*	soldier beetles, lacewings, earwigs, syrphid flies
yarrow	*Achillea* spp.	lady beetles, parasitic wasps of aphids, scales, and whiteflies

From R. Kourik's *Designing and Maintaining Your Edible Landscape Naturally* (Metamorphic Press, 1986).

Drawing birds to your garden can help reduce insect problems (and the birds are fun to watch). Installing a birdbath is one way to welcome birds to your garden, but remember to change the water weekly to prevent it from becoming a mosquito habitat. (Photo by Tim Gainey/GAP)

fertilization, because these all feed the soil. The old organic gardening adage is true: "Feed the soil and the soil will feed the plants."

3. CREATE AND PROTECT WILDLIFE HABITAT

A variety of desirable macro- and microorganisms live in the soil and in your garden. They not only add practical benefit, but the ones you can see are also fun to watch. Hover flies looking for aphids will lay an egg nearby when they find them. Birds can be seen eating insects. Butterflies and honeybees pollinate your vegetables and ornamentals.

If you live in an urban or suburban setting, you should be aware that protecting and maintaining a

(Photo by Steven Cominsky, courtesy of *Fine Gardening*)

ORGANIC MATTER AND COMPOST

Composting garden clippings and applying them to your garden improves the texture of your soil and its fertility.

An alternative to encourage soil fertility without composting is to bury organic kitchen wastes directly in the garden. Do not bury protein (meat), fats (animal or vegetable), or dairy products; these will attract scavengers. It is extremely important to bury waste quickly before it attracts flies, which lay eggs in it, and deeply enough so that it does not become a source of food for rats, raccoons, and other opportunists. Ideally, each day's waste should be taken to the garden and laid under 6 in. to 12 in. (15 cm to 30 cm) of earth so it doesn't accumulate. However, if there are rat burrows in the neighborhood, it is better to save the waste and start a hot composting bin yourself or use worms to make vermicompost. Vermicompost is a great source of nutrients and improves soil structure and texture.

Hot batch processing of organic wastes, in which the temperature rises to 160°F to 180°F (71°C to 81°C), is by far the best procedure for processing organic wastes that are high in nitrogen. If all parts of the batch are exposed to this temperature for a week or so, the weed seeds, pathogens that cause plant disease, and some pesticide residues are broken down into useful compounds. Hot composting, however, takes some knowledge of the process and tight wooden, brick, or cinderblock bins.

A warning about using herbicides and composting the killed weeds: Some herbicides are not broken down during composting. They are persistent, and when compost containing these herbicides is spread under plants, they can be injured or killed from the herbicide residue.

If you live in a community that recycles kitchen and green waste for composting, use this service. Compost what you can, and "donate" the rest to the community compost system.

variety of wildlife in the garden is not always easy. Domestic cats that roam from yard to yard are likely to prey on lizards, snakes, and toads, and they also hunt down larger insects, such as black ground beetles, that are very important predators of pests.

These larger predatory insects also need protection from the sun and from their own natural enemies. Unfortunately, the gardener's desire to have the garden neat and clean-looking, like a room in the house, may lead to the elimination of miscellaneous organic debris that serve as hiding places for larger insects and other predators. In order to provide wildlife with a variety of habitats, garden borders can be designed with rocks, thick organic mulches, or overturned flowerpots (particularly if their rims are uneven or they are placed on lumpy, uneven ground). Try artfully placed piles or low garden walls built from chunks of recycled concrete or stone to provide habitat for lizards.

If you have deer or rabbit problems, leave a section of your garden for them to graze if space permits. This makes them a garden "feature" rather than a pest. Put in owl boxes to reduce local rodent populations. Installing raptor perches can draw in hawks and even the occasional eagle. They'll use the perch as a vantage point to hunt rodents and other small animals.

4. LANDSCAPE FOR LESS TO THE LANDFILL

Space plants properly so they have room to grow in their natural size and shape. Properly spaced plants also allow better air circulation, which reduces disease problems and encourages beneficials and wildlife. Consider the mature height that your plants will get and make sure that when full grown the tallest plants will not shade out smaller plants.

If feasible, organic materials can be composted, such as shredded paper, vegetable and fruit peelings, scraps, cardboard, sawdust, arborist woodchips, and even organic fabrics like cotton and wool. Often these materials would wind up in the landfill, but they can provide nutrients for plant growth and help improve soil structure. Organic materials break down into humus, which has an electrical charge and can attract and release basic mineral compounds needed for plant growth into the soil.

5. CONSERVE WATER

Overwatering is the single biggest cause of both biotic and abiotic plant disorders. Too much water promotes the water-loving fungi, like *Pythium* spp. and *Phytophthora* spp., which are commonly called the water molds. Soggy soils inhibit or stop respiration by the roots; without respiration, the roots cannot absorb water and nutrients. As strange as it seems, a plant in waterlogged soil dies of drought. In the absence of air it cannot absorb the water.

Create hydrozones for your garden. Group plants together that have the same water requirements, especially if you have an irrigation system. Native plants shouldn't need additional water once they are established. Consider a drought-tolerant hydrozone. There are many beautiful drought-tolerant plants, in addition to cactus and succulent species, that make very attractive garden plants.

If you need to have an irrigation system, install drip irrigation. This system delivers water directly to the root system, and there is no "overspray" water for weed seeds. Drip systems also eliminate the wet foliage you get from overhead irrigation that promotes foliar diseases.

Watering deeply and infrequently conserves water. Shallow, frequent irrigation not only wastes water, but it is also unhealthy for the plant's root system, which will remain shallow, where the water is located. Shallow roots are more susceptible to physical and pest damage. Don't forget to use mulch to reduce evaporation from the soil surface.

6. PROTECT WATER AND AIR QUALITY

In the Bay-Friendly Sustainable Garden and Landscape model, IPM falls under the Water and Air Quality section. This is because pesticides are applied through the air and can become vapor, and their movement in the soil or from runoff can contaminate surface water and groundwater. As you've seen, IPM falls into each category in some way.

Some damage from pests is natural and desirable. Deliberately allow the presence of some pest insects, so their natural enemies will also be present. If there is no food in the form of pests, when the beneficials arrive, they will move on. Take pest control actions only if the amount of damage is or will become intolerable.

Avoid the area-wide use of any pesticide, no matter how selective or nontoxic it is to humans. Any material, even a fairly innocuous one such as soap or garlic spray, has the potential to kill organisms other than the target species. The sensible approach is to spot treat. In other words, confine your pest management action to only those areas and times where the pest population is rising to an intolerable level (see p. 38 for a discussion of spot treatment). As a rule, you should avoid preventive spray treatments.

(Photo by FhF Greenmedia/Gap)

THE VALUE OF LAWN CLIPPINGS

If you have a lawn, use a mulching mower (photo above). Grinding up clippings breaks them down and returns their nutrients to the soil. Collect and remove lawn clippings only when doing so is part of an IPM plan to deal with a turf pathogen, or if you are using the lawn clippings in your compost pile or as mulch. Hauling lawn clippings to the landfill is like throwing your fertilizer dollars away. Using a mulching mower can reduce nitrogen needs by one-third from the breakdown of clippings over the course of a year. The increase in soil fertility further reduces the need for supplemental fertilizer applications.

To discourage weeds, shade the soil surface. To do so, place plants so they grow an arching mat of foliage either at ground level or just above it, seed in a fast-growing temporary cover plant where you plan to place another plant in the future, or plant faster-growing annuals between slower-growing permanent plantings. The faster-growing annuals will cover the soil until the permanent plants shade them out. A multitude of other planting strategies can be used to ensure that one annual plant follows another in succession so the soil remains covered continuously. These methods are discussed in greater detail on pp. 174–175.

Unfortunately, there has been little research into which plants can be added to which settings to aid the home gardener in biological control of garden pests. But it is known that it is wise to include a number of shallow-throated flowering species in the garden, as many of the hymenopteran

ATTRACTING BENEFICIALS: A CASE STUDY

Many of the predatory and parasitic insects that feed on garden pests need nectar and pollen from flowers for nourishment in order to lay eggs. The California Department of Transportation capitalized on this fact in controlling a caterpillar pest on median strip plantings on roadways. The objective was to increase the number of parasitic miniwasp attacks on pest caterpillars. The parasitoids were already present in these plantings and did a good job of controlling the caterpillar through early June of each year, but after that the rate of parasitism fell dramatically.

In work carried out by Dudley Pinnock and James Milstead at the University of California, several plants were examined for attractiveness to the beneficial parasitic miniwasp and for a tendency to flower from June through the summer months. Ultimately one plant was selected and tested in field trials. The increase in parasitism was dramatic and effective, and the plants were added to the highway landscape at regular intervals where the pest problem occurred. This successful use of a flowering plant to enhance biological control of a pest insect was part of a larger biological control project that has saved the transportation department considerable amounts of time and money over the years.

parasitoids of aphids, scales, mealybugs, caterpillars, and other organisms are very tiny and compete poorly with honeybees and other larger hymenopteran insects for nectar from deep-throated flowers.

Fertile soil is teeming with simple life forms—yeasts, fungi, bacteria, actinomycetes, and others—which derive sustenance from the decomposition of organic matter. They in turn produce plant nutrients, in the form of relatively stable compounds, and are themselves the basis of many food chains within the soil. These organisms also compete with, or actively destroy, potentially destructive inhabitants of soil and root surfaces.

A complex soil community with many interlocking food webs provides the greatest resistance to invasion by exotic (non-native) organisms, including plant pathogens such as bacteria and fungi, root-feeding nematodes, soil-inhabiting insects, and other plant-feeding arthropods. Exotics blown in by the wind, carried in by birds and other mammals, or that travel in on their own will find a wealth of predators, parasitoids, and competitors already established. These make it difficult for the strangers to survive and multiply. Thus, encouraging a wide variety of soil life, even though most of it is hidden or too small to see, is an important part of creating diversity in the garden and protecting it from exotic invaders.

7. CONSERVE ENERGY

Plant locally grown native species because they are likely to have fewer pests than non-natives. The pests they do have often have a local predator or parasitoid that keeps them under control. Native plants can save energy because, once established, they are able to live on normal rainfall, need fewer pesticides, and live easily on compost and organic fertilizers.

Plants from nurseries in your area require less energy to transport. There may be food plants native to or naturalized to your area, such as berries and herbs, to include in your plans. Plant a variety of locally grown ornamentals, fruits, and

Companion planting in a vegetable garden creates a prettier garden where pests have more difficulty finding their host plants among the variety of species. The nasturtium plants not only help protect other plants but also provide flowers that are a delicious addition to your garden salad. (Photo by Elke Borkowski/GAP)

sider taking your plant list to the local county extension service office for their advice.

Consider reducing or eliminating your lawn and converting it to food and ornamental plants. Lawnmowers, edgers, lawn pesticides, and fertilizers make turfgrass the most energy- and labor-intensive plants you can have. Lawns also use more water, which requires energy to get it from its source, purify it, and pump it through miles of pipes to your turfgrass. Plant food and flowers, and while the neighbor is mowing you can kick back, eat some homegrown food, and enjoy your flowers.

Plastics and synthetic fabrics are petroleum-intensive products. Avoid using inorganic materials such as plastic sheets or synthetic fabrics to cover the soil. Although these materials do keep weeds down and unquestionably may have a small role to play in the overall garden scheme, they introduce yet more nonrecyclable plastic into the environment and do not provide the benefit of the best mulches: contributing organic material to the soil.

Avoid synthetic fertilizers. They require large amounts of energy to produce and they tend to promote lush growth that attracts insect pests and is easily attacked by pathogens. Synthetic fertilizers also raise water requirements because of their "salt" nature.

Use manual gardening tools and equipment; for the home gardener, hand tools are all that is usually needed. If you need power equipment, consider renting. If you need to purchase equipment, consider corded electrical or battery-powered tools.

vegetables. Select your plants, if possible, so that something is blooming year-round, even in the food garden. If you must plant non-native plants, choose plants from a locale that has a similar climate and are not invasive. California is in a Mediterranean bioclimate zone, with its winter rainfall and dry summers; the Midwest has a similar climate to northern Europe and the steppes of Asia; and the Gulf Coast states are subtropical. In all cases, con-

DEER AND IPM

Applying the IPM decision-making process to deer is a little different than lawn grubs or rose aphids, because deer are game animals, which can be pests. Game animals have laws to protect them, so you can't just wash them away with a soap solution. Traps and poisons of any kind are illegal and cannot be used.

Every situation is different, which is why we spend so much time on the concept of IPM.

- First, is the problem tolerable?

- If intolerable, estimate the budget to manage the problem. In deer situations, wildlife agencies may be able to help, depending upon where your house is located.

You want to be certain that deer are the culprit. Although large and easily seen, they are nocturnal, so check the garden at night with a flashlight. Also look for physical signs of deer, such as tracks, droppings, trails, and damage to foliage from deer browsing.

A small herd can take out a garden in one night; take action when signs of deer are first detected. If you know deer have caused problems nearby, consider using exclusion methods before damage occurs.

The goal is to prevent the damage, so barriers are best, and they can come in all sizes, costs, and designs. For the homeowner whose landscape is being gobbled up by deer, fencing is a big investment, but it's permanent. And if well constructed, a barrier may also work for other difficult animals like rabbits, turkeys, foxes, and so on. Compare the losses sustained by deer feeding to the cost of installing the barrier. On top of that, deer carry Lyme-disease-transmitting ticks. Skipping Lyme disease exposure is worth your life. In Lyme country, we would go for the best barrier possible.

Dogs, especially medium to large size, are effective.

We also have found deer netting useful. It comes in various sizes and is laid out over the tops of the plants. You must adjust as stems grow through the netting.

A border of so-called deer-resistant plants works very well if your neighbor has appetizing plants. They'll bypass your yard and go to the neighbor's. But deer will eat most deer-resistant plants if they get hungry enough.

Repellents, both egg-based and pepper-based, work quite well, but like all sprays need to be applied regularly to new "tasty growth" and after rain or irrigation washes them off of the foliage. Repellents often seem to be site specific, which is to say you need to experiment and find out which material works for your local deer population.

In some cases, using individual plant protectors may be more practical and economical than fencing an entire area.

Because deer rapidly adjust to noise-making devices, these devices are ineffective. And because deer can travel great distances to seek food and shelter, modifying their habitat to make it less desirable is impractical. Planting alternative attractive foods away from the garden will not prevent damage to more valued plants and might even make the whole area more attractive to deer.

We found two deer repellents to be effective: both the egg and blood meal formulations and the capsaicin hot-pepper sprays kept our plants protected. (Photo by Guy J. Sagi/iStockPhoto)

COMPANION PLANTING

Plants influence each other in the garden. They do this by producing substances that specifically inhibit or enhance the growth of other plants, by providing alternative food sources or habitats for beneficial insects and other organisms, and by discouraging the buildup of undesired organisms. They may do the latter by reducing the attraction for certain pests or by repelling them.

In response to this realization, there has been a search for specific companion plants and an increase in tolerance among gardeners for some adjacent or interspersed weed or wild plants among the garden plants. Unfortunately, the search has not yet resulted in a list of species that produce reliable results outside the specific varieties of plants in the specific soils and climates and under the particular horticultural regimes used in the original studies.

Nonetheless, the organic literature abounds in recommendations, nearly all of them unsubstantiated. The most widely publicized of these schemes is derived from a misunderstanding. We often hear gardeners say, "I have planted marigolds, but they don't do any good." Will marigolds keep pest insects away? The idea that they do apparently arose from the fact that both small marigolds (*Tagetes patula*) and large marigolds (*T. erecta*) produce a root exudate or secretion that discourages certain plant-infesting nematodes, such as the meadow or root lesion nematode (*Pratylenchus penetrans*). Nematodes are not insects; they are long, thin worms. Moreover, the kinds that infest plants are microscopic and not that common. Usually they become a problem when highly susceptible plants such as strawberries are grown season after season in the same soil, so that the nematode population can build up.

A study by the Connecticut Agricultural Experiment Station showed that when soils are infested with nematodes, planting the field solidly with marigolds for an entire season, then plowing them under, provides good nematode control for two to three years, better than any other method used for this purpose. They also found that planting marigolds for shorter periods or merely interplanting them among other crops does not have the same effect—it must be a solid planting and turned under, much as one would plant wheat. It should also be noted that although this technique has been proven effective against nematodes, there is no evidence that marigolds repel pest insects.

Because of growing interest in least-toxic controls, there have been various scientific studies of companion plantings. In *Designing and Maintaining Your Edible Landscape Naturally* (Metamorphic Press, 1986), Robert Kourik has made an outstanding effort to render these scattered reports understandable and usable. Although he suggests what might be worth experimenting with in your own garden, he does not promise panaceas. All his recommendations are fully documented, so you can read the original study if you want to know more about the precise conditions under which the plant association was found to be effective.

LEARNING TO LIVE WITH SOME VISIBLE PEST DAMAGE

If you adopt the attitude that some visible effects of pest activity are tolerable, you can provide a garden environment that encourages the buildup of natural enemies of the pests. This in turn reduces pest populations and ensures that the damage remains within a tolerable range. This is one of the most important and basic considerations in pest control, because there can be no natural enemy populations without pests being present in some number (see the discussions of injury level on p. 32 and biological control on pp. 45–46 for a closer look at this concept).

The most critical time in the garden's life is when it is first established. Without the complexity of plants and animals that a mature garden provides, the newly planted area is likely to suffer severely from pest damage as the season progresses. However, stability can be established gradually by patiently introducing greater and greater diversity into the planting scheme, by encouraging insect and animal communities above and below the soil surface, and by practicing a restrained form of spot treatment that uses hand removal and pruning as the primary tools for pest reduction.

It is particularly advantageous to leave the remains of heavily parasitized pests so that the beneficials can emerge to carry on their work. For example, a heavy infestation of aphids on Chinese cabbage is likely to be parasitized by beneficial miniwasps and will probably attract large numbers of egg-laying syrphid flies. If these first plantings are left to crumble where they stand, they will become the nursery for natural enemies that will control aphids on cabbage family plants grown later in the season. The natural enemies will also eat other aphids that attack a wide variety of vegetables and ornamentals.

CHAPTER 10

MEET THE WEEDS

f we were asked to rank the garden pests we are most frequently asked about, weeds would be highest on the list. No matter what the garden area—vegetable patch, lawn, path, fence line, drainage ditch, or shrub bed—weeds usually manage to gain a foothold. If left unrestrained, some species seem to envelop a garden almost overnight, often out-competing cherished vegetables or flowers for the nutrients, water, and sunlight necessary for vigorous growth.

The remarkable competitive edge that many weed species appear to have over edible and ornamental plants, coupled with their ability to intrude into even the most carefully placed brick pathways or other garden structures, mystifies and frustrates many gardeners and stimulates the "see 'em and spray 'em" attitude that is responsible for chronic overuse of herbicides.

A "weed" is commonly defined as a plant growing in a place where it is not wanted. Plants can be unwanted because they compete for resources with desired species; because they cause harm to people, pets, or structures; or simply because someone dislikes the way they look or smell. Thus, the designation "weed" can be quite subjective—the same species can be considered a weed in one setting and a wildflower or medicinal herb in another. When surveying the weed literature or discussing this topic with any group of gardeners, however, there appears to be some consensus on the weedy nature of certain plant species, such as thistles, docks, crabgrass, ragweed, poison oak, poison ivy, and many others. These species tend to have common characteristics that enable them to "take over" certain garden habitats when conditions are right.

To the degree that gardeners gain a better understanding of conditions suited to weed growth

"Nature . . . knows no plants as weeds." —Liberty Hyde Bailey, father of modern horticulture

and are able to design and maintain their gardens in ways that minimize such conditions, their battle with weeds will become briefer each year, and the need to resort to toxic weed control will be minimized or eliminated. To identify the conditions that promote weed growth, it helps to review some basic principles of weed biology and ecology. Because this information is usually omitted from conventional "recipes" for weed control, we cover it in detail here.

VEGETATION SUCCESSION

This drawing shows a simplified sequence of vegetation succession. At (A) bare, low-nutrient soil is colonized by broad-leafed plants such as thistles and some grasses. As the plants die and decompose, enriching the soil, grasses predominate (B). As the soil is further enriched, woody shrubs begin to appear (C), followed by trees (D). Eventually, the trees become the predominant vegetation type (E), shading out most competing vegetation.

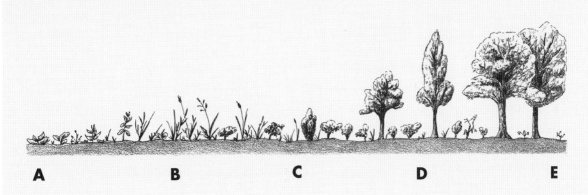

A   B   C   D   E

WEEDS: THE FIRST SOIL CONSERVATIONISTS

When a place where weeds grow is examined, a little detective work usually reveals that the soil has been subjected to a disturbance at some point. That disturbance may have taken the form of cultivation to prepare the ground for new plants, grading in connection with road maintenance, overgrazing of pasture, excessive trampling or close mowing of a lawn, or repeated use of herbicides to clear vegetation. Yes, the use of herbicides is considered soil disturbance, which is why you have to repeat applications on a regular basis if no other action is taken.

The correlation between disturbed soil and the appearance of weeds is part of a natural process called vegetation succession, whereby the first plant species to colonize a patch of bare, open soil will be displaced over time by other plant species in response to changes in the soil microhabitat. Thus, a meadow left undisturbed may eventually become a forest, as shown in the drawing on p. 177.

Plant ecologists explain the appearance of weeds this way. At the very beginning of the succession process there is an earthquake, volcanic eruption, landslide, flood, fire, or some other natural occurrence. Once the tremors stop or the floodwaters recede, an expanse of bare, exposed rock is left behind. After approximately 1,000 years of chemical and physical weathering, the rock is converted into an inch of topsoil. Left bare, these "young" soils are vulnerable to erosion by wind and water.

Certain plants have evolved to take advantage of these new or disturbed soils. As a consequence of their colonizing these areas, the soil is stabilized, erosion is reduced, and the environment becomes more conducive to the growth of other plants with less-weedy characteristics. Because these disturbed soils tend to be hot, dry, unshaded habitats whose mineral nutrients are tied up in chemical forms largely unavailable to most vegetation, the plant species able to colonize such soils can do so only because they have developed special biological and behavioral mechanisms that enable them to migrate to new areas and survive in hostile locations. These

NUMBER OF SEEDS PER PLANT FOR COMMON WEEDS

COMMON NAME	SCIENTIFIC NAME	SEEDS PER PLANT (PER YEAR)
barnyardgrass	Echinochloa crus-galli	7,160
black medic	Medicago lupulina	2,350
broadleaf plantain	Plantago major	36,150
Canada thistle	Cirsium arvense	680
common mullein	Verbascum thapsus	223,200
common ragweed	Ambrosia artemisiifolia	3,380
common sunflower	Helianthus annuus	7,200
crabgrass	Digitaria sanguinalis	8,246
curly dock	Rumex crispus	30,000
lambsquarters	Chenopodium album	72,450
mustard, black	Brassica nigra	13,400
mustard, white	Brassica hirta	2,700
Pennsylvania smartweed	Polygonum pensylvanicum	3,140
purslane	Portulaca oleracea	52,300
redroot pigweed	Amaranthus retroflexus	117,400
sandbur	Cenchrus incertus	1,110
shepherd's-purse	Capsella bursa-pastoris	38,500
spurge	Euphorbia esula	140
stinkgrass	Eragrostis cilianensis	82,100
wild buckwheat	Polygonum convolvulus	11,900
wild oats	Avena fatua	250
yellow foxtail	Setaria glauca	12,618
yellow nutsedge	Cyperus esculentus	2,240

Data from Klingman et al.'s *Weed Science: Principles and Practices* (John Wiley and Sons, 1975), and L. J. King's *Weeds of the World* (Interscience Publishers, 1966).

plants are the very same garden nemeses that appear on every weed list: thistles, dandelions, docks, knotweeds, plantains, certain grasses, sedges, and many others. Many of the worst weeds are introduced species, primarily from Europe.

WEED SURVIVAL STRATEGIES

One of the most important mechanisms many weeds utilize to compete against other plants is the production of large amounts of seed, which can give the weed a reproductive edge. A single curly dock plant *(Rumex crispus)* can generate up to 30,000 seeds in a single season. The chart on the facing page lists the seed-production records of some familiar weeds. Moreover, weed seeds can remain dormant in the soil for many years, awaiting the right conditions for germination. In seed-viability experiments conducted at the University of Michigan, curly dock seeds were found to be viable after 70 years of burial in sterile subsoil. But fortunately for us gardeners, seeds in soils are subject to microbial action, so many die before they can germinate.

Many weed species have developed special physical adaptations that allow them to use wind, water, wildlife, livestock, humans, and even vehicles to travel to habitats suited to their growth and survival. The drawing on p. 180 illustrates some of these interesting adaptations. Perhaps the most important agents of dispersal are migratory birds, many of which fly thousands of miles in their seasonal travels. According to a report in Mea Allan's *Weeds: The Unbidden Guests in Our Gardens* (Viking Press, 1978),

> Alfred Newton, a professor of zoology at Cambridge University, sent Charles Darwin the leg of a partridge with a hard ball of earth weighing 6½ oz. [184 g] adhering to it. Darwin kept the earth for three years, but when he broke it up, watered it, and placed it under a bell glass, no fewer than 82 plants grew from it.

The most successful of the early colonizer weeds tend to be annual broad-leafed plants, which have rapid life cycles that enable them to take advantage of brief periods of rainfall to germinate, shoot up, blossom, set seed, and die, often within the space of a few weeks or months. Some desert species can accomplish this entire life cycle in a matter of days, often after lying dormant for years before adequate rainfall occurs. These rapid life cycles minimize the amount of nutrients and water needed for growth. The grey or grey-green foliage characteristic of many of these species reflects the heat of the sun from tender plant tissues. Such plants may also have other adaptations, such as thick, waxy cuticles on leaf and stem surfaces that minimize water loss. Plants with these special characteristics include not only many of the common

> ## DID YOU KNOW?
> The seed viability record belongs to the seeds of the sacred lotus *(Nelumbo nucifera)*, found in the peat of a dried-up Manchurian lake and then germinated. It was determined by residual carbon-14 dating that the seeds were over 1,000 years old.

Stellaria media, also known as chickweed, is an annual broad-leafed weed. (Photo by Martin Hughes-Jones/GAP)

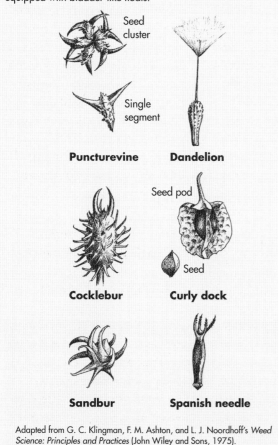
weeds listed in the chart on p. 178, but also many of the ephemeral wildflowers and herbs seen in abandoned fields and vacant lots.

Though perennial weeds also produce seeds, their main means of reproduction tends to be vegetative. They produce new top growth from buds located on the rootstalk. Using this method, a single perennial weed can cover large areas of soil in a short period. The vigorous underground rhizomes of Canada thistle (*Cirsium arvense*), for example, can spread laterally for a distance of 15 ft. (4.5 m) in a single season and produce dozens of new shoots.

WEEDS AND VEGETATION DYNAMICS

When the early colonizing plants die, they are converted by soil microorganisms into organic matter. This material, called humus, improves the soil habitat by increasing overall water retention. Humus also increases the CEC (cation exchange capacity), which is the soil's ability to hold onto nutrients and keep them from leaching or volatilizing. Humic acids help dissolve mineral nutrients into solution, thereby making them available for uptake by plants. Organic matter also improves the physical structure of the soil, making it easier for plant roots to penetrate hard-packed ground in their search for minerals, water, and anchorage. In sandy soil the organic matter acts like glue, holding sand particles together and trapping water and nutrients that otherwise would be leached away.

Over time, the organic matter and shade provided by the early, primarily broad-leafed colonizer plants improve the soil microhabitat enough to allow slightly less hardy species such as annual grasses to move in. In the improved soil, grasses usually hold a competitive edge over broad-leafed plants and gradually displace them. As long as the soil remains undisturbed, the fertile organic matter produced by the constant recycling of dead plant roots and top growth continues to enrich the soil and increase water retention, creating a habitat capable of supporting longer-lived biennial and perennial grasses and broad-leafed species. Eventually shrubs and trees dominate.

This ecological process can be seen in contemporary gardens by comparing the abundance of weeds sprouting in freshly turned soil in the vegetable garden with the relative absence of weeds in perennial borders where a thick growth of shrubs, trees, and groundcovers protects the soil from disturbance.

Sometimes this gradual process of succession gets stuck. For example, if the soil is frequently disturbed by flooding, cultivation, or trampling, the habitat will continue to support only the hardiest of pioneering plant species. And if certain seeds, such as those of thistles, are uncovered and exposed

VEGETATION DYNAMICS IN YOUR GARDEN

What does vegetation dynamics have to do with the weeds in your garden? After all, you probably haven't had any landslides or major floods lately. However, your rototiller, lawnmower, herbicide sprayer, fenced-in dog, and/or rambunctious children may be serving as surrogate acts of nature, trampling and compacting the soil, removing its vegetative cover, exposing it to the bright sun, and drying it out. In other words, if weeds are a problem in your garden, it's probably because you or your family are creating the soil conditions that encourage weeds to grow. The mix of weeds that emerges is primarily determined by the "seed bank" buried in your soil. The secondary source is seed that is moved onto the site by the wind, new soils, immature or worm compost, feet and clothing, flowing water, equipment, and wildlife. These weed imports can usually be spotted and removed quickly before they produce seeds themselves. Monitor your garden for new weed species and pull them out immediately.

Seeds from the common dandelion, *Taraxacum officinale*, can travel an average of 6 miles on the wind. (Photo by Pernilla Bergdahl/GAP)

to sunlight or are the first to blow in and land on newly bared soil, they may become established for very long periods, refusing to yield to competing grasses or other plants despite improvement of the soil habitat. This is due to a variety of reasons, including the fact that certain plants, including many thistles, can release toxins into the soil that prevent seeds of other plants—and sometimes even their own offspring—from germinating and becoming established. This ability to inhibit the growth of potential competitors is called allelopathy, and could be a promising new avenue in ecologically sound weed management. Allelopathy is discussed in detail in Chapter 11.

INTEGRATED WEED MANAGEMENT

Having learned about the connection between

weeds and disturbed soils, you are probably wondering how you are supposed to maintain your lawn, ornamental beds, vegetable garden, orchard, pathways, and fence lines without creating weed-favoring conditions. After all, isn't some tilling, mowing, hoeing, or spraying required to plant and maintain such areas?

The answer is quite simple. If you want to minimize weeds in the first place or prevent their return once you've pulled them out, dug them out, or spot-treated them with herbicides, you must be certain that any tactic you use to get rid of the weeds is combined with an action designed to modify the soil so it becomes unfavorable for future weed growth. It is this element of habitat modification that is missing from conventional weed control strategies (particularly those that rely exclusively on herbicides), dooming the gardener to an endless battle with weeds.

Habitat modification is a key element in an integrated approach to weed management that has three major components:

- Establishing *realistic* tolerance levels for weeds.
- Modifying the habitat to minimize conditions that produce more weeds than you are willing to tolerate (also called indirect suppression).
- Focusing direct suppression efforts on weed populations that threaten to exceed tolerance levels rather than on all weeds growing in the garden.

The first component of the integrated approach to weed management is discussed below; the other two components are described in detail in Chapter 11.

ESTABLISHING TOLERANCE LEVELS

Given the bad press that weeds have received over the years, many people find it difficult to develop realistic tolerance levels for weeds in their gardens. The importance of the key word "realistic" cannot be overstated. That said, keeping weed populations to a minimum is definitely important to the growth and vigor of ornamental and edible garden plants, as well as the overall appearance of the garden. Complete eradication of all weeds from your garden now and forever is a pipe dream; complete eradication is neither feasible nor desirable. However, some weeds, because of their rapid growth rate, can cause unnecessary trouble if you let them stay too long. Mallow is a favorite example here, as it grows a deep tap root quickly—too quickly. In our gardens, we are constantly on the lookout for mallow, and stop everything to pull out even the smallest seedling.

The oft-stated gardener's goal of a weed-free lawn, vegetable bed, or flower border is fostered by a barrage of advertising with the objective of selling all kinds of hardware and chemical products that aid in the war on weeds. Take, for example, those photos of velvety-smooth "weed-free" lawns depicted in the herbicide ads. You can be 99.9 percent certain that if you examined random transects across those lawns you would find that a number of

weed species had set up housekeeping, staying low to the ground to avoid the mower and blending into the overall greensward captured by the camera lens. (A transect is a line drawn across an area. By identifying and recording the range of plant species along

> ## "Complete eradication of all weeds from your garden now and forever is a pipe dream; complete eradication is neither feasible nor desirable."

that line, you arrive at an estimate of the number of species present in a given area of soil. See p. 289 for details on the use of transects in lawn weed control.)

An annihilate-the-weeds ethic is also nurtured by much of the popular and scientific garden literature, which tends to apply to the residential garden the same economic and aesthetic standards established for agricultural crops and putting greens.

Such rigid standards are not appropriate to the garden—nor, many would argue, are they realistic for agriculture or golf courses, given the large amounts of pesticides, fertilizers, water, and other resources required to maintain such standards. We feel that this "standard" is more expensive in every way, environmentally and in dollars, than the return.

The bottom line is to recognize that the presence of some weeds is not only inevitable, but actually good for your garden. In *Weeds: Guardians of the Soil* (Devin-Adair, 1964), Joseph Cocannouer describes the way in which deep-rooted weeds such as thistles, pigweeds (*Amaranthus* spp.), and nightshades (*Solanum* spp.) penetrate the subsoil, increasing openings for water and

Globe mallow, *Sphaeralcea munroana*, is a native of the western U.S. Along with a number of other mallow species, globe mallow is often considered a weed but its drought tolerance makes it a candidate for a dry climate garden. (Photo by Martin Hughes-Jones/GAP)

root movement and absorbing minerals such as phosphorus and potassium stored in the lower soil horizons. These minerals are brought up to the topsoil, where they are made available to less aggressive plant species upon the death and decay of the weed that "mined" them.

In addition to improving soil fertility and water-holding capacity, certain weeds provide a habitat for beneficial insects and should, therefore, be tolerated to some degree. For example, in California the common blackberry provides nectar and shelter for *Anagrus epos*, a tiny parasitoid of the grape leafhopper, which vectors a serious disease of wine and table grapes. It was discovered that by allowing hedgerows of blackberries to remain at the borders of vineyards, enough parasitoids develop to control the leafhopper. Moreover, at the East Malling Research Station in Kent, England, orchard specialists found that hedgerows of blackberries provide a habitat for a variety of beneficial organisms that control the two-spotted spider mite *(Tetranychus urticae)*, a serious orchard pest. Although we usually recommend plants that attract beneficials, blackberry is an exception to this rule. Blackberry is problematic as a weed because it is so invasive and difficult to control, especially when it becomes naturalized. It creates more problems as a weed than it solves in its role as an attracter of beneficials for two-spotted mite. Don't plant blackberry unless you plan on harvesting the fruit and spending a good amount of your gardening time keeping it under control and out of the rest of your garden. It is much easier to buy your blackberries at the farmer's market or supermarket.

Weeds in the sunflower *(Asteraceae)*, parsley *(Apiaceae)*, and mustard *(Cruciferae)* families are nectar sources for beneficial insects. These flowers have shallow throats whose pollen and nectar is easily available to beneficial wasp parasitoids that cannot compete with bees for these materials in deep-throated flower families such as the morningglories *(Convolvulaceae)*.

Sometimes weeds help gardeners in unexpected ways. A good example is provided in Mea Allan's *Weeds: The Unbidden Guests in Our Gardens:*

> F. C. King, for many years in charge of the famous garden at Levens Hall in England's Lake District, found that the best way to secure a good crop of sound onions was to allow weeds to develop in the onion bed after about the first week in July. The growing weeds, by denying the onions a supply of nitrogen, improved their keeping qualities, and by digging in the weeds in the autumn provided a supply of humus for the next crop.

Other weeds should be tolerated because they can assist the gardener by serving as "trap crops"

Field bindweed, *Convolvulus arvensis,* is also known as the wild morningglory. It is a tenacious and difficult-to-control weed that can sprout from seed and, more important, from roots left in the soil. (Photo by S & O/GAP)

for pest insects. By allowing these weeds to border your garden or grow in rows within the garden area, insects that otherwise would feed on your vegetables or ornamentals are attracted to the weeds instead.

For example, gardeners in South Dakota report that by encouraging weedy grasses and broadleafs such as the annual kochia *(Kochia scoparia)* to grow as a barrier between the garden and adjacent open fields, grasshoppers that normally migrate from the dry pastures into irrigated gardens in the summer stop instead to feed on the weedy trap crop. The trap crop is irrigated occasionally to keep it lush, and is cut back lightly several times during the growing season to keep the weeds from going to seed. The grasshoppers often complete their life cycles and die off without ever leaving the trap crop. Some gardeners monitor their trap crops. When they detect large numbers of eggs or young pest insect larvae, they spray the trap plants to kill the pests. This approach allows the food crops to remain unsprayed but still protected.

These examples of the beneficial role some weeds play in gardens are offered not as rationalizations for tolerating all weed growth, but rather as counters to the barrage of media information that makes you feel that all sorts of horticultural havoc will result if weeds are tolerated at any level.

In setting weed tolerance levels you need to ask the following questions:

- Which weed species are growing in the garden?
- How aggressively are they growing and spreading?
- Where in the garden are they growing and how visible are they?
- How much damage are they likely to cause to other plants, structures, or the overall aesthetics of the area?

For example, if the weed growing in your flower-

> **TIP** Consider lawn substitutes (wherever practical) where lawns aren't a necessity. We recommend the use of food and ornamental plants, the former because they give a useful return and the later because ornamentals are less demanding than lawns.

bed is the annual scarlet pimpernel *(Anagallis arvensis)*, a relatively slow-growing, prostrate weed that competes poorly with established plants, there's no need to rush right out and remove it. You might even find its tiny scarlet flowers attractive and appreciate the fact that its spreading habit will protect the soil from desiccation (drying out) by the sun until your flower or vegetable seedlings are large enough to shade the soil (and shade out the scarlet pimpernel).

If, on the other hand, the weed is *Convolvulus arvensis*, commonly known as wild morningglory or field bindweed, quick action is required. This perennial plant can send out 30 sq. yd. (25 sq. m) of stolons (underground stems) in a single season. Each of the many buds on these stolons can produce new top growth with twining stems seemingly dedicated to the singular task of choking out your prize dahlias or zucchini.

Of course, if the bindweed happens to be growing not in your garden but in another of its habitats—say, on a south-facing hillside where the combination of harsh sunlight, steep slope, water runoff, and little or no topsoil severely limits the growth of other plants—you should probably leave it alone and thank your stars that those bindweed roots are helping to hold the soil in place so your house does not go sliding downhill in heavy rains.

KNOWING YOUR WEEDS

The discussion of tolerance levels underscores the importance of identifying the weed species you are dealing with and knowing something about its biology. The more adept you become at recognizing garden weeds, particularly at the seedling stage, the better you can judge which weeds need immediate attention and which can be removed later or even allowed to stay.

For example, weeds that form deep, fleshy taproots such as dandelion *(Taraxacum officinale)* or sow-thistle *(Sonchus arvensis)* should be removed in the seedling stage. If you wait until they mature, you will find the roots tenaciously anchored in the soil and the weed very difficult to pull out or kill. Moreover, if you fail to remove every piece of live root from the soil, new top growth is likely to emerge from dormant growth buds present on even small pieces of mature root tissue.

Like most advice, one needs to fit the biology and potential uses of the plant into your particular management activities. Dandelion is desired by many people for tea, salad or cooked greens, and dandelion wine. When considering these uses, dandelion becomes a crop rather than a weed.

Quick action is not particularly necessary for weed species with shallow, fibrous root systems such as chickweed *(Stellaria and Cerastium* spp.) or lambsquarters *(Chenopodium album)*, as these are easy to pull out of most garden soils even when approaching maturity. Still, it is very important that these weeds be harvested before they set seed.

Another good reason for learning to identify weeds is that some serve as excellent indicators of garden conditions, including soil pH (acidity), salinity, and moisture. For example, patches of nutsedge *(Cyperus* spp.) indicate the presence of excessive water, perhaps due to a break in an irrigation pipe or the presence of an underground spring. Conversely, prostrate knotweed *(Polygonum aviculare)* in your lawn indicates dry, compacted soil and suggests the need for improved aeration and irrigation.

WEED NAMES

A particular weed may have many common names, but it has only one scientific name, which consists of the genus and the species. It is this scientific name that you should use when you search for information. The bad news is that even this scientific name can change, because botanists are forever moving plants from one genus or species to another as new information about them emerges. When looking up a particular weed, you may see it listed by different scientific names in different texts. For example, poison ivy is listed in some books as *Rhus radicans* or *Rhus toxicodendron* and in others as *Toxicodendron radicans.* If you want to know the scientific name currently in vogue, consult the most recent edition (2010, as of this writing) of the *Composite List of Weeds*, published by the Weed Science Society of America (www.wssa.net).

WEED KEYS

If you want to take the "Sherlock Holmes" approach to weed identification, you should acquire a key to the weeds or general flora of your region. First, however, we suggest you read Harrington and Durrell's gem of a book, *How*

Yellow nutsedge *(Cyperus esculentus)* indicates waterlogged soil, whereas prostrate knotweed *(Polygonum aviculare)* indicates dry, compacted soil. Certain weed species are good indicators of soil conditions. (Left photo: Thomas Alamy/GAP/Science Photo Library; right photo: Bruno Petriglia)

to Identify Plants (Swallow Press, 1957), in which they write, "Keys provide a convenient shortcut method of determining plants by outlining and grouping related types. There is a particular 'knack' in using keys, gained partly by certain native ability in weighing evidence in order to arrive at a correct decision, but obtained mostly by constant practice and experience." The book provides the necessary background in botanical terminology and field collection for using plant keys. Without a reference such as this, working through keys can be extremely frustrating.

Bear in mind that if all efforts at identification fail, you can always prepare a sample of your weed and take or mail it to a weed identification expert. Your local cooperative extension office or nearest state department of agriculture, university herbarium, community college botany department, or natural history museum may offer such assistance.

HELPFUL LITERATURE ABOUT WEEDS

Because there are thousands of species of plants that in one situation or another are considered weeds, describing all of them is far beyond the scope of this book. For aid in identifying your particular weeds and learning about their growth habits and other characteristics relevant to management, we offer the following suggestions.

The easiest way to identify weeds is to compare your live specimen with a good illustrated description of weeds common in your area. Such weed identification literature is often available from your local cooperative extension office.

Perhaps the best and most comprehensive photo-oriented identification tools are *Weeds of California and Other Western States,* vols. 1 and 2 (www.anrcatalog. ucdavis.edu/E-WeedControl/3488.aspx) and *Weeds of the West,* 9th ed. (www.anrcatalog.ucdavis.edu/ WeedsUnwantedPlants/3350.aspx). Both are cooperative extension publications. Most of the weeds in these two books grow throughout the United States and Canada. In both books plants are listed alphabetically by scientific family name, from Agavaceae to Zygophyllaceae.

KEEPING RECORDS

As long as you are taking time to identify the weeds in your garden and learning about their behavior and the beneficial and undesirable roles they play, it would be a shame not to record this information. Not only will it be useful in future seasons, but a written record means that the collected insights from your garden experience will not be lost due to the frailties of human memory.

One of the easiest and most practical methods we've seen for keeping a record of weeds and their management is to preserve samples on plastic-covered cardstock in a ring binder. This simple method results in a portable, easy-to-use reference. Notes on the weed's identity, behavior, and susceptibility to control efforts can be written on cards that are kept next to the specimen in the binder. By noting when weeds show up, how many appear, and what effect they seem to have on the growth of garden ornamentals and food plants, you will, in a season or two, have a reliable means of determining which and how many weeds you can tolerate without harming the functional or aesthetic performance of the garden.

A written record also helps you keep track of whether you are winning or losing the battle with weeds over the long term. Unfortunately, most gardeners we've worked with have not been able to state with any certainty whether the weed populations that show up every season are increasing, falling, or staying about the same. They are also unable to say whether the weeds are generally the same or are shifting to new species—a common result of weed control efforts. Without this information it is impossible to determine the long-term effectiveness of your management methods.

Written records also minimize weed surprises. There's nothing more irritating than having weeds spring up and choke out the petunias, sugar peas, or other plants you spent all weekend putting in the ground. By referring to your notes, you'll know which weeds to expect in various areas of your garden and be able to take preventive action accordingly.

CHAPTER 11

SAFE AND SANE WEED MANAGEMENT

Once you have acquired some biological background on the weeds that grow in your garden and have established realistic weed tolerance levels, you are ready to implement a variety of strategies that will rid your garden of weeds and prevent new ones from taking their place. The key concept here is "realistic weed tolerance levels."

Preventive approaches, called indirect management strategies, focus on reducing or eliminating the habitat that supports weeds. A direct management strategy, by contrast, is one that attacks the weed itself and reduces or eliminates its population, but not the habitat that allowed it to grow in the first place. For the most permanent reduction of weeds (and weeding!) it is wise to use a combination of direct and indirect strategies, as summarized in the chart below.

In IPM and sustainable landscaping, planning is the cornerstone of any project. Take your realistic weed tolerance levels and combine them with your garden/landscape management goals. These management goals include, but are not limited to, what the garden will be used for, time commitments you can realistically make for maintaining the garden, and the kinds of plants you want to grow. When using both indirect and direct weed suppression strategies, be sure to plan your activities thoroughly and assemble all of the tools and supplies necessary to complete the task before you begin your work. Timing is important in weed management, so be prepared to complete each phase of your task in a timely manner so that weeds don't gain the advantage in the garden.

INDIRECT WEED SUPPRESSION

The three major indirect strategies are design/redesign, habitat modification, and horticultural controls.

DESIGN/REDESIGN

The design/redesign strategy focuses on prevention by removing weeds' life supports. It "designs" weeds permanently out of the system, first by identifying current or potential weed habitats, then by creating long-term weed barriers in those habitats. Design is the most important first step in IPM and sustainable landscaping. The design decisions you make on plant selection, garden layout, pathways, hardscape, soil improvement, and other components will determine how much time you will have to spend combating weeds and other pests. Failing landscapes and high pest management inputs are almost always a result of poor initial planning.

Paths, Driveways, and Patios. To reduce the likelihood of weeds growing through permeable pavings of gravel, decomposed granite, brick, or stone, place several layers of heavy building paper or roofing paper on the soil before installing the paving material (as shown at A in the drawing on p. 191). This type of paper is very durable and does not decompose rapidly, as does black plastic material. It will prevent weed growth for many years. This technique is similar to sheet mulching used in new plantings (see the tip on the facing page).

Algae on garden walkways or greenhouse floors can be minimized or prevented by using porous concrete rather than the typical impervious mixture. The porous mix uses no sand and therefore allows water to pass through by gravity. Because

WEED SUPPRESSION

INDIRECT SUPPRESSION (MOST PERMANENT)	DIRECT SUPPRESSION (LEAST PERMANENT)
Design/Redesign Removes life supports, makes life impossible for weeds. **Habitat Modification** Reduces life supports, makes life difficult for weeds. **Horticultural Controls** Reduce life supports, crowd out weeds.	**Physical, Biological, and Chemical Controls** Kill pests directly but may not prevent reinfestation.

the pores are so large, this mixture also prevents water from moving upward through the concrete by capillary action. The formula for the mix (suggested by the staff of Cook College of Rutgers University) is given in the sidebar on p. 191. In sustainable landscaping, pervious concrete is considered the best option for sidewalks, driveways, and parking areas.

A bioswale is a landscape feature that is designed to remove particulate matter and chemical pollutants from surface stormwater runoff, primarily from paved surfaces. The vegetation that fills the swale is selected to slow the water's flow rate so that silt can settle out, pollutants can be absorbed by the plants, and stormwater can infiltrate into the soil. Bioswales reduce silt, pollutants, and the total amount of water flowing into stormwater drainage end points like bays, lakes, rivers, streams, and the ocean. When bioswales are combined with landscaping using pervious concrete, stormwater load in the sewer system is reduced, deep groundwater is supplied to plants during dry weather, and groundwater can even be recharged.

TIP In sheet mulching, recycled cardboard or other organic material is placed directly over weeds or prepared soil. Weed-free compost or topsoil is then distributed on top of the cardboard and overseeded. Plants up to 1 gal. can be planted on top of the cardboard/compost layers; plants larger than 1 gal. require planting through a hole, cut in the cardboard sheeting.

Fences. The soil under and immediately adjacent to wooden fence posts and rails is usually colonized by weeds. Such areas are hard to reach with most weed control equipment, and herbicides can disfigure the finish on the fence and damage garden plants growing nearby. The best solution is to eliminate this weed habitat at the time the fence is constructed by creating a "mow strip."

To do this, lay a 12-in.-wide (30-cm) strip of roofing paper in a line between the fence posts. Cover the paper with clean, coarse sand and lay brick pavers on top. Work sand or dry cement/mortar mix into the paver seams and wet down with a water spray to compact the sand or to wet down the cement. You can also dig a shallow trench about 2 in. deep and fill it with concrete to form your mow strip. The concrete mow strip is usually quicker to make, and there are no seams and joints from which weeds can sprout. Create the mow strip before nailing on the fence stringers and boards. The 12-in. width will cover the soil immediately

The red fescue in this swale slows down the flowing water during a rain event, allowing sediment to settle instead of being washed into the bay. The water also infiltrates into the soil better than faster-moving water. The grass absorbs many of the pollutants that the stormwater has picked up from the pavement. (Photo by Steven Ash)

under the fence and 6 in. (15 cm) either side of it (shown at B in the drawing on the facing page). That way weeds cannot grow up the sides of the fence. If a flower border abuts your fence, the strip will provide an edge against which flowers or vegetables can grow. Stray weeds growing near this edge can be removed easily by pulling or other methods.

Some sources recommend using gravel or bark mulches to cover the roofing paper. If the mow strip is indeed an actual "lawn mow strip," these are bad choices, as gravel and bark can be picked up by the mower and propelled considerable distances. One of us had a car windshield cracked by a lawn-mower-propelled rock from 30 ft. away.

Similarly, if you are building a stone or masonry wall, simply add a 4-in. to 6-in. (10-cm to 15-cm) strip of concrete or brick at the soil surface adjacent to the sides of the wall to create a mow strip. The small concrete strip serves as a surface for one wheel of your lawn mower, as shown at C in the drawing on the facing page; it allows you to keep a neat, flush edge between the lawn and the wall. Consider using recycled concrete pieces to construct walls and mow strips.

In recent years, a new material has become available for mow strips, and it can be used as a border or under a fence line. The mow strip/edging is made of recycled rubber tires that are made to look like bark mulch. The edging is permeable to air and water, and a weed-fabric backing stops weeds. It is quick and easy to install and the cost is competitive. The edging is held in place using landscape staples, available from landscape suppliers. When it comes to mowing along the edging, or mow strip, you can run the wheels along the rubber mat just as you would on concrete or pavers. Millions of tires are discarded every year, so this helps reduce a very serious waste-disposal problem. In fact, similar in one respect to composting, it

A brick mowstrip separates the lawn from the rest of the garden, making mowing much easier and keeping the turfgrass out of the flowers. One wheel of the mower rides on the mowstrip, which means there's no need for an edger or weed whip to tidy up the border. (Photo by Juliette Wade/GAP)

takes a waste product and turns it into a resource. We like the use of recycled rubber for edging and for tree rings on slopes. However, we do not think the use of loose ground-rubber mulches is an environmentally sound idea.

Vegetable and Flower Beds. Instead of growing annual flowers and vegetables in a large patch that provides a habitat for weeds in the spaces not occupied by the plants, consider constructing raised beds with permanent paths between them. You can use wood, brick, or stone to construct frames 8 in. to 10 in. (20 cm to 25 cm) high. Fill the beds with garden soil and nutrient-rich compost or other soil additives so that flowers and vegetables grow rapidly, shading out weeds. The rich, friable (easy-to-crumble) soil can be covered with a mulch to discourage weeds further. Any weeds that do make an appearance are easy to pull out of this moist, organically rich soil. We also recommend that you line the bottom of the raised bed with ¼-in. hardware cloth to prevent burrowing animals, like gophers and moles, from accessing your planters.

When there are gaps in your garden activity (such as during winter or long vacations), the bare soil in these raised beds should be covered with organic sheeting (cardboard or several sheets of newsprint) overlaid with mulch or fitted wooden covers. This helps keep wandering weed seeds from blowing into the soil. The paths between the raised beds can be "weed-proofed" by covering them with a deep layer of sawdust, wood chips, or more permanent paving material (as described in the section on paths on pp. 188–189). Our favorite mulch for paths is sawdust. Not only is it usually available free for the hauling, but microorganisms attempting to decompose the sawdust tie up soil nitrogen at the

FORMULA FOR POROUS CONCRETE

To make 1 cu. yd. of mix, use:

- 2,700 lb. of ⅜-in. aggregate
- 5½ sacks of cement, each 94-lb.
- 22 to 23 gal. of water

The mix is stiff and sets up quickly, so it should be kept damp, particularly when temperatures are high. However, resist the temptation to add too much water. The material should be screeded (finished and leveled on its surface) with a 2×4 board; it should not be hand-troweled, because this works the cement to the surface and creates an impervious layer, just the opposite of what you want. When poured in a 3-in. slab, the working stress of this mix is 600 lb. per sq. in., more than enough to carry foot traffic and garden or other light vehicles.

sawdust/soil interface, rendering it unavailable for weed growth. In this sense, sawdust acts as a very localized herbicide. Therefore, remember to use it only on paths, not on your planting beds. (For ways to design weeds out of lawns, see "Managing Weeds in Lawns," pp. 285–291.)

WEED-FREE GARDEN DESIGN

Good garden design keeps weed habitats to a minimum. An underlayer of roofing paper (A) keeps weeds from coming up through gravel paths. Combining roofing paper and gravel (B) keep weeds from growing along fence lines, and a concrete mow strip (C) makes it easy to mow those plants that would otherwise spring up right alongside a wall.

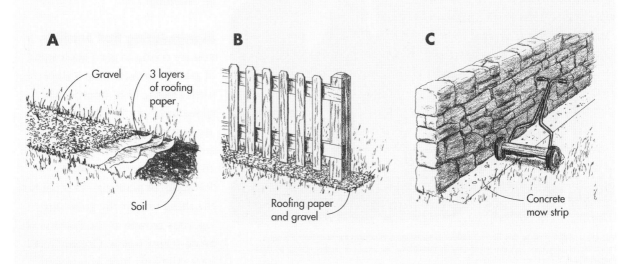

A
Gravel
3 layers of roofing paper
Soil

B
Roofing paper and gravel

C
Concrete mow strip

HABITAT MODIFICATION

When permanent removal of the life-support systems for weeds proves impossible or prohibitively expensive, the next most permanent strategy, habitat modification, should be considered. Modifying the habitat changes the biophysical environment to reduce its carrying capacity for weeds. This is achieved primarily by limiting or manipulating the water, fertilizer, and sunlight needed by weeds.

Limiting Water. Where feasible, use drip-irrigation systems that place water directly in the root zone of ornamental or edible plants. Drip systems apply water slowly enough for plants to absorb most of it soon after it reaches the roots; so little moisture is left over to support weeds. By contrast, overhead irrigation systems apply water indiscriminately over the soil surface, watering both garden plants and weeds.

Subsurface irrigation systems that rely on porous plastic hose are commercially available. This "ooze hose" can be placed 6 in. (15 cm) below the

> **TIP** Subsurface irrigation hoses can save a great deal of water but can be subject to gopher damage and can support fire ants. Experiment first to see if this is a problem.

soil in rows 12 in. to 18 in. (30 cm to 45 cm) apart. Garden transplants are set into the soil above the hoses. Because the moisture is released below grade, roots are encouraged to travel down to the water. The surface of the soil rarely becomes wet, and weed seeds in the top 2 in. (5 cm) of soil—the germination range—are unable to get the moisture required to germinate. Drip and ooze irrigation supplies are carried by many garden and landscape suppliers, nurseries, home improvement stores, and online.

The amount of water available to weeds can also be limited by planting vegetables on raised soil mounds and irrigating them via furrows dug beside the mounds. The furrows and the edges of the mounds where weeds get enough water to grow can be cultivated. Meanwhile, the tops of the mounds remain relatively dry, so few weeds germinate there. This technique may not be effective if the mounds are shallow—less than 4 in. (10 cm) high—or in clay soils or soils very high in organic matter, where water may move upward by capillary action. When this happens, the tops of the mounds become wet after a furrow irrigation, a phenomenon known as "subbing."

Manipulating Soil Fertility. If you are trying to get a good stand of grass to grow to stop a slope from eroding or to improve the appearance of a weedy lawn, an application of high-nitrogen fertilizer—for example, 11 lb. (5 kg) of 16-20-0 mix per 1,000 sq. ft. (93 sq. m) of planting—is often just the thing to spur the grass into vigorous growth at the expense of broad-leafed weeds. Organic fertilizers relatively high in nitrogen,

Burying a soaker hose or drip line will reduce evaporation and protect the hose from the sun's concentrated ultraviolet rays that will eventually breakdown the plastic or rubber. (Photo by Paul Debois/GAP)

A variety of natural and synthetic materials can be placed on the soil surface as mulch to exclude light, inhibiting the growth of weeds. Organic compost (A) must be at least 4 in. (10 cm) deep. Sawdust (B) not only obscures light but also robs nitrogen from the surface of the soil, denying weeds critical nutrients. A synthetic weed mat (C) provides long-term protection from germinating weed seeds and is superior to black plastic in that it allows air and water to penetrate to the soil.

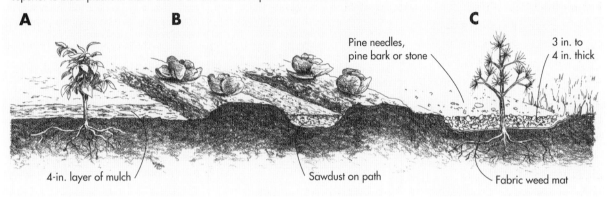

such as blood meal and fish emulsion, can also give turf a quick boost. If you prefer to see a mix of wildflowers and clover, weedy grasses can be discouraged in favor of broad-leafed plants by increasing the amount of phosphorus in the soil—say, 11 lb. (5 kg) of single superphosphate 0-20-0 mix per 1,000 sq. ft.—but not adding any nitrogen. The subject of manipulating soil fertility is dealt with in an interesting bulletin by T. E. Adams and B. Kay, entitled "Seeding for Erosion Control" (University of California Cooperative Extension, 1982). Our preference is to use organic fertilizers when we can; 8 lb. (3.6 kg) to 18 lb. (8 kg) of bone meal, depending on the nutrient analysis, is equal to 11 lb. (5 kg) of single superphosphate. In this case, one drawback is that the nitrogen content of bone meal can range from about 1 percent to 4 percent, whereas single superphosphate has no nitrogen.

Mulching to Limit Light. When weed seeds germinate, they have a finite amount of energy available to them to push up through the soil and reach sunlight. Sunlight is needed by most plants to manufacture, or photosynthesize, carbohydrates used to provide the energy for growth. If you can prevent the germinating seedling from reaching sunlight, it will die without ever making an appearance above the soil. The most practical way to do

this is to cover the soil with a mulch (as shown in the drawing above). Mulches can be composed of organic plant residues, gravel, or manufactured plastic or metal products. The chart on p. 194 lists the pros and cons of some common mulch materials. We recommend the organic mulches, because their breakdown over time adds to soil health and, by extension, to plant health. We discourage the use of plastics because of high-energy inputs and the inability to recycle these materials.

To be effective in preventing or limiting weed growth, mulches must be applied immediately after soil cultivation or other soil disturbance—for example, after pulling weeds or readying the soil for planting. This timing is critical to prevent sunlight from reaching weed seeds brought to the surface when the soil was disturbed; it also prevents migrating seeds from settling in. Thus, it is best to plan thoroughly and have mulch on hand before you begin digging or weeding so you can periodically cover cleared sections before moving on.

Organic mulches must be applied deep enough to overcome the attempts of germinating seeds to get to sunlight. But too much organic mulch can smother the roots of desirable vegetation and impede water penetration and gaseous exchanges in the soil. Thus, on garden beds, you can apply lightweight mulches, such as straw, small-particle

A COMPARISON OF MULCHES

MATERIAL	AREA	ADVANTAGES	DISADVANTAGES
aluminum foil	beds	increases soil temperature, which may increase yields; may inhibit frost injury; repels some insects	expensive; may produce too much heat for ornamentals; must be weighted down or will blow away; tears easily
bark products	beds, paths	come in several sizes—medium and coarse grades best for weed control; can be slow to decompose; attractive	somewhat expensive; small sizes blow away in windy areas; can migrate onto pavement areas
black plastic	beds	easy to apply: lay on soil, cut slits, insert seeds or plants; use at least 6-mil grade for maximum longevity; irrigate soil before laying plastic	nonrecyclable; must be weighted down; weakened by ultraviolet sun rays, breaks down in one season; unattractive; somewhat expensive; roots of plants develop in thin layer beneath plastic, so they are poorly anchored and susceptible to drought
cardboard/newspaper	beds, paths	inexpensive, readily available; use 3 to 6 sheets thick	must be weighted down; unattractive; potential habitat for slugs; inks may contain PCBs toxic to plants
carpet pieces (of natural fiber only)	paths	free or inexpensive; can be rolled up for tillage or planting; retain moisture; if laid with underside up, have brown, earthy appearance; decompose slowly	may become eventual disposal problem; can attract slugs and ants; do not use synthetic fiber
compost	beds	improves soil as it decomposes; free if homemade; attractive	decomposes rapidly
gravel, crushed stone	paths	decorative; packs densely to exclude light; can be used to cover plastic or paper	expensive; can reflect excessive amounts of heat onto plants (use dark colors to reduce heat); semi-permanent, difficult to move
leafmold	beds	free, available, attractive	can be used only with plants suited to acid soils; decomposes rapidly
pine needles	beds, paths	free, attractive; good on paths because leaching stops most plant growth	on beds can only be used with plants suited to acid soils; can be fire hazard when dry
recycled rubber mats (not loose recycled rubber)	Beds, mow strips, tree rings, paths	durable; air and water penetrate easily; can be lifted and moved easily; will not blow or wash away; can be staked down; recycles tires	not always recyclable; expensive; potential habitat for snails and slugs; can get hot on the surface, which can affect plants; do not use "loose rubber" mulch.
sawdust	beds, paths	free or inexpensive; excellent on paths because it depletes soil nitrogen, making weed growth difficult	must be stabilized with nitrogen when used on beds; decomposes fairly rapidly; blows away in windy areas unless kept wet; unstabilized sawdust should not be buried
straw/hay	beds, paths	inexpensive; enriches soil as it decomposes; lightweight, easy to apply; pleasant to walk on	can contain weed seeds; not easy to find in urban areas; unstable in wind; must be stabilized with nitrogen; fire hazard if dry
wood chips	beds, paths	slow to decompose; pack well to exclude light from soil; free from tree-care companies	can contain weed seeds; can be expensive to purchase; can be fire hazard; can migrate unless confined by retaining board
woven weed mats	beds, paths	allow water and air to penetrate soil but screen out light; available from nurseries	nonrecyclable; expensive if used on a large garden

This field of lavender has groundcover aisles between the rows. The aisles can be planted with a mixture of plants that attract beneficial insects. (Photo by FhF Greenmedia/GAP)

bark, or compost, up to 6 in. (15 cm) deep. But heavier mulches, such as wood chips, or mulches that pack densely, such as sawdust or leafmold, should be limited to a maximum depth of 3 in. or 4 in. (7.5 cm or 10 cm). Be careful to keep the mulch several inches away from the stems of plants; when mulch is mounded against plant stems, moisture is retained and disease is promoted. You can apply mulch on paths to a depth of 8 in. (20 cm) or more. Organic mulches decompose over time, so they must be replenished periodically to maintain optimum depth. The decomposition of organic mulches is a wonderful sign; it means that your soil is full of active microbes improving soil structure and fertility.

Bear in mind that most organic mulches are high in cellulose (carbon) and low in nitrogen. This is called the C–N (carbon to nitrogen) ratio. Soil microorganisms cannot get enough nitrogen from these materials to break them down to humus, so the microbes absorb additional nitrogen from the soil immediately adjacent to the mulch. When mixed into the soil, this raw organic matter can cause a temporary reduction in nitrogen available to garden plants and can stunt their growth. To avoid nitrogen deficiencies when using high-cellulose (C–N) mulches such as raw sawdust on garden beds, add 1 lb. (0.45 kg) of available nitrogen per 1,000 sq. ft. (93 sq. m) of mulched area. This is the amount contained in 100 lb. (45 kg) of poultry manure or 200 lb. (90 kg) of cow, hog, or steer manure, or in 10 lb. (4.5 kg) of commercial fertilizer such as a 10-10-10 or 12-12-12 mix. Spade the nitrogen source under with the mulch in the fall. On paths where no plant growth is desired, the addition of nitrogen is not recommended.

HORTICULTURAL CONTROLS

Horticultural controls involve manipulating plant selection, planting techniques, and cultural practices so that desired vegetation grows so densely and vigorously that weeds are crowded out.

Complementary Plantings. Oregon Extension Specialist Jim Green describes these as plantings that are designed "to occupy an environment or space not occupied by crop plants which would otherwise be open for invasion…by weeds…and other uninvited 'guests.' As opposed to pathogenic or competitive organisms that would invade this environment, complementary plantings actively improve the environment of the neighboring crop plant." Applications for this technique in typical gardens include the following:

    1. Sod Aisles. One example of complementary plantings is the use of perennial grass, clover, or other groundcover to provide a permanent cover on aisles between rows of trees, vegetable crops, or flowerbeds. These plants are sown from seed in the aisles; they are then irrigated and fertilized to get them established quickly. Sod aisles should be mowed periodically to control their height and make it easy to walk or move garden equipment along them. Once established, the grass or other plant is an effective barrier to weeds that would otherwise colonize the cultivated soil separating rows of plants. Grasses or other plants with allelopathic traits are excellent choices for sod aisles. Allelopathic plants produce toxins that prevent or stunt the growth of some plant species (see "Allelopathy" on p. 200).

    When creating sod aisles, a quick and efficient method of installation is to use the sheet mulching technique. As mentioned above, sheet mulching uses a layer of cardboard or other organic material directly over weeds or prepared soil. The cardboard is covered with 2 in. to 4 in. (5 cm to 10 cm) of mature weed-free compost and the seeds are sown directly into the compost. The organic sheet layer physically keeps weeds from emerging, and they die. The sheet layer (and covered weeds) eventually breaks down, usually within a few months depending on the season it is laid. The decomposing sheet layer and weeds add more organic matter to the soil. The compost and decomposing weeds provide enough nitrogen to compensate for the high C–N ratio of the cardboard. Avoid additional applications of nitrogen, as this could accelerate the decomposition of the sheet layer, allowing weeds to push through. For more information on sheet mulching, go to www.stopwaste.org.

    At one time sod aisles were standard features in orchards, but the practice of using them was largely abandoned with the advent of herbicides. It is now gaining new popularity as the financial, horticultural, and environmental limitations and hazards of conventional herbicides become clearer. Larger agricultural systems, particularly the efficient polycultures still found in the Third World, have been the traditional settings for complementary plantings, but the use of this technique is also increasing in urban and suburban gardens in the United States and Europe. Many residential and community gardens in Europe have sod aisles as permanent paths between beds containing ornamental and vegetable plants. According to Dr. Green, these paths provide a verdant alternative to gravel, concrete, or asphalt coverings, and they have additional benefits that include the following:

- minimizing freestanding water on the soil surface (the water can contribute to the spread of pathogens)
- facilitating biological control programs by providing host plants for predators and parasitoids and by serving as host sources for mycorrhizal inoculum (beneficial soil fungi that aid plant roots in absorbing mineral nutrients)
- contributing to the maintenance and renewal of soil organic matter and the soil structure, minimizing soil erosion
- removing excess moisture from the root zone in the winter
- conserving moisture in the summer through mulching action

- providing, through the mulching effect, soil temperature modification, thereby protecting roots against freezing in winter and against high summer temperatures
- improving the load-bearing capacity of the soil, which facilitates year-round maintenance

2. Overseeding. Another increasingly common application of the complementary planting technique involves heavily overseeding newly planted shrub beds or groundcover areas with fast-growing annual flowers. These include sweet alyssum *(Lobularia maritima)*, farewell-to-spring *(Clarkia amoena)*, and scarlet flax *(Linum grandiflorum var. rubrum)*. Such plants are colorful temporary fillers that germinate quickly and occupy the soil spaces between slower-growing shrubs or groundcovers. They later give way as the more vigorous landscape plants fill in. Consult your favorite seed catalog for fast-germinating annuals suited to your area.

3. Plant Succession. Perhaps the most imaginative use of the complementary planting concept in urban landscapes that we have observed is that developed by David Bigham, a landscape designer in Berkeley, California. Working almost exclusively with California native plants suited for use in ornamental plantings, Bigham developed a unique planting procedure in which he installs an entire plant succession at once. For each area to be planted, Bigham selects plant species that represent the major stages of a vegetative succession leading up to the final, or climax, planting designed for the site—usually a mixture of groundcovers, shrubs, and trees. This approach takes into account what nature will do to a freshly cultivated planting bed—colonize it with weeds—and essentially outwits nature by including in the design aesthetically pleasing wildflowers or grasses to colonize the typical weed habitat.

TIP It is apparent that some weedy plants, along with some other pest species, have started appearing noticeably earlier in the spring than they did a decade ago. Make allowances for these effects of climate change when scheduling planting dates.

For example, if the ultimate goal is a mature oak grove, Bigham plants the oaks and all phases of the understory at the same time. Such a planting might include a selection of ornamental grasses and wildflowers, semi-woody groundcovers, taller shrubs, and the oak trees. The plants interact with each other much as they would if they were growing under natural conditions. Thus, in the first year or two, colorful grasses, wildflowers, and groundcovers visually dominate. As the seasons pass and the shrubs and trees become well established, they eventually overtop and shade out the lower-growing plants. Finally, the mature oaks largely shade out the understory trees.

Bigham's planting and maintenance techniques work for small- and large-scale landscapes. Because the planting design itself keeps the need for weed control to a minimum, his company is able to maintain plantings even on large private estates in a cost-effective manner, despite the fact that no herbicides are used. Although Bigham developed this method in California, the concept should work in any part of the country as long as the plant species used mimic the local vegetation succession patterns.

When designing complementary plantings, it is critical to select plant varieties that can outcompete weeds but will not unduly compete for the nutrients, light, and water needed by the ornamental or food plants themselves. There isn't much documentation to guide the gardener through such selections, but a few useful resources do exist.

An exhaustive and delightfully written compendium of grasses and legumes (plants that cooperate with soil fungi to produce nitrogen) suited for use as complementary plantings in agricultural and ornamental systems can be found in *Feed the Soil* by Edwin McLeod (Organic Agricultural Research Institute, 1982). The description of each

SMOTHER CROPS IN YOUR GARDEN

If your garden is awash in perennial weeds, try mowing them down in early spring, irrigating, and then using a seed drill (a tool that pokes seeds into shallow pockets in the soil) to plant a smother crop of alfalfa, buckwheat, clover, or other legumes. Mow the smother crop twice during the summer to prevent it or any weeds that have managed to grow from producing seed. In the fall or spring, rototill the smother crop under and plant your garden.

plant species includes a discussion of habit, uses, range, soil preferences, and seeding rates. An excellent discussion of appropriate species and management programs for sod aisles in orchards appears in the handbook *Cover Cropping in Vineyards: A Grower's Handbook*, U.C. publication #3338, from the University of California. Much of the information in this guide appears to be appropriate to other areas of the United States as well.

Seed catalogs usually list appropriate times of the season to plant individual species, as well as the length of time it takes for seeds to germinate after planting. Using this information, you can select candidates for your complementary planting program.

Competitive Planting. Competitive planting entails growing a desired plant to reduce light, water, nutrients, or space available to another plant, in this case weeds.

1. Shading Out Weeds. Sometimes competitive planting is as simple as selecting a plant species that grows so large and rapidly that with just a little help in the beginning it can shade out weeds. An example is corn and common summer annual weeds. If you destroy weed seedlings by running your hoe alongside young corn plants a couple of times in the first two or three weeks after they have germinated, the corn soon grows so rapidly that most remaining weed seeds can't get enough light to germinate, let alone grow. The same is true of ornamental plants such as the daisy-flowered marguerites *(Chrysanthemum frutescens)*, euryops

(Euryops pectinatus), and gamolepis *(Gamolepis chrysanthemoides)*, which soon shade out competing weeds.

2. Using Smother Crops. One of the oldest competitive planting techniques uses smother crops to outcompete weeds. For example, large populations of perennial Canada thistle *(Cirsium arvense)* have been controlled by mowing or tilling and then planting the field in alfalfa or buckwheat. Alfalfa is a vigorous grower whose aggressiveness in exploiting the soil for moisture and nutrients provides severe competition even for the rugged thistles. The alfalfa's ability to colonize the soil environment is enhanced by periodic mowings. By cutting it several times a season, resurgence of thistle is prevented. Within as little as one season the thistle roots deplete their nutrient reserves and die. The alfalfa can be left in place or tilled under in late summer and allowed to decompose, enriching the soil with the nitrogen it produces. In the newly enriched soil, other crops or ornamentals have a competitive advantage over many weeds.

3. Using Barrier Plants. One ingenious use of competitive plantings has been reported from the island of Mauritius, where bermudagrass *(Cynodon dactylon)* is kept out of sugarcane fields by planting a dense row of turf lilies *(Liriope* spp.) at the borders of the cane fields. The lily plant is apparently aggressive enough to keep encroaching bermudagrass out of the cane. This strategy might also be employed at the edges of lawns to keep grass from creeping into adjoining flowerbeds. A number of *Liriope* species are sold in nurseries throughout the United States, particularly in the Southeast, where it is known as mondo grass.

4. Close Planting. If your garden soil is loose, well drained, and full of rich organic compost—which is easy to accomplish through the use of raised beds described earlier—you can plant your vegetables or flowering plants very close together without sacrificing yields. The close spacing will enable the transplants to occupy most of the soil habitat, inhibiting weed germination and shading out those weeds that do manage to lift their leaves above the soil line. This technique is clearly described in John Jeavon's interesting book, *How to Grow More Vegetables Than You Ever Thought Possible on Less Land Than You Can Imagine*, 8th ed. (Ten Speed Press, 2012).

5. Replacement Control. Replacement control involves manipulating the dynamics of natural vegetation to encourage desired species and discourage weeds. Plant ecologist Robert Piemeisel defines this method as that "which employs an indirect means of getting rid of pests through changes in vegetation." This concept has been employed on a large scale at a demonstration project conducted for several decades by the Connecticut College Arboretum in New London in an effort to reduce herbicide use in the management of vegetation growing under power lines and along other rights-of-way.

The focus of the project has been to selectively remove the tall-growing tree species such as oaks, poplars, and maples found under power lines to encourage the development of dense, stable stands of low-growing native shrubs such as huckleberry (G*aylussacia baccata*), low blueberry (*Vaccinium vacillans*), and greenbrier (*Smilax rotundifolia*), as well as herbaceous groundcovers such as little bluestem (*Andropogon scoparius*).

The project has been monitored for over three decades. Researchers have found that once existing trees are removed, there is little or no germination of new tree seedlings in areas where the shrub or grass cover is dense. Where the density of the cover is moderate, only a few tree seedlings manage to germinate. The researchers hypothesize that competition for light, moisture, and nutrients, as well as allelopathy (the ability of certain plants to produce toxic chemicals that prevent growth of other plants) probably account for the ability of well-established stands of shrubs and grasses to keep out trees. This pioneering concept was developed by researchers Frank Egler, William Niering, W. C. Bramble, and W. R. Burns, and has been adopted by a number of Northeast electric utility companies as a successful alternative to the blanket spraying of herbicides on rights-of-way.

If you live in the Northeast or other areas where tree seedlings seem to pop up overnight in your lawn or flowerbeds, replacement control might be a solution. Try covering these areas with a dense stand of attractive shrubs and/or groundcovers. Choose species that are adapted to the soils and climate and have a dense growth form. Many native shrubs that meet these criteria are very decorative and are readily available from commercial nurseries.

TIP If tree seedlings are a problem in a lawn area and you aren't interested in planting shrubs, try planting an allelopathic grass species. These produce toxins that prevent or stunt the growth of certain tree species.

Plant the new shrubs 18 in. to 24 in. (45 cm to 60 cm) apart and apply 3 in. to 4 in. (7.5 cm to 10 cm) of mulch between them, keeping the mulch a few inches away from the stems to prevent moisture and disease problems. In the first season or two while the shrubs are filling in, pull out the seedlings that emerge in the spaces between the shrubs. The mulch will keep the soil moist and friable, making it relatively easy to remove the seedlings (and their roots) by hand. Once the shrubs have fully covered the planted area, tree seeds will find it very difficult, if not impossible, to germinate. You will have to sacrifice some lawn or flower beds to this strategy, but the tradeoff may be worth it if it means you don't have to battle tree seedlings every year. You will find that shrubs require substantially less maintenance time than a lawn, a positive development that promotes more restful weekends.

6. Competition on Ditchbanks and Swales. The collection and transportation of excess water is often achieved through the use of drainage ditches or swales. Water flow in the ditches is frequently seasonal, rendering the ditch a muddy eyesore part of the year and a weed patch the rest of the time. In sufficient numbers, weeds can reduce the carrying capacity of the swale as well as the speed with which water can move along it. Using herbicides in response adds toxicants to the water and creates environments for new weeds by only killing certain weed species.

A very innovative solution was designed by Mike and Judy Corbett and others at the Corbetts' award-winning solar subdivision, Village Homes, in Davis, California (www.villagehomesdavis.org). Among the many energy-conserving features of this unique urban community is the use of swales and percolation ponds to conserve surface runoff and use it to recharge groundwater. This cuts down irrigation needs during the summer dry season, because many landscape plants can use groundwater for moisture.

There are many open swales and other catchment areas throughout the subdivision. Realizing these could become weedy eyesores, Corbett designed them to look like natural creeks and planted easy-to-manage ornamental vegetation that could outcompete weeds.

Varying grades of drain rock and sand were installed at the bottom of the swales to absorb and percolate runoff and recharge the groundwater. The rock layer is 12 in. to 18 in. (30 cm to 45 cm) thick, and serves as a barrier to weed growth. The ditch is intercepted at key points by intake pipes connected to the storm drain system, which acts as an emergency backup during peak water flows.

The sides of the swales were graded at a gentle 4:1 slope to facilitate the planting and mowing of grass. The grass, which outcompetes weeds that would otherwise colonize the ditch, is mowed to a height of 3 in. (7.5 cm) so it does not impede water flow and visually blends with the adjacent turf. Native riparian (stream-side) trees are planted in groves along the artificial creek to promote the effect of a natural stream and shade out undesirable plant species.

Allelopathy. Allelopathy is the ability of certain plants to produce toxic substances in the soil that inhibit the growth of other plants. In other words, this is a kind of biochemical warfare. The drawing at below shows the movement of allelopathic substances from source plant to target plant. The chart on p. 202 lists some plants that are known to have allelopathic effects on weeds.

In her 1978 article, "Allelopathy: Chemical Conversation between Plants," Linda Schenck describes allelopathy as "a process in which a plant adds a chemical compound to the environment that has a deleterious effect on others." She goes on to say that the allelopathic chemicals include:

Phenolic acids, flavonoids, coumarins, quinones and other aromatic compounds, terpenes, steroids, alkaloids, essential oils, and organic cyanides. They reach

---

ALLELOPATHY

Some plants exude toxic substances that inhibit the growth of competing vegetation, a phenomenon known as allelopathy. The source plant releases toxins that vaporize in the air, leach into the soil in rainwater, or are exuded from roots or decomposing tissue. Nearby seeds or plants that are susceptible either fail to germinate or are stunted or killed after contact.

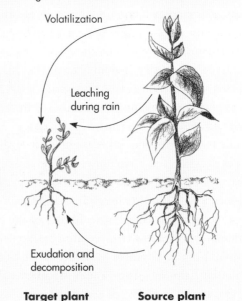

Volatilization

Leaching during rain

Exudation and decomposition

Target plant   **Source plant**

Redrawn from R. J. Aldrich's *Weed-Crop Ecology: Principles in Weed Management* (Breton Publishers, 1984).

the soil by a variety of routes: release by rain wash and fog drip from leaf surfaces and glands, by volatilization from leaves, by excretion or exudation from roots, and by decay of above- and below-ground plant parts directly or through the agency of micro-organisms.

Early plants recognized as having allelopathic properties were walnut trees *(Juglans* spp.) and aromatic shrubs such as sage *(Salvia* spp.). As described by Schenck:

> The principal allelopathic chemical of *Juglans* is juglone, found in a nontoxic form, hydroxyjuglone, in the leaves, fruits and other tissues. Washed by rain from living leaves and released with tannins from dead leaves and fruit, it is added to the soil in its oxidized form, juglone. It selectively inhibits many undergrowth species such as broomsedge, ericaceous shrubs and many broad-leafed herbs, while others, such as black raspberry and Kentucky bluegrass, are tolerant and may often be found as ground cover under walnut trees.
>
> The mechanism operating in the soft chaparral of low, aromatic shrubs is slightly different. In such an area, sage *(Salvia* spp.) and sagebrush *(Artemisia* spp.) often dominate, and some of the terpenes responsible for their fragrance (cineole and camphor) are allelopathic. They volatilize from the leaves into the atmosphere and from there into the soil, where they are adsorbed onto soil particles. Accumulated during the dry summer season, in the spring they show a strong inhibitory effect on the germination of grasses and herbs. By inhibiting respiration and the growth of seedlings that do germinate, terpenes increase the vulnerability of the seedlings to other environmental stresses.

The ability of some plants to inhibit others biochemically was reported as early as 1832 by Alphonse de Candolle, who observed that *Euphorbia* was inhibitory to flax, thistles to oats, and flax to wheat. That toxins accounted for this inhibition went counter to popular theories attributing plant competition solely to the cycling of soil nutrients. But scientific research that challenges conventional scientific or academic thought has often had a rough row to hoe.

> ## "Allelopathy is the ability of certain plants to produce toxic substances in the soil that inhibit the growth of other plants."

L. J. King, in *Weeds of the World* (Interscience, 1966), describes the battle over allelopathy:

> The early work, which touched off the controversy, goes back to the early part of the twentieth century to the studies of Whitney of the United States Department of Agriculture. He believed that unproductiveness of cropped soils was due to the accumulation of toxic substances excreted by each crop plant, which proved injurious to that species of plant (truly an allelopathic action).
>
> This was heresy to Cyril G. Hopkins, of the University of Illinois, who had reduced the soil fertility problem to a bank account system; and who held that nutrient depletion and reduction in crop yields would not occur if certain practices of rotating with leguminous crops, controlling the soil reaction with lime, and using fertilizers to replace the lost elements, were followed . . . . The issue was so sharply defined that it led to a Congressional investigation of the teachings of Whitney and his associates.

Theories about the existence of allelopathy remained controversial until recent years. Research into ways to make use of this aspect of plant behav-

PLANTS SHOWING ALLELOPATHIC EFFECTS ON WEEDS

ALLELOPATHIC PLANT COMMON NAME	SCIENTIFIC NAME	WEED AFFECTED COMMON NAME	SCIENTIFIC NAME
aster	Aster pilosus	common ragweed	Ambrosia artemisiifolia
		wild radish	Raphanus raphanistrum
barley	Hordeum vulgare	common ragweed	Ambrosia artemisiifolia
		redroot pigweed	Amaranthus retroflexus
		purslane	Portulaca oleracea
		foxtail	Setaria viridis, S. lutescens
besom heath	Erica scoparia	various grasses	
bracken fern	Pteridium aquilinum	barley	Hordeum spp.
broomsedge	Andropogon virginicus	pigweed	Amaranthus palmeri
		Japanese bromegrass	Bromus japonicus
		needlegrass	Aristida oligantha
		bluestem	Andropogon scoparius
cereal ryegrass	Secale cereale	green foxtail	Setaria viridis
		redroot pigweed	Amaranthus retroflexus
		purslane	Portulaca oleracea
		common ragweed	Ambrosia artemisiifolia
cucumber	Cucumis sativus	hog millet	Panicum miliaceum
		white mustard	Brassica hirta
dropseed grass	Sporobolus pyramidatus	bermudagrass	Cynodon dactylon
eucalyptus	Eucalyptus globulus, E. camaldulensis	various forbs (broad-leafed plants) and grasses	
Italian ryegrass	Lolium multiflorum	various forbs and grasses	
oats	Avena sativa	redroot pigweed	Amaranthus retroflexus
		wild mustard	Brassica spp.
		barnyardgrass	Echinochloa crus-galli
red fescue	Festuca rubra	various woody plants	
sage	Salvia leucophylla	wild oat	Avena fatua

ior for weed control has received serious attention from researchers; however, this research has not resulted in products available to gardeners.

1. Ryegrass Mulch. One body of research that has reached the stage of practical use for gardeners was conducted under the direction of Alan Putnam at the University of Michigan. First, a study was done to determine which species of cereal grains, such as rye, wheat, and sorghum, would not harm vegetable crops such as beans, peas, tomatoes, car-

rots, and cabbage, but would exhibit toxic effects on weeds generally found with those crops.

Next, a plan for using annual cereal rye (*Secale cereale*)—the most successful of the experimental plants—as an allelopathic mulch for controlling weeds in vegetable crops was tested. Rye was planted as a fall cover crop, keeping the soil from blowing or washing away when the snow melted and emerging in the spring. When it was 12 in. to 16 in. (30 cm to 40 cm) tall, the ryegrass was

ALLELOPATHIC PLANT COMMON NAME	SCIENTIFIC NAME	WEED AFFECTED COMMON NAME	SCIENTIFIC NAME
sagebrush	Artemisia tridentata	wheatgrass	Agropyron smithii
		spurge	Euphorbia podperae
		false pennyroyal	Hedeoma hispida
		pennycress	Thlaspi arvense
		yarrow	Achillea millefolium
		bromegrass	Bromus inermis, B. rigidus
sorghum	Sorghum bicolor	common ragweed	Ambrosia artemisiifolia
		redroot pigweed	Amaranthus retroflexus
		purslane	Portulaca oleracea
		foxtail	Setaria viridis, S. lutescens
sudangrass	Sorghum sudanense 'Piper'	common ragweed	Ambrosia artemisiifolia
		redroot pigweed	Amaranthus retroflexus
		purslane	Portulaca oleracea
		foxtail	Setaria viridis, S. lutescens
sunflower	Helianthus mollis	radishes, wheat	
sycamore	Platanus spp.	various forbs and grasses	
tall fescue	Festuca arundinacea	crabgrass	Digitaria sanguinalis
		various woody plants	
wheat	Triticum aestivum	common ragweed	Ambrosia artemisiifolia
		redroot pigweed	Amaranthus retroflexus
		purslane	Portulaca oleracea
		foxtail	Setaria viridis, S. lutescens

Data compiled from R. C. Anderson et al.'s "Allelopathy as a Factor in the Success of Helianthus Mollis" (*Journal of Chemical Ecology,* 1978); U. G. Bokhari's "Allelopathy Among Prairie Grasses and Its Possible Ecological Significance" (*American Botany,* 1978); M. M. Larson and E. L. Schwartz's "Allelopathic Inhibition of Black Locust, Red Clover, and Black Alder by Six Common Herbaceous Species" (*Forest Science,* 1980); R. H. Lockerman and A. R. Putnam's "Evaluation of Allelopathic Cucumbers (*Cucumis sativus*) as an Aid to Weed Control" (*Weed Science,* 1979); E. J. Peters and A.H.B. Mohammed Zam's "Allelopathic Effects of Tall Fescue Genotypes" (*Agronomy Journal,* 1980); A. R. Putnam and W. B. Duke's "Biological Suppression of Weeds: Evidence for Allelopathy on Accessions of Cucumber" (*Science,* 1974); and D. T. Walters and A. R. Gilmore's "Allelopathic Effects of Fescue on the Growth of Sweetgum" (*Journal of Chemical Ecology,* 1976).

mowed down or sprayed with a short-term herbicide; the residue was left on the soil as a mulch. After about a week, seeds of vegetables not affected by rye toxins were planted through the mulch with a seed drill.

Large-seeded crops such as beans and peas were found most compatible with the mulch. The vegetables germinate and grow up through the rye mulch. As the rye decomposes, toxins are released that inhibit the growth of such weeds as redroot pigweed (*Amaranthus retroflexus*), common ragweed (*Ambrosia artemisiifolia*), purslane (*Portulaca oleracea*), and green foxtail (*Setaria viridis*). Thus, the rye not only produces the usual benefits of mulch—increased soil moisture, greater microbial activity, and buffered soil temperature—but also provides biochemical weed control.

Home gardeners with large seasonal vegetable gardens could plant rye cover crops following the procedure developed at the University of Michigan, or grow a crop of rye in the back area of the garden, mow it monthly, and spread the clippings. Aisles between trees in home orchards might also be planted with rye and kept mowed.

The use of allelopathy for the control of weeds is at the cutting edge of environmentally sound pest management. In addition to looking at ways to use allelopathic plants as mulches, researchers are now trying to isolate the exact chemical toxin(s) responsible for the death of plants in the hope of developing plant-based organic herbicides. In recent years, some new herbicides have been developed that contain plant oils and derivatives. However, their action is physical rather than chemical.

"Early farmers recognized that by growing the same crop in the same place season after season, soil nutrients were used up, crop yields decreased, populations of insects and soil pathogens built up, and weeds became a problem."

2. Tree-Inhibiting Grasses.

Other research projects have looked into the tendency of certain grasses to inhibit the growth of tree seedlings. Botanists Frank Egler, William Nierling, and others in Connecticut and other parts of New England have observed the ability of little bluestem (*Andropogron scoparius*) to inhibit the germination of shrub and tree seedlings. This lovely perennial grass is native to the Midwestern and Northeastern United States, and is available from commercial suppliers of forage seed.

Recently, researchers at the University of Illinois have demonstrated that a common turfgrass, Kentucky 31 tall fescue (*Festuca arundinacea*), inhibits the germination of sweetgum (*Liquidambar styraciflua*) seedlings. In other studies conducted at the Ohio Agricultural Research and Development Center, tall fescue was found to inhibit the growth of black locust (*Robinia pseudoacacia*) and black alder (*Alnus glutinosa*) seedlings. Another turfgrass, Arizona fescue (*Festuca 'Arizonii'*), was shown by USDA Forest Service researchers to inhibit the germination of ponderosa pine (*Pinus ponderosa*).

Many varieties of tall fescue (*Festuca arundinacea*) exhibit allelopathy. This trait is beneficial when growing tall fescue as a turfgrass. In the Midwest the allelopathy of tall fescue has made it an invasive weed in native grasslands and prairie restoration areas. The fescue inhibits native grasses and forbs enough to outcompete them.

Gardeners with unwanted tree seedlings sprouting in their lawns might experiment by seeding tall fescue in the problem areas. It is widely available from commercial nurseries. The research cited above was conducted with the wild species of

A line of Clary sage was planted next to a row of purple Lactuca lettuces. Sage has allelopathic qualities. (Photo by Carole Drake/GAP)

tall fescue, which has a rather wide, coarse blade and is often considered a weed when found growing with finer-bladed turf grasses such as Kentucky bluegrass. Since the late 1970s, however, tall fescue cultivars with narrow leaves have been available. Although most of these cultivars have not been studied for their allelopathic effects, given their parentage, chances are excellent that most will carry the appropriate genes. Other advantages of these grasses are ability to survive drought, low soil fertility, and heavy trampling.

Crop Rotation. The ancient agricultural technique of rotating crops probably developed because early farmers recognized that by growing the same crop in the same place season after season, soil nutrients were used up, crop yields decreased, populations of insects and soil pathogens built up, and weeds became a problem. Weed species with life cycles most like that of the crop plant soon occupied any open soil niches. The same is true in small-scale plantings. Unless the crop plant or the management techniques are changed, weed populations become worse each year, seriously reducing crop yield.

As outlined in *Weed Control*, a report published by the National Academy of Sciences:

Most habitat-management techniques [e.g., crop rotation] rely on sometimes subtle differences between weeds and crops. They usually require more sophisticated manipulations than the simple recognition of differences in appearance and the direct application of physical control methods. Important differences are the life cycles of weeds and crops, specific growth habits, variations in plant morphology and physiology, environmental influences that affect weeds differently than crops, and biotic factors.

Simply put, crop rotation involves following one crop with another that differs in its life cycle and associated cultural practices. This change in crop and culture reduces the habitat for weeds com-

SUMMARY OF HORTICULTURAL WEED CONTROLS

COMPLEMENTARY PLANTINGS
- Using sod aisles.
- Overseeding annual flowers in spaces between immature groundcovers or shrubs.
- Installing an entire plant succession.

COMPETITIVE PLANTINGS
- Shading out weeds.
- Using smother crops.
- Using barrier plants.
- Close planting.
- Replacement control.
- Maintaining grass swards in drainage ditches.

ALLELOPATHY
- Using toxin-producing plants to inhibit germination or growth of weeds.

CROP ROTATION
- Rotating crops so that one crop is followed by a crop with a different life history and cultural requirements. Weeds suited to one crop will have difficulty growing with the following crop.

patible with the previous crop. With the habitat reduced, those weeds are less successful competitors. Though rarely completely eliminated by rotations, their numbers drop to such low levels that they inflict no significant damage on the crop.

Classic crop rotation usually includes strongly competitive crops grown in each part of the rotation. For example, summer row crops such as corn are followed by winter or early spring grain crops, which are drilled or broadcast. The grain crop and cultural practices associated with it suppress the summer annual weeds, such as pigweed (*Amaranthus* spp.), lambs-quarters (*Chenopodium album*), and common ragweed (*Ambrosia artemisii-folia*), which otherwise become pests in the corn. Likewise, the cultural practices used for the corn inhibit the growth of winter annuals, such as wild mustard (*Brassica* spp.), wild oats (*Avena* spp.), and various thistle species that occur in the grain crops.

DIRECT WEED SUPPRESSION

Often you find yourself confronting a weed problem that is too far along to be managed by indirect suppression alone. When quick action is needed, the following direct weed suppression strategies are available: physical or mechanical controls, biological controls, and chemical controls.

Before choosing a direct control strategy, determine whether you are dealing with young or mature weeds and whether they are annuals or perennials. All direct strategies are most effective on young seedlings generally no more than a few inches tall with only three to five leaves. Seedling weeds, whether annuals or perennials, are easy to remove by hand and other non-chemical methods, roots and all.

TIP Put weed seeds in a compost only if you are operating a hot composting system, because cool, slowly decomposing compost piles will not kill weed seeds. All areas of the compost pile must heat up to at least 160°F (71°C).

If annual weeds have grown beyond the seedling stage, it is important to remove them before they produce seeds. At the stage where you can see unopened flower buds, you can often kill annual weeds simply by cutting off the top growth, by hand, with a "weed-eater" or with a lawn mower. This is because weeds at the bud stage have channeled most of their energy into the formation of flowers and seed embryos and have little or no carbohydrates left in their roots to use for regenerating new top growth.

If you wait until the flowers on annual weeds have opened before removing the weeds, there is a danger that the seeds will ripen on the plant even though it has been pulled out of the soil. Therefore, you should not allow mature flowering weeds to lie on the soil. Instead, throw them on a ground tarp or in a wheelbarrow.

If perennial weeds have grown beyond the seedling stage, your efforts must focus primarily on the roots. This is because perennial roots—bulbs, tubers, rhizomes, stolons, crowns, and taproots—produce new top growth if the existing leaves and stems are damaged or removed. Moreover, if the perennial roots are themselves broken apart by the gardener trying to dig them out, each piece may be able to generate an entirely new plant. This is the reason behind the admonition "get the roots" when pulling out perennial weeds.

The energy used to make new top growth comes from nutrients that are produced by the photosynthesizing leaves and sent down for storage in the roots at the end of the growing season. Every time the roots are called upon to initiate new top growth, this store is diminished. Thus, there is a limit to the number of times roots can initiate new foliage in a single season.

Once three or four new leaves have developed, they begin photosynthesizing and take over the job of supplying the energy needed for further growth. During the rapid growth phase of the new plant, the carbohydrates being manufactured by the top growth are used up in the production of leaves, stems, flowers, seeds, and new root hairs. It is not until just after blossoming that surplus nutrients become available for storage in the roots. These nutrients are used to initiate new growth the next season.

This suggests that if your efforts to dig out or otherwise kill mature perennial weeds are insufficient, an alternative strategy is to exhaust nutrient reserves in the roots and prevent their resupply by repeatedly destroying new top growth as it emerges early in the growing season. This forces the roots to use up stored nutrients to develop new stems and leaves. Eventually the nutrient supply is exhausted completely and new top growth does not appear.

A weed knife (A) is used for cutting and digging roots of perennial weeds, short- and long-handled dandelion knives (B, C) for removing taprooted weeds, a long-handled trimmer (D) for chopping annual and perennial weeds, hoes (E, F) for chopping and scraping out seedling weeds, a weed popper (G) for pulling roots of perennial weeds, a briar hook (H) for removing large weeds without bending, a gas or electric weed trimmer (I) for mowing weeds, and a mattock (J) for digging out stubborn roots.

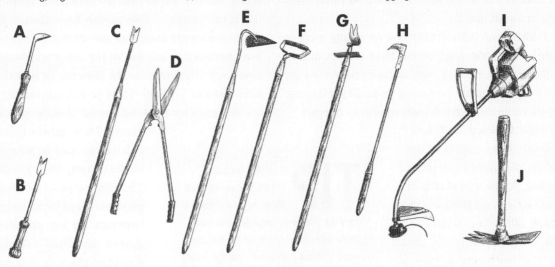

Without leaves to photosynthesize and supply new food, the roots die.

To achieve the greatest effect, top growth should be removed before the weed begins to translocate (move) food reserves down to the root zone for storage for the following season. This translocation occurs just before or during the early stages of flowering. Removal of top growth at this point also takes advantage of the fact that root nutrient reserves are already low, and thus the plant is less able to generate new leaves and stems. Resupply of nutrients also can be reduced by limiting the access of plant leaves to sunlight, water, or minerals.

PHYSICAL CONTROLS

Physical or mechanical controls comprise such familiar methods as hand-pulling, cultivation with various tools, mowing, and mulching, as well as some less familiar techniques such as flaming and soil solarization.

Hand-Pulling. When removing weeds by hand, be certain to get a good grip so that when you pull you get the roots along with the tops. Grip the plant as close to the soil as possible, rock it back and forth a few times to loosen its roots, then pull steadily upward. Failure to pull up the roots usually means the weed will soon push out new top growth and your efforts will be wasted. It is also a good idea to water the soil the day before you intend to weed, because weed roots are very difficult to remove thoroughly when the soil is dry.

When hand-pulling weeds such as dandelions (*Taraxacum officinale*) that have long, fleshy taproots, a hand tool with a 12-in.-long (30-cm) shaft and a V point (B and C in the drawing above) will help you get the entire root. Remember that roots of perennial weeds usually have growth buds along their lengths, and even small pieces left in the soil can produce new plants.

Cultivation. The objective of cultivation is to cut or loosen the weed's roots and expose them to the drying action of the sun and air. If done properly, the roots desiccate (dry out) and die, providing a mulch for the soil. If rainfall or overhead irrigation is plentiful, however, you may be wise to rake up and remove the weeds so that their roots don't become re-established.

Cultivation is most effective on young weed seedlings. At that stage, weeds have not yet developed extensive roots or tops and are relatively easy to control. If you are preparing an area for planting, one effective cultivation technique is to dig out any existing weeds and then cultivate, level, rake, and irrigate the soil where you intend to plant. Allow a new crop of weed seeds to germinate—this usually takes 7 to 10 days—then cultivate shallowly, about 1 in. (2.5 cm) down, and repeat the process, removing the weeds a second time. Plant your seeds or transplants after the second cultivation. This process decreases the supply of weed seeds in the top 2 in. (5 cm) of soil where weed seeds germinate, minimizing the need for subsequent weeding.

Another preventive cultivation method is described by Gene Logsdon, an organic farmer and regular contributor to *Organic Gardening* magazine, who recommends starting "preemergent rake cultivation" three to five days after planting seeds. According to Logsdon, you should:

> Watch the soil surface very closely after you have planted your seed. In about three days, you will notice (in most gardens) many tiny weeds beginning to sprout. A cursory cultivation with the steel rake will kill them.... Just rake gently over the whole planted space, including the rows, to about an inch depth. You won't hurt your seeds if you don't rake as deeply as you planted. You can rake across corn rows even when the plants are coming up if you are gentle about it.

TIP It often makes more sense to rent than to purchase a tool or piece of equipment you may use only once or twice per year. These "shared" rental tools also have less embedded energy of manufacturing when spread among many users.

After the initial raking, rake again once a week for several weeks or until you no longer see the green "fuzz," or "green carpet stage," of weeds. After that, your crop plants will be large enough to shade out any weeds that try to become established.

If the weeds in your garden have already passed the green carpet stage and are several inches tall, hoe them out or use one of the other weed cultivation tools illustrated in the drawing on p. 207. Be sure the tool is sharp. Some power cultivating tools are designed for working among closely spaced plants. These power tiller and cultivators may be powered by either electricity or gasoline. The electric-powered tools, some powered by rechargeable batteries, are less polluting, quieter, and often less expensive than gasoline-powered equivalent tools. Most of these lightweight garden tools are available from rental stores.

In addition to physically removing weeds, cultivating tools can be used to throw several inches of soil into a row of growing vegetables or flowers that are 3 in. (7.5 cm) or more above the ground to bury small germinating weeds.

A stand of established weeds, either annuals with deep, fleshy taproots or perennials with extensive root systems, can be removed with a sharp, pointed shovel or a four-tined digging fork (available from garden centers). These tools help get all the root, reducing the likelihood of new top growth appearing from pieces left in the soil. If perennial weeds are covering a large area, you might be wise to mow off the tops and then rotary-till the area to bring up as many roots for drying as possible. The pieces of root left in the soil after tillage will soon sprout new tops. As soon as they do, till the area again. By repeating the tilling every time you see new flushes of top growth, you will eventually exhaust the food reserves in the roots and the roots will die.

Mowing. Mowing is effective for preventing seed production on medium- to tall-growing annual and perennial weeds. It can also be used to enhance the competitive edge of certain desired species over unwanted ones. A familiar example is using a mower to encourage tillering (the growth of numerous grass blades from a single bud) of lawn grasses, which enables them to outcompete broad-leafed weeds (see chapter 12 on lawn care for further discussion). In addition to suppressing weeds, mowing leaves a vegetative cover that reduces erosion and keeps the soil habitat closed to migrating weed species. The timing of mowing in the life cycle of the plant is roughly the same for annuals and perennials.

The objective of mowing annual weeds is to time the mowing to prevent seed production. This is achieved best by mowing just before the weeds bloom to prevent seeds from forming. Just before blooming the weeds are well on their way to ending their life cycle and may not have enough energy left to produce a second flush of top growth. If you wait until after the blossoms have opened, you may be wasting your time, because many weed seeds are able to mature as long as pollination occurred prior to mowing.

Some weeds, such as yellow starthistle *(Centaurea solstitialis)*, horseweed *(Erigeron canadensis)*, or bitter sneezeweed *(Helenium tenuifolium)*, are able to sprout new stems below the cut. With such species it is best to keep the blade high at the first mowing, then lower it enough at the second mowing to cut off the sprouted stems. By the second mowing the stem is often hard and woody and cannot put out new sprouts below the cut.

The prevention of seed production is one objective of mowing perennial weeds, but an even more important goal is forcing the roots to use up their nutrients, which leads to their death. This is done best by timing the first mowing to coincide with the bud stage of the weeds just before blossoms open. At this stage, nutrient reserves in the roots are lowest, making regeneration of new top growth more difficult. The second and, if necessary, subsequent mowings should occur after regrowth is halfway between your ankle and knee. The mower blade should be set low so that as much top growth as possible is removed.

The number of times you need to mow to kill the weed population depends on which species you are dealing with, how many weeds there are, and how well established their root systems are. If you persist, even the toughest-to-control perennial weeds, such as Canada thistle *(Cirsium arvense)*, will succumb. Canadian botanist Dr. R. J. Moore, writing in the *Canadian Journal of Plant Science*, described a study conducted on a large field in Kansas that was completely covered with this thistle. A series of systematic mowings with the blade as low as possible, one month apart and four times a season, exhausted root nutrients and resulted in the removal of practically all the thistle in two to three seasons.

Weeds can be mowed with rotary mowers (heavy-duty models are available), gas- or electric-powered "weed-eaters," which come with string or blade attachments, or small-scale riding tractors with mower attachments. For slicing weeds

Flamers can be used to control seedling-stage weeds. The heat from the flame causes weed cells to rupture and the weeds dehydrate and die within a few hours. (Photo by Mary O'Malley)

by hand, a well-made, inexpensive, short-handled Japanese sickle called a "kama" is available at some nurseries and from online garden suppliers in the United States.

If mowing is the only strategy used against weeds at a site, there is of course a good chance that weed species adapted to mowed areas will simply move into the area vacated by the weed species killed by the mowing. Examples are weeds with prostrate growth habits and a tolerance for bright sunlight, such as annual bluegrass *(Poa annua)*, a lawn weed, or pigweed *(Amaranthus* spp.), a common garden weed. Thus, it is important that other tactics—smother-cropping and mulching, for

A thumbprint is clearly visible on this miner's lettuce leaf, a sign that the plant has been flamed properly. (Photo by Steven Ash)

FLAMING: THE THUMBPRINT TEST

Leaves that have been heated sufficiently to burst cell walls will feel very soft to the touch and may turn a purplish color before wilting and dying. Try flaming a smooth leaf, then grasp it firmly between your thumb and fingers. If you flamed it properly you should leave a visible thumbprint in the leaf (see the photo above). Thus, when you are first trying this technique, use this touch test on the weeds. With some experience you will learn how long to hold the flame to the plant. Remember that the hottest part of the flame is an invisible cone surrounding the visible portion—you should hold the flamer nozzle an inch or more above the weeds for optimum heating. Test your weed torch at twilight so that you can see the flame completely; it is very difficult to see the flame in full daylight.

example—be used in conjunction with mowing. See Chapter 12 on lawns for suggestions on ways to integrate mowing with other tactics.

Flaming. This technique has been popular in residential gardens in Europe for over 50 years and, in the last 10 years has finally received the attention it deserves in the United States. Before you conjure up an image of massive grass fires and "controlled burns," let us assure you we are not referring to these methods.

Flaming utilizes a propane-gas-fired torch to sear the tops of young weeds. The flame produces temperatures of 2,000°F (1,093°C), heating the sap in the cell walls of the plant tissue and causing the cells to expand and rupture. The weed wilts and dies. This technique is most effective on young annual and perennial weeds in the seedling (four- to five-leaf) stage, because at that point the fragile root system is killed along with the top growth. Weeds growing in dry areas tend to respond more quickly to flaming than those growing in moist habitats, although the reason why is not known. However, drought-stressed plants are less susceptible to flaming than are plants with sufficient moisture.

Mature perennial weeds such as johnsongrass *(Sorghum halepense)*, Canada thistle *(Cirsium arvense)*, and even wild morningglory *(Convolvulus arvensis)* also succumb to flaming, but only after a number of treatments spread over a season or two.

In the United States, flaming, or flame cultivation as it is called in agriculture, was used in cotton and corn fields in the 1930 before the advent of sophisticated herbicides. Its use petered out in the 1950s when the romance with herbicides was going strong. It experienced a revival in the mid-1960s when some of the shortcomings of chemicals, including shifts of weed species, herbicide damage to crops, and cost, made it attractive again. Today, flaming is used to control weeds in row crops, orchards, and along fence lines and waterways. A flamer has even been used to control stray weeds in the pavement in front of the Kennedy Center in Washington, DC. In Europe, flamers are experiencing a renaissance, on organic farms as well as in urban gardens and parks.

A number of hand-held and tractor-mounted flaming tools scaled to various garden sizes are available on the American market; all are powered by propane. Three small weed flamers that run on small bottles of propane are the Primus, Mini-Dragon, and Bernzomatic garden weed torches. The Mini-Dragon and medium to large handheld as well as tractor-mounted flamers are available from Flame Engineering (www.flameengineering. com). Green flaming, as it is now often called, is used extensively in the IPM Program for the City and County of San Francisco. They began using green flamers around 2000, primarily on weeds in paved areas and pathways made of decomposed granite or gravel. We have provided training in the safe use of green flamers to San Francisco City and County gardening staff for over 12 years. In planting beds, where organic matter such as leaves can accumulate, we recommend irrigating the night before flaming weeds to reduce the chances of fire. One gardener on staff at the Strybing Arboretum flames weeds during periods of light rain, because the rain reduces or eliminates any fire hazard. In smaller gardens, weed infestations in confined areas, such as pavement cracks, can be killed with one of the small green flamers.

There is an art and a science to flaming weeds. The mistake people often make is to assume that they must hold the flame on the weed until they see the plant burn up or at least look sizzled and scorched. Nothing could be farther from the truth. The whole point of flaming is to heat the cell sap, which is accomplished by slowly passing the flame over the plant. You may not see any evidence of wilting, let alone plant death, for several hours or even until the next day.

FOR YOUR SAFETY

Green flamer torches operate at around 2,000°F (1,093°C), and they can ignite dried organic matter quickly. Have a charged garden hose with a lever-action pistol-type nozzle handy at all times. If you suspect something is smoldering, or if you see open flame, you have a water source handy to extinguish it before it gets out of hand. It is common to see steam rising from properly flamed plants.

The process was stumbled upon by accident in the 1930s. As reported by Corkins and Elledge in the May 1940 issue of *Reclamation Era*, it happened like this:

John Hendreschke, county pest inspector in the Eden Valley, Wyoming, was burning a patch of bindweed [morning-glory] (*Convolvulus arvensis*), which had developed mature seed. The growth was heavy and thick and John was doing a good job of burning it up. In fact, he was doing such a good job that by the time it was half done, his burning fuel had been three-fourths used up. So it was a matter either of making a long trip after more fuel or taking a chance on getting the job done with a rapid, light burning. He chose the latter and proceeded to quickly sear the tops of the plants on the rest of the patch.

John got his surprise when he went back to treat this patch the next summer. The part, which he had given a "good job" of heavy burning, seemed to have been stimulated by the treatment and the growth was heavier and ranker than before. The part that he had given the "poor job" of light searing of the top foliage was thinned by at least half and the remaining plants were sickly and weak.

Broad-leafed weeds are far more susceptible to control by flaming than are grasses. The fact that grasses evolved in environments where fire was a natural component of the ecosystem may explain the relative heat-resistance characteristic of many grasses. It is also important to note that flaming is most effective on seedling-stage weeds; older plants are more difficult to kill. A final point: Annual weeds succumb to flaming more readily than perennials. One pass with a flamer may kill the tops of perennial weeds, but new growth will regenerate from the below-ground roots. Repeated flaming—several times in a season—eventually starves the roots and kills the weed.

We have used a technique in San Francisco, and in our own gardens, that we call "flame-igation." It is similar to the technique mentioned earlier, where a prepared bed is irrigated and then cultivated twice before planting. We prepare the bed fully for planting and then irrigate. Seven to ten days later we flame the weeds that are at the green carpet stage. We repeat this process and then plant. In newly cultivated areas, or where the soil seed bank is extensive, we may use flame-igation three times on the bed to ensure adequate weed control before planting.

Soil Solarization. Agricultural scientists in Israel developed a practical way to use sunlight to generate soil temperatures hot enough to kill weeds. A clear plastic soil tarp is placed over weeds or cultivated soil containing weed seeds. When daytime temperatures average 85°F (29°C) or more, the tarp traps solar energy, raising the soil temperature to 140°F (60°C) or higher, the thermal death point of the weeds. Black plastic is not used because it does not trap enough heat.

According to Hebrew University of Jerusalem plant pathologist J. Katan, possible mechanisms of weed control by solarization include "direct killing of weed seeds by heat; indirect microbial killing of seeds weakened by sublethal heating; killing of seeds stimulated to germinate in the moistened mulched soil; and killing of germinating seeds whose dormancy is broken in the heated soil."

In the pamphlet "Vegetable Plantings without Weeds," weed extension advisors Kathleen Hesketh and Clyde Elmore outline how this method can be used in cultivated beds in the home garden. First, they write:

Cultivate and rake the soil level, removing large clods. Irrigate the area 1 to 2 weeks before tarping to encourage weed seeds to sprout. An ideal irrigation method is to lay out a soaker hose because the plastic tarp can be placed directly over it as irrigation proceeds. Lightly work the soil to be sure it is level just before or while placing the tarp so that the soil is smooth enough that the tarp lies close to the soil surface. It is essential that the soil be relatively smooth: if there are furrows or large clods, poor

Solarization uses trapped solar energy to raise the soil temperature high enough to kill germinating weed seeds. After cultivating the soil, removing the clods, and irrigating, a plastic tarp is laid on as shown with its edges weighed down to seal in heat. (Photo © 2012 Felix Wong Felixwong.com)

control will result. A smooth, level surface maximizes the high soil temperatures necessary to render seeds unviable. Irrigate again to maximize soil moisture.

A clear plastic tarp should be [at least] 1 to 2 mils (0.001 to 0.002 inch) thick and can be purchased at most hardware stores and many nurseries. Anchor the tarp by burying its edges in a small soil trench around the plot. If a soaker hose is not used under the tarp, or if the area was dry before the tarp was put down, place a hose under the tarp and thoroughly soak the soil with the water on at very low pressure. Because moisture loss by evaporation is minimal under plastic, one soaking is usually sufficient (unless the soil is very sandy). Wait 4 weeks while the sun heats the soil. If tears or rips occur in the plastic, repair them with tape for an air-tight cover.

Once the plastic is removed and the soil has dried somewhat, it is ready for planting. However, if the soil must be worked again before planting, be sure to work it shallowly to 1 inch [2.5 cm]. Weed seeds can be deep in the soil and if the soil is cultivated deeply—down to 4 inches [10 cm] where soil temperatures are not high enough to kill weed seeds—viable seeds may be brought to the surface.

Weeds usually controlled well by this method are annual grasses such as barnyardgrass (*Echinochloa crus-galli*) and wild barley (*Hordeum leporinum*) and some broad-leafed plants such as purslane (*Portulaca oleracea*), pigweed (*Amaranthus* spp.), and cheeseweed (*Malva neglecta*). Even bermudagrass has been controlled if the grass and soil are worked up (incorporated) and irrigated prior to placing the plastic.

TIP Solarization can be used in late fall to warm the soil sufficiently to germinate weed seeds. The tarps could then be removed and the weed seedlings left to freeze.

Research has shown that soil solarization is effective during periods of high temperatures and high light intensity. This usually means keeping the treated area of your garden unplanted for four to six weeks during the prime growing season. However, this sacrifice may be more than offset by the high degree of weed control achieved and the bonus side effects: fewer disease problems and increased yields.

As well as controlling weeds, soil solarization kills many disease-causing soil microorganisms and nematodes while leaving beneficial soil fungi and bacteria unaffected. It also produces an increased growth response, a phenomenon noted at the turn of the century in soils disinfested of pathogens. Katan found that solarization can result in plant growth up to 56 percent greater than in untreated controls. He writes,

A number of mechanisms, not related to pathogen control, have been suggested for explaining increased growth response in disinfested soils: increased micro and macro elements in the soil solution; elimination of minor pathogens or parasites; destruction of phytotoxic substances in the soil; release of growth regulator–like substances; and stimulation of mycorrhizae or other beneficial microorganisms.

BIOLOGICAL CONTROLS

Biological control includes the use of herbivorous insects, pathogens, fish, geese, and livestock to suppress weeds. These tactics have been used since the turn of the century, when the Argentine mothborer (*Cactoblastis cactorum*) was employed in Australia to control prickly pear cactus (*Opuntia inermis* and *O. stricta*), a pest introduced into that country by settlers from South America.

In the United States, beneficial insects have been used successfully to control a number of range

Goats are being used more frequently by water departments to control weeds on watersheds where herbicide use is restricted or prohibited. Here a goat is eating invasive and weedy shrubs on uneven and steep terrain in San Francisco. (Photo by Steven Ash)

and waterway pests, such as St. John's wort *(Hypericum perforatum)* and waterhyacinth *(Eichhornia crassipes)*. Recently a number of fungi that kill certain weed species have been produced commercially for use on range weeds. These pathogens are being called mycoherbicides. At present, however, practical use of mycoherbicides as well as predatory insects and herbivorous fish is generally limited to large infestations of weeds in rangelands, pastures, open-space parks, rivers, and lakes, rather than in residential gardens. In other words, these biological controls are good for use on a community-wide basis but are not yet cost-effective for individual gardeners.

We summarized current information about the most important mycoherbicides in Chapter 8; check there if you want to learn more about them. However, there are other biological control agents that are ready and waiting to help you weed the garden.

Goats. When we first mentioned goats as a possible alternative to herbicides for the control of brushy weeds such as poison oak, the suggestion was met with great skepticism. Weren't goats ornery critters that eat everything off the clothesline and then start in on the dahlias? Well, there may be goats like that, but not the ones we're talking about.

For years, Spanish and Angora goats (Angoras are the small goats whose long shaggy hair is used by weavers) have been used to keep firebreaks cleared of brushy vegetation. These breeds prefer woody vegetation over grasses and forbs (broadleafed plants), and, if managed properly, can convert areas covered with dense brush back to an earlier stage of vegetation, such as grassland. Although goats do eat grasses and broad-leafed plants such as thistles, they look upon them as hors d'oeuvres, preferring for their main course the woodier species such as poison oak and ivy, bamboo, gorse, scotch broom, wild blackberry, and coyote bush.

One pioneer in the use of goats for weed control in urban settings is Dick Otterstad, who formerly operated a goat-based brush-clearing service in the San Francisco Bay area. The primary weed control "tools" of Otterstad's company were small, 125-lb. to 175-lb. (57-kg to 79-kg) Angora and Spanish goats and lightweight, flexible fencing reinforced with electrified wire. (A brief flirtation with dairy goats in the brush-clearing operation was abandoned because Otterstad found them to be "goof-offs" when it came to eating and in need of more care than the other breeds.)

Otterstad discovered the effective role goats could play in urban weed management when searching for ways to respond to customer requests for cost-effective alternatives to herbicides. He was also concerned about reducing the hazards of mechanical and chemical brush clearing on steep slopes, where workers were more susceptible to injury from poison oak, falling brush, chemical spray drift, chain saws, gas-powered weed-eaters, and other equipment. Because the majority of Otterstad's clients were residential property owners with large, steeply sloped, brush-covered lots who needed to comply with fire ordinances, the sure-footed goats were ideal.

Before moving the goats to the site, Otterstad's crew used chain saws, weed-eaters, and brush hooks to clear a fence line and install lightweight, electrified plastic fencing called Flexinet®. The fence keeps the goats in and predators out. It is 30 in. (76 cm) high, augmented by 18 in. (45 cm) of plastic bird netting, all supported on nonconductive fiberglass fence posts. It is pow-

ered by a 12-volt car battery or a solar-fueled battery, and a two-person crew can install 150 ft. (46 m) of it in about half an hour. It proved so effective that only one goat was lost (to a dog) in the four years Otterstad worked with this method.

Once the fence was installed, the goats were moved to the site; up to 20 goats were carried in the back of a standard pickup truck. If wanted trees or shrubs were located inside the area to be cleared, they were surrounded with more electrified fencing to protect them from the goats. This was not always necessary, because goats that were not corralled in one place for too long often showed little interest in munching on established trees as long as there were still woody shrubs around.

The number of goats used to clear a site is determined by such factors as the size of the area, the species of vegetation, the age, and density of weeds to be removed, and the degree of brush destruction desired. By carefully manipulating the size of the herd and the length of time it is corralled at the site, the brush can be reduced in height and volume or can be completely killed so that the species composition is forced to revert to grasses and forbs—an earlier stage of plant succession. The odorless goat pellets increase available nitrogen in the soil, which gives grasses a competitive edge over broad-leafed plants.

Otterstad usually put 10 goats to work at a typical residential site. He found this herd size to be sufficient to clear typical urban hillside lots and remain economically competitive with other brush-clearing methods. The herd and the state of the vegetation were assessed every two to three days. Although goats get all the water they need from vegetation during the winter, supplemental water is necessary in summer and fall.

Experience has shown that although goats can eventually trample and consume even very dense, mature woody vegetation in the initial clearing

TIP We do not recommend buying goats unless you can keep watch over them and protect them from predators, especially stray dogs.

Geese can keep vegetation in check. In one housing development, wild geese keep certain areas of turfgrass so short that it never needs mowing. (Photo by vinciber/Bigstock)

forbs. Some of Otterstad's clients wound up buying one or two goats as a more permanent means of keeping down the brush on their urban and suburban lots.

A 300-goat herd operated by Ken McWilliams with the aid of Australian sheepdogs is currently employed clearing firebreaks and trails for a number of large northern California regional parks and water districts that want to reduce their use of herbicides. For years, McWilliams's herd maintained the firebreaks in the Cleveland National Forest in Southern California; local fire marshals are some of the strongest advocates of goats for brush control. Presumably, this is because much of the fire hazard in their communities comes from weedy vegetation on steep hillsides and other spots easily accessible only to goats.

The City and County of San Francisco and many other Bay Area jurisdictions have used goats to clear brush from watersheds, wildlands, and parks to reduce fire fuel loads or just eliminate unwanted shrubs like poison oak. A few companies in northern California have been established that use goats exclusively for brush control. The goatherds often number 50 to 100 or more goats, depending on the size of the area to be cleared. These companies employ professional shepherds and trained dogs that look after the goats 24 hours a day. During the clearing, the goats don't leave until they are finished. One of the oldest companies is Goats R Us (www.goatsrus.com). Check out their website for more information.

Weeder Geese. Like many old techniques forgotten in the face of modern technology, the use of weeder geese has made a comeback with farmers and gardeners looking for safe and effective ways to control weeds. Geese are grass-eaters, and when placed in a garden or orchard where the crop is a broad-leafed plant, they keep it clear of such aggressive species as johnsongrass (*Sorghum halepense*), bermudagrass (*Cynodon dactylon*), nutsedge (*Cyperus rotundus*), watergrass (*Echinochloa crus-galli*), and crabgrass (*Digitaria sanguinalis*). They have

process, they are most cost-effective when clearing or suppressing 1- to 4-year-old regrowth of brush. When faced with mature brush, they defoliate twigs and strip off bark but leave the plant's superstructure, which is too old and tough to tempt them. In such cases, the goats must be followed by human crews that cut the remaining plant parts with power saws. If, on the other hand, you are removing a thick stand of young thistles or a patch of succulent poison oak or ivy, the goats will kill it quickly.

Once initial clearing has occurred, goats alone can be used periodically to keep the brush cover sparse, or to kill stump sprouts or young woody plants and encourage the growth of grasses and also been reported to eat puncture-vine *(Tribulus terrestris)*, indicating that they're not total "grassetarians" and underscoring the fact that they must be managed properly so they don't damage the crop they're assigned to weed.

Geese have been used extensively to weed cotton fields throughout the United States. Their use as weeders in vegetable and fruit crops and in tree nurseries is on the rise, particularly in organic farm and gardening systems. Any breed of goose can be used for weeding, but the preferred one is the white Chinese weeder goose, developed 2,000 years ago in China primarily for weed control. These geese are lightweight, grow rapidly, are good egg-layers, and appear to be more active than other breeds. Moreover, their light color may make them more adaptable to hot weather. White Chinese geese are available from hatcheries throughout the United States.

Be forewarned, however, that all breeds of geese are noisy honkers, and some adults can be aggressive toward other animals, including humans. These qualities may make them good substitutes for watchdogs, but they also suggest that a degree of caution is advisable when handling them.

Young geese at least 6 weeks old and well feathered are considered the best weeders, because they eat their own weight or more in grass every day. Older geese require food only for body maintenance and therefore aren't as voracious. You don't need a lot of geese to get the job done. In very weedy fields, three to five geese per acre (0.4 hectare) are recommended; in areas with low to moderate infestations, one goose per acre may be all that's needed. Thus, in a residential garden, one or two geese ought to do the job. At the end of the season you can decide whether you want to keep the geese as permanent weeders and egg-layers, or eat them and buy new young ones next year.

DID YOU KNOW?

During the Cold War, regular "infiltration" exercises were held at military installations. The "infiltrators" were able to get by every electronic security measure and even trained dogs. The one security measure they could never get past were "watch-geese" that patrolled between fencerows.

One Missouri gardener kept two adult Embden geese in a run adjacent to her 20-ft. by 60-ft. (6-m by 18-m) garden. The garden was divided by fencing into three areas connected by gates. In fall, the geese were turned onto the entire garden to eat the remains of that year's vegetables. What they didn't eat, they crushed, hastening the decomposition process. The geese remained in the dormant garden, keeping it weed-free until spring planting. They were excluded from one section of the garden while early crops were planted, then moved out of the second section into the run when the rest of the garden was ready for planting.

The geese spent the summer growing season in the run, with daily excursions on the grounds around the house. As soon as the seedlings were about 2 in. (5 cm) tall, mulch was applied between rows. When the crop was a foot tall, stray weeds were pulled and more mulch was applied. Any weeds that grew after that were left for the geese to deal with when they were turned into the garden in the fall. After several years of this routine, the soil in the garden was so friable that cultivation was rarely needed.

"The use of herbicides in home gardens is usually unnecessary."

Geese are most effective if introduced into the area to be weeded just after weed seeds sprout and plants are still young and tender. They can be left in the field or garden until 75 percent to 90 percent of the weeds have been devoured, but should be removed at that point because there is the danger they will begin munching on the crop plant, seeking diversity in their diet. In fact, the provision of extra feed in the form of poultry or rabbit pellets or grain helps keep the geese healthy and growing. In an article entitled "Management of Weeder Geese in Commercial Fields," cooperative extension agent Clarence Johnson recommends that 1 lb. (0.45 kg) of feed supplement per 10 birds be provided daily. When geese are confined overnight, some feed should be provided before they go into the field, because they do not have a crop for storing food as do most other birds. If they are allowed to get very hungry, they may develop digestive troubles after gorging themselves on grass.

Geese also need clean, fresh drinking water and shade from the hot sun. By moving the location of the water and shade structure, geese can be encouraged to weed a given area more thoroughly. Although they don't absolutely need water to swim in, in hot climates they will probably develop leg or foot ailments if they don't have access to a pond or a ditch. In return, they help keep grasses from clogging the waters.

Geese need to be protected from predators such as dogs, which can "playfully" kill a whole flock overnight, and from wildlife such as raccoons, coyotes, weasels, and foxes, which kill geese for food. The Flexinet electric fence (described on p. 215) is an inexpensive means of protection, or you can construct a fence of chicken wire topped with barbed wire. A 2-ft.-high (0.6-m) fence keeps the geese confined, but a 3-ft. or 4-ft. (0.9-m to 1.2-m) fence may be needed if dogs are a problem. The bottom 6 in. (15 cm) of the chicken wire should be bent into an L and buried at least 6 in. (15 cm) under the soil with the bottom of the L pointing outward. This helps prevent predators from digging under the fence.

CHEMICAL CONTROLS

The use of herbicides in home gardens is usually unnecessary. As stated by cooperative extension weed scientists Hesketh and Elmore in their pamphlet, "Vegetable Plantings without Weeds:"

> Chemical weed control is complicated. Most herbicides cannot be used to control all weeds safely in all crops....Residues of some herbicides may remain in the soil and affect the growth of a following crop....It takes much less time and effort in the small vegetable garden to hand-pull or hoe young weed seedlings than it does to read several chemical labels, decide on the proper chemical, check the sprayer, measure the needed amount of chemical, make the application, and then wash the sprayer.

There are the added problems of washing the protective equipment and disposing of the extra herbicide.

It is a testament to the skill of the advertising industry that it has made herbicides seem so easy to use. However, anyone trying to understand the labels on herbicide containers or the recommendations given in weed control literature quickly runs into a bewildering array of herbicide terminology— contact, translocated, selective, non-selective, pre-emergent, post-emergent, soil-applied, foliage-applied, residual, pre-plant, and so on. These and other terms (discussed in Chapter 6) refer, variously, to the ways in which the herbicide acts on the plant and to the point in the plant's life cycle at which the plant is susceptible to the herbicide. These concepts must be understood thoroughly in order to select the right chemical and apply it correctly.

But this is just the tip of the iceberg. An individual herbicide is usually effective only on a fairly limited range of weed species. Its ability to kill those species in a given location depends on a large number of variables, including soil type, climate, available moisture, equipment used, and application technique.

Plant Resistance to Herbicides. If the same herbicide is used year after year on the same weed species, the weeds develop resistance just as insects develop resistance to insecticides. The resistance phenomenon in weeds has been documented primarily for species treated with the triazine class of preemergent herbicides, including simazine (Princep®), atrazine (AAtrex®), and prometon (Pramitol®), which are commonly used on flower-

VINEGAR AS AN HERBICIDE

One interesting recent development has been the discovery that undiluted distilled vinegar is an effective contact herbicide. As an herbicide, vinegar works similarly to the way it does when too much is added to salad, it causes the greens to wilt. Vinegar needs moderate to high temperatures to be effective. Use above 70°F (21°C) for best results, although it can work at temperatures as low as 55°F (13°C). At temperatures above 85°F (29°C) you can almost watch the plants wilt. Some of the new least-toxic herbicides contain acetic acid (vinegar) along with some plant-derived materials, including clove oil, citric acid, lecithin, and lemongrass oil. They may also contain mineral oil and soaps in the form of sodium lauryl sulfate and others. Look for the OMRI symbol on the label; it means all of the materials are organic with minimal processing. And remember, *organic* does not mean nontoxic.

If you are making a homemade vinegar herbicide, mix a little liquid dishwashing soap (not automatic machine detergent) into the otherwise undiluted vinegar. The detergent breaks the surface tension of the water and allows for more uniform coverage of the foliage. Vinegar will wilt almost any leaf it comes in contact with, so be careful when using it around desirable vegetation.

Even though vinegar is a common household product, when used as an herbicide it is important to wear appropriate safety equipment, especially eye protection.

beds, paths, baseball diamonds, and roadsides. However, weed scientists are currently studying the resistance of certain weed species to other classes of herbicides. The failure of most people who use herbicides, including professionals, to understand the complexities of herbicide technology has no doubt contributed significantly to the chronic abuse of these chemicals that has exacerbated the resistance problem.

A brief but useful description of key herbicide terminology and explanations of the various classes of herbicides is provided in Chapter 6. The topic is explored in greater depth in Swan et al.'s *Weed Control on Rights-of-Way*. We recommend that

you read and understand the information in this bulletin before you use any herbicides. We also recommend that you thoroughly protect yourself with gloves, goggles, a respirator, and coveralls when applying these chemicals, because like other pesticides, they are poisons. See pp. 100–101 for a discussion of protective equipment.

Least-Toxic Pesticides. In those rare cases when herbicides are considered necessary, refer to pp. 113–120 for a discussion of soap-based herbicides such as Sharpshooter® and weed oils, which we consider the least-toxic chemical materials available for managing weeds. Information on the many other registered herbicides is available from your local cooperative extension office. Unfortunately, most of these herbicides, in our opinion, have undesirable characteristics, and we try to avoid their use.

Integrating Chemical Controls. Once you have chosen the chemical, it is important that you apply it as selectively as possible; that is, do your best to restrict it to the target weeds and keep it off other vegetation and the soil. This is known as spot treatment, and it is most successful when integrated with other control strategies. To limit the amount of herbicide you must store around your home, we suggest that you purchase herbicides in a ready-to-use (RTU) formulation. These have much lower percentages of the herbicidal active ingredient, which is safer to store. We recommend that you only purchase the amount of herbicide you will need for a particular application. When treating a cut stump (see p. 221), you will need to use a concentrated herbicide, rather than an RTU formulation. Purchase the smallest quantity possible, or even coordinate with neighbors, so that you can use all of the concentrate and will have no need to store the herbicide.

FOR YOUR SAFETY

Do not, under any circumstances, use herbicides containing arsenic compounds, 2,4-D, or 2,4,5-T, because they have been found to pose serious hazards to humans and to the environment.

CONTROLLING POISON OAK AND POISON IVY

Dick Otterstad, owner of Otterstad's Brush Control Service in Albany, California (whose use of goats for clearing was discussed on pp. 214–216), has perfected a technique for cutting out poison oak (*Toxicodendron diversilobum*), handling the debris, and protecting the workers doing the job. The technique will also work for the control of poison ivy (*Toxicodendron radicans*).

OVERVIEW OF THE METHOD

After mechanically flailing (chopping) the plants during the dormant season, Otterstad follows in early spring with a spot treatment of the re-sprouts with small amounts of a translocating herbicide. In contrast to conventional poison oak control methods, which are applied in spring or summer when the plants are in full leaf, Otterstad's method is undertaken largely during the cool winter months when the plants have shed their leaves. Without leaves, there is less surface area from which workers might pick up the toxic oil. Also, the woody structure of the plants is quite visible at that time, enabling the crew to see what they are cutting.

CUTTING

Poison oak is considered difficult to cut because of the springy nature of its many ½-in.-dia. (13-mm) branches, which can whip up and fly against workers. Otterstad solves this problem by carefully removing such growth with power hedge shears. Next he cuts wood up to 2 in. (5 cm) in diameter with a heavy-duty Husqvarna® mechanical clearing saw powered by a 65 cc, 2½-hp gasoline engine. Otterstad prefers this brand because it is well-balanced, maneuverable, and rugged, and the variety of blades available increases the saw's versatility as a brush-clearing tool.

An experienced operator can clear a 5-ft. by 30-ft. (1.5-m by 9-m) stand in about 10 minutes. The flailed material falls to the ground in lengths varying from 1½ in. to 12 in. (4 cm to 30 cm), depending on the operator's technique and the needs of the client. The worker must be careful to cut plants as close to the ground as possible without damaging the sawblade.

DISPOSAL OF DEBRIS

Once the dormant plants are chopped, there are a number of options for handling the debris. Otterstad prefers to flail it into fairly small lengths, compact it firmly on the soil, and leave it to decompose. In his experience, the woody stems do not sprout once they have been flailed, and the decomposing litter helps reduce erosion. It also saves clients hauling and dump fees, and eliminates the often fruitless search for a landfill that accepts poison oak.

To prevent pets or people from coming into contact with the still-toxic remains, Otterstad places logs on top of it or uses a 12-in.-deep (30-cm) mulch of wood chips collected from tree-trimming. The litter can also be buried on the site. Debris that makes good contact with the soil will decompose completely in a season or two, depending on how finely it was chopped.

One of the most significant benefits of integrating chemical controls with other direct and indirect control strategies is that the amount of herbicide needed to control the weeds is reduced. Take, for example, the task of removing a large clump of wild berries, bamboo, or other brush from your garden. Typically the gardener is advised to spray the entire clump of weeds thoroughly so the herbicide comes into contact with more surface area of each plant. But this approach makes it difficult to keep the herbicide from drifting onto nearby plants, including those located in neighboring gardens, or from coating the soil in which the weeds are growing.

An alternative method involves removing as much of the surface vegetation as possible by mechanical means and applying the herbicide to the remaining stems. This reduces the overall amount of herbicide needed to kill the weeds and enables you to use application techniques that confine the herbicide to the weeds. To do this, we recommend the use of a gas- or electric-powered "weed-eater" with a blade attachment to cut the brush as low to the ground as possible. Rake away the severed plant parts to expose the stems left protruding from the ground. Use a hand ax to chop gashes in the stumps to expose more of the internal stem tissue that normally carries nutrients down to the plant roots.

SUBSEQUENT TREATMENT

In early spring, stumps left in the ground after winter flailing put out a flush of leaf growth. At this stage, the live clumps are easy to spot among the dead plant litter and are spot-treated once or twice with an herbicide. By limiting herbicide applications to spot treatments, workers' exposure to herbicides is minimized, and the danger to wanted vegetation from drift is virtually eliminated.

Once the poison oak is removed it is important to alter the habitat to discourage recolonization by poison oak seedlings, which can sprout from seed reserves in the soil. Deep wood chip mulches or vigorous alternative vegetation is recommended.

PROTECTING WORKERS

Workers must be protected from the poison oak, as well as from accidents with power equipment and herbicides. The first step is to use a barrier cream. Otterstad recommends Marvelous Marianne's SkinSafer® Concentrated Barrier Cream to form a protective barrier on the skin. It is sold primarily by art supply stores because painters use it to protect their skin.

To minimize contact with the poison oil in the sap, flailing is scheduled for cool, cloudy, or foggy days when the air is less likely to contain the particulate matter to which droplets of the toxic plant resin can cling. Cool weather also makes workers more comfortable in the somewhat heavy protective clothing, and this in turn reduces exposure caused by wiping off perspiration with oil-contaminated sleeves or gloves. If the toxic oil makes contact with the skin, it can be washed off with a special cleanser such as Tecnu®, available in hardware stores or pharmacies.

Following the maxim "keep covered but cool," crews wear only one layer of clothing. Shirts and sleeves are fully buttoned, pant legs are tucked into boots, and heavy cotton or leather gloves are worn at all times. A helmet with full-face visor protects against flying wood chips. Noise abaters on the helmet guard against hearing loss.

Thigh and shin guards shield workers from poison oil and the occasional rocks and other debris thrown up as the saw moves through dense vegetation. The shin guards are the type made for baseball umpires, and contain a section that also protects the area between the ankle and the steel toe of the boot. The flexible covering over the kneecap is designed to move with the knee.

To protect the thighs, Otterstad and his crew developed a lightweight alternative to commercial equipment. Lengths of corrugated PVC drain pipe are cut with tin snips to fit the thighs of each crew member. Velcro® is used to strap on the guards securely. These homemade devices are flexible and lightweight enough not to impede movement, yet strong enough to provide protection against sharp objects. They can be dropped in a bucket of soapy water to remove any poison oils that collect on them.

This technique is called the cut-stump method of herbicide application.

Using an herbicide that translocates to the roots, apply the strongest solution permitted on the label to the cuts. For the most selective application, apply it with a paint brush or a wick applicator or with a standard 1-gal. or 2-gal. herbicide sprayer, available at nurseries or hardware stores.

For this technique to work, the herbicide must be applied within 30 minutes of cutting open the stumps, because you want the weed's internal plumbing system—the phloem cells—to absorb the herbicide and carry it to the roots. If you wait too long, the plant will place an invisible protective seal over cut surfaces. If you are treating a large area of brushy weeds, it might be difficult to chop down and rake all the foliage and get the herbicide on all surfaces within 30 minutes. Either work on small sections, completing all steps in one section before moving to the next, or simply hold off on chopping the stems with the ax until just before you are ready to apply the herbicide.

It will take several weeks for the underground parts of the plants to die. Some may send up new shoots, which will require spot treatment with the ax and/or herbicide. Resprouting can be prevented by covering the stumps with black plastic after applying the herbicide. However, it is not known to

The "hack and squirt" method of herbicide application (or injection) puts the herbicide directly into the cambial layers where it can be translocated throughout the plant. Another method is to drill holes into the wood and pour herbicide into the hole, which can then be plugged. Both of these methods prevent herbicide drift from the target area. (Photo by Steve Dewey, Utah State University, Bugwood.org)

what degree, if any, sunlight is required by the plant to stimulate the phloem cells into translocating the herbicide to the roots. If you want to try this procedure, wait a few days after applying the herbicide before covering the treated area with plastic.

The integrated methods described here work very well for the control of poison oak *(Toxicodendron [=Rhus] diversilobum)* and would probably also work on poison ivy *(Toxicodendron [=Rhus] radicans)*. The sidebar at on pp. 220–221 describes how they can be used and what precautions must be taken. The sidebar on the facing page tells you what to do if you are exposed to the sap of poison oak or poison ivy.

FOR YOUR SAFETY

In all cases, keep herbicides and other pesticides out of the reach of children and under lock and key.

Methods for Applying Pesticides Selectively.

There are a number of ways to apply herbicides to target weeds that minimize contact with nontarget organisms:

1. Wick Applicators. Wick applicators absorb the herbicide on a rope, sponge, or carpet wick and permit the worker to wipe the herbicide directly onto the target weed. They can be designed or retrofitted with long handles, allowing the worker to stand some distance from the target weed. Hand-held or machine-mounted wick applicators can be purchased from commercial sources online.

2. Injection, Frill, and Basal Application. When using herbicides to kill unwanted woody shrubs, trees, or vines such as poison ivy, use injection, frill, or basal spray techniques where possible. Frill application entails making shallow ax cuts around the circumference of the stem and applying herbicides in the cuts. Basal spraying involves coating the bark on the lower 12 in. to 24 in. (30 cm to 60 cm) of the trunk or stem with herbicide. Herbicide injection tools, which resemble either hatchets or hand guns and are attached by a tube to a pesticide container, are available from forestry equipment suppliers and from landscape and garden equipment sources online.

3. Large-Droplet Sprayers. When foliage sprays are required, use spray nozzles that produce fairly large herbicide droplets to limit drift of the herbicide. It may be helpful to include an anti-drift product in the spray tank. Drift is also minimized by using moderate pressure, which produces relatively large spray droplets. High pressure produces smaller, lightweight droplets that can remain airborne for longer distances.

If herbicides drift onto wanted vegetation or sterilized soil you want to grow plants in, quick action is needed. Detoxifying methods differ, depending on the type of herbicide you are using. Herbicides normally applied to a plant's leaves are usually less damaging to plants when that herbicide is inadvertently applied to the soil than when it drifts onto the desirable plant's foliage. You should rinse the plant foliage thoroughly with plain water for 5 minutes to wash off the herbicide. To minimize damage, rinsing of the foliage should occur as soon as possible following the accidental application. If you wait longer than 1 to 4 hours after contamination to rinse, it is probably too late to avoid damage to the desirable plants. Tainted lawns should be irrigated and then mowed as soon as possible after the accidental chemical exposure. Remove the herbicide-contaminated clippings from the garden.

For soil-applied herbicides, if drift has just occurred, rinse off plants with water. If rain or irrigation has moved the herbicide into the soil, apply as much compost or other organic matter as you can. Organic matter attracts and binds up some

WHAT TO DO IF YOU ARE EXPOSED TO POISON OAK OR POISON IVY SAP

Contaminated skin should be washed several times with water and a strong soap such as Fels Naptha®, tincture of green soap, Dr. Bronner's® Peppermint Soap, or one of the commercial poison oak and ivy preparations such as Tecnu, available in hardware stores and pharmacies and from mail-order suppliers. Cold water is recommended for washing because heat tends to open the pores and allows the sap to enter the lower layers of skin. If soap is not available, you can use vinegar (2 tbsp. in 1 cup of water) or alcohol (½ cup of alcohol to ½ cup of water).

To avoid spreading the dissolved sap over wider areas of skin, dab the vinegar or alcohol onto the contaminated area with a piece of absorbent cotton. Promptly remove the dissolved oil with a dry piece of cotton, discarding each piece as used. Repeat this procedure a number of times. Calamine lotion or a paste of baking soda can be applied to the rash to relieve itching. (Note: Cortisone shots or creams may have dangerous side effects and should only be used with the advice and supervision of a physician.) Healing time varies from a few days to several weeks, and healed sites often remain hypersensitive to further contact with the sap for several months.

herbicide residues, reducing their ability to damage plants. You can also cultivate powdered, steam-activated charcoal into the soil, which absorbs certain herbicides, particularly the triazines, such as simazine (Princep). Herbicide concentrations of 4 lb. (1.8 kg) of active ingredient or less per 100 sq. ft. (9 sq. m) can be counteracted with 1 lb. (0.45 kg) of activated charcoal over the same area. Thoroughly incorporate the charcoal to a depth of 6 in. (15 cm). This treatment should deactivate the herbicide, but it may take up to six months.

If these methods fail, it may be necessary to dig up and remove contaminated turf or soil. The contaminated soil should be composted in its own pile. Microbes will break down the toxicants to some degree, but there is no guarantee that the soil will again support plant growth. In any case, it should not be used to grow food plants.

CHAPTER 12

PREVENTING LAWN PESTS

We discussed changing the name of this chapter to "Preventing Lawns" because attitudes toward lawns have changed so dramatically since the publication of *Common-Sense Pest Control* in 1991. Even as the book went to print, water departments began offering incentives to reduce ornamental lawns, and local governments started passing ordinances limiting the size of lawns to about 10 percent to 20 percent of the total landscape footprint. Most of these changes were in response to drought conditions, especially in California in the late 1980s. The concept of Xeriscaping was emerging, which promoted reducing landscape water use by selecting native and/or water-conserving plants, reducing turfgrass, and hydro-zoning (placing plants with similar water requirements together in the same irrigation zone). We fully support these water-conserving efforts and programs not only from a water-conservation and IPM standpoint but also as a best sustainability practice. Simply put by the Northeast Organic Farming Association (NOFA), "Limiting the size of lawns to what is absolutely necessary reduces maintenance costs and is better for the environment."

Although we fully support the reduction or elimination of ornamental lawns, we understand that most people will want at least some turfgrass for kids, recreation, and/or utilitarian and aesthetic reasons. In this next chapter we will give you information that will help you maintain a healthy lawn while minimizing or eliminating the use of toxic materials. Then you and your family can lay and play on the lawn without being concerned about inadvertent contact with potentially poisonous lawn maintenance chemicals.

Most lawn pest problems can be solved safely by understanding which conditions favor the problem, then changing those conditions as much as possible. This approach—treating causes, not just symptoms—is not the traditional way of dealing with lawn pests. The technical literature or the expert being consulted more often focuses on the identity of the pest organism and on finding the "approved" pesticide for control. Too often the pest is not identified beyond its general appellation: insect, fungus, or weed. As a result, a broad-spectrum pesticide is selected to kill the pest. Thus, lawn pest control becomes a game of matching the pesticide to the pest organism. Unfortunately, this approach leads to the pesticide treadmill and associated problems outlined earlier in this book and ignores the central IPM question: Why is the pest problem occurring in the first place?

Unless this critical question is answered, any treatment, chemical or cultural, is likely to provide only short-term relief. If the conditions making the lawn hospitable to pests are not altered, the pests will return, requiring treatment again and again, season after season. The treadmill effect is worsened by the side effects on the lawn ecosystem of the pesticide regimens outlined in most lawn-care publications, especially the use of broad-spectrum

RESOURCES TO HELP YOU REDUCE YOUR LAWN

Many people are now raising edible plants and native ornamentals where lawns once stood. In her book, *Edible Landscaping,* 2nd ed. (Sierra Club Books, 2010), Rosalind Creasy shows how to create "home landscaping with food-bearing plants and resource-saving techniques" that can be adapted to all climates. If you are looking for primarily ornamentals, *Reimagining the California Lawn* (Cachuma Press, 2011) by Bornstein, Fross, and O'Brien is a great source for ideas. Another great source for garden planning and planting is Nicola Ferguson's *Right Plant, Right Place,* rev. ed. (Simon & Shuster, 2005). Information on over 1,400 plants will help you select the ones that will do the best in your location.

When perusing books from other parts of the country (or state), select the plants you like and go to your local county extension service and ask them to help you find similar plants that will prosper locally. Many extension offices also have master gardeners who can help with plant selection. Be sure to use the services of your local county cooperative extension service; your frequent use helps to ensure sufficient funding. The county cooperative extension service is a branch of your state's land grant university system.

products. Because the pesticide also damages soil organisms that benefit grass growth, grass vigor is reduced—and vigorous growth is the lawn's primary defense against pests, particularly weeds.

In order to explain what might be causing pest problems on your lawn and how you might alter the conditions conducive to pests, let's look at the evolution of a typical suburban lawn and see what lessons can be learned.

THE SAGA OF THE SUBURBAN LAWN

Once upon a time there was a tomato field—or orchard or forest or pasture or hillside—that was converted into a residential or commercial development. First the topsoil was scraped off the land, sold, and carted away. Then bulldozers and other heavy construction equipment ran across the bare subsoil, moving some of it and compacting all of it. The soil on the building pads (which includes the area around the house that many people use for gardens) was compacted to a density of 90 percent or more to meet building codes.

Then construction began. Foundations were poured and innumerable supply trucks drove over the soil, compacting it even more. The soil became the local dump for debris generated during construction, including old crankcase oil from the bulldozers and pickups, leftover cement, paint, solvents, nails, mastic, drywall, "mud" (unused mortar and drywall compound), and a host of other exotic substances.

Upon completion of construction, the soil, including these various "amendments," was either left bare for the prospective homeowner to tend, or a quick landscape "band-aid" was applied. Typically a few inches of imported loam are spread over the compacted subsoil, a layer of sod is rolled out, a few shrubs are planted, and someone is paid to water these doomed plants daily in the hope that they will stay alive until the property is sold. The newly arrived residents are faced with the difficult task of trying to maintain a lawn essentially designed to

die. Or, faced with bare soil, they often create their own version of a lawn band-aid in their eagerness to get something growing as soon as possible.

That lawns can, and often do, survive such

> "Most lawn pest problems can be solved safely by understanding which conditions favor the problem, then changing those conditions as much as possible."

careless installation results from their inherent ability as colonizing species to adapt to adverse conditions. However, lawns with such poor beginnings in life rarely thrive in the long run and require more maintenance than properly installed turf. Even with chemical help, the grass lacks vigor in soil abused by construction activities. It has few resources for warding off insect or disease attack or for competing with weeds. Next we look at why this is so.

HEALTHY SOIL: BUILDING BLOCK OF A HEALTHY LAWN

Grasses have descended from natural environments where they were constantly grazed. Thus, they can tolerate minor feeding by insects and fungi. If, despite this hardiness, your lawn lacks the color, density, vigor, and pest resistance you hoped for, the soil is the first place to look for causes. Grasses, like other living organisms, need food, water, and a hospitable habitat. Their habitat includes the soil in which roots can find the anchorage, air, water, and minerals that support stem and leaf growth.

The most vigorous lawn growth occurs in friable (loose), loamy soils that are teeming with beneficial microorganisms, insects, worms, and other invertebrates (see the drawing on the facing page). This active fauna is entertainingly described for the lay reader in Jeff Lownefels and Wayne Lewis's *Teaming with Microbes: The Organic Gardener's Guide to the Soil Food Web* (Timber Press, 2010) and in James Nardi's *Life in the Soil: A Guide for*

Naturalists and Gardeners (University of Chicago Press, 2007).

These organisms play critical roles in decomposing dead organic matter—such as blades of grass sheared off by a lawn mower—into an end product called humus. Humus increases soil aeration and water-holding and nutrient-exchange capacity, and it buffers the soil pH (its relative acidity or alkalinity). Soils rich in humus provide an environment with a wide margin for error in the growing of lawn grasses. The interaction of the soil flora and fauna with the decomposing organic matter creates a moist, nutrient-rich, buffered habitat where plant roots can survive short-term drought—such as when the family goes away for a summer weekend—or a lack of fertilizer.

THE FOOD WEB OF ORGANISMS IN HEALTHY SOIL

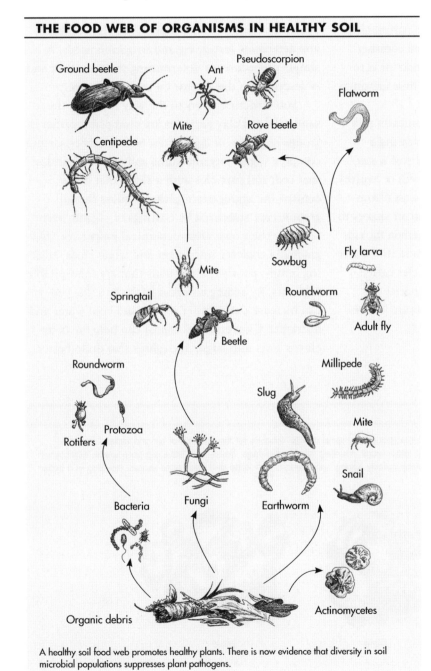

A healthy soil food web promotes healthy plants. There is now evidence that diversity in soil microbial populations suppresses plant pathogens.

Plant resiliency in organically rich soil is the result of abundant food, water, and a protective habitat. All higher plants, be they lawn grasses or trees, acquire food in two ways. Organic foods are manufactured in the leaves through the process called photosynthesis, whereas minerals (there are at least 17 mineral nutrients required by plants) are obtained from the soil by the roots.

To "mine" these minerals from the soil, plant roots need help from other constituents of the soil ecosystem, primarily microbes, especially the beneficial mycorrhizae. Most essential plant minerals are present in the soil in insoluble forms; plants cannot absorb them until microorganisms convert them into soluble states that can pass into the root hairs. Microbes produce many of the acid-forming compounds that break nutrient particles loose from bonds with other minerals, making them available for uptake by plant roots. Microbes are also necessary intermediaries in converting nitrogen from the gaseous state in which it is found in the atmosphere to water-soluble compounds that the plant roots can absorb.

Mycorrhizae, whose beneficial and often essential qualities were realized in the 1970s, have been found necessary for the very survival of many plants. Their presence always increases the health and vigor of the higher plants with which they are associated. There are two general types of mycorrhizae: endomycorrhizae and ectomycorrhizae. As you might suspect, the "endo" live in the plant's roots and the "ecto" live on the surface of the root. Most grass species build a mutualistic partnership with endomycorrhizae. Innoculants are commercially available, some sold as either endo- or ecto- and some as a combination of both. These are often labeled as landscape mixtures.

Soil organisms growing in an organically rich soil substrate also play a key role in creating a favorable balance between soil air and soil water, both of which are essential to the growth of healthy plants. Grasses and other plants take water from the soil through their roots and rely on air spaces to support the exchange of oxygen and carbon dioxide that occurs in root respiration. Soils hold this water and air in openings between soil particles called pore spaces. These vary in size and capacity depending on the soil's texture and structure (see the drawing below).

Soil texture refers to the classification of the rock or mineral portion of a soil by particle size. The largest particles are sand, silt particles are next in size, and clay particles are the smallest. These particles impart physical properties to soils that affect water- and nutrient-holding abilities. Different soils have different proportions of sand, silt, and clay, and thus vary in their moisture content and fertility. Knowing the basic texture of your soil (for example, "sandy," "silty loam," or "clayey") helps you determine fertilizing and irrigation needs. A simple procedure for determining the texture of soil is described in the sidebar on the facing page.

Soil structure refers to the way in which the sand, silt, and clay particles are clumped together in groups of grains, or aggregates. Soil microbes secrete complex sugars (organic gums and polysaccharides) that coat soil particles with a slime that helps cement the aggregates together. Unless the soil granules are stabilized by coatings of organic matter or by their own electrochemical properties, they gradually coalesce into larger and larger clods, creating lumpy, poorly drained soils that are inhospitable to plants. By adding compost to sandy soils, you can increase their ability to trap and hold water and nutrients. Conversely, compost can help break up clayey soils into larger aggregates that drain better.

PORE SPACES IN SOIL

The openings between soil particles are called pore spaces and serve as vital conduits for the passage of air and water. Clay soils have small pore spaces that contain little air but retain water, resulting in poor drainage. Sandy soils have big pore spaces that contain large amounts of air but allow water to drain away quickly. Loamy soils contain both large and small pore spaces, resulting in a better balance of soil, air, and water.

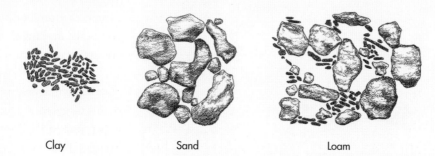

Clay   Sand   Loam

THE TOUCH TEST FOR SOIL TEXTURE

With practice, you can tell soil texture (the proportions of sand, silt, and clay) by touch. Try this touch comparison test with as many different soils as possible.

PREPARATION

Place about a tablespoonful of the soil in the palm of one hand. Then add a little water. (If water isn't handy, saliva works fine.) With the fingers of your other hand, work the water into the soil until the soil is thoroughly wet but still firm; don't use so much water that the mixture becomes runny.

Now perform these two tests:

Test 1: Texture. Rub the mixture out thinly against your palm and note what you feel and see.

- Clay soil feels slippery and becomes shiny when you press down firmly to spread it out. It may also stick to your fingers.

- Sandy soil feels gritty; you may be able to feel individual sand grains. It does not shine. Make sure you take time to mix and knead the soil thoroughly so you won't be deceived into thinking you are feeling sand particles when you are really finding hard clay lumps.

- Silty soil has a greasy feel and slips easily through your fingers as you work it. But it lacks the plastic (moldable) quality of clay soil.

Test 2: Plasticity. The ability of moistened soil to maintain its shape is called plasticity. Roll the wet soil first into a ball and then into a snake as long and thin as possible. Let the last inch or so of the snake overhang the edge of your palm. If the soil is very sandy, this portion of the snake will drop off due to its own weight. If this doesn't happen, try picking the snake up by the overhanging end. The greater the clay content of the soil, the thinner you can make the snake and still be able to pick it up this way. For example, when the clay content reaches about 35 percent, a snake ¼ in. (6 mm) in diameter can be picked up without breaking. Silty soil performs better in this test than sandy soil but not as well as clay soil.

To increase your understanding of how organic material influences soil performance, try mixing a small amount of sifted compost into the sample before you moisten it. The first thing you'll notice is how much more water it takes to moisten the more absorbent mixture thoroughly. If the soil is sandy, you'll see how the organic matter helps the soil maintain its shape; if it is high in clay, the organic matter will prevent it from becoming sticky and unworkable.

Soil Texture Triangle

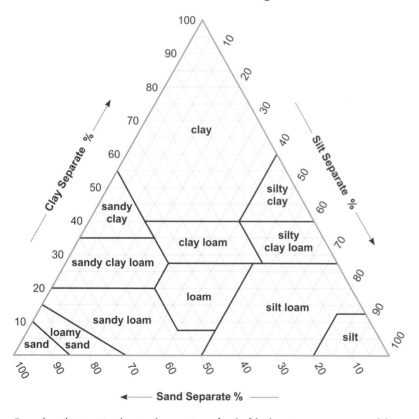

To use the soil texture triangle, enter the percentage of each of the three texture components and draw the appropriately angled lines from those percentages. For example, if your sample is 30 percent clay, 60 percent sand, and 10 percent silt, then your soil is a sandy clay loam, the point where all three lines intersect.

Sweet clover, *Melilotus officinalis*, and all other legumes work with symbiotic bacteria on their roots to fix nitrogen from the air and make it available to plants. Common white clover, growing in your turfgrass, can supply your lawn with as much as a third of its annual nitrogen requirement. (Photo by Dave Bevan/GAP)

TECHNIQUES FOR SOIL IMPROVEMENT

After the preceding discussion of soil composition, it should be clear why it is so difficult for lawn grasses to grow in the compacted, infertile, droughty soils found in typical subdivisions, condominium developments, and other post-construction landscapes. Thus, one of the best investments you can make in your lawn is improving the soil. Below we discuss several ways of accomplishing this.

Planting Clover. If you've just moved into a newly constructed home and are faced with an expanse of bare, compacted soil, you should consider rototilling it, adding as much organic amendment as you can afford, and then sowing sweet clover (*Melilotus* spp.) over the entire area. The clover sends down deep roots, breaking up the compacted soil and raising mineral nutrients such as phosphorus to the upper soil levels, where they become available to later stands of lawn grasses.

The clover has a rich green appearance, produces surplus nitrogen, and encourages the presence of beneficial soil microorganisms. After a season or two it will improve the soil enough so that it can be rototilled under and replaced by lawn grasses. If you don't want to become a slave to the mower, you might even consider keeping the clover.

Top-Dressing. If you already have a lawn and don't want to dig it up in order to improve the soil, you should begin a program of top-dressing. This involves periodically spreading a thin layer—about ¼ in. (6 mm)—of composted organic matter over your lawn. In the first edition of this book, we recommended mixing sand with compost for ease of application. Mixing sand is acceptable in "sandy soils," but in clay soils it acts like an aggregate in concrete. If you must mix something with compost, make it locally obtained topsoil instead of sand. The organic matter can consist of composted manure, sifted garden compost, pulverized fir bark, or other material.

The benefits of top-dressing are documented in a USDA study that found that a top dressing of composted sewage sludge applied to turf at a rate of 3,300 lb. to 6,600 lb. per 1,000 sq. ft. (180 to 360 metric tons per hectare) decreased the bulk density (compaction) of the soil, increased its water-holding capacity and air exchange, and improved the rooting environment for grasses. Increases in pH, phosphorus, and magnesium can also be expected with applications of sewage sludge. The sludge or other organic amendment is consumed by beneficial microorganisms, increasing their numbers and promoting all the benefits they provide, including suppression of weeds and diseases. Top-dressing is also the most effective method for reducing thatch (dead and dying roots and stems) in lawns. It should be applied at least twice a year—in spring and in early fall—particularly in combination with aeration (see pp. 239–240).

However, sewage sludge, derived primarily from municipal sewage treatment plants, is controversial because of potential contamination by heavy metals, pharmaceuticals, persistent organic compounds, and other pollutants not destroyed during the composting process. Questions also have been raised about a possible connection between sewage sludge used on baseball fields and Hodgkin's disease contracted by several athletes. However, there is as yet no documentation of any connection. It also turns out that dogs have an affinity for feces and are therefore attracted to and eat sludge and other manure-based products. Children tend to eat dirt of any kind and will also consume sludge if it is not properly incorporated into the soil. The Organic Materials Review Institute does not certify sewage sludge as an organic material. We suggest that you do a web search for "sewage sludge" and weigh the pros and cons of using this material in your particular situation. There are definitely general benefits to the soil from the use of composted sewage sludge, but we no longer feel we can recommend its use, especially if food crops are going to be grown in the application area. We recommend that you look at the New York state restrictions on the use of sewage sludge.

Pest-Suppressive Soils. By top-dressing your lawn with composted manure, garden debris, or pulverized tree bark, you are quite likely inoculating it with insect and disease-fighting microbes. Plant pathologists are now paying more attention to the role beneficial microorganisms play in suppressing soil-borne plant disease. One aspect of this research involves the identification of "antagonists," usually beneficial fungi, which either outcompete disease organisms in the soil for food and habitat, keeping their numbers low, or attack and kill pests directly by producing antibiotics or other toxic substances. Soils containing high numbers of these antagonists are known as *suppressive soils.* Most of the new lines of "complete" organic fertilizers incorporate beneficial microbes into their products, so that each time you fertilize you reinoculate your soil with beneficials. A "complete fertilizer" is simply one that contains the three familiar macronutrients: nitrogen (N), phosphorus (P), and potassium (K). If the fertilizer formulation doesn't contain all three (N, P, K), it's called an amendment, a nutrient, or a simple fertilizer.

Current research is focusing on beneficial actinomycetes, fungi such as *Gliocladium* spp., *Streptomyces* spp., and *Trichoderma* spp., and bacteria such as *Bacillus subtilis* and *B. penetrans.* A commercial formulation of *Trichoderma* known as BINAB-B has been sold in Europe for a number of years and is used to treat a variety of plant diseases, including Dutch elm

TIP If you use manure as top-dressing, you should be certain it has been through a "hot" compost system that kills seeds. Otherwise, you may find weeds growing in your lawn.

disease and utility-pole decay organism. Israeli studies have found that *Trichoderma* controls a variety of soil-borne diseases, including *Rhizoctonia*, *Fusarium*, and *Sclerotinia*. Many lawn diseases are represented by these genera. *Trichoderma* and other beneficial organisms have been isolated from aged compost (mostly from the centers of compost piles a year or more old) and from pulverized tree bark products sold in nurseries as soil amendments. RootShield® Home & Garden Biological Fungicide, which contains *Trichoderma harzianum* Rifai strain KRL-AG2, is commercially available online as a natural fungicide at the Bio-Works website (www.bioworksinc.com).

A large number of organic lawn fertilizers fortified with disease-fighting beneficial microorganisms are available in the United States. For example, Lawn Restore®, produced by Ringer Corp., contains bone meal, feather meal, soybean meal, and other protein sources plus actinomycetes and bacteria in the genus *Bacillus*. To increase the number of beneficial soil microbes, you can purchase (from garden centers and online sources) a combination of products that contain one or more beneficial species. Enzymatic-type and conventional wetting agents can be used to flush out and leach substances that inhibit high levels of microbial activity in thatch and soil. Use these in combination with products that contain nutrients and extracts from plants and microbes.

Michigan State University researchers led by plant pathologist J. M. Vargas tested these products on Kentucky bluegrass lawns heavily infected with necrotic ring spot, which is caused by the fungus *Leptosphaeria korrae*. Plots treated with the microbe-boosted organic fertilizers three

COMMON COOL-SEASON LAWN GRASSES

TEXTURE (LEAF BLADE WIDTH)

Fine → red fescue
↑ creeping bentgrass
colonial bentgrass
Kentucky bluegrass
↓ perennial ryegrass
Coarse → turf-type tall fescue

NITROGEN NEEDS

High → creeping bentgrass
↑ colonial bluegrass
Kentucky bluegrass
perennial ryegrass
meadow fescue
↓ tall fescue
Low → red fescue

HEAT TOLERANCE

High → tall fescue
↑ meadow fescue
Kentucky bluegrass
colonial bentgrass
red fescue
↓ ryegrass
Low → creeping bentgrass

COLD TOLERANCE

High → Kentucky bluegrass
↑ creeping bentgrass
colonial bentgrass
perennial ryegrass
red fescue
↓ tall fescue
Low → meadow fescue

DROUGHT TOLERANCE

High → tall fescue
↑ red fescue
Kentucky bluegrass
perennial ryegrass
meadow fescue
↓ colonial bentgrass
Low → creeping bentgrass

COMPACTED SOIL TOLERANCE

High → tall fescue
↑ Kentucky bluegrass
perennial ryegrass
meadow fescue
red fescue
↓ colonial bentgrass
Low → creeping bentgrass

WEAR TOLERANCE

High → tall fescue
↑ perennial ryegrass
meadow fescue
Kentucky bluegrass
red fescue
↓ colonial bentgrass
Low → creeping bentgrass

RATE OF ESTABLISHMENT

Fast → perennial ryegrass
↑ creeping bentgrass
meadow fescue
tall fescue
Kentucky bluegrass
↓ bentgrasses
Slow → red fescue

THATCHING POTENTIAL

High → creeping bentgrass
↑ colonial bentgrass
Kentucky bluegrass
fine fescues
↓ perennial ryegrass
Low → tall fescue

From W. Schultz's *The Chemical-Free Lawn* (Rodale Press, 1989).

COMMON WARM-SEASON LAWN GRASSES

TEXTURE (LEAF BLADE WIDTH)

Fine → Coarse

improved bermudagrass
zoysiagrass
centipedegrass
bahiagrass
common bermudagrass
meadow fescue
St. Augustinegrass
carpetgrass

NITROGEN NEEDS

High → Low

dichondra
common bermudagrass
improved bermudagrass
St. Augustinegrass
zoysiagrass
centipedegrass
carpetgrass
bahiagrass

HEAT TOLERANCE

High → Low

zoysiagrass
improved bermudagrass
common bermudagrass
carpetgrass
centipedegrass
St. Augustinegrass
bahiagrass
dichondra

COLD TOLERANCE

High → Low

zoysiagrass
common bermudagrass
improved bermudagrass
dichondra
carpetgrass
centipedegrass
St. Augustinegrass

DROUGHT TOLERANCE

High → Low

improved bermudagrass
zoysiagrass
common bermudagrass
bahiagrass
St. Augustinegrass
centipedegrass
carpetgrass
dichondra

COMPACTED SOIL TOLERANCE

High → Low

improved bermudagrass
common bermudagrass
zoysiagrass
St. Augustinegrass
dichondra

WEAR TOLERANCE

High → Low

zoysiagrass
bermudagrass
bahiagrass
St. Augustinegrass
carpetgrass
centipedegrass

RATE OF ESTABLISHMENT

Fast → Slow

bermudagrass
St. Augustinegrass
bahiagrass
centipedegrass
carpetgrass
zoysiagrass

THATCHING POTENTIAL

High → Low

bermudagrass
St. Augustinegrass
zoysiagrass
centipedegrass
carpetgrass
bahiagrass

From W. Schultz's *The Chemical-Free Lawn* (Rodale Press, 1989).

---

times a year completely recovered from the disease, whereas plots receiving synthetic nitrogen fertilizer experienced a 300-percent increase in disease during the same period. For more details on this research, see p. 280.

Some microbe-enriched products claim to help lawns recover from fusarium, dollar spot, brown patch, and other fungal diseases. We hope that independent research will confirm the effectiveness of these products on common lawn diseases and that the number of such products will increase.

PEST-RESISTANT LAWN GRASSES

Once you have improved the soil, the next item on the pest-prevention agenda is the selection of grasses that grow vigorously in your climate and soils and therefore have the best chance of resisting pests. This is an opportunity to check in with your county cooperative extension service for information on turf types best suited for your location and requirements.

SELECTING THE RIGHT SPECIES

The most commonly sold and advertised lawn grasses are varieties of Kentucky bluegrass (*Poa pratensis*). These grow well in certain climates, but they are not suited to all situations, particularly where rainfall is low and summer temperatures are high, or where lawn maintenance is sporadic and the lawn is frequently walked or played on.

When a grass is ill-suited to the soil, climate, maintenance practices, and other variables that affect lawn health, it does not thrive. Often pesticides are applied with the mistaken notion that these chemical cure-alls will revive the grass. Also, even when grass varieties are bred for disease- or insect-resistance, these qualities may hold true only for certain climatic regions. Yet the grasses are often advertised as having these qualities no matter where they are planted. To make sure that the grass varieties you choose are pest-resistant in your area, contact your county cooperative extension office. The office is in touch with field stations throughout the United States that test the performance of lawn grasses. The National Turfgrass Evaluation Program (www.ntep.org) also evaluates 17 species of turfgrass around the United States and Canada and has great information on turfgrass trials.

Before selecting a species of grass, consider which grasses are suited to the soils and climate in your area, how much maintenance effort you are willing to expend on the lawn, how much and what kind of use the lawn is going to get, what the common lawn pests in your area are, and how much time you are willing to spend on planting and maintenance.

The charts on pp. 232–233 rank lawn grasses on a relative scale according to various horticultural characteristics.

PLANT BLENDS OR MIXES OF SPECIES

To achieve a uniform lawn appearance, homeowners often plant a single grass species. However, if that species happens to be susceptible to a particular disease or insect or cannot tolerate a sudden change in temperature or the availability of water or nutrients, the entire lawn can be lost. Furthermore, single-species lawns grow vigorously only under the seasonal conditions to which they are adapted. There are cool-season turfgrasses and warm-season grasses. If your grass likes the cool conditions of early spring and fall, it may not perform well in the heat of summer unless you maintain it within the narrow range of irrigation, fertilization, and mowing regimens required to keep it growing when it would otherwise become partially or fully dormant.

If a uniform lawn appearance is extremely important to you and if you have the time and resources to maintain the lawn regularly, plant a blend of two or three varieties of the same species

of grass. These blends are composed of varieties that have different levels of pest resistance, color, drought tolerance, and so forth. An interesting phenomenon concerning disease has been observed in such blends. When a disease-susceptible variety is planted with one or more varieties that are resistant to that particular disease, there is an overall reduction in disease that is greater than expected on the basis of the percentage of the varieties in the blend. Thus, if 'Merion' bluegrass, which is notoriously susceptible to stem rust, is planted 50/50 with a resistant bluegrass variety, rust infestations are very slight. Some researchers think the resistance is passed through the roots, but the phenomenon remains largely unexplained.

If you live in a climate with major seasonal temperature fluctuations, or if you don't have the time or resources for regular lawn maintenance, a mix of at least two different species of compatible lawn grasses may be a better choice. Combinations of bluegrass and perennial ryegrass or tall fescue and perennial ryegrass are popular. With multiple grass species, a pest organism may attack one species but

Kentucky bluegrass, *Poa pratensis*, has always been a popular turfgrass. It is usually mixed with other turf species because of its cultural limitations and susceptibility to diseases. (Photo by jlsohio/iStockphoto)

leave the other alone. The unaffected grasses will grow more vigorously, usually masking the damaged grass and providing the overall appearance of a healthy, green lawn. In the past 15 years, we have seen the use of seed mixes containing tall fescue, red fescue, ryegrass, and bluegrass. They are often chosen when broadcasting seed in an area that has several microclimates, a variety of geological features, shade, or other variables. Usually two or three of the species will dominate a particular area, while the other one or two become minor players in the mix.

The importance of planting multiple species where resources for lawn maintenance are low was demonstrated to us as we developed Integrated Pest Management programs for the National Park Service and a number of municipal park systems throughout the United States. Park operators were often caught in the bind of ever-increasing use of lawn areas in the park while suffering budget cuts that reduced labor, equipment, and supplies.

Most of the lawns we observed originally had been planted with Kentucky bluegrass. Although this species flourishes under optimum conditions, it is not very tolerant of neglect, particularly when subjected to heavy use. One of our first recommendations was to change the species of grass to types that could tolerate low maintenance, drought, and heavy wear. One such mix is composed of a fine-bladed tall fescue (*Festuca arundinacea*) cultivar and a perennial ryegrass (*Lolium perenne*) cultivar in a ratio of 80 percent tall fescue to 20 percent ryegrass. Select cultivars of tall fescue and ryegrass based on local performance. Check with your cooperative extension for more information.

Because the parks' low budgets also reduced their use of fertilizer, we recommended adding white Dutch clover (*Trifolium repens*) or strawberry clover (*T. fragiferum*) to the grass mix. Clover, a plant that is maligned as a weed in most lawn-care publications, fixes nitrogen from the air and passes it to grasses via bacteria (*Rhizobium*) that live on its roots. Clover is far more drought-tolerant than most grasses and remains green under the droughty conditions that turn grasses brown.

There are, however, two potential drawbacks to clover. The first is that clover flowers attract bees to the lawn. However, regular mowing usually keeps flushes of bloom to a minimum. Turf specialist John Madison notes that strawberry clover has only a short season of bloom, and bees do not seem highly attracted to it. A second complaint is that clover usually grows in clumps, reducing the uniform look many people desire. Here, the use of strawberry clover may help. Madison found that when strawberry clover is grown with perennial ryegrass and/or tall fescue, it becomes loosely distributed throughout the lawn rather than growing in clumps. He attributes this to the fact that both perennial ryegrass and tall fescue are allelopathic; that is, they release toxins in the soil that weaken the clover enough to prevent it from forming clumps.

One of the most significant results of changing the park lawns from primarily Kentucky bluegrass to a tall fescue/perennial ryegrass/clover mix was significantly reduced weed problems. The drought tolerance, high resistance to wear, and self-fertility of this mix enabled the grasses to grow vigorously. The tall fescue grew well in spring and summer. When it went into a resting stage in fall and winter, the perennial rye grew actively. Thus, there were few opportunities for weeds to invade the lawn despite low maintenance and high use.

GRASSES THAT REPEL INSECTS

In addition to outcompeting weeds, certain tall fescue and perennial ryegrass varieties also resist insect attack. Called endophytic grasses, these varieties contain a symbiotic (beneficial to both organisms) endophytic fungus in their tissues that repels or kills common leaf- and stem-eating lawn insects

DID YOU KNOW?

Some turf researchers estimate that over 30 percent of the annual nitrogen needs of lawns can be provided by clover in the turf mix.

ENDOPHYTE LEVELS IN PERENNIAL RYEGRASSES

Mark Mellbye, Tom Silberstein, and William Young III, scientists at Oregon State University, compiled a list of commercially available perennial ryegrasses and tall fescues by levels of endophytes. The information was obtained from turfgrass seed companies and was not verified experimentally. The collected information is partially summarized below.

VERY HIGH (90 PERCENT TO 100 PERCENT)
Applaud II
Manhattan 3
Paradigm

HIGH (75 PERCENT TO 89 PERCENT)
Imagine
Kokomo 2
Omni
Wizard

MODERATELY HIGH (50 PERCENT TO 74 PERCENT)
All Star 3
Citation III
Indy
Omega 3

MODERATE (25 PERCENT TO 49 PERCENT)
Allaire II
All Sport
Arrival
Charger
Continental
Icon
Rodeo II

LOW (0 PERCENT TO 24 PERCENT)
Buccaneer II
Galileo
Linn
Michelangelo
Newton
Phantom
Quickstart II
Sky Hawk

From M. Mellbye, T. Silberstein, and W. Young III's "Level of Endophyte Infection in Tall Fescue and Perennial Ryegrass" (Oregon State University, 2006). Available at cropandsoil.oregonstate.edu/seed-ext/publications/endo-lev.

such as sod webworms, armyworms, cutworms, billbug larvae, chinch bugs, certain aphids, and Argentine stem weevil larvae. However, root-feeding lawn pests such as "white grubs," a blanket term that includes the larvae of the Japanese beetle and European chafer, do not appear to be repelled by endophytic grasses, probably because the endophytic fungi apparently do not live in the roots of grasses.

The endophyte phenomenon was first discovered by researchers in New Zealand, who found that certain forage grasses harbor fungi that maintain an intercellular relationship with the leaf tissue of the host grass. These endophytic fungi are the source of toxins that accumulate in infected grasses and cause physiological disorders in grazing sheep and cattle. On the other hand, these same endophytic fungi do not harm the grass plant, and, in fact, contribute to the plant's resistance to attack by certain pests. If the grass or clippings are going to be grazed or fed to livestock, it is best to avoid the use of endophytic grasses.

Product literature from the Lofts Seed Company, which markets endophyte-bearing perennial ryegrass, contains the following comments on endophytes and the grasses they inhabit:

An endophyte is a fungus that lives within a plant but is not necessarily parasitic on another plant. The presence of an endophytic fungus produces no known adverse effects to the host plant, but provides many advantages that enhance turf grass performance. Upon seed germination the endophyte grows into the seedling and continues to live in the tissues of the mature grass plant....Resistance has been found with insects, which typically feed on the lower stem, and crown of plants, as these areas normally have the highest concentration of endophytes. Plants containing endophytes may show improved disease resistance, drought tolerance, persistence and seedling vigor. Certified seed of 'Repell' perennial ryegrass is produced to insure that over 80 percent of seed will contain viable endophyte at the date of testing.

Endophyte viability can be lost through normal seed storage within two years, so you should use only freshly harvested seed for insect-resistant turf. Seeds of ryegrass and tall fescue are specially tagged to ensure the presence of the endophyte; to ensure the highest viable endophyte level, the seed should be used within nine months of the test date listed on the package. Cold storage at 40°F (4°C) prolongs endophyte viability.

Endophytes are often present in high numbers in some varieties of tall fescue (*Festuca arundinacea*), and there is scientific documentation of these varieties' resistance to sod webworms, armyworms, and certain aphids. Unfortunately, the level of endophytes varies from one seed lot to the next, and the labels on the seed packages do not contain any information on endophyte content. Turf Seed, Inc. produces commercial varieties of tall fescue that are known to contain endophytes. Plant specialists at the company are currently breeding varieties of tall fescue to increase the endophyte level to 100 percent.

Planting endophyte-bearing grass won't eliminate all insect pests from a lawn, but it will substantially reduce their numbers. As more endophytic grasses reach the market in the next few years, opportunities to reduce pesticide use on lawns will increase accordingly.

DISEASE-RESISTANT GRASSES

Disease-resistant cultivars of most common lawn grasses are available from seed suppliers and nurseries. Once you have selected the species and cultivars you intend to use, you can do a web search to see if those varieties are resistant to the turfgrass diseases common in your area. Remember, however, that resistance can diminish or be lost entirely in the presence of high numbers of disease spores and the temperatures and humidity levels that support them, particularly when these conditions are combined with poor horticultural practices.

Remember that lawn grass seed that shows disease resistance in one location may not retain it under the conditions in your area. To find out which diseases are prevalent locally and which grass cultivars appear to be resistant, consult with your local cooperative extension specialist, the turfgrass department and experts at your state's land grant university, local sod producers, or a local nursery. Their recommendations are based on real observations under local conditions. Note, too, that planting blends of one grass species or a mix of different species—discussed on p. 234—further enhances disease resistance.

GRASS SUBSTITUTES

One important alternative to lawn maintenance is not having a conventional lawn at all. As mentioned earlier, if you want the look of a greensward without the maintenance of a typical lawn, you can achieve a lawn-like look with low-growing ground covers. Clovers, Irish or Scotch moss, creeping thyme (*Thymus serpyllum*), chamomile (*Anthemisnobilis*), Lippia (*Phyla nodiflora*), and creeping mint (*Mentha requienii*) are but a few of the many ground covers that can substitute for lawns. When selecting a turf-grass alternative, check with your cooperative extension service to make sure that you are not buying and planting an invasive weed species for your lawn substitute. You, your neighbors, and local invasive species managers will be happy that you checked first.

Another possibility is to plant grasses that can remain unmowed and still look wonderful. One candidate is creeping red fescue (*Festuca rubra 'Ruby'*). Although its blades grow up to 14 in. (35 cm) long, they lie on their sides, creating glorious swirls and ripples when left uncut. The so-called no-mow fescue is very popular along the west coast, especially where IPM and sustainable landscape practices have been adopted. Some people use a string trimmer to clip off the seed heads and cut the grass down to 4 in. to 6 in. (10 cm to 15 cm) every few years to reduce the buildup of thatch; others just let the new blades of grass cover the thatch. The uncut

This bioswale uses no-mow fescue, *Festuca rubra*, which successfully competes with weeds. Formerly a difficult to mow and weedy drainage ditch, it is now a green swale that requires almost no maintenance. (Photo by Steven Ash)

tufts look particularly good on slopes, where they resemble tumbling ocean waves. These waves of grass also crowd out and smother weeds, eliminating the need for herbicides. Creeping red fescue can tolerate a moderate amount of traffic, and the tufts are wonderful to sunbathe on.

Before planting, you should cultivate the soil and irrigate it to germinate weed seeds. Hoe the weeds out and repeat the process to ensure minimum weed competition with the grass seedlings. Then sow 1 lb. to 2 lb. (0.45 kg to 0.90 kg) of fescue seed per 1,000 sq. ft. (93 sq. m). Once the fescue is well established, it can easily outcompete any weeds that attempt to germinate.

Another grass that can be left uncut is fountain grass (*Pennisetum setaceum*, often sold as

P. ruppelii). It resembles a small-scale pampas grass, with 2-ft.-tall (0.6-m) fountains of leaves and 3-ft. to 4-ft. (0.9-m to 1.2-m) pinkish flower plumes. Once established, it needs little or no summer water.

The most controversial alternative to the conventional suburban lawn is creating a "meadow" by letting an existing lawn go unmowed most of the year and incorporating wildflowers into the grass. You may have seen such meadows on highway median strips, where this technique has become popular. To achieve the meadow effect, cut the present grass as low as possible, or "scalp" it, in early fall or spring, rake up the clippings, scarify (scratch) the soil with a rake, and sow wildflower seeds over the cut grass. The flowers will spring up in the spaces normally colonized by weeds.

You can either let the fall or spring rains germinate the flower seed or you can irrigate. In most areas the meadow will need only a few long, slow soakings during the summer. Mow the meadow down to a 6-in. (15-cm) height at the end of summer, or whenever the wildflowers lose their aesthetic appeal, and spread compost over the mown area in fall. Be warned, however, that some communities have ordinances that require that lawns be mowed and maintained in a conventional manner.

REDUCING STRESS ON LAWNS

If your lawn is attacked by insects, disease, or weed pests, the first thing you should do is determine whether the lawn is under some kind of horticultural stress. A vigorous lawn can usually tolerate significant numbers of pest organisms without showing excessive damage. But if it is suffering from insufficient water or fertilizer, excessive compaction, improper mowing, or other stresses, it generally lacks the resiliency to regenerate portions damaged by pests.

Most significant pest damage results from poor lawn maintenance. The following suggestions for general lawn care will help you keep pest problems to a minimum.

AERATION, THATCH MANAGEMENT, AND INTERSEEDING

When lawns are used heavily or are simply mowed on a regular basis, the soil eventually becomes compacted and the pore spaces that allow water and gases to pass through the soil become compressed. As a result, water is unable to penetrate easily to the root zone, and oxygen used by plants during respiration cannot escape from the soil. These adverse conditions in turn inhibit vigorous plant growth and create an environment that pest organisms exploit.

One way to counteract compaction is to punch holes in the soil once or twice a year using an aerator. Aerators remove soil cores ¼ in. to ½ in. (6 mm to 13 mm) in diameter approximately 3 in.

"FLAME-IGATION"

A somewhat unusual preplant weeding method is to use a combination of green flaming and irrigation, a process we call "flame-igation." Irrigate the finished soil and wait a few days for the weed seeds to germinate and reach the "green carpet" growth stage. Then use a green flamer to kill the weeds. Repeat this two to four times, being sure not to disturb the soil and bring up new weed seeds. Because the weeds are so young they do not have enough reserves in their roots to resprout.

If, however, you wait for the weeds to have two or three sets of true leaves, the perennials among them will resprout. Hold the flame on the plant only long enough to rupture the cell walls, like blanching vegetables. The ruptured cells lose water/sap and collapse. Do not burn the weeds to a crisp, as this can actually increase the weed resprout problem.

(7.5 cm) deep at 4-in. (10-cm) intervals. These openings allow water and air to enter the soil. Such coring, or aeration, also cuts holes through thatch and helps relieve that problem as well.

Coring tools that are pressed into the soil by foot pressure are available from nurseries and hardware stores. They should have hollow tines that remove a core of soil, because spiking the soil with solid tines only worsens the situation by further compacting the soil. Power coring equipment can be rented or the work can be contracted for.

To avoid encouraging weed growth in the aerated lawn, aerate when the grasses in your lawn are growing most vigorously. Sow some grass seed over the lawn after coring, then drag the entire lawn surface with a metal door mat or piece of cyclone fence to break up the soil cores. This is also a good time to apply a top dressing of organic matter, as discussed on pp. 230–231. The dressing helps fill the holes created by the coring and provides a good seed bed for the lawn grasses.

Thatch is an accumulation of dead but undecomposed roots and stems that collects in a layer at the soil surface. If the thatch becomes excessively deep—greater than ¾ in. (19 mm)—water and nutrients do not penetrate the soil adequately. When water puddles on thatch, it enhances the habitat for disease organisms. Regular aeration keeps thatch at an acceptable level, and the use of organic fertilizers such as compost or composted manure promotes thatch decomposition. Synthetic chemical fertilizers, on the other hand, actually enhance thatch development. Excessive layers of thatch can also be removed with de-thatching rakes sold in garden centers, or with power de-thatchers available from the equipment rental firms found in most communities.

Wherever lawns are thinned by aeration, de-thatching procedures, insect or disease attack, or environmental problems such as drought, it is wise to sow seed of desired turfgrasses. The seeds can be mixed into the top dressing of soil amendment or organic fertilizer that is customarily applied to thinned lawns. The grass seedlings usually outcompete weeds that attempt to occupy the openings.

IRRIGATION

Poor irrigation practices encourage a variety of pest problems. Too often, automatic sprinklers are timed to water lawns for brief periods on a daily basis. Although this may be a good idea during the first few weeks that a lawn is getting established, ongoing daily irrigation usually leads to problems. Light, frequent irrigations produce very shallow root systems that make grass completely dependent on artificial watering, and one or two missed irrigations can doom the lawn. In addition, daily irrigations may cause leaching of minerals, resulting in weakened grass plants with a yellowish-green appearance that are more susceptible to invasions by weeds, insects, and diseases.

It is best to irrigate only when the water supply in the soil has been depleted by the lawn sufficiently to require replacement. It is also a good idea to irrigate during the morning in warm weather, because nighttime irrigation encourages fungus diseases. Automatic systems can be set to start irrigating around dawn, when the disease hazard is less, the lawn is not in use, the water pressure is highest and most stable, and there is usually less wind. The morning sun will dry the surface of the lawn before temperatures become high, reducing the likelihood of disease outbreak. Avoid irrigating during daytime hours, especially midday, unless establishing a new lawn. Evaporation is high during the heat of the day and

Weeds and other pests thrive in lawns where there is excessive soil compaction and/or buildup of thatch. Foot- or gas-powered aerators remove plugs of soil, improving aeration and drainage. Under these conditions, thatch is decomposed more easily by soil arthropods and microbes. (Photo by Leigh Clapp/GAP)

AVERAGE DAILY WATER USE BY LAWN GRASSES IN CALIFORNIA

IRRIGATION SEASON	HOT INTERIOR VALLEYS	COASTAL VALLEYS
summer	0.25 in. to 0.35 in.	0.15 in. to 0.20 in.
spring or fall	0.10 in. to 0.20 in.	0.10 in. to 0.15 in.

Note that water use is slightly higher during dry, windy periods or when temperatures are abnormally high.

WATER-HOLDING CAPACITY OF VARIOUS SOIL TYPES

SOIL TYPE	WATER-HOLDING CAPACITY In. per ft. of soil depth	WATER-HOLDING CAPACITY Gal. per cu. ft. of soil
sand	0.8	0.5
loam	1.6	1.0
clay	2.4	1.5

See the sidebar on p. 229 to determine what type of soil you have.

winds are usually higher, so an appreciable amount of your irrigation water will be lost to the air.

To determine when to irrigate and how much water to use, you must first understand a few basic facts about how soils hold and give up water. The following information is abstracted from an excellent pamphlet on this subject entitled "Soil and Water Management for Home Gardeners" by soil specialist B. A. Krantz. The texture and structure of a soil determine the amount of available water the soil will hold at any one irrigation. The bottom chart above gives the approximate water-holding capacities of various soil types.

The depth from which a plant normally extracts water depends on the rooting depth of the plant. Appropriately irrigated lawn grasses normally root in the top 6 in. to 12 in. (15 cm to 30 cm) of soil; lawns irrigated on a daily basis often root only in the top 1 in. (2.5 cm) of soil. The amount of water a plant uses in one day depends on the air temperature and the wind velocity. The top chart above is a general guide to average daily water use in two typical climatic areas of California. Similar informa-

tion for your area can be obtained from your county cooperative extension office or local weather bureau. Ask specifically for the evapotranspiration (Et) rate (the average amount of water that evaporates from the soil on a daily basis).

For example, during the summer, a lawn growing in loamy soil in an interior valley would use approximately 0.3 in. (8 mm) of water per day. Because the top 12 in. (30 cm) of a loam soil holds about 1.6 in. (4 cm) of water, the plants would deplete most of the available water from the main root zone in about five days (1.6 in. divided by 0.3 in.). Thus, irrigation would be required every four or five days.

If you have a sprinkler that applies about 0.5 in. (13 mm) of water per hour and no runoff occurs, a three-hour irrigation would be required to replenish the lost water. In spring and fall, the amount of water required per irrigation would be the same, but the number of days between irrigations would be almost twice as many in fall as in spring.

On vigorous, well-fertilized lawns, the first indication that you need to water is when the imprint

CALIBRATING YOUR SPRINKLERS

To determine evenness of water distribution from the sprinklers, place four or more straight-sided cans (all the same size) at regular intervals in a line running out from the sprinkler. Now run the sprinkler system for a period of time (a 1-hr. period simplifies your calculations). Ideally, when you shut the system off after that time, all the cans should contain the same amount of water, indicating that the water is being distributed evenly across the area served. If they don't, the problem could be any or all of three things: the sprinkler head(s) is spraying unevenly and needs cleaning, the spacing among sprinklers needs adjustment, or there is a drop in water pressure among the sprinklers in the system that must be corrected.

To determine how much water is reaching the lawn on average, add together the measurements you took for the depth of water in each can. Then divide by the number of cans to get the average depth of water per can. If you ran the sprinkler system for 1 hr. and the total amount of water in all four cans was 1 in. (25 mm), the average depth of water in each can is ¼ in. (6 mm). Thus, if you wanted to apply ½ in. (13 mm) of water to the lawn, you would have to run your system for two hours. Generally, the amount of water delivered by sprinklers, known as the precipitation rate (PR), ranges from ⅒ in. (2.5 mm) to 1 in. (25 mm) per hr. Check the specifications for your sprinkler heads (nozzles) to find the manufacturer's listed precipitation rates.

of your foot remains visible in the grass for a few minutes or if the grass in areas that dry out fastest becomes dull and turns a bluish-green or yellow. You can also determine when to irrigate by poking a sharp metal rod such as a screwdriver into the soil. If it penetrates easily to a depth of 6 in. to 8 in. (15 cm to 20 cm), the soil is probably wet and irrigation is not needed. If you can't get the rod to sink more than an inch or so, the soil is probably dry. Tensiometers, available from garden suppliers, are more sophisticated tools that can be used to measure available water in the soil; some versions can be incorporated into an automated irrigation system. Hand-held models are available, but they are expensive and require some expertise to use.

To decide how long to leave your sprinklers on, you must know how much water they deliver over a given period. The sidebar at left explains how to determine this. Check with your local water department to see if they offer irrigation water audits or other assistance in conserving landscape water. The audit process will provide you with information on the efficiency of your irrigation system and its distribution uniformity. An irrigation schedule will be provided that will show how long you should run your system, based on the evapotranspiration rate for your area.

You should irrigate a lawn slowly enough that the water soaks into the soil immediately without runoff. If runoff occurs, stop watering for an hour or two, then continue until enough water has been applied. Remember to irrigate thoroughly but as infrequently as possible. Frequent, shallow irrigation causes more water to be lost from the surface through evaporation than does infrequent, deep watering.

If your lawn is over- or under-watered, it not only invites pest insects and diseases, but it can also mask the symptoms of pests for a longer period than would otherwise be the case, preventing you from taking early remedial action. This is especially true of lawns that receive too little water.

In *Turfgrass Insects of the United States and Canada* (Cornell University Press, 1987), H. Tashiro writes:

> Two groups of insects, the chinch bugs and sod webworms, do most of their damage during periods of high temperature and moisture stress, with the grass going into dormancy. The dormancy of the turfgrass makes it impossible or very difficult to detect early symptoms of damage. Only after heavy precipitation and greening of the healthy grass does the insect damage become apparent, often after irreversible damage has taken place . . . . When the turf is growing steadily at adequate moisture levels, symptoms of early insect damage are much more

readily detected in the form of yellow leaves and small patches of brown.

FERTILIZING

The type and amount of fertilizer applied to a lawn plays a significant role in determining the presence or absence of pests. Because nutrition is such an important variable in lawn pest management, it is worth spending a little time learning about the below-ground food factory your grass relies on.

Calcium. Calcium is the key to balanced soil fertility. If you have read about basic lawn fertilization, your reaction is probably, "Hey, wait a minute! I thought nitrogen was the key to healthy lawns." It is true that modern lawn-care literature is dominated by an emphasis on nitrogen fertilization, but we do not agree with this approach.

Our emphasis on the key role of calcium is based upon the pioneering work of Dr. William A. Albrecht, microbiologist and soil scientist at the University of Missouri, who earned his Ph.D. in 1919 and whose career spanned more than 60 years. The fruits of his insights into soil fertility are collected in a book entitled *The Albrecht Papers,* vols. 1 and 2, edited by Charles Walter (Acres USA, 2005, 2011), which we recommend for anyone who grows plants.

Albrecht studied the cation exchange capacity of soils. This is the process whereby plant nutrients containing positive electrical charges (cations) are held on particles of clay soil or organic matter that have a negative charge. Cations are loosened from their electrical bonds to the clay or organic matter particles only in the presence of hydrogen ions, which knock them off the soil colloid, enabling them to be absorbed by plant roots.

Albrecht's study convinced him there was a critical proportion of calcium relative to other mineral nutrients. By artificially stripping all nutrient cations off a particle of clay soil in the laboratory and then slowly adding them back, he adjusted the proportion of the cations until he achieved optimum growth of laboratory plants. The proportion of cations that worked best was as follows:

Calcium	60 percent to 75 percent
Magnesium	10 percent to 20 percent
Hydrogen	10 percent
Potassium	2 percent to 5 percent
Sodium	0.5 percent to 5 percent
Others	5 percent

To the degree that you can reproduce this balance of cations in the soil supporting your lawn, the healthier and more vigorously the lawn will grow. To determine the relative proportions of these cations in your soil, send a sample to a professional soil testing lab and request an analysis of the cation exchange capacity (CEC). Because most soil labs focus on the amounts of nitrogen, potassium, and phosphorus (NPK) in the soil, be sure you make it clear you want to know the CEC in the detail described above.

"Calcium is the key to balanced soil fertility."

Note that the proportion of calcium in Albrecht's guideline is as much as 10 times greater than the other nutrients. Many soils do not naturally contain that much calcium, particularly in areas of high rainfall, heavy irrigation, or high sand content. Under these conditions, calcium is leached out of the soil. When calcium is deficient, soils become acid, as represented by a pH level of less than 7. When calcium is excessive, the soil is alkaline, with a pH above 7.

Lime. The common recommendation in conventional lawn-care literature that lime (calcium carbonate) should be added to soils on a regular basis is usually based on a desire to raise the pH of the soil. Albrecht maintains that this is far too simplistic a view of soil fertility. He suggests that it isn't the acidity of soils that should be of concern. Rather, we should recognize that acid soils are deficient in calcium, and the calcium balance should be restored as suggested in his formula. If this is done, he says, the soil pH will adjust itself to an appropriate level.

Viewed this way, the question of whether or not to add lime and which type to use becomes part of the overall question of soil fertility rather than merely a matter of tinkering with the pH. A soils laboratory report can tell you how much lime or other fertilizers to add to achieve the balance of cations recommended by Albrecht. Again, be sure to specify to the soil lab that you want this information, because it is not customarily spelled out.

Albrecht argues strongly in favor of using natural organic and inorganic forms of fertilizers when adding nutrients to the soil rather than the highly soluble synthetic forms that came into vogue in the 1930s and 1940s and still cause major environmental problems today. Limestone (calcium and magnesium), gypsum (calcium and sulfur), rock phosphate (phosphorus), and bone meal (phosphorus and calcium) are mineral sources that have evolved with the microorganisms that break them down into forms that move first into the clay soil and organic matter soil particles and later into plants.

This highly efficient, symbiotic relationship is a system that conserves soil nutrients by keeping them bonded to soil particles (or in the bodies of microbes) until they are sought out and absorbed by plant roots. It minimizes leaching out of nutrients by rainfall or irrigation. By contrast, when synthetic chemical fertilizers are applied to the soil, they are in large part immediately available for uptake by plants. This can result in plant tissue being burned by toxic amounts of the nutrients, or in a rapid deficiency of nutrients after the soluble fertilizer is leached out of the soil.

The two most common symptoms of nitrogen deficiency in seedlings are that leaves develop a light or pale yellow color and plants become stunted, showing little growth and vigor. Similar symptoms may develop from a lack of water during dry weather. (Photo by R. J. Reynolds Tobacco Company, Bugwood.org)

Nitrogen. The greatest disservice you can do to your lawn is to load the soil with nitrogen, particularly the highly soluble forms such as nitrate or urea found in most commercial chemical fertilizer packages. Nitrate and urea forms leach easily from the soil. Studies at Alabama Polytechnic University showed that at least 50 percent of quickly soluble nitrogen applied to soil leaches out before plants can use it. The remainder, when taken up in large doses by plants, tends to encourage attack by insect pests such as aphids and various disease organisms that are attracted to the succulent growth resulting from excessive nitrogen.

Quickly soluble nitrogen also causes grass to grow more quickly, which means that you have to mow the grass more frequently. In addition, soluble nitrogen fertilizers are usually formulated with highly soluble forms of potassium and phosphorus salts. Many soils already have high natural levels of these nutrients, and when more are added, the natural nutrient levels are thrown out of balance. This imbalance can in turn reduce the availability of other nutrients to plants.

The best way to tell when to apply nitrogen to your lawn and how much to use is by watching it. When the lawn begins to look grey-green or yellowish, it is time to fertilize. Turf expert John Madison advises applying the least amount of nitrogen consistent with good results and use. He notes that one of the best ways to supply nitrogen and other nutrients is to allow grass clippings to remain on the turf after mowing. Microorganisms decompose the clippings, returning the nutrients to the soil solution to be recycled by plant roots. Another option is to apply chelated iron to the lawn, preferably as a liquid foliar spray. This will result in a quick green-up, without the use of excess nitrogen. A word to the wise: All iron compounds will stain porous surfaces such as wood, concrete, masonry, clothing, paint, and even metal in some cases.

In experiments with grass clippings, Madison found that when starting new lawns on former agricultural soil in California, which presumably is severely nitrogen depleted, nitrogen fertilizer was needed the first year at a rate of 8 lb. to 10 lb. (3.6 kg to 4.5 kg) actual nitrogen per 1,000 sq. ft. (93 sq. m). ("Actual" nitrogen is the amount of nitrogen by weight in a fertilizer bag; for example, 10-percent N in a 25-lb. bag = 2½ lb. of actual N.)

But the second year, with clippings left on the lawn, only 4 lb. (1.8 kg) to 5 lb. (2.3 kg) of actual nitrogen were needed, and the third year, 1 lb. (0.45 kg) to 3 lb. (1.4 kg). By the fourth year, the nitrates present in irrigation water alone were sufficient to augment the nitrogen available from the clippings. Madison also noted, however, that "sometime during the spring flush some rust will appear and a little nitrogen needs to be added to control rust. In October, another light application helps that spreading growth that enables the turf to compete with the germinating winter annual weeds."

When you must apply nitrogen, use an organic nitrogen source and split its application between fall and spring for best results. Irwin Brawley, groundskeeper at Davidson College in Davidson, North Carolina, used only organic fertilizers to maintain the college's extensive lawns and athletic fields. He applied 7½ lb. (3.4 kg) of Zook and Ranck's Nitro-10 (made from leather tankage, or dried animal residue), 2½ lb. (1.1 kg) of rock phosphate, and 10¾ lb. (4.9 kg) of greensand (potassium) per 1,000 sq. ft. (93 sq. m) of lawn in the fall and spring. This is the organic equivalent of a 10-10-10 NPK fertilizer, and it provides approximately ¾ lb. (340 g) each of nitrogen, phosphorus, and potash to

TIP If you plan to allow your clippings to remain on the lawn, be certain the mower you buy does not contain an automatic bagging device that forces you to collect clippings. Consider buying a "mulching" mower, which automatically grinds clippings into fine pieces and spits them back out onto the lawn, where they quickly sift down into the turf and decompose.

Clover in your lawn not only helps you meet your turf's nitrogen needs, but it also gives your lawn a meadow-like appearance, which has a much nicer feel to it than a monoculture lawn without flowers. (Photo by Geoff Kidd/GAP)

Other good organic fertilizers include stabilized, weed-free compost or stable manure, cottonseed meal, soybean meal, bloodmeal, and castor bean pomace. Organic fertilizer blends are now available at almost all home and garden centers. When comparing the prices with inorganic fertilizers, remember that you do not need to make as many applications per year with organic fertilizers. Organic fertilizers increase soil health, whereas synthetic fertilizers do not. This benefit alone would make any additional expense cost effective. When the time saved and fewer applications are considered, organic fertilizers are usually very competitive. If you have a small lawn, the difference in cost is not significant.

If you use the proportions described above, watch your lawn for a few weeks after applying the organic fertilizers. If the lawn looks healthy and has a good green color, continue with the program. If it develops a yellowish look, it may need more nitrogen. Add more compost, or perhaps bloodmeal, which contains a higher percentage of nitrogen. Keep a record of your fertilizing program, and compare notes from year to year. After some experimentation you will find a nitrogen program that is right for your lawn. Remember to consider the "intensity" of green that your turfgrass species and variety should have when healthy. Don't try to make a tall fescue lawn look as dark green as a dark Kentucky bluegrass.

In *Principles of Turfgrass Culture* (Van Nostrand Reinhold, 1971), Madison cautions that a lawn's fertilizer needs change as the growing season changes and pest problems occur:

> When seasonal stresses reduce growth, reduce [fertilizer] applications. When grass is thinned out, by insects for example, thin

the lawn. You can purchase organic fertilizer already blended at this ratio to avoid having to do the mixing yourself.

For warm-season grasses such as bermudagrass, centipedegrass, and St. Augustinegrass, apply the 10-10-10 fertilizer when the grass begins active growth in May and again in late fall before it goes dormant. The fall application feeds the annual ryegrass that is usually overseeded to keep the lawn green in winter and also stimulates growth of the roots of the warm-season grasses long before new top growth is evident in late spring.

down the fertilizer applications until recovery is well along. Grass in shade can use a fraction of that in sun. Soil supplies much of the needed minerals. Your program only needs to supply the difference between what plants need and what the soil supplies. At times soil can supply minerals for heavy grass growth with no need for fertilizer.

Soil minerals are usually highest in spring, lowest in fall. When a steady fertilizer program has been followed for several years, soil reserves are often restored and needs decreased…. If grass fails to respond to an application of nitrogen, don't add more nitrogen. First look for other problems.

If you do decide to use a synthetic nitrogen fertilizer, we suggest a slow-release form of urea or IBDU (iso-butyldiene diurea) formulation used in combination with calcium. A study of synthetic lawn fertilizers conducted at Texas A&M University found that fertilization with four parts urea to one part calcium nitrate produced turf with better color, verdure (health), and root and rhizome production than did fertilization with various nitrogen sources that did not contain calcium. The researchers concluded that calcium enhanced the ability of grass roots to absorb nitrogen.

Clover can contribute as much as 30 percent of the yearly nitrogen needed by a lawn; by including clover in your lawn mix, you reduce the lawn's nitrogen requirement. Significant nitrogen amounts can also be obtained by allowing grass clippings to remain on the lawn after mowing. We like the meadow look for home lawns, so clovers and wildflowers are a feature, not a problem.

We should also mention that many professionals who manage golf courses and other high-maintenance turf keep the lawn looking good by simply fertilizing lightly and irrigating grass that shows signs of pest damage. We call this the "chicken soup" approach, because it is comparable to the attentive feeding of someone with an ail-

ment. Because grasses are such resilient organisms, special but moderate feeding or watering when their roots or tops have suffered damage often gives them just the extra edge they need to recover. If you nurse the patient along with needed minerals, which, by the way, grass can absorb through its leaves when its roots are damaged, it will often put out a burst of new growth and repair the visual damage.

MOWING

One of the best ways to guarantee pest problems in a lawn is through improper mowing. Most lawns are mowed too short too often. As a result, the grass becomes weak and falls prey to invasion by weeds and infection by various pathogens. In fact, the USDA often lowers the cutting height of the

"One of the best ways to guarantee pest problems in a lawn is through improper mowing. Most lawns are mowed too short too often."

mowers on its experimental lawn plots to incite lawn diseases for use in experiments!

In *Practical Turfgrass Management*, John Madison provides some explanations for our national penchant for closely mowed lawns:

Early mowing of ornamental turf was without doubt patterned after grazing and hay-making practices, cuts being made from three to four times a year to monthly during the growing season. Such a schedule is still followed in some European parks. In crowded U.S. suburbs, there is a kind of mind that finds even a little disorder disquieting. This, combined with an early 20th century passion for sanitary sterility, demands uniform lawns, free of weeds, evenly edged, and mowed as quickly as any new growth mars the uniformity of clipped ranks and rows.

Whenever a blade of grass is cut there are a number of predictable stress responses: Root and rhizome growth temporarily stops, carbohydrate production and storage is reduced, there is water loss from the cut ends, and water uptake decreases. As long as lawn grasses have enough nutrients, water, and soil aeration, as well as moderate temperatures, most can tolerate the temporary stress caused by mowing and bounce back with new growth. The spurt of top growth occurs in two phases. The first ranges from three to four days and involves the elongation of existing cut leaves; the second includes the development of new leaves. In addition, under optimal horticultural conditions mowing increases the number of individual grass plants in a lawn, making a tighter, more weed-resistant turf.

Unfortunately, few lawns are maintained under optimal conditions. If repeated close mowings occur in conjunction with one or more additional stresses such as drought, insufficient nutrients, or a spell of unusually hot or cold weather, grass plants become smaller and fewer. This creates openings for weed invasion. Moreover, the cut ends provide ideal ports of entry for such disease organisms as leaf spot, rust, and dollar spot. So always wait for the driest, or at least dryer, conditions to mow your lawn. Disease microbes prefer wet conditions, and your lawn mower is the perfect transport to new locations.

Mowing Height. To minimize problems caused by mowing, cut the grass as high as is consistent with satisfactory growth and appearance and as infrequently as possible. How high and how often you cut depends on the growth habit of the grass, the horticultural condition of the lawn, the climate, and the purpose for which the lawn is used.

TIP To establish the height of the cut on a rotary mower, measure between the cutting edge of the blade and a smooth, level surface such as a pavement or patio. A small 2×4 wood block can be used to estimate height. For a reel-type mower, measure between the cutting edge of the stationary bed knife and the pavement.

The key to judging appropriate mowing height is knowing something about the growth habit of the type(s) of grass in your lawn. Most lawns outside the southern United States are composed of a mixture of two or more grass species. Kentucky bluegrass (*Poa pratensis*) mixed with perennial ryegrass (*Lolium perenne*) or tall fescue (*Festuca arundinacea*) and perennial rye are popular in most parts of the Northeast, Midwest, and West, where they are hardy. Bentgrasses (*Agrostis* spp.) are common in the Pacific Northwest. Bermudagrass (*Cynodon dactylon*), centipedegrass (*Eremochloa ophiuroides*), St. Augustinegrass (*Stenotaphrum secundatum*), and zoysiagrass (*Zoysia* spp.) are popular in the Southwest and southern states.

Prostrate, low-growing grasses such as bermudagrass and creeping bentgrass tolerate fairly low mowing heights—about ¾ in. to 1 in. (1.9 cm to 2.5 cm). Erect-growing grasses such as the fine-bladed, drought-resistant tall fescues or Italian ryegrasses respond better if cut higher, about 2 in. to 3 in. (5 cm to 7.5 cm).

Kentucky bluegrass lawns also fall within the latter mowing-height range, depending on the cultivar. For example, 'Park,' 'Kenblue,' and 'Baron' have a more erect growth habit and a higher growing point than the more prostrate 'Gnome,' 'Merit,' and 'Rugby.' These prostrate cultivars can tolerate mowing as low as 1 in. to 1½ in. (2.5 cm to 3.8 cm), whereas the others should be mowed no shorter than 2 in. (5 cm).

Seasonal Adjustment of Mowing Height. The mowing height of cool-season grasses such as Kentucky bluegrass and the fescues, bentgrasses, and ryes should be raised during periods of prolonged high temperature. Recent research at Mississippi State University with the increasingly popular tall fescue grasses found a noticeable advantage to raising the mowing height during midsummer, when tall fescue suffers most from heat and drought stress and is most susceptible to weed invasion and disease.

In the Mississippi study, the highest turf density and darkest color were obtained by using a split mowing schedule: a 2½-in. (6.5-cm) mowing height from September to May and a 5-in. (12.7-cm) mowing height from June through August. Raising the mowing height from 2½ in. to 3 in. (6.5 cm to 7.5 cm) during the summer is probably warranted on Kentucky bluegrass/perennial ryegrass mixes as well. However, grasses with very prostrate growth habits, such as the bentgrasses, probably should not be mowed higher than 1 in. (2.5 cm) to avoid drought stress, excessive accumulation of thatch, and other problems.

Warm-season grasses such as bermudagrass or centipedegrass, which grow vigorously during periods of high temperature, can tolerate lower summer cutting heights. Bermudagrass should be cut as low as ¾ in. (1.9 cm) in summer when it is growing vigorously, to prevent thatch buildup. During the cool season, when it is semi-dormant, the mowing height can be raised to 1½ in. (3.8 cm). Generally, when temperatures cool in fall, the mowing height of most grasses can be reduced. Seasonally adjusted optimum mowing heights are listed in the chart below.

Mowing Frequency. Most lawn-care books warn against long intervals between mowings because too much grass is cut off in a single cutting, leading to a severe setback in subsequent growth. Although there is some merit to this argument, studies by Madison and others indicate that as long as not more than 30 percent to 40 percent of the grass blades are removed at any one cutting, the setback is minimal. Thus, if the mowing height is set at 2 in. (5 cm), you can let the grass grow 3 in. (7.5 cm) tall before you need to mow it again.

In summary, lawn grasses can tolerate frequent mowing as long as the mowing height is not too low for the species of grass. Mowing must be more frequent when grasses are growing vigorously and less frequent when they are semi-dormant. An interval of 7 to 10 days between mowings may be appropriate for bluegrass or tall fescue/perennial rye mixes during their growing season; this extends to 14 to 21 days or longer when growth slows. The right interval between mowings allows grasses to recover from the previous cut and enter the second growth phase wherein new blades, called tillers, are produced from the growing points. "Tillering" keeps lawns growing in a tight, dense manner that discourages weeds.

RECOMMENDED MOWING HEIGHTS

GRASS	RELATIVE HEIGHT	MOWING HEIGHT (IN INCHES) Spring/Fall	Summer
bentgrass	very short	0.75	1.0
bermudagrass		1.5	0.75–1.0
zoysiagrass		1.5	1.0
buffalograss	medium	2.0	2.5
red fescue		2.0	2.5
centipedegrass		2.0	1.5
carpetgrass		2.0	1.5
Kentucky bluegrass		2.0	2.5–3.0
perennial ryegrass		2.0	2.5–3.0
meadow fescue		2.0	2.5–3.0
bahiagrass	high	2.0	3.0
tall fescue		2.5	3.0
St. Augustinegrass		2.0	3.0 (West), 2.0 (South)
Canada bluegrass		3.0	4.0

CHAPTER 13

LEAST-TOXIC LAWN PEST MANAGEMENT

n this chapter we describe complete IPM programs for major insect, disease, weed, and rodent pests of lawns. The solutions are based on the horticultural strategies for producing healthy lawns discussed in the previous chapter, so we encourage you to review that material before implementing the methods described here.

We wish to reemphasize the importance that healthy soil plays in turfgrass vigor and insect and disease resistance. There is evidence that mature compost and compost tea have very positive effects on turfgrass health and resilience. There is anecdotal evidence that compost tea application to turfgrasses (and other plants) suppresses fungal diseases and improves overall health. Compost and compost tea contain small amounts of macronutrients and micronutrients, both of which can be absorbed through the leaves and taken up by the roots. Importantly, mature compost and tea made from mature compost feed the soil.

CATERPILLARS: THE SOD WEBWORM

(Order Lepidoptera, *Crambus* spp.)

The larval stages of butterflies and moths are called caterpillars or worms. The chart on p. 252 lists the major caterpillar species that are considered lawn pests. Although the list of potential caterpillar pests is long, only a few, including sod webworms, armyworms, and cutworms, are serious pests of residential lawns. And of the 60 to 80 species of webworms in the United States, most are pests of grain crops and wild grasses, not of lawns. Because detection and management of all three are essentially the same, we confine our detailed discussion to sod webworms. If armyworms or cutworms are problems in your lawn, follow the recommendations here. For more detailed information on these and other insect lawn pests not covered in detail in this chapter, we recommend *Turfgrass Insects of the United States and Canada* by P. Vittum, M. Villani, and H. Tashiro (Comstock Publishing Associates, 1999).

BIOLOGY

A sod webworm is the larval, or caterpillar, stage of a small whitish or dingy-brown moth. The caterpillar is ¾ in. to 1 in. (1.9 cm to 2.5 cm) long and, depending on the species, greyish-brown to greenish to dirty white with four parallel rows of dark brown spots on the abdomen. The adult moths have a habit of folding their wings closely about their bodies when at rest, earning the group the name "close-winged moths." The two finger-like horns protruding from the head give them their other common name, "snout moths." If disturbed during the day, the moths fly erratically for a short distance before settling again on the lawn or adjacent shrubbery. The adult moths do not feed on grass.

Armyworms are larger than sod webworms in the moth and caterpillar stages. Mature armyworm caterpillars are 1½ in. to 2 in. (3.8 cm to 5 cm) long and vary in color from grey to yellowish green. Light stripes run the length of their bodies. The fall armyworm usually found in the southern states has a characteristic white or yellow inverted "Y" on the front of its head capsule. Adult armyworm moths are three times larger than the sod webworm moth, with a 2-in. (5-cm) wingspan.

Cutworms are also larger than sod webworms, reaching 1½ in. to 2 in. (3.8 cm to 5 cm) in length and varying in color from pale grey to brownish black, often with a lighter-colored underside. Adult moths are brownish tan to greyish, with a wingspan of 1½ in. (3.8 cm). The front wings are darker than the hind pair and usually have various light and dark markings.

In late spring and early summer, female sod webworm moths fly over lawns at dusk, dipping down to drop as many as 200 eggs in the grass. The eggs resemble tiny cream-colored beads, and are preferentially dropped in humid areas of succulent grass. According to John Madison, writing in *Practical Turfgrass Management* (PWS Publishers, 1971):

> The eggs need moisture to develop, and if the area dries, mortality will be high. The eggs hatch in about 4½ days at 75°F [24°C]. The small worm produced leads a precarious existence. With its small mouth it can only

CATERPILLARS THAT DAMAGE LAWNS

COMMON NAME	SCIENTIFIC NAME
Lawn moths	
sod webworms	*Crambus* spp.
Skippers	
fiery skipper	*Hylephia phylaeus*
Essex skipper	*Thymelicus lineda*
Armyworms	
common armyworm	*Pseudaletia unipuncta*
fall armyworm	*Spodoptera frugiperda*
beet armyworm	*S. exigua*
Cutworms	
granulated cutworm	*Agrotis subterranea*
black cutworm	*A. ipsilon*
turnip moth	*A. segetum*
hart and dart	*A. exclamationis*
variegated cutworm	*Peridroma saucia*
yellow underwing	*Triphaena pronuba*

From J. H. Madison's *Practical Turfgrass Management* (PWS Publishers, 1971).

skeletonize the soft interveinal surface parts of a leaf. If the leaf is tough and hard it may starve to death at this stage. If a drop of rain or irrigation water hits the larva, it may wash off the leaf to the soil and be lost. The first and second instars [stages of caterpillar growth] are usually spent on a single grass leaf. By the third instar the worm is large enough to take bites from the edge of the leaf and leaves appear notched.

During the fourth, fifth, and sixth instars, the worms construct little burrows or tunnels in the thatch layer of lawns. The burrows are covered with bits of dirt, lined with silk, and reinforced with excrement and pieces of grass. Then the worms cut off the grass blades entirely and drag them into their burrows, where they feed in safety at leisure. When the larvae have completed their growth and are about ¾ in. (1.9 cm) long, they leave their burrows and construct cocoons of silk and bits of earth on the nearby soil. In 10 to 14 days, the moth emerges from the pupa and forces its way from the cocoon into the open air. Within a few minutes the moth's wings have spread and dried and the moth is ready to mate and produce a new generation. Adult moths live only a few days. Because adults take no solid food, it is only in the larval stage that these insects are harmful.

Nearly mature caterpillars overwinter in the soil and resume feeding in late April to early May as soon as soil temperatures begin to rise. In northern and midwestern states, adults begin to emerge in early June and can be seen flying across lawns at dusk. Pupation occurs in late June to early July, and second-generation adults are observed shortly thereafter. New eggs are deposited and second-generation larvae reach peak activity in mid- to late August, which is when most damage is observed. As temperatures drop in fall, the larvae burrow deeper into the soil to overwinter. In warmer areas, webworms may produce up to three generations. In Western and Southern states, the generations may overlap, with all life stages occurring simultaneously.

DAMAGE

All webworm feeding occurs at night. While the worms are small, the injury resulting from their feeding is likely to pass unnoticed. It appears first as small, irregular brown patches in the grass. As the worms grow older and begin eating entire leaves, often consuming twice their own weight nightly, large areas of grass can be severely damaged if the population is high. According to Madison:

> A hundred larvae per square yard [or 11 per sq. ft.] at this stage can thin turf out at a rate where it seems to disappear overnight. As green leaves are removed, the brown duff is exposed and the infested areas are straw-colored. The worms stay close to their burrows and so tend to thin the turf in a circular area the size of a quarter or half dollar. From above the turf, these feeding areas appear as pock marks in the lawn and can be readily recognized.

DETECTION AND MONITORING

Because the brown patches caused by webworm damage can superficially resemble those caused by other pest insects or diseases, accurate diagnosis is important. Webworms live in the thatch layer of the lawn rather than in the soil, so you should check for them in the layer of dead grass just above the soil line. Webworms are present if grass blades in the damaged area are actually missing and not just dead, there are green fecal pellets in the thatch, you find larvae in silk-lined tubes in the thatch (you can use a small hand trowel to loosen the thatch), or you find holes pecked by birds, which indicate the birds are searching for webworms.

TIP Because webworms prefer to live in layers of deep thatch, you should reduce the thatch level if it is thicker than 1/2 in. to 3/4 in. (1.3 cm to 1.9 cm). The optimum thatch thickness runs from 1/4 in. to 1/2 in.

Soap drenches, whose use as a monitoring tool is outlined in the sidebar at right, can also help you detect thatch-dwelling insects such as webworms, cutworms, and armyworms.

If your lawn is in good condition and growing vigorously, the presence of two or three webworm larvae per sq. ft. is probably not cause for concern. If your lawn is under stress through compaction, infrequent irrigation, or under-fertilization, the presence of as few as one larva per sq. ft. usually indicates the need for treatment. Because factors such as grass vigor, temperature, and moisture play major roles in the number of webworms a lawn can tolerate without significant damage, it may take a season or two for you to decide what the action level is.

TREATMENT

INDIRECT STRATEGIES

Indirect strategies for webworm control include planting resistant grass varieties, managing horticultural stresses on your lawn, and conserving native biological controls.

1. Webworm-Resistant Grass Cultivars.

There are Kentucky bluegrass varieties that show some tolerance for webworms. If webworms are a chronic problem, however, you should consider replacing your turf with endophytic grasses (grasses that contain beneficial fungi within their tissues), discussed on pp. 235–237. Most lawn seed companies are introducing endophytic fungi into a wide variety of their lawn grasses, so many varieties with high percentages of endophytes are now available.

2. Habitat Management.

Webworms like areas of the lawn that are hot and dry during the day. Damage may coincide with areas that are insufficiently watered or

USING A SOAP DRENCH TO MONITOR FOR WEBWORMS

Mark off two or three 2-ft.-sq. (0.6-m by 0.6-m) sections of lawn in both damaged and undamaged areas. Mix 2 Tab. of liquid soap or detergent in 1 gal. (3.8 l) of water in a sprinkling can, then pour the mix evenly over each area to be sampled. You can also make this kind of drench by mixing 1 tsp. of 1-percent to 2-percent pyrethrin in 1 gal. of water.

The soap irritates the caterpillars, causing them to crawl to the surface. Keep a close watch on each test area for about 10 minutes, because brief movements alone may indicate webworms are present. Where the thatch is thick, it may be necessary to pour several more gallons of soap solution on the test area to reach the webworms. If the thatch is saturated but no caterpillars appear, the damage is probably due to disease or another type of insect. If insects do surface, check to see that they are webworms.

Even if there is no damage, you can use the soap method to check your lawn periodically for developing insect problems. Because many such problems begin in the hot, dry edges of lawns, particularly near concrete driveways or sidewalks, it is a good idea to select several such areas and monitor them once a month during spring and summer with the soap drench.

compacted (compaction interferes with the soil's ability to absorb water). Correction of these conditions enables the grass to resume vigorous growth and replace damaged blades (see Chapter 12 for a more detailed discussion of stress reduction methods). Once the grass is growing vigorously, a moderate amount of feeding by webworms will not be noticeable.

3. Conservation of Native Biological Controls.
Good lawn management should encourage the presence of the natural enemies of webworms. Four species of ants, particularly *Pheidole tysoni*, and the mite *Macrocheles* feed on webworm eggs. The robber fly (*Erax aestuans*) captures webworm moths. Spiders, vespid wasps, native earwigs, carabid beetles, and rove beetles prey on various stages of the pest. Birds, including poultry, as well as a number of parasitoids and a pathogen eat the caterpillars.

For example, the parasitoid *Apanteles* ssp., a small wasp-like insect in the family Braconidae, deposits its eggs inside webworms. The tiny parasitoid maggots emerging from these eggs feed on the internal tissues of their hosts, eventually causing death. Several parasitoids may develop in a single host larva. When full grown, they emerge from the host and spin their small white ellipsoid cocoons in a mass on the ground. The adult parasitoids emerge from the cocoons to lay their eggs in other webworms. Two species of flies, *Phorocera claripennis* and *Zenillia caesar*, also parasitize webworms to some extent. These flies deposit their eggs on the skin of the webworm larvae. The maggots hatching from them burrow into the bodies of the host larvae and feed, eventually killing the worm.

Where moisture and temperature are high and infestations are heavy, the fungus *Beauveria bassiana* attacks webworms. The infected larvae turn dull pink and become flaccid. The fungus provides good control, but unfortunately only after the larvae have already caused significant damage to grass. The impact of the fungus is not really seen until

the following year, when there are fewer over-wintering webworms due to the kill of larvae the previous fall. Commercially available protozoans *Nosema* ssp. and *Thelohania* ssp. attack webworms.

TREATMENT
DIRECT PHYSICAL CONTROLS
In areas where webworm presence has been confirmed, you can drench the soil under and adjacent to the damaged grass with the soap solution described in the sidebar on p. 253. As soon as the caterpillars wriggle to the surface, rake them into piles with a flexible lawn rake, scoop them up with a shovel, and drop them into a bucket of soapy water.

TREATMENT
DIRECT BIOLOGICAL CONTROLS
Poultry and the microbial insecticide *Bacillus thuringiensis* can be used to control webworm infestations.

1. Poultry. If you keep chickens, which is increasingly common in urban and suburban neighborhoods, let them roam the lawn for a day or two. They can clean out a webworm infestation more quickly and safely than any other method. After

(Photo by Scott Phillips, courtesy of *Fine Cooking*)

removing the poultry, irrigate the lawn thoroughly. If you are raising the chickens for food, it is best not to give them names.

"Chickens can clean out a webworm infestation more quickly and safely than any other method."

2. *Bacillus thuringiensis* (BT). For those of you who don't have chickens handy, *Bacillus thuringiensis* is the next best thing (see pp. 138–143 for a detailed discussion of this microbial product). Sold in nurseries, hardware stores, and online under many brand names, this naturally occurring bacterium affects only caterpillars, acting as a stomach poison when ingested. It has no known damaging effects on other species.

Bear in mind, however, that BT also has no effect on the moth stage of sod webworms. Many people apply BT as soon as they observe large numbers of moths flying over the lawn. Moths do not feed on grass and therefore do not ingest the material. If you see moths and therefore anticipate a large infestation of caterpillars, especially during abnormally hot, dry summer weather, wait approximately two weeks before applying BT to allow time for the eggs deposited by the moths to hatch.

It is the youngest caterpillars, the first and second instars, which are the most susceptible to BT. They ingest the BT spores when they eat grass sprayed with it. To maximize BT contact with the larvae, mow the lawn before you apply it; don't mow again until you absolutely must to delay removal of the sprayed leaves. It is recommended that you mix a good surfactant, sometimes called a "spreader-sticker," in the spray tank with the BT to ensure that the insecticide adheres to the blades of grass and/or penetrates the thatch. We recommend using surfactants, soil penetrants, and spreader-stickers listed by the Organic Materials Review Institute.

3. Nematodes. Beneficial nematodes are effective parasitoids of webworms. Research with com-

SUMMARY: LEAST-TOXIC WEBWORM CONTROL

- Monitor for webworms by visually examining the thatch layer or by using a soap drench to flush them out.

- Plant webworm-resistant grass varieties.

- Reduce thatch and other horticultural stresses on lawns.

- Conserve native biological controls.

- Use soap drenches and raking to remove moderate populations.

- Apply the microbial insecticide *Bacillus thuringiensis* if high populations threaten the lawn. Beneficial nematodes may also control the infestation.

- If a chemical treatment is necessary, use a pyrethrum product or insecticidal soap.

mercially available *Heterorhabditis* and *Steinernema* nematodes indicates that they reduce webworm populations when watered into the thatch. Rincon-Vitova Insectaries is one supplier of beneficial nematodes (www.rinconvitova.com/nematode.htm). For more information on these biological controls, see pp. 150–152 and the discussion of white grubs on p. 263.

TREATMENT
DIRECT CHEMICAL CONTROLS

Natural pyrethrum and pyrethrin (see Chapter 7 for details) are effective against the sod webworm, although they also kill beneficial insects in treated portions of the lawn. Therefore, if you use pyrethrum products, confine them to those areas where you are certain webworms are present to minimize damage to the webworm's natural enemies. Pyrethroids, synthetic pyrethrum mimics, are also effective and broad-spectrum, but are now controversial because they are suspected endocrine-disrupting chemicals.

Insecticidal soap can be effective for controlling webworms if the thatch layer is thoroughly saturated. Read labels carefully and follow directions whenever using any pesticidal product. It is illegal and hazardous to exceed the labeled dilution rates. Insecticidal soaps can damage plants when the dilution rate is too high or the interval between applications is too short. Test spray a small portion first; if you see plant damage wash the plant thoroughly to dilute the soap and reduce damage. Damaged plants will recover.

Neem-based insecticides, many of which are OMRI listed, are also effective against webworms and some other lawn insect pests. Neem's repellent qualities reduce feeding by pests immediately, even though insect death may be delayed. Neem also has fungicidal properties.

From left to right, the three species of white grubs are: Japanese beetle *(Popillia japonica)*, European chafer *(Amphimallon majalis)*, and June bug *(Phyllophaga spp.)*. (David Cappaert, Michigan State University, Bugwood.org)

BEETLES (WHITE GRUBS): THE JAPANESE BEETLE

(Order Coleoptera, family Scarabaeidae)

The larvae, or grubs, of a number of beetles can become serious lawn pests when present in high numbers. The most important of these are listed in the chart on the facing page.

Although the adults of various beetle species differ from one another in life cycle and appearance, the grubs of all species look very similar. Fully grown larvae are ½ in. to ¾ in. (1.3 cm to 1.9 cm) long, and white to greyish with brown heads and six legs. When you see the grubs in the soil, their bodies are usually curved in a characteristic C shape. The particular species can be identified on the basis of the pattern of hairs, or rasters, found on the

underside of the last abdominal segment. They are visible with a 10× hand lens.

Because prevention and treatment are quite similar for these various beetles, we will provide detailed instructions for the most widespread, the Japanese beetle *(Popillia japonica)*. If irregular patches of your lawn begin wilting and dying in late spring or summer, it might indicate the presence of the larvae, or grubs, of this beetle. Although the adult beetles are common, familiar feeders on leaves, flowers, and fruits of ornamental and orchard plants, the grub stage prefers the roots of lawn and pasture grasses. In many parts of the United States, Japanese beetle grubs (one species of a number of lawn-dwelling beetle larvae known collectively as "white grubs") are considered the single most damaging insect pest on lawns.

As the name suggests, this beetle originated in Japan, where it is only a minor pest. It was first discovered in the United States at Riverton, New Jersey, in 1916. In the mid-Atlantic states, the beetles found a climate similar to that of their native Japan and large expanses of lawns and pastures in which to develop. But the natural enemies that kept the beetles below damaging levels in Japan were not present in New Jersey, and this allowed populations to build to extremely high levels. Their spread into neighboring states was rapid, despite concerted efforts to contain them. Today, the Japanese beetle is found in practically all states east of the Mississippi, and is a periodic invader in California and other states.

BIOLOGY

Adult Japanese beetles are approximately ¼ in. to ½ in. (6 mm to 13 mm) long. The head and prothorax are greenish bronze, and the wing covers are brownish bronze with green along the sides and center. Twelve white tufts of hair are present along the sides of the abdomen and at the tips of the wing covers. The adults' long legs have large claws. Adults live four to six weeks, and their maximum abundance occurs in early July in most infested areas. They are active during daylight, leaving their earthen cells to feed and mate in the morning and returning to the soil in late afternoon.

Mated females lay approximately 60 eggs during their lifetime, usually burrowing about 3 in. (7.6 cm) into the ground late in the afternoon to deposit the eggs. Favored egg-laying sites are grassy areas such as turf, pastures, and meadows in close-cropped grass. Because the eggs must absorb water to support the embryo, moist soil is essential.

The white, elongate eggs hatch into grubs in about two weeks. The grubs feed approximately eight weeks until they are nearly full grown. Most feeding damage on lawns is seen in September and October. Mature grubs are about 1 in. (2.5 cm) long, and have three pairs of legs. The thorax and most of the abdomen are white. The head is tan, with large, brown-black chewing mouthparts, or mandibles. The grubs hibernate over the winter, assuming a curled C position in earthen cells 4 in. to 8 in. (10 cm to 20 cm) below the ground.

The grubs feed in early spring, pupate in May or June, and emerge as adults in summer (mid-May in North Carolina, mid-June in Maryland and Dela-ware, and by early July in New York, New Jersey, Connecticut, Pennsylvania, Ohio, Indiana, and Michigan). The life cycle, which usually takes one year, is shown in the drawing on p. 258. In high elevations and northern latitudes the cycle may take as long as two years.

DAMAGE

The grubs inhabit the soil or subsurface layer of turf beneath the thatch (the accumulation of dead grass stems and roots at the soil line). They feed on the roots of a wide variety of grasses, cutting the roots and loosening the sod, which can then be rolled up like a carpet. Lawns attacked by grubs will show irregularly shaped patches of wilted, dead, or dying grass in April and May and August to mid-October. The fall grub population is the most damaging because it feeds when all but warm-season grasses tend to be in a semi-dormant stage in the hot weather and moisture stress is common. Grass usually does not recover from severe grub injury, but it can regrow if the injury is moderate. An attack by even small numbers of grubs can cause yellowing and slowing of grass growth.

Once grubs complete their life cycle in the lawn, they emerge as adults in late spring and move to adjacent vegetation. They are known to feed on close to 300 different species of plants. Generally, they consume leaf tissue between the veins, as well as portions of blossoms and fruits. Skeletonized leaves eventually wilt and fall from the plant. The beetles are most active and feed most extensively between 9 a.m. and 3 p.m. on warm, clear summer days, because they prefer areas exposed to direct sunlight; plants in densely wooded areas are rarely attacked.

DETECTION AND MONITORING

The presence of large flocks of blackbirds, tunneling of moles,

MAJOR BEETLE PESTS OF LAWNS

COMMON NAME	SCIENTIFIC NAME	NATIVE/EXOTIC
black turfgrass ataenius	*Ataenius spretulus*	native
May or June beetles	*Phyllophaga* spp.	native
northern masked chafer	*Cyclocephala borealis*	native
southern masked chafer	*C. immaculata*	native
Asiatic garden beetle	*Maladera castanea*	exotic
European masked chafer	*Amphimallon majalis*	exotic
Japanese beetle	*Popillia japonica*	exotic
oriental beetle	*Anomala orientalis*	exotic

or digging up of the lawn by skunks, raccoons, and other mammals in search of grubs are signs that grub populations may be high. But the most accurate way to estimate grub populations is by examining several areas of soil underneath the grass. Because disease, adverse temperature, and other factors greatly reduce the beetle population between the egg and adult stages, the most accurate surveys are made just prior to adult emergence in late May to mid-June (somewhat later farther north).

It is best to sample three or four locations on your lawn before you see any damage. This enables you to detect a developing problem and intervene. If you already see signs of damage, check those areas as well as undamaged grass nearby. Use a spade to cut three sides of a 1-ft. (30-cm) square of turf to a depth of 4 in. to 5 in. (10 cm to 12.7 cm). Carefully fold back the turf, using the uncut edge as a hinge. Pick the dirt from the roots and count the number of grubs exposed. Then fold the grass back into place, tamp it, and water it with a small amount of fish emulsion or other fertilizer containing organic nitrogen and phosphorus.

Because there are several species of scarab grubs in turf that superficially resemble Japanese beetle grubs, it is imperative that sampled grubs be positively identified if species-specific controls are to be used successfully. Checking the rasters is one way of identifying the larvae; another is taking any large larvae found during sampling, placing them in a jar, and waiting until the adults emerge. The jar can then be taken to a cooperative extension office for identification.

The number of beetle grubs your lawn can tolerate without showing significant damage is largely a matter of how well it is maintained and how vigorously it is growing. Well-maintained turf normally does not show signs of injury when spring grub populations are below 15 per sq. ft., whereas poorly maintained turf may show significant damage at that level. In late August or September, when grasses are semi-dormant and thus more suscep-

THE LIFE CYCLE OF THE JAPANESE BEETLE

The Japanese beetle grub (A) overwinters in a cell 4 in. to 8 in. (10 cm to 20 cm) below the soil surface. The grub comes nearer the surface to feed in early spring (B), then pupates (C). An adult (D) emerges in summer, feeds on foliage and fruit (E), then lays eggs in the ground (F). The eggs hatch in about two weeks, and the young grubs (G) grow and feed rapidly. This is the stage at which they inflict the most damage on roots.

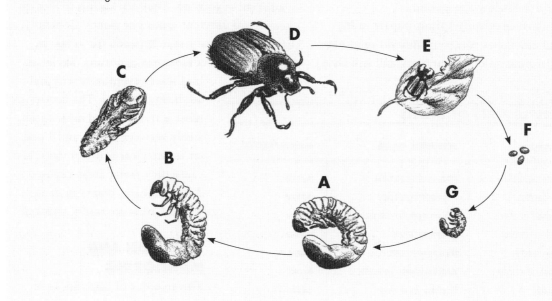

tible to damage, as few as 6 to 10 grubs per sq. ft. may call for some form of treatment. A couple of seasons of monitoring will enable you to gauge how many grubs per sq. ft. your lawn can tolerate.

Remember that a low population of grubs may actually be advantageous, because the grubs ensure that a naturally occurring disease of Japanese and certain other pest beetles called *Bacillus popilliae* (BP) is maintained in the grass from year to year. The presence of this bacterium protects your lawn from extensive damage by infecting grubs, causing them to stop feeding and die without reproducing (for more information on these beneficial organisms, see "Direct Biological Controls" on pp. 261–264). In addition, low populations of grubs help the lawn by decomposing the dead stems and roots of grass that accumulate at the soil line. When this layer of thatch is too thick, water cannot penetrate to the soil and lawns become drought-stressed.

TIP Beetles prefer to lay eggs in closely cropped lawns, so you should raise the summer mowing height to 2½ in. to 3 in. (6.4 cm to 7.6 cm).

TREATMENT
INDIRECT STRATEGIES

Vigorously growing lawns can tolerate more grubs without showing damage. Thus, part of Japanese beetle control involves managing horticultural stresses on your lawn. Another indirect strategy is to conserve natural enemies of Japanese beetles.

1. Habitat Management. The first step in habitat management is to check for excessive thatch, compacted soil, or other conditions that might impede proper flow of water and nutrients to the grass. These problems can often be corrected by aerating the soil. You can rent a power aerator that removes cores of soil from the lawn, or you can use a hand-operated aerator. You should then apply a top-dressing of 50 percent composted steer manure and 50 percent river sand, overseeding it with a mix of grasses suited to the microclimate of your yard (see Chapter 12 for details).

Appropriate irrigation can also help make lawns less hospitable to grubs and beetles. Japanese beetles prefer to lay eggs on soil that is constantly moist. When females are seeking a place to lay eggs—early July in most areas—deep, infrequent irrigation discourages them because the soil surface dries between waterings. Eggs that do get laid often desiccate (dry out) and fail to hatch. Deep, infrequent irrigation also encourages deep-rooted, drought-tolerant lawns and reduces lawn diseases fostered by heavy summer watering.

In the spring and fall (September), irrigation should be used to maintain sufficient soil moisture to keep the lawn from becoming drought-stressed. This watering regime encourages the spread of milky spore disease in grubs (see "Direct Biological Controls") and encourages damaged grass to regrow. In many areas, spring and fall rains keep lawns sufficiently moist during these periods. In an unusually dry spring or fall, however, supplemental irrigation should be applied.

2. Conservation of Natural Enemies. A number of native bird species, including grackles, starlings, cardinals, meadowlarks, and catbirds, feed on adult beetles. Native insect predators include pentatomids, such as *Podisus* spp., and wheel bugs (*Arilus cristatus*). Between 1919 and 1936, soon after Japanese beetles were discovered in this country, a large-scale effort to import biological control agents was launched by the former U.S. Bureau of Entomology. Of the 26 species imported, five became established (see the chart on p. 260). Two of these five, *Istochaeta aldrichi*, which parasitizes adults, and *Tiphia popilliavora*, which parasitizes larvae, show promise for providing good control in areas with high beetle infestations. The best way to protect these natural enemies is by keeping the use of conventional broad-spectrum garden pesticides to a minimum.

DIRECT PHYSICAL CONTROLS

Direct physical controls for Japanese beetles include hand removal, vacuuming, trapping, and spiking.

1. Hand Removal of Adult Beetles.
Hand picking can be effective in reducing light infestations of adult beetles on shrubs bordering the lawn. Any method that reduces the number of adult females, particularly early in the season, will tend to reduce the grub population and therefore the adult population the following year.

One simple, effective method for collecting significant numbers of adult beetles is to shake the plants over a drop cloth placed under the plants. The beetles feign death and drop downward when the plant is shaken. Pick up the drop cloth and empty the beetles into a bucket of soapy water solution. For smaller areas, hold a large funnel under the plant and over the soap solution to send the falling adults directly into the soapy water. This is best done on cool mornings when the beetles are still sluggish.

2. Vacuuming Adult Beetles.
A small handheld vacuum with a disposable bag can also be used to collect adult beetles. This method is commonly used by scientists to collect insects for research. Again, early morning is the best time for collection. Kill the beetles by placing the paper vacuum bag in a plastic bag and leave it in the sun, or put it in a bucket of soapy water, or in the freezer for 24 hours.

3. Trapping Adult Beetles.
Japanese beetle traps baited with food and/or sex pheromones have been on the market for many years. However, a recent study indicates that if only a few traps are used they can actually attract more beetles than they catch. Researchers at the University of Kentucky tested the effectiveness of the traps in capturing adult beetles and reducing the number of grubs in the soil. They found that if only one or two traps are used in a garden, as few as 54 percent of the beetles are captured and there is a net increase in beetles in the area around the traps. This is true despite the fact that a single trap often captures as many as 20,000 adult beetles in a single day. The experiment also revealed that the number of Japanese beetle grubs in the soil around the traps did not change, despite the large numbers of adult beetles found in the traps. The researchers concluded that the advice on the trap packages suggesting that only one or two traps are needed to protect an average-size yard is wrong.

Other studies have shown mass trapping to be effective at reducing adult beetle populations when large numbers of traps are used throughout an entire neighborhood. The traps should be placed every 200 ft. (60 m) around the perimeter of the area to be protected. In this way, the beetles are captured as they fly into the protected zone.

4. Spiking Beetle Grubs.
In studies at Colorado State University, a pair of lawn aerator sandals, sold for use in lawn aeration at online garden suppliers, was equal to or more effective than some insecticides

IMPORTED NATURAL ENEMIES OF JAPANESE BEETLES ESTABLISHED IN THE UNITED STATES

GENUS/SPECIES	ORDER/FAMILY	ASSOCIATION WITH HOST	ADULT FOOD SOURCE
Istochaeta aldrichi (=*Hyperecteina alcrichi*)	Diptera/Tachinidae	parasitizes adults	honeydew, nectar
Tiphia vernalis	Hymenoptera/Tiphiidae	parasitizes larvae	honeydew
T. popilliavora	same	parasitizes larvae	wild carrot
Dexilla ventralis	same	parasitizes larvae	nectar
Prosena siberita	same	parasitizes larvae	nectar of umbelliferous plants

Lawn aerator sandals are also known as the "spikes o' death" because they are so efficient at killing grubs and caterpillars that live in the top few inches of soil, the thatch, and the turf rootzone. (Photo by Gennady Kudelya/Shutterstock)

at controlling Japanese beetle grubs. Called "Spikes O' Death" by entomologists Whitney Cranshaw and Rick Zimmerman, the sandals are fitted with 3-in. (7.6-cm) nails and strap onto the wearer's shoes.

Wearing the sandals, the researchers walked over well-irrigated plots of lawn three to five times to achieve an average of two nail insertions per sq. in. (6.5 sq. cm). Two weeks later, flaps of turf in the plots were cut on three sides and pulled back so the grubs could be counted. Fifty-six percent of the grubs were killed by the spikes—a statistically significant level of control. The researchers concluded that this mechanical grub control technique, which can be used in late spring or late summer when grubs feed near the soil surface, shows promise. They plan to refine the method to increase penetration density, uniformity, and the depth reached by the spikes. A mechanized aerator with spikes in place of plugs is another possible avenue of research.

TREATMENT
DIRECT BIOLOGICAL CONTROLS

By far the most important natural enemies of the Japanese beetle are the milky spore disease bacteria *Bacillus popilliae* and *Bacillus lentimorbus*. These bacteria, particularly *B. popilliae*, have been largely responsible for the widespread reduction in beetle populations over the last 40 years. These and other biological controls are discussed below. The best way to apply these organisms is through a neighborhood effort, as one small affected lawn can infest the entire neighborhood. Treating one lawn amongst many will not reduce adult numbers appreciably.

1. Milky Spore Disease. *B. popilliae*, first isolated in 1933 from diseased grubs, was soon found to be virulent to Japanese beetle grubs and several other scarab grubs even though it is harmless to other organisms, including humans. Between 1939 and 1951, the USDA applied 178,000 lb. (80,740 kg) of spore dust containing 100 million spores/gram to 101,000 acres (40,875 hectares) in 14 states and the District of Columbia. To date, there is no evidence that beetle grubs have developed resistance to the disease.

Commercial formulations of milky spore disease are available for application to infested soil. The commercial spore dust is made by inoculating beetle grubs with the disease and then extracting the spores, which resemble dust or powder when dry. Each commercial formulation contains 100 million viable spores of *Bacillus popilliae* per gram. The spores can be applied any time except when the ground is frozen or a strong wind is blowing. It makes sense to apply the dust as soon as you detect grubs in the spring or late summer.

One producer recommends using the material in early August, when grubs are young and sunlight, which can damage BP spores, is less intense. It is usually applied at a rate of 10 lb. per acre (11 kg per hectare) in spots 4 ft. (1.2 m) apart. Roughly speaking, this comes to about one level teaspoon per spot. At this rate, approximately 20 oz. (567 g) of the spore dust is enough to treat 5,000 sq. ft. (465 sq. m) of lawn.

EFFECTS OF TOPICAL APPLICATIONS OF AZADIRACHTIN ON IMMATURE JAPANESE BEETLES

STAGES TREATED	PERCENT DEAD AND DEFORMED
larvae (unfed from storage)	100
larvae (after feeding for 14 days)	100
larvae (feeding complete)	92
pre-pupae (immobile)	92
pupae (24 hours after molt)	79
pupae (72 hours after molt)	0
pupae (just prior to adult emergence)	0

From T. L. Ladd, J. D. Warthen Jr., and M. G. Klein's "Japanese Beetle (*Coleoptera: Scarabaeidae*): The Effects of Azadirachtin on the Growth and Development of Immature Forms" (Journal of Economic Entomology, 1984). Data for 2 micrograms per insect.

According to producers of milky spore products, grubs become infected when they feed on the thatch or roots of grass where the spores have been applied. As the infected grubs move about in the soil, then die and disintegrate, they release one or two billion spores back into the soil. This spreads the pathogen to succeeding generations of grubs. Thus, tolerating a low population of grubs in your lawn helps keep the spores regenerating over the years, providing decades of protection.

> **"Keep in mind that microbial pesticides are fundamentally different in action than a quick-knockdown insecticide. It may take a season or two before they have a substantial impact."**

How quickly milky spore disease alone brings a grub infestation under control depends on many factors, including the size of the beetle population, the amount of milky spore dust applied, and the temperature of the soil. When grub populations are very high and feeding vigorously and the soil is at least 70°F (21°C) and very moist, the pathogen can spread through the grub population in a week or two. Keep in mind, however, that microbial pesticides are fundamentally different in action than a quick-knockdown insecticide. It may take a season or two before they have a substantial impact.

The high soil temperature required for rapid buildup of the spores makes the disease less effective north of New York City and through central Pennsylvania (latitude 40°N), where soil temperatures seldom reach 70°F (21°C) during the period when grubs are feeding. If you live in an area where soil temperatures seldom, if ever, reach 70°F, check with your county extension service for advice on the use and timing of applications of milky spore disease powder.

You can tell whether a grub has been infected with the disease by pulling off a leg and giving the grub a slight squeeze. If the blood has a milky color, the disease is present; if it is clear or slightly amber, the grub has not been infected.

Remember that adult Japanese beetles can migrate into your garden from as far away as ⅛ mile (0.2 km). They climb to the top of tall trees, then coast on wind currents until they find moist lawns on which to lay eggs. Thus, new generations of grubs can appear in your lawn in the fall even though the milky spore disease effectively suppressed grubs the previous spring. If the lawn is kept moist in the fall, the new grubs will probably become infected before they do much damage.

2. Parasitic Nematodes. The parasitic nematodes *Heterorhabditis bacteriophora* (formerly *H. heliothidis*) and *Steinernema carpocapsae* are effective against grubs of the Japanese beetle as well as against the masked chafers (*Cyclocephala* and *Amphimallon* spp.). These beneficial nematodes attack only certain insects; they do not feed on plants or infect mammals. These microscopic worms kill their host by introducing a bacterium that causes a disease that attacks only susceptible insects. Many soil-inhabiting insect larvae are susceptible. Field tests with *H. heliothidis* have shown that over 70 percent of the spring grub population was killed by the nematodes. This is considered quite acceptable for control of low to moderate grub populations, meaning 10 to 15 grubs per sq. ft. (0.1 sq. m). It is not yet known whether the nematodes produce an acceptable level of control if grub populations reach high levels of more than 25 to 30 grubs per sq. ft. When grub populations are high it may be advisable to treat the area twice; monitor between applications to be sure a second treatment is necessary. Following the nematode application, make sure you water the nematodes deeply enough into the soil so they will come into easy contact with the target grubs.

Nematodes can be purchased at many local garden centers and nurseries and from online suppliers. They arrive in damp packing material. They should then be mixed with water and applied to the lawn with a sprinkling can or through an irrigation

SUMMARY: LEAST-TOXIC BEETLE AND GRUB CONTROL

- Ideally, begin monitoring your lawn before you see damage. Learn how many grubs your lawn can tolerate before treatment is necessary.

- Improve the soil to promote strong, healthy grass.

- Minimize irrigation to reduce the moist habitat preferred by the beetles during egg laying.

- Conserve the natural enemies of the beetle by minimizing use of conventional pesticides.

- Hand-pick, vacuum, or trap adult beetles.

- Apply milky spore disease or beneficial nematodes to kill grubs.

- If chemical control is warranted, apply neem or an insecticidal soap/pyrethrin mix.

system. Adequate soil moisture is essential, because the nematodes need a film of water in which to migrate to and penetrate a grub. It is important to irrigate before and after applying nematodes. As much as ¼ in. to ½ in. (6 mm to 13 mm) of water may be needed to ensure that the nematodes are washed down through the grass to the soil, and that the soil is moist enough to provide a suitable habitat in the root zone.

Although nematodes can survive when grass is at the wilting point, they are far less mobile under these conditions. Proper irrigation is particularly critical when controlling grubs that appear in late summer and early fall, when soil moisture deficits are common.

TREATMENT
DIRECT CHEMICAL CONTROLS

The active ingredient azadirachtin, an extract of the neem tree (*Azadirachta indica*), has been shown in laboratory tests to kill the grubs and some pupal stages of Japanese beetles, as indicated in the chart on p. 262. Pyrethrum-based products are also effective.

1. Neem. Neem-based pesticides have become readily available in the United States under a number of brand names. In a study by a major distributor of microbial and other pesticides with low toxicity to mammals, 99 percent of the adult Japanese beetles given leaves sprayed with neem oil refused to eat and starved to death. This is evidence that neem acts as an antifeedant as well as an insecticide, so it could probably be used on foliage adjacent to lawns to discourage adult beetles from remaining in the area.

2. Pyrethrum-Based Products. Pyrethrins and synthetic pyrethroids can be used as soil drenches to kill grubs. See pp. 123–125 for details on these materials. A product containing insecticidal soap plus 0.01 percent pyrethrins extracted from the pyrethrum chrysanthemum flower is registered for use against adult beetles. Insecticidal soaps (see pp. 113–116) and pyrethrin extracts are among the safest insecticides for nontarget organisms currently available, and their combination in the new product promises to enhance their effectiveness against target pests.

The product, called Safer Brand Yard and Garden Insect Killer, is available at garden centers and online. Safer says that this product will suppress adult Japanese beetles, preventing egg laying. This, in turn, will reduce grubs in lawns the following year. But the product is not very effective if applied to the soil to kill grubs. This is because the soil is a very biologically active medium, and when soap or pyrethrin is placed in such an environment it is rapidly degraded by microorganisms.

CHINCH BUGS

(Order Hemiptera, family Lygaeidae)
Chinch bugs (*Blissus* spp.) are the most important of the "true bugs" (order Hemiptera) that become pests on lawns. Many other insects in this family, especially the big-eyed bug (*Geocoris bullatis*), are beneficial predators of pest insects such as the chinch bug.

Several species of chinch bug are serious pests of a variety of lawn grasses. The southern chinch bug (*B. insularis*), prevalent in the warm climates of the Southeast, South, and parts of the West, feeds primarily on St. Augustinegrass, but it also feeds on bermudagrass and zoysiagrass. The hairy chinch bug (*B. hirtus*), a pest in the Northeast, particularly from New Jersey to Ohio, feeds on bentgrasses, bluegrass, and red fescue.

BIOLOGY
Adult chinch bugs overwinter in dry grass and other debris that offers them protection. In spring or early summer, depending on temperature and moisture, overwintering females lay from 200 to 300 eggs on leaves of grass, or push them into soft soil and other protected places. Young nymphs (the immature stages) emerging from the eggs are bright red with a distinct white band across the back. The red changes to orange, orange-brown, and then to black as the nymph goes through five growth stages, or instars.

Nymphs range from about 1/20 in. (1.25 mm) long soon after hatching to nearly the size of the

---

THE CHINCH BUG

Chinch bugs are often found on drought-stressed lawns, where they suck juices from the leaves of grasses through needle-like beaks. Nymphs are easily recognized by their bright red color and white band across the back. Adults are black with shiny white wing covers. Big-eyed bugs feed on chinch bugs, which they superficially resemble. Their large eyes, wider bodies, and rapid movements help distinguish them from the pests. (Actual length of adult bugs, 1/4 in./6 mm)

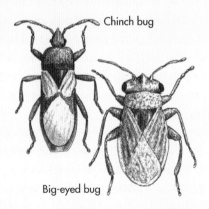

Chinch bug

Big-eyed bug

¼-in.-long (6 mm) adult. The nymphs mature into adults, which are black with a white spot on the back between their wing pads. The adult stage of the southern chinch bug can live 70 days or more, whereas hairy chinch bug adults live only 8 to 10 days. Adult southern chinch bugs tend to move by walking, whereas hairy chinch bug adults fly. In spring the adults can be seen flying to new areas.

The development time of eggs, nymphs, and adults is directly dependent upon temperature, and thus varies from one part of the country to another. Development of one generation, from egg to adult, can take 6 weeks at 83°F (28°C) and 17 weeks at 70°F (21°C). Chinch bugs produce up to seven generations per year in southern Florida, but only three to four generations in northern Florida, two generations in Ohio, and one in New Jersey.

The degree-day model concept of monitoring for pests uses temperature and development over time to predict when pests will be present at various stages. In Marin County, California, we've used the elm leaf beetle degree-day model to time treatments for the greatest benefit. Information on degree-day models can be found at UC IPM Online (www.ipm.ucdavis.edu/WEATHER/index.html). The degree-day template found at this website can be adapted to any pest whose developmental temperature range is known and where accurate temperatures can be recorded.

DAMAGE

Chinch bugs suck the juices from grass leaves through their needle-like beaks. They also inject toxic saliva into the plant that disrupts the plant's water-conducting system, causing it to wilt and die. Most damage is caused by nymphs that concentrate

The term *chinch bug* can refer to three different species in the Lygaeidae family; *Blissus insularis* (shown above)—the southern chinch bug; *B. leucopterus*—the true chinch bug; and *Nysius raphanus*—the false chinch bug. (Photo by Graham Montgomery)

in limited areas together with the adults and feed on the same plants until all the available juice has been extracted from the grass. This feeding pattern results in circular patches of damaged grass that turn yellow and then brown as they die. In the yellow stage, the grass superficially resembles grass that is drought-stressed. As it dies, the chinch bugs work outward from the center of the infestation, destroying a larger area as they advance.

Populations of chinch bugs are increased by hot, dry conditions. In wet, cool years, or when lawns are kept properly irrigated and not over-fertilized, the chinch bug populations decrease significantly.

DETECTION AND MONITORING

You can best protect your lawn from damage by chinch bugs (or any other pest) through regular monitoring. The objective is to detect pests while their populations are still small and determine whether their natural controls—such as adverse weather, other insects, and diseases—will keep the population low enough to prevent damage. Early detection allows you the option of using least-toxic controls.

Any lawn can tolerate a low population of chinch bugs and most other pests without sustaining significant damage. If the monitoring techniques described below indicate that there are fewer than 10 to 15 chinch bugs per sq. ft., generally no action is needed.

It is a good idea to begin monitoring as early as mid-April in south Florida, mid-May in Ohio, and early June in New Jersey, before overwintering adults have laid their full complement of spring eggs. A quick check of the lawn once a month through September should be sufficient in most areas.

COUNTING CHINCH BUGS
FLOTATION METHOD
If you see damage you suspect has been caused by chinch bugs but you cannot see the bugs themselves, try the flotation method. Cut the ends off a 2-lb. (0.9 kg) coffee can or 5-in.-dia. to 7-in.-dia. pipe, then push one end of the can a few inches into the sod. If this is difficult, use a knife to cut the ground around the perimeter of the can. Fill the can with water; if it recedes, top it off.

If chinch bugs are present, they will float to the surface in 5 to 10 minutes. If you are monitoring before you see any sign of chinch bug damage, the flotation method should be used in four or five random locations around the lawn. If damage has already occurred and you are trying to diagnose the cause, place the can at the edge of the damaged area to detect nymphs that have moved to the perimeter of the damage to feed on fresh grass.

SOAP-AND-FLANNEL-TRAP METHOD
Put 1 fluid oz. (30 ml) of dishwashing soap in a 2-gal. (7.5 l) sprinkling can and drench a 2-sq.-ft. (0.2 sq. m) area of lawn where you suspect there are chinch bugs. Watch the area for two or three minutes. Larger areas can be covered by putting the detergent in a hose attachment designed to hold pesticides for spraying the lawn. If chinch bugs are present, they will crawl to the surface of the grass.

Next, lay a piece of white cloth, such as an old bedsheet or a piece of nappy white flannel, over the area treated with the soapy water. Wait 15 to 20 minutes, then look under the cloth to see if chinch bugs have crawled onto it as they attempt to escape the soap. Their feet tend to get caught in the flannel's nap. Pick up the cloth and either vacuum it or rinse it off in a bucket of soapy water to remove the bugs. The vacuum bag should be disposed of so that the bugs will not return to the lawn.

This method can also be used to monitor for other insects such as lawn caterpillars, mole crickets, and beneficial insects that feed above the soil, but it will not bring soil-inhabiting grubs or billbugs to the surface.

Chinch bugs produce an offensive odor that advertises their presence, especially when populations are high or when they are crushed by foot traffic. Because nymphs tend to congregate in groups, it is important to check several areas of the lawn. Infes-tations often begin on the edges of lawns, particularly in sunny, dry spots, so check these areas carefully. Spread the grass apart with your hands and search the soil surface for reddish nymphs or black adults. Chinch bugs may also be seen on the tips of grass blades, where they climb during the day. Be certain to distinguish between the pest chinch bugs and their predators, the big-eyed bugs, which they superficially resemble. The sidebar at left describes two methods of counting chinch bugs.

TREATMENT
INDIRECT STRATEGIES
Indirect strategies for chinch bug control include planting resistant grass varieties, habitat management, and conserving native biological controls.

1. Chinch-Bug-Resistant Grass Cultivars.
If chinch bugs are a chronic problem, consider replacing your existing grass with a type that is resistant to chinch bugs. In southern states where St. Augustinegrass is the grass most often attacked by this pest, plant a variety that resists chinch bug or switch to centipedegrass, which is not attacked. In other parts of the country, try planting an endophytic variety of tall fescue or perennial ryegrass (see the discussion of insect-resistant endophytic grasses on pp. 235–237).

The Floratam variety of St. Augustinegrass was originally developed in the 1970s to resist chinch bug and St. Augustine Decline Virus (SADV). In the 40 years since its introduction it has lost its ability to resist chinch bugs, which are now considered a pest of the Floratam variety. This is a classic case of insect resistance developing over time.

2. Habitat Management.
Chinch bugs are attracted to lawns that have an excessive buildup of thatch, are insufficiently irrigated (often due to soil compaction), or have either too little nitrogen or too much in a highly soluble form that forces grass to grow too rapidly. Review the discussion of good lawn culture on in Chapter 12 for suggestions on overcoming these problems. Proper habitat

management will go a long way toward controlling the bugs.

3. Conservation of Native Biological Controls.
At least two beneficial organisms often move in to feed on chinch bugs. One is a predatory insect called the big-eyed bug (*Geocoris* spp.), which often appears where chinch bug populations are high and feeds on them. Big-eyed bugs superficially resemble chinch bugs, so you must learn to distinguish between the "good guys" and the pests. According to Ohio State University turf specialist Harry Niemczyk, "The body of the chinch bug is narrow, the head small, pointed, triangular-shaped, with small eyes, while the body of the big-eyed bug is wider, the head larger, blunt, with two large prominent eyes. Big-eyed bugs run quickly over the turf surface and are much more active insects than the slower-moving chinch bugs." *Geocoris* spp. are commercially available.

In addition, a tiny wasp, *Eumicrosoma beneficum*, can parasitize up to 50 percent of chinch bug eggs under favorable conditions. If the lawn is moist when the weather turns cool in fall, a beneficial fungus, *Beauveria* spp., often moves in and kills chinch bugs. Infected bugs become coated with a greyish cottony mass of fungal hyphae, which can be seen easily with the unaided eye. It should be noted that common broad-spectrum

"You can best protect your lawn from damage by chinch bugs (or any other pest) through regular monitoring."

insecticides, such as the organophosphates (malathion) and herbicides such as simazine, significantly reduce populations of these biological control organisms in lawns, thus triggering repeated pest outbreaks.

TREATMENT
DIRECT PHYSICAL CONTROLS
Small populations of chinch bugs can be removed from the lawn physically using the soap solution and white flannel cloth method described in the sidebar on the facing page. This is particularly appropriate when damage is just beginning to appear, because at this stage chinch bug nymphs are still congregated in specific locations and can be collected efficiently. Small vacuums may also be helpful.

TREATMENT
DIRECT CHEMICAL CONTROLS
If pesticide use seems necessary to bring a serious chinch bug infestation under control, consider using insecticidal soap, pyrethrin, or neem products. See pp. 113–116 and pp. 123–126 for information on these materials.

SUMMARY: LEAST-TOXIC CHINCH BUG CONTROL

- Aerate your lawn in the spring and fertilize with a slow-release form of nitrogen. During hot summer months, irrigate as needed to maintain adequate soil moisture. Repeat the aeration and fertilization in fall.

- Monitor once a month beginning in May to detect developing chinch bug infestations. Check several areas of the lawn, particularly borders.

- Conserve native biological controls.

- Remove small infestations with soap-and-flannel traps.

- Treat large infestations with insecticidal soap or pyrethrum/pyrethroids.

- Begin a long-term program of replacing existing grass with varieties that show a high resistance to chinch bugs.

LAWN DISEASES: OVERVIEW
Lawn diseases are caused primarily by fungi that live in the soil or thatch layer. Over 400 species of fungi are known to live in the lawn habitat, but less than 25 percent are potentially harmful. Even the

disease-causing fungi can live in association with grass plants without damaging them as long as environmental conditions and cultural practices do not create opportunities for attack.

The disease-causing fungi are often saprophytes, meaning they can feed on decaying organic matter. Thus, they act as decomposers of dead plant parts, such as lawn clippings and thatch, helping recycle plant nutrients. Other fungi that cause disease can remain in the soil for a long time in the inactive spore stage; they attack only when the lawn ecosystem is thrown out of balance by various stresses, such as high temperature combined with excessive irrigation and fertilization. The overall health of soil organisms is one of the key components in disease avoidance.

This suggests why good cultural management, which involves proper irrigation, fertilization, aeration, and mowing, and the avoidance of pesticides whenever possible, are the best defense against lawn disease. These preventive management practices are described at length in Chapter 12; if you want to avoid lawn diseases or solve an existing problem, read that chapter before proceeding.

DISEASE IDENTIFICATION

To manage a disease problem effectively in the least-toxic manner, it is essential that you identify the disease organism correctly. Often this can be done by learning to recognize the characteristic damage symptoms that pathogenic fungi cause on grasses. The sidebar on pp. 272–273 describes common lawn disease symptoms.

Photographic keys to common lawn diseases are often available from county cooperative extension offices. For example, the Nebraska Cooperative Extension Service publishes an inexpensive booklet called *Turfgrass Disease and Damage Prevention and Control: A Common-Sense Approach* (University of Nebraska Cooperative Extension Service Publications, 1985). The O. M. Scott Company sells an excellent pocket-size guide, *Scott's Guide to the Identification of Turfgrass Diseases and Insects* (O. M. Scott and Sons, 1987). The photos and descriptive information in these booklets are very useful for identifying common lawn diseases. A more scholarly disease atlas with excellent illustrations is the *Compendium of Turfgrass Diseases* (American Phytopathological Society, 2005). Conducting an online photo search

"Good cultural management, which involves proper irrigation, fertilization, aeration, and mowing, and the avoidance of pesticides whenever possible, are the best defense against lawn disease."

for the disease can also be helpful in disease identification. Be specific in your search, using scientific names whenever possible. We still frequently make use of the county extension service to confirm our diagnoses. When you bring a good sample to the county extension office, you are helping the specialists and master gardeners better understand the pests that affect your locale. Several county extension agents that we know always thank us for bringing in samples so that they know what is happening around the county.

One difficulty in disease identification is that attack by pathogens often occurs as a secondary affliction. That is, something else so weakens the grass that a pathogen is able to attack it. A classic example involves a leaf spot disease on Kentucky bluegrass caused by the fungus *Drechslera* (=*Helminthosporium*) *sorokinianum*. Normally this fungus is a very weak competitor with other microorganisms and is unable to get a foothold and attack plants. However, when the thatch layer of the lawn is allowed to dry out due to improper or nonexistent irrigation and is then re-moistened, the normal population of beneficial microorganisms drops, and the thatch leaks more sugars and amino acids than it normally would. *Drechslera* utilizes these nutrients in the absence of the competing microbes and rapidly becomes a problem. In this case, simply identifying the symptom—the disease-causing pathogen—would not give you enough information to solve the problem in the long term. One option when turfgrass and thatch dry out is to wet the lawn with compost tea made from mature high-quality compost. This re-wets the area while providing an instantaneous supply of beneficial microbes. This tactic could reduce or prevent a pathogen from taking hold.

Another complication is that some disease symptoms resemble symptoms produced by insect damage. For example, damage by young sod webworms is often mistaken for a leaf spot disease. Alternatively, the disease symptoms can resemble cultural problems. The discoloration of large grass areas due to iron deficiency is sometimes mistaken for the disease caused by *Drechslera*. If you aren't certain how to identify the symptom you are observing, collect a sample of the damaged grass as described in the sidebar on p. 270 and take or mail it to your local county cooperative extension office. Plant pathologists at the nearest land-grant university will culture the sample and determine whether a disease is present.

Keeping records is very important. In general, a lawn does not contract every disease it is susceptible to, nor is it attacked by a different disease every year. Usually, a single disease or a few diseases occur on a particular lawn from year to year. If your lawn has a disease now, chances are it has occurred before and that it coincides with certain weather patterns or lawn maintenance practices. Keep a record of when you water, mow, and fertilize, and of weather just before and during disease outbreaks. It will help you identify the conditions triggering the disease so you can modify them to the degree possible. When weather is forecast that favors a fungal attack, you can then take preventive

measures to reduce the severity of the disease or possibly prevent it from becoming established. This is only possible if you have kept records and know how the disease expresses itself in you particular locale.

TIP Smartphones and computers have the ability to alert you to weather conditions based on parameters that you set. This early warning system can assist you in catching disease outbreaks early, when they are most easily managed.

FACTORS THAT TRIGGER LAWN DISEASE

Although disease spores may be present at any time in your lawn, an epidemic will not occur unless all of these factors are present:

• a host plant (i.e., the grass susceptible to attack by the specific fungus)

• a disease organism (i.e., the fungus that attaches itself to host plants and extracts nutrients from them)

• favorable environmental conditions (including the natural and man-made conditions and practices that encourage the development of disease, such as temperature, moisture, watering, fertilizing, mowing, and soil compaction)

• a means of spore distribution (i.e., the means by which spores are transported from plant to plant, such as lawn mowers, foot traffic, wind, water, and infected grass clippings)

Howard Ohr, plant pathologist with the University of California Cooperative Extension Service, lists the following factors as significant in whether or not diseases attack lawns:

1. Water. Most disease fungi need free water or very high relative humidity to germinate, grow, and infect grasses. Water movement over the surface of the grass helps spread some pathogens. For example, the *Pythium* fungus thrives in warm, wet conditions, especially if the soil has been fertilized recently with nitrogen. It grows rapidly and releases its zoospores, which are capable of swimming in water to new plants. More important, the movement of water over the grass surface rapidly transports these spores over wide areas, where they infect more host plants.

HOW TO COLLECT AND PREPARE A SAMPLE OF DISEASED LAWN FOR IDENTIFICATION

Take the sample from an area that is just beginning to show symptoms. Turf layers about 1 ft. (0.3 m) square and 2 in. (5 cm) deep are recommended. If the disease occurs in patches, half the turf in the sample should be from the diseased area, the other half from adjacent healthy turf. If large samples cannot be collected, cut several samples about 4 in. (10 cm) square and 4 in. deep. Do not soak the samples with water before or after collection or expose them to heat or sunlight.

If the sample is to be mailed, wrap it in several layers of paper or foil (not plastic, which retains too much moisture, causing the sample to rot). Pack samples tightly in boxes, and include a note providing as much of the following information as possible:

- species and cultivar(s) of grasses affected

- age of the lawn

- overall symptoms, answering these questions: Is the disease uniform throughout the area, or is it in low, wet areas only? Do symptoms occur in circular or irregular patches? How large are they? What color are they?

Does the disease pattern suggest the involvement of your lawn mower or other equipment? Are there holes in the affected turf? Can the plants be pulled out easily, or are they firmly rooted?

- specific symptoms and signs on leaves of affected plants: spots, yellowing, water-soaking, banding, shape and color of lesions, presence of fungal mycelia and/or fruiting bodies, color of fungal signs

- general background information on the lawn environment: soil type; drainage; air movement (free or blocked by buildings?); the irrigation program for the past month; fertilization dates, types, and amounts; the record of pesticide applications

- weather conditions just before and at the time the disease symptoms appeared

- dates symptoms were first observed and the date the sample was collected

Take digital pictures, both long shots and close-ups (macro), of the diseased area. Take several "landscape" shots, covering a full 360 degrees, so that the extension specialist will understand how the site is situated in terms of wind, slope, compass direction, sun exposure, building location, and other important site characteristics. Put these pictures on a flash drive, CD, or DVD and include them with your sample.

Take or overnight-mail the sample to the local cooperative extension office or state university plant pathology department. Remember that grass is a living system subject to decay as soon as it is removed from its "natural" environment. Be sure to collect samples early in the week. If possible, always mail samples between Monday and Thursday so that the package does not sit in a warehouse or mailbox over the weekend. It is common courtesy when sending a sample to alert the recipient by phone or email that a sample is coming to them. Accurate identification requires prompt examination so that secondary pathogens and other organisms present in the sample but not related to the problem will not overgrow the sample and make diagnosis impossible or inaccurate. Include your telephone number, email, and street addresses, so the diagnostician can reach you.

The water or high relative humidity must be available over a long enough period to permit spores to germinate and infect grasses. This is usually 18 hours or more. Water applied in late evening or at night often remains on foliage for long periods, giving pathogens the maximum opportunity for infection, whereas water applied in the early morning usually dries rapidly, preventing pathogens from becoming established. Too much water on grass plants may also increase their succulence or stress them by preventing oxygen uptake by the roots, both of which result in increased susceptibility to disease. Too little water can trigger disease outbreaks as described on p. 269 for *Drechslera* leaf spot.

2. Temperature. All grasses have a temperature range in which they grow most vigorously. Within this range they are most resistant to many pathogens; below or above it they become more susceptible.

The disease organism also has an optimum temperature range, but it may be able to grow sufficiently above or below this range to cause a serious problem. In addition, many lawn disease fungi are active at temperatures that may stress the grass. For example, several fungi known as snow molds are active under a blanket of snow. The fungus *Pythium* is capable of rapid growth and spread during 85°F to 95°F (29°C to 35°C) weather, when cool-season grasses such as Kentucky bluegrass and perennial ryegrass are under heat stress. The disease "spring dead spot" evidently occurs when bermudagrass is dormant. The most effective means of minimizing the effects of temperature on disease development is to choose grass species and varieties that are best adapted to your area.

3. Fertilizer. The effects of fertilizing on disease development vary with the disease. For example, when bentgrasses are grown with low but balanced levels of fertilizer, they are less susceptible to attack by *Pythium*. However, when calcium is deficient or out of balance in the soil relative to other nutrients, the plants are more susceptible to attack. Brown patch, caused by *Rhizoctonia solani*, is more severe if nitrogen levels are too high while phosphorus and potassium levels remain normal. If all three nutrients are lower than normal, disease severity increases. The effects of *Sclerotinia* dollar spot are more severe on nitrogen-deficient turf and may be reduced by increasing nitrogen fertilizer. This reduction is due to an increased growth response by the plants. (See the discussion of lawn fertilization in Chapter 12 for an overview of practices that ensure sufficient lawn fertility.)

4. Mowing. Mowing inflicts a large number of wounds on grass through which pathogens may enter. Brown patch is more severe on grasses that are cut short, possibly because the mowing wounds provide openings for pathogens. Mowing also appears to lower disease resistance by removing some photosynthesizing portions of the plant. The consequent reduced supply of sugars and starches results in a weakening of disease resistance. Kentucky bluegrass plants cut below 1½ in. (3.8 cm), for example, show a marked increase in incidence and severity of diseases caused by *Drechslera*.

5. Aeration. Coring the soil improves the ability of gases and water to move in and out of the soil. This reduces the anaerobic (oxygen-deprived) conditions in the soil that promote certain disease organisms. It also allows the grasses to grow more vigorously, enhancing their innate disease resistance. Aeration has the added bonus of killing grubs in the soil when it is done while grubs are near the surface for feeding.

6. Thatch Management. Thatch is the tightly intermingled layer of living and dead stems, leaves, and roots of grass that develops between the green vegetation and soil surface. When the thatch is thick enough—greater than ½ in. to ¾ in. (1.9 cm) —grass roots develop in it rather than in the soil. Plants rooted in thatch are more subject to drought and inadequate nutrition, and thus become weakened. In addition, thatch is colonized by fungi that may, under suitable conditions, become pathogenic and attack growing plants, especially those in a weakened state. A reduction of thatch reduces the food base for disease organisms, thereby reducing the opportunity for pathogens to produce disease.

7. Pesticides. The application of common lawn pesticides can increase disease problems. For example, in a study at the University of Illinois it was found that frequent applications of two pre-emergent herbicides, calcium arsenate and bandane, increased the incidence of *Drechslera* (=*Helminthosporium*) disease on Kentucky bluegrass. The researchers concluded that the herbicides killed off earthworms. In the absence of these earthworm decomposers and the microorganisms

DAMAGE SYMPTOMS AND LIFE CYCLES OF COMMON LAWN DISEASE ORGANISMS

WARM-SEASON DISEASES (70°F TO 100°F, 21°C TO 38°C)

Brown Patch (*Rhizoctonia solani*)

Brown patch generally appears as roughly circular brown patches from a few inches to several feet across. Infected leaves first appear dark and water soaked, then eventually dry, wither, and turn brown. Brown to black fungal fruiting bodies may be found on stolons or under sheaths. The patch may be surrounded when humidity is high by a "smoke ring" of fungal mycelium. It disappears as the foliage dries. A musky odor may be perceptible 12 to 24 hours before the first appearance of the disease. In some cases, centers of damage may recover, resulting in a brown ring that surrounds healthy grass.

Brown patch can survive unfavorable periods as inert hyphal masses (fungal threads) or mycelia in infected plants and debris, or as growing saprophytic hyphae in soil. Under warm, humid conditions, hyphal masses germinate, and mycelia spread through leaf thatch or soil, infecting any roots or leaves contacted. Infected tissues collapse and shrivel rapidly when exposed to sun or wind. Hyphal masses (sclerotia) form on or in infected tissues, and are released into the soil as dead tissues decompose. The sclerotia are highly resistant to fungicides.

Fusarium Blight, Summer Patch (*Fusarium culmorum* and *F. tricinctum; Magnaporthe poae*)

The symptoms of these two diseases are so similar that we group them together. Infected turf has small, circular, 2-in. (5-cm) spots of dead and dying grass that often enlarge to 24 in. (60 cm) in diameter. Spots begin as dark blue to purple wilted turf and turn straw-colored to light tan when dead. The grass in the center of each spot may remain healthy and become surrounded by a band of dead turf, a symptom called "frog eye." Both leaf blades and the basal crown may be affected; summer patch tends to produce leaf die-back from the tip down, whereas fusarium blight tends to kill the basal crown. Pinkish fusarium mycelium can be seen on the surface of the crown when soil moisture is high.

These fungi overwinter as mycelia in infected plants and debris, and as thick-walled, microscopic chlamydospores in thatch or soil. When favorable conditions occur, mycelia grow rapidly and spores germinate. The fungi sporulate freely in moist thatch; spores are carried by wind and water to host plant leaves, roots, or crowns, although main entry is via the roots. All parts of the plant can be infected. Sporulation may occur on infected plant leaves.

Pythium Blight (*Pythium* spp.)

Early symptoms are circular red-brown spots from 1 in. to 6 in. (2.5 cm to 15 cm) across. When dew-covered, infected leaves are water soaked, dark, and may feel slimy. Leaves shrivel and turn red-brown as they dry. Dew-moistened spots may contain cottony purple-grey to white mycelium at the margins. Infected plants collapse quickly. In hot, moist weather, infected areas enlarge rapidly. The disease spreads along drainage patterns, thus it may appear in long streaks.

These fungi are soil saprophytes, and thus are common in soil, thatch, and the roots of mildly infected hosts. In the presence of high nitrogen, water, and heat, motile zoospores or mycelia may penetrate host plants, producing new mycelia. The fungi spread from leaf to leaf by mycelial growth. Resting spores (oospores) are produced in or on dead tissues. All spore forms may be transmitted by water or in infected soil on shoes and equipment.

MODERATE-SEASON DISEASES (60°F TO 80°F, 16°C TO 27°C)

Dollar Spot (*Lanzia* and *Moellerodiscus* spp., formerly *Sclerotinia*)

Dollar spot appears as round, bleached to straw-colored spots ranging from the size of a quarter to that of a silver dollar sunken in the turf. Individual spots may coalesce to destroy large areas of turf. Fresh spots may show fluffy grey-white mycelium in the early morning, when grass is wet. Leaf spots appear as bleached-out or light-tan lesions over the entire width of the blade, and have red-brown margins (in all hosts except annual bluegrass).

These fungi survive unfavorable periods as dormant hyphae in infected plants, and as mycelial masses (stromata) on the surfaces of leaves. When conditions become favorable, the hyphae begin growing out into humid air, infecting any moist leaf they contact (roots and rhizomes are not infected). No spores are formed by these fungi in nature, so fungal distribution to new hosts is by movement of infected grass by people, animals, water, wind, and equipment.

Necrotic Ring Spot (*Leptosphaeria korrae*)

Symptoms resemble those of fusarium blight and summer patch. However, necrotic ring spot occurs primarily in cool, wet weather, whereas the others are warm-season diseases. Dead patches of grass can reach 12 in. (30 cm) in diameter, with the characteristic "frog eye" frequently present.

COOL-SEASON DISEASES (40°F TO 75°F, 5°C TO 18°C)

Drechslera Melting Out or Leaf Spot (*Drechslera sativus,* formerly *Helminthosporium sativum*)

Early symptoms are small dark-purple or black leaf spots occurring primarily during cool weather in spring and fall. The centers of the spots may become light tan as the spots enlarge. The entire blade may become involved, appearing dry and straw-colored. Cool, drizzly weather promotes infection of roots and crowns, producing the "melting out" phase that can severely thin out turf. Similar symptoms can occur in summer when temperatures exceed 85°F (29°C), but this melting out is cause by another fungus, *Bipolaris sorokinianum.*

Fungi can survive unfavorable conditions as spores and dormant mycelium in infected plant tissue and debris. They are saprophytes, and will grow and sporulate when dry debris is moistened. During cool, wet weather, when moisture films can occur on leaf surfaces, spores produce germ tubes, which penetrate grass leaves. Lesions occur, and sporulation may occur on the larger lesions. Infection may continue until the cold weather returns.

Fusarium Patch, or Pink Snow Mold (*Microdochium nivale,* formerly *Fusarium nivale*)

In the absence of snow, fusarium patch occurs as reddish-brown, circular spots from 1 in. to 8 in. (2.5 cm to 20 cm) across in infected turf. Under snow cover the spots are tan to whitish-grey or red-brown and expand from 2 in. to 3 in. (5 cm to 7.5 cm) to 1 ft. to 2 ft. (0.3 m to 0.6 m) in diameter. Immediately after the snow has melted, pink mycelia may be visible at the margins of the spots.

Fungi survive unfavorable periods as mycelia in infected debris or as spores in the soil. Under cool, wet, overcast, or shaded conditions, mycelium infects leaves, spreading rapidly in temperatures between 32°F and 61°F (0°C to 16°C). If overcast skies are broken by sufficient sun to keep up carbohydrate levels in grass, there is rarely a problem. Or if the turf dries and warms up after a prolonged overcast period, the fungus becomes inactive.

Grey Snow Mold (*Typhula spp.*)

Infected turf develops circular, grey-straw to brown spots 3 in. (7.5 cm) to 2 ft. (0.6 m) across as the snow melts. Fuzzy, grey-white mycelia may be visible, especially at the margins of the spots immediately after the snow melts. The color of the mycelium gives the disease its name.

These fungi oversummer as dark-colored, small sclerotia on infected leaves. When temperatures reach 50°F to 64°F (10°C to 18°C), sclerotia may germinate if the humidity is high. Mycelium may be produced directly or may be preceded by sexual-spore production. Mycelia may infect grass plants under snow cover. When the snow melts, light causes the mycelia to go from the infective stage to production of sclerotia. New sclerotia are produced in infected leaves and crowns, and are released into the soil as dead plants decompose.

Note that temperature ranges are approximate; some diseases may occur at higher or lower temperatures.

that process thatch initially broken down by earthworms, the thatch layer grew, stressing the grass and making it more susceptible to disease. There are many other studies in the scientific literature describing how increased disease incidence is associated with the use of insecticides, herbicides, and even fungicides.

GENERAL BIOLOGY OF LAWN DISEASE FUNGI

The fungi that cause most lawn diseases live in the soil and in the dead leaves, stems, and decaying roots that form thatch. Fungi are low, thread-like forms of plant life that are incapable of manufacturing their own food. Instead, they live off living or dead plant or animal matter. It is important to inoculate and to provide conditions that maintain the highest levels of beneficial microbes in the soil. These may not only be antagonists of pathogens, but their sheer numbers might also crowd out pathogens and/or provide the plant with a last line of defense.

Most fungi produce spores (seed-like units) or other resistant forms (sclerotia or stromata), which can be spread by wind, water, or mechanical means. Under ideal conditions, the spores germinate and produce branches (hyphae). These grow and multiply into masses of thread-like appendages called mycelia, which are sometimes visible with the naked eye. The hyphae penetrate the plant tissues through natural openings or wounds such as those caused by mowing. They grow, drawing their sustenance from the plant and breaking down its tissues until they destroy its normal functioning.

At maturity, the fungus gives off more spores (which are sometimes produced on mushrooms, the fruiting bodies of fungi). These spores start the life cycle over again. In a few cases, spores are not created, and perpetuation of the life of the fungus is carried on by parts of the mycelium scattered about the lawn or soil. The sidebar on pp. 272–273 describes the life cycles and damage symptoms of

a number of the most common lawn disease organisms and indicates the seasons of the year each disease usually occurs. We have limited our discussion to lawn disease organisms that are common throughout most of North America for which there are effective management strategies that involve little or no use of conventional fungicides.

Given the major role temperature plays in the development of lawn diseases, specific turf diseases usually are associated with the cool, moderate, or warm seasons of the year, depending on geographic location. Thus, we begin the following

"The application of common lawn pesticides can increase disease problems."

sections on treatment of lawn diseases with those associated with the warm season (generally June, July, and August), and end with those that generally appear during the cool seasons (fall through early spring).

BROWN PATCH OR RHIZOCTONIA BLIGHT

(*Rhizoctonia solani*)

Humid weather with temperatures above 85°F (29°C) during the day and 60°F (16°C) at night, in combination with leaf surfaces that remain wet for 6 to 8 hours, creates ideal conditions for the onset of brown patch. Unbalanced soil fertility and excessively low mowing heights exacerbate the disease. Susceptible grasses include bentgrasses, bermudagrass, bluegrasses, fescues, ryegrasses, and zoysia. Damage symptoms are described in the sidebar on pp. 272–273.

TREATMENT

INDIRECT STRATEGIES

Indirect strategies for controlling brown patch focus on planting resistant grass cultivars or blends and on horticultural controls. See pp. 233–237 for details on resistant cultivars and Chapter 12 for background information on the horticultural controls discussed in this section.

1. Water Management. During periods of drought or heat, give the lawn a long, slow irrigation to keep adequate water in the soil. Irrigate as infrequently as possible while temperatures are high and ripe for brown patch development. Improve water infiltration into the soil by aerating and top-dressing (see p. 239) so water does not puddle on the grass.

> **TIP** Water only in the early morning to ensure that the grass dries before nightfall. Avoid overhead sprinkling during windy and/or hot conditions to keep waste and evaporation to a minimum. Water deeply, to thoroughly wet the turfgrass rootzone.

2. Fertility Management. High levels of nitrogen in combination with low levels of phosphorus, potassium, or calcium exacerbate disease. Avoid heavy early spring and summer fertilization with highly soluble nitrate fertilizers. Apply only moderate levels of nitrogen, and make sure potassium and phosphorus levels are in balance with other nutrients, especially calcium. Use organic or slow-release fertilizers and do not fertilize during hot periods.

3. Mowing and Thatch Management. Avoid frequent, low mowing of the grass. Raise the mowing height to 2½ in. (6.5 cm) or higher and remove diseased grass clippings. A dull mower frays the edges of cut grass blades and serves as a point of entry for the fungus. Excessive layers of thatch favor the disease, so use the methods discussed on p. 239 to keep thatch in check.

4. "Poling" and Syringing. One study found that dew and other nutrient-bearing free water on grass leaves is a key factor in the development of brown patch. Dew or "guttation water" contains high amounts of nutritious sugars that wash out of grass leaves. This food source attracts fungi such as *Rhizoctonia*. Initial infection of the above-ground grass blades was observed to take place through a lower leaf that is in contact with the soil. The fungus then grew over and through this leaf to others, eventually reaching the uppermost clipped ends.

During a brown patch attack, the fungus multiplied in the drops of dew and spread rapidly to adjacent plants by bridging the drops of water on grass blade tips in spider-web fashion.

Given the major role dew appears to play in the spread of this pathogen, it is wise to remove dew from the lawn in the morning, either by dragging a hose or a flexible bamboo pole across the lawn, a procedure called poling, or by squirting the dew off with water from a hose, which is called syringing. Studies at the University of Rhode Island indicate that spraying turf with a wetting agent such as soap or detergent helps prevent the accumulation of water drops on the grass blades for a number of days, thereby effectively controlling brown patch. Another strategy is to syringe with an active compost tea; this not only washes off the guttation and dew but also provides a beneficial microbial boost to both above- and below-ground plant parts.

5. Hydrated Lime. On golf courses, hydrated lime is used to keep the surface of the leaves relatively dry, reducing *Rhizoctonia* damage. The procedure is described by Houston Couch, author of *Diseases of Turfgrasses* (Krieger Publications, 2000). According to Couch, at the first sign of the disease you should broadcast the lime at the rate of 10 lb. (4.5 kg) per 1,000 sq. ft. (93 sq. m) of grass. To reduce the possibility of plant injury, apply the lime only when the grass is dry. Pole the limed grass immediately after application, and do not irrigate for 24 hours. Repeat the application at roughly three-week intervals as long as the disease is present.

TREATMENT

DIRECT PHYSICAL CONTROLS

The effectiveness of covering soil with thin sheets of clear plastic so sunlight heats it enough to kill disease organisms is well documented. This disease control practice, called solarization, is being adopted increasingly by farmers for the control of many agricultural disease organisms that also attack lawns. If a brown patch outbreak has killed extensive areas of your lawn, necessitating renovation of the lawn, we recommend solarizing the soil first. Details are provided on pp. 212–213.

Solarization, done in sunny, warm weather, heats the soil to temperatures in the range of 113°F to 122°F (45°C to 50°C) at a depth of 4 in. (10 cm), and 100°F to 113°F (38°C to 45°C) at a depth of 8 in. (20 cm). Most lawn pathogens are present in the top 2 in. to 4 in. (5 cm to 10 cm) of soil, and are killed at these temperatures. Fortunately, many beneficial microorganisms such as *Trichoderma* (discussed below) can survive. Thus, solarization "pasteurizes" the soil, tipping the balance in favor of the beneficials. This contrasts with chemical fumigation, which sterilizes soils, killing virtually all microbes and creating a biotic vacuum that can be recolonized by pathogens just as readily as beneficials.

Israeli researchers have found that the beneficial *Trichoderma* spp. are even more effective at suppressing *Rhizoctonia* and other pathogens if introduced into solarized soils. You can probably achieve the same effect by solarizing the diseased portion of your lawn, then incorporating large amounts of aged compost or pulverized tree bark into the soil before replanting the lawn.

TREATMENT

DIRECT BIOLOGICAL CONTROLS

Recognition of the important role played by benefi-cial microorganisms in suppressing disease organisms is growing (see the discussion of suppressive soils on pp. 231–233). The best-studied microbe antagonistic to species of *Rhizoctonia* is *Trichoderma*. This beneficial fungus is present in homemade compost and in the tree-bark-based soil amendments sold in nurseries.

Trichoderma is a very strong competitor in the soil habitat and has demonstrated its ability to outcompete a wide variety of disease organisms. In Europe it is being used to control problems ranging from Dutch elm disease, caused by the fungus *Ceratocystis ulmi*, to decay organisms that attack utility poles. In Israel, scientists have demonstrated the ability of *Trichoderma harzianum* to control tomato fruit rot caused by the same species of *Rhizoctonia* that attacks lawns.

In observing the behavior of *Trichoderma*, researchers found that when it moves into the vicinity of *Rhizoctonia* it forms more branches (mycelia) and grows toward the disease organism. This directed growth is apparently the result of a chemical stimulus released by the *Rhizoctonia*. Once in contact with the *Rhizoctonia* fungus, *Trichoderma* coils around it. Scientists think that once *Trichoderma* is in the proximity of a host organism like *Rhizoctonia*, it produces antibiotics that damage or kill the other fungi.

This and other research linking *Trichoderma* to control of *Rhizoctonia* suggests that inoculation of a lawn with *Trichoderma* might slow or prevent development of brown patch. Although there are as yet no scientific studies of the effect of *Trichoderma* on lawns, we have some suggestions if you want to experiment on your own.

Commercial sources of *Trichoderma harzianum* are available in the United States. One current brand is RootShield Home and Garden biological fungicide. Another convenient source of *Trichoderma* is your backyard compost pile or a bag of commercial pulverized tree bark, which usually contains these beneficial organisms. Researchers at Ohio State University found that composted hardwood bark aged at least one year contains high numbers of *Trichoderma*, and that these beneficials suppress *Rhizoctonia* when compost constitutes 40 percent to 50 percent of the soil mix. *Trichoderma* have also been found to colonize compost piles.

Thus, if your lawn is showing damage from brown patch, you can try poking some holes in the damaged turf and adding a ¼-in. to ½-in. (6-mm to 13-mm) layer of composted tree bark (which is available from nurseries) or compost. Be sure that the bark you buy is well composted, because poorly aged bark does not work as effectively. If you are using your own compost, take it from the middle of an aged, stabilized pile. You can also try making a compost or bark "tea" by soaking a burlap bag full of the organic matter in a bucket of water for several days, then watering the damaged area with the solution. Laboratory studies have found that leachates of composted bark suppress disease, so we suggest trying the tea as a means of inoculating the lawn with *Trichoderma*.

If you try incorporating these compost materials or use the tea, leave at least one section of lawn untreated so you have a "control" to compare the treated area with. This will help you decide whether or not the method worked. Remember that lawn diseases are so temperature- and moisture-dependent that a sudden change in the weather can start or stop a disease outbreak. Keep records, and don't jump to any conclusions about the method until you have tried it a few times.

A number of organic fertilizer products enhanced with beneficial microorganisms (actinomycetes, fungi, and bacteria) have been shown to prevent or halt some lawn diseases, including brown patch. These products are discussed in Chapter 12.

TIP Inoculation of seeds with *Trichoderma* before planting has produced high levels of protection from the "damping off" forms of *Rhizoctonia* responsible for the death of many grasses at the seedling stage. Thus, you might try coating grass seed with sifted compost dust before sowing. Top-dress the seed with weed-free topsoil or compost and water in with compost tea.

One of the recent microbial additions is the actinomycete *Streptomyces lydicus*, which is labeled to suppress or prevent *Rhizoctonia*. It is also said to prevent or suppress *Pythium*, *Fusarium*, *Phytophthora*, and root decay fungi. Currently this microbe is available in two formulations. One is Actino-Iron, a dry formulation with iron and humic acid. Another, Actinovate SP, is a water-soluble powder labeled for the following soil-borne fungi: *Pythium*, *Rhizoctonia*, *Phytophthora*, *Verticillium*, *Fusarium*, and others. The label also claims that it suppresses and controls foliar diseases such as powdery mildew, downy mildew, greasy spot, *Botrytis*, *Sclerotinia*, *Monilinia*, *Alternaria*, *Erwinia*, and others.

For additional information on microbial soil amendments, see the discussion of necrotic ring spot on pp. 278–280.

TREATMENT
DIRECT CHEMICAL CONTROLS

Least-toxic chemical controls for brown patch include neem oil, garlic oil, and fungicidal soap. It should be pointed out that the microbial preparations we discussed under biological controls are technically and legally pesticides. These usually go by the name "bio-pesticides."

1. Neem Oil. Neem oil, a product extracted from India's neem tree (*Azadirachta indica*), acts as a fungicide as well as an insecticide. Indian scientists testing the ability of neem oil to prevent or suppress diseases of gram, a type of bean, found that when soil is drenched with neem oil, *Rhizoctonia solani* as well as other pathogens do not form sclerotia and therefore do not reproduce.

In addition to other active ingredients, neem oil contains large amounts of sulfur compounds. Sulfur has been used as a fungicide for centuries, and it is thought that the sulfur compounds play a role in neem's toxic effects on certain fungi. Neem is available for use as an insecticide under various brand names. It is also registered by the EPA for use as a fungicide. Household neem soap is sold in many import stores that carry products from India, and it might be worth experimenting with if you are inclined to use homemade rather than commercial preparations.

2. Garlic Oil. In laboratory studies in India, oil from the common garlic plant (*Allium sativum*) used as a soil drench at a concentration of 150 to 200 ppm (0.02 oz. to 0.03 oz. per gal.) completely inhibited sclerotium formation and mycelial growth in *Rhizoctonia solani.* In laboratory studies at the University of Hawaii, extracts from the roots of 1-month-old garlic seedlings were ground up in water and diluted (1.5 g wet weight of root per l ml of water). A solution of 30-percent garlic root extract applied to the soil (at 100 ml per 1,000 g of soil) held losses of papaya seedlings from damping off disease to only 3 percent, compared to 53 percent in the untreated soil. The success of these trials and others has led to a number of commercially prepared garlic pesticides.

3. Fungicidal Soap. See the discussion under dollar spot (p. 282).

TIP When using homemade preparations for any purpose, be careful mixing materials. Always test the material on an inconspicuous area of the plant to make sure it is not toxic to the plant in any way. This is especially true when using any type of oil in hot weather.

FUSARIUM BLIGHT, SUMMER PATCH, AND NECROTIC RING SPOT

(*Fusarium culmorum* and *F. tricinctum; Magnaporthe poae;* and *Leptosphaeria korrae*)

For many years, fusarium blight symptoms were thought to be caused by a single disease. However, it was discovered that fungi in three separate genera are involved, each of which has been given separate disease status, as listed above.

Fusarium blight and summer patch are warm-weather diseases that can occur from late June through early September, depending on location. They usually appear after a week or two of dry weather following a heavy rain, and are associated with shallowly rooted grass, which is highly vulnerable to drought stress. Symptoms often appear first along sidewalks and in poorly drained areas, and primarily attack Kentucky bluegrass when it is kept in a lush, overfertilized state in summer. Necrotic ring spot is primarily a cool, wet-weather disease occurring in spring and fall, and attacks the roots of Kentucky bluegrass.

Damage symptoms for all three diseases are similar (see the sidebar on pp. 272–273). Some Kentucky bluegrass varieties are particularly vulnerable. Annual bluegrass and some fine-leaf fescues are also affected.

TREATMENT
INDIRECT STRATEGIES
Indirect strategies for controlling fusarium blight,

summer patch, and necrotic ring spot focus on planting resistant grasses and on various horticultural controls.

1. Planting Resistant Grasses.
Consider modifying or replacing highly susceptible Kentucky bluegrass lawns with a mix of species such as the tall fescues, perennial ryegrasses, or warm-season grasses (such as bermudagrass and St. Augustinegrass) that are less susceptible to the disease.

One study found that adding as little as 10 percent to 15 percent perennial 'Manhattan' or 'Pennfine' ryegrass to a 'Park' Kentucky bluegrass lawn eliminated summer patch. A seeding of 15 percent or more perennial ryegrass and 85 percent or less Kentucky bluegrass by weight resulted in approximately a 50/50 bluegrass/ryegrass plant count after three years. The increased drought- and heat-tolerance of perennial ryegrass, tall fescue, and other varieties is one of the factors thought to explain the suppression of disease. Check with your local county cooperative extension service for cultivars that grow well in your area.

TIP If you have a Kentucky bluegrass lawn, remember that it naturally slows its growth during summer because it does not tolerate high temperatures well. So don't overfertilize; if you do, the lush, soft growth produced by the grass is more vulnerable to attack by diseases.

2. Fertility Management.
Maintain a moderate but balanced fertilizing program so the lawn can produce growth to cover damage. Organic slow-release fertilizers, composted garden material, or composted manure should be used. Avoid the highly soluble fast-release nitrogen fertilizers. (Note: Important background information on lawn fertility is presented in Chapter 12.)

3. Aeration.
Fusarium blight, summer patch, and necrotic ring spot are exacerbated by compacted soils, excessive thatch, and soil layering, all of which inhibit the percolation (seeping) of water into the soil. Puddles of standing water create anaerobic conditions in the thatch that allow summer patch fungi to become active.

Diseased turf should be aerated with a coring tool (see the discussion of aeration on pp. 239–240) to reduce compaction and thatch and increase infiltration and soil air movement. Coring also helps integrate the dissimilar soil layers that occur when imported topsoil or sod rather than seed is used to establish the lawn. When one soil type is laid on top of another, water tends to collect at the interface, moving laterally rather than vertically. Grass roots tend to stop growing when they reach this interface, and can be killed by the excessive water at that point. By coring into the layered soil and incorporating compost, both water and roots are encouraged to move more deeply into the soil, producing more vigorous grass growth.

4. Water Management.
Supplemental irrigation will help drought-stressed grasses outgrow fusarium blight, summer patch, and necrotic ring spot. You may need to water daily at the hottest times of the day until the grass resumes vigorous growth.

Thatch management and mowing are also effective controls; for information on these strategies, see the discussion of melting out on p. 283.

For details on soil solarization, a recommended physical control for these three diseases, see pp. 212–213.

TREATMENT
DIRECT BIOLOGICAL CONTROLS
Because fusarium blight, summer patch, and necrotic ring spot primarily attack roots, the more you can do to increase the number of beneficial soil fungi and bacteria antagonistic to the pathogens, the fewer problems you will have. In studies conducted by J. M. Vargas and colleagues at Michigan

State University, several microbially enriched commercial soil amendments allowed existing necrotic ring spot patches to recover and prevented the development of new ones.

According to these researchers, when microbes are used for the biological management of soil-borne disease, two mechanisms are at work:

The first is competition for nutrients in the thatch and soil between the beneficial microorganisms and the pathogens. By utilizing available nutrients, they can deny the pathogens the nutrients needed to stimulate germination of resting structures (spores or sclerotia), and, after germination, they can deny them the nutrition needed to grow saprophytically to reach the root of the host plant for infection. The second feasible mechanism is the production by beneficial microorganisms of substances that are antagonistic to the germination and growth of soil-borne pathogens.

Vargas et al. used two categories of commercial products to manage necrotic ring spot. The first improves the thatch and soil environment to encourage higher levels of beneficial microbial activity, whereas the second adds beneficial microbes to the thatch and soil. Products in the first category used in the study were Soil Aid®, an enzymatic wetting agent that flushes thatch and soil of substances toxic to beneficial microbes, and Green Magic® or Strengthen & Renew®, which contain major and minor nutrients as well as extracts of plants and microorganisms. In the second category, the researchers used Lawn Restore, an organic fertilizer consisting of bone meal, feather meal, soybean meal, and other protein sources supplemented with actinomycete fungi and *Bacillus* spp. bacteria. These microbes have been shown in laboratory cultures to produce substances antagonistic to necrotic ring spot fungi. Unfortunately, Soil Aid, Green Magic, and Strengthen & Renew are no longer available, although Lawn Restore is available online and at nurseries and home and garden centers.

The experimental information is still timely, even if the actual products are no longer made. These experiments demonstrate that a complete complement of plant nutrients in combination with beneficial microbes can reduce disease symptoms and may be antagonistic to pathogens. We suggest using mature active compost and organic fertilizers fortified with microbes in place of the discontinued products.

In one series of plots on a condominium lawn in Novi, Michigan, Soil Aid plus either Green Magic or Strengthen & Renew was applied twice in summer and once in fall at a rate of 1 lb. per 100 sq. ft. (48 g per sq. m). In another series of plots, Lawn Restore was applied at the same frequency and dose. These treatments were repeated for three seasons. When the researchers compared the number of necrotic ring spots on the treated lawn at the end of the experiment in 1986 with the number of spots apparent in 1984 when the experiment began, they found 100-percent recovery of the lawn. In untreated areas of the lawn the number of ring spots had increased over 300 percent during the three-year period.

These researchers stress the importance of frequent treatment when using biological approaches to managing lawn diseases:

These products are not like fungicides that can be applied one time, halting the spread of the fungus and allowing the grass to recover. In order to be effective, [such products] must be applied on a regular basis, either monthly or bi-monthly throughout the growing season to change the biological makeup of the thatch and soil environment.

For more on the use of beneficial microbes against lawn pathogens, see pp. 231–233 and the discussion of *Trichoderma* on pp. 276–277.

Direct chemical controls for fusarium blight, summer patch, and necrotic ring spot include neem, garlic oil, and fungicidal soap. For a discussion of the first two materials, see pp. 277–278. The use of fungicidal soap is described under dollar spot on p. 282.

PYTHIUM BLIGHT (COTTONY BLIGHT, GREASE SPOT)

(*Pythium* spp.)

Pythium fungi survive in thatch and soil. They become active in warm, wet weather when daytime temperatures exceed 85°F (29°C), nighttime temperatures are above 68°F (20°C), and the relative humidity is close to 100 percent. The disease may occur to a limited extent under cooler conditions. Poorly drained, heavily used grasses are particularly vulnerable.

Disease symptoms are described in the sidebar on pp. 272–273 and shown in the photo at right. All common turfgrasses are susceptible.

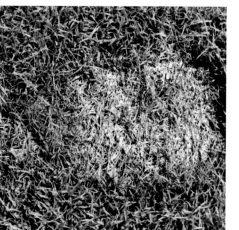

Pythium blight on bentgrass. (Photo courtesy of Clemson University—USDA Cooperative Extension Slide Series, Bugwood.org)

TREATMENT
INDIRECT STRATEGIES

Indirect strategies for controlling *Pythium* blight include the following:

1. Planting Resistant Grasses. For information on disease-resistant grasses, see p. 237. Also, check with your local county cooperative extension office for recommendations on resistant grasses in your area.

2. Fertility Management. Grasses growing on soils with a calcium deficiency or excessive alkalinity are more susceptible to *Pythium* blight. Make sure the soil nutrients are in balance, and avoid applications of highly soluble nitrogen fertilizers just prior to or during the onset of warm weather. (For an overall discussion of lawn fertility, see pp. 243–247.)

3. Water Management. Because *Pythium* blight first appears where water forms puddles on the lawn, make sure all sprinkler heads are working properly. Fill in any low spots on the lawn where water collects. Irrigate the lawn infrequently and deeply during warm weather, and water early in the day so the grass dries before nightfall.

4. Aeration. Poor drainage exacerbates *Pythium* blight, so aerate with a coring tool and top-dress with compost (see pp. 239–240).

5. Thatch Management. Reduce excessive thatch buildup. (See the discussion of thatch on pp. 239–240.)

6. Mowing. Remove infected grass clippings to reduce sources of disease. Rinse the mower and the soles of your shoes with a bleach solution, as described below, before walking on undamaged parts of the lawn.

For information on direct physical controls, see the discussion of solarization on pp. 212–213; for biological controls, see brown patch (pp. 275–278) and fusarium blight (pp. 278–280).

TREATMENT
DIRECT CHEMICAL CONTROLS

In an experiment on a bowling green chronically infested with *Pythium* fungi, we found that drenching the affected areas with a solution of household bleach at 1 oz. bleach (5.25 percent available chlorine) per 4 gal. of water, or 100 ppm, reduced the incidence of the disease (but did not eliminate it). We got the idea when we learned that soils high in chloride ions suppress certain *Pythium* species.

For information on the effectiveness of neem and garlic oil, see pp. 277–278; for fungicidal soap, see dollar spot, p. 282.

DOLLAR SPOT

(*Lanzia* and *Moellerodiscus* spp., formerly *Sclerotinia*)

Dollar spot overwinters in thatch. It is encouraged by nutritionally deficient grasses and by warm days and cool nights that produce dew. It is easily spread by infected grass clippings, foot traffic, and mowers. Damage symptoms are described in the sidebar on pp. 272–273 and shown in the photo below.

TREATMENT
INDIRECT STRATEGIES

Treatments for dollar spot are the same as those listed for pythium blight. Similarly, direct physical controls (soil solarization) are identical to those given for brown patch (p. 276). For biological controls (microbial soil amendments), see brown patch (pp. 276–277) and necrotic ring spot (pp. 279–280). Direct chemical controls for dollar spot include the use of bleach (see *Pythium* blight, p. 281), neem, and garlic oil (see brown patch, pp. 277–278), and fungicidal soap.

Field tests of a commercial fungicidal soap available from Safer against dollar spot and other lawn diseases looked very promising. The soap killed the fungi; however, when used as a spray on lawns, the microbes broke the soap down so quickly that there was little residual protection of the grass. Therefore, researchers were trying to develop a method for encapsulating the soap in a slow-release formulation that remains active on the lawn for some weeks. Unfortunately, this did not result in a commercially viable product. However, using the soap as a drench spot treatment on discrete areas of damaged lawn, with repeat applications every four

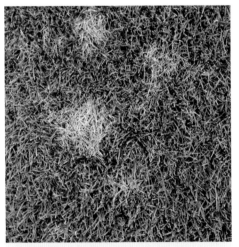

Dollar spot on Kentucky bluegrass. (Photo by Mary Ann Hansen, Virginia Polytechnic Institute and State University, Bugwood.org)

to five days, might work on home lawns, but there are no documented tests of such a procedure at present.

FUSARIUM PATCH (PINK SNOW MOLD) AND GREY SNOW MOLD

(*Microdochium nivale* [formerly *Fusarium nivale*], and *Typhula* spp.)

Fusarium patch or pink snow mold (see the photo on the facing page) can develop whenever the temperature drops below 60°F (16°C), whether or not snow is present. The greatest activity occurs when snow falls on unfrozen ground. The disease is most serious in areas where air movement and soil drainage are poor, skies remain overcast for long periods, and the grass stays wet for extended periods. Lush, tall growth in late fall and plant injury due to frost promote damage.

Grey snow mold occurs when the ground is unfrozen, soil moisture is plentiful, and the temperature is between 32°F and 40°F (0°C and 4°C). Initial development takes place in the absence of light, which is usually brought about by snow cover.

Symptoms of grey snow mold are described in the sidebar on pp. 272–273. Most turfgrasses that grow where temperatures are cool are susceptible. Such grasses include bluegrass, fescues, and ryegrass.

INDIRECT STRATEGIES

Indirect treatment strategies for fusarium patch and grey snow mold include the following:

1. Planting Resistant Grasses.

For information on this strategy, see the discussion of disease-resistant grasses on pp. 233–237. Also, check with your local county cooperative extension office for recommendations on resistant grasses in your area.

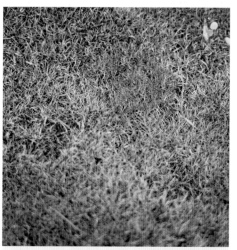

Fusarium patch is a disease in turfgrass settings. (Photo by William M. Brown Jr., Bugwood.org)

2. Fertility Management.

Lawns should not be allowed to enter cold weather in an actively growing condition. A light application of fertilizer in early fall encourages grass to grow and fill in bare spots, which is important for weed management. Fertilization in late fall near the time of potential snowfall may encourage active growth too late in the season, leading to damage from cold or disease. For this reason we recommend the use of organic fertilizers, because the availability of nutrients is determined by microbial activity in the soil, which is temperature dependent. (Note: Background information on cultural practices is provided in Chapter 12.)

3. Aeration.

Because poor drainage exacerbates these two diseases, you should aerate in fall with a coring tool and top-dress with compost.

4. Thatch Management.

Reduce excessive thatch buildup (see the discussion of aeration and thatch on pp. 239–240) and remove grass clippings at the last mowing of the season. These practices will reduce the nutrients from decaying organic matter available to the disease organism.

DIRECT CONTROLS

Physical controls include soil solarization (see brown patch, p. 276) and the use of snow barriers. The latter entails the proper placement of barriers, snow fences, or landscape plantings to reduce snow build-up on the lawn. Do not mulch the grass with straw, which is often done to try to prevent winter-kill of the grass. The straw creates an ideal environment for the disease.

For information on biological controls for fusarium patch and grey snow mold, see the discussion of microbial soil amendments under brown patch and necrotic ring spot.

Chemical controls include the use of neem and garlic oil (see brown patch, pp. 277–278), fungicidal soap (see dollar spot, on the facing page), and iron sulfate. An iron sulfate solution made from ¼ oz. (7 g) of ferrous iron sulfate mixed in ½ gal. (1.9 l) of water (enough to cover 1 sq. yd./0.84 sq. m) is used by the Royal Horticultural Society in England to drench areas afflicted with snow mold. This mix must be used immediately, because it takes only 30 minutes for the ferrous form of the iron to change to the ineffective ferric form.

DRECHSLERA MELTING OUT OR LEAF SPOT

(*Drechslera* spp., formerly *Helminthosporium* spp.)
A complex of leaf spot fungi survive in thatch and are most active during cool, moist weather. Symptoms of melting out are described in the sidebar on pp. 272–273. Overfertilized grass that

produces lush, succulent growth is most likely to be attacked. Watering in the evening allows water to remain on grass blades for long periods, which provides disease spores with enough water for germination. Close mowing also stresses the grass and encourages the disease to move down to attack grass crowns and roots.

TREATMENT

INDIRECT STRATEGIES

Indirect strategies for controlling melting out include the following:

1. Planting Resistant Grasses.
Melting out primarily attacks Kentucky bluegrass. Check with your local county cooperative extension office for recommendations on resistant grass species that grow well in your area, or consult pp. 233–237.

Drechslera leaf spot on orchardgrass. (Photo by Mary Ann Hansen, Virginia Polytechnic Institute and State University, Bugwood.org)

2. Fertility Management.
Contrary to earlier recommendations against spring fertilizing, recent research at Michigan State University indicates that a good, balanced level of soil fertility in the spring helps protect grass during this potential infection period. For a more detailed discussion of this topic, see pp. 243–247.

3. Mowing.
Grasses mowed to a height of 1½ in. (3.8 cm) or lower are more susceptible to melting out. If the disease is a problem in your lawn, raise the mowing height to 2½ in. to 3 in. (6.4 cm to 7.6 cm), keep the mower blades sharp, and collect infected grass clippings. If only a small area is affected, drench the mower blades and wheels and the soles of your shoes with a 1-percent solution of bleach (about 1.25 oz. bleach in 1 gal. of water) to disinfect them before mowing the rest of the lawn. Bleach reduces the spread of the disease.

4. Thatch Management.
Because the fungus lives in thatch, management of this habitat is important in disease control. Turf scientists have discovered that by keeping thatch moist, large numbers of antagonistic microorganisms develop and hold *Drechslera* fungi at low levels.

It may seem strange to water the lawn during the season of spring or fall rains, but remember that we are not talking about irrigation, only a brief sprinkling to wet the thatch. If the thatch dries out, even for a few days, the beneficial organisms become inactive, the thatch begins leaking out highly nutritious sugars and starches from decomposing tissues, and the normally weak *Drechslera* fungi are able to grow in numbers great enough to damage the grass. A brief daily irrigation—just enough to keep the thatch layer moist but not enough to waterlog the soil—has been shown to reduce the incidence of the disease radically. If you water using a compost tea solution in a hose-end sprayer it will supplement the beneficial microbial population. Remember to thoroughly filter the compost tea to prevent clogging the hose-end sprayer. If the thatch is excessively deep, aerate it in early spring or fall to reduce harborage for the disease. Following aeration, be sure to top dress with a mature compost that will also help breakdown the thatch layer.

TREATMENT

DIRECT BIOLOGICAL AND CHEMICAL CONTROLS

Because this fungus is only a weak competitor in the presence of antagonistic fungi such as *Trichoderma*, careful lawn maintenance according to the directions in the preceding chapter, which are designed to enhance the habitat for beneficial organisms, should go far toward preventing or solving the problem of melting out. Regular application of organic matter (see the discussion under brown patch and necrotic ring spot, above), which enhances microbial diversity and activity, encourages the presence of antagonists of *Drechslera*.

Although there are no published studies of the use of neem, garlic oil, or fungicidal soap against *Drechslera* species, they have proven effective against other lawn diseases that behave similarly. Thus, they are worth considering. Refer to the sections on brown patch and dollar spot for details on these chemical controls.

MANAGING WEEDS IN LAWNS

The good news about weed management is that if you follow the cultural recommendations for preventing lawn pest problems described in the previous chapter, you are not going to have significant weed growth in your lawn. This statement is based on our many years' experience in lawn pest management. Every time we have been called in, we have been able to correlate the presence of weeds with stressful lawn maintenance practice—usually mowing too short and/or too frequently, fertilizing with excessive soluble nitrogen (or lack of any fertilization program), and irrigating too frequently. Soil compaction also contributes to weediness. Once cultural practices were improved, weed populations subsided, with many weed species disappearing altogether.

The direct relationship between optimum growing conditions for grasses and the relative absence of weeds results because vigorously growing grass can outcompete most broad-leaved weeds and many grass weeds. It is only when optimum conditions do not prevail that grass becomes stressed and thins out, enabling weeds to gain a foothold. More information on why this is so is provided on pp. 179–181.

When weeds invade lawns, they are responding to something that is out of balance in the lawn ecosystem. By identifying the weed, you can often tell what kind of stress is occurring. For example, prostrate knotweed (*Polygonum aviculare*) grows in compacted, droughty soils; yellow nutsedge (*Cyperus esculentus*) grows best in waterlogged soils. The chart on p. 287 lists soil or other stress conditions indicated by the presence of certain common lawn weeds. Use this information to help diagnose what is stressing the grass and enabling weeds to colonize your lawn.

WEED TOLERANCE LEVELS

Before proceeding any further, let's dispense with the notion of a "weed-free" lawn. This goal is rarely feasible or desirable. A lawn is a very dynamic ecosystem, and even under optimum grass-growing conditions, some weeds will become established. In many cases, weeds fill areas that simply cannot be made to suit vigorous lawn growth. Examples are a very shady spot next to a pine tree, whose leaf litter acidifies the soil, or an area with a very high water table.

As long as the weeds stay green, they blend in with the grass and help provide a uniform appearance. Some so-called lawn weeds, such as clover, move into compacted, insufficiently fertilized areas of lawn where the grass has thinned. The clover's deep roots break up the compacted soil and form associations with beneficial nitrogen-fixing soil bacteria (*Rhizobium*). This enables the clover to provide surplus nitrogen to the soil, enhancing the growth of surrounding grass. After a time, the soil becomes so improved that the adjacent grass moves in and displaces the clover. The presence of some flowering weeds, such as dandelions or English daisies, also helps attract the beneficial insects that help control lawn and garden insect pests.

Thus, your goal in lawn weed management should not be to eliminate all weeds; rather, you should try to keep weed numbers low enough to prevent significant visual damage. Obviously this is a subjective aesthetic decision. Most people can and do tolerate 5-percent to 10-percent weed growth in their lawns without even knowing it. At those levels, weeds are hard to detect. Even when weeds are quite visible, tolerance levels vary widely depending on the weed. For example, many people like the way English daisies (*Bellis perennis*) look and will tolerate high populations of this "weed." When confronted with plantain (*Plantago* spp.), however, these same people may show a very low tolerance because it has coarse leaves and lacks showy flowers.

How many and which type of weeds you are willing to tolerate in your lawn is up to you. If you have more weeds than you want, identify them. Two inexpensive, handy photographic reference tools are *Turfgrass Weed Identification and Control: A Common Sense Approach* (University of Nebraska Cooperative Extension Publications, 1983), and *Turfgrass Pests* (University of California Co-operative Extension Service, 1980). You can also contact your local county cooperative extension office for publications and advice. This is one area where use of the web is not that satisfactory. To find weed photos on the web you must know the name of the weed in order to do the search. Web resources that can help are the county extension service websites or the website for your state's land grant university. The IPM website at the University of California, Davis (www.ipm.ucdavis.edu/PMG/menu.weeds.html) is one good example.

There is, however, a caveat to using university and extension publications. Many of the fact sheets published by them are directed more toward agricultural situations than toward the home gardener. These agricultural fact sheets make pesticide recommendations for treating hundreds or even thousands of acres, not a few hundred or thousand sq. ft. of home garden. In fact, they often recommend pesticides that are only legal for agricultural use and are illegal to use around the home and garden. They recommend those products and procedures that are

legal, not just those that are environmentally based. When perusing university and extension fact sheets we recommend that you concentrate on the excellent biology, the great photos, and the nonpesticidal recommendations they make for pest control. When you get to the section on pesticides, consider only those that are truly least-toxic materials. In IPM, the choice of least-toxic pesticides is always a last resort, when the combination of all other measures has failed to provide adequate control of the pest.

The next step is to estimate the percentage of lawn that is occupied by weeds. A good way to make this estimate and measure the rise and fall of weed populations from season to season is with a lawn transect. This is simply a line drawn through one or more representative areas of a lawn. By peri-

"When weeds invade lawns, they are responding to something that is out of balance in the lawn ecosystem. By identifying the weed, you can often tell what kind of stress is occurring."

odically recording the percentage of weeds versus grass along the transect, the level of weed growth can be quantified.

The sidebar on p. 289 describes the use of the transect method to estimate weed populations on a home lawn. Once you know the percentage of weeds you are not willing to tolerate, you can begin management practices to enhance the competitiveness of grasses, thereby reducing weed growth to a level you can tolerate. For large lawn areas such as those in parks or athletic fields, several random transect lines should be used to ensure that the weed count is representative.

WEEDS THAT IDENTIFY WHAT IS WRONG WITH YOUR LAWN

COMMON NAME	SCIENTIFIC NAME	LAWN PROBLEM
annual bluegrass	*Poa annua*	low fertility, compaction, low mowing, high moisture
barnyardgrass	*Echinochloa crus-galli*	thinned, wet grass
black medic	*Medicago lupulina*	drought, low fertility
broomsedge	*Andropogon virginicus*	low fertility
buttercup	*Ranunculus* spp.	excessive moisture
carpetweed	*Mollugo verticillata*	drought, thin grass
chickweed	*Stellaria media*	thin grass, excessive moisture
clover	*Trifolium repens*	low nitrogen, drought, compaction
crabgrass	*Digitaria* spp.	compaction, low fertility, drought, thin grass, hot spots
cutleaf geranium	*Geranium dissectum*	drought
dallisgrass	*Paspalum dilatatum*	low mowing, wet areas
dandelion	*Taraxacum officinale*	thin grass, low mowing, low fertility, drought
dock	*Rumex* spp.	excessive moisture
English daisy	*Bellis perennis*	low fertility, low pH, excessive moisture
goosegrass	*Eeusine indica*	compacted soils
ground ivy	*Glechoma hederacea*	excessive moisture and shade
hawkweed	*Hieracium* spp.	excessive moisture
kochia	*Kochia scoparia*	drought
lambsquarters	*Chenopodium album*	disturbed soil, insufficient lawn seed
lippia	*Phyla nodiflora*	drought
mallow	*Malva* spp.	disturbed soil, thin grass
morning glory	*Convolvulus arvense*	disturbed soil, drought, low mowing, low fertility
moss	various genera	low fertility, poor drainage, drought, low pH, compaction, heavy shade
mouse-eared chickweed	*Cerastium vulgatum*	low mowing
pennywort	*Hydrocotyle* spp.	excessive moisture, shade
pigweed	*Amaranthus* spp.	bare, drought, low mowing, compaction
plantain	*Plantago* spp.	low fertility, low mowing
prostrate knotweed	*Polygonum aviculare*	compaction, drought, thin grass
puncturevine	*Tribulus terrestris*	dry, sandy soils
purslane	*Portulaca oleracea*	excessive fertilizer, thin grass
red sorrel	*Rumex acetosella*	low fertility, poor drainage, tolerates acidity
sandbur	*Cenchrus longispinus*	sandy soil, drought, low fertility
speedwell	*Veronica* spp.	low fertility, poor drainage, shade
spotted spurge	*Euphorbia maculata*	low mowing
thistles	*Cirsium* spp.	low fertility, drought, heavy clay compaction
wild garlic	*Allium vineale*	wet, heavy soil
woodsorrel	*Oxalis* spp.	drought
yarrow	*Achillea millefolium*	low fertility

INDIRECT STRATEGIES

The only way to achieve long-term weed control is to do everything you can to grow healthy, vigorous grass. If you succeed, the grass will perform its own weed control. The cultural methods for reducing stress on grasses outlined in Chapter 12 can produce an amazing turnaround in lawn weediness in a season or two.

It is dramatic what simply raising the mowing height can do to weeds. In a study at the University of Maryland on 2-year-old lawn grass, crabgrass and broad-leaved weeds accounted for only 8 percent of the overall lawn cover in plots where the grass was mowed at a height of 2½ in. (6.4 cm), whereas weeds occupied 53 percent of the area in plots where grass was mowed at 1½ in. (3.8 cm). In this experiment, all other variables—such as watering and fertilizing—were the same.

Fertilization can also be used to reduce crabgrass incursions into lawns. A study by Ohio Extension Service researchers in the 1940s showed that an application of 20 lb. (9 kg) of composted poultry manure per 1,000 sq. ft. (93 sq. m) of lawn in late fall and early spring stimulated early spring growth of lawn grasses, enabling them to crowd out the crabgrass. In this study, crabgrass was reduced by up to 75 percent within one year. We have seen similarly dramatic reductions in weed growth in response to improved cultural practices in our work with parks departments throughout the United States and Canada. So before you consider other methods, revise your lawn maintenance practices to conform to the recommendations in Chapter 12. That may be all that is required to solve your weed problem.

Another fertilization technique used successfully by Ralph Montana, IPM Coordinator for San Francisco Recreation and Parks Department, is a mixture that uses a combination of two forms of iron and a liquid humate. It appears that the formula invigorates turfgrass to the point that it out competes broadleaf weeds. To treat 1,000 sq. ft., mix 2 oz. of dry 10-percent chelated iron, ½ lb. of ferrous sulfate, and 4 oz. of liquid humate in enough water to cover the area uniformly (it normally takes about 3 gal. to 4 gal. in a sprayer to cover 1,000 sq. ft.). Apply this mixture once weekly until weeds are under control, usually 5 or 6 weeks. Reapply as necessary to obtain desired control.

When designing a lawn area, install a mow strip—a line of bricks or a strip of concrete, for example—to separate the edge of the lawn from adjacent shrub beds or other planting areas (see the photo on p. 190). This prevents grass from growing into the planter bed and becoming a "weed." You can roll one wheel of the mower along the mow strip, cutting off the adjacent grass. Another benefit is the elimination of the need to edge the lawn.

In those instances where you feel you need to remove weeds more rapidly than can be achieved by improving cultural practices alone, consider the least-toxic options outlined below. If you are planting a new lawn, use the repeated cultivation technique described on pp. 207–208 to reduce weed seeds in the soil before you sow the grass seed.

TIP If there are areas of your lawn that are chronically trampled and therefore prone to weeds, cover the area with turf blocks. These are concrete blocks with holes in them where grass can be planted. They are sold in most garden centers. The concrete reinforcement reduces the impact of the footwear while allowing the grass to grow.

DIRECT PHYSICAL CONTROLS

Direct physical weed control focuses on cultivation, smothering, solarization, flaming, and mowing.

1. Cultivation. Whenever people balk at cultivating out weeds we feel compelled to point out that even when an herbicide is used, it leaves a bare

USING TRANSECTS TO MONITOR WEED POPULATIONS IN LAWNS

A transect is one line or a series of lines drawn across the surface of a lawn (or other surface). By walking along the line and recording the presence or absence of weeds, you can get a rough determination of the percentage of lawn taken up by weeds.

STEP 1

Lay a length of rope or garden hose in a straight line across your lawn. Try to have the line cross all representative areas of your lawn (e.g., dry and wet spots, heavily used and lightly used areas, areas near concrete, shady areas). You may need to establish two or more transect lines if your lawn is large and conditions vary significantly. Place some sort of identifying markers such as small stakes or marks on a fence post at each end of the transect so you can repeat the process in the same location at the end of the season.

STEP 2

Clamp a sheet of lined paper onto a clipboard and begin walking along the line. Each time you take a step, write a consecutive number on the paper to represent the step, then look down at the 3-in. by 3-in. (7.6-cm by 7.6-cm) area of lawn at the tip of your toe. Next to the number, write W if there is either a weed (even if it is mixed in with grass) or a bare spot (which is likely to become weedy even though there are no weeds yet). If you happen to know the name of the weed, write it down. Write G if all you see is grass. Continue taking this data until you reach the end of the transect. If you do more than one transect, use a separate column for each.

STEP 3

Add up the total number of Ws in the column (or in each column, if there were several transects) and divide this number by the total number of steps you took on that transect. The resulting number represents the rough percentage of weeds in the lawn. Although this method would not satisfy a statistician, the data it yields is perfectly adequate for lawn care.

By collecting data from the transects at the beginning and end of each season, you can spot emerging problems. For example, if several steps in succession are marked W, a closer look at that area is warranted.

A length of rope or hose laid across the lawn can be used to mark a transect for estimating weed populations. By walking along the marker and recording the presence or absence of weeds, you can arrive at a ballpark estimate of the percentage of weeds in the lawn. (Photo by Mary O'Malley)

Such a concentration of weed growth generally indicates compacted soil, heavy wear, too much or too little water (perhaps from a faulty sprinkler), or related conditions. If these conditions are spotted soon enough and corrected, the weeds will be displaced by grass.

spot where the weeds die. This bare spot must be dug up and improved or another round of weeds will grow in the same place. So why not cultivate in the first place? You can dig out small groups of weeds with a trowel or sharp pointed tool. Large areas of weeds should be irrigated to loosen the soil first, then dug out with an appropriate tool. Incorporate compost and a slow-release phosphorus source such as bone meal to promote root growth in the bare soil. Level the area so it blends with the adjacent lawn, then sow lawn seed suited to your area.

If you are battling crabgrass (*Digitaria* spp.), consider planting a fine-bladed tall fescue or perennial rye cultivar. These grasses are reported to release toxins that repel crabgrass. Cover the seed with a very light dressing of compost and keep the area moist until the seeds germinate. This approach not only removes the weeds, it improves the soil, maximizing the chance of the new grass achieving vigorous growth.

There are many new weeding tools available, and it seems that new ones appear every spring.

Some of these tools actually make hand-weeding enjoyable, or as enjoyable as hand-weeding can be. Try some of them out and, once you get a handle on the weed population, hand-weeding can be a relaxing outdoor activity. A colleague of mine once said that he would go to a job site when no one else from the company was there and weed by hand. He said it was a "sort of Zen meditation experience." He paused and added, "But you can only spend so much time in Nirvana."

2. Smothering. If you have large expanses of lawn weeds, irrigate and then cover the area with a layer of black plastic. Anchor the plastic with stones or bricks and leave it in place over the weeds for four to six weeks. This is usually sufficient to kill even the toughest perennials. You can cover the plastic with decorative bark mulch if you want to make the area look more aesthetically pleasing while the smothering is underway.

3. Solarization. If your lawn is so far gone that you need to renovate it completely, consider solarization. This technique not only kills the weeds, it kills the seeds buried in the top 4 in. to 6 in. (10 cm to 15 cm) of soil as well. Solarization takes about six weeks. It has the added benefit of killing many soil pathogens, whereas beneficial microbes are actually promoted through the process. Moreover, plants grown in solarized soil show better growth. Complete details on how to use this method are spelled out on pp. 212–213.

4. Flaming. This technique involves the use of a gas-powered torch to heat the cell sap of weeds enough to cause the plant cells to burst, killing the plant. Note that we are not talking about wildfires here. The flame is used only to heat—not burn— the weeds. Flamers are used widely in Europe for weed management in home and municipal gardens as well as on organic farms. Weed flamers are used extensively in the San Francisco IPM program, especially for weeds in pavement joints and cracks.

Flamers should also be considered for weed control on lawns. Grasses are far more heat-resistant than broad-leaved weeds, probably because grasses evolved on prairies, where fire is an integral part of the ecosystem. The growing points from which grass stems originate are contoured at the ground-hugging base of the plant, and are protected by leaf sheaths whose succulence helps protect the growing points from the heat of fire. Thus, even if the grass blades are damaged by the heat, the plant will bounce back.

Flamers work best on seedling-stage weeds, but can also be used to kill even deeply rooted perennials if several applications are made. They can also be used to spot-treat individual patches of weeds in a lawn, much as an herbicide is used. Both the herbicide and the flamer leave a dead patch of vegetation. The advantage of the flamer is that there is no toxic residue in the soil to pollute the groundwater and kill beneficial organisms. If the bare spot where the weed was killed is less than 12 in. (30 cm) in diameter, use a rake to scratch open the soil, then add some compost and irrigate. Adjacent grasses will soon grow in and cover the spot. If the spot is more than 1 ft. in area, sow grass seed.

Information on buying and using flamers is provided on pp. 210–212. For small jobs, you can use the type of small, hand-held propane torch sold in hardware stores for stripping paint.

5. Mowing. In addition to the suggestions made on pp. 247–249, you can use the mower to cut off flowers of lawn weeds before they set seed. That way you reduce the number of weed seeds in the soil.

DIRECT CHEMICAL CONTROLS

A number of producers have introduced nonselective contact herbicides based on essential oils, vinegar, and soap technology; new formulations are being introduced all the time. These herbicides, derived primarily from plant oils, are nontoxic to people, pets, and wildlife. When sprayed on plants, the cell membranes are disrupted, causing vegetation to shrivel and die. The active ingredients biodegrade, so grass can be replanted 48 hours after application. Many of these new contact herbicides are OMRI listed and many meet the criteria to be rated as 25b food-grade materials.

These new herbicides can be spot-sprayed on seedling-stage weeds in lawns. Because they are broad-spectrum herbicides, they damage or kill most vegetation they hit. To protect wanted grasses, you must apply it directly to weeds with a wick applicator (see p. 222). If you use a sprayer, cover the grass surrounding the weeds with cardboard or plastic. Once the weeds are dead, remove them and re-seed the bare spot with grass. These contact herbicides do not translocate to the roots, so they won't kill mature taprooted weeds such as dandelions, although they will burn their tops back. Repeated burning back of the tops ultimately starves the taproot and thus kills the plant. However, work is currently underway to make biologically based herbicides that do translocate. It is our hope that these systemic bioherbicides are on the market by the time you read this.

Many annual weeds growing in lawns can be killed by spraying with a high dose of nitrate fertilizer (e.g., ammonium nitrate 20-0-0 NPK or ammonium thiosulfate 12-0-0-26 NPKS). The fertilizer acts as a contact herbicide, burning the tissue of the weed and killing it. This technique is most effective if used as a spot treatment on young weeds (the two- or three-leaved stage) in the heat of day when no moisture is on the leaves.

Weeds that can be controlled this way include mallow (*Malva* spp.), chickweed *(Stellaria media)*, groundsel *(Senecio vulgaris)*, London rocket *(Sisymbrium irio)*, mustard *(Brassica* spp.), deadnettle *(Lamium* spp.), nightshade *(Solanum* spp.), purslane *(Portulaca oleracea)*, and shepherd's-purse *(Capsella bursa-pastoris)*. Many other weeds are no doubt also susceptible to this treatment.

FOR YOUR SAFETY

When flaming, remember to follow all safety recommendations to prevent starting a wildfire. We recommend irrigating prior to flaming, and having a charged garden hose at the ready in case of an emergency.

MOLES

(Order Insectivora, family Talpidae)

Moles are much maligned, delicate creatures that improve the soil, eat many pest insects, and get blamed for damage they do not cause. At one time they were prized for their velvety fur, and a farmer angered by mole activity could sell the pelts for a good price. Although mole skin is no longer in vogue, killing moles is still popular. Yet it is best if moles can be tolerated, because in the long run their insectivorous diet is beneficial to the gardener. As discussed below, grass damaged by moles often recovers quickly, and moles rarely stay in lawns for long periods unless poor cultural practices are encouraging high insect populations.

Moles are classified as insectivores, and the largest part of their diet is usually composed of insects. Of interest to gardeners is the fact that they eat many troublesome beetle larvae such as the white grubs found in lawns. They may also eat earthworms, spiders, and centipedes. Occasionally, moles eat a small amount of vegetable matter, especially if it has been softened by water. Townsend's mole, found in the Northwestern United States, eats more vegetation than do the other common mole species. Still, it has been shown that the mole will starve to death if offered only plant food.

People most often object to the sight of mole tunnels or molehills because they ruin their "perfect lawn." Certainly the tunnels make it more laborious to mow the grass. Mole runways may also be used by rodents, such as voles, white-footed mice, and the common house mouse, that eat seeds, bulbs, and roots, and do cause direct damage to the garden. There may be the unfounded fear that mole tunneling will damage nearby trees or cause permanent damage to the turf. In fact, the only real damage caused by moles is indirect, as a result of their shallow tunnels lifting up the turf or garden soil and allowing the plant roots to dry out. The best immediate response while you are trying to decide whether mole control is warranted is to press back the soil with your foot and water the area thoroughly.

A great variety of folk remedies have been recommended. If they seem to work, it is largely by coincidence or because of indirect effects that could be achieved through other, less picturesque methods. For example, castor bean plants have been touted for mole control, the recommendation being that the plants be grown around the garden and the seeds, which are poisonous to people, be placed in the mole runways. But moles do not eat seeds. In an article that appeared in *Organic Gardening* magazine in July 1949, Paul Scott suggested that if castor bean plants have any effect at all, it might be because they are fast-growing and quickly develop a large root system that requires large amounts of water. "This reduces the water content of the soil to such an extent," he writes, "that there are no pests, no earthworms, and, therefore, no moles."

A rarely seen, but common, black mole. (Photo by torasnapsfr/Bigstock)

In the past few years, commercially available formulations of castor oil have been developed as mole and gopher repellents. These appear to work when used conscientiously. It seems that moles and gophers don't like the smell, the taste, or maybe the "feel" of the soil when it is treated with castor oil mixtures. We have had some success with these materials, and although the mechanism seems unclear, they are worth trying.

Knowing something about the biology of moles and how to distinguish them from problem rodents such as gophers will help you in planning control strategies.

BIOLOGY

There are seven species of moles (*Scapanus* spp.) and shrew-moles (*Neurotrichus* spp.) in the United States, four on the West Coast and three on the East Coast. The lack of species in the Great Basin, Rocky Mountain, and western Great Plains regions in part reflects the fact that these areas are largely too arid and rocky to provide good mole habitat. Moles require the rich, moist, friable soil that also supports the insects and earthworms upon which they feed.

The mole's body shows many impressive adaptations to a life lived largely in narrow tunnels underground: a streamlined skeleton 5 in. to 7 in. (12.7 cm to 17.8 cm) long, fur that can point forward as easily as aft for ease of movement, a narrow snout, no external ears, eyes much reduced and covered with skin, and outwardly pointing claws and feet, with the front claws large and strong for digging.

These stout front claws are the mole's only means of digging through the soil. The mole uses them alternately to push the soil away from its face and along the sides of its body. A rodent's foot, by contrast, can be used to manipulate materials or dig like a dog. Because a rodent's feet can be placed flat against the ground when walking or running, the rodent is as agile above ground as below. This is not so with the mole, which shows off its unique adaptations best when "swimming" through soft, moist earth.

If you compare the shape and arrangement of the mole's teeth with those of a gopher, a typical burrowing rodent, you will see that they also reflect important differences in digging style and abilities. The mole has pointy little incisors, or front teeth, that generally are too weak to dig through the soil or gnaw through vegetable matter, bulbs, or roots.

The gopher has sharp, strong incisors that continue to grow throughout its life. It uses these teeth to gnaw through tough materials. Behind these front teeth is a gap into which the rodent can suck its cheeks, preventing the entry of dirt into its mouth while it is gnawing and digging. A gopher uses its jaws to lift and remove rocks and pebbles from its path as it advances.

Whereas rodent skulls are comparatively tough, the mole's skull is delicate. The mole cannot use its head in digging, which is why it prefers soft, un-compacted soil. In fact, the mole's head is so fragile and sensitive to vibrations that it can easily be stunned or killed by a sharp tap on the snout or by slapping the broad side of a shovel down on a tunnel where it is active.

Although the mole's eyes are virtually useless, probably only able to distinguish between light and dark, its hidden ears are remarkable in their acuity, making it possible for the mole to locate its prey through many inches of earth. Its sense of smell is also excellent. The mole with the most remarkable nose, the star-nosed mole (*Condylura cristata*), has a ring of 22 fleshy appendages at the tip of its snout, which it uses not for smelling but for feeling its environment. This mole, common on the East Coast in damp soils near swamps, streams, and lake edges, wanders above ground more than many other species, and is also an excellent swimmer.

Moles build two types of tunnels (see the drawing below). Their permanent tunnels may be quite deep and not detectable from the surface. Their nests, located in these permanent tunnels, may be 1 ft. to 2 ft. (0.3 m to 0.6 m) deep. Within these tunnels the moles are active year-round. It is their shallow feeding runways, sometimes used only once, that concern gardeners.

MOLE TUNNELS

Moles build two types of tunnels, or runways. Their permanent tunnels are often 1 ft. (0.3 m) underground and lead to nests that can be 2 ft. (0.6 m) deep. Connected to these permanent tunnels are runways that are closer to the soil surface, where moles can feed on root-dwelling insects. These runways may be used only once. Moles push excavated soil to the surface, creating their familiar molehills.

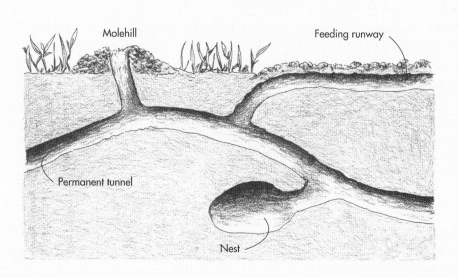

Molehill

Feeding runway

Permanent tunnel

Nest

Molehills (shown here) are cone-shaped, like a volcano, while gopher mounds have a distinct crescent shape. (Photo by Maxine Adcock/GAP)

If you are faced with an elaborate series of tunnels in your lawn, it probably does not mean that you have more than one mole. Moles may tunnel extensively at any time of day or night just to obtain enough food to satisfy their enormous appetites.

Moles also cause problems by throwing out excavated soil in large or small mounds or hills, depending on the species. These mounds can be distinguished from those of gophers by their shape and the texture of the soil used to build them. A Washington State University Cooperative Extension Service leaflet points out that a molehill is built like a volcano by the thrusting up of earth plugs through the center that then roll down all sides, whereas a gopher mound is fan or crescent-shaped with loose dirt pushed out and away from the exit hole on one side. The charac-

teristics that distinguish molehills from gopher mounds are shown in the drawing on p. 321.

DETECTION

If you are planning to use direct methods to kill the mole, you must determine which of the many runways are in use, because some of the shallow tunnels may be dug once for feeding and then abandoned. There is more than one method of doing this; which you use depends on the species you are dealing with.

East Coast moles do not leave telltale signs that betray the location of their deeper tunnels, so you must examine the shallow surface ridges of soil they thrust up. Ignore ridges that twist and turn; instead, look for the straight runs, particularly those that seem to be connected to two or more other

DID YOU KNOW?

Most species of mole are not gregarious; in fact, they are highly territorial and will fight to the death with other moles attempting to enter their burrow system.

tunnels. Also look for ridges at the edge of the area along hedges or where the tunnels appear to enter the yard or garden from adjacent areas.

Moles repair their tunnels immediately if they are disturbed, so you can determine which tunnels are active by pressing down the earth with your foot and watching to see which ridges are rebuilt. Or you can poke a number of holes in the ridges you think may be active and check to see which are repaired. Repairs should be made within a few hours or at most within a day. Any tunnel that is not repaired is not active enough for use in direct mole control.

The larger mole species of coastal Washington, Oregon, and California (*Scapanus* spp.) betray the presence of their deeper, permanent burrows by pushing up numerous molehills. You can locate the main runway leading away from these holes by probing the ground in a circle around them. Push a rod into the soil at 2-in. (5 cm) intervals 3 in. or 4 in. (7.6 cm or 10 cm) from the edge of the mound. When the rod is directly over a runway you will feel a sudden give as it breaks into the tunnel. These deeper tunnels are used year-round.

TREATMENT
INDIRECT STRATEGIES

Because beetle larvae such as white grubs are a favorite food of moles, one strategy for reducing the attractiveness of an area to the mole is reducing the number of these lawn pests. For ways to do this, consult the discussion of white grubs such as the Japanese beetle on pp. 256–264.

Another approach to managing mole pests focuses on the fact that they cannot dig through soil that is severely compacted, stony, or heavy in clay. Consequently, building borders of stone-filled, clay, and/or compacted soil around the areas you want to protect discourages mole invasion. These barriers must extend at least 2 ft. (0.6 m) into the ground. Introduced and compacted materials should be at least 6 in. (15 cm) wide, although 12 in. (30 cm) is even better. The barrier area can be paved over, creating a mow strip or a path around the lawn or garden.

Of course, there is always the chance that a mole will cross such a barrier above ground. A fence that is mainly buried but also reaches a short distance above ground helps prevent such crossings. If the barriers can be kept relatively dry all year they are even more effective. See the discussion of buried fences below.

TREATMENT
DIRECT PHYSICAL CONTROLS

Physical controls for moles include flushing with water, installing buried fencing, and trapping.

1. Flushing with Water. Spring flooding, where it occurs in low-lying areas or along streams, is a natural control for moles. The adults may manage to climb out of their tunnels and wait for the water to subside on elevated ridges or drifting material, but the young are extremely vulnerable in their nests. Even a heavy rain can drown them.

Flooding can be used to a similar end by the gardener. It is probably most effective against West Coast moles that betray their deeper nests by pushing up large molehills. Flooding will likely have the greatest impact in the spring when the young are still in the nest. To drown them, open the molehill, poke a garden hose into the tunnel and turn on the water. Expect it to take about 10 or 15 minutes before there is enough water in the tunnels to flush out the adult mole. Watch for its emergence from one of the other exits; you can dispatch it with a small shovel. This method is likely to be effective only if the tunnel system is confined to small and fairly level areas.

2. Buried Fencing. Fencing a small area either with small-mesh, tightly woven hardware cloth or with low cement walls has been shown to protect the area against the common eastern mole (it also protects against mice). The fence should begin slightly above the soil surface and extend into the soil at least 18 in. to 24 in. (45 cm to 60 cm). If it is bent outward underground in an L shape, it is even more effective. The base of the L should point away

MOLE TRAPS

Trapping is the most successful and practical method of getting rid of moles. There are three excellent mole traps on the market. If properly handled, all give good results. All depend on the same type of mechanism for releasing the spring: The trap is triggered as the mole upheaves the depressed portion of the surface burrow over which the trap is set. Brand names of these traps are Out O'Sight®, Victor® mole trap, and Nash® (choker loop) mole trap. The Out O'Sight trap has scissor-like jaws which close firmly across the runway, one pair on either side of the trigger pan. The Victor trap has sharp spikes that impale the mole when driven into the ground by the spring. The Nash trap has a choker loop that tightens around the mole's body.

These traps are well suited to moles because they capitalize on the mole's natural habits. They can be set without exciting the animal's suspicions by entering or introducing anything into its burrow, and they are sprung by the mole as it attempts to reopen obstructed passageways. Success or failure in the use of these devices depends largely on the operator's knowledge of the mole's habits and of the mechanism of the particular trap chosen.

MOLE TRAPS

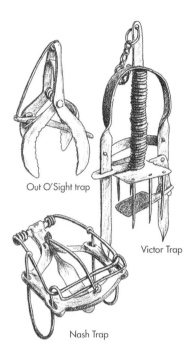

Out O'Sight trap

Victor Trap

Nash Trap

SETTING A TRAP

To set a trap properly, select a place in the surface runway where there is evidence of fresh work and where the burrow runs in a straight line. A satisfactory way to place the trap is to dig out a portion of the burrow, locate the tunnel (drawing A above), and replace the soil, packing it firmly beneath where the trigger pan of the trap will rest (drawing B above).

If the trap is the harpoon or impaling type, raise the spring, set the safety catch, and push the supporting spikes into the ground, one on either side of the runway. The trigger pan should just touch the earth where the soil is packed down. Now release the safety catch and allow

SETTING A SCISSOR-TYPE MOLE TRAP

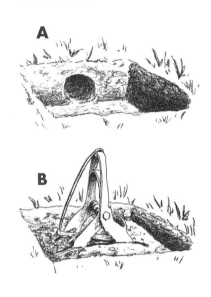

A

B

the impaling spike to be forced down into the ground by the spring. This will facilitate their penetrating into the burrow when the trap is sprung. Set the trap and leave it. Do not tread on or otherwise disturb any other portion of the mole's runway.

(If a trap fails to catch the mole after two days, it can mean any of three things: The mole has changed its habits, the runway was disturbed too much during trap placement, or the trap was improperly set and was detected by the mole. In any event, you must move the trap to a new location.)

Adapted from F. Robert Henderson, *Prevention and Control of Wildlife Damage* (University of Nebraska Cooperative Extension Service, 1983).

from the area being protected. Joints or connections in the fence should be overlapped and tightly closed with staples or wire.

3. Live Trapping. You can capture moles live in a pit trap and then release them some short distance away. First, dig through a mole tunnel that is likely to be in active use. Excavate deep enough so that the mouth of a large-mouthed jar or a 3-lb. (1.4-kg) coffee can will be flush with the floor of the mole tunnel when the container is sunk into the hole you have just made. Then cover the top of the tunnel with a board so no light can enter. The mole will not be able to hoist itself out of the container.

Check the status of the trap daily by removing the cover board. Bear in mind that if you wait too long before checking, the mole may starve to death, defeating the purpose of the live trap. If several days pass with no sign of the mole, the runway has probably been abandoned and you should repeat the procedure in a different tunnel.

Please take note that it is illegal in California and many other states to transport or relocate live wild animals. There is the concern of spreading disease from one location to another. Another problem is that when animals are relocated to strange surroundings they are likely to die of starvation or be attacked by predators because they have no shelter. Moles and gophers are wild animals. To determine if relocation is an option in your area, contact your state's fish and game department. They will be happy to provide you with the necessary information.

4. Lethal Trapping. The most effective method for removing moles from the garden is to use one of the commercially available mole traps. For a discussion of the three main types of traps, see the sidebar on the facing page.

5. Natural Predators and Baits. There are a number of natural predators of moles and other small animals. Raptors, like hawks, owls, and falcons, feed on moles as well as on gophers, rats,

mice, ground squirrels, and other small animals. Other natural predators include coyotes, dogs, and cats. All of these animals help keep moles and other small animal populations low when allowed to flourish. All of these natural predators are also susceptible to the strychnine and anti-coagulant poisons used in baits for moles and other small animals. Secondary poisoning, when a predator or scavenger eats a poisoned animal, is a very serious issue and is becoming more common because baits are so widely available and seem so convenient to use. Strychnine and anti-coagulant baits are also poisonous to people, especially children because of their small size. We think that poisonous baits for all small animals should be unavailable to the general public. Small-animal baits should only be available for use by licensed professionals under very strict and specific limitations. The hazards these baits pose to people, pets, and wildlife is too great for their use by the general public.

SUMMARY: LEAST-TOXIC MOLE CONTROL

Remember that moles are primarily beneficial: They eat pest insects and improve the soil through aeration. Do not kill them unless their damage is becoming intolerable. If the latter is true, do the following:

- Reduce the number of white grubs (beetle larvae) in the soil with the selective bacterial spray *Bacillus popilliae,* sold for Japanese beetle control.

- Apply beneficial nematodes to the soil to reduce white grubs and certain other soil-dwelling insects.

- Where feasible, create dry, compacted, and/or stony soil barriers.

- Use buried fencing or concrete barriers to protect small areas.

- Catch live moles in pit traps and release them away from garden areas.

- Flush moles out of their tunnels with water from a garden hose.

- Use strategically placed lethal traps.

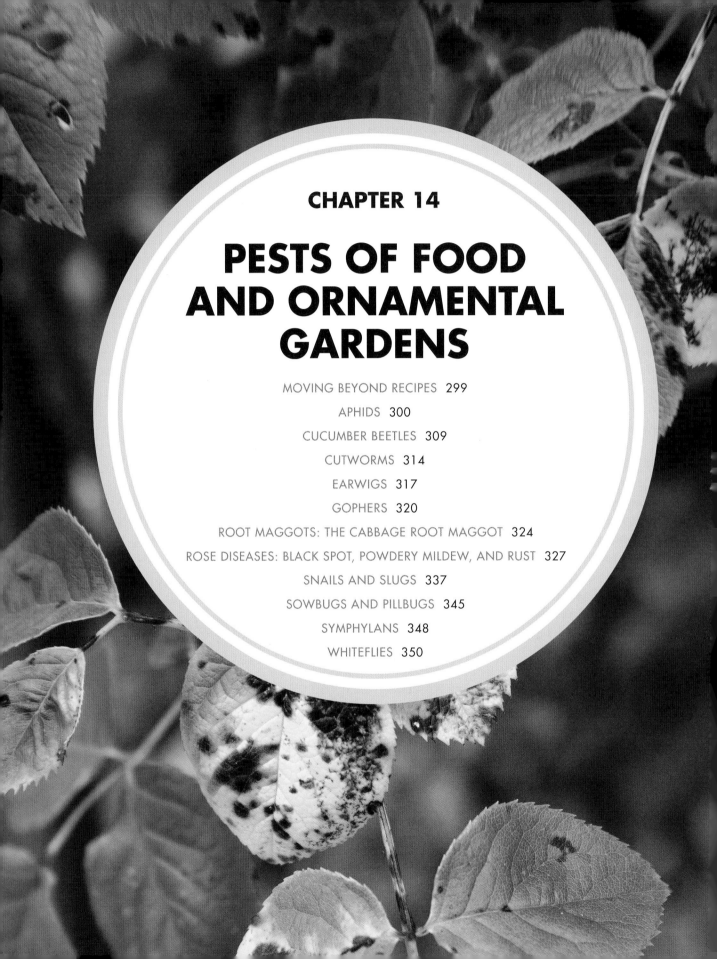

CHAPTER 14

PESTS OF FOOD AND ORNAMENTAL GARDENS

The number of potential pest insects and other animals in gardens is so large that nothing less than an encyclopedia could begin to discuss them all. This contrasts with indoor environments, where only a limited number of serious pests are common in temperate climates.

Much of our garden wildlife falls into the pest category, but only because of limited human tolerance for minor plant damage and the visible presence of certain species. We prefer to think of these organisms as potential pests. Although some of them may be capable of eating garden plants, their presence does not necessarily mean they are causing damage worth worrying about. Other organisms may not be causing any damage at all; it's simply that the gardener finds them visually unappealing.

Even if we eliminate such cases from consideration, however, the list of pests that can become truly damaging remains enormous. The selection of books, pamphlets, and magazine articles on garden pests is almost as large as the number of pests. Many take a partially or completely encyclopedic approach. *The Encyclopedia of Natural Insect and Disease Control*, edited by Roger B. Yepsen (Rodale, 1984), is among the best of these.

One difficulty with such an approach, however, is the simplification required to keep the book to a manageable size. This usually means reducing a problem's solution to a "recipe." It is a popular approach that most people welcome because it requires little thought. (That a recipe—usually pesticides—is popular because it requires little thought is disturbing in and of itself.) However, relying on recipes has two drawbacks in addition to the obvious one of limited information. One is that you may encounter new pests to which the instructions do not apply, because recipes tend to be very specific. The other is that if new developments in the control of a pest occur after the book has been produced, you have learned little that will help you judge the merits of the new approach or its compatibility with the previously recommended procedure.

The solution to the first problem is to provide yourself with some basic information about the garden ecosystem and the role the specific pest plays within it. This is not so difficult, because information on the biology of these animals is usually available through a variety of educational materials. However, make sure you supplement your book research with first-hand observation, which we discuss below.

Solving the second problem takes the kind of time and resources most people do not have. The field of nontoxic pest control is changing so rapidly

"Learning about the species you are trying to control is the surest route to finding least-toxic ways of preventing the damage they cause."

that you really need regular updates to keep abreast of the newest and best methods available. That is one of the main purposes of our periodical for the general public, *Common-Sense Pest Control Quarterly*. Readers can look through its indexes to keep up with the latest developments in the management of whichever garden pests concern them.

MOVING BEYOND RECIPES

Throughout this book we have tried to arouse your curiosity about the insects and other animals you find in your garden. We believe that learning about the species you are trying to control is the surest route to finding least-toxic ways of preventing the damage they cause. Another benefit of increased knowledge is decreased fear of pests.

Some of this kind of information can be found in books such as this one and the others we recommend at the end of the book. But often the most valuable insights are those you acquire through your own patient observation. You might even dis-

THE IMPORTANCE OF BATS

Bats are probably one of the most important predators of night-flying insects. Bats in your attic, or your belfry, are problematic, but bats in a cave or bat house are an enormous benefit to the neighborhood or farm. Bats spend the night eating flying insects, primarily moths and mosquitoes. Help to preserve these important beneficial mammals. Directions for making bat houses can be found online. Check with your county extension service agent for bat preservation groups in your area or state. (For more information on bats, see p. 77.)

cover something about the pest or its natural controls that is not yet known to others.

So let us encourage you to spend some peaceful moments in your garden looking at the wildlife. You can learn to distinguish the plant-feeders from the carnivores, the potentially serious pests from those that are infrequent problems, and the beneficial organisms that are worth encouraging from those that are not.

In this chapter we have chosen to discuss a number of specific pests (organized alphabetically by group) of food and ornamental gardens for which our recommendations may be at variance with the abundant literature on the subject. For instance, we advise against importing lady beetles to control aphids, and suggest conserving rather than killing earwigs whenever possible. Sometimes we offer something in addition to the popular knowledge on the subject—we suggest, for example, that in residential-size gardens you use traps, hand-picking, and vacuuming for catching cucumber beetles and yellow sticky traps and vacuuming for collecting white-fly adults.

In our minds there is a distinct difference between pests such as termites or mosquitoes that can have a serious economic or medical impact on the household and those that are primarily an annoyance, because, for example, they chew holes in cabbage or disfigure a few flowers. Our hope is that by refraining from pest control in the garden

unless the situation is serious enough to warrant it, many more of the visitors to our gardens will be spared and allowed to establish a complex, stable environment.

Usually a mix of direct and indirect tactics is required to achieve the desired effect and derive a lasting benefit. You may want to review Chapter 4, which describes these general strategies for controlling pests and some criteria for selecting treatments. The discussion is particularly applicable to garden problems.

Assuming you have done your best to select and site the plants appropriately, we recommend that you apply physical controls first, particularly in emergencies. Squash the pest, pick it off the plant, prune it out, grub it out, trap it, or create a barrier between the plant and the pest. Then examine the potential for modifying your horticultural practices such as fertilizing and watering. Next, decide whether releasing biological control organisms is appropriate. Finally, if none of the above is adequate by itself, follow the advice given in Chapter 6 on the use of chemical controls.

> **"The first rule of aphid management is to conserve the many natural enemies of aphids present in most gardens."**

APHIDS

(Order Hemiptera [Homoptera], superfamily Aphidoidea)
Aphids are a common garden problem, particularly at the beginning and end of each plant's growing season. Given that aphids have an abundance of natural enemies, you might wonder why this is so. Part of the answer is that the predators and parasites of aphids generally are not available to help control the pests until large numbers of their prey are already present. It makes good sense if you think about it. If the beneficial insects arrived on the scene too early, they would starve to death before they had a chance to propagate themselves.

The interval between the appearance of the aphids and that of their natural enemies may be as short as a day or two or as long as several weeks if the temperature is low. It is this predator-prey lag that you must bridge to control most aphids.

The first rule of aphid management is to conserve the many natural enemies of aphids present in most gardens, because the potential for good biological control of aphids improves as the season progresses. You do this by confining any treatments against aphids to just those times and places where aphids are intolerable, and by using only methods that do not harm the beneficial predators and parasitoids when they do arrive in the aphid colonies.

Another reason aphids are so visible at certain times and not at others, and on certain parts of a plant but not elsewhere, is that they respond to nitrogen levels in the plant. When and where nitrogen levels are high, aphids can multiply very rapidly. Nitrogen levels are generally very high when a plant begins active growth. For most plants in temperate climates this is in the spring. Nitrogen is particularly high in the portions of the plant that grow the most rapidly, such as the buds and tips of the stems. The nitrogen level drops during the middle of the growth period, only to rise again to a smaller peak in the fall or when the leaves begin senescence (their decline) and prepare to drop off the plant.

Thus, the second rule of good aphid management is to follow horticultural practices that maintain nitrogen at a level just adequate for slow to moderate growth. This is where the use of organic fertilizers and amendments comes into play. It is much more difficult to have excess available nitrogen when you have a healthy soil food web, and feed it only organic fertilizers and amendments.

Rose aphids, *Macrosiphum rosae*, shown here feeding on the tender bud growth, also like succulent vegetative shoots. (Photo by Steven Ash)

BIOLOGY

At least 4,000 aphid species have been described, and probably many more remain to be discovered and named. Within each species there may be considerable variation in color, size, other aspects of appearance, response to environmental conditions, and/or food preference. Thus, it is very difficult to generalize about aphids in a way that is useful for the particular species you find in your garden.

Most of the known aphid species are quite restricted in their host range; that is, they feed on one or a few closely related species of plants. On the other hand, approximately 10 percent of aphid species can and do feed on many different types of plants because they are blown from plant to plant by the winds, sometimes for hundreds of miles.

Some species alternate between two host plants each year, leaving their spring environments to fly to other species of plants during the summer, and returning to their initial hosts at the end of the growing season. For this reason, it is not uncommon to find a heavy infestation on one type of plant and then, just when you think you must do something about it, the aphids disappear, as if by magic. They have gone off to their summer host. In many cases, the alternate hosts of common aphids have not yet been discovered. Other aphid species remain all season on the same species, although they may be lifted by the winds from one patch of it to another.

The superfamily of aphids is divided into two major groups. One of the differences between the groups is defined by the ability to bear live young. Although there are a number of root and conifer aphid pests that only lay eggs, the aphids seen most commonly in gardens are more unusual. Their remarkable life cycle helps explain how they can appear in large numbers quickly when there were few before, and how variation within the species occurs.

In temperate climates, females lay their eggs toward the end of the growing season in protected places on their favorite plant species. Such places include cracks and crevices in the bark or bud scales. When spring arrives, plump, distinctive-looking aphids emerge from these eggs. These are called "stem mothers," and they give live birth to daughters, and they to more daughters, all without mating. As each new female is born, she already has her partially formed daughters within her. Essentially, she is born pregnant. This is called telescoping generations. Thus, each female can rapidly replicate any genetic peculiarities originally passed on by her. It is very interesting to take a 10× hand lens and watch the baby aphids being born alive. Meanwhile, the mother goes on calmly feeding on the host plant, her pointed, stylet-like mouthparts inserted into the leaf or stem from which she sucks nutritious sap.

At the end of the growing season, males are finally produced in the aphid colonies. Females born at the same time have eggs rather than live young inside them. Mating occurs, the eggs are fertilized, and the overwintering eggs are again laid in protected areas on the plants. One exception occurs among those species that live in subtropical or tropical environments, including greenhouses. Such aphids may never produce either males or females that lay eggs.

The sap that aphids imbibe from the plants is sweet, like maple syrup. They take more in than they can assimilate and excrete the excess, called honeydew. Honeydew is also produced by other common insects in the order Hemiptera, including scales, whiteflies, and mealybugs.

Honeydew's high sugar content soon grows a sooty mold, much like a black fungus growing in an old jelly jar. This may be considered undesirable because it makes the plant's leaves look sooty or dirty. Some tree-feeding aphids produce such copious amounts of honeydew that it falls off in great drops on cars parked beneath or on sidewalks, where it causes leaves and other debris to stick to the feet of pedestrians. In this way, honeydew can become a problem even when aphids are not doing any appreciable damage to a tree.

An aphid group often referred to as the woolly aphids produce filaments of fine wax around themselves, a trait shared with the closely related Hemiptera. One common species, the woolly apple aphid (*Eriosoma lanigerum*), is found worldwide on some species of apple, pear, quince, and closely related plants. The aphid is under such good control by its natural enemy, a chalcid wasp, that gardeners notice it only when large numbers of its parasitoid have been temporarily eliminated through pesticide use, ant interference, or unfavorable environmental conditions.

APHIDS

Adult aphids can be winged or wingless, and can produce living young at various times of the year without mating. The paired tubular structures on the abdomen are called cornicles, which produce an alarm substance when the aphids are disturbed by predators. The size and shape of the cornicles help distinguish aphid species. (Actual size of adult, ⅛ in./3 mm)

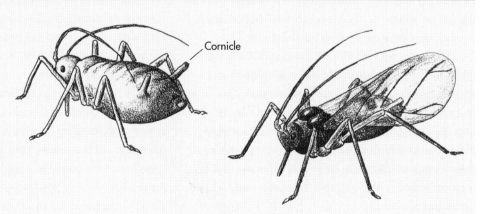

Cornicle

NATURAL ENEMIES OF APHIDS

The natural enemies of aphids are so numerous and varied that it is as difficult to generalize about them as it is about the aphids themselves. The enemies fall into three major groups: pathogens, predators, and parasitoids.

Certain aphids can transmit plant-infecting viruses from plant to plant, but the aphids themselves are not harmed by these. Fungi are the important pathogens causing disease in aphids, and close examination of any aphid colony often reveals the fruiting bodies of a fungus emerging from dead individuals.

Predators are the most familiar of the natural aphid enemies. They differ from parasitoids in that one predator consumes many prey, often of many different species. Examples are lady beetles, brown and green lacewings, and various flies. The best-known of the flies are the syrphid flies and the aphid-eating gall midges.

Numerous species exist in each of these families of predators, and in the case of lady beetles, lacewings, and gall midges, all three species are available commercially for aphid control. No species of syrphid or flower fly is commercially available. For more information about these beneficial insects, see Chapter 5.

The difficulty in using aphid predators outdoors is that they tend to skim the top off whatever local aphid population is largest, then, because they can feed on so many different species of aphids, move on to find a more abundant colony elsewhere. Thus, rather than purchasing commercially available predators for outdoor use, we urge you to encourage native predators by growing a variety of plants so a variety of aphid species will also be present. (Seed mixes that are designed to attract beneficials are available from insectaries from online sources, and sometimes from local nurseries.) That way the predators will stay nearby, feeding on each aphid population in turn according to which is most abundant. In addition, if you grow flowering plants you can attract those predator species, such as syrphid flies, in which the adult is dependent on pollen and nectar for egg laying.

The parasitoids of aphids generally are no larger than the head of a pin (about $\frac{1}{10}$ in. or 2.5 mm). They resemble parasites of mammals in that they reside either within the host or on its skin, living off just one host during their larval life. Unlike true parasites, however, parasitoids kill the host. Four parasitic wasps are commercially available: *Aphidius colemani, A. ervi, A. matricariae,* and *Aphelinus abdominalis.* If you decide to purchase these parasitoids, be sure that you have properly identified the aphid species, because these beneficials are relatively specific in their host choices.

The most important aphid parasitoids—all members of the large order Hymenoptera to which the honeybees and paper wasps also belong—are highly species-specific. The significance of this fact is that they can keep the population of aphid hosts very low, because they often live off no other species. The minute female parasitoid searches diligently for individual aphids in which to lay her eggs. After the egg hatches inside the aphid, the larva of the

APHID RANCHING

Certain ant species are so fond of honeydew that they jealously guard the aphid colonies producing it, killing such natural aphid enemies as the larvae of lady beetles, lacewings, syrphid flies, and gall midges. The ants tend the aphids as though they were livestock, not only protecting them from predators, but also carrying them to new succulent growth (new pastures), and even taking them into their nest (barn) when the weather turns foul. Ants will even use their antennae to massage (milk) the aphids to get them to produce honeydew more quickly and in greater quantities, like dairy farmers and cattle. This can lead to an aphid pest problem, and ant-exclusion measures become essential.

DID YOU KNOW?

There are some species of aphids for which no males have ever been identified.

miniwasp eats the aphid from the inside out, then pupates within or just below the dead body. Parasitized aphids are easy to detect, because their bodies become stiff, shiny, and hard, with a color varying from black to tan, cream, or brown, often with a metallic or bronzy appearance.

Once you have taught yourself what the parasitoids look like, you will begin to recognize them when you see them in the garden walking on leaves or flowers while hunting their prey. The ovipositor, or egg-laying apparatus, by which the female places her egg within the aphid can be seen clearly on the abdomen of the larger parasitoids.

In addition to laying eggs within the aphids, some of these miniwasps also feed upon the aphids directly, behaving like predators. Although it is difficult to quantify the effect of direct feeding by parasitoids on an aphid population, the combination of both methods of attack means that some of these beneficial insects can have a very significant impact upon the potential pest problem and may be underappreciated as predators.

INDENTIFYING APHID PARASITOIDS

If you discover aphid "mummies" on your plants and would like to know what the responsible aphid parasitoid looks like, place the leaf with the mummy in a small pill jar stoppered tightly with cotton. Check it daily for the emergence of a small black, yellow, or brown flying insect and the appearance of a small round hole in the aphid where it has emerged. Some parasitoids are very tiny and difficult to see without a hand lens, but larger ones are the size of a very small ant with wings. Because there are also parasitoids of the parasitoids (secondary parasitoids), you have no way of knowing whether the insect that emerges is a first- or second-level carnivore. One clue is that the common secondary parasitoids of aphids are very small, uniformly dark, and fairly chunky looking. They also make ragged emergence holes, whereas primary parasitoids make smooth, round holes. Any small, light-colored or yellow miniwasps are probably primary parasites. The movie *Alien* was based on this parasitoid behavior; egg implantation in the host, larva growth inside the host while eating it, and eventual emergence. In this instance, the movie was scarier than nature.

DETECTION AND MONITORING

Because all plants can tolerate some number of aphids without sustaining significant damage, the trick is to determine what number is tolerable. By carefully observing your roses or other plants in early spring, you can note when aphids first appear. Check the stem ends and buds weekly on those varieties that have proven most susceptible to aphids in the past. By watching the aphid colonies you locate, you should be able to spot the arrival of lady beetles, lacewing larvae, and the tiny slug-like larvae of the syrphid flies. The aphid-eating gall midges, another species of small flies, are usually late to arrive in the colonies. They have a brilliant orange-yellow color, which may make them stand out from their surroundings in certain settings. Also watch for the mummies, described earlier, that signal the presence of parasitoids.

For each susceptible plant, you need to determine whether the amount of damage that occurs between the hatching of the aphids and the arrival of sufficient natural enemies—the lag time—is tolerable. For example, in a municipal rose garden in coastal northern California, our staff determined that most of the rose species could tolerate up to 10 aphids per bud before damage was significant. This tolerance was based on a number of factors, such as temperature, that affect how rapidly aphids multiply and how quickly beneficial insects appear. By making similar observations, you can determine your own aphid tolerance levels.

TREATMENT
INDIRECT STRATEGIES

Indirect strategies for aphid control include nitrogen control, strategic pruning, allowing aging plants to decompose in place, the use of ant barriers, and attracting predators and parasitoids with flowering plants.

1. Nitrogen Control. Because aphid reproduction is enhanced by high nitrogen levels in plants, you should avoid using heavy doses of highly soluble nitrogen fertilizer. Instead, use less soluble forms of nitrogen—for example, organic or coated slow-release—and space the feedings over the growing season. Compost or decomposed manure is ideal for general garden use; fish emulsion or liquid seaweed can be used for individual ornamental plants. Timed-release urea-based formulations such as Osmocote® can also be used for cole (cabbage family) crops, which require a substantial nitrogen input. If you are growing plants primarily for flowers or fruit, use fertilizers that are relatively high in phosphorus relative to nitrogen. For example, rock phosphate combined with composted manure provides adequate nourishment when supplied in a slow but constant stream over the growing season.

2. Pruning. Pruning can also play a role in encouraging aphids, because a flush of high-nitrogen new growth follows the old growth. If the plant is a variety that is susceptible to aphids in your area, encouraging an abundance of new growth early in the season before most of the aphids' natural enemies are present can cause a serious aphid problem. It may even lead to stunting or distortion of the new growth.

On such plants, prune more moderately in winter and early spring, saving more severe pruning for after the aphids arrive. Then plan your cuts strategically to remove heavily infested areas. Space out thinning and shaping over the remainder of the season, a very little at a time. End all pruning well before fall so you don't encourage a sudden flush of new growth and increased nitrogen when the plant should be starting its process of hardening off for the approaching cold season.

3. Letting Aging Plants Linger. When you observe an aging annual plant with aphid colonies that are heavily parasitized or are attracting many predators, save its foliage so natural enemies that

TIP Specimen plants particularly susceptible to aphids that are being protected by ants can be raised in large tubs or planters. Either the sides of the planter should have ant (and slug and snail) barriers built in, or the container should be placed on an ant stand that is similarly protected.

are nonspecific in their aphid prey can move from it to younger foliage or other plants. When possible, as in the case of successive plantings of vegetables, simply let the aging plant linger until it falls over and decomposes in place. Where you find the appearance of the aging plant unattractive, you may be able to bend it down and out of sight behind other plants. Alternatively, you can cut off the aphid-infested material and use it as a mulch under other plants to build up the beneficial insect population in the garden.

4. Ant Barriers. As discussed earlier, in some areas of the country, certain ant species protect aphids from their natural enemies to ensure that the aphids continue to excrete the honeydew the ants feed upon. If you see ants on aphid-infested plants, assume they are playing this protective role. The application of a band of sticky material (such as Tangle-foot®, available at nurseries) to stalks of roses and other woody plants keeps the ants away. Be certain the foliage of the banded plant is not touching anything the ants can use as a bridge to the plant foliage. For more on ant control, see the discussion under "Direct Chemical Controls" on pp. 307–309.

5. Encouraging a Continuum of Flowers. Try to ensure that there are some plants flowering in your garden all season long, because many predators and parasitoids of aphids are dependent on obtaining nectar and pollen for egg laying.

TREATMENT
DIRECT PHYSICAL CONTROLS
A time-honored physical means of controlling aphids is washing them off a plant with a strong stream of water. A certain number of aphids are destroyed by this process, and others are eaten

LADY BEETLES FOR APHID CONTROL: YES OR NO?

Lady beetles sold commercially are collected in the areas where they hibernate in large numbers. In California, the popular convergent lady beetle (*Hippodamia convergens*) gathers yearly by the millions in the same sites along river valleys in the foothills of the Sierra Nevada. These are the beetles that are collected by the dealers. After collection, which is usually in winter, the beetles are placed in cold storage and sold in the spring. When you release them in your garden, they fly away, just as they would from their hibernation sites, especially when the temperature reaches 65° (18°C) or above.

Because releases of purchased beetles are usually made at the same time the native convergent lady beetles are flying in and they all look the same, you have no way of knowing whether the beetles in the garden are the ones you released. This was demonstrated to us conclusively when we participated in a study in which the beetles purchased were marked with blue paint. A day after release, there were many beetles in the garden but very few with blue marks. If they had not been marked, we might have thought the release was a success.

While the beetles hibernate (more accurately "diapause," a state of arrested development often compared with the hibernation of mammals), they must burn up fat deposits in their bodies before they can feed again. Beetles collected after May from mountain aggregations may remain in the area where they are released, but their feeding activity is not normal, apparently because they are still subsisting on their stored fat. Moreover, the process of collection and release results in the unavoidable death of large numbers of these beneficials through shipping and storage. For this reason, we discourage the practice of purchasing lady beetles for aphid control.

by predators such as spiders once they are on the ground. The disadvantage is that water-washing must be repeated fairly often, sometimes every three or four days, until the natural enemies of the aphids make their appearance in the garden and take over. On the positive side, water poses no hazard to humans and leaves no toxic residue on the plants that might harm the beneficial organisms.

You can wipe small colonies of aphids from leaves and buds with your hands, which should be covered by a pair of cloth garden gloves. Severely infested sections can be pinched off or pruned out. If it is early in the season and no natural enemies of the aphids seem to have arrived yet, dispose of the prunings in a hot compost. They can also be dropped in a bucket of soapy water, then drained and left to decompose as mulch or in a slow compost pile.

TREATMENT
DIRECT BIOLOGICAL CONTROLS

Although lady beetles and praying mantids are listed in nursery and other mail-order catalogs for aphid control, in our opinion, they are not appropriate for outdoor control of garden aphids.

As far as we can tell, the "success" that people claim when using lady beetles and mantids for aphid control is really the result of their refraining from using conventional pesticides for fear of harming the beneficials. When you refrain from using conventional pesticides, particularly in the conventional manner—that is to say, spraying everything in sight—you allow the survival of a large number of native predators and parasitoids. These become active about the time the commercially available lady beetles and mantids arrive. The result is good biological control, but not particularly from the insects that were purchased and released.

Praying mantids are fascinating insects and make good pets for children. You can keep one in a small terrarium and feed it flies and other insects appropriate to its size. Such close observance of a mantid may inspire a lifelong interest in insects. If you do this, one thing you will observe is that mantids are general feeders, totally indiscriminate in what they eat. They are as likely to feed on a beneficial insect as they are on a pest. In fact, if you release enough mantids, they will eat each other.

In the past, we generally discouraged people from releasing mantids, in the garden for pest control. However, literature translated from Chinese has broadened our sense of how these predators might find a role in a biological control program if the right procedure were followed. The mantids would have to be hatched in time to grow large enough to handle the pest in question. In that case, buy the "cocoon" egg case in the spring and store in a cold place. Wait for a good number of aphids to develop on one of your garden plants. Then place the case close to the aphids so the hatchlings can eat them, and consequently grow into adult mantids that can eat many other garden pests.

TREATMENT
DIRECT CHEMICAL CONTROLS

A variety of home brews for aphid control can be found in the organic gardening literature, but we do not recommend them. Now that reliable insecticidal soaps that are nontoxic to mammals are available commercially, we suggest you become familiar with their use. Other chemical controls focus on the ant species that protect aphids, but spraying for ants is usually ineffective. Exclude the ants with barriers or use ant baits to reduce numbers. Keeping the ground moist by watering can deter many ants, but keeping the soil surface moist can promote weeds and can only be used in areas not under drought restrictions.

TIP If the aphid colonies are already parasitized or are attracting lady beetles and other predators, cut prunings to a small size and leave them in an inconspicuous place beneath a shrub to decompose.

1. Insecticidal Soap. When water alone is ineffective at reducing aphid numbers, either because the plant cannot sustain the force of a stream strong enough to wash them off or because the leaves are so sticky the aphids won't wash off, we suggest using insecticidal soap. First, however, make some careful observations. Treatments should be made only when and where aphid numbers are really intolerable and there is no sign that natural predators and parasitoids have arrived. If you feel you must apply insecticidal soap, read pp. 113–116 for details.

2. Insecticidal Baits. Where ants cannot be controlled with sticky barriers, you might want to try a boric acid bait, available from hardware stores in plastic bait stations. You can also make your own boric acid bait. Ant species in the garden, and sometimes ant colonies within a species, may vary greatly as to what foods attract them, so the secret to baiting is discovering what attracts the colony you are trying to kill. Once you know what food they prefer over the other potential foods around them, mix this with the boric acid. The proportion of poison to food should be great enough to kill the colony, but the poison should not be so strong that the ant scouts die before they have an opportunity to carry the food back to their queen in the nest.

We suggest placing the bait inside a small jar, about the size of an old plastic 35 mm film canister. Make holes in the lid, then tighten it securely. The holes allow ants to enter and enable you to re-liquefy the bait with additional water as necessary, because the bait should be kept moist. Make sure the jars are not in sunlight at any time and cover partially with mulch to shade. Direct sunlight not only dries out the bait but also makes the interior of the container too hot for the ants to enter. Several containers will be needed to surround the plant or the entrance to the ant colony you are trying to kill. Use plastic plant stakes to mark the location of the bait containers so you can check and refill them as needed.

If you mix the bait yourself, make certain that your bait holders are out of the reach and sight of children and pets. Be sure to mark the containers "poison," with a skull and crossbones. Although boric acid is much less of a hazard than the commercial arsenic ant baits that have been popular for so long, it nevertheless can harm a child or pet that eats it. Warn your children of the danger; if they are simply too young to understand and have access to

FIRE ANT CONTROL

We have found silica aerogel to be extremely useful in field tests where native fire ants *(Solenopsis xyloni)* are a problem. These are not to be confused with the red imported fire ant *(Solenopsis invicta)* that is infamous across the southern United States and Mexico. The native fire ant kills eggplants and peppers by girdling their stems and branches. In as little as two days, a mature plant can be injured beyond recovery. Usually the ants affect just one plant at a time or occasionally two adjacent plants.

When we discover an infestation early enough, we can usually destroy it by spraying the compound on about 6 in. (15 cm) of the stem beginning at the base and in a circle about 12 in. (30 cm) in diameter around the plant. If lower branches touch the ground, we prune them off so the ants have no other access to the upper portions of the plant. Because the pesticide breaks down in a few days, it is often necessary to repeat the application several times at intervals of 5 to 7 days before the attack subsides.

The fire ant is a problem only in extremely dry areas. Thus, an alternative to using this pesticide is watering plants by soaking the ground between rows as well as around the crops themselves. When we did this at the field station, fire ants were never a problem. But water is very scarce there, and we now use underground irrigation to minimize water consumption. In this case, we decided that water conservation was essential and elected to spot-treat periodically with the pesticide.

your garden, we suggest you tolerate the ants rather than take any risk.

Hydramethylnon and fipronil are also effective against ants. They are available as Combat® bait stations, which are sold in most hardware stores. Combat also has a boric acid bait. Most commercial single-use bait stations are very secure and almost impossible to open. One of the authors cut his hand twice trying to cut one open and take it apart using pliers, tin snips, and wire cutters. Despite the difficulty in opening them, keep these and all bait preparations out of the reach and sight of children and pets.

Insecticidal baits must be renewed periodically, because as fast as you kill one ant colony, another

seems to replace it. Where the aphid-infested plant has one or only a few woody stems, we advise combining sticky barriers (see p. 305) with the use of baits.

Remember, however, that ants are generally very beneficial, eating many pest insects and aerating the soil with their tunneling. So don't kill them wherever you find them in the garden, but confine ant control to those areas where they are a serious problem. Spiders, some birds, and lizards eat ants.

3. Silica Aerogel/Pyrethrin. If none of the techniques suggested above is adequate and the problem is serious, you can spot-treat with a silica aerogel/pyrethrin mix, as described on p. 110. This material is available in an aerosol can with an applicator tip that allows you to confine the material to a small area such as a plant stem. The silica aerogel leaves a white residue so you can see exactly where it has been applied.

4. Least-Toxic 25b Generally Recognized as Safe (GRAS) Insecticides. A number of new, very low toxicity insecticides have been coming on the market in recent years. Many are labeled for aphids, ants, and other pest insects. A few of the common active ingredients in these pesticides are garlic oil, mint oil, eugenol, vegetable oils, neem oil, lemongrass, and clove oil. Many of these insecticides are OMRI listed, and some are in the 25b, or "food grade," category of GRAS pesticides. That is, a large group of these pesticides, made of organic ingredients, are considered "food grade" materials. Although these materials are considered much safer than synthetic pesticides, they are not without hazards. Some of these concentrated materials can cause substantial eye irritation and/or skin reactions. They may also be problematic for persons with food allergies because these pesticides are primarily made from concentrated food oils, the part of the plant most likely to cause an allergic reaction in sensitive individuals.

The 25b GRAS pesticides do not carry an EPA registration number, a unique number assigned to all pesticides not in this group, and they do not go through the testing to which conventional pesticides are subjected. We think every pesticide should be assigned an EPA registration number so that its use can be tracked. The EPA registration number is also used by doctors and poison control centers to identify all of the ingredients in a pesticide and to determine a treatment regimen in the case of accidental exposure or poisoning.

CUCUMBER BEETLES

(Order Coleoptera, family Chrysomelidae)

Cucumber beetles (*Diabrotica* spp.) are serious agricultural pests that also bother home gardeners, although not necessarily on the same crops. The adults feed mostly on pollens and floral parts, especially on corn but also on other garden vegetables, flowers, weeds, and native plants. At certain times during the season, they may be highly visible on members of the cucurbit family, as the name cucumber beetle implies. The adults of pestiferous species are a conspicuous yellow or green, some marked with black spots or stripes. They fly or drop from the plant quickly if the leaves are touched.

Farmers are primarily concerned with the damage these beetles inflict on corn, beans, and alfalfa. The adults lay their eggs in the ground and the larvae feed on the roots; thus, they are also called corn rootworms. They probably cause more agricultural loss than any other pest, and more insecticide is used against them than against any other pest. About $1 billion is lost each year to the beetle and its con-

Some years, the spotted cucumber beetle, *Diabrotica undecimpunctata* is everywhere you look, with lots of visible damage. Traps and handpicking may help. (Photo by Elliotte Rusty Harold/Shutterstock)

trol in the United States alone. Research indicates that much of this insecticide use is probably ineffective, and new research is underway to develop other means of control. Some of the early results already have implications for the home gardener. We summarize them here.

BIOLOGY

Only 7 of the 338 known beetle species in the genus *Diabrotica* occur in the United States; of these, 6 are serious pests (see the chart on p. 310). Overall, the most damaging species in the corn belt are the western corn rootworm and the northern corn rootworm.

Diabrotica are divided into two groups. Species in the *furcata* group overwinter as adults and have more than one generation per year (they are multivoltine) in the north temperate zone. Those in the *virgifera* group have only one generation per year (they are univoltine) and overwinter as resting or hibernating (diapausing) eggs. Thus, they would appear to be controllable through crop rotation.

Research indicates, however, that at least one species, the northern corn rootworm, has eggs that can diapause in the soil for two years. This is discussed further below.

Beetles developing on corn probably account for most of the *Diabrotica* in any particular area. The adults feed on corn tassels, leaves, and silk, as well as on the pollen of corn, grain crops, legumes, and weeds. The adults can keep the corn silks chewed back to the ear tip during the period of pollination, resulting in poor grain set; they can also feed directly on the terminal kernels of corn. The larvae can cause poor grain set through excessive root feeding, which reduces water intake and produces symptoms that mimic drought damage.

CUCUMBER BEETLE (*DIABROTICA*) PEST SPECIES (NORTH AMERICAN TEMPERATE ZONE)

COMMON NAME	banded cucumber beetle	western spotted cucumber beetle	northern corn rootworm	southern corn rootworm (spotted cucumber beetle)	western corn rootworm	Mexican corn rootworm
SCIENTIFIC NAME	*D. balteata*	*D. undecimpunctata*	*D. barberi*	*D. undecimpunctata howardi*	*D. virgifera virgifera*	*D. virgifera zeae*
DISTRIBUTION	South America, Central America	West Coast	Midwest to East, not South	Midwest to East, South and Southwest	Midwest and Southwest	Texas and Oklahoma, Mexico

Banded cucumber beetle, western spotted cucumber beetle, and southern corn rootworm are in the *furcata* group, have more than one generation per year, and overwinter as adults. The remaining species are in the *virgifera* group, have a single generation per year, and overwinter as eggs.

The yellow-orange rootworm eggs are deposited in the moist soil at the base of corn plants from about August to October. The larvae feed on the roots of grasses, legumes, and six other plant families. They also transmit plant pathogens through their feeding. Larvae-infested plants grow slowly and can topple in wind or heavy rain. After leaving the roots, the larvae pupate in the soil.

DAMAGE AND DETECTION

A heavy rootworm infestation can completely destroy the roots of corn. The loss of primary and brace roots greatly weakens the support system of the plant and can reduce plant growth and production. Weakened or fallen plants should be pulled or dug out and inspected for larvae feeding on the roots. After feeding, the larvae can be found in small cells in the soil where they prepare themselves for pupation. Mature larvae are white, slender, and about ½ in. (1.3 cm) long with brown heads. They can move at most 20 in. (50 cm) to another corn plant after hatching or during their larval lives.

Adults may tunnel into or completely destroy the corn tips, resulting in a browning and rotting of the injured areas. When present on the corn plant above ground, or on other vegetable plants, the adults are easy to spot because of their light color.

TREATMENT
INDIRECT STRATEGIES

For many years it was believed that yearly crop rotations with legumes such as soybeans was completely effective in reducing the opportunities for these beetles to lay eggs and reproduce. It has now been found that annual crop rotations are not always helpful, apparently because at least one species, the northern corn rootworm, has eggs that can diapause in the soil for two years. Thus, a non-host crop would have to remain in place for two or more years if rotation were the only technique being used to manage the problem. This is not economically feasible for most large-scale growers, but it could certainly be used on a small scale.

TREATMENT
DIRECT PHYSICAL CONTROLS

In years when adult beetle numbers are overwhelming, hand-picking may seem tiresome and ineffective. In most years, however, repeated hand-picking in small plots or vacuuming in larger plots can greatly reduce adult damage. Other physical controls include the following:

1. Funnel-and-Bag System. An effective way to collect relatively large numbers of adults is to adapt the funnel-and-bag system used by researchers. They use a bag measuring 16 in. by 24 in. (40 cm by 60 cm) that is sewn from plastic window screen (18 mesh) with a drawstring at the opening. A small, #10, ½-in. rubber stopper is fitted into the stem of the funnel. The bag is then tightened over the funnel stem with the drawstring. We have also used plastic bags and masking tape to hold the bag to the funnel. The small producer or gardener can set up a similar system with plastic bags and rubber bands.

Place the funnel beneath leaves with beetles. Slightly jar the foliage to cause the beetles to fall into the funnel and slide down into the bag. Once they are in the bag, put the rubber stopper into the funnel stem to keep them in the bag when going from plant to plant. When collecting is finished, pull the funnel stem out of the bag and close the bag with the drawstring. In corn fields, one person can collect 15,000 to 20,000 beetles in three or four hours. Daily collections when beetles are particularly numerous may help prevent excessive damage. Captured beetles can be kept in the freezer until they are dead or can be placed in the sun to "cook" in a tightly closed plastic bag.

2. Sticky Traps. Trapping may also be effective if enough of the proper type of traps are used. This is speculative, because no studies have been conducted yet, but the usefulness of traps as monitoring tools has been proven. Because trapping methods are currently being researched, it is possible that a cheap, convenient, mass-produced trap will soon appear on the market. Before that occurs, however, small-scale growers may want to experiment with their own models.

Researchers have used yellow sticky traps made from pieces of fiber board 6 in. (15 cm) wide and 8 in. (20 cm) high coated with an adhesive such as Tanglefoot. The traps can be attached to stakes at ground level or about 12 in. (30 cm) above. Researchers found that when these traps were baited with eugenol emanating from dental wicks (tube-shaped pieces of gauze) attached to the boards, the number of females captured was much greater than with unbaited boards. Eugenol is available in a pure form as a laboratory material at drugstores, health-food stores, or online and is also found in natural form in many plants. For example, allspice oil from *Pimenta dioica* is composed of 60 percent to 80 percent eugenol. Bay oil from the West Indian bay plant (*P. racemosa*) contains up to 56 percent eugenol. Similarly, clove bud oil from *Syzygium aromaticum* contains 60 percent to 90 percent eugenol.

These trap designs went through many changes before a commercially available product was marketed. One currently on the market is the Tomcat® eugenol trap. The small producer or home gardener may want to experiment to find designs that are easy to service and last many seasons. Plywood or Masonite® pieces or plastic boards should be better than fiber board because they last longer, particularly after repeated exposure to sunlight, heat, and the solvents used to remove the adhesive and trapped beetles. Alternatively, traps could be made from recycled cardboard painted yellow and covered with adhesive. When full of beetles, these traps can be discarded.

A trap with a detachable sticky yellow sheet may prove even more effective. Larger boards should capture more beetles overall than smaller ones. No studies currently indicate how large such traps should be, but there must be some point of diminishing return where further increases in trap size are not effective relative to the size of the plot being protected. Wind should also be considered when sizing traps, because larger traps are more vulnerable to buffeting.

CUCUMBER BEETLES: WHAT THEY EAT

Adult cucumber beetles feed on more than 280 plants in at least 29 families. They have been reported as a pest of 61 different crops, but they primarily attack corn, cucurbits, sweet potatoes, and legumes, including peanuts, common beans, cowpeas, and broad beans.

Although sticky traps generally are inexpensive and easy to construct, they are hard to manage unless designed so that the adhesive does not interfere with transport, servicing, and storage. Anyone who has worked with these adhesives can attest to the nuisance factor. In addition, the trap described previously is inherently limited in its effectiveness because eugenol primarily attracts the northern corn rootworm and not the western corn rootworm. Combinations of lures and traps may prove effective once sex pheromones that attract both major rootworm species have been isolated, identified, and tested. For example, indole has been identified as the active attractant in squash blossoms, which are highly attractive to rootworm adults.

Yellow sticky traps, or sticky cards, are used to monitor insect populations. The yellow color attracts many flying insects, especially whiteflies. (Photo by FhF Greenmedia/GAP)

3. Attractant/Poison Traps. Studies have shown that attractant/poison traps can be effective at catching beetles without broadcasting the poison into the environment. This type of trap uses the attractiveness of certain cucurbits with high levels of the bitter compound cucurbitacin. Cucurbitacin acts like an arrestant rather than a classical pheromone, causing beetles to stay where they are rather than pulling them in from a considerable distance, as classical sex pheromones do. The sidebar on the facing page (aimed primarily at professionals) describes how these traps are made.

TREATMENT

DIRECT BIOLOGICAL CONTROLS

There are two promising new areas of biological beetle control, both involving nematodes. A mermithid nematode, *Hexamermis* spp., was discovered to be infesting and killing adults of *D. speciosa vigens* in Peru. Over a four-year period, parasitism rates varied, but included up to 90 percent of the adults in some samples. Laboratory testing indicates a relatively wide host range for this nematode, so it looks hopeful. After further evaluation, the beneficial nematode may be introduced into *Diabrotica* populations in North America.

With luck, this nematode will establish itself and become an important natural control of cucumber beetles. However, as with other classical biological control attempts, there is no guarantee that it will work.

The other nematodes, *Heterorhabditis bacteriophora*, *H. indica*, and *H. marelatus*, are available commercially. These species can be applied much like conventional pesticides. They are poured or sprayed in liquid solution onto the soil about the same time immature beetles are hatching. Appropriate strains, dosages, application times, and delivery systems are available from commercial suppliers to enable home gardeners and professional landscapers to use them.

Inoculation of the soil with 90,000 nematodes per linear foot at planting time has proven effective in controlling rootworm in small test plots.

A LESS-TOXIC ATTRACTANT/POISON TRAP FOR CUCUMBER BEETLES

A commercially available source of cucurbitacin is a product called CideTrak®. Available from Rincon-Vitova Insectaries, this material is mixed with Entrust® brand 80-percent Spinosad WP, which is OMRI listed.

If you prefer to make your own cucurbitacin, the first step in making the attractant is selecting the most bitter fruits of cucumber (e.g., 'Marketer') or bitter squash (e.g., 'Calabazilla' or 'Hubbard') that result from a cross of *Cucurbita andreana* and *C. maxima*. You can do this by touching small pieces of the fruits to your tongue. The most bitter fruits are then cut up into small pieces, air-dried, and powdered in a food-processing mill.

The CideTrak powder, or your home-made cucurbitacin, is usually mixed with spinosad insecticidal dust (wettable powder). It is dusted onto sheets of 3M® infrared transparency film, which are cut into 21 strips per sheet. The arrestant/insecticide strips are then placed in small amber 16-dram vials 1 in. (2.5 cm) in diameter and 3 in. (7.6 cm) high. These vials have white locking caps that have had the solid bottom portions removed. The opening made in the cap is covered with 14 by 18 mesh wire screening to prevent water vapor from condensing inside the trap. Five $1/5$-in. (5 mm) holes are then drilled at equal intervals around the vial.

The vials are hung over the corn ears with a piece of wire. The beetles enter the traps, and while attempting to feed on the cucurbitacin are killed by contact with the insecticide. These traps have been used successfully to trap both the northern and western corn rootworms. If a more benign poison than carbaryl can be used, this sort of trap could be very useful in the future for small producers and gardeners.

For larger areas, Rincon-Vitova suggests a bait mix containing the following:

- 1 oz. Entrust 80-percent Spinosad WP
- 3.1 oz. CideTrak cucurbitacin bait
- 10 gal. water.

Mix ingredients in a sprayer and "spray large droplets on 1 acre crop or surrounding vegetation." The ingredients, Entrust and CideTrak, represent a fairly substantial monetary investment. Use of these products is probably limited to farmers and pest management professionals who have sufficient acreage to use all of the materials in a season. Avoid the need to store pesticides; buy only the amount of pesticide you will use.

From J. L. Krysan and T. A. Miller's *Methods for the Study of Pest Diabrotica* (Springer-Verlag, 1986) and Rincon-Vitova Insectaries, 2010.

Because the susceptible rootworm stages are not present for up to three weeks after planting, even better results may be obtained if the nematodes are applied at that time. Current research indicates that the nematodes are lost from the root zone soil rapidly, so multiple applications may be necessary. Nematodes (*H. bacteriophora*) are commercially available for cucumber beetles from Rincon-Vitova Insectaries.

Cucumber beetles are attacked by a variety of natural enemies, the most important being a parasitic tachinid fly, *Celatoria diabroticae*. Other predators that attack *Diabrotica* are soldier beetles, lacewings, and ladybugs.

DIRECT CHEMICAL CONTROLS

Until recently, it was not possible to determine infestation rates for cucumber beetle eggs in fields accurately, because egg and larval numbers were difficult to obtain. Further developments now suggest that most previous insecticide use was probably ineffective. Although disturbing from the viewpoint of efficiency and environmental pollution, this news suggests that preventive drenches with insecticides aimed at the larvae in the soil probably represent a dead end, and that new approaches and techniques must be searched out, tested, and applied. The problem can usually be handled by trap cropping, using beans or alfalfa. Direct control by regular vacuuming can be effective enough to keep adult numbers low.

CUTWORMS

(Order Lepidoptera, family Noctuidae)

Nearly all caterpillars encountered in the garden can be controlled either by simple hand-picking or with the use of a bacterial spray of *Bacillus thuringiensis,* described at length in Chapter 8.

One group of caterpillars, the cutworms on the facing page, warrant additional discussion, because you may not be able to use either hand-picking or BT against them. Cutworms are common in grassy areas and may become severe in a garden that has just been converted from lawn or wild grass. Certain species are particularly damaging to young seedlings, and these are among the hardest pests to control.

Cutworms are hard to control with hand-picking or BT because they are most likely to inflict their damage at night; they spend the day buried in the soil somewhere near the plants they have been eating. Often, gardeners plant their seedlings one day and return the next to find a row of little stems cut an inch or less above the ground. No doubt this is the source of the name "cutworm."

BIOLOGY

The word "cutworm" is used loosely to designate about 200 species in the family Noctuidae, the largest family in the Lepidoptera. There are 2,925 species of this family in North America. Most of the cutworms occur in one of the 16 subfamilies, the Noctuinae. The chart on p. 316 lists some common species. The different groups of cutworms can be distinguished by their feeding habits.

Tunnel-making cutworms feed at or below the soil surface and eat only enough to topple the seedling. Examples are black, bronzed, and clay

Cutworm is a term used to describe the larvae of about 200 species in the family Noctuidae. These caterpillars feed at night and get their name from their habit of eating completely through the stems of seedlings. (Photo by pitrs/Fololia.com)

cutworms. Climbing cutworms climb plants and eat buds, leaves, and fruits. Examples are variegated and spotted cutworms. Army cutworms may move in large groups from field to field and can consume all parts of the plant. Examples are the several species of army cutworms. Subterranean cutworms remain in the soil and feed on underground stems and roots. Examples are the pale western and glassy cutworms.

There is an unfortunate overlap in the use of the common names cutworm and armyworm, and sometimes "army cutworm." Some people call a particular species an armyworm, others may call it a cutworm. The term *army cutworm* refers to the characteristics of both groups: the cut-stem plant damage and the army-like larval foraging behavior. This can cause confusion unless the scientific name is used.

In general, cutworm larvae start feeding in early spring. They eat at night and spend the day under surface litter near plant stems or in burrows in the top few inches of soil. Pupation occurs in the soil. Eggs are laid mostly on broad-leafed weed stems and leaves. Some species overwinter as eggs, others as larvae or adults. There can be up to four generations per year. Wood, used as stepping stones, can be used to trap larvae, as they prefer to curl up under these boards. Premade stepping stones can also harbor caterpillars underneath if the soil under them is rich, moist, and even in texture.

DETECTION AND MONITORING

If seedlings are cut off at ground level or slightly higher (as shown in the drawing on the facing page), cutworms should be suspected. You can verify their presence by searching just below soil surface debris in concentric circles around several remaining stems. Frequently you will find the C-shaped cutworm. Searches should be made at night with a flashlight and pencil or small stick. Make sure the C-shaped worm is a cutworm, and not misidentified as a beetle grub.

Farmers can use ultraviolet or black light traps (as shown in the photo on p. 317) to capture adult moths to determine the peak periods of egg laying and subsequent emergence and growth. There are also numerous pheromone traps available for many adult stages of cutworm species that are used to determine peak activity periods. Light traps and pheromone traps should be evaluated as potential mass-trapping systems.

If these techniques are used by the small-scale gardener, however, there is a danger that the pheromones will attract more adults into the garden than would occur if no traps were set. This is more of a danger when too few traps are used. The position of the traps in relation to the potential food sources is also important. Traps should be as far away from the crop as possible to minimize the number of insects attracted into the core growing area. You will have to experiment. At this time we can give no clear guidelines for the small-scale producer and cannot yet recommend these traps for home gardens.

TIP A foolproof method to control cutworms is to use seedling-size or plant-bed-size screened enclosures. These enclosures also protect against root maggots, the young of flies that burrow into the roots of cabbage family plants and onions (see the directions for constructing cone-shaped enclosures under "Root Maggots" on p. 325).

TREATMENT

INDIRECT STRATEGIES

One approach we have used successfully is starting seedlings inside on windowsills, then transplanting them when they are large enough to withstand a little damage. On the West Coast, where we garden, there are other pests that are particularly hard on seedlings, including birds, snails, slugs, mice, and sowbugs. Putting in larger plants instead of seedlings reduces the time spent in the seedling stage and provides greater production per unit of area once transplantation shock has been overcome. Moreover, a new batch of seedlings can be started before the crop has been harvested. We realize, however, that this is not practical in many situations.

In large gardens, you may reduce cutworm damage by minimizing the amount of weeds, particularly grass or grass-like weeds, where the seedlings will grow. The timing of spring cultivation is important. If you can eliminate all weed food for developing cutworm larvae for 10 days or longer (depending upon the cutworm species) before the emergence of crop seedlings, you will starve the newly hatched larvae. A weed-free period prior to planting also minimizes cutworm egg laying in the immediate area. Small gardens may experience less benefit than larger ones from this tactic, because cutworms do migrate in the larval form, some species more than others. Cutworms can visit small gardens one evening, then retire to neighboring areas before morning.

CUTWORMS

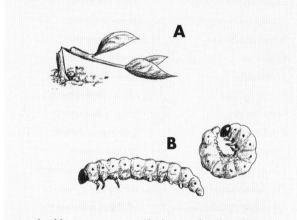

You should suspect cutworms (the larvae of moths) when seedlings have been snipped off near the ground (A). Search for them at night on the plants or during the day when they lie curled up nearby in the mulch (B). (Actual length, up to 1¼ in./32 mm)

THE BASICS OF PEST CONTROL

With each specific pest, keep in mind three things:

1. Basic information on the biology of the pest is crucial to successful control.

2. Control efforts work best when confined to the precise time and place where the pest is a severe problem.

3. It is rare that you can do just one thing to solve a pest problem.

DIRECT PHYSICAL CONTROLS

The use of barriers to control cutworms may have potential for small-scale gardeners.

Although it is popularly recommended that you place tar paper squares flat on the ground around the plant, this control is only somewhat successful. This is probably so because modern "tar" or roofing paper is not actually impregnated with "real tar" as it used to be, and the repellent effect on caterpillars is considerably less than in the past.

Yet the general tactic of constructing barriers against these caterpillars makes sense due to the caterpillar's habit of biting off seedlings at ground level. In our experience, paper collars, such as the cardboard tube inside a roll of toilet paper, provide a bit more protection than tar paper squares.

Although sticky barriers are of no help in protecting seedlings, on sturdier plants they prevent the larvae from moving up the stems to feed on buds, fruit, and leaves. This is particularly true if the barrier is wide enough to prevent the passage of the worms en masse, if the particular species shows this behavior.

The possibility of success with sticky barriers in larger field applications has increased with the availability of a Tanglefoot spray product called Tangle-Trap® Aerosol, which allows the quick application of a sticky barrier to many stems in a short time. We have no experience with this aerosol on succulent plants, so we cannot recommend it without encouraging you to test it first on a few plants to make sure

no phytotoxic reactions result. We should also caution that methylene chloride, the propellant in this product, poses a hazard to the user. If a substitute propellant can be found, this method of Tanglefoot application will find many uses.

DIRECT BIOLOGICAL CONTROLS

Many organisms feed on cutworms, including microbes, birds, bats, insect predators such as ground beetles, and hymenopteran parasitoids. Thus, any control aimed at cutworms must not pose a simultaneous threat to these species that prey on them. Fortunately, baits containing BT as the active ingredient are effective specifically against caterpillars without harming these other organisms.

SOME IMPORTANT DAMAGING CUTWORM SPECIES

SCIENTIFIC NAME	COMMON NAME
Agrotis gladiaria	claybacked cutworm
A. ipsilon	black cutworm
A. malefida	pale-sided cutworm
A. orthogonia	pale western cutworm
A. venerabilis	dusky cutworm
Amathes c-nigrum	spotted cutworm
Chorizagrotis auxiliaris	army cutworm
Crymodes devastator	glassy cutworm
Euxoa auxillaris	army cutworm
E. detersa	sandhill cutworm
E. messoria	dark-sided cutworm
E. ochrogaster	red-backed cutworm
Feltia ducens	dingy cutworm
F. subterranea	granulate cutworm
Lacinipolia renigera	bristly cutworm
Loxagrotis albicosta	western bean cutworm
Peridroma saucia	variegated cutworm
Spodoptera eridania	southern armyworm
S. exigua	beet armyworm
S. frugiperda	fall armyworm
S. praefica	western yellow striped armyworm

Older entomological literature has many references to bran baits for controlling cutworms. The arsenic compounds used in these baits are fortunately now obsolete and unavailable, but BT can be mixed 12 percent by weight with wheat bran and either grape or apple pomace, the residue left after juicing. The mixture should be placed on the soil surface or on boards or cardboard.

There is so little research on the use of baits for cutworm control that we cannot make more precise recommendations on bait placement and renewal. It is unclear from the literature whether it is the bran or other ingredients that attract the cutworms, or whether these substances merely cause the cutworms to stop and feed. In any case, the bait should be broadcast around the entire plant to be protected, not just piled in one spot, to ensure that the cutworms encounter it before they reach the plant.

Electric black light (ultraviolet) traps attract a variety of night-flying insects such as moths and beetles. They are useful monitoring tools, and can be purchased from entomological suppliers or made from standard parts available at hardware stores. (Photo by Jerry A. Payne, USDA Agricultural Research Service, Bugwood.org)

EARWIGS

(Order Dermaptera, family Forficulidae)

Despite the fact that earwigs are now known to be largely beneficial, most of us are still trying to control them in our vegetable and flower gardens and occasionally in our homes. This is partly because of the damage they cause when they eat small holes in the leaf margins of seedlings of plants such as radishes. But the desire to kill earwigs is also due to the fact that people simply don't like the way they look, whether encountered in the garden or indoors.

The appearance of their posterior pincers seems frightening. These pincers, or forceps, are used by females to defend their families against predators. Earwig mothers are very protective of their eggs and young. If these are scattered, the mother collects them and stays to defend them with her pincers. Earwigs also use their pincers to fold away their wings after flight. Occasionally, two adjacent females with young will use the pincers to fight over food. As threatening as they may look, however, the pincers are not a menace to people.

The European earwig (*Forficula auricularia*), which was accidentally introduced into North America in 1907, is native to Europe, western Asia, and possibly North Africa. The species is omnivorous; it eats plants, other animals, and decaying material. When it enters homes looking for a nice dark place to hide, it becomes a household pest.

Research has demonstrated that earwig predation is significant in suppressing pests such as aphids in apple trees. It is our first-hand experience that, given a diverse soil surface of compost mulch on which to feed and hunt, earwigs can be present in the vegetable garden in enormous numbers and cause negligible damage to seedlings and larger plants. By contrast, when plants are set out in neat rows with bare soil between them and boards, pieces of broken sidewalk, or other inedible debris that can serve as earwig hiding places nearby, the earwigs may feed on the seedlings because there isn't much else available.

When abundant, earwigs are often blamed for damage caused by snails, slugs, cutworms, and other garden pests, because during the day when gardeners are active, the earwigs may choose damaged tomatoes or other fruits as handy, dark, moist hiding places. Nighttime checks with a flashlight reveal quite a different picture as the true culprits emerge to feed and the earwigs are busy foraging in the mulch.

We recommend that you keep in mind the beneficial predatory role earwigs can play in the garden, and make an effort to reduce their numbers only when nighttime checks definitely show them to be causing intolerable damage to your horticultural plants.

The European earwig, *Forficula auricularia*, is omnivorous and a beneficial generalist predator that also eats plants. The pincers on the abdomen are used to capture prey. (Photo by artist_as/Fololia.com)

BIOLOGY

Earwigs are reddish-brown and approximately ¾ in. (19 mm) long. The young are similar in appearance to the adults. The male's pincers are large and curved; the female's are smaller and nearly straight. As explained earlier, the pincers help females defend their eggs and clean their nests but pose no threat to humans. These insects have wings but rarely fly.

The female may lay up to 60 round white eggs in small nests in the upper few inches of soil. Ear-wigs are often referred to as semi-social insects, because the female guards the eggs and tends the young during their first two weeks of life. The first batch of eggs hatches in the spring, and the insect takes about 70 days to mature. A second batch may be laid during the summer. Earwigs live about a year, and many die the winter following their birth. A few, mostly females, survive to the following spring to raise another generation.

Earwigs forage at night, eating the eggs, young, and adults of small organisms such as insects, mites, and nematodes, as well as algae, fungi, and tender plant tips. During the day they hide in any tiny crevice they find near or on the ground, on plants, in piles of debris, in the cracks and crevices of the bark of trees, or in houses, sheds, and other structures.

EARWIG PHOBIA

Perhaps the worst fear people have of earwigs, and the one that is least founded, is that they crawl into the ear and bore into the brain. The old Anglo Saxon word "earwicga" literally means "ear creature," and in nearly all European languages the name for earwig suggests a connection with the ear. Apparently, present-day Americans have inherited this ancient European fear. Perhaps when people slept on dirt floors, straw, or hay, earwigs explored human ears as a place to hide. It is not inconceivable, though there are no records of this actually happening.

DAMAGE, DETECTION, AND MONITORING

Earwig damage to plants can consist of small holes in the leaves or entire new growth on seedlings that is nibbled away. Because earwig damage is similar to that of other pests, nighttime checks with a flashlight are the only sure way to determine whether earwigs are the cause. Check on a number of successive nights for actively feeding earwigs where you have noticed plant damage.

Rolled-up newspapers or other traps (see "Direct Physical Controls" on the facing page) can catch large numbers of earwigs even when they are not causing a problem, so we do not consider trapping by itself a good monitoring strategy. However, where nighttime checks reveal that earwigs are causing damage, traps can indicate where they are most heavily concentrated. When damage is the case, consider barriers as well.

INDIRECT STRATEGIES

The most frequent complaints we receive about earwigs come from gardeners planting a newly landscaped area and starting with relatively bare, unmulched soil. In such cases, we recommend first putting down a mulch of compost to provide a complex soil surface with many organisms on which the earwigs can feed.

Where earwigs are causing damage in an already mulched older garden, the best strategy is to raise seedlings indoors and transplant them to the outdoors when they are large enough to withstand some damage. You can also raise them outdoors on a protected surface such as a table with ant excluders around its legs (see p. 305). If you see earwigs eating flowers or damaging larger plants, trapping them to reduce their numbers may be the best approach (see below).

We also receive complaints about earwigs getting into the house. They do not cause any damage there, but people do not like to see them. For suggestions on what to do about earwigs in the house, refer to the sidebar above. Vacuuming is the least-toxic and simplest method for such invasions.

DIRECT PHYSICAL CONTROLS

Earwigs are easy to trap. In the home garden, containers such as tuna-fish cans that hold ½ in. (13 mm) of vegetable oil or moistened bread crumbs can serve as traps without any poison. Because of the earwigs' predilection for crawling into small spaces, bamboo tubes or rolled-up newspapers are also good traps. The traps, baited or not, should be placed on the soil near plants just before dark and checked with a flashlight 12 hours later or in the morning. Shaking the trapped insects into a pail of soapy water drowns them.

DIRECT BIOLOGICAL CONTROLS

The European earwig, like many insect pests not native to the United States, left its natural enemies

WHAT TO DO IF EARWIGS, OR OTHER CRAWLING PESTS, ARE GETTING INTO YOUR HOUSE

- Caulk cracks and crevices.
- Screen and weatherstrip windows and doors to eliminate access routes.
- Remove piles of debris or organic materials that lean against the house.
- Prune foliage that touches the walls of the house.
- Create a clean, dry border directly adjacent to the house foundation.
- Vacuum up stray earwigs found indoors and plug entrance cracks.

in its country of origin. Beginning in 1924, efforts were made to import a parasitic tachinid fly, *Bigonicheta spinipennis,* into the United States from Europe in the hope that it would control the earwig. Because the parasitoid depends upon the earwig alone for its sustenance, there was no danger it would attack other prey and become a nuisance itself.

This effort is considered to have been moderately successful in the northwestern United States and very successful in British Columbia. Today, one usually does not need to do anything to obtain the effects of this biological control except know that it exists. The parasitoid has now spread widely, but there still may be places without it. In such cases, contact your local cooperative extension service for assistance. Note also that specialists working on earwig control draw attention to the beneficial predatory habits of the earwig, and emphasize that control should be carried out only when confirmed earwig damage is beyond tolerable levels.

GOPHERS

(Order Rodentia, family Geomyidae)

Gophers feed on a wide variety of roots, bulbs, tubers, grasses, and seeds, which makes these burrowing rodents a threat to cultivated gardens and lawns. The pocket gopher *(Thomomys* spp.) is the type most often found around the home. Gophers live alone in the extensive underground burrow systems they create by tunneling through the soil and disposing of the excavated dirt above ground in crescent-shaped (or fan-shaped) mounds. The shape of these mounds can be used to distinguish gophers from moles, whose hills tend to be circular (volcano-shaped) with a plug in the middle (see the drawing on the facing page). Moles are considered beneficial in some instances because they eat subterranean insects. However, they also eat earthworms and their tunneling can sever the plant roots from the aboveground shoot, resulting in death of the plant.

A pocket gopher, *Thomomys bottae*, peeks from his hole. (Photo by South12th/Dreamstime.com)

ing their lips behind the exposed teeth. The name "pocket" refers to the external reversible fur-lined cheek pouches they use for carrying food and nest materials. Gopher fur is a mottled brown. This also distinguishes them from moles, which have very dark velvety fur, spade-like front paws, and no visible ears. Gophers use their keen sense of smell to locate foods such as bulbs, tubers, roots, grasses, seeds, and occasionally tree bark.

Gophers do not hibernate, although they do spend most of their lives underground, coming to the surface only for brief periods to push soil out of their burrows, forage, disperse to new areas, and seek mates. Except when mating or rearing a brood, gophers live alone in their burrows. They are fiercely territorial and solitary, and will fight to the death with any other gophers they encounter in their burrow systems.

Gophers mate and produce young only from January to April, depending on the location. They generally have one litter per year, with an average of five offspring per litter. Their lifespan is up to 12 years.

BIOLOGY

Pocket gophers are thick-bodied rodents that range from 6 in. to 12 in. (15 cm to 30 cm) long. In the western hemisphere there are some 33 species in five genera. The differences between them are discussed in an excellent article on gopher control by Ronald Case in *Prevention and Control of Wildlife Damage,* 2nd ed. (University of Nebraska Press, 1994).

Gopher adaptations for life underground include powerful forelegs with long claws, small eyes, and small ears set far back on the head. Their exposed chisel-like teeth are used for digging, and grow continuously 9 in. to 14 in. (23 cm to 36 cm) a year. Gophers keep dirt out of their mouths by clos-

DETECTION

Gopher control is not very successful when carried out at the mound, because the mound is located at the end of the lateral tunnel the gopher regularly plugs. Instead, you must locate the main burrow that runs perpendicular to the lateral tunnel below the ground at a depth of 4 in. to 18 in. (10 cm to 45 cm).

You can find the main burrow by probing the soil with a long, thin screwdriver, sharp stick, or wire or with a probe sold commercially (see the drawing on p. 322). Locate a fresh mound and look for a small circle or slight depression on the "unfanned" side of the mound. This indicates the location of the plug in the lateral tunnel. Begin probing 8 in. to 10 in. (20 cm to 25 cm) from the plug side of the mound. Repeated probing may be required before you find the burrow. When the probe hits the burrow, it suddenly drops 2 in. to 3 in. (5 cm to 7.5 cm).

DIRECT PHYSICAL CONTROLS

Direct physical controls for gophers include the construction of barriers, flooding, and the use of traps.

1. Barriers. As with any pest problem, the safest and most effective management method is to "design the pest out" of the system. Sometimes gophers can be excluded from a garden by burying ½-in. (1.3-cm) mesh fencing 24 in. (60 cm) below ground and extending it the same distance above ground. This might be effective around raised vegetable beds or small flower gardens and lawns. Bulb beds or individual shrubs or small trees can be pro-

GOPHER MOUNDS AND MOLEHILLS

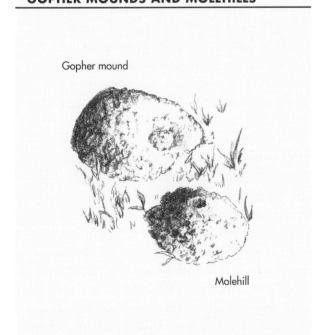

A gopher mound is fan-shaped with an offset plug and an indentation in its circumference; a molehill is circular with the plug at its center.

tected by ½-in. (1.3-cm) mesh wire if it is laid on the bottom and sides of the planting hole. Be sure to place the wire deep enough so it does not restrict root growth.

Barrier trenches that exclude gophers may be used to protect large lawns, gardens, and orchards. They are steep, vertical-walled ditches 18 in. (45 cm) wide and 24 in. (60 cm) deep that contain open-topped 5-gal. cans spaced at 25-ft. (7.6-m) intervals and sunk so their tops are level with the ditch bottom. When gophers burrow or move on the surface, they fall into the trench and follow it until they tumble into the cans, from which they cannot escape. The trenches can be dug with a shovel or spade.

Encircling the garden with plants such as oleanders that are unpalatable to gophers is another exclusion tactic that might be tried. Foraging gophers that encounter oleander roots would presumably be deterred from tunneling into the garden. There is quite a body of anecdotal literature on the use of plant barriers against gophers, but there are no scientific studies confirming their effectiveness.

2. Flooding. Once you have located the main burrow, you can insert a garden hose into it. The water will flow in both directions in the burrow, and the gopher will try to escape from one of the mounds. When you spot it, you can dispatch the gopher with a shovel. However, this requires fast action because gophers move quickly when above ground. A whole area such as a field can be flooded by raising dikes around it and filling it with water.

3. Trapping. You can trap gophers with a Macabee or other pincer trap, or a box trap such as the Gopher Getter. You need two or more traps, and you must set them with care. Wear gloves to prevent human smells from contaminating the devices. You can also wash the traps in soapy water. Trials in British Columbia re-forested sites demonstrated that trapping is far more effective than toxic baiting.

Open an active main burrow enough to allow insertion of two traps, one facing in each direction

A gopher's main burrow can be located by probing with a long screwdriver, wire, or commercial probe, shown here. Look for a slight depression in the "unfanned" side of the mound indicating the plug to the lateral tunnel, and begin probing 8 in. to 10 in. (20 cm to 25 cm) out from that point. The probe suddenly drops a few inches when it finds the burrow.

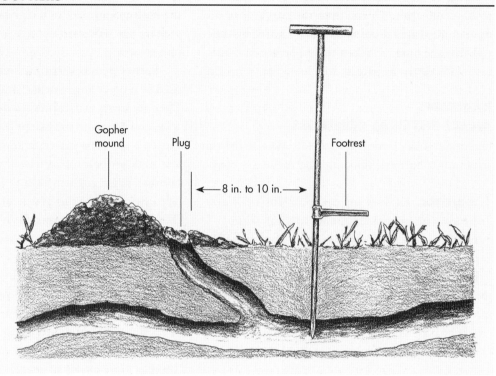

Gopher mound

Plug

Footrest

8 in. to 10 in.

(as shown in the drawing on the facing page). This ensures that no matter which direction the gopher moves in, it will run over a trigger. Attach strong twine or rope to the trap and to a stake to prevent the rodent from pulling the trap deep into its burrow. Use a board, cardboard, or other material to cover the trap, and be sure to sift dirt around the edges of this cover to exclude light. If the gophers see light, they will push soil toward it, tripping the trap without getting caught. If no gopher is caught within three days, pull out and reset the traps in a new location.

TREATMENT
DIRECT CHEMICAL CONTROLS

Unfortunately, the most commonly available rodenticide for gopher control is strychnine-baited barley. In California, a licensed pest control operator or advisor must apply this if more than 1 lb. (0.45 kg) is used. Strychnine-baited grain for gopher control is placed underground, but it can cause secondary kill. This means that if another predatory animal such as a gopher snake, owl, or hawk eats a gopher that has taken in strychnine-baited grain, then it too dies. Consequently, we do not recommend the use of strychnine-baited grains, especially around the home, because strychnine is so toxic.

Another group of potentially hazardous baits are anti-coagulants. They fall into two main categories, single-feed and multi-feed baits. The single-feed baits are the most toxic, as you might expect. The anti-coagulant chemicals used in these baits are similar to, and sometimes the same as, blood-thinning pharmaceuticals taken by humans. It is this similarity that makes them hazardous to humans, pets, and wildlife. The anti-coagulants are toxic, at various doses, to predators and scavengers that eat poisoned gophers, including dogs, cats, hawks, coyotes, falcons, and owls. We do not recommend the use of anti-coagulant baits for gophers.

One strategy we do recommend for gopher control is fumigation. Gopher burrows can be fumigated with the exhaust from a gas-powered riding mower, rototiller, or other vehicle. This is done by slipping a 10-ft. (3-m) length of flexible metal exhaust pipe, available at automotive shops, over the rigid exhaust pipe on the mower. Be sure the diameter of the flexible pipe is such that it fits snugly over the rigid pipe. Non-riding mowers may require the addition of a metal elbow to the rigid exhaust pipe to facilitate attachment of the flexible pipe.

Before attaching the pipe, squirt a few drops of oil into the end to be fitted to the mower pipe. Place the free end of the pipe at the mouth of the excavated runway and pack soil around it to create a seal. To avoid the possibility of the heated pipe scorching the lawn or ground cover, prop it on a shovel. Let the mower engine idle for 15 to 20 minutes. The carbon monoxide exhaust acts as a fumigant, killing the gopher quickly in the tunnel. Smoke created by the oil squirted into the mower end of the flexible hose will escape from any exit holes available to the gopher. If you spot escaping smoke, quickly seal the exit or dispatch the emerging gopher with a shovel.

Two points of caution regarding this procedure: First, in some states it is illegal for licensed pest control professionals to use this method because carbon monoxide is not a registered pesticide; second, engine exhaust from vehicles made after 2000 contains fewer toxic materials than it once did, thanks to the Clean Air Act. This doesn't mean that the exhaust fumes aren't toxic; it just may take longer to kill the gopher than it used to.

TIP Because gophers occasionally feed on the bark of certain trees, particularly stone fruits such as almonds and cherries, it is wise to protect the trunks of these trees during planting with cylinders of ½-in. (1.3-cm) galvanized hardware cloth sunk 12 in. (30 cm) underground and rising 12 in. above the surface.

TRAPPING GOPHERS

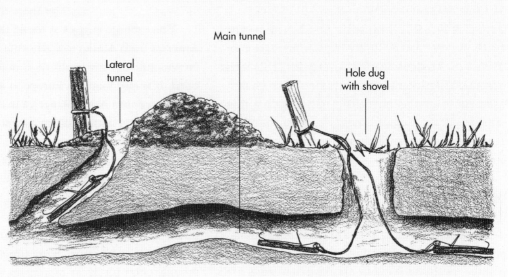

Place two traps in opposite directions in the main gopher tunnel and a single trap in the lateral tunnel. Stake traps so they can be retrieved easily and pack dirt loosely in the hole to exclude light. Check the traps daily.

Lateral tunnel

Main tunnel

Hole dug with shovel

ROOT MAGGOTS: THE CABBAGE ROOT MAGGOT

(Order Diptera, family Anthomyiidae)

Imagine that your seedlings of broccoli, turnips, or other members of the cabbage family are growing nicely. Then suddenly one day, although no insects or other pests are visible, many of the young plants begin to wilt and die. When you pull them up you find small, fat, white, worm-like maggots tunneling into the roots. Or perhaps the roots are so damaged the plant appears not to have any at all. You have just had your first close encounter with the cabbage root maggot *(Delia brassicae)*, the larval stage of a small fly.

Closely related species attack carrots, onions, and seed corn, which show similar damage. All the flies belong to the genus *Delia* (formerly *Hylemya*), on which there is extensive literature. We might also mention that another member of the genus, *Delia (=Hylemya) seneciella*, has been introduced into the Pacific Coast states from France to control the noxious weed tansy ragwort. This latest introduction is a supplement to the earlier establishment of another biological control against this same weed, the cinnabar moth *(Tyria jacobaeae)*. This is a classic case of human interests labeling one creature a pest and its close relative a beneficial.

BIOLOGY

Cabbage root maggots are usually less than 1/3 in. (8.5 mm) long when fully grown. The head end is pointed and the rear is blunt with a dozen short, pointed, fleshy projections arranged in a circle

Root maggots are flies in the genus *Delia*, the larvae of which tunnel into cabbage family plants such as broccoli and cauliflower. (Photo by Dave Bevan/GAP)

around two brown, button-like spiracles, or breathing holes. The larvae are usually found eating feeder roots and boring into the taproot. As many as 100 larvae can be collected from a single root. The maggot attacks cabbages, Brussels sprouts, cauliflower, radishes, rutabagas, and turnips.

The adult is an ash-colored fly slightly smaller than a housefly. It has black stripes on the thorax and black bristles over its body. This is not the only species that may be found in the root zone of a cruciferous (cabbage family) plant. There are up to 30 others, but the cabbage root maggot *(Delia brassicae)* is the most common. Two other common and related species are *Delia (=Hylemya) crucifera* and *D. (=Hylemya) planipalpis*.

The females lay their small white eggs within 2 in. (5 cm) of the stem of a cabbage-like plant. They hatch in a few days and the larvae tunnel into the roots. They feed for three to five weeks, then pupate in the roots or surrounding soil. Later they emerge as adults and mate, and the females begin oviposition. There can be as many as three generations during a single season. Some pupae can diapause (hibernate) for more than one season.

The cabbage maggot is found throughout North America from Alaska to California and Manitoba to Newfoundland, and south to Illinois and North Carolina. It is also found in Europe. It was accidentally introduced into North America from Europe; fortunately, certain natural enemies were introduced at the same time. The discussion of control of these root maggots is applicable to any of the species that attack vegetable crops in the home garden.

DAMAGE

Injury is seldom serious in the southern part of the cabbage maggot's range. Sometimes the maggots provide entry for decay organisms so that infested roots are rotten and riddled with burrows. Infested plants can appear yellowed, stunted, and wilted, especially during the hottest part of the day. Young plants are the most susceptible; healthy, larger plants that are well established can tolerate moderate infestations and usually outgrow the damage.

Winter and spring crops suffer the most. The greatest damage is experienced during wet years, especially in cool, moist areas. Because cauliflower and Brussels sprouts are less vigorous than the hybrid cultivars of broccoli that are now grown, they sustain more damage.

DETECTION AND MONITORING

To sample for eggs, mark a circle 5 in. (12.7 cm) in diameter around the plant's stem. Dig out the soil within the circle to a depth of 1 in. (2.5 cm), then drop the soil in a container of water. After mixing and allowing the soil to settle, small white eggs will float to the surface if the maggots are present.

Although one source document indicated that adults are attracted to purple sticky traps, no further information about this monitoring technique is available. Yellow sticky traps are currently recommended for trapping adults.

Because injury levels are very site-specific, it is difficult to say what number of individuals at a particular stage of development will cause damage. However, *Integrated Pest Management for Cole Crops and Lettuce* (University of California Division of Agriculture and Natural Resources, 1992), a manual published by the University of California, suggests that "when using the above-mentioned egg-sampling procedure, if [there are] more than 25 eggs per cauliflower plant or more than 50 eggs per cabbage plant, economic damage may occur." This level of damage in the garden is unlikely to occur in a normal year. If, however, the problem is substantial, consider the use of nematodes for control.

TREATMENT
INDIRECT STRATEGIES

One way to minimize losses of young seedlings is to start them on sunny windowsills indoors or

HOW TO CONSTRUCT A CONE SCREEN BARRIER
MATERIALS

To make a cone screen 18 in. (45 cm) tall and 12 in. (30 cm) in diameter, you need a pair of good household scissors or tin snips, a sturdy stapler, some aluminum screen (which is stronger than nylon and won't rust), and some short, thin wood strips, such as pieces of commercially available lath.

PROCEDURE

Cut a length of screen into a rectangle approximately 18 in. (45 cm) by 24 in. (60 cm). Bend it into a cone shape, overlapping the edges, then close the two edges by stapling them together against the lath strip. Let the thin wood strip extend a few inches below the opening of the cone base so you can force it into the soil until the cone is flush with the ground, anchoring it firmly. The lower edges of the cone should be completely covered with mulch or soil. If you need multiple cone enclosures, make a paper model of the cone to facilitate duplication.

Once the seedlings are too big for the cones, their roots are tough enough to withstand any root maggot invasion. Remove the cones and place them over the second planting. At the end of the season, clean the cones and store them. They will serve you season after season and can reduce your root maggot losses to zero; the investment you make will repay you for many years.

within tightly screened greenhouses or cold frames. It is essential that the seedlings be protected from egg-laying flies at all stages, particularly during the hardening-off period when they are between the house or greenhouse and the growing plot and are getting used to outdoor temperatures. When the seedlings are several inches tall, transplant them into protective screened cones, as described below.

TREATMENT
DIRECT PHYSICAL CONTROLS

The most effective reusable device for controlling root maggots in the home garden is a cone-shaped protective screen barrier that is placed over seedlings immediately upon transplanting. It is described in the sidebar above.

Tightly constructed cold frames or similar structures would also presumably be effective in preventing egg laying by root maggot flies, but we have no experience using them. A less permanent but simple barrier can be created by protecting plants with plastic row covers. However, where slugs are also a problem, unacceptable damage is likely to occur under the covers, making this approach impractical.

Although it seems reasonable to use traps to capture the flies before they have an opportunity to deposit their eggs near the plants, there are no studies documenting the efficacy of this approach. A few years ago, some of our students tried unsuccessfully to attract adults into standard fly traps baited with various crucifers (cabbage family plants). We suspect that root maggot populations may have been too low at that time to provide enough adults to validate these initial tests, and we have not had the opportunity to pursue the matter further.

DIRECT BIOLOGICAL CONTROLS

One of the most important natural enemies of the cabbage root maggot and other related *Delia* species is the rove beetle *Aleochara bilineata* (family Staphylinidae). This small beetle is parasitic on the pupae of the cabbage maggot and predatory on its eggs. It was one of the species introduced into Canada probably at the time the cabbage maggot invaded; it now occurs widely throughout North America.

The staphylinid rove beetle attacks many *Delia* species, so it is important in helping to protect a number of crops. There has been some work directed at developing a method of mass-rearing it. Unfortunately, field tests have found that the rove beetle is not as reliable and prodigious a predator/parasitoid in the field as it is in the laboratory. These trials also discovered that timing is crucial in the success of rove beetle releases. A little too early or a little too late in the life cycle of the root maggot, and the beetles leave the area.

Two of the *Steinernema* spp. beneficial parasitoid nematodes that can be used against the cabbage maggot are commercially available. The nematodes are poured in solution around the base of the seedling stems so that they attack any maggots that hatch. The exact timing, dosage, and frequency of application must, of course, be adapted to local conditions. We recommend that you contact the distributor or producer and ask how many nematodes to buy and how often to use them.

Cabbage root maggots feed on the roots of broccoli and other members of the cabbage family, thereby limiting water uptake. Root damage can be severe enough that the plant may die. (Photo by Dave Bevan/GAP)

TREATMENT

DIRECT CHEMICAL CONTROLS

There are many other natural enemies of the cabbage root maggot. Some of these are ground beetles (family Carabidae). Unfortunately, when most insecticides are applied to the soil in an attempt to control the cabbage maggot, they also kill these natural enemies. There are as yet no insecticides that kill only the cabbage maggot and leave these natural enemies. Consequently, we do not recommend the use of any insecticides for suppression of cabbage maggot populations. It is up to us as gardeners to keep the use of broad-spectrum pesticides to an absolute minimum, to conserve the native predators in your areas. Zero use of broad-spectrum insecticides is the ideal.

ROSE DISEASES: BLACK SPOT, POWDERY MILDEW, AND RUST

(Diplocarpon rosae; Spaerotheca pannosa; and Phragmidium spp.)

A few years back while strolling through our local municipal rose garden and enjoying the riot of colors and shapes of the hundreds of cultivars on display, we became aware of a strong, unpleasant odor that masked the roses' perfume. A chat with the rosarian revealed that the odor was the residue of 200 gallons of pesticides sprayed on the acre of rose shrubs each week from spring to fall. Because we knew that if we could smell the pesticide we were absorbing it into our lungs, we decided to leave.

As a result of this experience we pondered the unhappy fact that roses—one of the most aesthetically rewarding and popular flowering shrub groups in the world—are also among the most heavily sprayed. Is this heavy use of pesticides an unavoid-

able tradeoff for the enjoyment of roses, or are there less toxic ways to manage rose pests?

To answer this question, we reviewed the scientific literature on rose pests and talked with researchers, commercial rose growers, rosarians, and rose gardeners in different regions of the United States. This investigation has produced a wealth of information on alternative methods for managing rose pests. Some methods have been used successfully for years, whereas others have proven effective in research programs but need further testing in the home garden. This book cannot be a manual for the cultivation of roses, but we hope that the information on aphids, snails, and slugs in this chapter, plus the following summary of recent research on three rose diseases, will help reduce some of the pesticide load that both gardeners and gardens currently endure.

Three fungi top virtually any list of rose diseases: black spot, powdery mildew, and rust. The sidebar on pp. 328–329 describes common symptoms and provides other clues useful in identifying these diseases on your roses. All three diseases may occur in the same garden, but their severity usually depends on the prevailing climate. In general, black spot is most severe in the eastern United States, which has warm, wet summers. Powdery mildew grows best where summers are cool and dry, and is particularly prevalent in the coastal regions of the West. Rust is a major problem in areas such as the Pacific Northwest, where cool summers and high moisture levels prevail.

BIOLOGY

Studies of the life cycles of these three pathogens have shown that local temperature and humidity levels are limiting factors in disease development. Each disease begins as a microscopic spore that is transported by wind, water, animals, or garden tools to a susceptible rose host. When enough heat, moisture, and possibly light are available, the spores germinate, inserting a small germ tube into the plant tissue and absorbing nutrients from the plant. In the process, the plant tissue is damaged or killed.

(Photo by Dave Bevan/GAP)

(Photo by Geoff Kidd/GAP)

BLACK SPOT (DIPLOCARPON ROSAE)

Optimum conditions for infection. 64°F to 75°F (18°C to 24°C), 95 percent RH. Spores must be wet continuously for seven hours before infection can occur. Symptoms become visible 3 to 10 days after infection. New spores can be reproduced every three weeks.

Symptoms. Circular black spots 1/16 in. to 1/2 in. (1.5 mm to 13 mm) in size with fringed margins on canes and both leaf surfaces. Spots may coalesce to produce large, irregular lesions. Young leaves 6 to 14 days old are most susceptible. In mild infections, spots may remain as small black flecks, causing little damage. In severe cases, entire leaves may yellow and drop from plant, and plants may be defoliated by mid-summer.

Overwintering/dispersal. Spores overwinter on fallen leaves and in infected canes. Spores are dispersed in drops of splashing rain or irrigation water, by people during cultivation, by wind, or by contact with sticky parts of insect bodies.

Distribution. Most common in Northeast, Southeast, and some Midwest states with warm, moist summer climates.

Monitoring. Begin in spring when temperatures approach the mid-60s and rainfall and humidity are high. Look for signs of dark-colored spots on the surfaces of leaves near the ground and on young leaves, stalks, and flower buds at the top of the plant. If damage is seen, prune it off and/or begin treatments described in the text. Continue periodic monitoring during flushes of new growth.

RUST (PHRAGMIDIUM SPP.)

Optimum conditions for infection. Temperatures between 64°F and 70°F (18°C and 21°C) and continuous moisture for a period of two to four hours. Spores reproduce every 10 to 14 days in summer.

Symptoms. Small orange or yellow pustules appear on any green portions of the plant. Infections usually occur first on the undersides of leaves and may be inconspicuous. Later, pustules develop on upper leaf surfaces and stems and are quite visible throughout the summer. Some cultivars drop infected leaves.

Overwintering/dispersal. Black overwintering spores are visible on leaves and canes in fall, and pass the winter inside the infected canes, which are distinguished by dark, corky blotches at points of infection. Spores are distributed by wind and water.

Distribution. Severe infestations are usually limited to the Pacific Coast; cold winters and very hot summers limit its development elsewhere.

Monitoring. Begin to check for pustules on undersides of new foliage in early spring. Prune off damage. When temperatures optimal for rust coincide with heavy dew, rain, periods of cloud cover, or periods of fog near the coast, preventive surfactant or other sprays may be needed.

POWDERY MILDEW (SPAEROTHECA PANNOSA)

Optimum conditions for infection. Night—61°F (16°C) and 95 percent to 99 percent RH; day—81°F (27°C) and 40 percent to 70 percent RH. Drop-like humidity from fog or dew is more damaging, because germination and growth are inhibited by films of water on leaves. Powdery growth is visible two days after infection; thousands of new spores are produced every four days. Growth appears to be enhanced by low light levels that accompany cloudy or foggy periods.

Symptoms. Starts on young leaves as raised blister-like areas that cause leaves to curl, exposing lower surface. Infected leaves become covered with a greyish-white powdery fungus growth; unopened flower buds may be white with mildew and may never open. Disease prefers young, succulent growth; mature tissue is usually not affected.

Overwintering/dispersal. Spores overwinter inside leaf buds on canes and are dispersed by wind.

Distribution. Pacific Coast and other coastal areas with moderate temperatures, high cloud cover or fog, and minimal rainfall in summer.

Monitoring. Begin in spring when temperatures are in the mid-60s without any rainfall. Check growing tips and young leaves for signs of powdery growth. Prune off infected parts. Begin water washes and other treatments and continue monitoring.

(Photo by Thomas Alamy/GAP)

Some infection can occur at lower temperatures and humidity, but most occurs when conditions approach the figures cited here. Remember that if the leaf is in the sun, the temperature of the leaf surface will be higher than the ambient air temperature. If the leaf is shaded (e.g., when located in the interior of the bush), the temperature will be lower and the humidity may be higher than that indicated by garden wet and dry bulb maximum/minimum thermometers.

Compiled from J. L. Forsberg's *Diseases of Ornamental Plants*, (University of Illinois College of Agriculture, 1975) and R. K. Horst's *Compendium of Rose Diseases* (American Phytopathological Society, 1983).

Management of these diseases involves a mix of tactics designed to prevent spores from over-wintering, prevent germination of those spores that survive the winter, and kill germinated spores before they cause excessive plant damage.

TREATMENT
INDIRECT STRATEGIES

Indirect strategies for control of rose diseases include planting disease-resistant rose varieties, manipulation of moisture, and nitrogen control.

1. Planting Disease-Resistant Roses. You
should plant rose varieties with genetic features that make them resistant to or tolerant of (meaning they show only minor injury) the diseases prevalent in your area. For example, some species and cultivars have thick wax-like material in the outer layers of their leaves and stems. These coatings act as natural barriers against the penetration of plant tissue by pathogens. A high level of wax on leaves also repels water, limiting the germination of fungus spores with high water requirements. It is also thought that some rose species produce toxins that repel or kill germinating spores.

Species known to have high levels of disease resistance include *Rosa majalis, R. multiflora, R. rugosa,* and *R. wichuraiana.* These old-variety roses can still be found in many public and private rose gardens, and are noted for their hardiness, profusion of blossoms once or twice a season, array of colors, petal arrangements, and scents. Many communities have old-rose societies whose members open their gardens for public viewing. For help locating local societies and for lots of information on growing roses, visit the American Rose Society (www.ars.org).

The modern hybrid tea, floribunda, and grandiflora roses have been bred to enhance the frequency and size of bloom, diversity of color, prominence of scent, and other features rather than to increase pest tolerance. Fortunately, many modern hybrid roses have retained some of their ancestral resistance or tolerance of disease despite the indifference of breeders to these characteristics. Bright spots for future rose research include disease-resistant roses, which are easily found in a web search.

2. Manipulation of Moisture. Because black
spot and rust spores must be immersed in a film of water for a number of hours before they germinate, disease prevention involves keeping susceptible foliage as dry as possible. This can be achieved in a number of ways: by planting roses in full sun and spacing them at least 3 ft. to 4 ft. (0.9 m to 1.2 m) apart to encourage good air circulation; by pruning roses so that they have open centers, reducing the density of the interior foliage; by using bubbler heads or soaker hoses when irrigating to avoid wetting the foliage; or (if irrigating with sprinklers) by watering during periods of sunlight and ceasing irrigation in time for the foliage to dry before nightfall.

Powdery mildew, on the other hand, cannot survive if there is a film of water on leaves or stems. In one university study conducted in the 1930s, powdery mildew on the highly susceptible Dorothy Perkins rose was kept to very low levels simply by syringing the bushes with a heavy stream of water from a garden hose. The water was applied for a few minutes through an ordinary spray nozzle that raised the normal 40 psi household water pressure up to 70 psi. Care was taken to wash both the upper and lower surfaces of the leaves. The wash was timed for early afternoon, because that is when powdery mildew spores are most likely to be moving on air currents on their way to infecting new leaves.

This research demonstrated that if spores were wetted within six to eight hours after landing on a leaf, infection could be prevented or kept to a very low level. The washing was begun two weeks after spores were sprinkled on the leaves of test plants. The bushes were washed every three days for four weeks. At the end of the test period, 72 percent of the leaves on unwashed roses were infected with powdery mildew, compared to only 21 percent of the leaves on water-washed plants. When the mildewed leaves from washed and unwashed plants were compared, damage on washed leaves was much less severe than on unwashed leaves.

Water-washing appears to suppress mildew in several ways. First, the force of the water physically removes ungerminated spores resting on the leaf; it also removes spores that have already germinated and have inserted their tubes into the leaf tissue. Once the powdery growth is separated from the infective tube already stuck in the plant, the tube atrophies and causes no further damage. Spores that are not removed by the spray of water are prevented from germinating by the film of water left on the leaf. The bead of water may elevate the spore high enough to prevent the germ tube from reaching the leaf tissue for penetration.

For the home gardener, the research suggests that as soon as weather conditions are right for powdery mildew (see the sidebar on p. 329), you should begin a program of hosing the foliage with a heavy stream of water for a few minutes once or twice a week, preferably in the early afternoon. Concentrate on tender new growth, because powdery mildew does not appear to attack mature foliage. Keep water-washing until the flush of new growth matures. Watch for the onset of new flushes of growth that coincide with optimal weather conditions for powdery mildew, and resume periodic water washes during the growth spurt. After a season or two of experimentation, you will be able to time your water-washing with increasing accuracy.

Because wetting the leaves can enhance black spot and rust in regions where these diseases occur along with powdery mildew, syringe the foliage in strong sunlight to speed drying. Fortunately, the temperature levels and other variables necessary for the development of black spot and, to some degree, rust often do not prevail in areas where powdery mildew is severe. The studies described above do not cite any secondary disease problems generated by water washes.

We recommend that you try using compost tea to wash down roses. It appears that the fungi, bacteria, and other microbes in the compost tea are

FINDING RESISTANT ROSES

The degree of disease resistance of any cultivar can vary from site to site due to variations in environmental conditions or cultural practices. It can also vary over time, as disease pathogens sometimes develop new races able to overcome resistance factors. To identify roses with a long history of disease resistance in your area, talk to knowledgeable gardeners, members of rose societies, or municipal rosarians. If you see a variety you like that seems to be disease free, ask if it has been sprayed. If it hasn't and it remains healthy throughout the summer, it's probably resistant to local pathogens. If roses in your garden have constant disease problems, consider replacing them with varieties you have observed to be resistant.

antagonistic toward many pathogens. The worst that can happen is that the compost tea provides a light foliar feeding. Be sure to use only fully mature compost for making the tea. As is always the case when washing down plants, do it early in the day so that the leaves will be dry by nightfall.

3. Fertilizing. Moderate applications of compost, stabilized manure, or slow-release fertilizers in late fall and early spring are recommended. Our preference is composted cow manure; roses seem to love it and we know rosarians that swear by it. Strange that something with so sweet a fragrance would thrive on something that has, what can only be described as, an "odor."

DIRECT PHYSICAL CONTROLS

Pruning and mulching are effective physical controls for black spot, powdery mildew, and rust.

1. Pruning. All three pathogens overwinter inside leaf buds formed on canes. In addition, spores of black spot and, to a moderate degree, rust also overwinter on or within the tissue of canes or fallen leaves. Thus, removal and destruction of infected leaves and canes is effective in limiting overwintering disease spores as well as in minimizing the spread of infection from spores active in spring and summer. Roses are fairly tolerant of heavy pruning and usually bounce back in the spring with strong new canes.

Researchers at England's Imperial College Field Station have found that powdery mildew spores tend to overwinter in leaf buds located just below infected flowers. They recommend that roses be lightly pruned in fall, with particular attention paid to the removal of infected flowers as well as stems and portions of canes directly below the damaged blooms. This removes newly forming buds that may already have become infected, preventing the carryover of inocula that might infect roses the next spring.

Overwintering black spot and rust spores are particularly common on fallen leaves; thus, proper disposal of all leaves and flower petals that have accumulated on the ground also helps prevent the spread of these diseases. The debris should be burned or composted. The spores will survive in compost piles unless they are hot-composted.

Infected canes should be pruned off and removed from the garden as early in winter as the climate allows to ensure that infected buds are removed before an unexpected warm spell forces them open and activates the dormant spores. It is relatively easy to identify black spot infections by the dark blotches on the wood. Rust damage appears as dark, corky lesions on the canes, but powdery mildew is invisible inside protective leaf buds.

Dr. Bob Raabe, professor emeritus in plant pathology at the University of California, Berkeley, notes that the level of rose disease in mild climates along the Pacific Coast is often increased by the fact that roses rarely go fully dormant. The pruning and garden cleanup that normally would reduce the carryover of disease spores from season to season does not occur. He recommends that in mild climates roses be "pruned into dormancy." Such pruning occurs in mid-January, and consists of removing all leaves and pruning off infected canes. This allows mild-climate gardeners to have the best of two worlds: a bloom for the winter holidays and reduced disease problems the following summer.

Some spores will evade removal despite all your efforts; others will blow in from adjacent gardens or may be imported on new rose bushes. Once the growing season has begun, watch for signs of infection when roses begin leafing out. Prune out damaged foliage, canes, and flowers as they appear. Early removal of disease may reduce or prevent further outbreaks. Continue light pruning whenever you see signs of disease. As long as you do not remove enough foliage to hamper photosynthesis you can continue light, preventive pruning throughout the season.

TIP Excessive application of highly soluble nitrate fertilizer should be avoided because it generates frequent flushes of lush, weak growth that is very susceptible to attack by powdery mildew and, to a lesser degree, black spot and rust.

As with any pruning for disease, be sure to disinfect your clippers and shears between cuts. We find that either isopropyl (rubbing) alcohol or a 1-percent solution of chlorine bleach is effective. We prefer alcohol because the drops or spills don't ruin clothing or shoes. Disinfectant sprays, such as Lysol®, can also be used and are easier to apply to larger tools like loppers or saws.

2. Mulching. Applying mulch under your rose bushes is another way to limit infection from disease spores that overwinter on fallen plant debris. After raking up the dead rose leaves in fall, apply a few inches of compost or other mulch material under the bushes. Apply another layer of mulch after mid-winter pruning. The mulch will form a barrier between the rose foliage and the black spot and rust spores overwintering on organic soil debris.

DIRECT BIOLOGICAL CONTROLS

The potential for using natural enemies to control powdery mildew is under study in Israel and at the University of Oregon. These projects have been initiated in response to the growing resistance of pathogens to chemical controls as well as the tendency of fungicides to cause secondary outbreaks of pests such as mites. In Israel, the fungus species *Ampelomyces quisqualis* has been effective in destroying powdery mildew. In Oregon, eight species of fungi have shown considerable promise as biological disease control agents. In the case of *Ampelomyces quisqualis,* an effective product called AQ10® Biofungicide was developed and marketed for a few years. It has now been pulled off the market.

A biofungicide called Serenade has *Bacillus subtilis* as its active ingredient and is effective against powdery mildew. It is available in concentrate and RTU formulations. Because this is a biological material, be sure to check the expiration date on the package and don't purchase more of this biofungicide than you need. Improper storage can render the fungicide ineffective.

Encourage your local land grant university to fund research on biological controls for rose pests and to assist commercial rose nurseries in using natural enemies in their pest management programs. If a market among commercial rose growers can continue to be developed for these organisms, home gardeners, too, may be able to purchase more of these natural enemies for release on their roses.

DIRECT CHEMICAL CONTROLS

The conscientious use of the nonchemical tactics described above will probably result in a significant

TIP If your garden had high levels of disease the previous summer, prune roses that showed severe damage to within 4 in. to 6 in. (10 cm to 15 cm) of the graft union. This increases the likelihood of destroying overwintering inocula. As with infected leaves, infected canes should not be composted unless you have a hot compost system.

reduction of disease in your roses. However, some cultivars may be so susceptible and some environments so optimal for disease development that these measures must be augmented by spot treatments with chemical controls. When such chemical controls seem necessary, it is wise to confine them to individual shrubs. Most roses can tolerate some level of disease without major damage. Experiment with spraying just those plants that you know from previous experience suffer intolerable damage.

Most of the available fungicides are more effective at preventing infections. In fact, most fungicides are actually fungistats; they stop the pathogen from growing rather than actually "curing" the disease. Thus, to protect roses and keep use of fungicides to a minimum, it is important to time treatments to coincide with periods of optimum temperature, humidity, and rainfall, as well as with the growth stage of the rose. The sidebar on pp. 328–329 provides most of this information.

Remember that roses are most susceptible to infection when they are in a state of rapid growth. By becoming aware of the growth cycles of your plants—rapid growth in spring and early summer, moderate growth in mid-summer, and a possible surge of growth in late summer—and by correlating

WHEN ALL ELSE FAILS, REPLACE THE PLANT

If you have a plant or plants that are constantly infested by disease or insect pests regardless of what you do, it is time to remove and replace the plant. You are spending time and money trying to control a problem that will probably not go away. When replacing disease- and insect-prone plants, choose varieties that are relatively pest free in your area. Design pests out of your garden and landscape.

these cycles with weather patterns that encourage disease development, you will learn how often it is necessary to apply fungicides.

1. Surfactants. Surface-active agents, or surfactants, are used daily in most homes in the form of dishwashing soaps and detergents. Gardeners know them as the wetting agents that are added to pesticide solutions to ensure even coverage of leaf surfaces and increase the ability of the pesticide to penetrate the waxy coatings on insect bodies. Chemically, surfactants are composed of fatty acid salts and have been known to have insecticidal properties for 200 years. Studies in the United States, Canada, and Great Britain indicate that surfactants show great promise as fungicides against powdery mildew and other plant diseases.

In the case of powdery mildew, researchers speculate that the surfactants work by disrupting the water balance inside ungerminated spores, by blocking certain fungal metabolic functions, and by increasing the "wettability" of the leaf surface so that spores are either killed or fail to germinate due to the presence of too much water. The effects on other fungi are probably similar.

A commercial rose fungicide based on fatty acid technology is available in the United States and Canada. In the United States, the product is called Safer 3-in-1 Garden Spray; in Canada, it is known as Safer Natural Garden Fungicide. The 3-in-1 Garden Spray prevents and eradicates powdery mildew or rust. For black spot control, however, it works only to prevent the onset of the disease.

In areas where black spot is a problem, the soap must be applied to all new growth every 10 to 14 days to prevent infection. Once black spot symptoms have appeared, the fatty acid is unable to arrest its growth on the infected leaf. When used as directed, this product is not phytotoxic to roses, nor

"Roses are most susceptible to infection when they are in a state of rapid growth."

is it toxic to mammals. It also kills pest mites but does not harm beneficial mites.

If powdery mildew is the major problem, you should probably apply the surfactant every 7 to 14 days during cool, dry weather. Because powdery mildew tends to infest only immature plant tissue, you may need to spray only when roses are undergoing growth spurts. Black spot is generally most active in hot, rainy weather, and it is during these periods that you should make weekly or biweekly applications of surfactants. Rust appears to be most infective when temperatures are in the low 70s (about 20°C) and humidity is high. Treat the plants every 7 to 14 days when these conditions prevail.

2. Antitranspirants. These are waxes, silicones, and other plastic polymers used on food crops and ornamental plants to decrease the loss of water (transpiration) through microscopic openings (stomata) in the leaves. They are also commonly used on agricultural products to delay desiccation (drying out) during storage or transportation.

In the early 1960s, Israeli agricultural scientists noted that sugar beets coated with antitranspirants remained largely free of powdery mildew. Tests by plant pathologists in Israel and Texas have shown that antitranspirants are effective at preventing infection of certain agricultural and ornamental plants by a number of mildew, rust, fusarium, and other pathogens.

TIP A note of caution. If powdery mildew is the major disease in your garden, take care not to prune any single bush too heavily during the growing season, because the roses will respond with spurts of succulent growth that are particularly susceptible to mildew.

Antitranspirants work as disease control agents by forming a barrier between the infective disease spore and the plant tissue that the spore must penetrate. When the stomata and other microscopic openings in leaf tissue are covered with air-permeable plastic or wax coatings, germ tubes from fungal spores seem to be discouraged from entering the leaf tissue. There is also evidence that the antitranspirants repel the film of water on the leaf surface needed by black spot, rust, and other pathogens to germinate.

In one test, the antitranspirants Wilt Pruf® and StaFresh® 460 were as effective as the fungicide benomyl (Benlate®) at controlling powdery mildew on wheat. In another test, control of powdery mildew on hydrangea and crape myrtle was as effective or better with the antitranspirants Vapor Gard® and Wilt Pruf than with the systemic triazole fungicide Tilt®. StaFresh 460 is no longer available. Benomyl (Benlate) was withdrawn from the market in 2001 amidst lawsuits for product contamination resulting in plant damage and allegations that benomyl caused birth defects.

Although no experiments investigating the effectiveness of antitranspirants on roses have reached the scientific literature, experiments reported to us on greenhouse roses at Longwood Gardens in Pennsylvania proved they were effective at preventing unacceptable levels of powdery mildew. Further experimentation is needed to determine when and how often the materials need to be applied. Dr. Bob Raabe notes that coatings applied to young foliage thin out or crack as the foliage expands and lose their effectiveness as a barrier. Repeated applications may be required. Other researchers note that these materials may not be suited to humid climates with frequent cloud cover because photosynthesis may be unduly inhibited. Further research is also needed to determine the ultimate fate of the antitranspirants in the garden ecosystem. The fact that some are biodegradable is hopeful.

A RECIPE FOR HOUSEHOLD SURFACTANTS

If you want to experiment with household surfactants, we caution you to use a solution no stronger than 1 percent, or 2 Tbs. (1 oz. or 30 cc) of surfactant per gallon of water, to minimize the chance of damaging the leaves. You can try any organic or all-natural liquid household soap or detergent, such as Seventh Generation™. You can purchase a cation surfactant from a local nursery, online, or from a pesticide dealer. Apply the surfactant as soon as weather conditions for disease development are optimal or as soon as you spot the first symptoms.

3. Baking Soda (Sodium Bicarbonate and Potassium Bicarbonate).
The use of common baking soda, or bicarbonate of soda, to control powdery mildew is mentioned in old gardening books. It turns out that they were right: sodium bicarbonate does control powdery mildew. If you have clay soil, you know that sodium is bad for soil texture and structure. Enter potassium bicarbonate, which controls powdery mildew better than sodium bicarbonate, without the ill effects of sodium on the soil. Potassium bicarbonate is available to the gardener as Bi-Carb Old-Fashioned Fungicide and to the professional as Kaligreen® fungicide, both from Monterey (www.montereylawngarden.com).

> "Plant replacement is recommended over the use of broad-spectrum fungicides."

4. Conventional Fungicides.
In the 1950s, broad-spectrum rose fungicides were adopted with enthusiasm by rose growers. The fungicides seemed to protect roses from heavy damage most of the growing season and appeared less likely to burn plant leaves than some of the inorganic fungicides available, such as copper or sulfur. By the 1970s, however, it had become evident that fungi were developing a tolerance or resistance to many of these fungicides. It was also recognized that some fungicides were highly toxic to nontarget organisms, particularly predators of spider mites. As a result,

mite outbreaks on roses were increasing following fungicide use. The lack of data on health effects of long-term exposure to fungicides also caused concern.

In an effort to overcome the negative effects on nontarget organisms, new selective fungicides have been developed. They are an improvement over the broad-spectrum materials, but the very mechanisms that make them selective also increase the likelihood of target diseases developing resistance. They will work for a while, but probably not for long. If the plant continues to have disease problems, plant replacement is recommended over the use of broad-spectrum fungicides. When choosing a replacement plant, make sure that it is not susceptible to the same pathogen as the plant being removed.

SUMMARY: LEAST-TOXIC BLACK SPOT, POWDERY MILDEW, AND RUST CONTROL ON ROSES

- Plant rose varieties that are tolerant of or resistant to the diseases prevalent in your area.

- Plant roses in full sun and space them a minimum of 3 ft. to 4 ft. (about 1 m) apart to encourage air circulation.

- In fall, rake up and discard all fallen leaves and other plant debris that may contain overwintering spores.

- In winter, prune off and discard all diseased canes and any remaining foliage.

- Before buds swell in spring, apply 2 in. to 3 in. (5 cm to 7.6 cm) of organic mulch under the bushes to cover any overwintering disease spores on the ground.

- When foliage emerges in the spring, monitor for signs of disease and prune off infected parts. Continue light pruning of infected parts throughout the growing season.

- If powdery mildew appears, apply weekly water washes during periods of active growth.

- If disease levels seem to be increasing despite your conscientious use of the tactics described above, spray with a surfactant, antitranspirant, potassium bicarbonate, sulfur, or baking soda.

Another development is the use of systemic fungicides to control rose disease. On many crops, systemics are applied to the soil. They are then absorbed by the roots and dispersed throughout the vascular system of the plant. Theoretically, this provides perfect coverage of the plant, avoiding the problem of rain or irrigation washing the chemical off and minimizing human exposure (although not that of beneficial microbes and insects), because the chemical is poured on the soil rather than sprayed in the air.

However, available systemics do not translocate readily in the woody tissues of roses. The major products used on roses are locally systemic on leaves, and are applied as sprays. Because roses put on rapid growth, the systemics become diluted by the expanding cell tissue and must be reapplied every 7 to 10 days to protect against disease. Information on the long-term health effects of these systemics on humans and beneficial organisms is difficult to obtain. Recent research suggests that some of the newer systemic fungicides may damage organisms that feed on the diseased plant tissue; avoid these chemicals if possible.

5. Sulfur-Based Fungicides. If you feel you must use a conventional fungicide, sulfur is probably safest to the applicator and beneficial organisms. When used in conjunction with the other tactics described in this section, sulfur should be quite effective in controlling the three rose pathogens. It has been used to suppress powdery mildew since at least 1820, and was probably used for hundreds of years before that. It also has a long history as a standard control for both black spot and rust. It comes in liquid or dust formulations and is easy to apply using conventional garden spray equipment. Both formulations are sold in garden stores, and directions for use, including the addition of surfactants, are on the label.

When applying the sulfur, be certain to cover the tops and undersides of leaves, paying special attention to the growing tips. It is best to begin applications early in the season, because sulfur is more effective at preventing disease than at curing it. Follow the directions on the label for dosage and timing. A word of caution: If the temperature exceeds 85°F (29°C), do not apply sulfur because it may burn the leaves. Fortunately, in areas where temperatures frequently reach that level, powdery mildew and rust are generally not significant problems as it is too hot for them. Although black spot can tolerate a fair amount of moist heat, disease growth is apt to come to a standstill when the temperature hits the high 80s (around 30°C). Thus, the temperature constraints on the use of sulfur may not unduly hinder disease control.

Some rose manuals recommend applying lime-sulfur sprays when roses are dormant. Presumably this kills overwintering spores lodged in unopened buds or on canes. Unfortunately, we could find no documentation of the efficacy of this treatment.

A garden snail, *Helix aspersa*, ready to snack on a yellow marigold. (Photo by StevenRussellSmithPhotos/Dreamstime.com)

SNAILS AND SLUGS

(Order Stylommatophora, families Helicidae and Limacidae)

Snails and slugs are more closely related to shellfish, such as clams, than they are to insects. Where conditions are favorably moist, either or both animals may become serious garden and commercial crop pests. Slugs and snails can eat up to six times their weight in your plants per night. Some of the most troublesome mollusks (from "Mollusca," the phylum to which they belong) are those that have been introduced. One example is the brown garden snail (*Helix aspersa*), which was deliberately brought to California in the 1850s as a potential food source (escargot).

There are several hundred species of snails and at least 40 species of slugs in the United States. The native snails and slugs tend to be solitary in habit, whereas the introduced species are gregarious or colonial.

The use of poison baits is popular for controlling these pests, and it is possible to use baits in such a way that contamination of the environment is greatly reduced. However, the large number of snails and/or slugs in areas where they are a serious problem often leads to the use of large amounts of poison scattered widely and repeatedly. This may lead to the production of local populations of snails that ignore or are resistant to the baits, as well as the possibility of poisoning domestic pets and humans. Some predatory insects may also be damaged. These are some of the reasons we recommend that you do not use metaldehyde snail and slug baits.

Whether or not you feel you must include poison baits in your campaigns against these pests, it is important to learn something about their biology. Then you can use a variety of tactics based on their behavior to reduce their numbers.

BIOLOGY

Both snails and slugs have shells, but the shells of slugs are much reduced and are hidden by the fleshy mantle on their backs. Snails and slugs rely on their large foot for locomotion and the secretion of a mucus, or slime, trail upon which they can glide. The snail's head has two pairs of retractable tentacles. The long pair has an eye on the end of each stalk, and the smaller pair is used to smell. The snail's mouth is below its tentacles and contains a horn-like rasping organ with which it scrapes away at food. The rest of the snail's body is curled up inside its shell. Variations in size, color, and pattern are common within as well as among species.

The brown garden snail may take from four months to two years to mature, depending on the abundance of moisture and food. Individual snails may lay up to 100 eggs, depending on the species, but usually the number is smaller. For example, the eggs of the brown garden snail, which are white and spherical, are laid in masses 1 in. (2.5 cm) in diameter and contain an average of 86 eggs each. Slugs lay fewer eggs, which may remain unhatched for long periods under dry conditions. They hatch when they receive moisture.

Young snails remain in the nest for several days, then stay close to the area in which they hatched for a number of months. This is important in management, because a large number of young snails in one area is a clue to where the snails are laying eggs.

Both slugs and snails require a damp environment and fairly humid air to survive; they avoid the sun and come out primarily at night or on cloudy days. They are not pests in dry climates. During the day, slugs pull themselves into the ground through crevices or available holes made by other animals such as earthworms, or they hide under boards and rocks or in other damp, shady places. The shady side of boards and rocks is favored by snails, too, along with damp leaves and other moist materials. They may return to the same place each night using the same route each time, unless their usual resting place dries out.

TREATMENT
INDIRECT STRATEGIES

Indirect strategies for slug and snail control focus on reduction of their favored habitat. Because both slugs and snails favor moist, shady areas for resting

DID YOU KNOW?

One fascinating aspect of the biology of snails and slugs is their hermaphroditism. Each animal has both male and female sex organs. Cross-fertilization is most common, though cases of self-fertilization have been reported.

and laying eggs, a wise first step in their control is reducing such sites in the immediate neighborhood of the flower or vegetable garden. Remove boards, bricks, and other piles of damp debris that are in contact with the ground. Either store them so that air can circulate around and under them, or place some moisture-reducing material under them (see the discussion of barriers under "Direct Physical Controls" on the facing page).

Snails and slugs also favor certain vegetation, so check around your yard to find the small young snails. Ivy and succulents are among their favorites, particularly when grown as dense ground cover. Once you determine that certain planted areas are harboring snails or slugs, you have several options. One is to thin the plants so sunshine can penetrate to ground level, wind can circulate, and the bed has an opportunity to dry out.

However, thinning out may cause new problems in the form of weeds—probably the reason the ground cover was planted in the first place. In this case, mulches 6 in. (15 cm) thick or more can be used to replace plants removed from the beds. Some mulches do not seem particularly attractive to snails. For example, although brown garden snails are severe horticultural pests here in the San Francisco Bay area, rough-cut cedar chips are used in some of our city parks without much problem. We have also read anecdotal reports of crushed eggshells and cocoa hulls discouraging snails. You will have to observe conditions in your neighborhood to see which ground covers and which mulches are unattractive to these pests.

Where thinning is not appropriate, you can shift to a ground cover less favored by snails and slugs or surround the area with a barrier that discourages them from migrating into parts of the garden containing seedlings or other plants particularly attractive to them.

DIRECT PHYSICAL CONTROLS

Direct physical controls for slugs and snails include hand-picking, trapping, and the construction of barriers.

1. Hand-Picking. Hand-picking remains an important control that is usually combined with some other tactic. Despite the ability of slugs and snails to produce large numbers of young and migrate long distances in damp weather, conscientious hand-picking concentrated in the area to be protected and the immediate surrounding areas provides immediate relief. If hand-picking is combined with barriers, the relief is reasonably long-lasting.

Hand-picking is most productive at night, when these animals are active. The best time is two hours after sunset. Use a flashlight and carry a container for captured specimens. If you are squeamish about picking up slugs, use thin plastic gloves or tweezers with broad ends, or just cut them in two with a pruning shear or scissors. If the captured mollusks are crawling out of the container before you have a chance to dispose of them, try adding a mixture of water and soap to kill the slugs and snails. Dispose of dead mollusks in the compost pile, squash them and then use them to bait your traps (see below), or leave them in the garden where the remains will be eaten and returned to the soil.

2. Trapping. If hand-picking at night is inconvenient, try trapping. Overturned flowerpots make excellent traps for daytime collection. We use unglazed pots and are careful to place them on the shady sides of the plants. Snails will not retreat into pots that are heated and dried by the early sun; pots must make a cool, dark resting place. Make sure the ground beneath the pots is uneven so snails and slugs can crawl under the rim.

You can destroy the trapped snails by shaking them from the flower pot onto a board and stepping on them, you can scrape out the inside of the pot with a stick and dispose of the snails later, or you can crush them against the sides of the pot with a stick and replace the pot without removing the bodies. Crushed snails and slugs make the pots particularly attractive to other snails and increase your catch.

Inverted grapefruit halves (after you have enjoyed the contents) can be used in a similar way. The animals like the citrus, moisture, and shady refuge. Beer, as most people have heard, is an attractant for snails and slugs. Apparently, the yeast is what the animals like, and many people have had success with a simple mixture of water and commercial yeast. The problem with these baits is that they must be monitored and renewed on a regular basis.

Garden writer Gene Logsdon, author of numerous publications on farming, describes an ingenious beer-baited pit trap made from a ½-gal.-size container, such as a plastic milk bottle. The entrance is

SNAILS AND SLUGS

Slug

Snail

Slugs and snails rely on a large, fleshy "foot" for locomotion and secrete a mucus or slime trail on which they glide. (Actual length, up to 2 in./5 cm)

a rectangular opening cut a third of the way up the side of the container. The trap is sunk into the ground to the level of the opening. The plastic cap, or other cover, is left on the container and cuts down on evaporation of beer and prevents larger animals from getting into the bait. (Those of us with beer-loving pets know this is not an unusual occurrence.)

Two other simple traps used by researchers, one for slugs and one for snails, can be adapted for home use. For monitoring slugs in grassy areas, use a white board or asphalt shingle covered on top with aluminum foil (as shown at A in the drawing at right). The foil or white surface reflects light, which keeps the board cool. Moisture, which accumulates under the trap, attracts snails and slugs. The rough surface of the shingle is covered with the foil, and the foil edges are folded and glued to the smooth side. The shingle is then placed on the ground with the foil side up and a nail driven through the center into the ground to keep the shingle in position. Monitoring and collection must be done in the early morning because the high temperature and the evaporation of moisture force snails away later in the day.

Dr. Theodore Fisher of the University of California, Riverside, uses 12 in. sq. (30 cm) boards on 1-in. (2.5-cm) risers as monitoring traps in his citrus orchard experiments (see B in the drawing at right). He has found that when trap counts are above 300 snails per board there is usually heavy damage to leaves and fruit; when there are fewer than 20, virtually no damage is evident. In a separate study of the effect of trap color in attracting snails, green was best, followed by red.

We also made a trap using 1-ft. sections of plastic rain gutter we bought at a building supply store. Once we cut the 1-ft. sections, we drilled a ¼-in. hole in each end so we could insert 12-in. nails

(these were sold as tent pegs) to hold the gutter section in place. We inverted the gutter so it looked like a little Quonset hut, used the nails to secure it to the ground, and covered the top with mulch to keep it cool. The first night we used a few drops of liquid snail bait to entice the slugs and snails into the mollusk motel. After 24 hours, we checked the trap and had about a dozen snails in it, and only three had actually eaten the snail bait. From then on we used no baiting materials at all, and it didn't

DID YOU KNOW?

If the air or the surface the snail is traveling on becomes too dry, a snail can pull its entire body into its shell and seal the opening with a sheet of mucus, which then hardens, forming a secure closure. It can remain dormant in this condition for as long as four years (the brown garden snail normally is not active below 50°F/10°C).

HOMEMADE SLUG AND SNAIL TRAPS

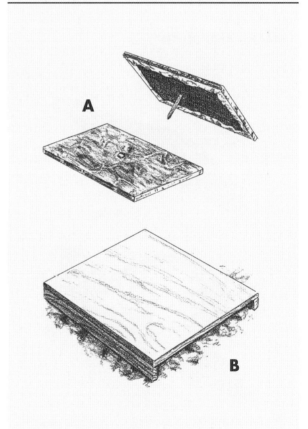

The simplest trap is a board or asphalt shingle (smooth side down) covered with aluminum foil and staked to the ground with a 3-in. (7.6-cm) galvanized nail in the center (A). Alternatively, a 12-in.-sq. (30-cm by 30-cm) board can be elevated on 1-in. (2.5-cm) rails (B).

Strips of copper can be fastened around tree trunks, flower pots, or seedlings. When slugs or snails make contact with the barrier, there is a toxic reaction—similar to an electric shock—and they are turned away. (Photo by Matt Anker/GAP)

researchers at the University of California showed that hardwood and softwood ashes and diatomaceous earth were all effective if kept dry. This is a big "if," because snails and slug migrations are usually a problem when the ground is wet from rain, dew, or irrigation. A commercial product, Snailproof® (no longer available), that consists of ground incense cedar by-products, did less well than other materials. However, this may be because in the tests the product was spread more thinly than it is by those who claim success. In these same tests, sand, which is sometimes suggested as a barrier, was found to be completely ineffective.

In our own vegetable gardens, we lay a 3-in. to 6-in. (7.6-cm to 15-cm) layer of fine sawdust on the paths surrounding each growing bed as a deterrent. Then, during our winter rainy season, we cover these paths with boards to walk on. This system has many advantages and we highly recommend it. The boards keep the sawdust dry and off your shoes; they also keep your feet dry when the ground is wet. The sawdust is an excellent herbicide. It shades the soil, and its slow decomposition takes nitrogen from the soil, depriving weed seedlings of nutrients. The thick mulch prevents compaction of walkways, making reuse of those areas for planting easier once the sawdust has totally decomposed. Slugs and snails do not like to cross the sawdust when it is dry, and they will not lay eggs beneath the boards. Best of all, we get the sawdust free from local cabinet shops and lumberyards. School woodworking shops are another good source. Do not use sawdust made from pesticide-treated (pressure-treated) woods. Pressure-treated

affect our trap counts. We like these traps because they are narrow, about 4 in. or 5 in. (10 cm or 12.7 cm) wide, so they fit anywhere. They are sturdy, and because the nails are driven 8 in. into the soil, animal and bird activity doesn't disturb them. The mulch hides them from kids and pets. In every area we used the traps, they were more effective than metaldehyde snail baits, without the hazard. Snails and slugs that hung onto the interior of the "Quonset hut" were scraped into a bucket of soapy water. Those on the ground were picked up by hand and tossed into the bucket.

3. Barriers. A number of snail and slug barriers have been popular for some time. Testing by wood contains chromated copper arsenate (CCA), and sawdust from this type of wood must be treated as a hazardous material.

The best barriers against these mollusks are strips of copper-backed paper stapled to boards around a bed. This material is sold commercially for this purpose and is used extensively in California to ring citrus trees. You can make your own strips out of the thin sheets of pliable copper sheeting or foil sold at hardware stores and online. Copper screening works well, too, but does not last as long. The eventual oxidizing of the copper, which turns green, does not affect its effectiveness as a barrier. The copper strips can be mounted on wooden frames or attached to existing benches with nails, glue, or other materials. Make sure no foliage bridges the copper or the mollusks will cross over and colonize the protected area. This takes vigilance, because plants grow and lean more as the season progresses.

No barrier is effective against the snails and slugs already hiding in the area you want to protect. Snails are easier to clean out of an area than slugs, because slugs usually hide in soil crevices. Slugs can move down earthworm tunnels and openings left by root decay, and are sometimes found more than 1 ft. (30 cm) below the surface in soils high in clay. The only way to deal with this problem is to go out at night during the first weeks the barriers are in place and remove the slugs by hand.

TIP Certain plants in the garden (for example, clumps of iris leaves) are excellent snail and slug traps in themselves because of their great attractiveness to snails. By observing which these are, you can focus your hand-picking effort on them in the daytime.

TREATMENT
DIRECT BIOLOGICAL CONTROLS

Biological controls for slugs and snails include ducks and other animals, rove beetles, protozoans, snails themselves, and humans.

1. Ducks and Other Animals. Many animals like to eat snails and slugs. A neighbor's dog crunches up the brown garden snail as if it were a chocolate-covered raisin; he likes to have them fed to him one by one. Many species of toads are very fond of slugs, as are other reptiles and amphibians. Ducks and chickens are often allowed to clear an area of snails, but they are so destructive to most plants that we do not recommend them for this purpose once the garden is planted.

However, first-hand experience with ducks has convinced us that in certain settings they can contribute to easy, safe snail control. Because ducks eat seedlings, newly planted areas should be protected with chicken wire. Also, if they are kept too long in one spot, the ducks mash down low vegetation. Rotation is the answer. The best system is to keep them in a pen except when being used for snail control. You can use low movable fences such as wooden picket fence sections for herding them around the property. They tend to stay near their water pans, so moving the pans encourages the ducks to move, too. Because they eat tender weed seedlings, they can be used to weed among perennials while they are hunting for snails and slugs.

Some people object to the ducks' loud quacking, even though they are not quite as loud as geese. We happen to like the noises made by domestic animals such as ducks, chickens, and geese, and live in a city that is remarkably tolerant of most sorts of farm animals in its midst. After borrowing a neighbor's three ducks as often as she would part with them one summer, we decided that they make comical, charming pets as well as handy snail catchers. If you can provide the right circumstances, we recommend them. Be forewarned, however, that not all urban communities are as open-minded as ours.

Ducks can be used to clear an area of snails but precautions must be taken to protect plants. (Photo by Zara Napier/GAP)

2. Rove Beetles. Two natural enemies of these pests have been considered for rearing as biological control agents: a rove beetle predator and a ciliate protozoan. The rove beetle *Ocypus olens* was accidentally introduced into California from Europe and has been gradually increasing its range. It has been observed feeding on slugs in England. The beetle is large and dark-colored, with strong jaws that enable it to cut through a snail's shell. An empty shell with a telltale jagged hole in the side is evidence of beetle attack. Although the beetles are long-lived, they reproduce very slowly, which unfortunately makes commercial rearing less economically attractive. In addition, the rove beetle's large size (about 1 in./2.5 cm) may frighten people into killing the beetle.

3. Protozoans. The literature on the protozoan *Tetrahymena rostrata* indicates that it has potential as a biological control agent for certain species of slugs and snails due to its ability to persist in the environment and its virulence for the grey garden slug. However, this possibility has not yet been fully evaluated.

4. Snails as Snail Predators. An important snail predator is another snail: the decollate snail (*Rumina decollata*), shown in the photos on p. 344. It is currently being used for control of the brown garden snail in southern California citrus groves. This predator evolved in North Africa and is found in countries around the Mediterranean. According to Ted Fisher, the University of California researcher who has studied this snail predator for

Rumina decollata, the predatory decollate snail, is feeding on the larger brown garden snail. Predatory snails will feed on eggs, small snails, and injured adults, as well as decomposing plant material. (Photos on left courtesy of Rincon-Vitova Insectarie. Photos on right by Sandara Star.)

many years, it was first reported in South Carolina in 1813, and has since been found in Alabama, Arizona, California, Florida, Georgia, Louisiana, Mississippi, New Mexico, North Carolina, Oklahoma, Texas, and Virginia.

As efficient as this predator is in eliminating the brown garden snail, it is not entirely beneficial, because it feeds on seedlings and on a few succulent ground covers such as *Dichondra*, baby's tears, and violets, as well as on flower petals. Once most plants are past the seedling stage, however, the snail shows no further interest. In some areas, it may become a threat to native snails that are not pests and should be conserved. Therefore, it is difficult to recommend this snail for gardens outside

the area in which it already occurs naturally.

5. Humans. For the brown garden snail, originally introduced here for food, and larger slugs such as the "banana" slug of the Northwest, humans are the ideal predator. Periodically the west coast media blossoms with recipes for the preparation of these delicacies, and there are reports of cooking contests to judge the results. Rumor has it that many an escargot entree in high-priced San Francisco–area restaurants is actually composed of local snails stuffed into shells of the "the genuine article" imported from France.

At least one enterprising snail farmer sells his product in the United States and overseas in pre-

DINING ON GARDEN SNAILS

If you are planning to experiment with your own brown garden snails (see p. 344), be advised that culinary experts recommend that they be allowed to feed on clean lettuce for a few days before consumption to rid them of grit. This should be followed by washing in vinegar to remove the slime. Unfortunately, the amount of meat per snail is not great in view of the effort expended, and one would have to be more inclined than are the authors to a diet heavy in melted butter to make snails and slugs a regular part of the fare. As a side note, if you have used metaldehyde bait for snails, wait at least 30 days after you have stopped using the bait before you begin collecting your snail harvest.

pared form and ready to pop into the oven. Having tasted it, we can report that it is delicious; the snail meat itself is indistinguishable from the butter, garlic, and other spices in the dish!

We knew a nursery owner who used to hand-pick snails from her plants and benches and toss them into a wading pool that had clean greens and shelter. Once a month she would "harvest" the snails from the pool, and she and several friends would get together for an escargot, wine, and cheese dinner. A great evening together with friends, with nontoxic snail control as the bonus.

TREATMENT
DIRECT CHEMICAL CONTROLS

If you feel it necessary to use baits to control slugs and snails, we urge you to use the iron phosphate baits, such as Sluggo® Snail & Slug Bait, rather than the more toxic metaldehyde snail and slug baits. If you use metaldehyde baits, you are also faced with the problem of keeping these poisonous baits away from dogs and other pets. Dogs find metaldehyde baits attractive and will eat them if they have the chance, and metaldehyde is very toxic to dogs. We think that iron phosphate is superior to metaldehyde baits both in performance and safety. Iron phosphate also breaks down into elements plants can use as fertilizer. In our opinion, metaldehyde snail bait is another material that should be prohibited for use by the general public and professionals.

SOWBUGS AND PILLBUGS

(Order Isopoda, families Porcellionidae and Armadillidiidae)
Sowbugs and pillbugs are the only crustaceans adapted to spending their entire lives out of water. In this way they are quite unlike their familiar relatives the crabs, shrimps, and lobsters. On the other hand, they are tied closely to damp environments and where it is hot and dry they do not become a problem.

In general, these animals are beneficial decomposers in the garden, breaking down complex plant material so its constituents are available to other plants as food. If you mulch your garden with organic matter, you are certain to see sowbugs in abundance because the decaying organic matter provides them with a source of food. Because they eat rotting material, these crustaceans can become a problem whenever garden vegetables remain damp and their outer cells begin decaying. This is particularly common where vegetables such as pumpkins and other winter squashes or fruits such as strawberries rest on damp ground. These isopods may severely damage succulent bean and other seedlings that are slow to unfold and grow in cool,

Sowbugs and pillbugs eat fruits and vegetables when they touch the ground and become moist. Tolerate what damage you can from these crustaceans, as they are the main decomposers of compost and, like earthworms, are critical for garden production. (Photo by Nicholas Piccillo/Dreamstime.com)

moist weather. Similarly, they quickly take advantage of damp seedlings that are kept covered with overturned flower pots too long after transplanting.

BIOLOGY

According to Dr. Arnold Mallis's *Handbook of Pest Control* (GIE Media, 2011), the common pillbug (*Armadillidium vulgare*) and the dooryard sowbug (*Porcellio laevis* and *P. scaber*) are worldwide in distribution. You can separate the pillbugs from the sowbugs by noting whether your specimen can curl into a ball that looks like a pill. The sowbug cannot manage this trick, but it does have two tail-like appendages the pillbug lacks.

The bodies of these crustaceans are oval when viewed from above. In cross section, they are convex above and flat or concave underneath. The head and thorax are small, but the abdomen is comparatively large and is composed of hard, overlapping plates. They have seven pairs of legs.

The female deposits her eggs in a membranous pouch called a marsupium or vivarium on the underside of her body. Here the embryos develop, the young emerging on their own about 44 days later for the pillbugs and in almost half that time for sowbugs. The females may have one or two generations per year, depending on the environmental conditions. Except in greenhouses, these crustaceans generally become inactive during the winter. Sowbugs may live as long as two years.

TREATMENT
INDIRECT STRATEGIES

Indirect strategies for control of sowbugs and pillbugs focus on modification of their favored habitat and horticultural controls.

1. Reduction of Favored Habitat. Try to create drier conditions where these animals cause problems. If sowbugs occasionally get into your house, this means there is damp, decaying vegetation adjacent to the building. Piles of wood, miscellaneous debris, decomposing leaves, and clippings should be moved away from the structure. Prune

vegetation back from the walls of the house so a space is created through which air can flow easily and dry out the area after a rain. Determine where the bugs are getting into the house and caulk or repair those cracks and crevices. Any space that gives sowbugs access to a house may also be a path for other undesired wildlife.

SOWBUGS AND PILLBUGS

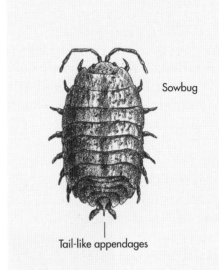

Sowbug

Tail-like appendages

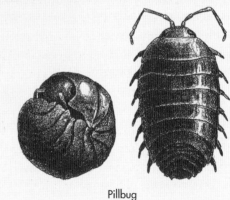

Pillbug

Sowbugs and pillbugs are small decomposers that closely resemble each other. However, sowbugs have two small tail-like appendages that pillbugs lack. The easiest way to tell them apart is by the fact that only pillbugs are able to roll up into a ball. (Actual size, ½ in. to ¾ in./13 mm to 19 mm)

2. Watering. Water early in the day so plants have an opportunity to dry before evening. Select mulch materials that are coarse enough to let water pass through, particularly when you are mulching plants that are susceptible to damage from these animals. If you are using compost mulch, do not sift it; instead, use it in its coarsest state. Or use mulch composed of large bark pieces or other materials that do not pack down to create a constantly damp mat at the soil surface.

Many squashes can be grown on fences or trellises, where the drying effect of the wind is enough to reduce pest damage. Old leaves that are beginning to fade can be removed by hand to improve air circulation. Maturing squashes that are resting on the ground can be elevated slightly by placing a small piece of wood beneath them. If the skin on the squash or melon remains dry, it is unlikely to be attacked.

Strawberries grown over a mulch present a different kind of problem. In areas where dew is heavy or rains are frequent, the sowbugs have a tendency to move from the mulch to any ripe berries that lie directly on the ground. One solution for small gardens is to make several dozen supports for the stems with tie wire (sold in most hardware stores). These should be stuck into the ground directly below each fruit-bearing frond just before the berries turn ripe; it should hold them above the mulch through the picking phase. As you harvest the strawberries, you can move these supports to newly ripening stems nearby.

Another approach is to grow the strawberries in step-like tiers of narrow raised beds constructed of wood. This lifts the plants off the ground into breezier, drier air. If these beds are not much more than one plant wide, the ripening berries will hang over the edges and dry off after each shower or irrigation. This helps reduce slug and snail damage and makes the berries easier to pick.

TREATMENT
DIRECT CHEMICAL CONTROLS

Sowbugs can be very damaging to bean and pea

PROTECTING SEEDLINGS

Seedlings such as beans that are particularly susceptible to sowbug and pillbug damage can be started indoors in peat pots or in open-bottomed cardboard containers. The seedlings can then be transplanted outdoors, container and all, which minimizes disturbance of sensitive roots. The level of the soil in the container should be slightly above the level of the garden soil after transplanting to ensure that the surface of the soil directly around the seedling does not collect moisture and promote disease. Pull mulch away from seedlings when you plant them, then return it after the plants have grown a few inches.

seedlings that are just emerging from the soil, particularly where heavy early morning condensation adds to the normal succulence of the seedlings. Thus a way must be found to protect them for the first day or two after they emerge.

A 2-in.-wide (5-cm) strip of pesticide-grade diatomaceous earth sprinkled directly over the row where the seeds have been placed will dry the area enough to discourage sowbugs if no rain or overhead irrigation wets the area in the meantime. One problem, however, is that too thin a layer of diatomaceous earth doesn't discourage the sowbugs, and a thick layer that becomes wet accidentally can harden to a plaster-like consistency that makes it very difficult for seedlings to poke through. Therefore, you must experiment with the thickness of the application, which will depend on the evenness of the soil surface and the likelihood it will get wet. Be certain that you use the pesticide grade of diatomaceous earth. Do not use the swimming-pool grade, which is processed in a way that makes it a respiratory hazard associated with silicosis.

Where the mortality (death rate) of unprotected seedlings is high and diatomaceous earth is impractical because it cannot be kept dry, a 2-in.-wide (5-cm) band of silica aerogel/pyrethrin spray (see p. 110 for more information) can be applied directly on the soil over the planted seeds. The white residue from the silica aerogel marks the treated area. Because this material breaks down rapidly, it must be renewed until the seedlings emerge. During the emergence and elongation period and until the true leaves have opened, you may need to spray the material at the base of the seedlings as well.

Usually two or three applications of the pesticide over 7 to 10 days confined to the narrow strip where the new bean or pea plants will emerge allows seedling survival even if sowbug populations are high in adjacent beds. Monitor for sowbugs in the daytime by disturbing the surrounding soil and mulch with your finger to see if they are curled up near the plant.

SYMPHYLANS

(Order Symphyla, family Scutigerellidae)

Symphylans are delicate, small white creatures that resemble centipedes. Because of this similarity they are sometimes called garden centipedes, although they are not related to centipedes. But you should get to know the difference, because centipedes are beneficial predators that prey on many pest insects, whereas symphylans feed primarily on microbes and plant materials in the soil as well as the roots of horticultural plants. Symphylans can become a problem in moist soils that are high in organic material; thus, increasing soil fertility by adding large amounts of manure and/or compost may increase their presence and make a minor problem worse. An effective control program for these organisms still remains to be developed. Our efforts are summarized below.

Scutigerella immaculata, is one of the better-known symphylan species and is a pest of many agricultural crops. However, just because you see

"Garden centipedes" (Order Symphyla, family Scutigerellidae) are not really centipedes but primitive insects. They can be most troublesome, especially in dry areas where the soil cracks give them access to roots. (Photo by Henrik Larsson/iStockphoto)

symphylans in your garden soil, don't assume they are the cause of root damage unless there is clear evidence. The section on detection should help you make that determination. If the symphylans are not harming the plants you are trying to cultivate, leave them alone.

BIOLOGY

Symphylans are small, ⅓ in. (8.5 mm) long at most. You need a magnifying glass to distinguish them from the other soil-inhabiting animals with which they may be confused. These include springtails, young millipedes, and centipedes. Symphylans are very active and very fragile.

The female symphylan lays about a dozen pearly white eggs in the soil and remains with them during the 10- to 23-day incubation period. The 6-legged young mature after about three months into 14-segmented adults with 12 pairs of legs, long antennae, and a pair of cerci (hair-like appendages) that arise from the last segment. They have a relatively long life, four years or more. Eggs and small larvae can be found in the soil year-round, but breeding is at its peak in the spring and early summer.

The vertical distribution of symphylans in the soil varies with the season. They are nearest the surface in bare soil in May and are deepest in July (in England, where most of the research has been done, although the findings apply to parts of America, as discussed on the facing page). Some individuals have been found as far as 5 ft. (1.5 m) below the surface. They do not tunnel; instead they follow earthworm tubes and natural soil crevices. In greenhouses, where they are commonly found near paths, walls, pipes, and pillars, they can reproduce and cause damage all year. Their optimal temperature range is 59°F to 68°F (15°C to 20°C), and they prefer 100-percent relative humidity in the soil air.

The damage that symphylans inflict on roots and root hairs may initiate root rots caused by bacteria and fungi. Symphylans may also eat yeasts, bacteria, fungi, and dead soil animals.

DAMAGE AND DETECTION

Symphylan damage varies, but it is usually associated with the fact that symphylans, by eating the roots, have reduced a plant's ability to absorb water. The precise symptoms may be slightly different in different plant species. The damage is described in "Symphylids," a bulletin of the British Ministry of Agriculture from 1981. Note that the bulletin uses "symphylid" when referring to symphylans:

> Several crops are susceptible to symphylid attack; young plants can be killed but the survivors usually outgrow the damage. The main type of damage is the removal of root hairs from young growing roots, leading to the disappearance of many small roots and consequent stunting of the plants. In the glasshouse [greenhouse], severely damaged plants wilt readily. Damage is sometimes mistaken for that caused by other problems such as excess salts, water-logging or acidity.
>
> On many crops damage shows as tiny black marks on the roots where a hemispherical piece of tissue has been scooped out. These small lesions may aid attack by fungi and other organisms, causing root rots. Where this occurs, the original cause is liable to be overlooked.

In addition to these general symptoms, there are some that are specific to the crop. The leaves of tomato take on a bluish tinge and the plants become very stunted. Lettuce plants do not develop a heart, and an injured plant often dies as a result of secondary root rots and botrytis. Chrysanthemum roots become thickened and gnarled, sometimes with a reddish tinge.

If garden plants appear to be suffering from root damage, there is only one way to determine whether symphylans are the source of the problem. The same British bulletin describes this technique:

> The extent of symphylid attack can be determined by lifting poorly growing plants and quickly lowering them, together with the soil surrounding the roots, into a bucket of water. The soil should then be gently

"Because symphylans are so fragile, any technique that vigorously disturbs the soil is likely to kill them."

> kneaded or stirred under the surface of the water, so that the symphylids come out of the soil and float up to the surface of the water where they can be counted.
>
> Soil that is suspected of being infested before being sown or planted up can be examined by the same method. When there is no crop present the symphylids will be below the soil surface, so a few spades full of soil should be taken to a depth of about 18 in. (46 cm) and each dropped into a bucket of water. The numbers of symphylids coming to the water surface after the soil has been broken up will give a useful indication of the degree of infestation.

Be sure that you examine the floating animals carefully to distinguish symphylans from springtails and other organisms. Symphylans tend to have a spotty distribution in the soil. Some areas of the

SYMPHYLANS: WHAT THEY EAT

Among the crops that symphylans attack are tomato, lettuce, sugar beets, chrysanthemum, asparagus, beans, brassicas, celery, cucumber, parsley, peas, pepper, potato, and strawberries. They are primarily a problem where soils are moist, friable, and high in organic materials.

garden bed or field may have high populations, whereas others have few or none. Thus, you must sample soil in several areas to know where to direct control efforts and whether they are working. Several references suggest that 10 or more symphylans found among the roots of a single plant are enough to cause concern and may signal the need for control.

TREATMENT
INDIRECT STRATEGIES

Although crop rotation is frequently suggested as an alternative to pesticides for controlling symphylans, the same literature is notably deficient in providing a list of specific rotations that have been shown to be successful. To the contrary, it was demonstrated that in some cases a crop of tomatoes following a crop of lettuce actually made matters worse.

TREATMENT
DIRECT PHYSICAL CONTROLS

Because symphylans are so fragile, any technique that vigorously disturbs the soil is likely to kill them. Much of the literature on symphylan control contains the recommendation that you pulverize the planting area with a power disc when it is dry just prior to planting. A rototiller, used when the soil is not too soggy to be worked, might have the same effect. Populations are likely to build up again, but not in time to harm the crops before they are harvested and the soil is turned and mixed vigorously again.

In the USDA Cooperative Extension Office literature, artificial flooding is the most frequently mentioned non-pesticide control. The references they cite suggest flooding for three weeks in winter or in summer just before planting. One expert suggested that flooding even for as short a period as 24 hours is helpful. This is a difficult technique to carry out unless temporary dikes can be created around the infested area.

In one letter we received, an organic gardener pleaded for information on how to "fry the little critters." Doing so might not be so easy. Steam sterilization of the soil in the fall is reportedly in-effective, but spring treatment after crop removal does have some effect. Heating the soil by covering it with sheets of clear plastic, a technique called soil solarization that is discussed on pp. 212–213, has been used successfully against certain soil-borne pathogens, nematodes, and weeds. Unfortunately, symphylans are more mobile than either weed seeds or microbes, and are likely to migrate away from areas made inhospitable to them.

TREATMENT
DIRECT BIOLOGICAL CONTROLS

The most promising alternative control we have found is a reference to the fact that the nematode *Steinernema carpocapsae* may be effective against *Scutigerella immaculata.* This nematode is sold commercially. There are two genera of beneficial nematodes available, *Heterorhabditis* spp. and *Steinernema* spp. It may be worth experimenting by applying a mixture of the species in these genera. Mixtures of these nematodes are available commercially.

Work in Oregon mentions the use of potato slices as a monitoring tool. The slices are placed in the soil where the plant damage is found and covered to prevent drying. After a few days they are checked for symphylans. Many can be killed by then shaking the slices over soapy water. Otherwise, nematodes and transplanting should be tried. For small-scale projects, insecticides with short-lived ingredients may be helpful, such as pyrethrins or a silica acrorogel/pyrethrin mix.

WHITEFLIES

(Order Hemiptera, family Aleyrodidae)
"Whiteflies are a more serious pest of plants indoors than in the garden, where they are more visible than damaging." When we wrote that sentence in the original *Common-Sense Pest Control* back in the late 1980s it was more or less true: You had to disrupt the predators/parasitoids in some way to have a whitefly problem outdoors.

Well, in 1988 the Ash whitefly (*Siphoninus phillyreae*) showed up in California and then was found in Florida in 2010. Also in 1988, the silver-leaf whitefly (*Bemisia argentifolii*), originally found in Florida, was described as a separate species from the sweetpotato whitefly (*B. tabaci*). The giant whitefly (*Aleurodicus dugesii*) was found in San Diego in 1992. The Ficus (fig) whitefly (*Singhiella simplex*) was found in Miami, Florida, in 2007, with a host range beyond the tremendous number of fig trees and vines growing there. These four whiteflies have caused their own little bits of havoc in the landscape, gardens, greenhouses, nurseries, and agriculture in general.

In the case of the Ash whitefly, we were in the forefront, called to landscape sites where the whiteflies were so thick we had to wear dust masks to keep from breathing them into our lungs. One gardener likened the whitefly population flying around the trees to a snowstorm, which is exactly what it was like. The Ash whitefly was easy to disturb; the lightest breeze or a person walking by would result in the air filling with whiteflies. Air filters on power equipment used in affected areas would clog with whitefly adults. Like all whiteflies, the Ash whitefly didn't respond well to pesticide applications. Spraying affected plants with soap, horticultural oil, pyrethrins, and even organophosphates (not on our recommendation) had no discernible effect on populations. Thanks to federal, state, and local government scientists within various departments of agriculture, two important beneficials were imported, tested, and released in California. These two insects, a parasitoid wasp (*Encarsia inaron*) and a lady beetle (*Clitostethus arcuatus*), have been spectacularly effective. We were fortunate to participate in the release of the

Encarsia inaron wasps in Marin County. Although we know they are still around, we haven't seen an Ash whitefly since 1992.

BIOLOGY

Whiteflies are sucking insects, more closely related to scales, aphids, and mealybugs than to most other insects. They undergo a complete metamorphosis, meaning they make a complete transformation in appearance between their young and adult forms, passing through a pupal stage. The host range of the four species of whitefly discussed above is huge. Many ornamental plants and agricultural crops are affected.

Shown here are greenhouse whiteflies, family Aleyrodidae, on the underside of a tomato leaf. Whiteflies have good natural enemies, but many species are exotic invaders in need of further research. (Photo by Dave Bevan/GAP)

Most whiteflies exhibit a reproductive characteristic known as arrhenotoky. This is a process by which males arise from unfertilized eggs and are haploid (having one set of chromosomes), whereas females are produced from fertilized eggs and are diploid (with the usual two sets of chromosomes). The life cycle of a whitefly starts out as an egg, either a male or female. A crawler (first instar) stage emerges from the egg and moves a short distance before settling down to feed. The next three instars, sometimes called whitefly scales, do not move but increase in size. The fourth instar, sometimes referred to as the "pupa," is the stage of whitefly development when it is easiest to identify the various species. At this pupal stage the whiteflies show the greatest differentiation between species. Use a 10× hand lens to look at the whitefly scales, and use photos or drawings to determine the species you have found.

DAMAGE

Honeydew, a sticky sugar-rich secretion, is a concern in interior plantscapes, along sidewalks, on

REPORTING A WHITEFLY PROBLEM

If you have tried everything listed here and can't control the whitefly, it is time to report the problem to the local county extension agent or county agricultural commissioner. You may have a new species or strain, and the authorities will want to know as soon as possible. Take a sample of the leaves (with adults if you can manage it), place the sample in a plastic bag, and put it in the freezer overnight to kill the adults. Then take it to the local county offices for them to identify. Give them as much information as you can regarding your control efforts and the plants affected. This will help them in identifying the species.

benches, under trees, and where cars are parked. The honeydew is annoying, can be damaging, and draws ants and flies. Leaves of affected plants often turn yellow to brown and fall off of the plant, weakening it in severe cases. This can reduce fruit and vegetable yields for gardeners and farmers alike. The primary concern with whitefly is the ability of some species to carry viruses from one plant to the next. This is especially problematic in agriculture.

DETECTION AND MONITORING

Whiteflies are strongly attracted to yellow sticky traps (see the photo on p. 312). This attraction is so strong that small infestations can sometimes be controlled by using sticky traps alone. Place the sticky trap at the same level as the whitefly infestation, tap the branch, and about half of the whiteflies that get airborne will go to the sticky trap instead of returning to the plant. If whiteflies are detected on sticky traps, inspect the foliage of nearby plants using a hand lens. Look for signs of parasitoids and other beneficials. One sign is the exit hole in the whitefly nymphal case (pupal case). If the exit hole is "T" or "Y" shaped, a healthy adult whitefly has emerged. If, however, the exit hole is round, it is a sign that the pupa was parasitized and an adult wasp has emerged.

INDIRECT STRATEGIES

Remove dust from plants with a water wash-down. Dust on foliage heavily favors whiteflies and inhibits and discourages their predators and parasitoids. In one interior plantscape where greenhouse whiteflies were a problem, the parasitoid *Encarsia formosa* was released regularly to little effect. Similarly, the addition of *Delphastus catalinae* (=*D. pusillus*) had little or no effect. It was recommended that all of the plants, including some interior trees nearly 20 ft. tall, be washed down. One weekend we went in and washed down all of the plant material. At first everyone was impressed with the aesthetic improvement; all the plants just looked better. Within eight weeks the greenhouse whitefly problem that had gone on for years was over. The site manager has reported to us that whitefly is no longer a problem and that he now schedules at least two wash-downs per year.

Control nitrogen in plants. This is a common tactic when dealing with any of the Hemiptera pest species, and with certain diseases, for that matter. We recommend the use of compost, worm castings, and/or organic fertilizers, especially for indoor plantscapes. These three nutrient sources also contain beneficial microbes, some of which may contain entomopathogenic (insect-killing) microorganisms such as *Trichoderma* spp., mentioned earlier.

DIRECT PHYSICAL CONTROLS

If you find evidence of a nascent whitefly infestation, remove the affected leaves; place them in a plastic bag in the sun until the insects are dead. Then put them into the compost. If on inspection you find evidence of parasitoids, wash the dust off of the plants and prune out damaged branchlets. Leave the prunings on-site so that the parasitoids can emerge. If the infestation is small enough, you can rub the whitefly scales off of the few affected leaves with your hand or with a toothbrush.

A strong, fine spray of water can dislodge whitefly nymphs and crawlers from leaves. Did we mention that this will also remove the dust from the plants? As mentioned earlier, dust on plants, whether indoors or outdoors, is advantageous to insect pests and detrimental to beneficials.

Vacuuming is another tactic that can be effective. The adult whiteflies can be sucked off the tops of plants with a hand-held vacuum in the cool hours of the early morning. The emphasis here is on "cool hours of the early morning." Once the temperature starts to rise, the adults are too active and they will take flight as you approach with the vacuum. Most of the whiteflies will be mortally injured during their quick trip through the vacuum hose, but we still recommend either freezing the vacuum bag or putting it in a clear plastic bag and letting it sit out in the hot sunshine to kill the insects.

TIP Remove any dust from your plants; it always favors pests of all kinds, not just whiteflies.

DIRECT BIOLOGICAL CONTROLS

Thankfully, there are many predators and parasitoids that can help you manage whiteflies, some of which are available commercially. Among the beneficials that attack whiteflies are lacewing (*Chrysoperla* spp.), several ladybug (lady beetle) species, big-eyed bug (*Geocoris* spp.), minute pirate bug (*Orius insidiosus*), and, of course, the parasitoid wasps in the *Encarsia* genus. There are a number of other predators of scale, aphid, and mealybug that will occasionally feed on whitefly. Be sure plants have been washed down and ants have been controlled before releasing beneficials.

To ensure a constant supply of beneficials, consider installing plants that will attract beneficials to your garden. Sweet alyssum (*Lobularia maritime*) is a good choice because it grows everywhere, germinates quickly, and is attractive. Seed mixes that attract a variety of beneficial insects are available online and often at local nurseries. This is a very worthwhile investment of time and money, and a great favor to your garden.

DIRECT CHEMICAL CONTROLS

Whiteflies are notorious for their ability to avoid insecticide applications and to build up a quick resistance to insecticides. If all other tactics, applied in a conscientious manner, prove ineffective, there will be the temptation to use insecticides. If you get to this point you should consider replacing the plant. If you simply must use an insecticide, we recommend that you limit yourself to soap, neem oil, or light horticultural oil. Be certain that you cover the leaf surfaces thoroughly, especially the underside of the leaves, where 99 percent of the whitefly life cycle stages are located.

The use of insecticides for whiteflies is likely to increase the problem rather than bring it under control, because most pesticides will also kill the predators and parasitoids that normally keep whitefly in check, while doing little to affect the whiteflies. The label recommendations for whitefly insecticides often direct you to apply the pesticide every 7 to 10 days until control is achieved. This puts additional pressure on the whitefly to develop resistance more quickly. It is commonly recommended that you rotate insecticides from different chemical classes (different chemistries and modes of action) to try to avoid insect resistance. But doing so means buying more pesticides that you must keep

"The primary concern with whitefly is the ability of some species to carry viruses from one plant to the next."

around and store. This is the pesticide treadmill that we have mentioned throughout this book and in our other publications.

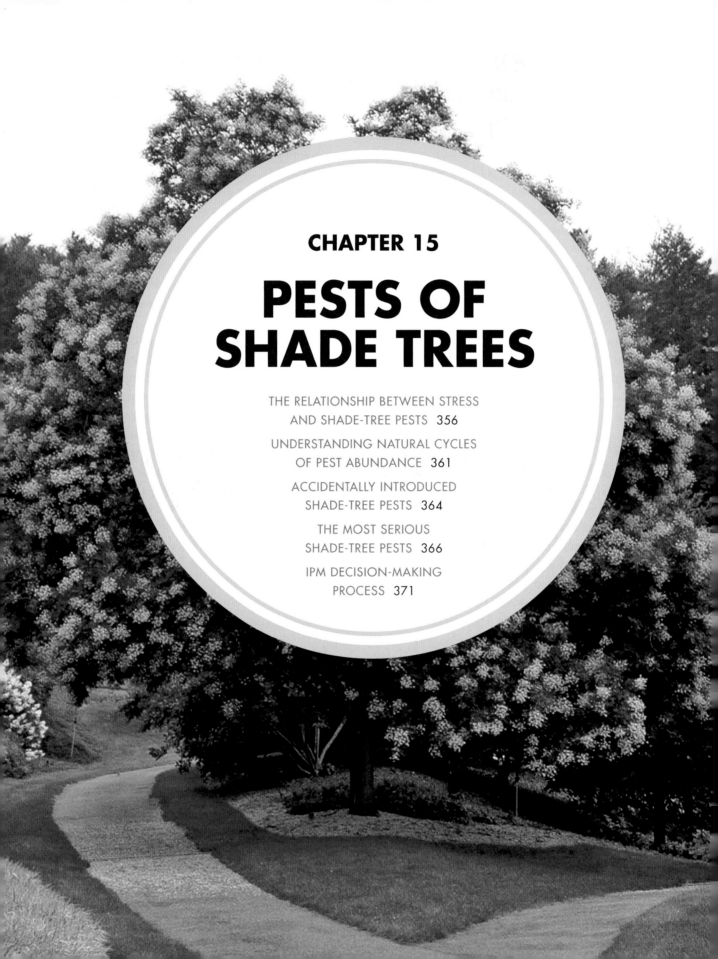

CHAPTER 15

PESTS OF SHADE TREES

Shade trees provide welcome protection from the sun and wind. They also humidify dry air, screen us from undesired sights and sounds, and gracefully frame our homes and gardens. Shade trees are often the most significant landscape element in any neighborhood. Ecologically they produce oxygen and sequester carbon, helping reduce planetary warming.

From a biological perspective, a shade tree is a world within a world. The birds, squirrels, and tree frogs hosted by shade trees enhance the value of the trees to us. Along with these animals come a multitude of less-appreciated forms of wildlife. But the microbes, fungi, other parasitic plants such as mistletoe, insects, mites, and spiders, together with their more admired, better-recognized companions, the moths and butterflies, are integral and essential parts of the shade-tree community.

In a way, each shade tree mimics in miniature the larger ecosystem of the forest that was its evolutionary home. The vegetarians, or herbivores, include the birds and squirrels that eat berries and nuts, the mites and aphids that suck plant juices, the caterpillars, beetles, and flies that eat leaves, and the microbes and fungi that decompose the bark and wood itself. The carnivores, which include insect-eating birds, insects, spiders, and mites, depend on the herbivores for their sustenance.

Unfortunately, several factors make it difficult for humans to take a calm, philosophical approach to the presence of all this shade-tree wildlife. One is the powerful image projected by the tree care and maintenance industries that a healthy, desirable tree is a sterile one with nary a bug or a blemish. Although a moment's reflection upon the natural forest scene tells us this is sheer nonsense, we may still fall for the misguided notion that complete

Trees along the street not only provide shade but also habitat for birds and other beneficial wildlife. (Photo by Miguel Malu/iStockPhoto)

elimination of these organisms is necessary, whatever the cost.

Then there is the fact that many people are afraid of insects or simply find them nasty—especially if they are overhead—whether they are causing problems or not. Or people fear that the life of the tree is threatened, or that the pests in the tree will spread to other plants in the garden. Finally, people who have lived through sieges of gypsy moths or Dutch elm disease understandably may have become gun-shy over new tree pest problems. Whatever the reason, the war against shade-tree wildlife has turned many a lovely, tree-shaded neighborhood into a battleground, with toxic materials being used as ammunition and, in some cases, citizens and their public officials in opposing camps.

An excellent example of an old tree being broken down and providing nutrients for a new tree. (Photo by Kfletcher/iStockPhoto)

To get a sound perspective on the problem of shade-tree pests, it helps to understand the role they play in the life cycle of the tree. It is also worth examining the natural rise and fall of pest populations and the special situation posed by exotic pest invaders. We examine each of these issues below.

THE RELATIONSHIP BETWEEN STRESS AND SHADE-TREE PESTS

Old trees in naturally wooded areas are decomposed and returned to the soil by certain insects, fungi, microbes, and other organisms. In this way the minerals locked up in tree tissues are recycled for use by other plants, an essential natural process in the forest. But the spread of insects and pathogens is a response to or a symptom of stress or weakness in trees. In a way, this is analogous to our "catching" a cold. Under stress, the same cold-producing pathogens our bodies normally ward off may trigger a full-blown cold, paving the way for more serious secondary infections. Similarly, a tree may be showing signs of stress when it becomes pest infested. Stressed trees may not produce as many pest-repellent or pest-killing compounds in their leaves and other parts. In addition, they may become more susceptible to wind or snow injury, which can expose inner bark areas and invite pests. And when the pests attack, stressed trees may show a decreased ability to recover.

With this in mind, there are three questions to ask when faced with a serious shade-tree pest problem: Is the tree under stress? Can the stress be alleviated? How can the tree's vigor be restored?

STRESS REDUCTION THROUGH APPROPRIATE SPECIES SELECTION

Stresses to shade trees can be grouped into two broad categories: those resulting from human activities and those caused by natural events. Of all the ways human activities adversely affect shade trees, none is more common or more tragic than the selection of the wrong species or the wrong variety of a particular species. Unfortunately, many landscape architects are more concerned with the appearance of a tree than with its ecological appropriateness to the site. They rarely take responsibility for maintaining the plants they design into a setting or the consequences of their choices. This is unfortunate. It is during the design process that pests are either designed into the system or out of it. There are landscape designers who take plant selection and sustainability seriously. They are the ones who design landscapes that work well for those who use the landscapes and those who maintain them over the years.

In addition, it is all too human to surround ourselves with vegetation that evokes childhood environments, status, or romance. Thus, in the semi-arid, mild winter climate of many western states, people attempt to re-create the landscapes of well-watered English country estates or the cold-winter birch forests of the Great Lakes region. Conversely, residents of the East and Midwest often try to establish exotic plantings that are neither winter-hardy nor adapted to local soils.

The ideal approach to landscaping your home is to select tree species that are native to the area or to similar ecosystems elsewhere on the planet. Select species that are suited to your site's climate, soils, water table, winds, and sun exposure. Avoid species that obviously do not do well in your neighborhood. This means looking around to see which trees are the oldest in your area; if you admire something planted locally, ask if it is comparatively maintenance-free. Seek advice from local arboricultural experts and horticultural manuals as to the tree varieties that are the most pest- and disease-resistant in your locale. Most county cooperative extension offices publish lists of trees suited to the area.

When selecting a tree that is relatively pest-free in your area, consider not only the type of tree—*Acer*, or maple, for example—but also the species—

Acer saccharum, or sugar maple—as well as the cultivar, such as 'Goldspire', which is the horticultural variety of that tree in the case of many commercially available plants. When purchasing trees from a plant nursery, you should ask for a cultivar that is best suited to the type of setting in which you intend to plant it.

Research has shown that the geographical origin of the tree seed affects pest management. Apparently through genetic selection, each species adapts to the climate and soils of its native area. These adaptations may not be visible, but they influence the tree's ability to withstand disease, insect pests, winter chill, summer scorch, different soil depths, varying soil moisture, and other conditions. This native quality, or provenance, of the tree is not affected by the location of the nursery where the tree happened to be raised; it depends solely on seed origin. It is always a good idea to check with the closest chapter of the Native Plant Society or a local knowledgeable environmental group. They often have seed, and sometimes even plants, that are the "local genotype."

If you live in a concrete-covered urban area, consider planting "pioneer" tree species. These are fast-growing trees with fairly short lifetimes. In

> **"The ideal approach to landscaping your home is to select tree species that are native to the area or to similar ecosystems elsewhere on the planet."**

nature, these are the first species to colonize arid, infertile environments, and they include the hawthorns *Crataegus crus-galli* and *C. phaenopyrum*, the tree-of-heaven (*Ailanthus altissima*), honey-locust (*Gleditsia*), cork tree (*Phellodendron*), and many others. Pioneer species can be quite attractive, and they tolerate the hostile planting sites of cities more readily than many popular shade trees grown in more horticulturally benign suburban settings.

HOW TREES RESPOND TO WOUNDS

Trees do not replace injured tissues as animals do. Instead, they compartmentalize or "wall off" injured tissue. After being wounded (see the drawing below), the tree reacts. Chemical barriers develop around the injured tissue, preventing many decay organisms from gaining a foothold in the damaged area. But some wood-inhabiting microorganisms surmount these barriers and begin to interact with the tree, moving from compartment to compartment. When the walls of the compartments begin to succumb to the invaders, the top and bottom of the compartment (Wall 1 in the drawing below) go first, followed by the inner wall (Wall 2) and then the side wall (Wall 3). But most of the time the barrier zone (Wall 4) holds up, confining the invaders to the wood present at the time of wounding. Eventually a ring of new, healthy wood surrounds the decayed area.

Recognition of this response mechanism was the outcome of a decade of research by Dr. Alex Shigo, a USDA forest pathologist. His insights into the response of trees to wounds have necessitated changes in the way trees are pruned and repaired.

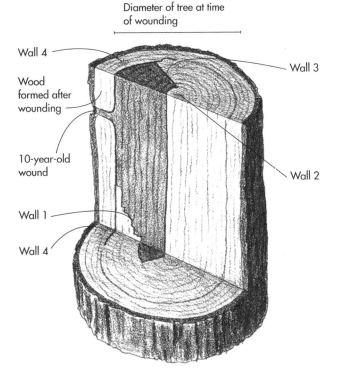

Diameter of tree at time of wounding

Wall 4

Wood formed after wounding

10-year-old wound

Wall 1

Wall 4

Wall 3

Wall 2

There are fads in plants just as there are in fashion and popular music, so you may find it difficult to locate the trees most suited to your area if they are out of vogue. Even local nurseries frequently propagate unsuitable varieties if they are selling. A classic example of this occurred in California, where the Modesto ash (*Fraxinus velutina* var. Modesto) was planted as a street tree in communities throughout the state long after it had been observed to be severely susceptible to the plant disease anthracnose and heavy infestations of the ash aphid (*Prociphilus fraxinifolii*). The result has been decades of heavy pesticide use in an attempt to control these two pests, which were "designed into" the neighborhoods when the tree species was selected. Ironically, an equally attractive species, the Shamel ash (*Fraxinus uhdei*), is quite resistant to both problems, but it was difficult or impossible to locate it in nurseries when the Modesto ash was first popular.

The lesson is that you must be persistent in your efforts to locate appropriate species. Do not overlook plant sales by local botanical gardens and arboretums or catalogs from nurseries specializing in plants native to your area. The native plant societies found in many communities often provide lists of such nurseries.

We realize that many of you are looking for less-toxic ways of managing pests of trees already in your care. Nevertheless, if it takes pesticides to keep your current shade tree alive, you should consider whether replacing it with a tree more suited to the site might not be more satisfactory in the long run.

STRESS REDUCTION THROUGH PROPER HORTICULTURAL CARE

Next in importance to appropriate species selection is proper care of the tree when it is young and as it grows. There are several horticultural factors you can monitor and control in this effort.

1. Drainage. Good drainage is essential. One common error is to sink a young tree in a hole to make irrigation easier. In fact, the top of the root ball should be elevated 1 in. to 2 in. (2.5 cm to 5 cm) above the soil grade when the tree is first planted to prevent water from collecting around the base of the trunk as it settles. Otherwise, because there are no feeder roots close to the trunk to absorb the collecting water, the base of the trunk is kept moist and becomes susceptible to penetration by various disease-causing pathogens. Slope the soil away from the trunk in all directions, then place a berm for establishment, watering 6 in. to 12 in. (15 to 30 cm) or more out from the trunk. Once the tree is established in its new location, usually about a year if planted correctly, remove the berm.

2. Staking. Trees develop the strongest resistance to wood damage if the ties to stakes permit some movement of the young trunk when the wind blows. If the stake that comes with the tree is not replaced at planting time with a different staking system, the plant will tend to rub against the stake and sustain bark injuries. These injuries invite beetle damage or attack by microorganisms. The drawing at right illustrates the proper staking of a tree.

3. Pruning. Improper pruning is also a major cause of tree decay and can trigger insect attack. The pioneering work of Dr. Alex Shigo, retired plant pathologist for the U.S. Forest Service, has demonstrated that trees have effective systems for defending themselves against disease organisms that enter the trunk through dead, dying, or improperly pruned branches. His basic theory is presented in the sidebar on the facing page.

The front line of the tree's defense system is located in a swollen collar of wood located at the point where the branch grows out of its supporting limb or trunk (see the drawing and photo on p. 360). When a tree is wounded, tissues in this collar form the chemical barriers that wall off decay organisms. Not only does the collar tissue enable most trees to contain the decay organisms rapidly, it also speeds up the external closure of the wound by stimulating the cambium tissue into forming new bark and sapwood.

Thus, when tree branches are pruned off flush against the supporting trunk or limb, the branch collar is removed and the tree is less effective in implementing its defense system against the microorganisms that inevitably colonize the cut surface. Although compartmentalization does eventually occur in the absence of the collar, it is much slower and the extent of decay is greater. Delay in compartmentalization also occurs when a branch is not pruned close enough to the collar and a stub is left to die back.

HOW TO STAKE A TREE

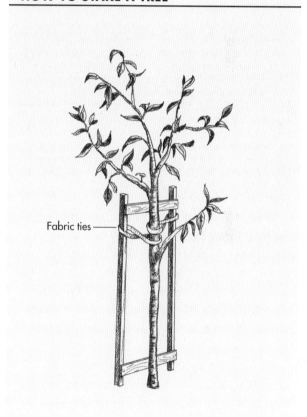

Fabric ties

This method works well for staking young trees. Note that two stakes are used, spaced so they do not touch the trunk. The fabric or rubber ties are loose enough not to restrict growth. Arrange and tighten the ties enough to allow the tree to bend in the wind without bumping the wooden stakes, even when the wind is gusting.

THE SHIGO PRUNING TECHNIQUE

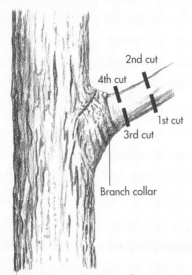

To maximize quick healing and minimize decay organisms access to pruning wounds, you must employ a two-step process. First, use a bottom cut (1st cut) to cut through the bark and cambium (no more than ¼ of the branch diameter), then join the first cut with a top cut (2nd cut) to remove most of the branch. This double cut prevents splitting of the branch's bark and cambium through the collar and into the trunk by removing over 95% of the branch weight. With all but about 6 inches of the branch removed, you then bottom cut (3rd cut) the stub and then remove the remaining branch end as closely as possible to the branch collar (4th cut), as indicated. Do not leave stubs, and do not paint the cuts.

The finished cut should be made just outside the branch collar; this is where the "healing" tissue forms to eventually cover the wound. (Photo by Alex A. Shigo, Shigo and Trees, Associates LLC)

Whenever sewer lines are dug, driveways renewed, or house foundations built or repaired, the roots of nearby shade trees may be damaged severely. The tree needs its roots not only for anchorage but also to draw in the water it requires. This water is transpired largely through the leaves. If the roots are injured, the only way you can offset the fact that more water is being lost through the leaves than is being taken in through the roots is by promptly reducing the leaf area through pruning. This can be very tricky, because removing too much of the foliage will slow the tree's ability to heal. Because the tree cannot photosynthesize sufficiently to repair itself. Prior to pruning to compensate for the root injury, call in a trusted certified arborist for advice. The arborist should be able to advise you regarding root anchorage concerns and water and nutritional absorption issues.

Digging sewer lines up for repair, often because tree roots have invaded fractured pipe, is most traumatic for nearby trees. A system currently in use is to auger out the inside of the existing damaged pipe in order to remove tree roots and any other obstructions. Then a new flexible plastic pipe-liner is inserted into the existing sewer line from the street and run all the way to the house. This provides a new seamless sewer line that will keep tree roots and other obstructions, such as soil and burrowing animals, out of the sewer line, giving it a new and extended life. Most important, the only tree roots disturbed are those that are growing into the seams and cracks of the original sewer line. Because there is no trenching involved with this pipe-repair method, it is neater and faster than traditional "dig and cover" pipe installations.

4. Soil Aeration. Tree roots need small empty spaces in the soil into which they can release carbon dioxide and from which they can obtain oxygen. Thus, a mulch of organic material should be placed over the soil to prevent compaction where human traffic passes beneath the drip line of the tree.

Aeration in already compacted soils can sometimes be improved with a special probe powered by water pressure from a garden hose or from compressed air. The compressed-air equipment is large and expensive, and usually available only by hiring a tree-care company to perform the task. First, the probe is placed into the soil at a predetermined depth, usually 12 in. to 30 in. (30.5 cm to 76 cm) Then air, with an organic or inorganic amendment (often compost or perlite), is forced into the soil in a burst of high pressure that fractures the surrounding soil and inserts the amendment into the spaces. This improves aeration and infiltration of water and nutrients into the root zone and allows the roots to spread out into the surrounding soil.

5. Weed Control. The application of herbicides to lawns and ground covers often harms nearby trees. Herbicides volatilize (vaporize) in warm temperatures and rise to damage the tree's leaves. Most herbicides are also water-soluble and can move to lower levels of the soil where spreading tree roots, often located as far as 30 ft. (9 m) from the tree, absorb them.

Organic mulch "weed mats," sheet mulching, and tree rings made from recycled car tires can replace herbicides for weed control under or around shade trees. Tree rings made from recycled tires are great for lawn trees on slopes where organic mulches may be washed away during rain events. Planting dense ground covers (competitive planting) under the tree's dripline is another weed control option. Your ground-cover choice should have cultural requirements, especially water needs, similar to the tree under which it is being planted. Weeds can also be controlled through proper lawn care, including periodic soil aeration, proper mowing height and frequency, the use of grass species suited to the site, deep and infrequent irrigations, and the use of compost, organic, or slow-release fertilizers (see the discussion in Chapter 13 on lawn management).

6. Fertilizer. The overuse of nitrogen fertilizer can encourage the growth of aphid and scale populations. If needed at all, an organic fertilizer or compost should be used to meet the tree's nutrient needs. If you want to plant a ground cover beneath a tree, bear in mind that in natural areas a slowly decomposing mulch of leaves and other organic debris provides the fertilizer the tree needs. The requirements of any plants grown beneath the tree should not interfere with the needs of the tree itself. Remember, you should be feeding the soil and keeping it healthy. The soil will provide for the tree.

7. Protection against Road Salt. Another serious stress results from the application of salt to icy roads in winter, which then burns nearby trees during spring thaws. The sidebar on p. 362 addresses this problem.

8. Protection against Natural Stresses. Stresses from natural causes also can reduce tree vigor. Most important among these are spells of unusual cold, periods of extreme dryness and heat, and successive years of attack by exotic (non-native) insects. Young trees can be wrapped to protect them against cold, and any tree benefits from periodic deep irrigation in unusually dry years. Whitewashing the bark of young trees helps prevent sunburn, which also invites insects and disease.

UNDERSTANDING NATURAL CYCLES OF PEST ABUNDANCE

Even the most vigorous of shade trees experience fluctuating levels of insect pest abundance. These cycles occur during the season and from year to year. Each season there is a lag between the appearance and growth of the herbivorous (plant-feeding) pest population and the arrival and suppressive actions of these pests' natural enemies.

PROTECTING YOUR PLANTS FROM ROAD SALT

In an excellent short article in the December 1989 issue of *Horticulture*, Ellen M. Silva suggests these practical steps if you feel your trees and shrubs may be suffering from salt burn:

- Take a soil sample to your county extension service and request a soluble salt test. Silva notes that in sandy soil, salt levels greater than 1,000 parts per million indicate potential trouble. The clay, silt, or humus portion of the soil has a higher water-holding capacity than the sand fraction. The presence of these non-sand components helps dilute high concentrations of salt. A pH of 7.5 or more may indicate a sodium overload.

- Find out whether local road maintenance crews can do anything to direct salty runoff away from your property.

- Leach the salt from the affected area in early spring. Apply 2 in. (5 cm) of water over a period of two to three hours. Wait three days, then repeat the procedure. You may want to add a surfactant to the leaching water to improve percolation.

- Where salt spray from passing traffic is the problem, wash the affected leaves and branches with a large volume of water whenever the spray is heavy and again in early spring.

- When shoveling walks or driveways around your home, avoid piling up snow or ice that may contain salt where the melting water can run into the root zones of trees and shrubs. Leave this salt-containing material where runoff can enter curbside ditches or rainwater catchments.

- Use sand or sawdust instead of salt to improve traction on your driveway and walks. Perhaps you can convince your local community to switch to one of these materials. Non-saline rock dust is popular in Europe for this purpose, but no similar product is as yet commonly available in the United States.

- Incorporate large quantities of mature compost, or other organic amendments, into the soil in the fall. This will improve soil texture and water-holding ability. It will also help buffer the soil, preventing large swings in soil pH. The application of gypsum (calcium sulfate) can also help mitigate the effects of sodium, because calcium displaces sodium in the soil. Compost combined with gypsum and spring leaching will go a long way in counteracting the effects of road salt on your soil and plants.

- Select salt-tolerant species for roadside plantings. Silva recommends honeylocust, juniper, Norway maple, roses, scotch pine, and red or white oak; she suggests avoiding such salt-sensitive plants as black walnut, red or sugar maple, and red or white pine.

- Build a low wall or grow a hedge of salt-tolerant evergreens along the road to deflect salt spray away from sensitive plantings.

Even more dramatic, however, are the large yearly differences in the size of the pest population. Year-to-year changes in the weather and in the abundance of predators, parasitoids, and pathogens that feed upon the pests play a significant role in these population changes. Periods of extreme winter cold or a very rainy or dry spring, for example, may cause high mortality among the overwintering forms of the pest. Even with small yearly differences in the weather pattern the pest may increase in abundance for two or more years, then suffer a population crash, usually from an outbreak of a disease. After the crash, sparse pest populations for a year or two swiftly starve the natural enemies that rely on the pest for food. The lack of natural enemies enables the pest gradually to build up its population again, and the cycle repeats.

Such pendulum-like swings in the size of animal populations are common in the natural world. (We humans, with our world population doubling in ever-shorter intervals, are the only animal to have temporarily escaped this natural cycling.) These observations of natural cycles translate into several practical suggestions:

- Avoid preventive sprays, because it may be a year in which the pest population never becomes large enough to be a problem even if left untreated. Don't treat ahead of time because a certain problem occurred last year. In the case of gypsy moth infestations, treating high populations may actually prolong the outbreak (see the discussion on pp. 368–370).

- When the pest makes its appearance, don't panic. A small pest population does not constitute a crisis. If you cannot admire wildlife, at least tolerate a few insects— the birds will have something to feed their young, and the beneficial insects and spiders will have a chance to build up their numbers.

TIP Use microbial insecticides when possible and chemical pesticides only as a last resort. By reducing the use of chemical insecticides, you delay the development of pesticide resistance in the insect population and more natural enemies of the pest will survive to help suppress the pest population in the future.

- Learn to recognize the natural enemies of pests, because you need to know when they are present and when their numbers are about to catch up with the pest population. Also, it is important not to mistake them for the pest organisms. An excellent source for information and identification of beneficials is the *Natural Enemies Handbook* by Mary Louise Flint and Steve Dreistadt (University of California Press, 1999). The excellent photographs, by the renowned biological photographer Jack Kelly Clark, make identification much easier.

- When the pest population appears to be reaching levels you find intolerable, select methods of suppression that are the least harmful to the pest's natural enemies. Where possible, mimic nature, and use physical and biological controls first. Examples are pruning out the pest, crushing egg masses, using water or compost tea washes, and applying microbial insecticides. These and other techniques are discussed briefly below under the various categories of pests for which they are applicable.

- If toxic materials must be used, spot-treat; that is, confine treatment to just those areas where the pest problem is intolerable. For example, applying pesticide in a band around the trunk of an elm tree for the control of elm leaf beetle instead of spraying the foliage of the entire tree canopy is one way to confine pesticides to a specific location. Treating only those trees that are about to experience intolerable damage rather than spraying all the trees in an area is another example.

- Where you are dealing with a large number of trees of the same species, as on a city block or a large estate, initiate a monitoring system to keep track of the pest population over the season. It helps to design a monitoring sheet that contains such information as date, location of specimen, type of tree, number and type of pests per leaf, and notes on treatments. Make photocopies of the blank form so you can use it repeatedly. You will probably find great differences between individual trees of the same species in natural resistance to pest attack. Only certain trees are likely to be so severely affected that treatment is warranted.

- Encourage city landscape planners to select a diversity of tree species for each neighborhood. This diversification reduces the likelihood of large numbers of trees simultaneously suffering high pest populations, and it reduces the amount of pesticide exposure in each neighborhood from street tree treatments. Although diversity of species seems like a common-sense approach, be advised that people have very strong feelings about "uniformity" when it comes to street trees. One need only remember what Dutch elm disease, chestnut blight (see below), and other insects and diseases have done to same-species plantings.

ACCIDENTALLY INTRODUCED SHADE-TREE PESTS

The most notorious pests of shade trees in the United States are those that were introduced accidentally from other geographic areas, leaving their natural enemies behind. Freed from the restraints provided by complexes of predators, parasitoids, and pathogens in their homelands and finding defenseless plant populations in the new environment, these exotic pests increased relatively unchecked.

The best-known examples of exotic shade-tree pests are the pathogens that cause Dutch elm disease and chestnut blight, as well as the gypsy moth, the elm leaf beetle, and the Japanese beetle. There

are many others, including the mimosa webworm, the smaller elm bark beetle (which carries the fungal pathogen that causes Dutch elm disease), and the European elm scale.

Although most people are aware of the large-scale disasters caused by these imported pests, it is still commonplace to find people attempting to circumvent the strict quarantine laws that regulate the movement of plant materials into the United States. A similar quarantine exists for the importation of plants into California, which is an "ecological island" separated by desert and mountains from neighboring states. The monthly reports from the agricultural inspection stations along California's borders with Oregon, Nevada, and Arizona provide insight into the unfortunate human affinity for smuggling, whether motivated by greed, self-importance, or the excitement of taking a risk. Many of the invasive species problems we have

The gypsy moth is the common name for *Lymantria dispar*, of the tussock moth family, native to Europe and Asia. Its caterpillars, or larvae, defoliate deciduous and evergreen trees and shrubs. Introduced from Europe into Massachusetts c. 1869, the European gypsy moth became a serious pest within 20 years. Asian gypsy moths were introduced to the Northwest by Russian ships in 1991 and to North Carolina by a ship returning from Germany in 1993. (Photo by John H. Ghent, USDA Forest Service, Bugwood.org)

today are the result of plant and animal smuggling. This includes the pest "stowaways" on these ill-gotten imports.

The breeding of genetically resistant plant materials has been the first line of defense against exotic plant diseases. But breeding is slow and uncertain, as those who have been following the progress of efforts to find resistant elms and chestnuts are well aware. More recently, direct assaults have been made against plant pathogens using other microbes that appear to be antagonists or competitors of the disease-causing organism. As the field of microbial controls develops, we can expect this technology to be applied to an increasing number of tree pathogens, including some of the exotic ones.

Plant breeding is very different from genetic engineering and the resultant genetically modified organisms (GMOs). In plant breeding, two plants from the same genus are bred and the resultant seedlings are grown out to see if they exhibit the desired traits. This method of altering plant characteristics has been going on since the very beginning of agriculture, and in nature since the beginning of life itself. In nature, it is very rare for plants of different genera to be able to breed successfully, let alone organisms from completely different kingdoms. In genetic engineering, genes from one organism are spliced into the chromosomes of what is very often a completely unrelated species.

For example, BT corn combines genes from the bacteria *Bacillus thuringiensis* (kingdom Eubacteria) with those of corn (*Zea mays,* kingdom Plantae) to produce a corn plant that is toxic to caterpillars. It is the BT toxins now produced in the corn plant that kill the larvae. One attraction for the farmer is that no spraying of the BT crop is required for caterpillars, and protection is good for the entire growing season from seedling to harvest. The potential downside for the rest of us is that this puts pressure on caterpillars (moth larvae in this case) to build up resistance to BT toxins. The worst-case scenario, and probable outcome, is that we will eventually

have populations of pest moths that are unaffected by BT, and we lose a biorational tool (see the discussion on p. 134). The question of whether the corn plant is affected in other ways because of this genetic tinkering is a discussion for another time. Genetic engineering and GMO crops are very controversial topics. We encourage you to search the web for information from a variety of sources, so that you can make your own informed decision on the subject.

BIOLOGICAL CONTROLS FOR ACCIDENTALLY INTRODUCED INSECTS

The most important, cost-effective, and underfunded effort for suppressing exotic insects is the search for natural enemies of the pest in the area in which the pests originated. Projects in this kind of classical biological control of shade-tree pests are what gave us our first taste of pest management. In

"The most important, cost-effective, and underfunded effort for suppressing exotic insects is the search for natural enemies of the pest in the area in which the pests originated."

fact, all of our subsequent work in IPM began with the realization in the early 1970s that these imported biological controls of shade-tree pests could not succeed unless they were part of a larger, more systematic, and environmentally sensitive approach to horticultural pest control. We describe one of these biological control projects briefly on pp. 52–53.

Since the time when we were focusing exclusively on biological controls for urban shade-tree pests, there has been further work by others on finding natural enemies of the elm leaf beetle. An extensive effort to find natural controls for the gypsy moth *(Lymantria dispar)* has been ongoing since 1906; however, these efforts have not been spectacularly successful.

Pests of agricultural trees, including citrus, walnuts, and olives, as well as pests of forest trees,

Poor cultural conditions predisposed this willow oak tree to infestation by scales. (Photo by William Fountain, University of Kentucky, Bugwood.org)

have commanded more biological control research dollars than urban shade trees (with some exceptions, because many forest trees are also common in cities). One notable example is the introduction of a parasitoid for the control of the winter moth (*Operophtera brumata*), an accidentally introduced caterpillar pest of oaks, maples, fruit trees, and other deciduous trees. It has been very successful on the east and west coasts of Canada.

Predators and parasitoids have a role to play in the biological control of certain native shade-tree pests, too. Canadian scientists and foresters have been releasing a small wasp in the genus *Trichogramma* that parasitizes the eggs of the eastern spruce budworm (*Choristoneura fumiferana*), which is a native caterpillar. Because the wasps do not overwinter in the Canadian release sites, they are reared in large numbers and put out each year as a biological insecticide. In China, there are many examples of rearing or collecting natural enemies such as parasitoids, spiders, and nematodes and releasing them against tree pests.

Perhaps future work on the biological control of shade-tree pests will follow along these lines. However, even as a private citizen you can protect the natural enemies of insect pests already on your trees, as well as additional pests that may be imported, by following conservation policies, and particularly by reducing or eliminating toxic and non-specific (broad-spectrum) insecticides in your garden and neighborhood.

THE MOST SERIOUS SHADE-TREE PESTS

The following discussion of organisms that cause disease in trees focuses on arthropods rather than on pathogens. This is because the best management for tree pathogens is horticultural and involves proper species selection, watering and cultural practices, and pruning techniques. By contrast, special techniques must be used in controlling arthropod pests. The exceptions are the non-native pathogens such as Dutch elm disease and chestnut blight. Finding a resistant variety of tree—one that has survived the attack of the pathogen—and the selection and propagation of antagonist microorganisms both offer hope for restoring the American elm and the chestnut to urban landscapes. Anyone who is observant may come across resistant trees. In contrast, the selection and propagation of antagonist organisms is not a technique that is easily pursued by the average tree-lover, so we will not discuss it in this book.

An enormous number of species of plant-feeding insects and mites exist in shade trees (see the drawing below). Most are of no consequence in terms of their damage and visibility, and most of the rest cause only minor annoyance as a result of human fear or slight visible changes in tree foliage. Of those that have the potential to become a problem, most problems occur in response to improper species selection or tree management, environmental stress, or human activities such as treatment of one pest with compounds that kill the natural enemies

of another. These problems can be corrected thorough the horticultural and ecological practices suggested above.

However, there are a few pests that pose a serious danger to shade trees. These are often exotic insects or plant pathogens. Very little can be done to control them, even with the use of toxic materials. However, some are good candidates for classical biological control projects (as discussed on pp. 46–53).

KEY SHADE-TREE PESTS

The three main categories of pest arthropods are mites, aphids, and scales. Management strategies for all three are discussed below.

Mites. In trees, mites are usually a secondary pest triggered by pesticide use against other pests or by dust from unpaved roads, which kills the mites' predators. They may also be a symptom of a lack of water due to inadequate rain, insufficient irrigation,

INSECTS THAT ATTACK TREES AND THE DAMAGE THEY CAUSE

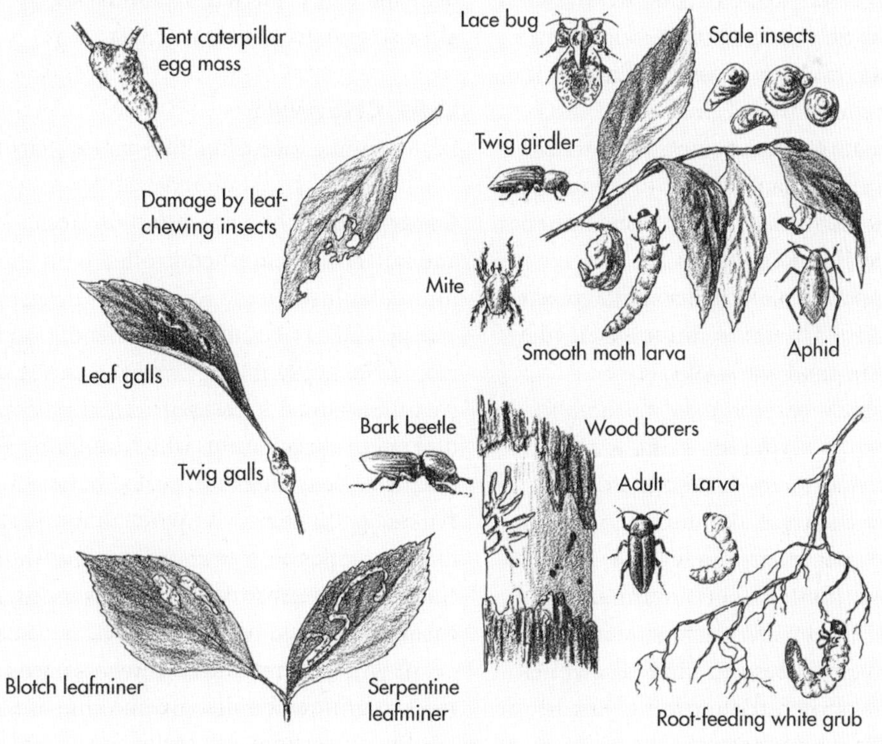

Tent caterpillar egg mass

Damage by leaf-chewing insects

Leaf galls

Twig galls

Blotch leafminer

Serpentine leafminer

Bark beetle

Lace bug

Twig girdler

Mite

Smooth moth larva

Wood borers

Adult Larva

Scale insects

Aphid

Root-feeding white grub

or plant pathogens that infect the tree's water-conducting tissues. In other words, a mite-infested tree can be presumed to be under some kind of stress if prior pesticide use is not involved.

For management of mites, switch to the selective microbial insecticides used in caterpillar control (see below). Increase irrigation, and try washing the tree periodically with water. It may gradually restore the balance between predatory and pest mites. Insecticidal soap may be helpful in emergencies. Use a hose-attached sprayer to get adequate water pressure for washing a medium-size tree. A truly large specimen may require washing by professionals with special equipment. If washing with plain water or insecticidal soap does not help, identify the mite or have it identified for you and check with insectaries about commercially available mite predators. Select tree species that are resistant to local soil-borne pathogens such as oak root fungus (*Armillaria mellea*), *Phytophthora* spp. root rots, and verticillium wilt.

Aphids. Aphids may be a symptom of excess nitrogen fertilizer, perhaps due to the use of lawn food. They can also be attracted to the succulent sucker growth that results from overly drastic pruning. The pesticides used against other pests can kill aphid predators and parasitoids, or there can be a temporary rise in aphid numbers in spring before the natural enemies catch up, a phenomenon called predator-prey lag. Sometimes the damage is primarily visual, such as black sooty mold growing on honeydew produced by the aphids or honeydew falling on parked cars and sidewalks.

To manage aphids, try to control the ants that protect aphids by ringing the tree trunk with a non-toxic sticky band. Apply the band early in spring before the rise in ant activity. If ants are already in the canopy, use soap and water to wash as many ants as possible out of the tree before banding. Another tactic can be used when ants move into the tree during the day and return to their nest at night. In the coolest time of the early morning, just before sunrise, band the tree before the ants move back in

during the day. We have seen sticky bands applied in the late afternoon, and thousands of ants that were up in the tree during the day were gathered just above the band, trapped in the tree.

Switch to organic or at least slow-release fertilizers beneath the tree, and prune out the inner canopy if it is severely infested. Use water washes, horticultural oils, or insecticidal soap to clean off aphids and honeydew.

Scales. Scales can be triggered by pesticides used against other pests (for example, fogging for mosquitoes), by excess nitrogen, or by environmental stresses, such as too much or too little water.

Prune out severely infested limbs and switch to compounds that do not kill parasitoids. Because parasitoids are usually small wasps, select pesticides whose label shows no adverse effects on Hymenoptera such as honeybees. Control ants if they are protecting the scales (see aphids, above). Use dormant oils (see pp. 117–118) during winter and/or insecticidal soap washes (see pp. 113–116) when scale crawlers (the young stages) are moving over the bark. Horticultural oils (see pp. 116–117) are also effective against scales.

LEAF CHEWERS
Leaf chewing insects include caterpillars and beetles.

Caterpillars. Most pestiferous larvae of moths and butterflies can be controlled with the selective microbial insecticide *Bacillus thuringiensis*, or BT (see pp. 138–143). Our recommendation for the control of the gypsy moth, however, is not to use any treatment at all. This approach maximizes the natural enemy population, which shortens the pest outbreak and lengthens the period between outbreaks. We recognize that this approach may cause changes in the composition of the forest, but in the long run it may be the most resource-conserving approach because repeated treatments will not be needed.

If you feel treatment is necessary on special trees or groups of trees surrounding homes or other areas, there are several things you can do. Where

Burlap bands wrapped around tree trunks trap gypsy moth larvae as they crawl down at night. The distinctive, hairy gypsy moth caterpillars collect under the bands and must be scraped off daily. They can then be stepped on or dropped into a pail of soapy water. (Photo by H C Ellis, University of Georgia, Bugwood.org)

An excellent pamphlet by K. Boyd, *Controlling Gypsy Moth Caterpillars with Barrier Bands* (University of Maryland Cooperative Extension Service, 1989), describes exactly how to apply and maintain sticky barriers and burlap bands (both discussed below).

The sticky barriers deny access to the tree to the many caterpillars that drop out of the tree or crawl in from neighboring trees. Because sticky materials may injure the bark of some trees, it is prudent to use duct tape between the bark and the sticky band. Circle the trunk with the tape, then place the sticky material on the tape. Check periodically (every week or two) to make sure that squirrels and other animals have not pulled the tape away from the bark or that dirt, other debris, or silken strands deposited by the caterpillars have not adhered to the band so thickly that caterpillars are using them as a bridge across the barrier.

A burlap band provides an excellent trap for large caterpillars that crawl down from the tree to rest or pupate. Adult moths will also be attracted to the burlap as a protected place in which to lay eggs. Daily cleaning of this band is necessary if it is to remain effective.

The use of cloth bands to protect trees from caterpillar pests that seek such sheltered places to pupate or overwinter is a well-known strategy and was once widely used in this country. Li Lianchang, an expert on pest control in fruit trees in China, has commented that they have found the larvae that collect beneath such barriers to be heavily infested with a species of *Beauveria*, a fungal disease of insects. *Beauveria* is used worldwide to control a number of pests of agricultural, urban, and forest trees. Scientists in China are studying ways to impregnate the bands with the fungus so that cater-pillars pupating in the bands or laying eggs there become diseased and die.

cocoons or egg masses are accessible on trunks or lower limbs, simply rub them off. Shake off larvae and sweep them up, then kill them by putting them in a sealed plastic bag in the sun. Use BT on the foliage during periods when larvae are feeding.

If you only need to protect a small number of trees from gypsy moth caterpillars, you may want to use special barriers that trap or exclude the pests from the foliage (see the photo above). Using barriers is less expensive than having your trees sprayed with BT and other nontoxic materials recommended for large tree stands. However, maintaining barriers requires time and attention once they are in place.

If you decide that a pesticide must be used, we recommend neem or BT, the least-toxic products that are effective against caterpillars. Neem-based insecticides (see pp. 125–126) are registered for the control of gypsy moths. Follow the directions on the label. Prune out tents of fall webworm or similar tent-making caterpillars when possible. Pyrethrin insecticides, although more costly than commonly used organophosphates and carbamates, are also safer for humans and degrade quickly (see pp. 123–125).

Beetles. The elm leaf beetle *(Pyrrhalta luteola)* travels down the trunk to pupate once during each generation. You can reduce pesticide use against this beetle by placing a 24-in.-wide (60-cm) band of insecticide around a portion of the trunk high above the heads of passersby. This technique requires community-wide participation to be effective, and you can request that your local street tree department or professional arborists use it.

Use traps and milky spore disease on turf areas to control the Japanese beetle (see pp. 260–263 for details). Neem is also effective as a repellent against this beetle.

BARK BEETLES AND TRUNK BORERS

Bark beetles and trunk borers are the insects most closely associated with stressed trees. Extensive tunneling and/or holes can overwhelm a tree's defenses and kill it directly. Beetles and borers can also carry pathogens—Dutch elm disease, for example—that can kill trees.

Build tree vigor and reduce stress through the horticultural and ecological practices suggested earlier. Protect young bark from sunburn with whitewash. Prune and repair limb injuries by cutting back just to the outer edge of the branch collar of the limb (see p. 360). Provide deep irrigation during droughts. Arrange trees appropriately (for example, aspen, birch, or eucalyptus should be grown in clusters and dogwoods should be grown as an understory to mimic their respective native forest conditions).

Sanitation is also very important in managing bark beetles and trunk borers. If nearby trees are stressed and heavily infested, remove the infested limbs or dead or dying trees quickly. De-bark them (in case of bark beetles), and burn the debris. A solution of insect-eating nematodes can be injected into borer holes. These nematodes are nontoxic to humans and do not feed on plants. Certain pine oil compounds have been found effective in repelling bark beetles and are being studied further for this use. Commercial products, however, have not been realized.

Elm leaf beetle larvae scrape the tissue from the surface of leaves, whereas the adults (shown) chew holes through the entire leaf. A 24-in.-wide (60-cm) band of insecticide sprayed high up on the trunk kills migrating larvae, which must cross the band on their way down to the soil to pupate. (Actual size of adult, ¼ in./6 mm) (Photo by Whitney Cranshaw, Colorado State University, Bugwood.org)

SUMMARY OF THE SHADE-TREE SYSTEM FOR THE URBAN BIOLOGICAL CONTROL PROJECT, UNIVERSITY OF CALIFORNIA, BERKELEY

CITY NAME	YEARS IN PROGRAM	CITY POPULATION	TREE POPULATION	TREES TREATED BEFORE IPM INITIATED	1976 BT TREATMENTS	1976 TOTAL INSECTICIDE TREATMENTS	PERCENTAGE REDUCTION IN TREATMENTS DUE TO IPM PROGRAM
Berkeley	6	107,500	35,000	11,500	32	35	99.7
San Jose	3	557,700	250,000	42,000	4,307	4,310	90.0
Palo Alto	2	54,900	80,000	1,600	369	375	77.0
Modesto	1	85,000	85,000	8,000	8	4,600	91.0
Davis	1	32,800	12,000	2,000	0	817	92.0
Totals		**837,900**	**462,000**	**65,100**	**4,716**	**10,137**	**89.3 (average)**

This chart presents data on some of the shade-tree systems for which we developed IPM programs, and shows how effective such programs can be. Don't be sidetracked by the dates in the table; similar IPM effects would be seen today when switching from a conventional pest control program to an IPM program.
City population based on January 1976 census. Percentage reduction in treatment calculated by dividing total 1976 treatments by number of trees treated before the IPM program was initiated and subtracting from 100 percent.
A total of 4,490 of the Modesto treatments occurred prior to the initiation of the IPM program. Only 350 trees were treated (twice) during the IPM program. These are estimates, as no records were kept prior to the IPM program. All of the Davis treatments, except 12, were carried out prior to the introduction of the IPM program. Only *Bacillus thuringiensis*, water-washing, and pyrethrin treatments were used.

Some pheromones, or behavioral chemicals, are being used experimentally. One such chemical, Verbenone, is an "overcrowded" pheromone that says to nearby borers, "This tree is full, find another susceptible tree." It is a chemical "No Vacancy" sign. This pheromone has been shown to be effective in some cases with some species.

IPM DECISION-MAKING PROCESS

IPM is an ideal approach to tree-pest management, as well as all other pest management. You can apply it in your own backyard, professional arborists can use it in their work, and the city tree-maintenance department can make it standard operating procedure.

1. IDENTIFY THE PEST (LOCATE FOCUS AREAS) AND DEFINE MANAGEMENT OBJECTIVES.

- Rank garden areas and plants in descending order of importance, with the most significant areas and plants at the top of the list.
- Determine presence or absence of *potential* pest species.

- Define your management objectives for the various garden area uses, plants, and the pests present.

2. MONITOR.

- Inspect the area two or more times to establish a comparison on which to judge whether the situation is getting better, worse, or remains the same.
- Record all pertinent monitoring information and maintain records.

3. SET INJURY LEVEL TO DETERMINE DAMAGE AND TREATMENT THRESHOLDS.

- *Set Injury Level:* Set the point at which the plant or location will be injured, damaged, or made unusable.
- *Damage Threshold:* What is the maximum pest level that the site can tolerate before damage levels are reached?
- *Treatment Threshold:* Determine the point at which an action or combination of actions must be taken in order to keep the injury level from being reached.

IPM DECISION-MAKING PROCESS

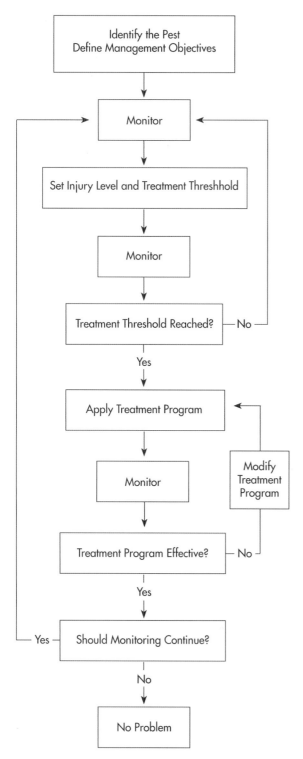

Adapted from Bio-Integral Resource Center (BIRC), "IPM Training Manual for Land-scape Gardeners" (BIRC, 2004).

4. MONITOR.
- Compare pest populations with treatment threshold levels.
- Are beneficials present?
- Is population rising, falling, or remaining the same?

5. IS THE TREATMENT THRESHOLD REACHED?
- If NO, then continue monitoring.
- If YES, then proceed to Step 6.

6. APPLY TREATMENT PROGRAM.
- Implement treatment program using the least-disruptive action or combination of actions available.
- You will often need to use more than one method or tactic at a time; this is the "integrated" in IPM.

7. MONITOR.
- Monitor for efficacy.

8. WAS THE TREATMENT PROGRAM EFFECTIVE ENOUGH TO PREVENT DAMAGE?
- If NO, modify the treatment program by incorporating additional methods and/or tactics. Return to Step 6 and implement the changes in your treatment program.
- If YES, go to Step 9.

9. SHOULD MONITORING CONTINUE?
- NO, if the problem has been solved for the near future or the long term.
- YES, if the pest will remain present or active in the near future.

10. NO PROBLEM.
- The pest is no longer problematic for this season.
- The pest has been controlled for the present.

AFTERWORD

As we hope this book has shown, most pesticide use is unnecessary, based on misinformation and fear. The simplest and least toxic approach to pest control is first of all to do nothing. Next on the spectrum of approaches are the truly least toxic methods such as hand pulling, hand picking, and applying soap and vinegar solutions. The microbial insecticide Bt would also be considered least toxic because it is so selective. The last option is to spot-treat with low-toxic, commercially available substances like pyrethrins, which are broad-spectrum but only last a day or so. Even with more toxic substances, spot treatment can reduce the use rates by 90% or more in most cases. This toxicity gradient is what common-sense pest control, and this book, is all about.

But common-sense pest control is only one aspect of sustainable gardening. Our gardens must be designed with a focus on sustainability and an understanding of their impact on our future. To achieve, first we must rethink the idea of *what a garden is*. Then we must employ sustainable gardening tactics at every step of the gardening process.

For example, most people today take it for granted that their landscape must be dominated by lawns. Lawns, however, require considerable care and maintenance. In some places lawns are regularly sprayed with insecticide, herbicide, and fertilizer combinations. It is a deluge of chemicals most of us wouldn't welcome in our homes and shouldn't welcome in our outdoor living areas. One solution is to convert much of these spaces to food gardens or maintenance-free landscapes.

For the most part, food plants in your own garden don't need pesticides. If you lose some of your crop, it's not the end of the world. Think of it as a learning experience, a way to discover another food plant better suited to your garden and not susceptible to your pest problem. Processing your own food at any level saves money, conserves transportation energy, and reduces all kinds of pollution. The whole food chain is improved, if even in a small way, when you grow something you previously purchased. Those small ways add up over time and can make a real difference for our future.

With this approach you not only want to avoid wasting resources, but when you can, create them. You can learn to produce your own fertilizer and mulch from compost, be it with the less labor intensive cold compost pile or the hot compost system. Composting creates the best fertilizer, even better than what is available at the local nursery, keeps garden waste out of the landfill, and saves money on expensive petroleum-based synthetic fertilizers.

In a sustainable garden, plants are chosen for more than their color; they may be chosen because they attract beneficial insects or outcompete weeds or tolerate the climate well. Plant selection requires careful observation, and knowledge, sometimes knowledge even beyond what is known by most local nursery folks. This book can help. For example, planting milkweed provides a food source for the developing monarch butterfly. This is critical right now, for GMO crops and loss of habitat are threatening this species, in particular. But by planting the milkweed you not only help protect a threatened species, but you also bring some beautiful wildlife into your garden. If you can't tolerate defoliated plants, just place them in areas where they won't interfere with your aesthetic. Don't worry, the butterflies will find them. There are a wide variety of plants for exploration, many discussed in this book, which feed beautiful butterflies and bugs.

Visit the ecology section of my website at www.WHO1615.com for lots more information.

—William Olkowski

CASE STUDY: SAN FRANCISCO

Public agencies across the United States have been a driving force in urban IPM adoption, primarily in response to outside pressure from citizen activists and environmental advocates. Especially active have been cities, counties, and school, park, and water districts at the local level. Local agencies have instituted system-wide IPM programs that have paid off in improved and affordable pest management and significant reductions in the use of conventional toxic pesticides. Their collaborative approach and generous information sharing continue to provide IPM models and guidance to others in the public and private sectors.

SAN FRANCISCO'S CITYWIDE IPM PROGRAM

San Francisco is the 12th largest city in the United States, with a population of 812,000 (2011) and over 96,000 acres of land: 5,600 acres within the city limits, and another 90,400 acres located along 150 miles of rights-of-way between the city and its water and power resource in Yosemite Valley.

The following summary describes how this large city established and has operated a successful IPM program for over 15 years. It is offered here as an inspiration to our readers who would like to see an IPM program established in their community. It is also directed to pest management professionals interested in qualifying for the growing number of IPM contracts available from public agencies who have adopted IPM.

IPM ORDINANCE

In 1996, the San Francisco City Council passed an IPM ordinance requiring IPM practices on all city-owned land and buildings. One of the authors of this book, Sheila Daar, was on the team that assisted city staff in the design and implementation of its trailblazing IPM program, which is operated by the San Francisco Department of the Environment.

The IPM concepts and many of the strategies and products described in *Common-Sense Pest Control* were incorporated into the initial program. Over time, they were adapted and added to as the visionary IPM program managers established a firm footing in city government culture. They created a sound IPM program infrastructure and secured reliable funding. They slowly but surely achieved IPM buy-in from city gardeners, maintenance staff, department managers, environmental activists, and the general public. Resulting IPM successes have lead to substantial pesticide reduction with improved pest control. This has created a positive profile and long-term backing for IPM from city leaders, citizens, and the press.

THE CITY'S IPM APPROACH

To quote the city's IPM brochure, "In San Francisco, IPM means regular monitoring to determine if and when treatments are needed, and employing biological, cultural, mechanical, physical, and educational strategies to keep their numbers down. We emphasize non-chemical control methods. But when pesticides are necessary, we have an approved list of reduced-risk chemicals to meet the need."

THE IPM TEAM

Operation of the city's IPM program is a team effort, coordinated by the IPM program managers in the Department of Environment and including the following:

- Citywide IPM program staff
- City building and grounds maintenance staff
- Structural pest control contractor
- IPM Technical Advisory Committee (TAC)

TAC members include staff from a wide variety of city departments involved with IPM. The city's IPM consultants and structural pest control contractor are also members. Participation from nearby public agencies is encouraged, including the San Francisco School District, the National Park Service, California State Parks, and environmental advocates.

Hosted by the citywide IPM program staff, the TAC is one of the most important components of the IPM program. Its monthly meetings and community-building atmosphere promote peer-to-peer information exchange, problem solving, and collegial decision making. It is a venue for IPM training in subjects requested by TAC members; IPM "how-to" information presented at TAC meetings and hands-on training programs are often incorporated into the annual pest-specific IPM plans produced by field staff.

It is also a place where emergency planning occurs during a pest emergency, such as the advent of mosquito-borne West Nile virus into California. The fact that city gardeners and building maintenance personnel have continued to participate in TAC meetings for over 15 years speaks to the value of this forum to those on the front lines.

Deshelia Mixon, the IPM Specialist for San Franciso Department of Public Works, uses a steam weeder at City Hall Plaza. (Photo by Steven Ash)

IPM PROGRAM HIGHLIGHTS
1. REDUCED-RISK PESTICIDE LIST

Since its inception, the objective of the city's IPM program has been to reduce pesticide use by maximizing pest prevention and non-chemical methods, and using "reduced-risk" (least-toxic) pesticides as a last resort.

Any pesticide considered for use on city property is first screened by a toxicologist against a list of criteria related to health and environmental hazards. The pesticide is then placed into one of three tiers: Tier 1: highest concern; Tier 2: moderate concern; Tier 3: lowest concern. The city's IPM program managers and its IPM Technical Advisory Committee use the hazard tier data, combined with assessments of likely use patterns and exposure to the pesticide, to decide whether a pesticide will be approved for city use and which, if any, limitations will be imposed.

Most pesticides still used fall into the Tier 3 (lowest concern) category. Use of Tier 1 or Tier 2 products requires a written request to the Citywide IPM Program Director with a justification and a plan for finding an alternative in the future. A guide to the hazard-assessment process and a copy of the Reduced-Risk Pesticide List is available at www.sfenvironment.org.

Weed barriers are one of the IPM methods used by the San Francisco program. (Photo by Brandi Spade, courtesy of *Fine Gardening*)

2. IPM INCENTIVES AND TRAINING

IPM program managers encourage awareness and use of non-chemical methods in a number of ways, including inviting suppliers of IPM compatible products and methods to demonstrate them at a TAC meeting, sponsoring hands-on training for field staff in the use of IPM products and methods, and providing small grants to field staff so they can test promising new alternatives. Another significant training opportunity is the biennial IPM conference sponsored by the Department of the Environment. The conference is also the venue for official recognition of IPM accomplishments by selected city IPM field staff and others. Awards are presented by the mayor of San Francisco.

3. ADOPTION OF NON-CHEMICAL METHODS

A small sample of methods used by city staff includes the following:

- Goat herds
- Propane flamers
- Weed barrier cloth and mulch
- Competitive plantings
- Compost tea
- Biological controls
- Insect-sniffing beagle
- Vacuums and heaters

The most hazardous pesticides were banned from use shortly after the IPM program was established in 1996. Between 1996 and 2005, the IPM program **reduced gallons of pesticides used by 85 percent, pounds of most common herbicide ingredients by 87 percent, and pounds of all pesticides used by 55 percent.** In 2009, approximately 80 percent of pest management treatments to buildings were conducted without the use of any pesticides.

4. IPM PRACTICES ARE EMBEDDED

IPM practices are integrated into the city's ongoing maintenance and pest management programs.

REFERENCES AND READINGS

For additional references and readings visit FineGardening.com/Common-Sense-Pest-Control.

CHAPTER 2: NATURAL PEST CONTROLS

Agrios, G. N. 2005. *Plant Pathology.* San Diego: Academic Press. 952 pp.
This comprehensive text on plant diseases provides in-depth background on how pathogens attack plants. It is essential reading for anyone who wants to maximize the use of non-chemical controls for plant diseases.

Flint, M. L., S. H. Dreistadt, and J. K. Clark. 1998. *Natural Enemies Handbook: The Illustrated Guide to Biological Pest Control.* Richmond, CA: Statewide IPM Project and the University of California Division of Agriculture and Natural Resources Communication Services #3386. 154 pp.

CHAPTER 3: INTRODUCTION TO INTEGRATED PEST MANAGEMENT

Most of the recommended readings listed below were taken from the leaflet *What Is IPM?* by Helga Olkowski, published by the Bio-Integral Resource Center, P.O. Box 7414, Berkeley, CA 94707.

Flint, M. L., and R. van den Bosch. 1981. *Introduction to Integrated Pest Management.* New York: Plenum Press. 240 pp.
This text is the best introduction to the concept of IPM in print. It covers basic ecological principles, the early history of pest control, the economic, social, and environmental costs of pest control, and the philosophy of IPM. It then moves to practical procedures like monitoring and decision-making before discussing case histories and the role of the IPM specialist. Finally, there is a chapter on future possibilities for IPM implementation.

Olkowski, H., and W. Olkowski. 1976. Entomophobia in the urban ecosystem. *Bulletin of the Entomological Society of America* 22(3):313–317.
This paper grew out of Bill Olkowski's experiences on the staff of the California State Bureau of Vector Control and Solid Waste Management, where he encountered a number of cases of public hysteria regarding real or imagined insect problems. Such hysteria is the basis for a great deal of unnecessary pesticide use. This phenomenon needs to be understood better if pesticide reduction is to occur.

CHAPTER 4: PEST TREATMENT STRATEGIES AND TACTICS

Anderson, E. 2005. *Plants, Man and Life.* Mineola, NY: Dover Publications. 272 pp.
An inspiring account of the author's adventures as a botanist in the United States and Central America. He describes the diverse garden designs found among Central America's food-producing plots.

van den Bosch, R. 1989. *The Pesticide Conspiracy.* New York: Doubleday. 226 pp.
A hard-hitting polemic by a man alarmed about the lack of attention given to the most powerful pest control strategy—biological control—and the logical framework for its implementation—IPM.

van den Bosch, R., P. S. Messenger, and A. P. Gutierrez. 1982. *An Introduction to Biological Control.* New York: Plenum Press. 247 pp.
A readable textbook-like introduction that is useful for the layperson but can also serve as an introduction for high school and college students.

CHAPTER 5: MEET "THE BENEFICIALS"

Flint, M. L., S. H. Dreistadt, and J. K. Clark. 1998. *Natural Enemies Handbook: The Illustrated Guide to Biological Pest Control.* Richmond, CA: Statewide IPM Project and the University of California Division of Agriculture and Natural Resources, Publication #3386. 154 pp.

CHAPTER 6: CHOOSING THE RIGHT CHEMICAL AND MICROBIAL TOOLS

Carson, R. 1962. *Silent Spring.* Greenwich, CT: Fawcett. 304 pp.

Hailed as a great book by the lay press and condemned by pest control academics and professionals, this book marked a turning point in public awareness of the side effects of pesticide use. It still makes very interesting reading, since much of what was written then still applies today.

Marer, P. J. 1999. *The Safe and Effective Use of Pesticides,* Second Edition. Davis, CA: University of California Statewide Integrated Pest Management Project, Division of Agriculture and Natural Resources, Publication #3324. 342 pp.

This is the best basic discussion of pesticide composition, behavior, toxicity, and appropriate methods of use currently in print. Written for professionals but accessible to the layperson, it contains practical advice for the use of pesticides in an integrated pest management framework.

Olkowski, W., and H. Olkowski. 1983. *Delivering Integrated Pest Management Services: Pest Control Services for Cockroaches, Mice, Rats and Flies in Public and Private Buildings.* Berkeley: Bio-Integral Resource Center. 50 pp.

This booklet is written for the pest control professional interested in providing a high level of pest control with minimal use of pesticides. It describes monitoring methods and the use of least toxic-control tactics.

CHAPTER 7: SOME USEFUL INORGANICS, ORGANICS, AND BOTANICALS

Davidson, J. A., S. A. Gill, and M. J. Raupp. 1990. Foliar and growth effects of repetitive summer horticultural oil sprays on trees and shrubs under drought stress. *Journal of Arboriculture* 16(4):77–81.

This paper was the source of the information on plant species that tolerate oil sprays while under drought stress in hot summer weather.

Ebeling, W. 1975. *Urban Entomology.* Los Angeles: University of California, Division of Agricultural Sciences. 695 pp.

A very useful source of information on silica aerogel, boric acid, other urban/suburban pesticides, and the biology and management of urban pests.

Grossman, J. 1990. Horticultural oils: New summer uses on ornamental plant pests. *The IPM Practitioner* 12(8):1–9.

This review brings together information about the uses of horticultural oils on ornamental plants and their pests.

Johnson, W. T. 1980. Spray oils as insecticides. *Journal of Arboriculture* 6(7):169–174.

A thorough discussion of modern horticultural-oil formulations and how to use them.

Johnson, W. T. 1982. Horticultural spray oils for tree pest control. *Weeds, Trees, and Turf* May: 36–40.

This paper clears up many misconceptions about the formulation and application of horticultural oils.

Kahn, I. A. and E. A. Abourashed. 2009. *Leung's Encyclopedia of Common Natural Ingredients Used in Food, Drugs, and Cosmetics.* New York: John Wiley and Sons. 810 pp.

A basic reference work that covers the common natural food ingredients, some of which are used in pesticidal products. The short general descriptions provide information on chemical composition, pharmacological or biological uses, and commercial preparations. The book is thoroughly referenced.

Ware, G. W. 1991. *Fundamentals of Pesticides: A Self-Instruction Guide.* Fresno, CA: Thompson Publication. 207 pp.

An excellent introduction to pesticides and their chemistry.

CHAPTER 8: NEW FRONTIERS: MICROBIALS, PHEROMONES, AND INSECT GROWTH REGULATORS

Daar, S. 1985. Microbial control for grasshoppers. *The IPM Practitioner* 7(9):1–6.

This article reviews the use of *Nosema locustae* by the National Park Service. It provides background information on the pathogen and its effectiveness and points out how this potentially useful grasshopper control agent has been neglected by the Animal Plant Health Inspection Service (APHIS), the USDA's agency responsible for grasshopper control.

Daar, S. 1987. New federal IPM program for grasshoppers. *The IPM Practitioner* 9(4):1–3.

A description of a five-year demonstration IPM program, along with a summary of other developments since the earlier article (see previous listing).

Liebman, J. 1989. IPM and the genetic engineering of plants. *The IPM Practitioner* 11(10):4–7.

This was the source for the sidebar on biotechnology on p. 136.

Lipa, J. J. 1990. Microbial pest control in Eastern Europe. *The IPM Practitioner* 12(2):1–5.

This article reports that microbial control in Eastern Europe is well developed, and documents developments with BT, *Beauveria bassiana*, nematodes, various antibiotics, *Trichoderma* spp., and various viruses.

Olkowski, W. 1988. Great expectations for non-toxic pheromones. *The IPM Practitioner* 10(6/7):1–9.

This article reviews early developments in pheromone synthesis and the literature to date concerning field studies on pheromones as trap components and mating disruptants. It speculates about the future of pheromones, and describes the need for changes in the USEPA registration process for them.

CHAPTER 10: MEET THE WEEDS

DiTomaso, J. M., and E. A. Healy. 2007. *Weeds of California and Other Western States,* Volumes 1 & 2. Richmond, CA: University of California Agricultural and Natural Resources Communication Services. Volume 1: 834 pp., Volume 2: 974 pp.

This two-volume set is available through UC-ANR. Visit their catalog website for these and other publications (anrcatalog.ucdavis.edu). While these excellent volumes are aimed primarily at the Western States, there are many weeds listed that are present elsewhere in the United States and Canada. Excellent photographs and text.

Ingels, C. A., R. L. Bugg, G. T. McGourty, and L. P. Christensen. 2002. *Cover Cropping in Vineyards, A Grower's Handbook.* Oakland, CA: University of California Agricultural and Natural Resources Communication Services. 162 pp.

McClure, S., and S. Roth. 1994. *Rodale's Successful Organic Gardening: Companion Planting.* Emmaus, PA: Rodale Press. 160 pp.

Miller, P. R., W. L. Graves, and W. A. Williams. 1989. *Covercrops for California Agriculture.* Richmond, CA: University of California Agricultural and Natural Resources Communication Services. Publication #21471. 24 pp.

Whitson, T. D., L. C. Burrill, S. A. Dewey, D. W. Cudney, B. E. Nelson, R. D. Lee, and R. Parker. 2000. *Weeds of the West,* 9th Edition. Newark, CA: Western Society of Weed Science. 628 pp.

CHAPTER 11: SAFE AND SANE WEED MANAGEMENT

Daar, S. 1991. Vegetation management on rights-of-way: An ecological approach. *The IPM Practitioner* 8(2):1–7.

This article describes techniques used by utility companies to establish low-growing, stable shrublands under power lines to replace problem trees. The techniques substantially reduced use of herbicides, and can be used along roads, park trails, and other rights-of-way.

DiTomaso, J. M., and E. A. Healy. 2007. *Weeds of California and Other Western States,* Volumes 1 & 2. Richmond, CA: University of California Agriculture and Natural Resources Publication #3488. Oakland, CA: 1,808 pp.

Ingels, C. A., and R. L. Bugg, G. T. McGourty, and L. P. Christensen, Editors. 2005. *Cover Cropping in Vineyards, A Grower's Handbook.* UC-ANR Publications #3338. Richmond, CA: University of California Agriculture and Natural Resources Communications Services. 162 pp.

Jeavons, J. 2012. *How to Grow More Vegetables Than You Ever Thought Possible on Less Land Than You Can Imagine,* Eighth Edition. Berkeley, CA: Ten Speed Press. 256 pp.

This groundbreaking book introduced American gardeners to the French intensive method of gardening. It details strategies for maximizing yields on small garden plots using ecologically sound techniques.

Turner, N. J. and P. von Aderkas. 2009. *The North American Guide to Common Poisonous Plants and Mushrooms.* Timber Press, Portland, OR. 376 pp.

CHAPTER 12: PREVENTING LAWN PESTS

Creasy, Rosalind. 2010. *Edible Landscaping,* Second Edition. San Francisco, CA.: Sierra Club Books. 384 pp.

The first edition (1982) was titled *The Complete Book of Edible Landscaping.* It and the new edition take you through planning, design, site preparation, plant selection, installation and planting, IPM, and harvest. The ideas she espouses will sound even better after you have gotten up on a Saturday or Sunday morning and mowed the lawn, knowing that you could have been harvesting homegrown produce instead.

Ferguson, N. 2005. *Right Plant, Right Place.* Revised Edition. New York: A Fireside Book by Simon & Shuster. 368 pp.

Glick, P. 2007. *The Gardener's Guide to Global Warming: Challenges and Solutions.* Reston, VA: National Wildlife Federation. 36 pp.

Help battle climate change in your own backyard with this short report, which can be downloaded for free at www.nwf.org.

Hayes, A., C. Nelson, and J. Nader. 2008. *Bay-Friendly Gardening,* Second Edition. Oakland, CA: StopWaste.Org (Alameda County Waste Management Authority and Source Reduction & Recycling Board). 82 pp.

Sustainable gardening manual.

Kennedy, G., M. Cahill, and M. Mwangi. 2006. *A Homeowner's Guide to Environmentally Sound Lawncare.* Boston: Massachusetts Department of Agricultural Resources Pesticide Bureau. 26 pp.

Lownefels, J., and W. Lewis. 2010. *Teaming with Microbes: The Organic Gardener's Guide to the Soil Food Web,* Revised Edition. Portland, OR: Timber Press. 220 pp.

The authors, self-described "typical suburban gardeners," have written a book that is easy for the casual gardener to read and yet has enough science to please the geekiest of gardeners and landscapers. A foreword by Dr. Elaine Ingham, Ph.D., president of Soil Foodweb, Inc., shows support of one of the pioneers in defining and promoting the living soils concept. An informative and fun read.

Nardi, J. 2007. *Life in the Soil: A Guide for Naturalists and Gardeners.* Chicago: The University of Chicago Press. 293 pp.

A very readable introduction to the flora and fauna found (at least we hope they are found) in your soil.

Stoner, K. 2011. *NOFA Standards for Organic Land Care,* Fifth Edition. Stevenson, CT: Northeast Organic Farming Association of Connecticut. 81 pp.

Tukey, P. 2007. *The Organic Lawn Care Manual.* North Adams, MA: Storey Publishing. 271 pp.

Excellent resource for organic lawn care, from design to installation to enjoyment. Visit their website at www.SafeLawns.org.

TURFGRASS IDENTIFICATION:

University of California Davis:

www.ipm.ucdavis.edu/TOOLS/TURF/TURFSPE-CIES/index.html. This is probably the best single source because of the wide variety of climates in California; both cool-season and warm-season turfgrass are used in the state and are identified in this key.

Purdue University:

www.agry.purdue.edu/turf/tool/index.html

Kansas State University:

www.ksre.ksu.edu/library/hort2/mf2031.pdf

Penn State University:

http://plantscience.psu.edu/research/centers/turf/extension/factsheets/cool-season-turfgrass-ID

Ohio State University:

http://buckeyeturf.osu.edu/pdf/01_turfgrass_identi-fication.pdf

Texas A&M University:

http://aggieturf.tamu.edu/answers4you/selection.html

CHAPTER 13: LEAST-TOXIC LAWN PEST MANAGEMENT

Couch, H. B. 2000. *The Turfgrass Disease Handbook.* Malabar, FL: Krieger Publishing. 209 pp.

DiTomaso, J. M., and E. A. Healy. 2007. *Weeds of California and Other Western States:* Volumes 1 and 2. Oakland, CA: University of California Agriculture and Natural Resources. Volume 1: 834 pp. and Volume 2: 974 pp.

McCarty, L. B., J. W. Everest, D. W. Hall, and T. R. Murphy. 2008. *Color Atlas of Turfgrass Weeds.* New York, NY: John Wiley and Sons. 432 pp.

Tashiro, H., P. J. Vittum, and M. G. Villani. 1999. *Turfgrass Insects of the United States and Canada.* Ithaca, NY: Cornell University Press. 448 pp.

An invaluable guide to the biology and behavior of turfgrass insect pests. This excellent volume includes information on cultural and biological controls, monitoring data, and other elements of an Integrated Pest Management approach. Many color photos aid in identification.

INDEX

A

Aeration
  compaction and lawn stresses, reducing, 239–240
  lawn diseases and, 270, 279, 283
  shade-tree stress and, 361
Aerator sandals ("Spikes O' Death"), 260–261
Agrobacterium radiobacter, 147
Allelopathy, 200–205
  description of, 181
  plants showing effects on weeds, 202–203
  ryegrass mulch, 202–204
  in sod aisles, 196
  tree-inhibiting shrubs and grasses, 199, 204–205
Anthracnose, 26, 109, 358
Ants
  aphids, associations with, 70, 303, 305
  as beneficial organisms, 69–71
  in biological control program, 46
  fire, 308
  subfamilies of North American, 71
Aphids, 300–301
  ants, associations with, 70, 303, 305
  ash, 19–20, 358
  biology of, 301–302
  detection and monitoring of, 304
  direct biological controls, 306–307
  direct chemical controls, 307
    insecticidal baits, 307–308
    insecticidal soap, 307
    least-toxic 25b generally recognized as safe (GRAS) insecticides, 308–309
    silica aerogel/pyrethrin mix, 308
  direct physical controls, 305–306
  fears regarding, 31
  garlic oil to control, 128
  indirect strategies to control
    ant barriers, 305
    let aging plants linger, 305
    nitrogen levels, 304–305
    plant flowering, encouraging, 305
    pruning, 305
  lady beetles and, 61–62, 306

natural enemies of, 303–304
parasitized, 23
parasitoids and, 52, 304
population peaks of, 19
rose, 301
as shade tree pest, 368
Syrphid flies and, 21–22
waterlily, 37
woolly apple, 302
Arsenic, 106–107

B

Bacillus, bacterial insecticides based on, 137–138, 231–232
Bacillus popilliae (milky spore disease), 131, 137, 141, 143, 259, 261–263
Bacillus subtilis, 147
Bacillus thuringiensis (BT), 138–143
  BT corn, development of, 132, 365
  caterpillars, controlling, 140, 141–142, 368–370
  cutworms, use against, 314, 316–317
  to kill mosquito larvae, controversial proposal, 29
  M-One® based on, 133
  mosquitoes, blackflies, and fungus gnats, treating, 142–143
  resistance to, 134, 137, 365
  sod webworm control by, 255
  timing of application, 37
  transgenic plants and, 136
  var. israelensis (BTI), 139, 142–143
  var. kurstaki (BTK), 132, 137, 139, 140, 141–142
  var. tenebrionis (BTT), 143
Baits
  for aphids, 307–308
  for slugs and snails, 337
Barrier plants, 198
Barriers
  burrowing animals, preventing damage from, 32
  cone screen for cabbage root maggot, 325
  direct suppression of pests by, 46
  against gophers, 321
  for gypsy moth caterpillars, 369
  as natural pest control, 19
  against slugs and snails, 341–342
Bats, 77–78, 300

Beauveria bassiana, 137, 144–145
Bees, 71–72, 96–97
Beetles
  bugs and, distinction between, 60
  Colorado potato, 133
  cucumber (see Cucumber beetles)
  elm leaf, 133–134
  flea, 109
  ground, 62–63
  grubs as larvae of, 256
  Japanese (see Japanese beetles)
  lady (see Lady beetles)
  predacious, prey of, 59
  rove, 63–64, 326, 343
  as shade tree pests, 370–371
Beneficial organisms, 55
  actinomycetes, 231
  ants, 46, 69–71
  attracting, case study in, 172
  bats, 77–78
  bees, 71–72
  centipedes, 58–59
  geese, 216–218
  goats, 214–216
  ground beetles, 62–63
  hover flies, 66–67
  Hymenoptera order, 68–69, 70
  installing plants to attract, 353
  lacewings, 49, 64–66
  lady beetles (see Lady beetles)
  mites, 50
  nematodes (see Nematodes)
  parasitic wasps, 76–77
  parasitoids (see Parasitoids)
  plants that attract, 168–169
  predators (see Predators)
  predatory mites, 21, 57–58
  rove beetles, 63–64
  social wasps, 72–75
  solitary predatory wasps, 75–76
  spiders, 21–22, 31, 56–57
  weed control by, 213–214
  weeds, 182–184
Big-eyed bugs, 264, 267
Biofungicides, 147–148, 333
Biological controls
  for aphids, 306–307
  augmentation of natural enemies, 50
  for brown patch, 276–277
  for cabbage root maggots, 326
  for chinch bugs, 267
  conservation of, 48–50
  for cucumber beetles, 312–313